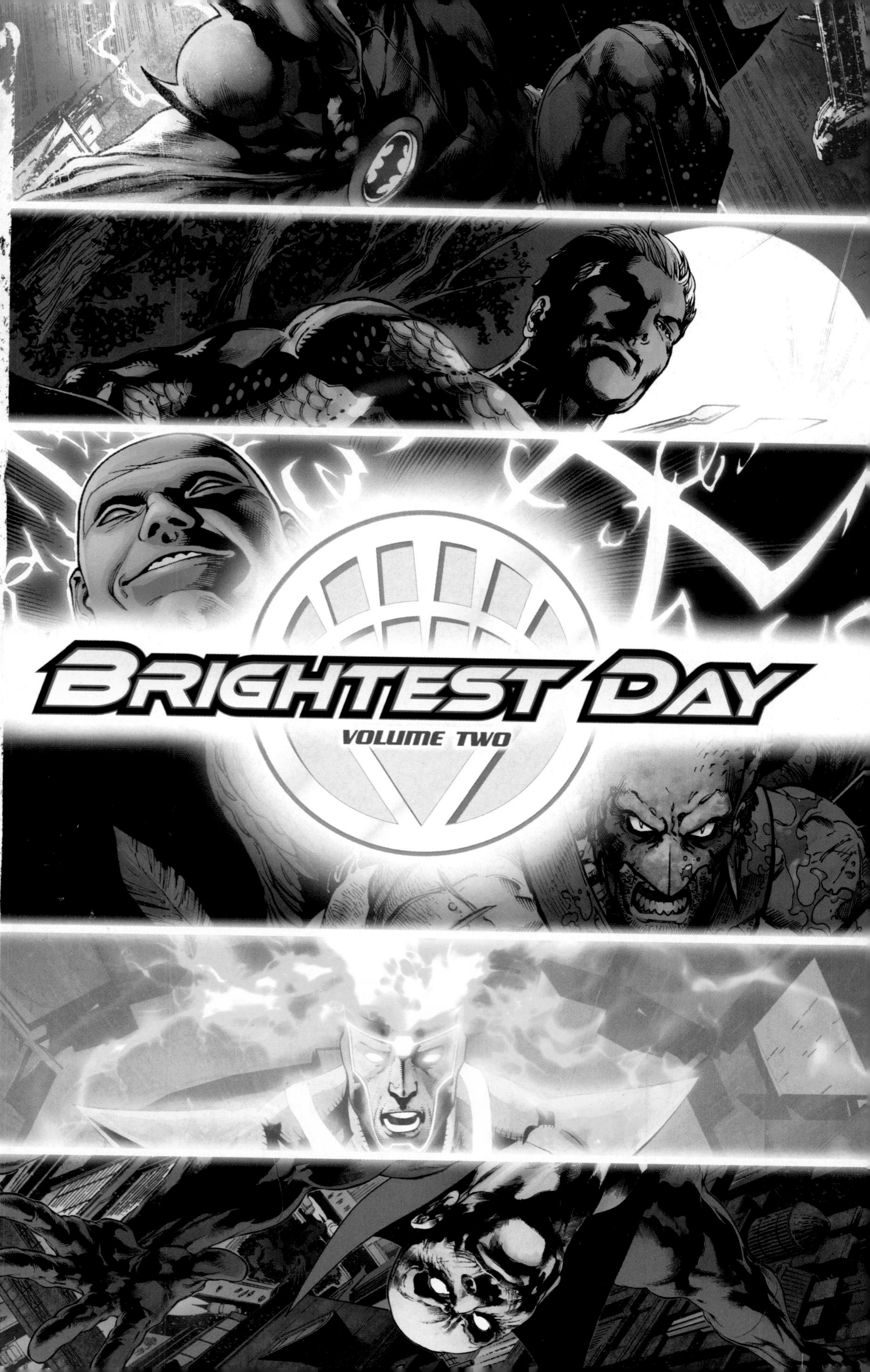
BRIGHTEST DAY
VOLUME TWO

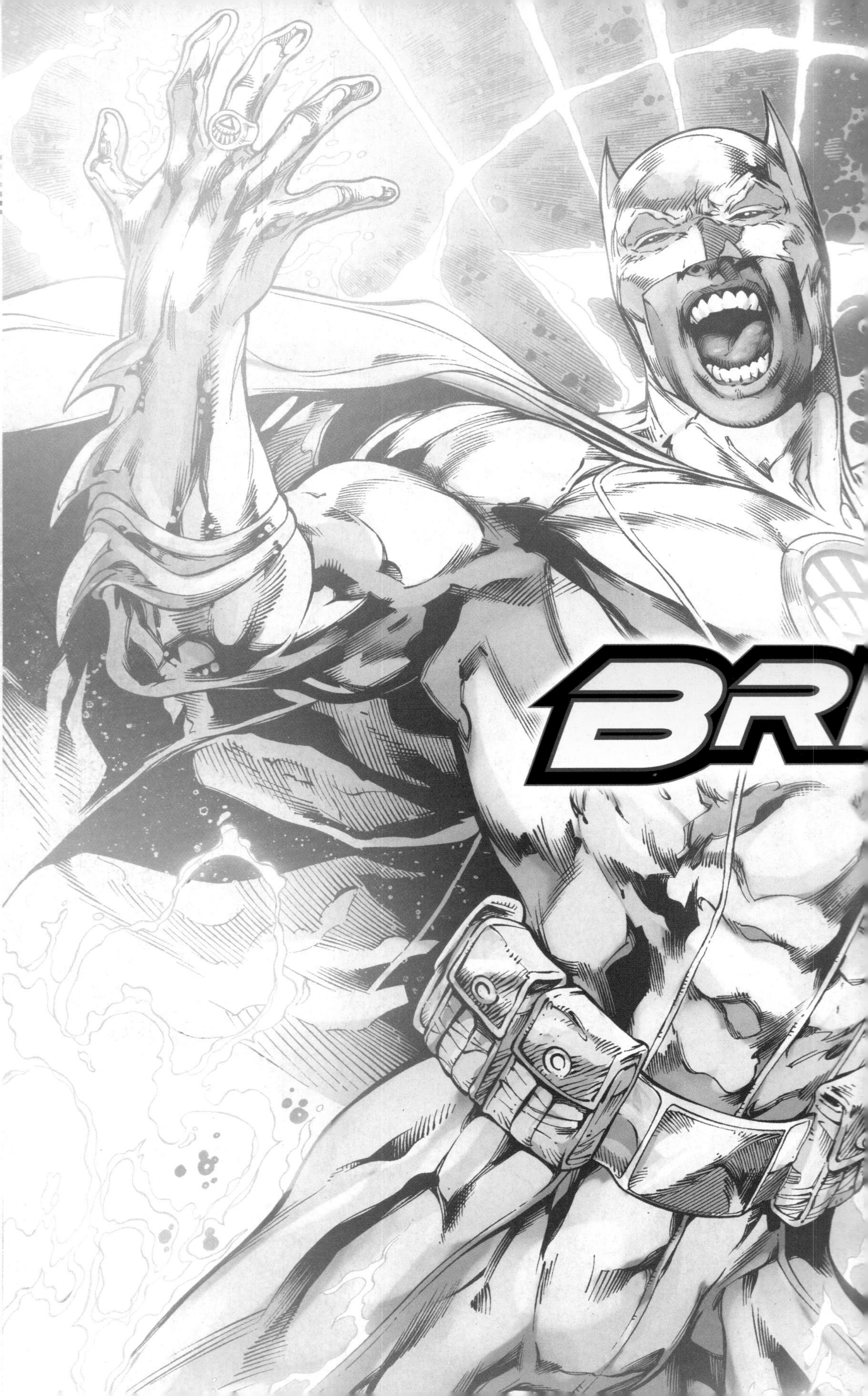

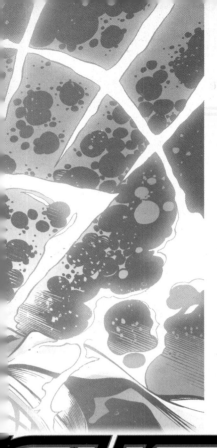

# GEOFF JOHNS & PETER J. TOMASI
WRITERS

# IVAN REIS
# PATRICK GLEASON
# ARDIAN SYAF
# SCOTT CLARK
# JOE PRADO
ARTISTS

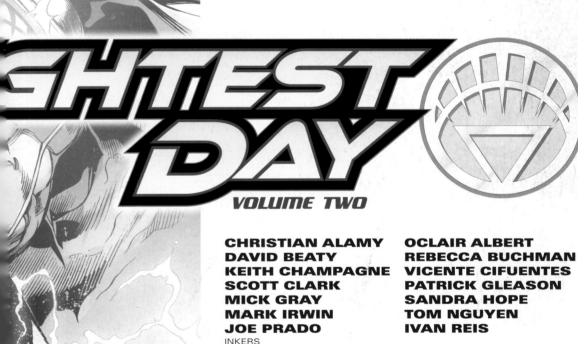

GHTEST DAY

VOLUME TWO

CHRISTIAN ALAMY
DAVID BEATY
KEITH CHAMPAGNE
SCOTT CLARK
MICK GRAY
MARK IRWIN
JOE PRADO
INKERS

OCLAIR ALBERT
REBECCA BUCHMAN
VICENTE CIFUENTES
PATRICK GLEASON
SANDRA HOPE
TOM NGUYEN
IVAN REIS

ASPEN MLT'S PETER STEIGERWALD
WITH BETH SOTELO, JOHN STARR & RAY DILLON
BRIAN BUCCELLATO
COLORISTS

ROB CLARK JR.
KEN LOPEZ
LETTERERS

DAVID FINCH, SCOTT WILLIAMS
& PETER STEIGERWALD
COLLECTION COVER

Eddie Berganza & Adam Schlagman  *Editors-original series*
Rex Ogle  *Associate Editor-original series* | Bob Harras  *Group Editor-Collected Editions*
Robbin Brosterman  *Design Director-Books* | Curtis King Jr.  *Senior Art Director*

**DC COMICS** | Diane Nelson  *President* | Dan DiDio and Jim Lee  *Co-Publishers*
Geoff Johns  *Chief Creative Officer* | Patrick Caldon  *EVP–Finance and Administration*
John Rood  *EVP–Sales, Marketing and Business Development* | Amy Genkins  *SVP–Business and Legal Affairs*
Steve Rotterdam  *SVP–Sales and Marketing* | John Cunningham  *VP–Marketing*
Terri Cunningham  *VP–Managing Editor* | Alison Gill  *VP–Manufacturing* | David Hyde  *VP–Publicity*
Sue Pohja  *VP–Book Trade Sales* | Alysse Soll  *VP–Advertising and Custom Publishing*
Bob Wayne  *VP–Sales* | Mark Chiarello  *Art Director*

SUSTAINABLE
FORESTRY
INITIATIVE
Certified Chain of Custody
Promoting Sustainable
Forest Management
www.sfiprogram.org
Fiber used in this product line meets the
sourcing requirements of the SFI program.
www.sfiprogram.org SGS-SFICOC-0130

**DC COMICS**  1700 Broadway, New York, NY 10019
A Warner Bros. Entertainment Company
Printed by Quad/Graphics, Versailles, KY, USA. 4/1/11. First printing.
HC ISBN: 978-1-4012-3083-8
SC ISBN: 978-1-4012-3084-5

Library of Congress Cataloging-in-Publication Data

Johns, Geoff, 1973-
  Brightest day volume two / writer, Geoff Johns ; pencils, Ivan Reis.
     p. cm.
  "Originally published in single magazine form in Brightest Day 8-16."
  ISBN 978-1-4012-3083-8 (hardcover)
  I. Reis, Ivan. II. Title.
  PN6727.J57B76 2011
  741.5'973--dc22
                              2011008700

BRIGHTEST DAY 8
Cover by David Finch

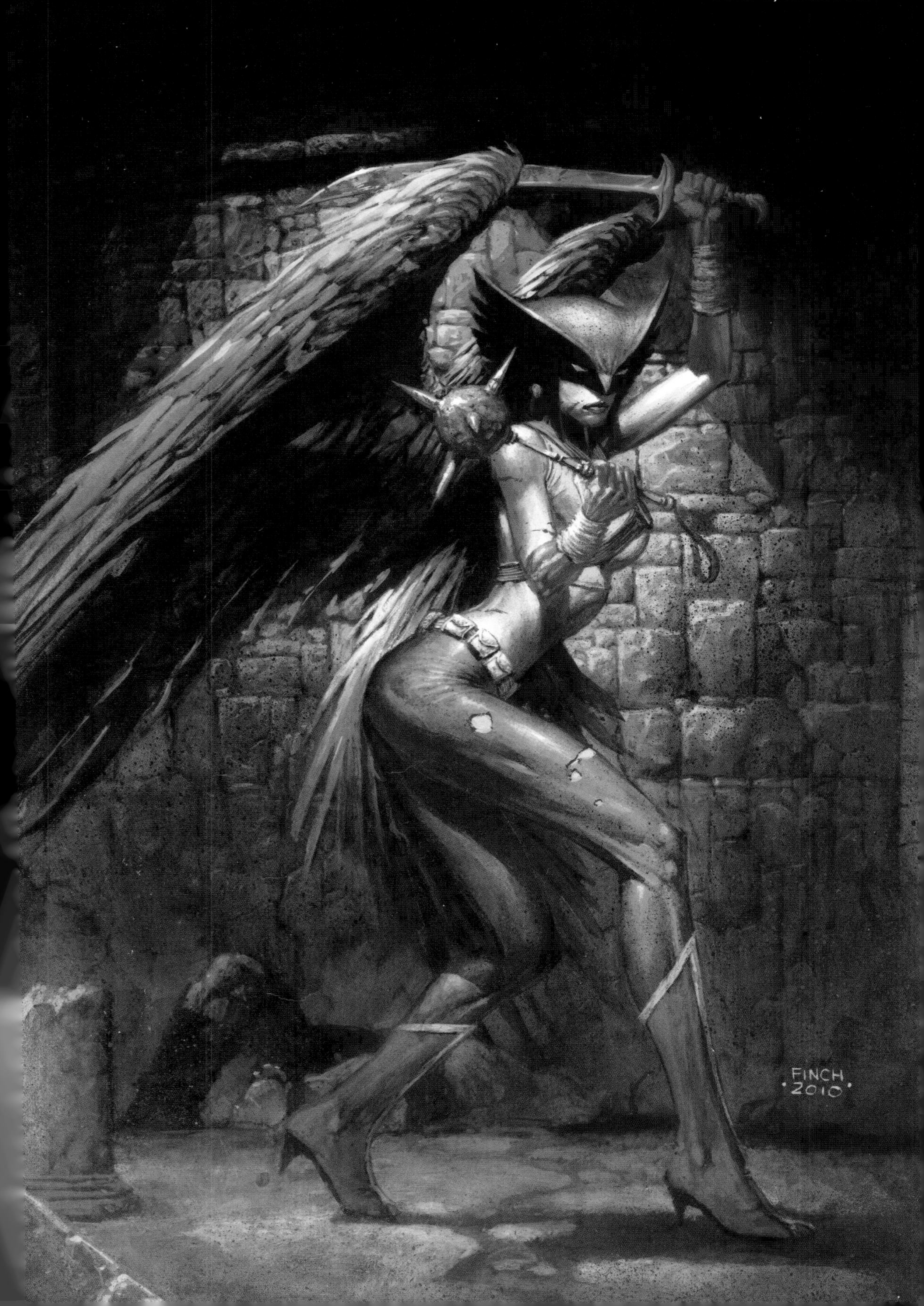
FINCH 2010

DEFIANCE

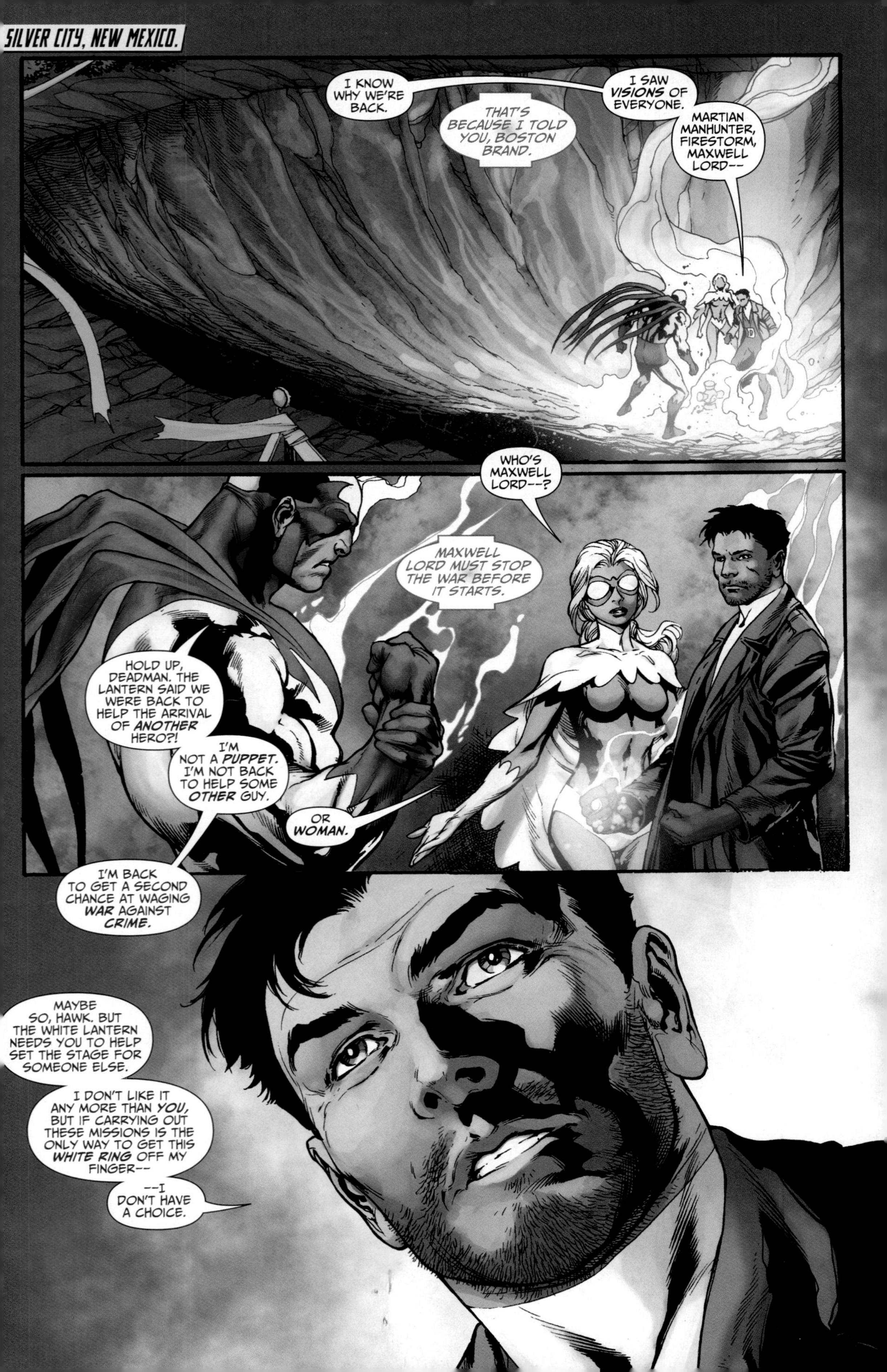
SILVER CITY, NEW MEXICO.
I KNOW WHY WE'RE BACK.
I SAW VISIONS OF EVERYONE.
THAT'S BECAUSE I TOLD YOU, BOSTON BRAND.
MARTIAN MANHUNTER, FIRESTORM, MAXWELL LORD--
WHO'S MAXWELL LORD--?
MAXWELL LORD MUST STOP THE WAR BEFORE IT STARTS.
HOLD UP, DEADMAN. THE LANTERN SAID WE WERE BACK TO HELP THE ARRIVAL OF ANOTHER HERO?!
I'M NOT A PUPPET. I'M NOT BACK TO HELP SOME OTHER GUY.
OR WOMAN.
I'M BACK TO GET A SECOND CHANCE AT WAGING WAR AGAINST CRIME.
MAYBE SO, HAWK. BUT THE WHITE LANTERN NEEDS YOU TO HELP SET THE STAGE FOR SOMEONE ELSE.
I DON'T LIKE IT ANY MORE THAN YOU, BUT IF CARRYING OUT THESE MISSIONS IS THE ONLY WAY TO GET THIS WHITE RING OFF MY FINGER--
--I DON'T HAVE A CHOICE.

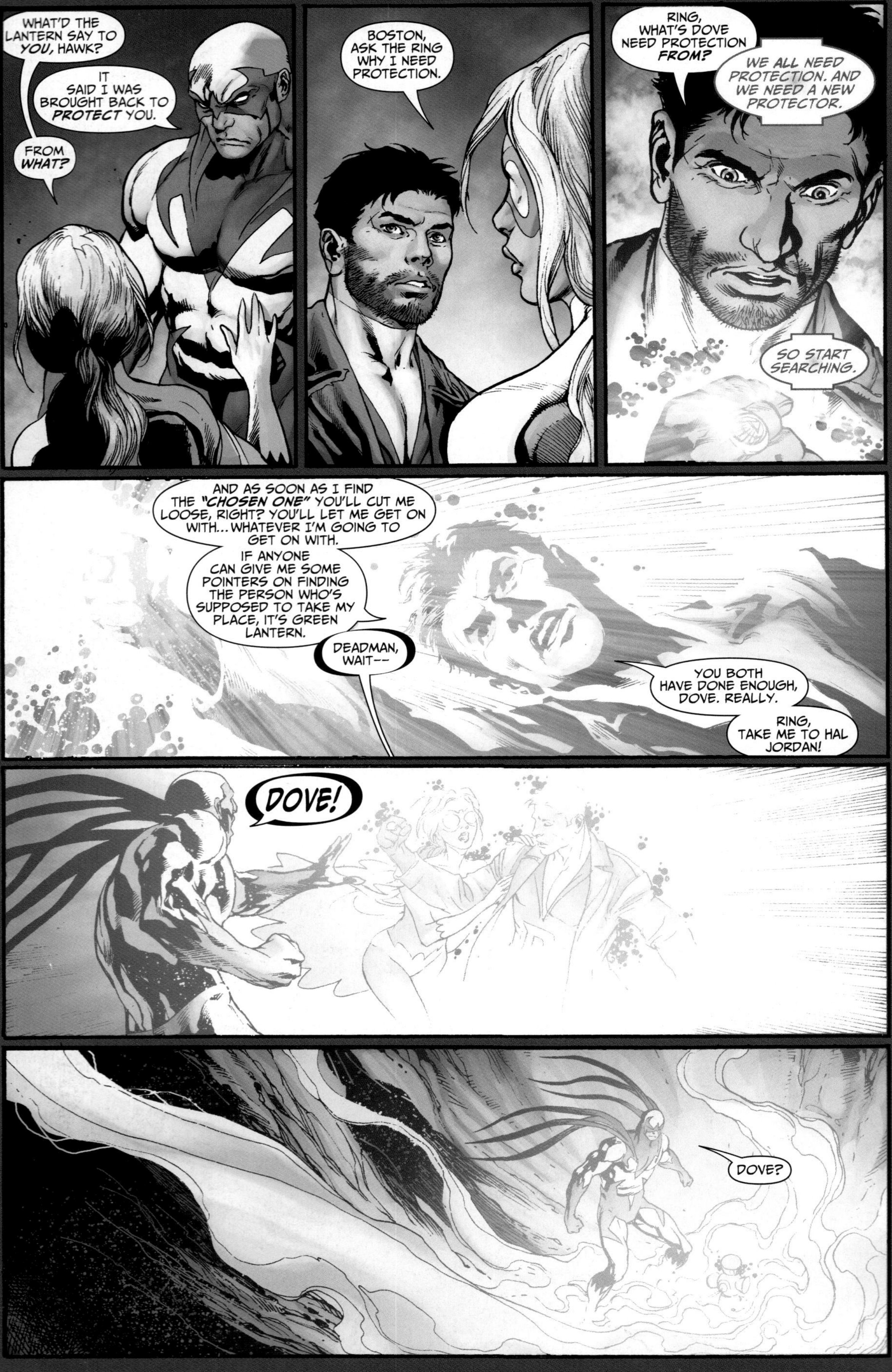
WHAT'D THE LANTERN SAY TO YOU, HAWK?
IT SAID I WAS BROUGHT BACK TO PROTECT YOU.
FROM WHAT?
BOSTON, ASK THE RING WHY I NEED PROTECTION.
RING, WHAT'S DOVE NEED PROTECTION FROM?
WE ALL NEED PROTECTION. AND WE NEED A NEW PROTECTOR.
SO START SEARCHING.
AND AS SOON AS I FIND THE "CHOSEN ONE" YOU'LL CUT ME LOOSE, RIGHT? YOU'LL LET ME GET ON WITH... WHATEVER I'M GOING TO GET ON WITH.
IF ANYONE CAN GIVE ME SOME POINTERS ON FINDING THE PERSON WHO'S SUPPOSED TO TAKE MY PLACE, IT'S GREEN LANTERN.
DEADMAN, WAIT--
YOU BOTH HAVE DONE ENOUGH, DOVE. REALLY.
RING, TAKE ME TO HAL JORDAN!
DOVE!
DOVE?

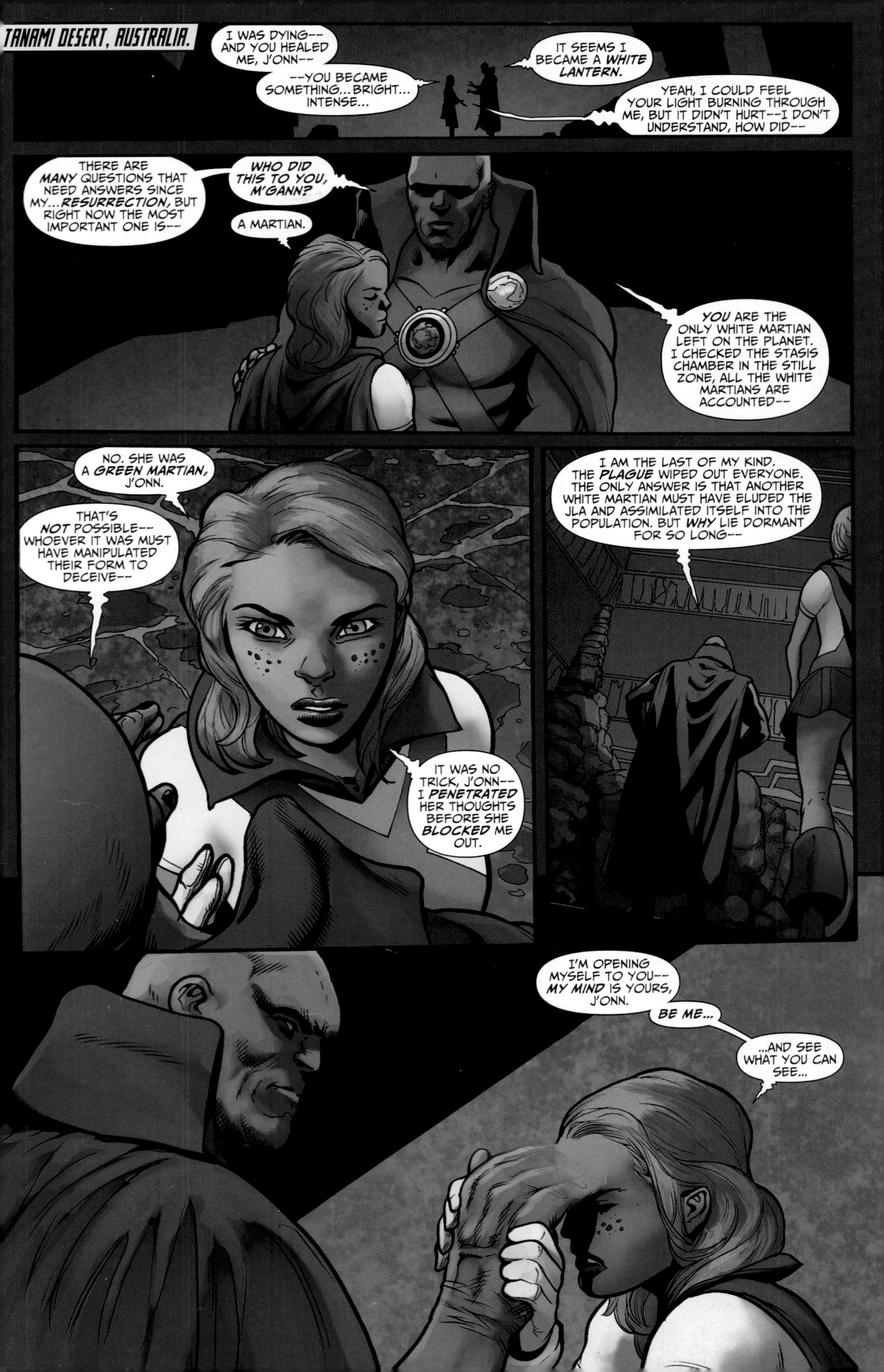
TANAMI DESERT, AUSTRALIA.
I WAS DYING-- AND YOU HEALED ME, J'ONN--
--YOU BECAME SOMETHING... BRIGHT... INTENSE...
IT SEEMS I BECAME A WHITE LANTERN.
YEAH, I COULD FEEL YOUR LIGHT BURNING THROUGH ME, BUT IT DIDN'T HURT--I DON'T UNDERSTAND, HOW DID--
THERE ARE MANY QUESTIONS THAT NEED ANSWERS SINCE MY... RESURRECTION, BUT RIGHT NOW THE MOST IMPORTANT ONE IS--
WHO DID THIS TO YOU, M'GANN?
A MARTIAN.
YOU ARE THE ONLY WHITE MARTIAN LEFT ON THE PLANET. I CHECKED THE STASIS CHAMBER IN THE STILL ZONE, ALL THE WHITE MARTIANS ARE ACCOUNTED--
NO. SHE WAS A GREEN MARTIAN, J'ONN.
THAT'S NOT POSSIBLE-- WHOEVER IT WAS MUST HAVE MANIPULATED THEIR FORM TO DECEIVE--
IT WAS NO TRICK, J'ONN-- I PENETRATED HER THOUGHTS BEFORE SHE BLOCKED ME OUT.
I AM THE LAST OF MY KIND. THE PLAGUE WIPED OUT EVERYONE. THE ONLY ANSWER IS THAT ANOTHER WHITE MARTIAN MUST HAVE ELUDED THE JLA AND ASSIMILATED ITSELF INTO THE POPULATION. BUT WHY LIE DORMANT FOR SO LONG--
I'M OPENING MYSELF TO YOU-- MY MIND IS YOURS, J'ONN.
BE ME...
...AND SEE WHAT YOU CAN SEE...

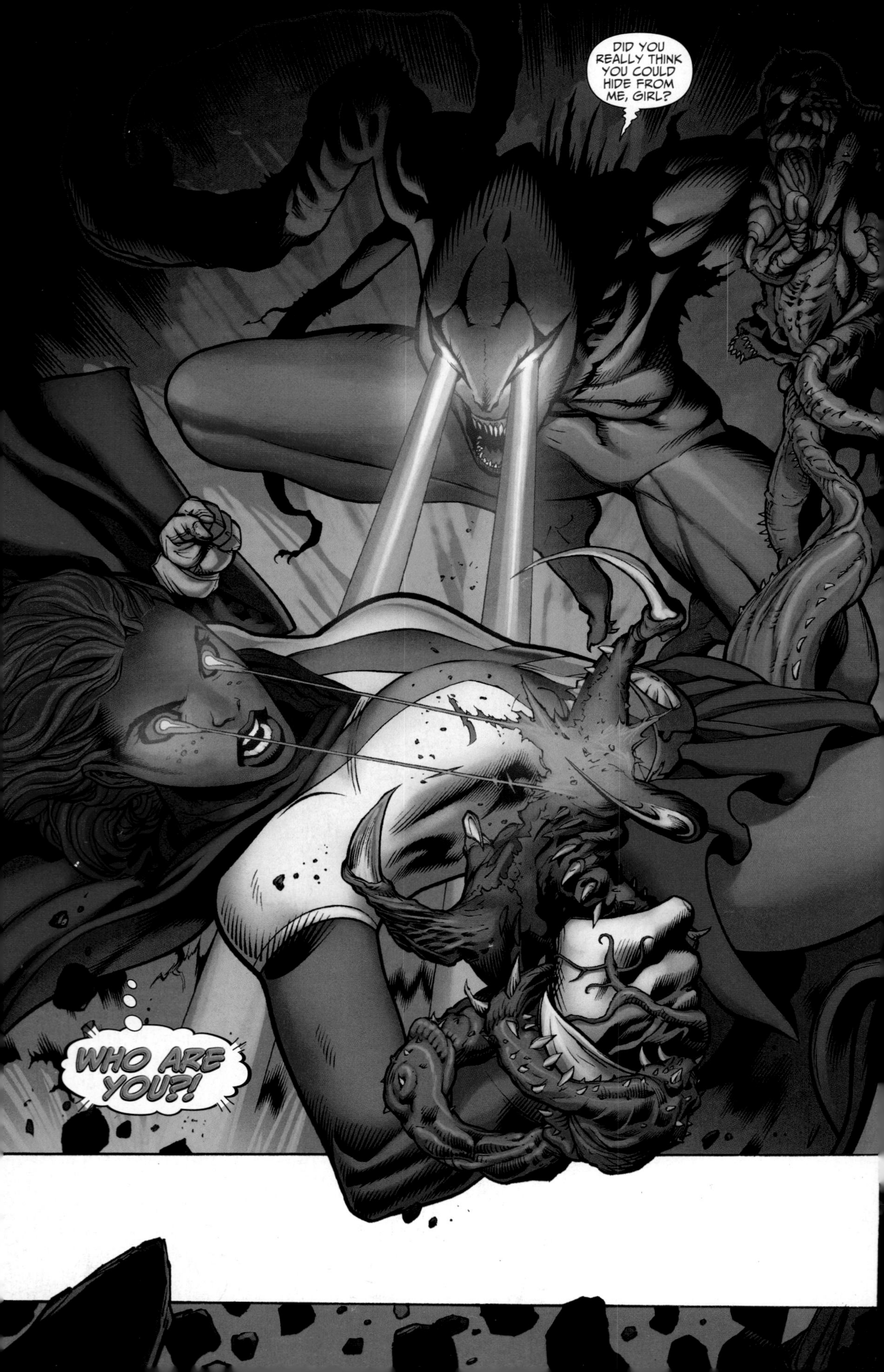
DID YOU REALLY THINK YOU COULD HIDE FROM ME, GIRL?
WHO ARE YOU?!

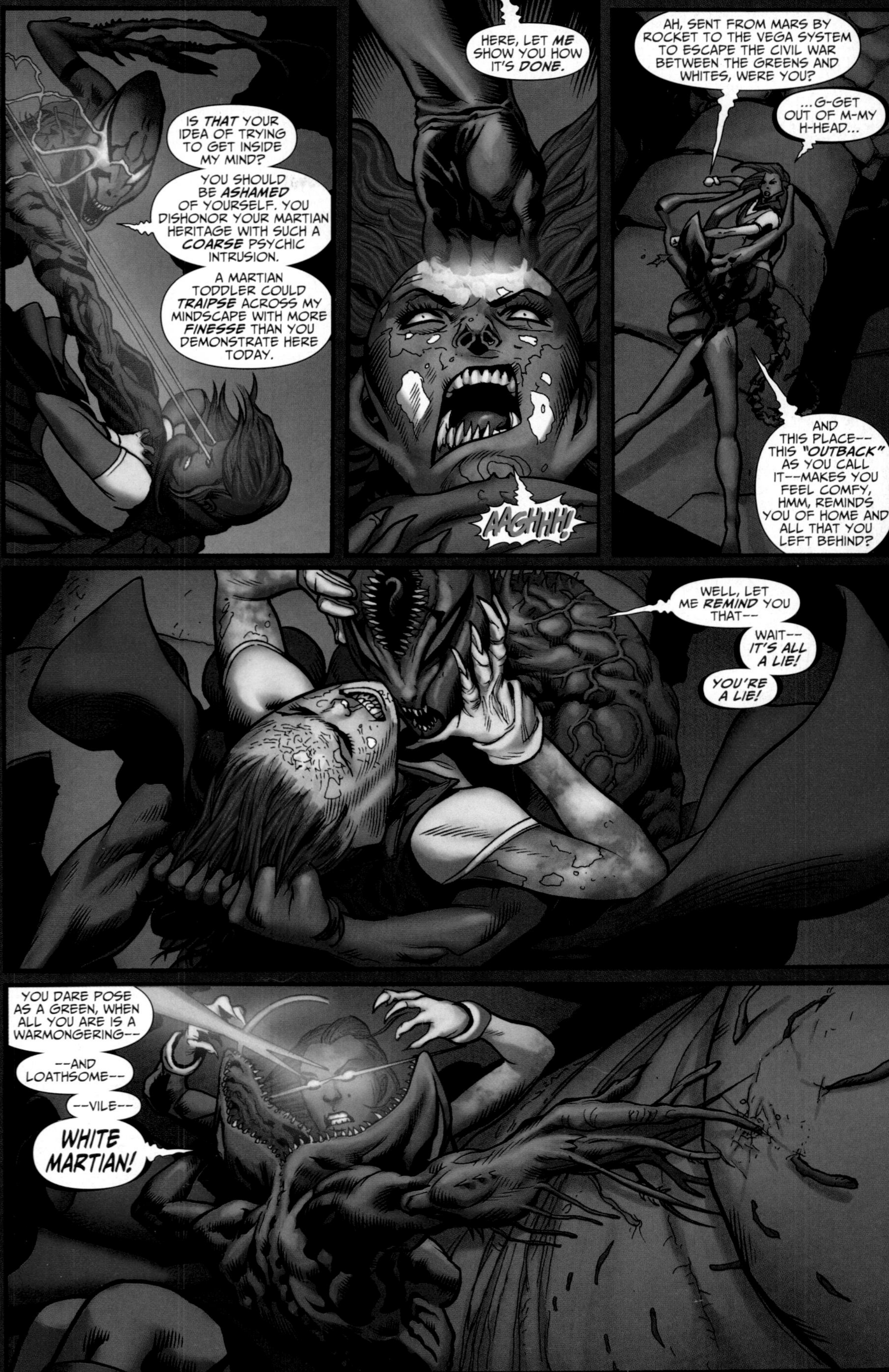
IS THAT YOUR IDEA OF TRYING TO GET INSIDE MY MIND?
YOU SHOULD BE ASHAMED OF YOURSELF. YOU DISHONOR YOUR MARTIAN HERITAGE WITH SUCH A COARSE PSYCHIC INTRUSION.
A MARTIAN TODDLER COULD TRAIPSE ACROSS MY MINDSCAPE WITH MORE FINESSE THAN YOU DEMONSTRATE HERE TODAY.
HERE, LET ME SHOW YOU HOW IT'S DONE.
AAGHHH!
AH, SENT FROM MARS BY ROCKET TO THE VEGA SYSTEM TO ESCAPE THE CIVIL WAR BETWEEN THE GREENS AND WHITES, WERE YOU?
...G-GET OUT OF M-MY H-HEAD...
AND THIS PLACE-- THIS "OUTBACK" AS YOU CALL IT--MAKES YOU FEEL COMFY, HMM, REMINDS YOU OF HOME AND ALL THAT YOU LEFT BEHIND?
WELL, LET ME REMIND YOU THAT--
WAIT-- IT'S ALL A LIE!
YOU'RE A LIE!
YOU DARE POSE AS A GREEN, WHEN ALL YOU ARE IS A WARMONGERING--
--AND LOATHSOME--
--VILE--
WHITE MARTIAN!

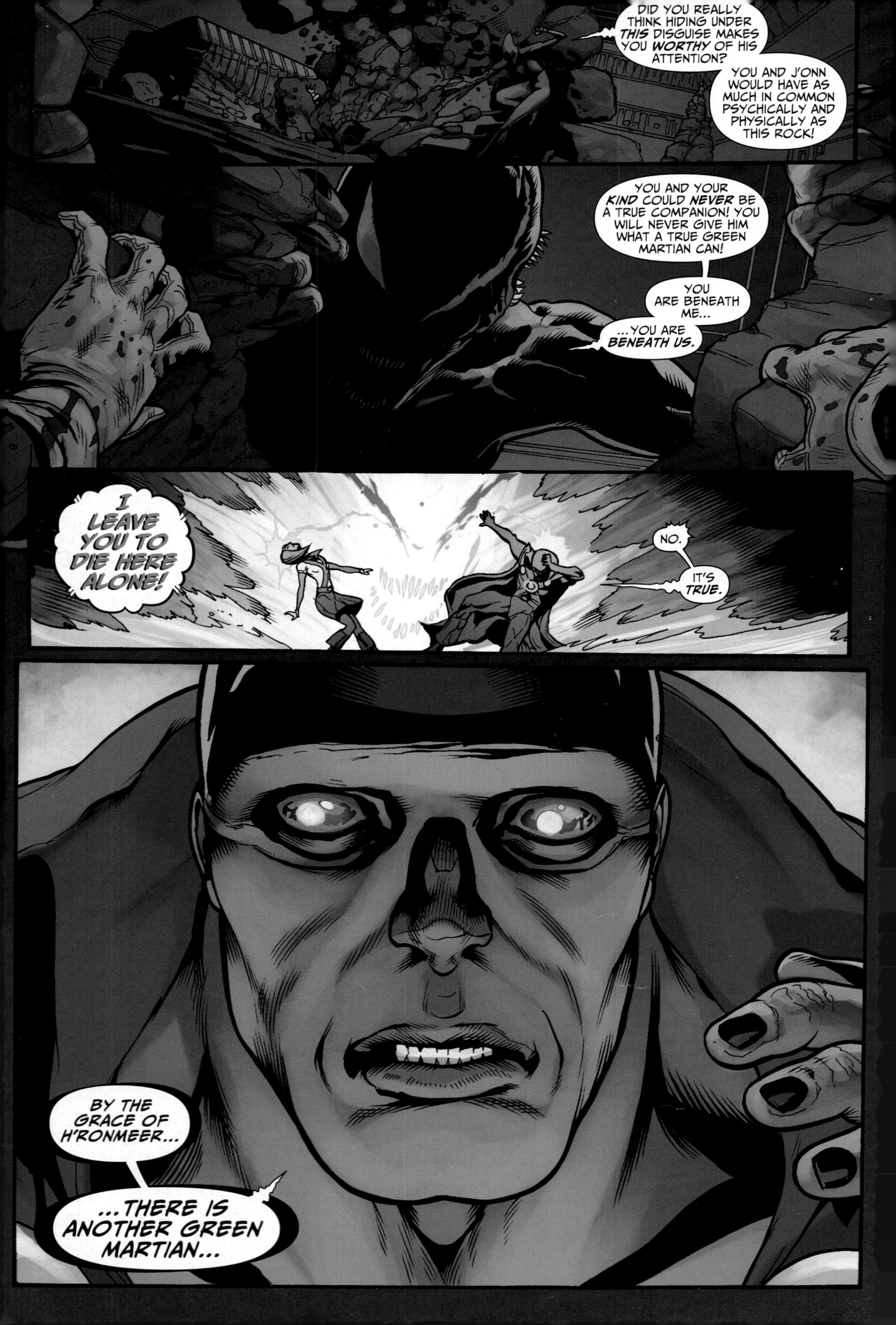
DID YOU REALLY THINK HIDING UNDER *THIS* DISGUISE MAKES YOU *WORTHY* OF HIS ATTENTION?
YOU AND J'ONN WOULD HAVE AS MUCH IN COMMON PSYCHICALLY AND PHYSICALLY AS THIS ROCK!
YOU AND YOUR *KIND* COULD *NEVER* BE A TRUE COMPANION! YOU WILL NEVER GIVE HIM WHAT A TRUE GREEN MARTIAN CAN!
YOU ARE BENEATH ME...
...YOU ARE *BENEATH US.*
I LEAVE YOU TO DIE HERE ALONE!
NO.
IT'S *TRUE.*
BY THE GRACE OF H'RONMEER...
...THERE IS ANOTHER GREEN MARTIAN...

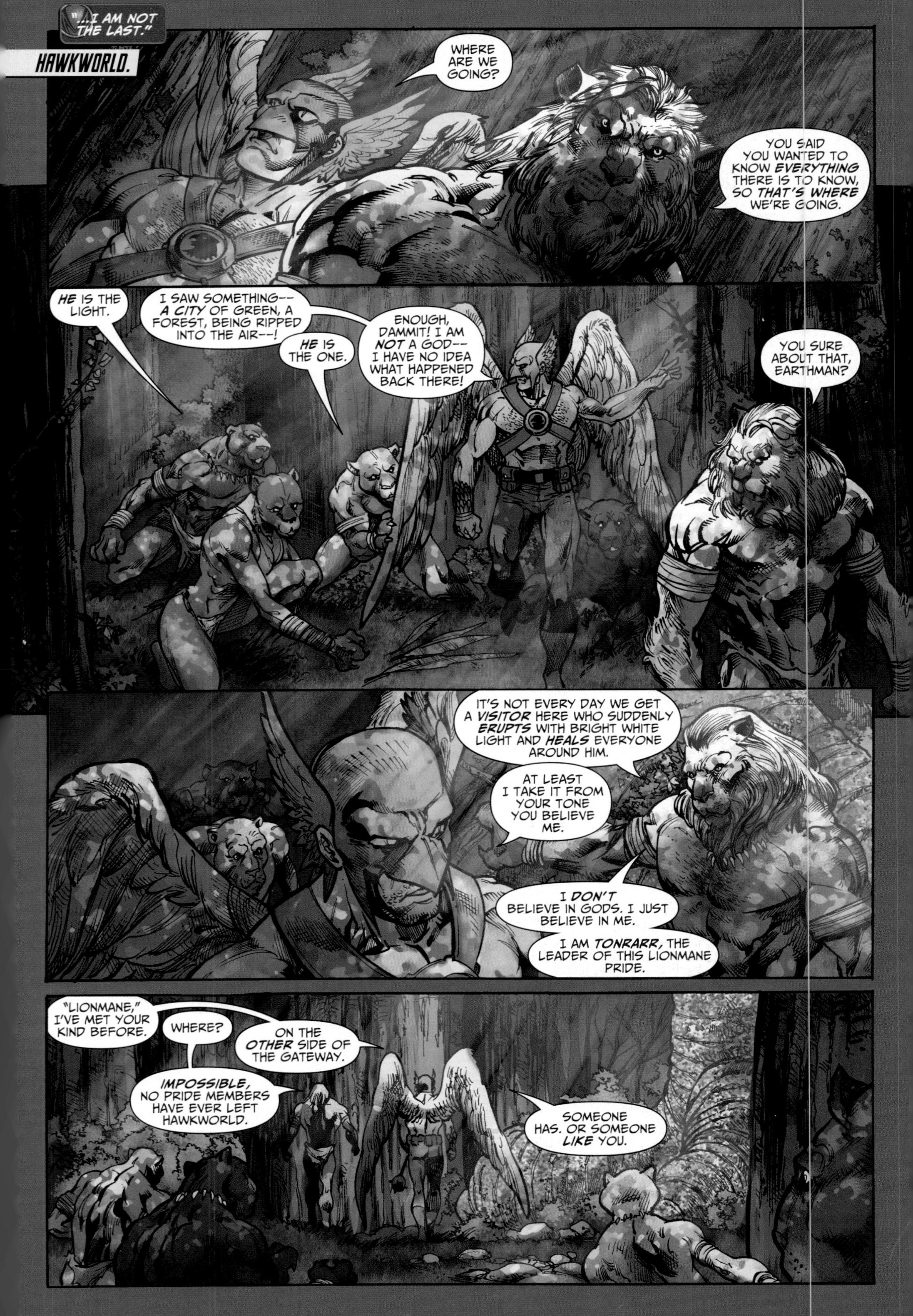
"...I AM NOT THE LAST."
HAWKWORLD.
WHERE ARE WE GOING?
YOU SAID YOU WANTED TO KNOW EVERYTHING THERE IS TO KNOW, SO THAT'S WHERE WE'RE GOING.
HE IS THE LIGHT.
I SAW SOMETHING-- A CITY OF GREEN, A FOREST, BEING RIPPED INTO THE AIR--!
HE IS THE ONE.
ENOUGH, DAMMIT! I AM NOT A GOD-- I HAVE NO IDEA WHAT HAPPENED BACK THERE!
YOU SURE ABOUT THAT, EARTHMAN?
IT'S NOT EVERY DAY WE GET A VISITOR HERE WHO SUDDENLY ERUPTS WITH BRIGHT WHITE LIGHT AND HEALS EVERYONE AROUND HIM.
AT LEAST I TAKE IT FROM YOUR TONE YOU BELIEVE ME.
I DON'T BELIEVE IN GODS. I JUST BELIEVE IN ME.
I AM TONRARR, THE LEADER OF THIS LIONMANE PRIDE.
"LIONMANE," I'VE MET YOUR KIND BEFORE.
WHERE?
ON THE OTHER SIDE OF THE GATEWAY.
IMPOSSIBLE, NO PRIDE MEMBERS HAVE EVER LEFT HAWKWORLD.
SOMEONE HAS. OR SOMEONE LIKE YOU.

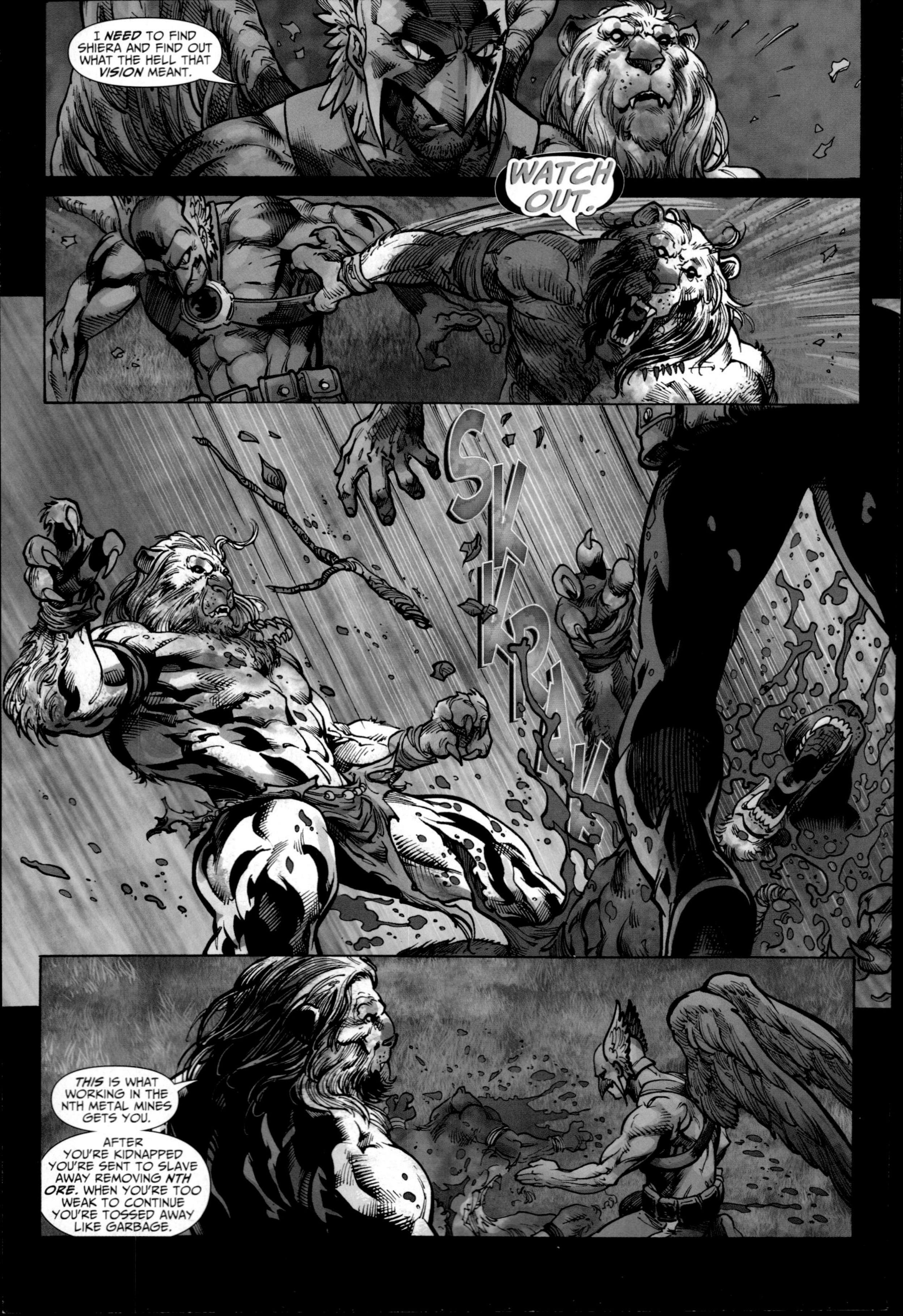
I NEED TO FIND SHIERA AND FIND OUT WHAT THE HELL THAT VISION MEANT.
WATCH OUT.
SKRAK
THIS IS WHAT WORKING IN THE NTH METAL MINES GETS YOU.
AFTER YOU'RE KIDNAPPED YOU'RE SENT TO SLAVE AWAY REMOVING NTH ORE. WHEN YOU'RE TOO WEAK TO CONTINUE YOU'RE TOSSED AWAY LIKE GARBAGE.

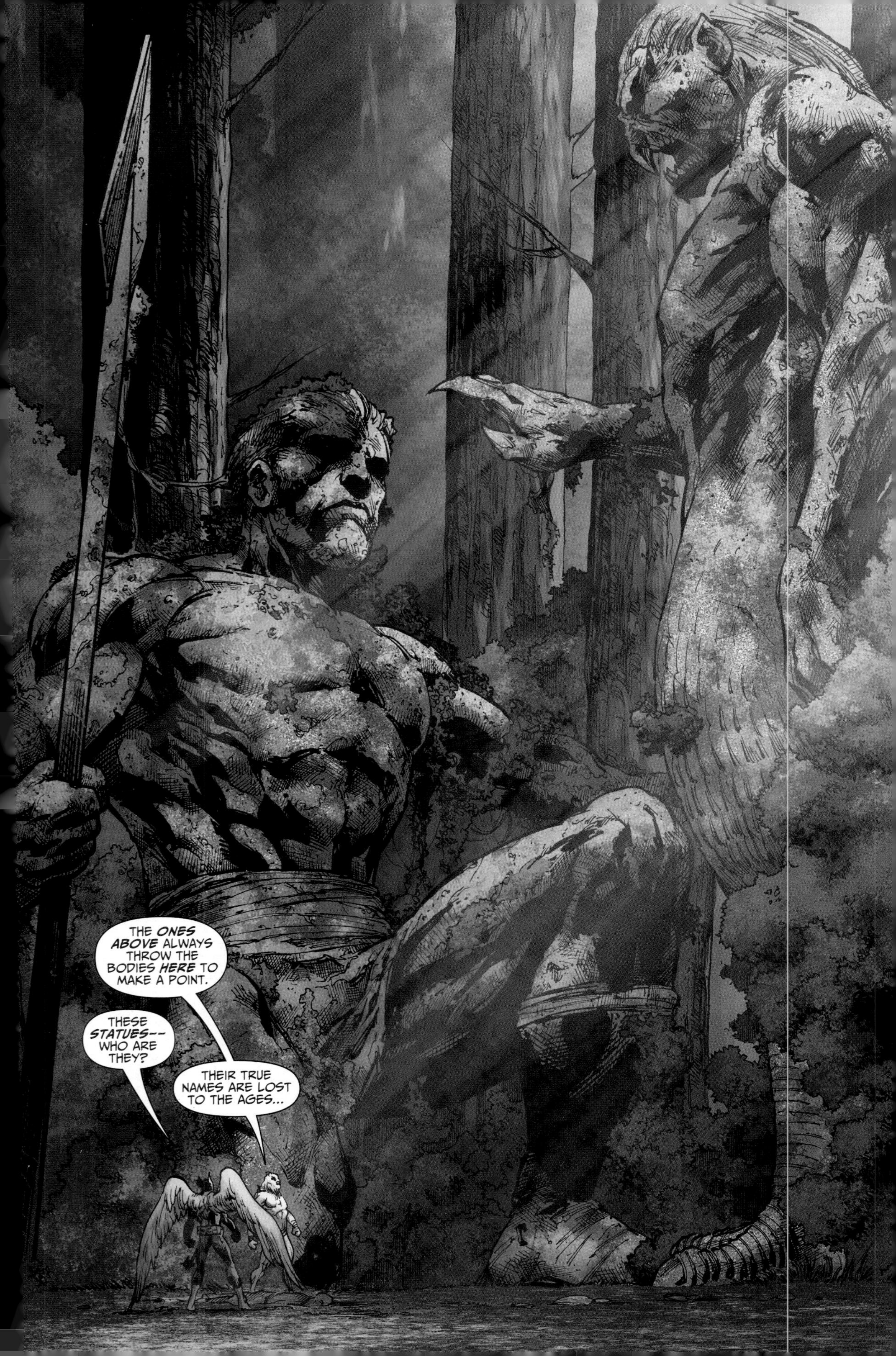
THE ONES ABOVE ALWAYS THROW THE BODIES HERE TO MAKE A POINT.
THESE STATUES-- WHO ARE THEY?
THEIR TRUE NAMES ARE LOST TO THE AGES...

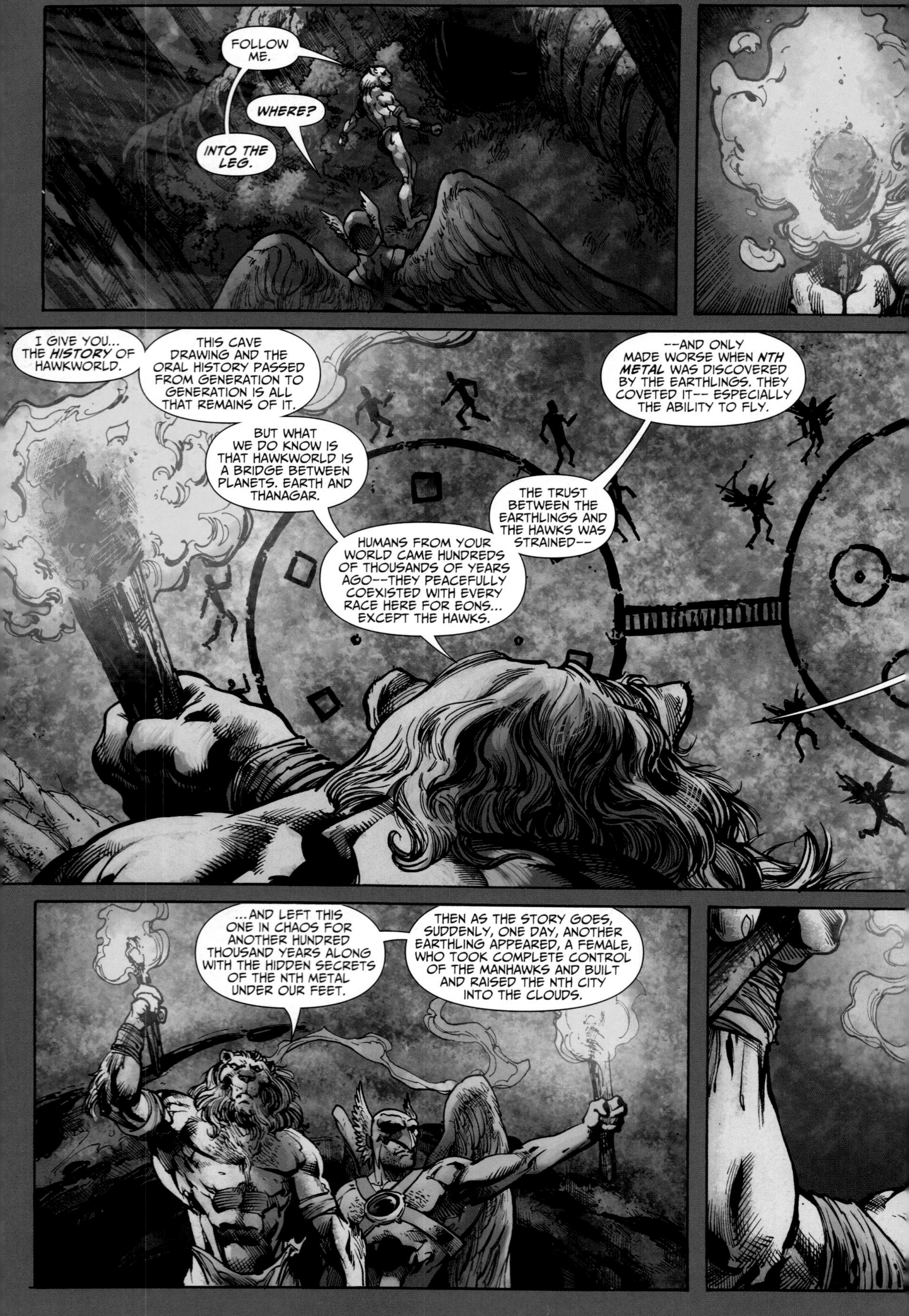
FOLLOW ME.
WHERE?
INTO THE LEG.
I GIVE YOU... THE HISTORY OF HAWKWORLD.
THIS CAVE DRAWING AND THE ORAL HISTORY PASSED FROM GENERATION TO GENERATION IS ALL THAT REMAINS OF IT.
BUT WHAT WE DO KNOW IS THAT HAWKWORLD IS A BRIDGE BETWEEN PLANETS. EARTH AND THANAGAR.
HUMANS FROM YOUR WORLD CAME HUNDREDS OF THOUSANDS OF YEARS AGO--THEY PEACEFULLY COEXISTED WITH EVERY RACE HERE FOR EONS... EXCEPT THE HAWKS.
THE TRUST BETWEEN THE EARTHLINGS AND THE HAWKS WAS STRAINED--
--AND ONLY MADE WORSE WHEN NTH METAL WAS DISCOVERED BY THE EARTHLINGS. THEY COVETED IT-- ESPECIALLY THE ABILITY TO FLY.
...AND LEFT THIS ONE IN CHAOS FOR ANOTHER HUNDRED THOUSAND YEARS ALONG WITH THE HIDDEN SECRETS OF THE NTH METAL UNDER OUR FEET.
THEN AS THE STORY GOES, SUDDENLY, ONE DAY, ANOTHER EARTHLING APPEARED, A FEMALE, WHO TOOK COMPLETE CONTROL OF THE MANHAWKS AND BUILT AND RAISED THE NTH CITY INTO THE CLOUDS.

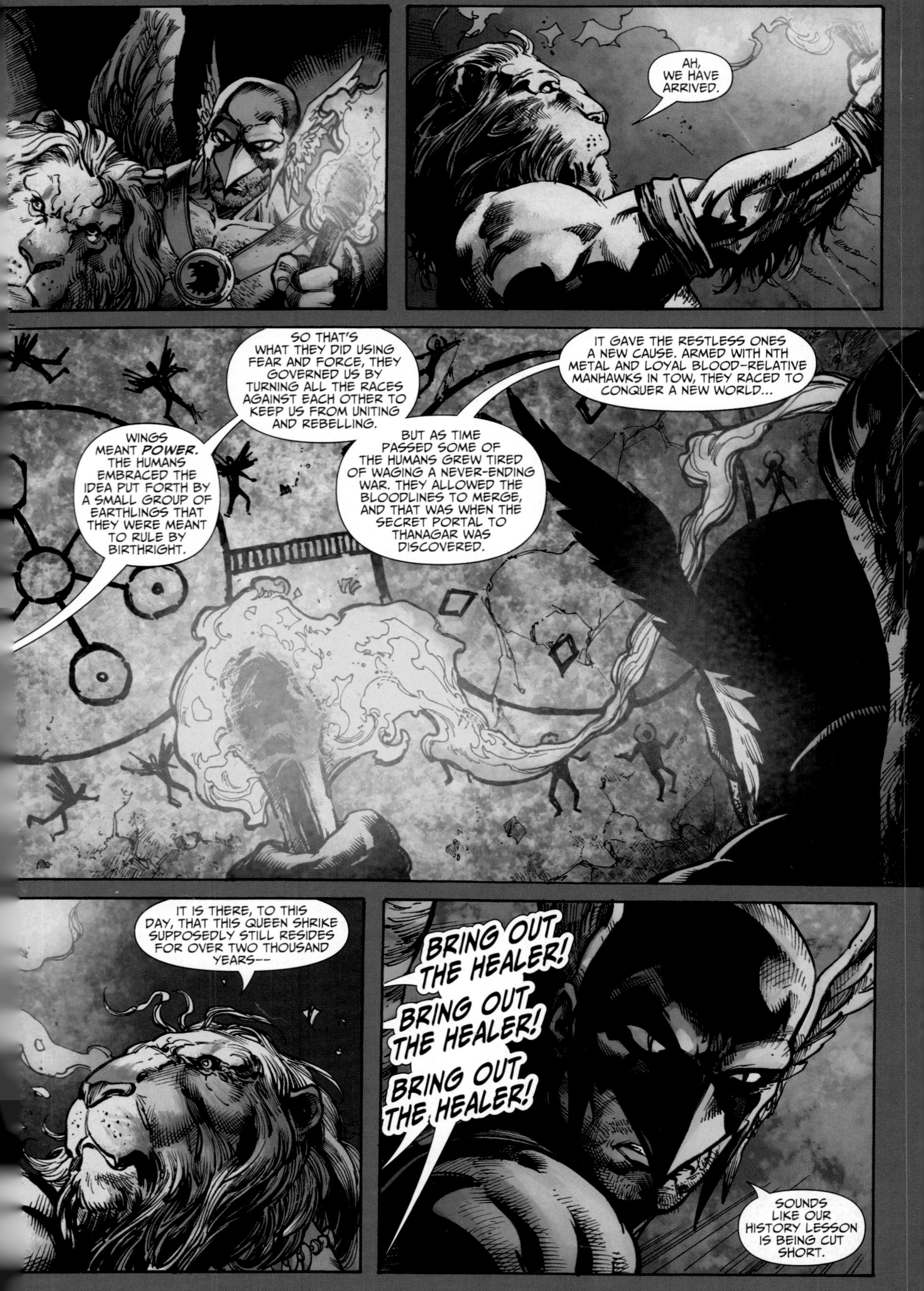
AH, WE HAVE ARRIVED.
WINGS MEANT POWER. THE HUMANS EMBRACED THE IDEA PUT FORTH BY A SMALL GROUP OF EARTHLINGS THAT THEY WERE MEANT TO RULE BY BIRTHRIGHT.
SO THAT'S WHAT THEY DID USING FEAR AND FORCE, THEY GOVERNED US BY TURNING ALL THE RACES AGAINST EACH OTHER TO KEEP US FROM UNITING AND REBELLING.
BUT AS TIME PASSED SOME OF THE HUMANS GREW TIRED OF WAGING A NEVER-ENDING WAR. THEY ALLOWED THE BLOODLINES TO MERGE, AND THAT WAS WHEN THE SECRET PORTAL TO THANAGAR WAS DISCOVERED.
IT GAVE THE RESTLESS ONES A NEW CAUSE. ARMED WITH NTH METAL AND LOYAL BLOOD-RELATIVE MANHAWKS IN TOW, THEY RACED TO CONQUER A NEW WORLD...
IT IS THERE, TO THIS DAY, THAT THIS QUEEN SHRIKE SUPPOSEDLY STILL RESIDES FOR OVER TWO THOUSAND YEARS--
BRING OUT THE HEALER!
BRING OUT THE HEALER!
BRING OUT THE HEALER!
SOUNDS LIKE OUR HISTORY LESSON IS BEING CUT SHORT.

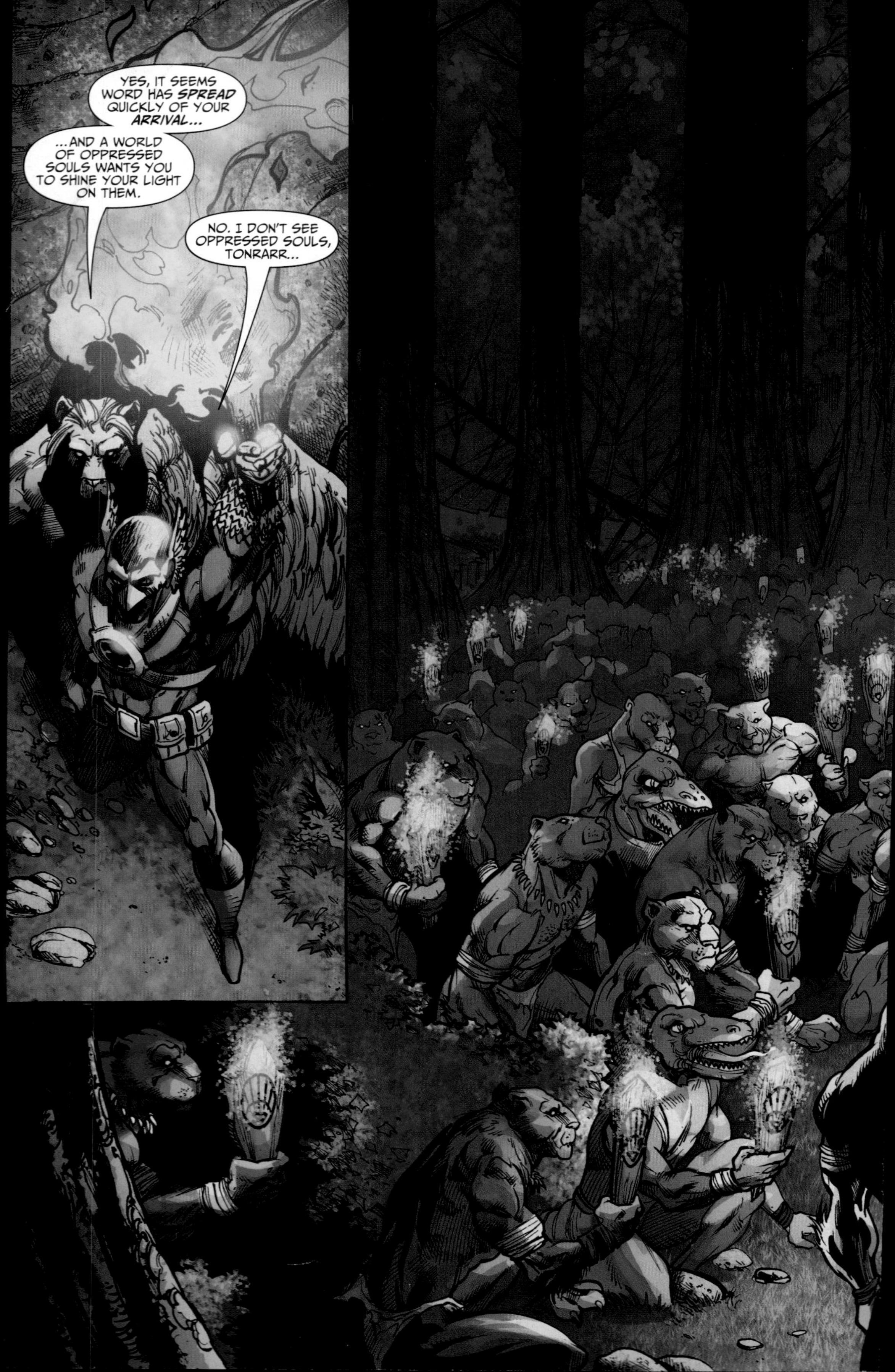
YES, IT SEEMS WORD HAS SPREAD QUICKLY OF YOUR ARRIVAL...
...AND A WORLD OF OPPRESSED SOULS WANTS YOU TO SHINE YOUR LIGHT ON THEM.
NO. I DON'T SEE OPPRESSED SOULS, TONRARR...

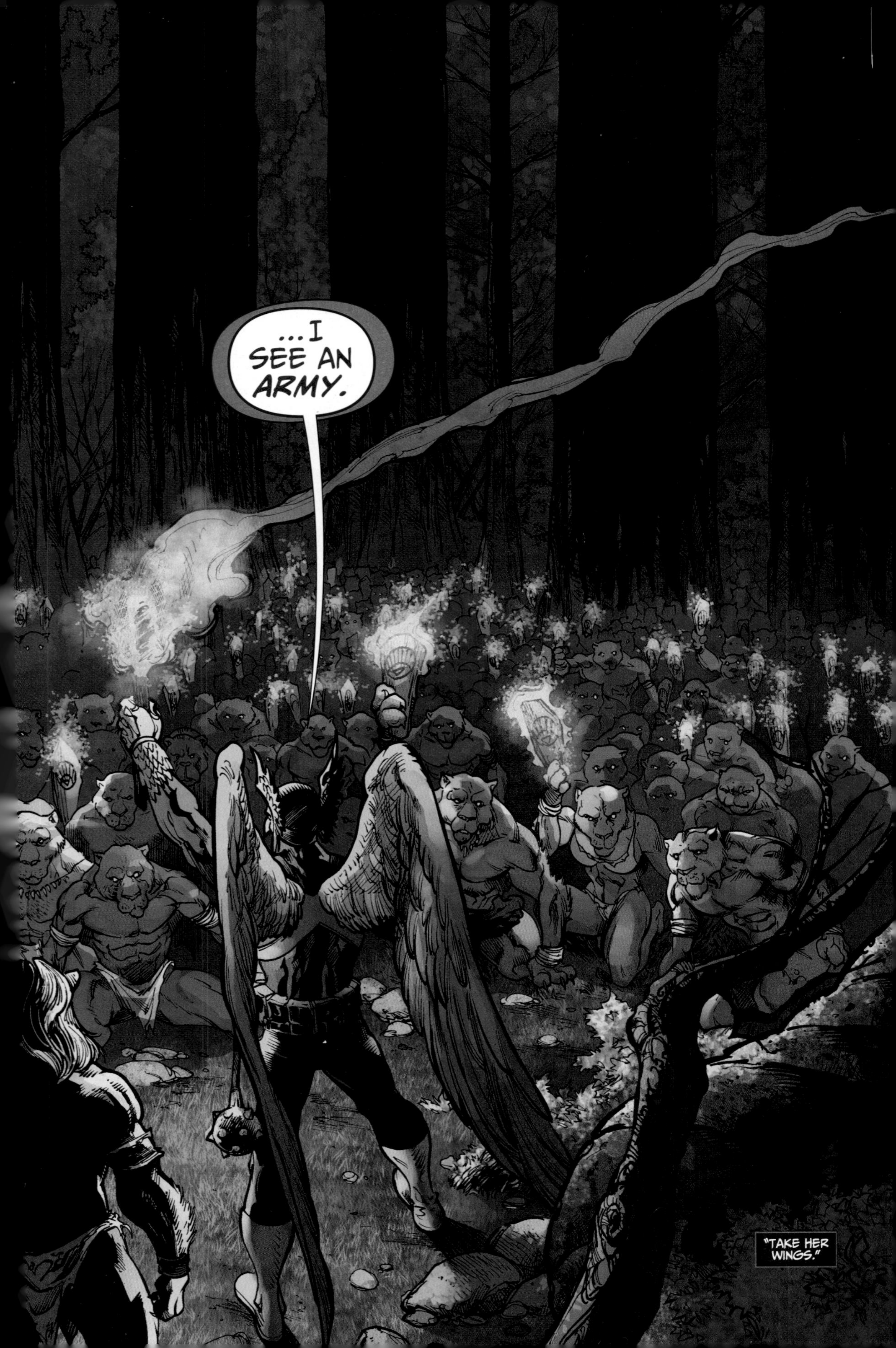
...I SEE AN ARMY.
"TAKE HER WINGS."

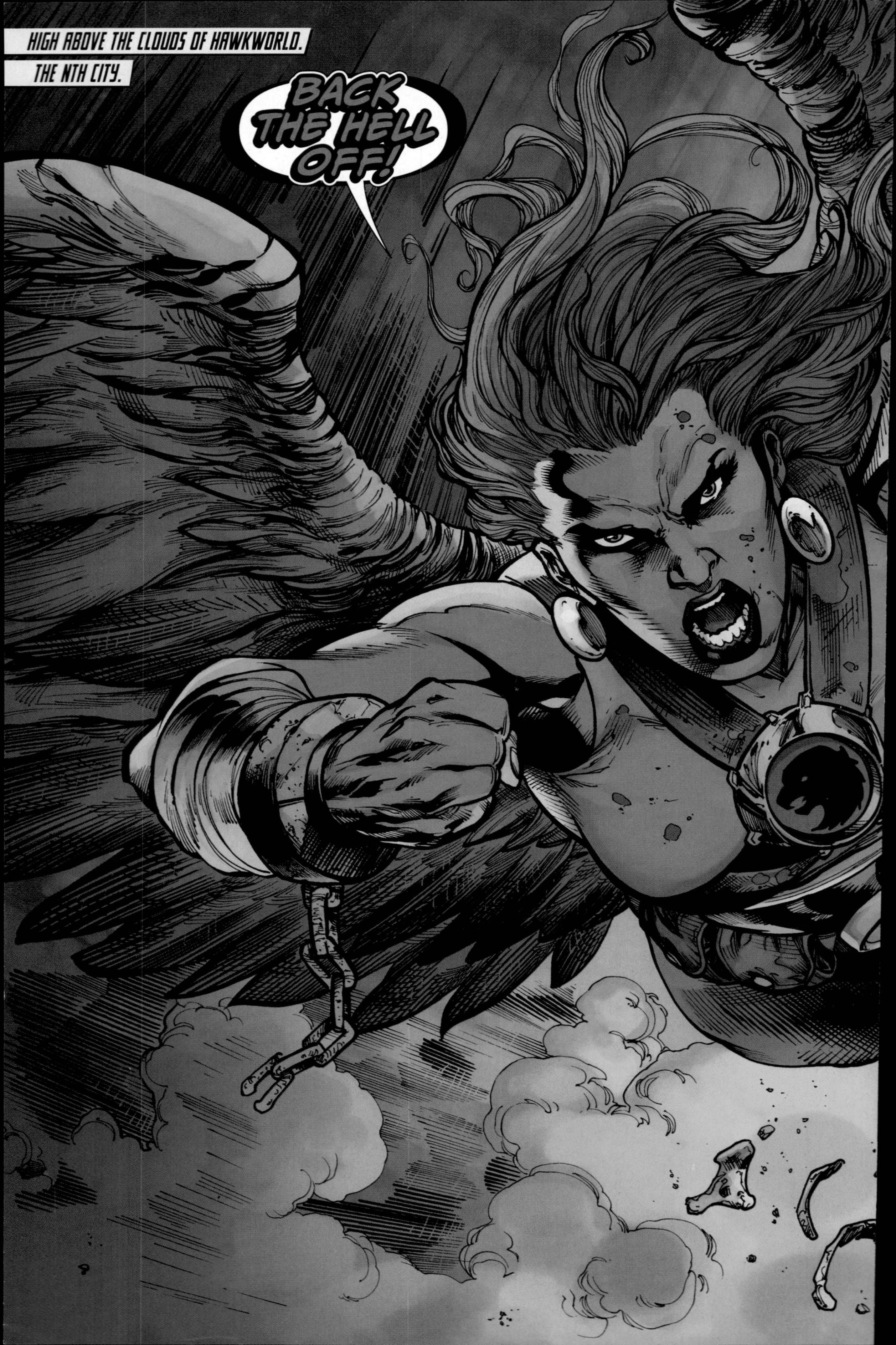
HIGH ABOVE THE CLOUDS OF HAWKWORLD.
THE NTH CITY.
BACK THE HELL OFF!

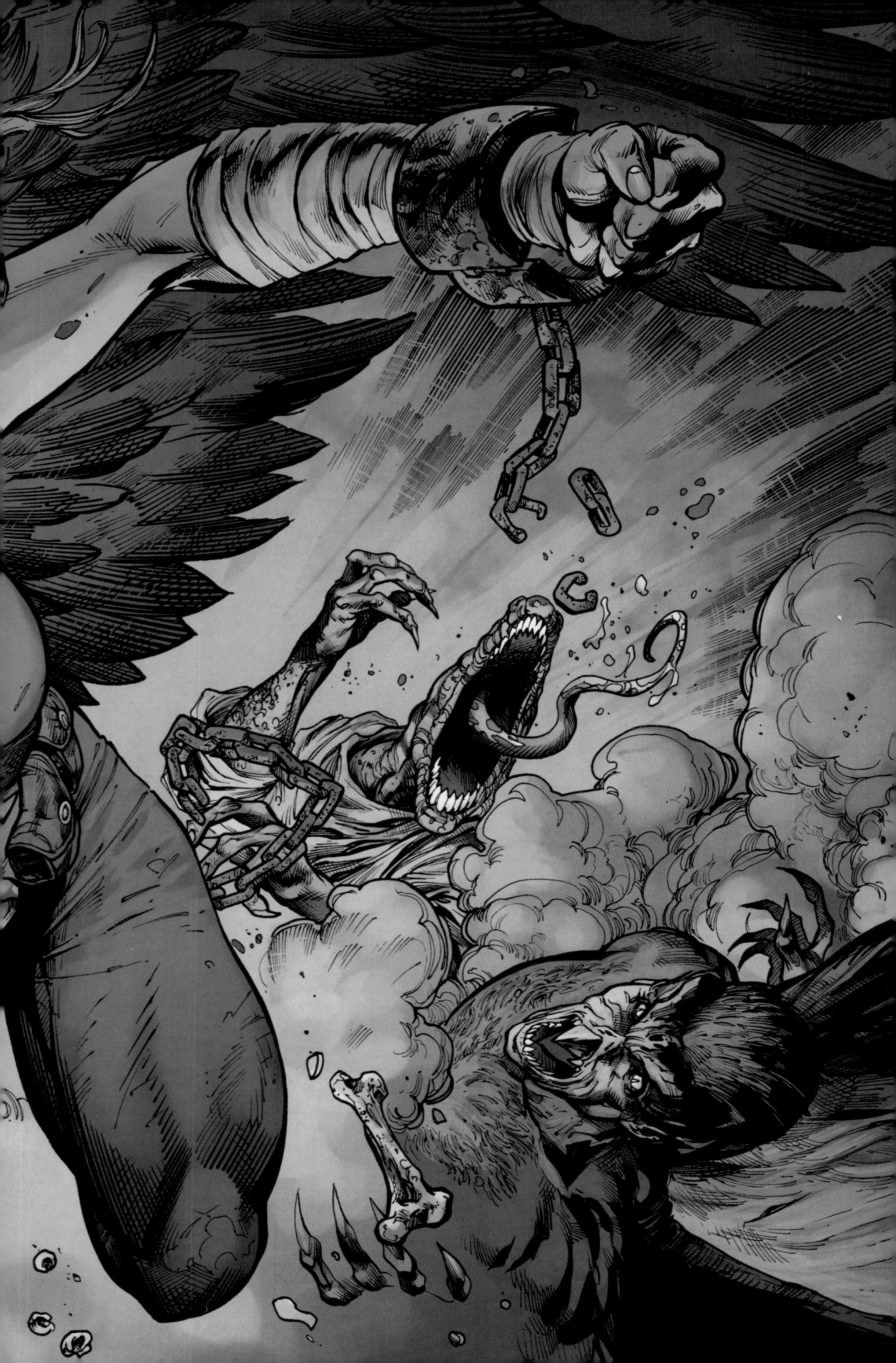

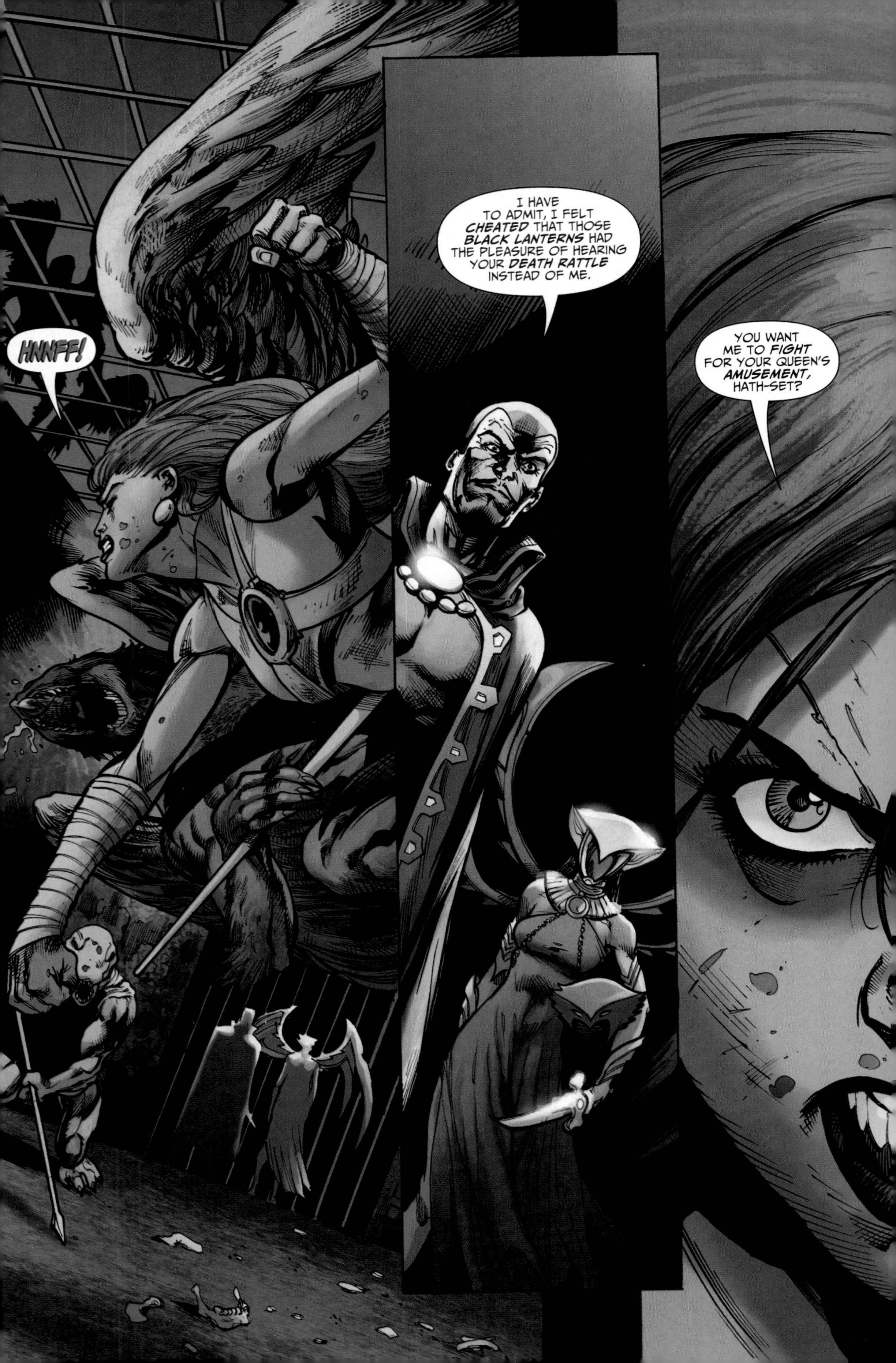
HNNFF!
I HAVE TO ADMIT, I FELT CHEATED THAT THOSE BLACK LANTERNS HAD THE PLEASURE OF HEARING YOUR DEATH RATTLE INSTEAD OF ME.
YOU WANT ME TO FIGHT FOR YOUR QUEEN'S AMUSEMENT, HATH-SET?

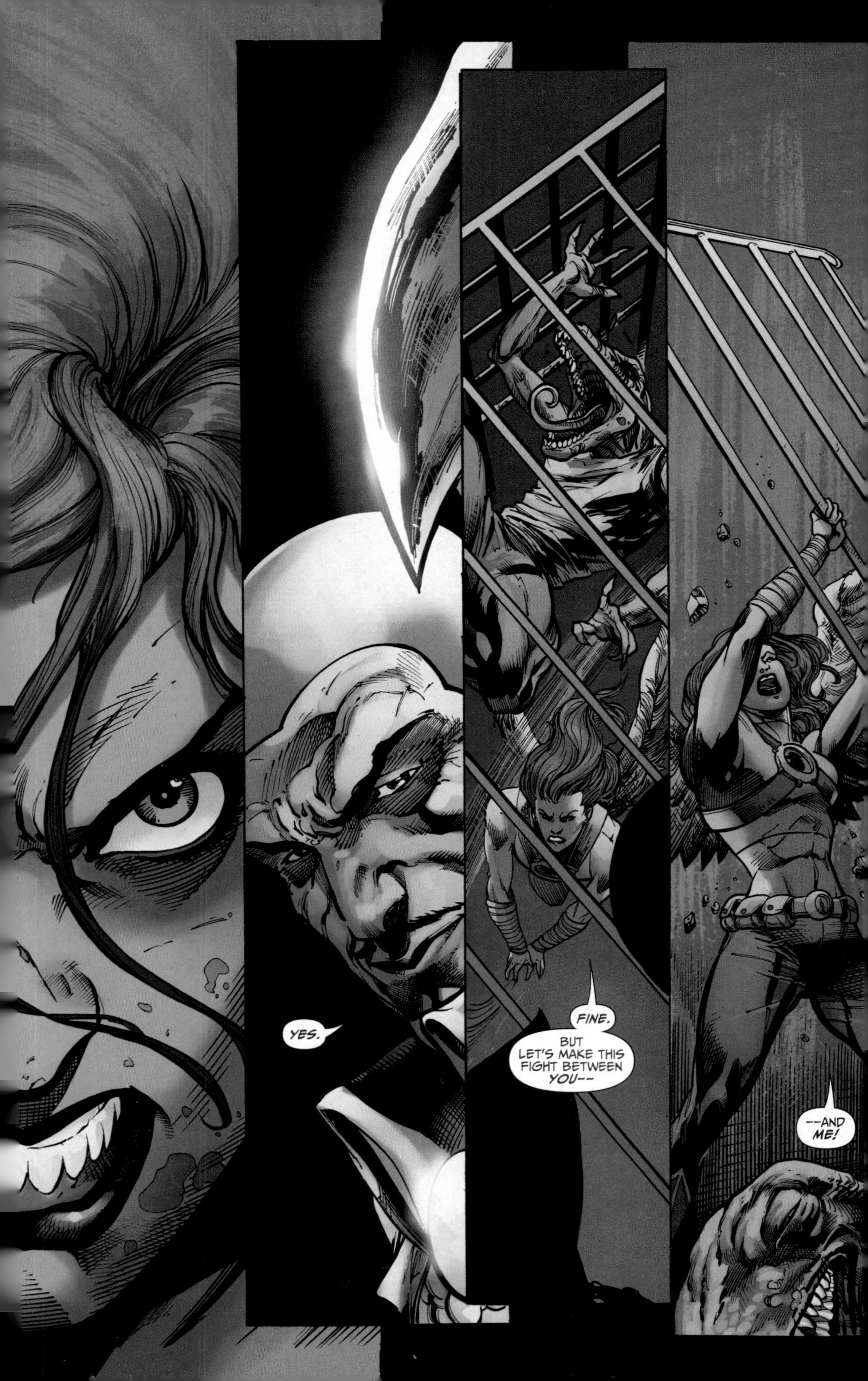
YES.
FINE.
BUT LET'S MAKE THIS FIGHT BETWEEN YOU--
--AND ME!

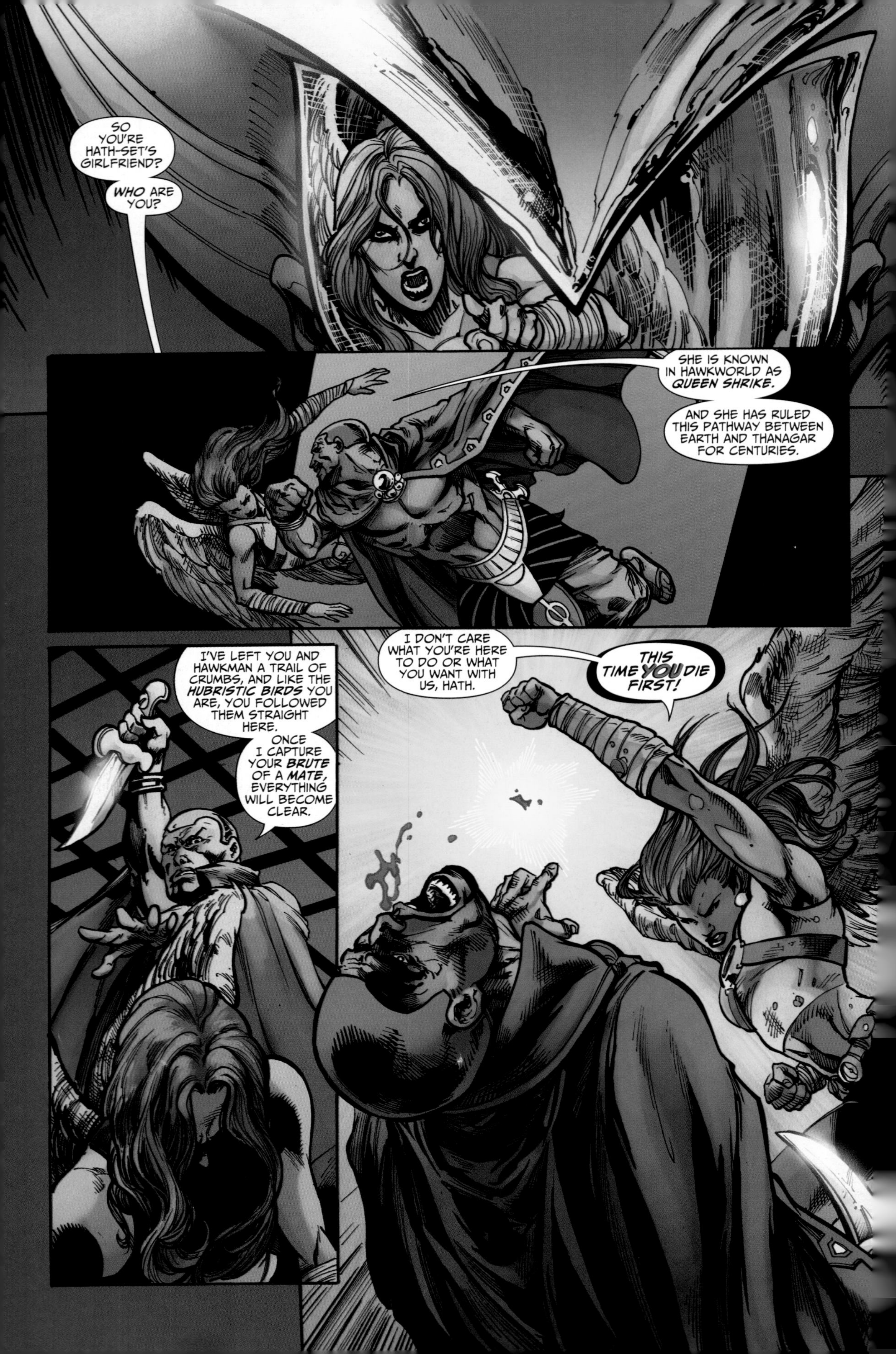
SO YOU'RE HATH-SET'S GIRLFRIEND?
WHO ARE YOU?
SHE IS KNOWN IN HAWKWORLD AS QUEEN SHRIKE.
AND SHE HAS RULED THIS PATHWAY BETWEEN EARTH AND THANAGAR FOR CENTURIES.
I'VE LEFT YOU AND HAWKMAN A TRAIL OF CRUMBS, AND LIKE THE HUBRISTIC BIRDS YOU ARE, YOU FOLLOWED THEM STRAIGHT HERE.
ONCE I CAPTURE YOUR BRUTE OF A MATE, EVERYTHING WILL BECOME CLEAR.
I DON'T CARE WHAT YOU'RE HERE TO DO OR WHAT YOU WANT WITH US, HATH.
THIS TIME YOU DIE FIRST!

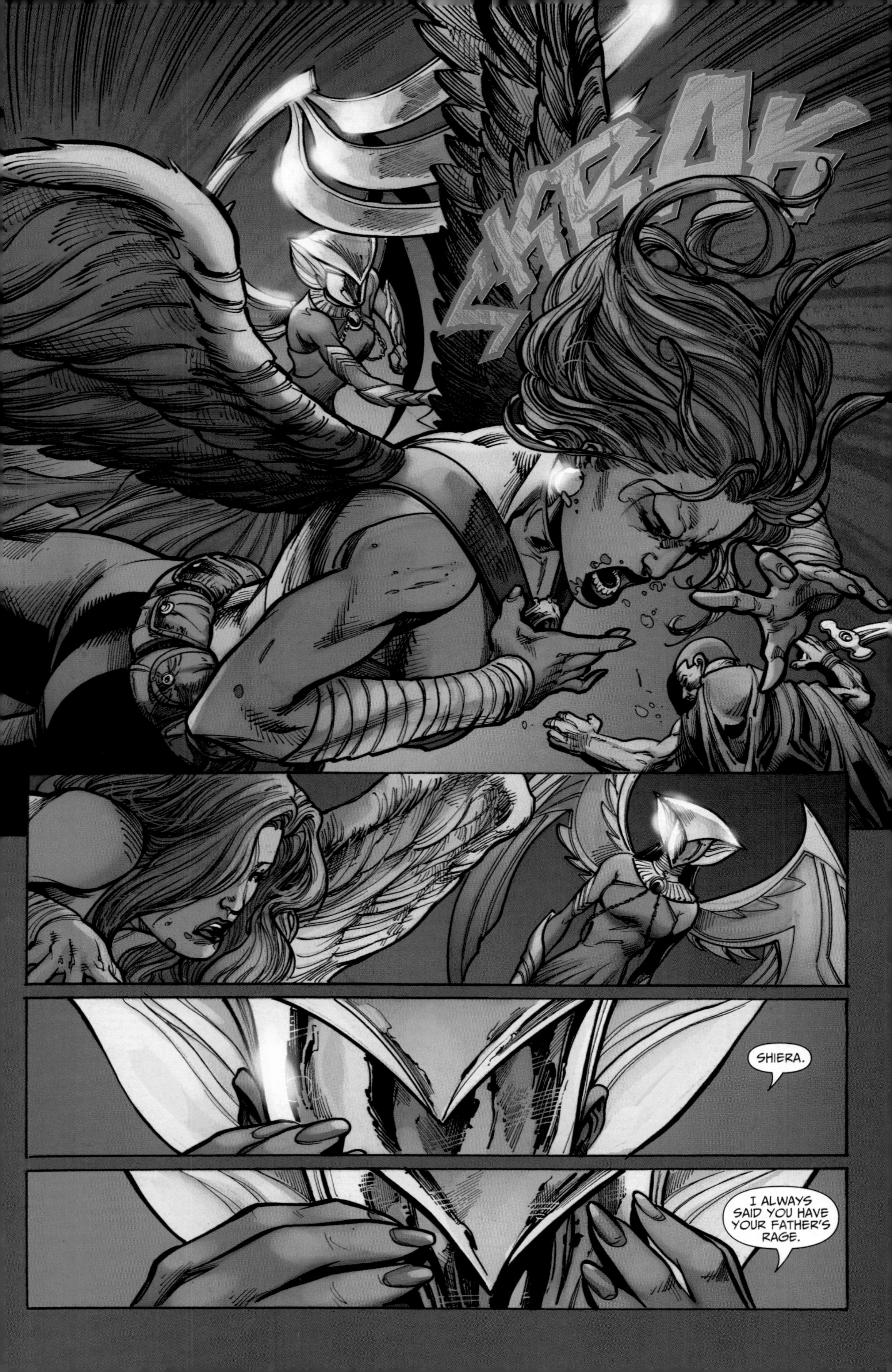
SKRAK
SHIERA.
I ALWAYS SAID YOU HAVE YOUR FATHER'S RAGE.

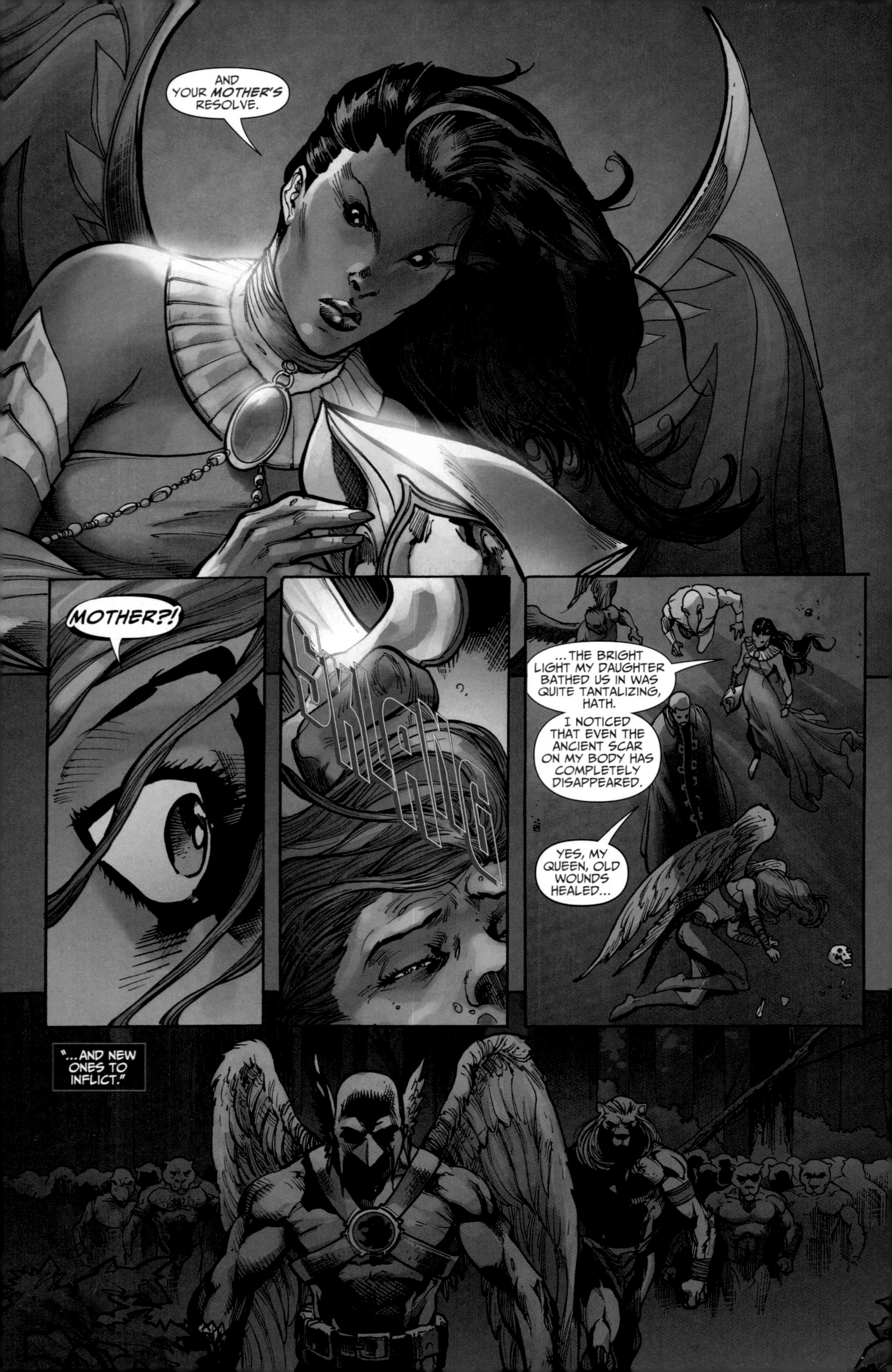
AND YOUR MOTHER'S RESOLVE.
MOTHER?!
SKLANG
...THE BRIGHT LIGHT MY DAUGHTER BATHED US IN WAS QUITE TANTALIZING, HATH.
I NOTICED THAT EVEN THE ANCIENT SCAR ON MY BODY HAS COMPLETELY DISAPPEARED.
YES, MY QUEEN, OLD WOUNDS HEALED...
"...AND NEW ONES TO INFLICT."

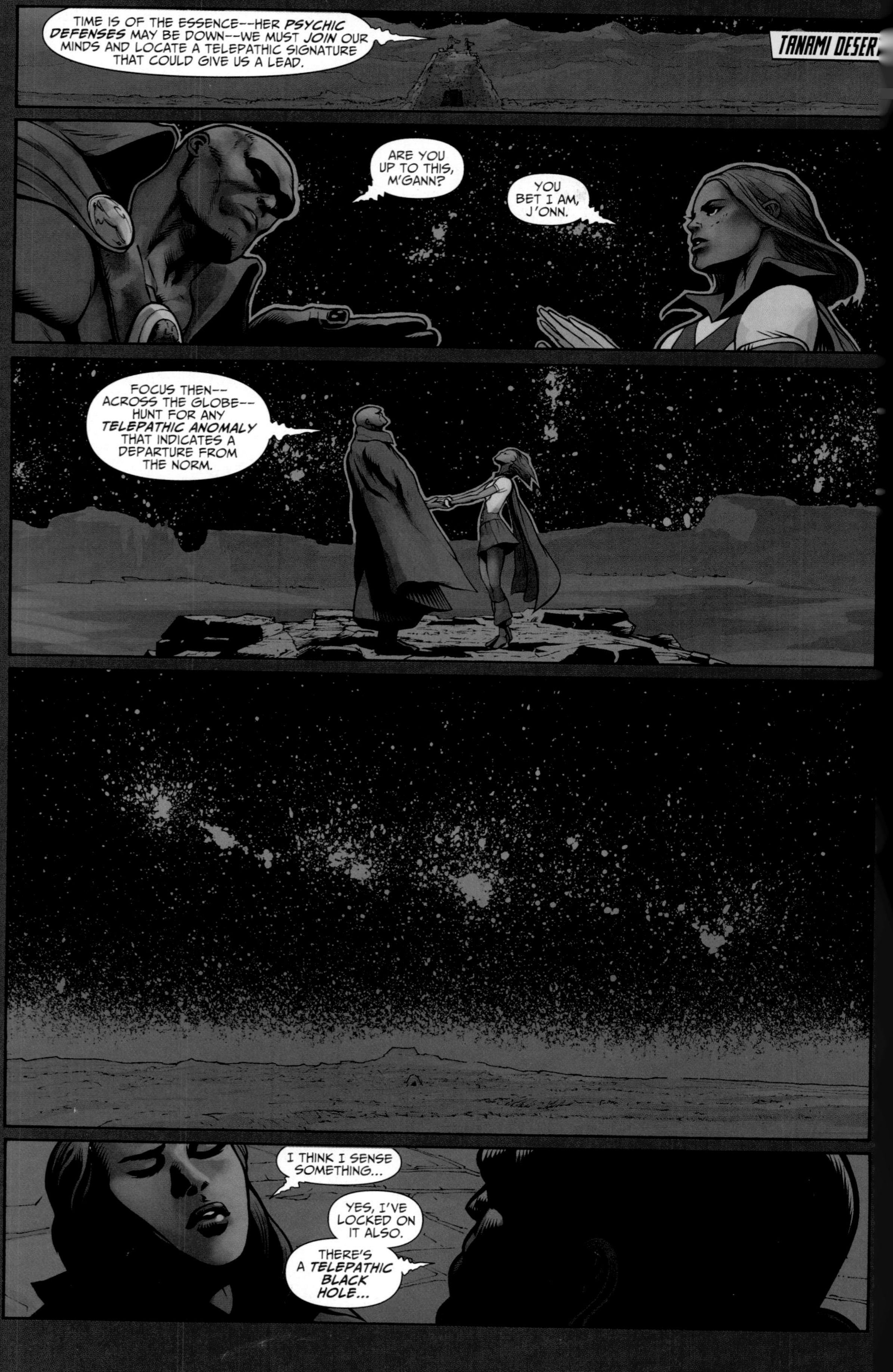
TANAMI DESERT
TIME IS OF THE ESSENCE--HER PSYCHIC DEFENSES MAY BE DOWN--WE MUST JOIN OUR MINDS AND LOCATE A TELEPATHIC SIGNATURE THAT COULD GIVE US A LEAD.
ARE YOU UP TO THIS, M'GANN?
YOU BET I AM, J'ONN.
FOCUS THEN--ACROSS THE GLOBE--HUNT FOR ANY TELEPATHIC ANOMALY THAT INDICATES A DEPARTURE FROM THE NORM.
I THINK I SENSE SOMETHING...
YES, I'VE LOCKED ON IT ALSO.
THERE'S A TELEPATHIC BLACK HOLE...

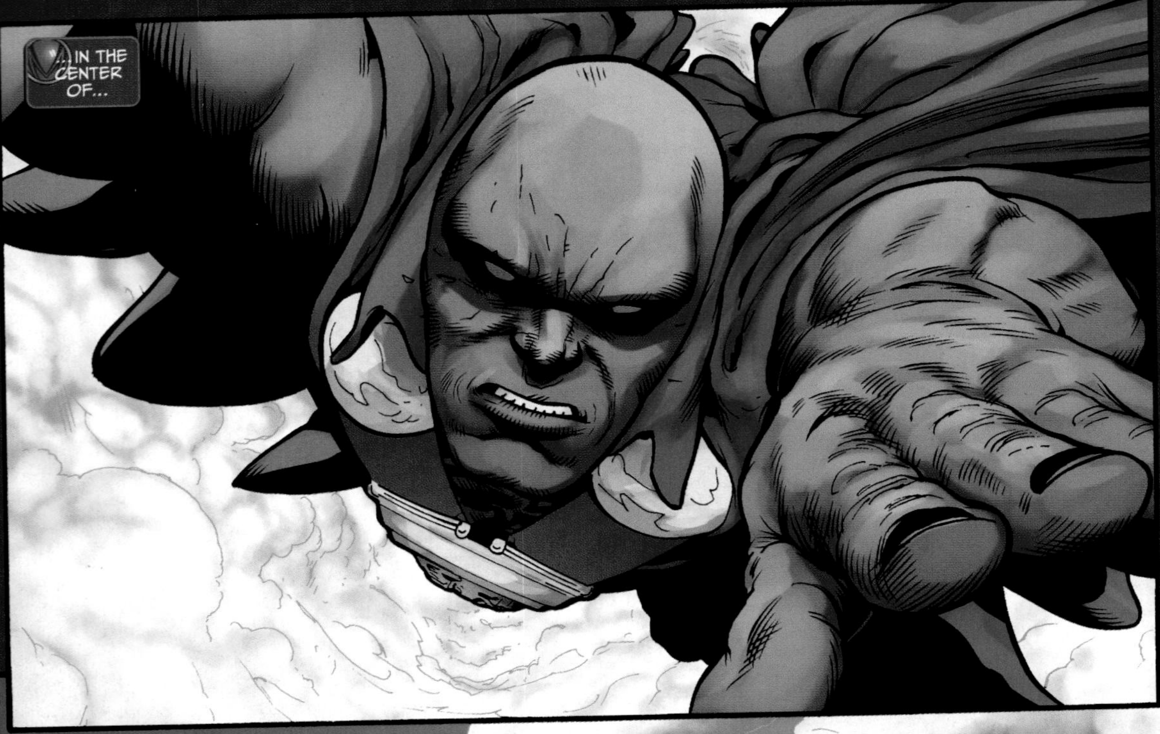
"...IN THE CENTER OF...

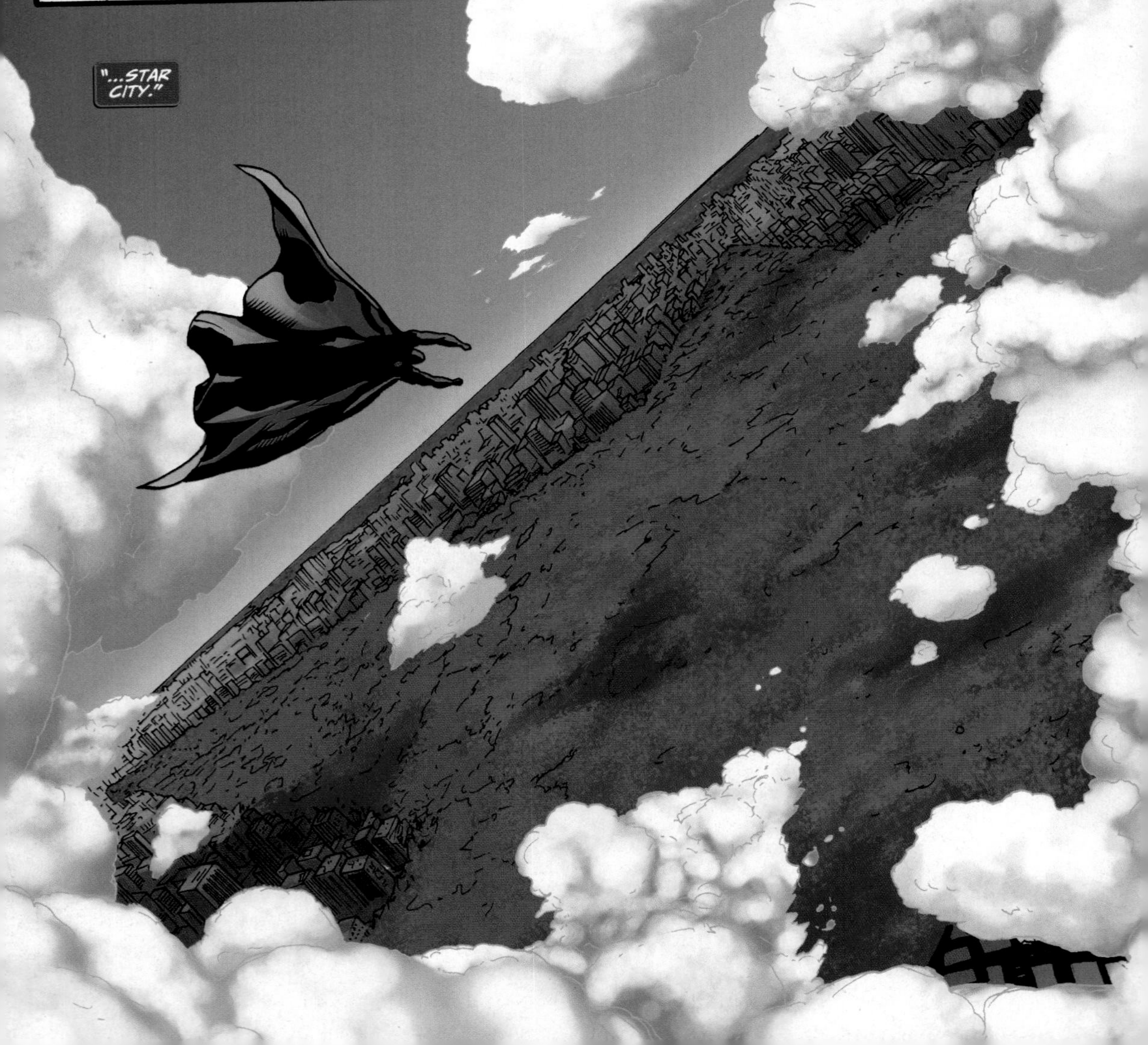
"...STAR CITY."

**BRIGHTEST DAY 9**
*Cover by David Finch*

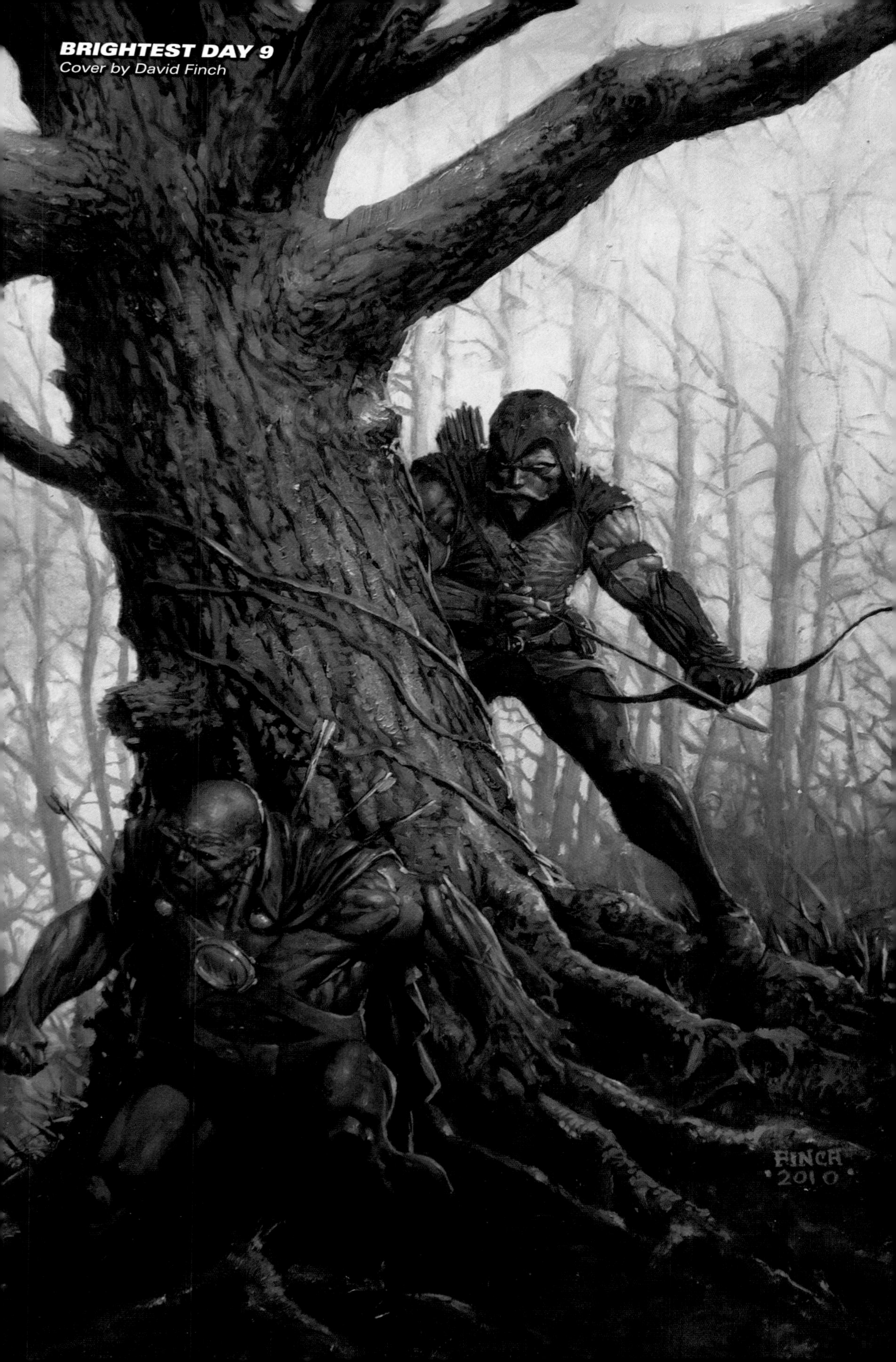
FINCH
2010

# LOST & FOUND

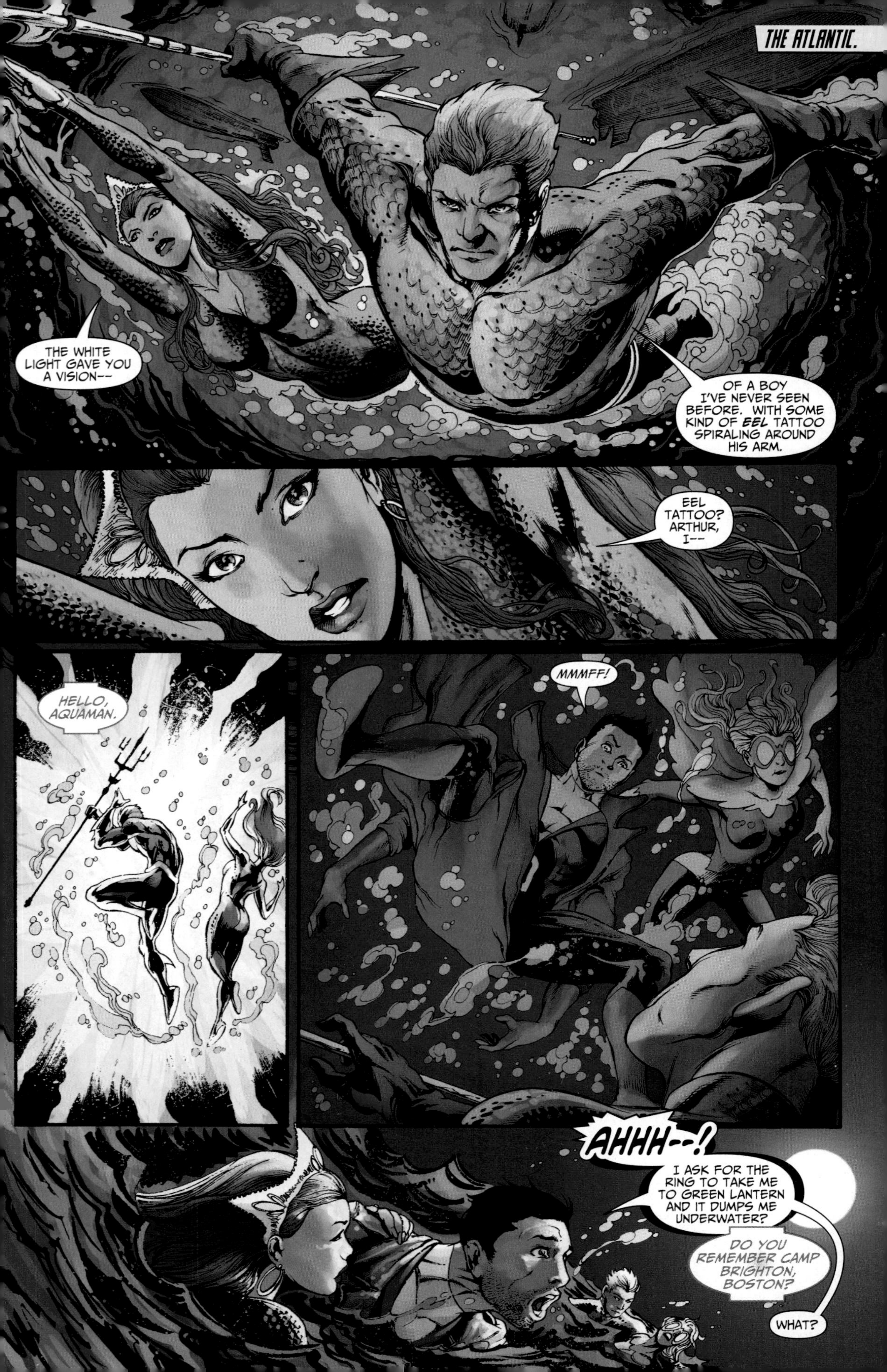
THE ATLANTIC.
THE WHITE LIGHT GAVE YOU A VISION--
OF A BOY I'VE NEVER SEEN BEFORE. WITH SOME KIND OF EEL TATTOO SPIRALING AROUND HIS ARM.
EEL TATTOO? ARTHUR, I--
HELLO, AQUAMAN.
MMMFF!
AHHH--!
I ASK FOR THE RING TO TAKE ME TO GREEN LANTERN AND IT DUMPS ME UNDERWATER?
DO YOU REMEMBER CAMP BRIGHTON, BOSTON?
WHAT?

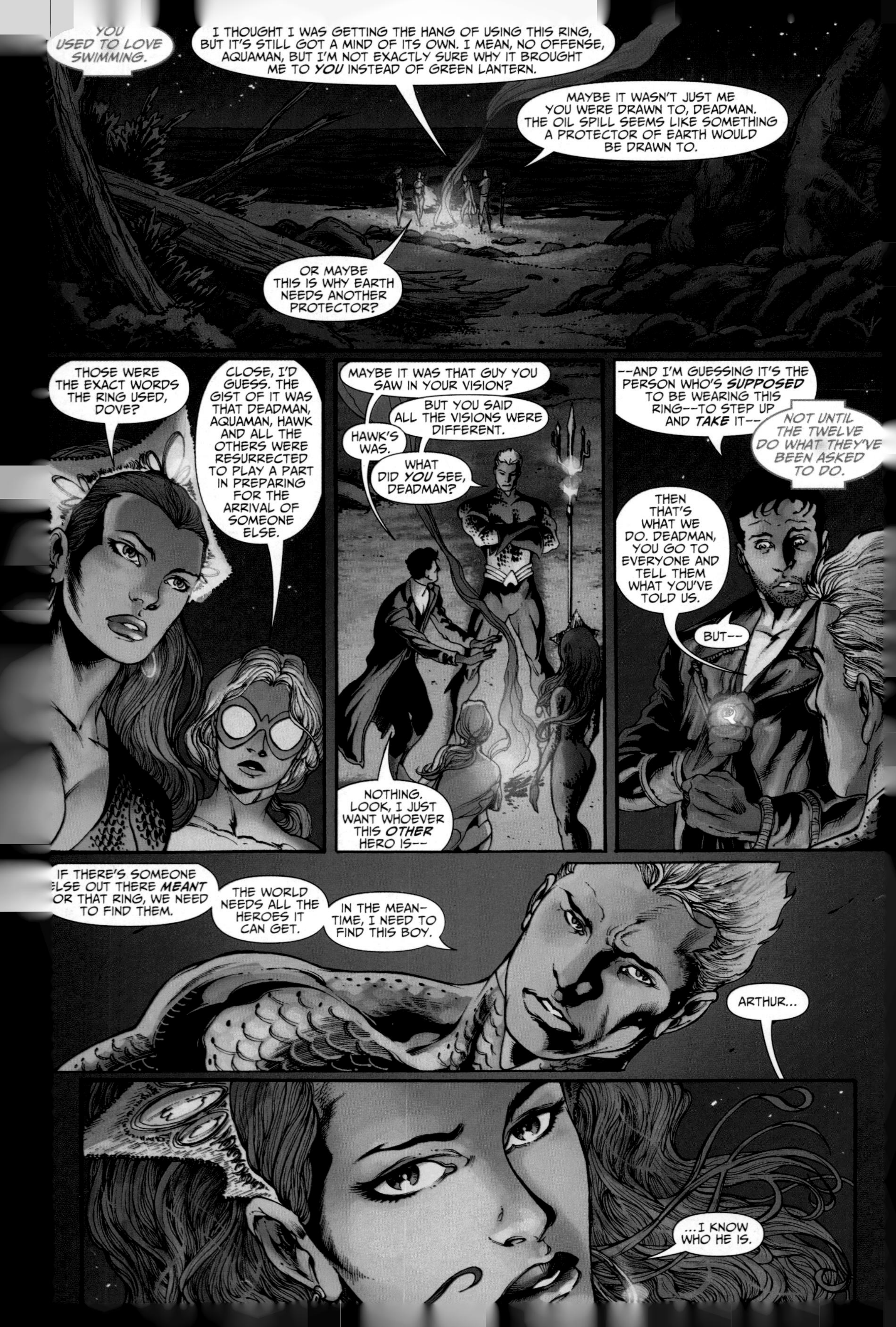
YOU USED TO LOVE SWIMMING.
I THOUGHT I WAS GETTING THE HANG OF USING THIS RING, BUT IT'S STILL GOT A MIND OF ITS OWN. I MEAN, NO OFFENSE, AQUAMAN, BUT I'M NOT EXACTLY SURE WHY IT BROUGHT ME TO YOU INSTEAD OF GREEN LANTERN.
MAYBE IT WASN'T JUST ME YOU WERE DRAWN TO, DEADMAN. THE OIL SPILL SEEMS LIKE SOMETHING A PROTECTOR OF EARTH WOULD BE DRAWN TO.
OR MAYBE THIS IS WHY EARTH NEEDS ANOTHER PROTECTOR?
THOSE WERE THE EXACT WORDS THE RING USED, DOVE?
CLOSE, I'D GUESS. THE GIST OF IT WAS THAT DEADMAN, AQUAMAN, HAWK AND ALL THE OTHERS WERE RESURRECTED TO PLAY A PART IN PREPARING FOR THE ARRIVAL OF SOMEONE ELSE.
MAYBE IT WAS THAT GUY YOU SAW IN YOUR VISION?
HAWK'S WAS.
BUT YOU SAID ALL THE VISIONS WERE DIFFERENT.
WHAT DID YOU SEE, DEADMAN?
NOTHING. LOOK, I JUST WANT WHOEVER THIS OTHER HERO IS--
--AND I'M GUESSING IT'S THE PERSON WHO'S SUPPOSED TO BE WEARING THIS RING--TO STEP UP AND TAKE IT--
NOT UNTIL THE TWELVE DO WHAT THEY'VE BEEN ASKED TO DO.
THEN THAT'S WHAT WE DO. DEADMAN, YOU GO TO EVERYONE AND TELL THEM WHAT YOU'VE TOLD US.
BUT--
IF THERE'S SOMEONE ELSE OUT THERE MEANT FOR THAT RING, WE NEED TO FIND THEM.
THE WORLD NEEDS ALL THE HEROES IT CAN GET.
IN THE MEAN-TIME, I NEED TO FIND THIS BOY.
ARTHUR...
...I KNOW WHO HE IS.

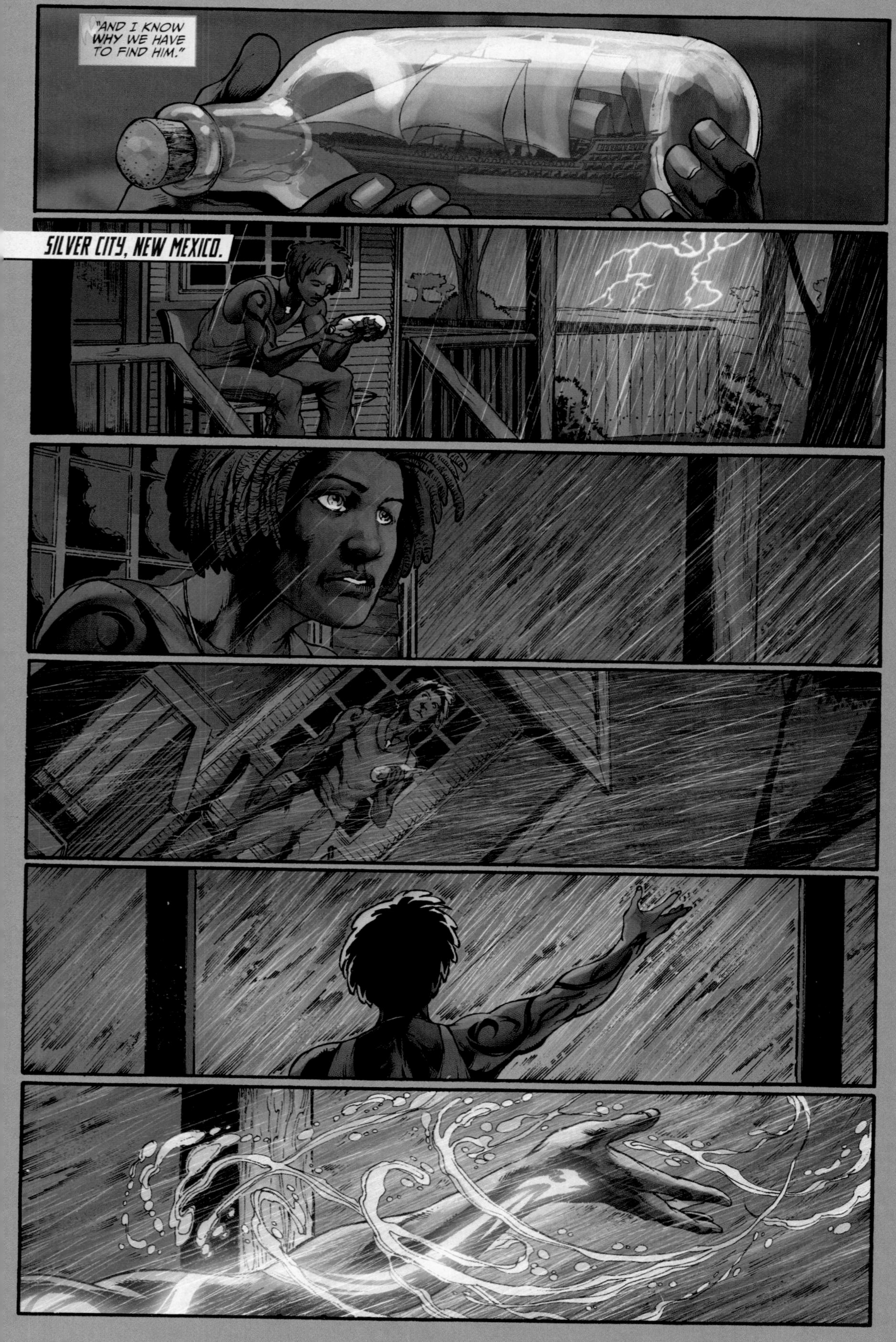
"AND I KNOW WHY WE HAVE TO FIND HIM."
SILVER CITY, NEW MEXICO.

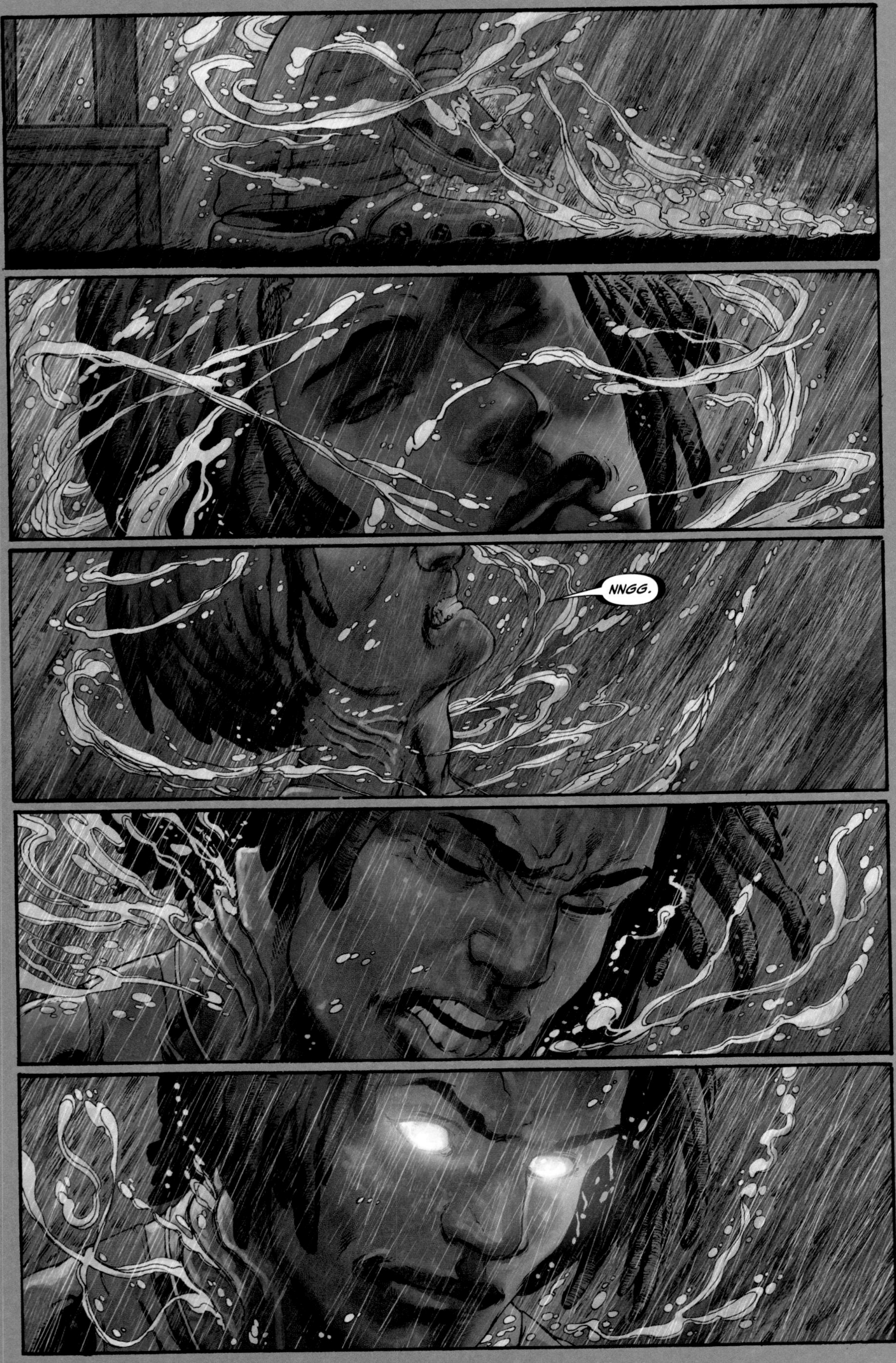
NNGG.

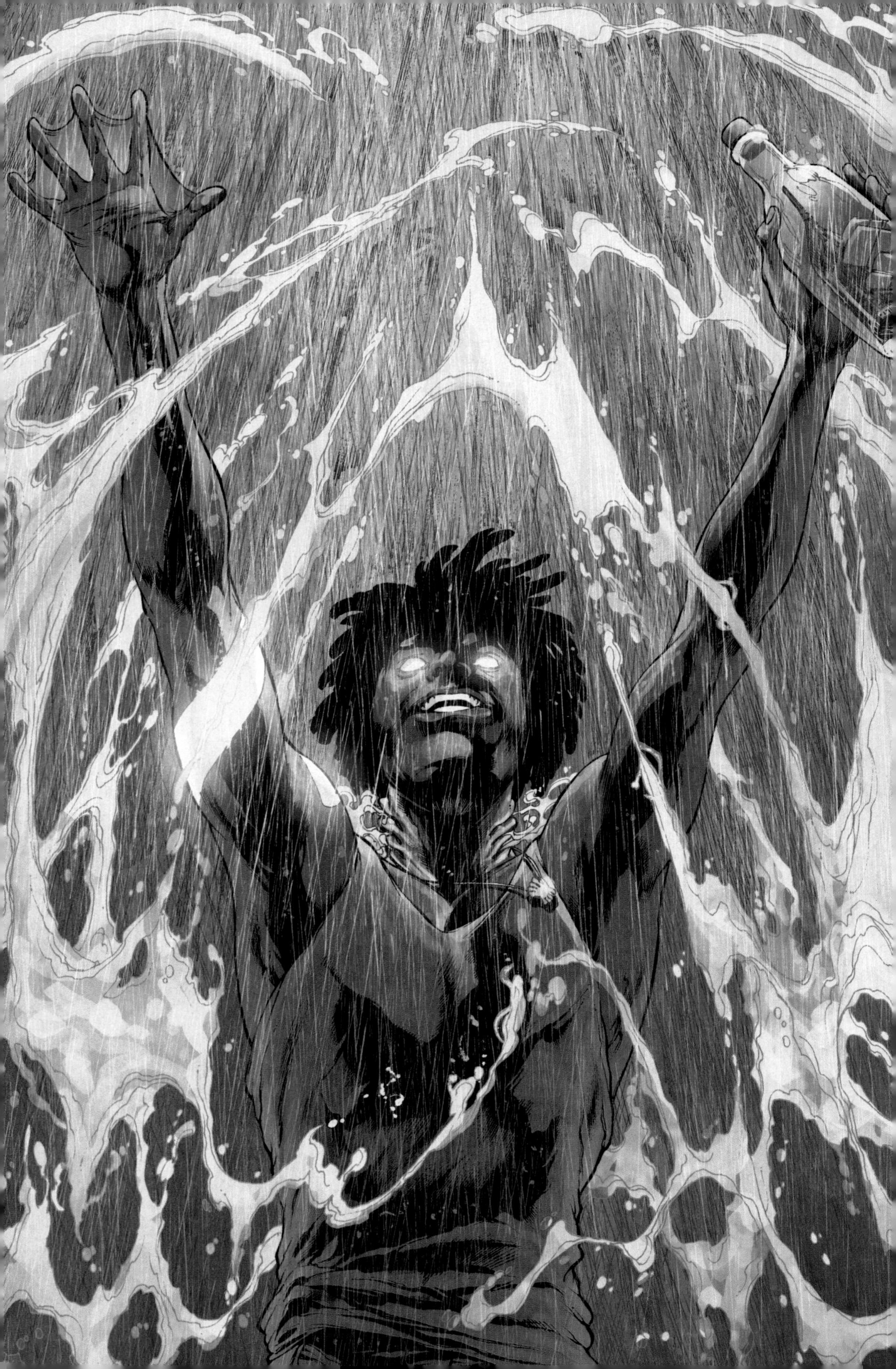

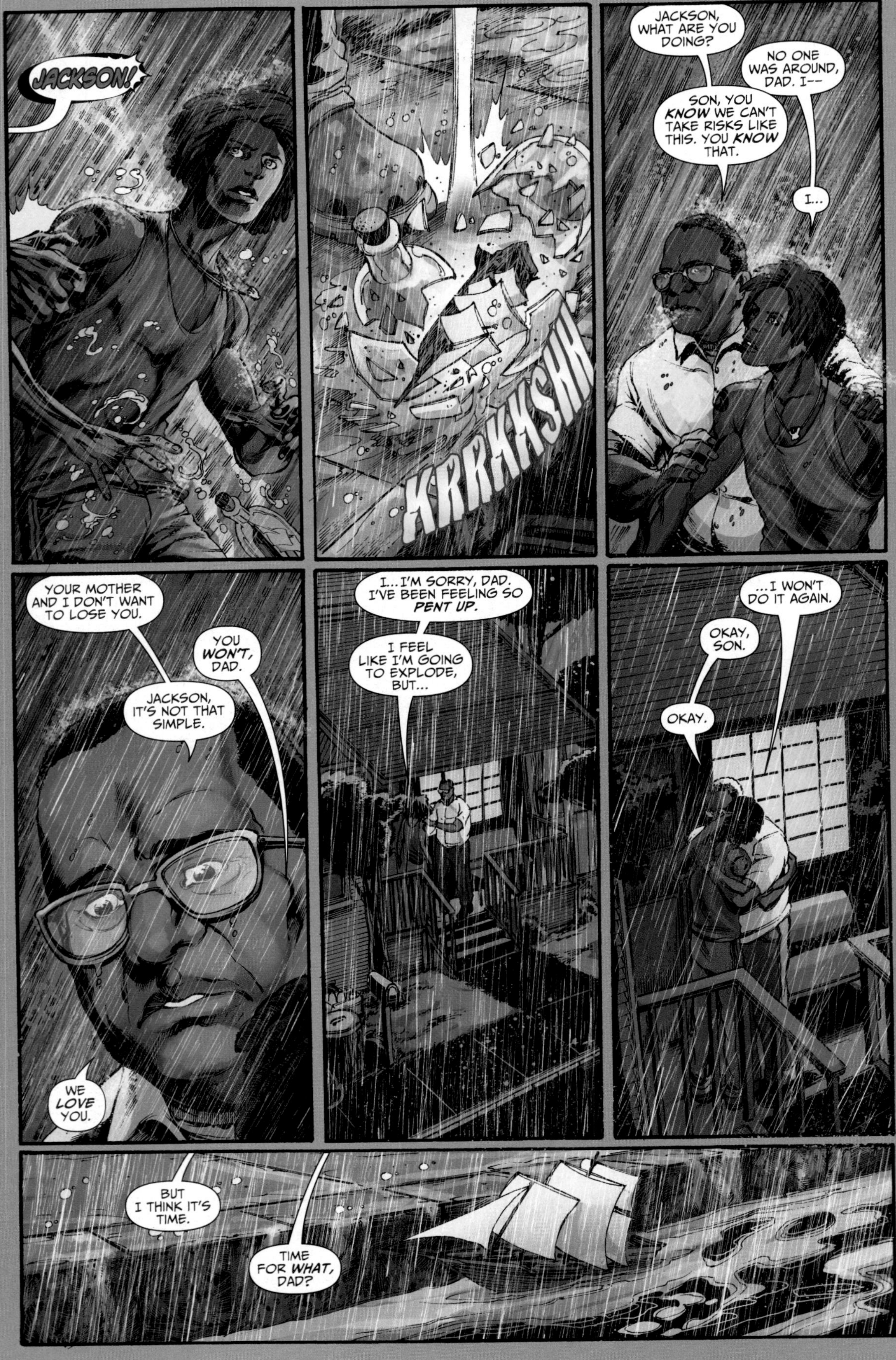
JACKSON!
KRRKKSHH
JACKSON, WHAT ARE YOU DOING?
SON, YOU KNOW WE CAN'T TAKE RISKS LIKE THIS. YOU KNOW THAT.
NO ONE WAS AROUND, DAD. I--
I...
YOUR MOTHER AND I DON'T WANT TO LOSE YOU.
YOU WON'T, DAD.
JACKSON, IT'S NOT THAT SIMPLE.
WE LOVE YOU.
I...I'M SORRY, DAD. I'VE BEEN FEELING SO PENT UP.
I FEEL LIKE I'M GOING TO EXPLODE, BUT...
...I WON'T DO IT AGAIN.
OKAY, SON.
OKAY.
BUT I THINK IT'S TIME.
TIME FOR WHAT, DAD?

"TIME FOR THE TRUTH."

STAR CITY.

ASTOUNDING.

SIMPLY ASTOUNDING.

BUT IF THE *VISION* I WAS GIVEN BY THE *WHITE LANTERN* IS CORRECT...

...I WILL HAVE TO *BURN* DOWN THIS PLACE OF MIRACULOUS GROWTH...

...TO *DESTROY* THE ONLY OTHER *GREEN MARTIAN* LEFT IN THE UNIVERSE.

BUT THERE IS NO WAY I WILL ALLOW MYSELF TO BE CONTROLLED BY SOMETHING I DO NOT COMPLETELY UNDER--

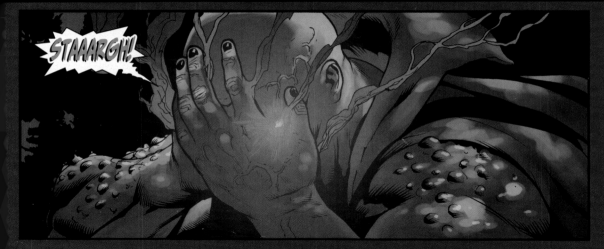

STAAARGH!

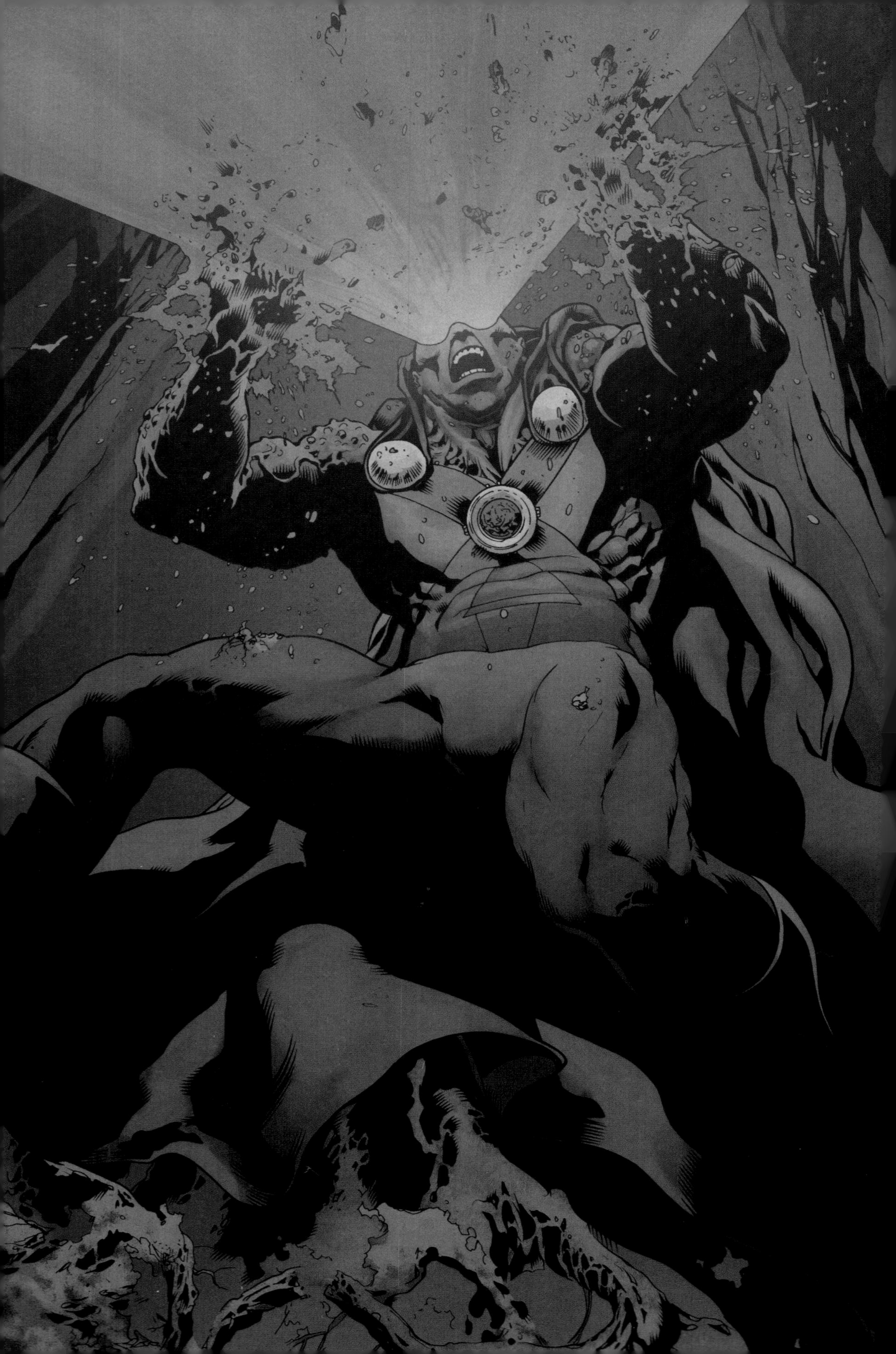

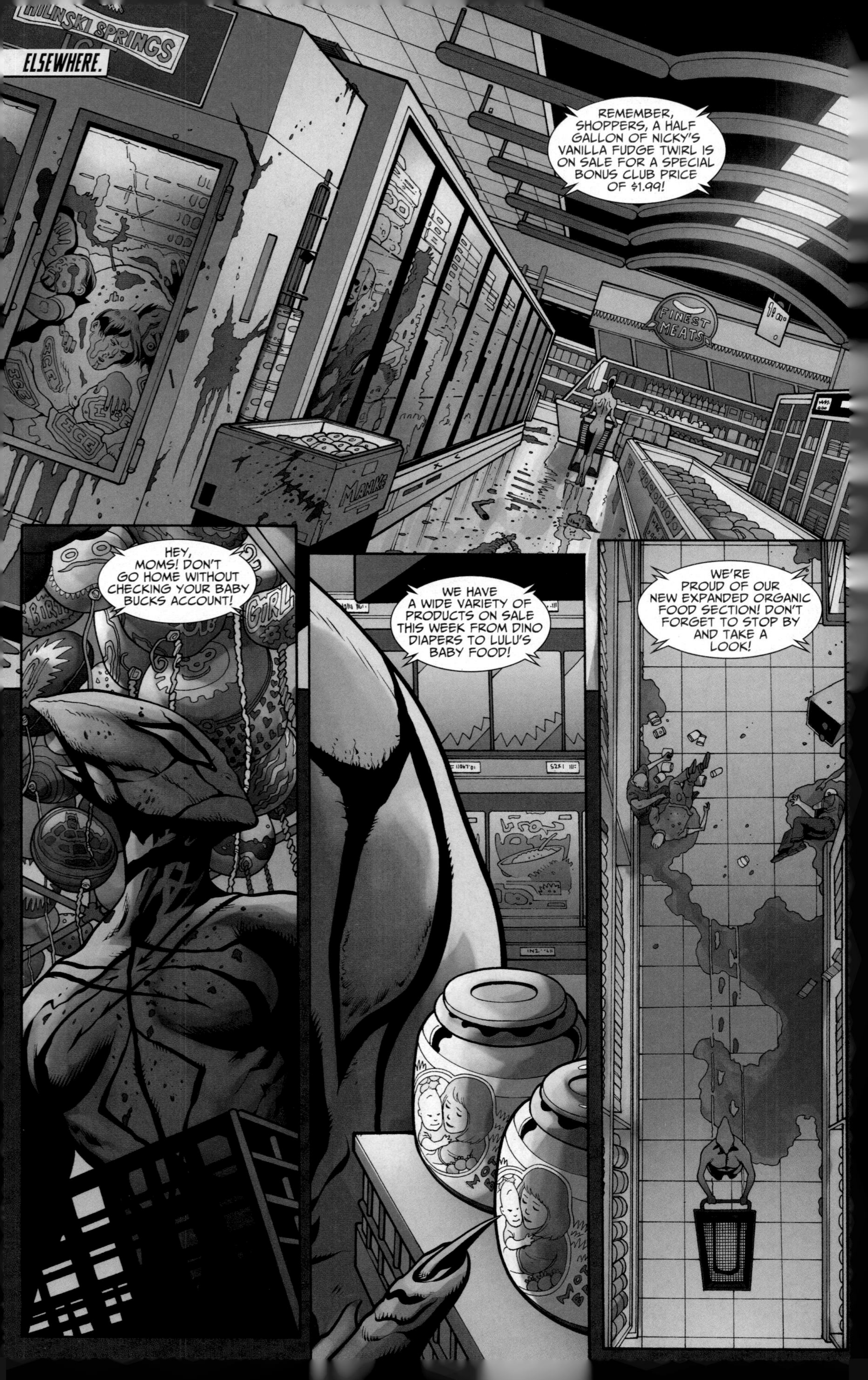

ELSEWHERE.
REMEMBER, SHOPPERS, A HALF GALLON OF NICKY'S VANILLA FUDGE TWIRL IS ON SALE FOR A SPECIAL BONUS CLUB PRICE OF $1.99!
FINEST MEATS
HEY, MOMS! DON'T GO HOME WITHOUT CHECKING YOUR BABY BUCKS ACCOUNT!
WE HAVE A WIDE VARIETY OF PRODUCTS ON SALE THIS WEEK FROM DINO DIAPERS TO LULU'S BABY FOOD!
WE'RE PROUD OF OUR NEW EXPANDED ORGANIC FOOD SECTION! DON'T FORGET TO STOP BY AND TAKE A LOOK!

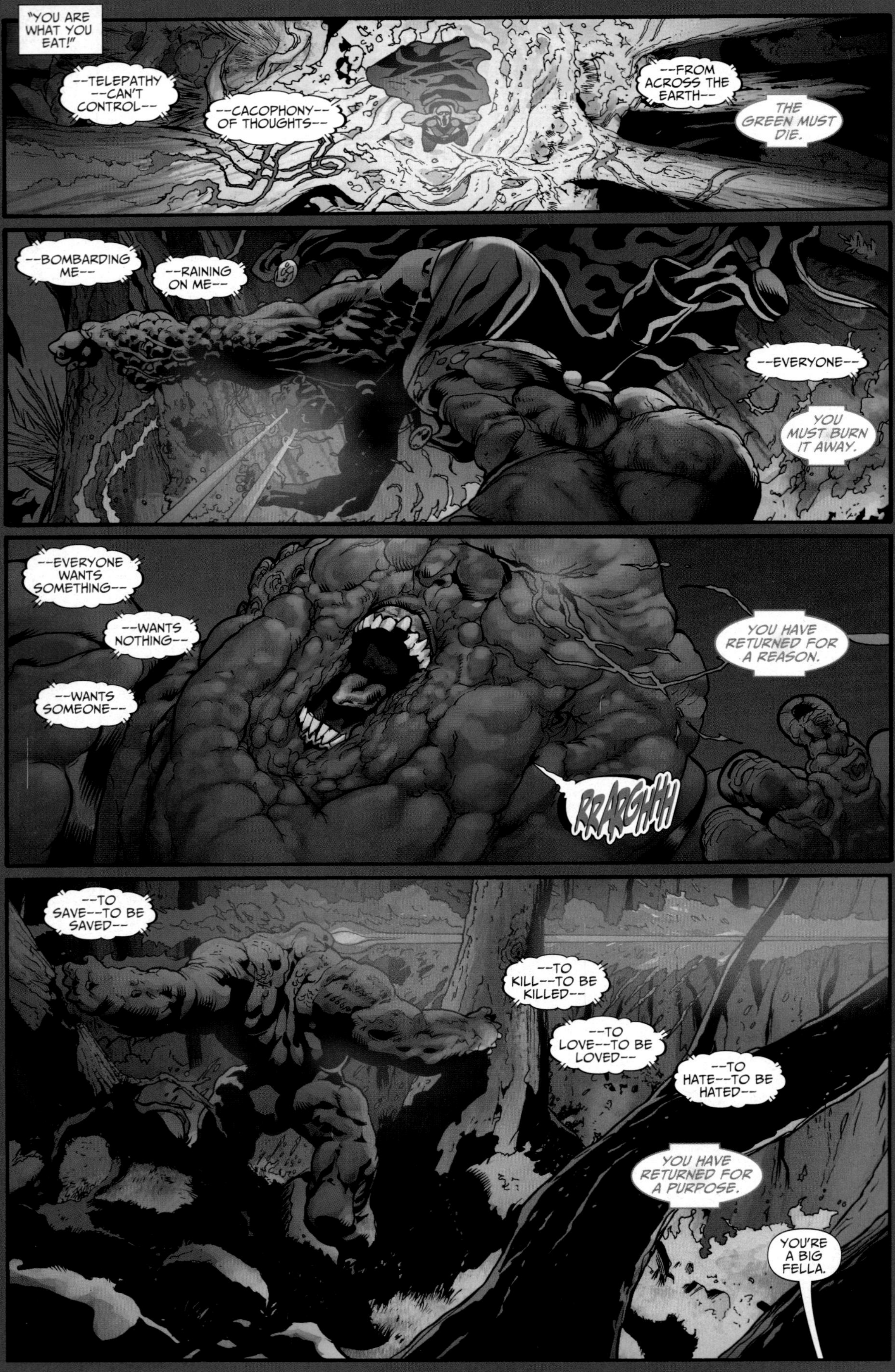
"YOU ARE WHAT YOU EAT!"
--TELEPATHY --CAN'T CONTROL--
--CACOPHONY-- OF THOUGHTS--
--FROM ACROSS THE EARTH--
THE GREEN MUST DIE.
--BOMBARDING ME--
--RAINING ON ME--
--EVERYONE--
YOU MUST BURN IT AWAY.
--EVERYONE WANTS SOMETHING--
--WANTS NOTHING--
--WANTS SOMEONE--
YOU HAVE RETURNED FOR A REASON.
RRARGHHH
--TO SAVE--TO BE SAVED--
--TO KILL--TO BE KILLED--
--TO LOVE--TO BE LOVED--
--TO HATE--TO BE HATED--
YOU HAVE RETURNED FOR A PURPOSE.
YOU'RE A BIG FELLA.

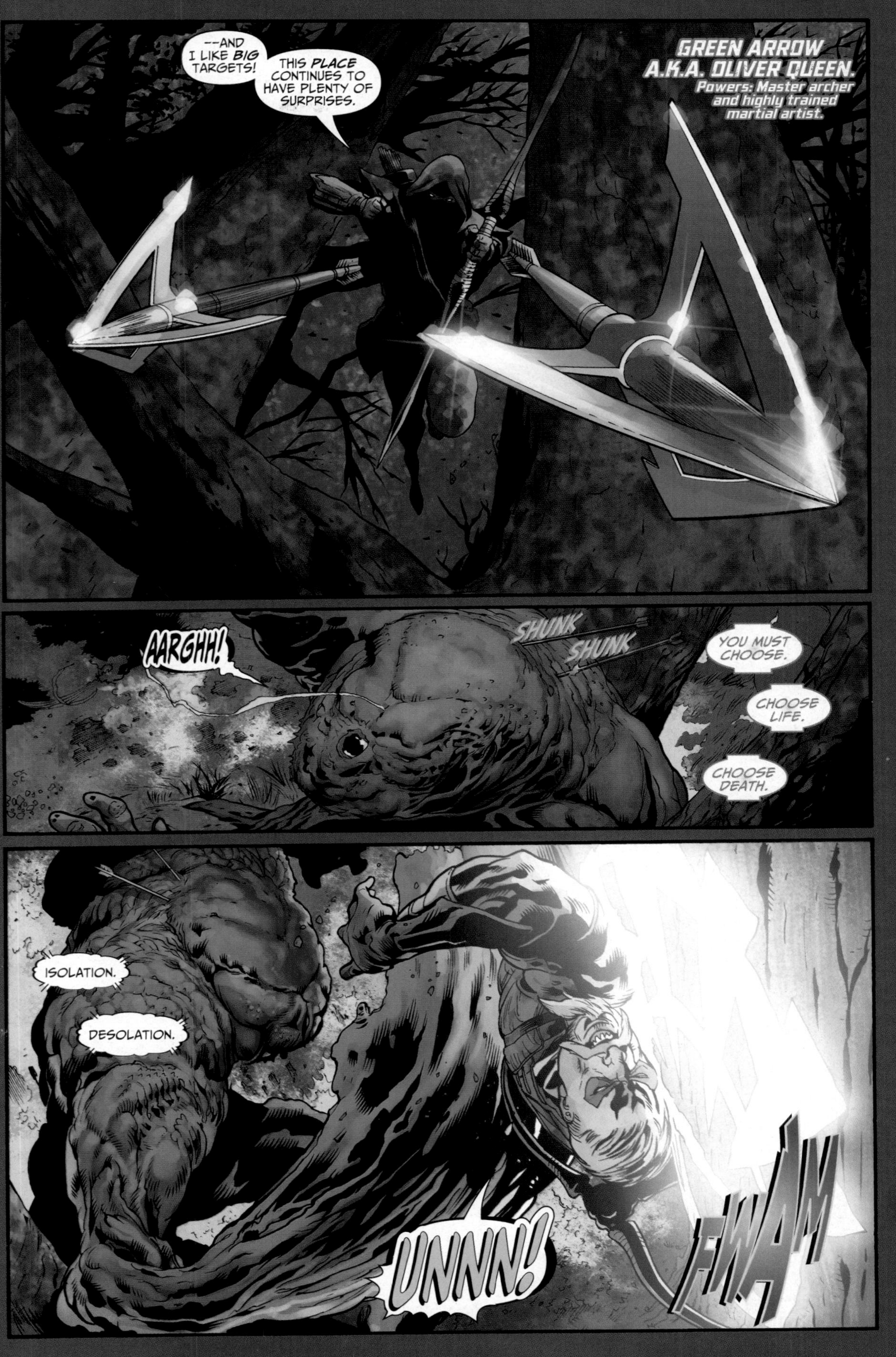
--AND I LIKE BIG TARGETS!
THIS PLACE CONTINUES TO HAVE PLENTY OF SURPRISES.
GREEN ARROW
A.K.A. OLIVER QUEEN.
Powers: Master archer and highly trained martial artist.
AARGHH!
SHUNK
SHUNK
YOU MUST CHOOSE.
CHOOSE LIFE.
CHOOSE DEATH.
ISOLATION.
DESOLATION.
UNNN!
FWAM

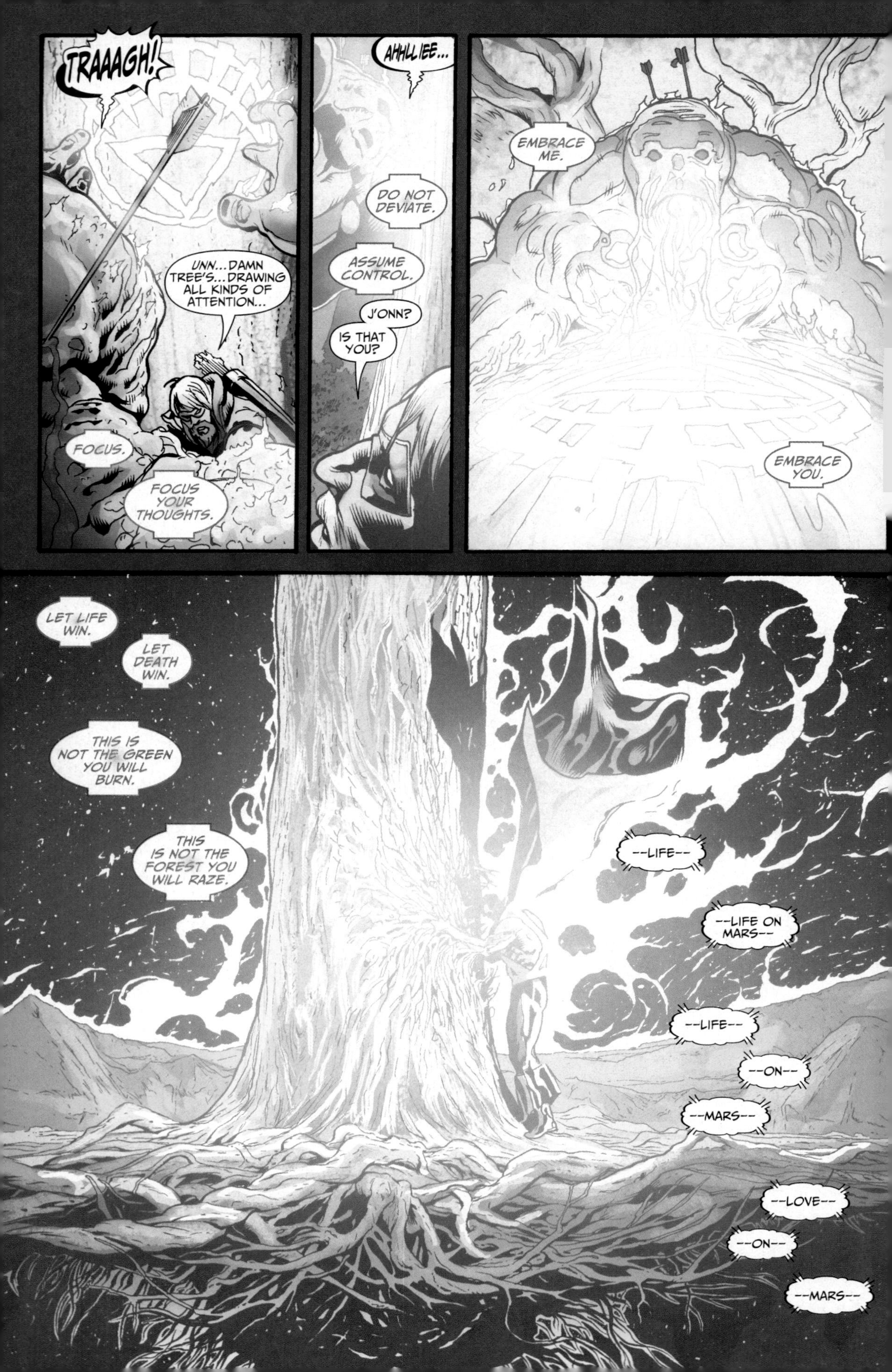
TRAAAGH!
UNN...DAMN TREE'S...DRAWING ALL KINDS OF ATTENTION...
FOCUS.
FOCUS YOUR THOUGHTS.
AHHLLIEE...
DO NOT DEVIATE.
ASSUME CONTROL.
J'ONN?
IS THAT YOU?
EMBRACE ME.
EMBRACE YOU.
LET LIFE WIN.
LET DEATH WIN.
THIS IS NOT THE GREEN YOU WILL BURN.
THIS IS NOT THE FOREST YOU WILL RAZE.
--LIFE--
--LIFE ON MARS--
--LIFE--
--ON--
--MARS--
--LOVE--
--ON--
--MARS--

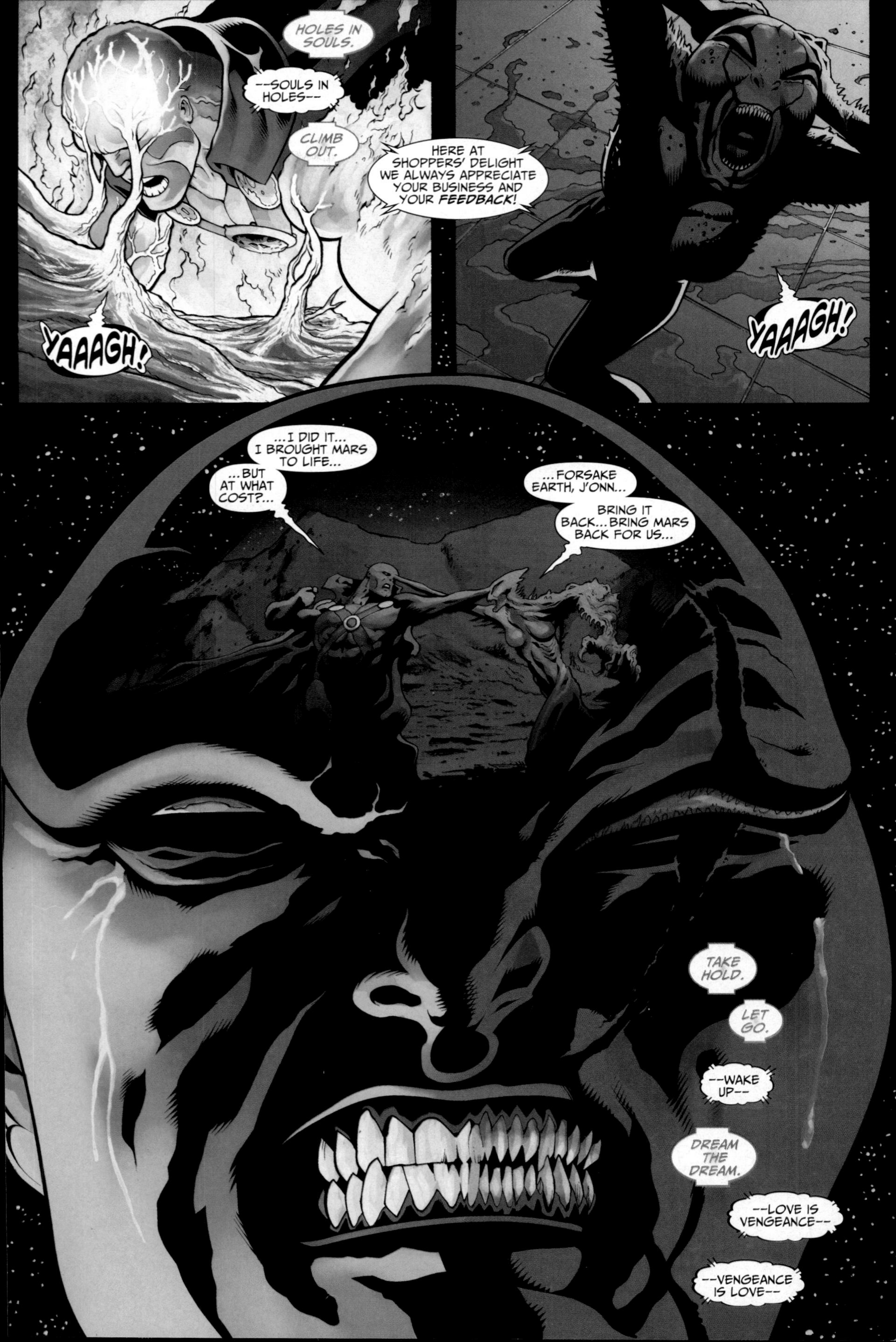
HOLES IN SOULS.
--SOULS IN HOLES--
CLIMB OUT.
HERE AT SHOPPERS' DELIGHT WE ALWAYS APPRECIATE YOUR BUSINESS AND YOUR FEEDBACK!
YAAAGH!
YAAAGH!
...I DID IT... I BROUGHT MARS TO LIFE...
...BUT AT WHAT COST?...
...FORSAKE EARTH, J'ONN...
BRING IT BACK...BRING MARS BACK FOR US...
TAKE HOLD.
LET GO.
--WAKE UP--
DREAM THE DREAM.
--LOVE IS VENGEANCE--
--VENGEANCE IS LOVE--

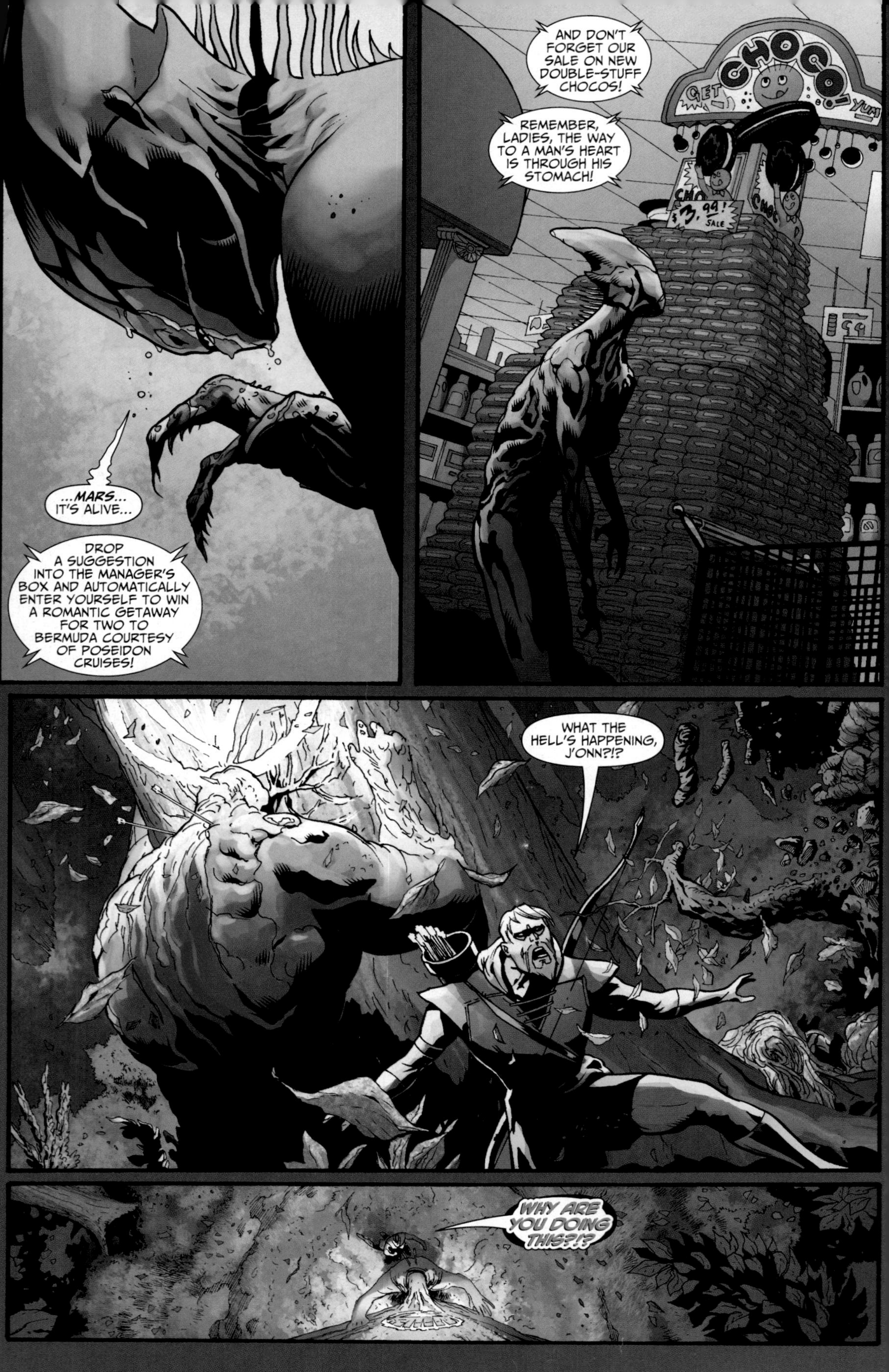

...MARS...
IT'S ALIVE...
DROP A SUGGESTION INTO THE MANAGER'S BOX AND AUTOMATICALLY ENTER YOURSELF TO WIN A ROMANTIC GETAWAY FOR TWO TO BERMUDA COURTESY OF POSEIDON CRUISES!
AND DON'T FORGET OUR SALE ON NEW DOUBLE-STUFF CHOCOS!
REMEMBER, LADIES, THE WAY TO A MAN'S HEART IS THROUGH HIS STOMACH!
GET CHOCO YUM
$3.94 SALE
WHAT THE HELL'S HAPPENING, J'ONN?!?
WHY ARE YOU DOING THIS?!?

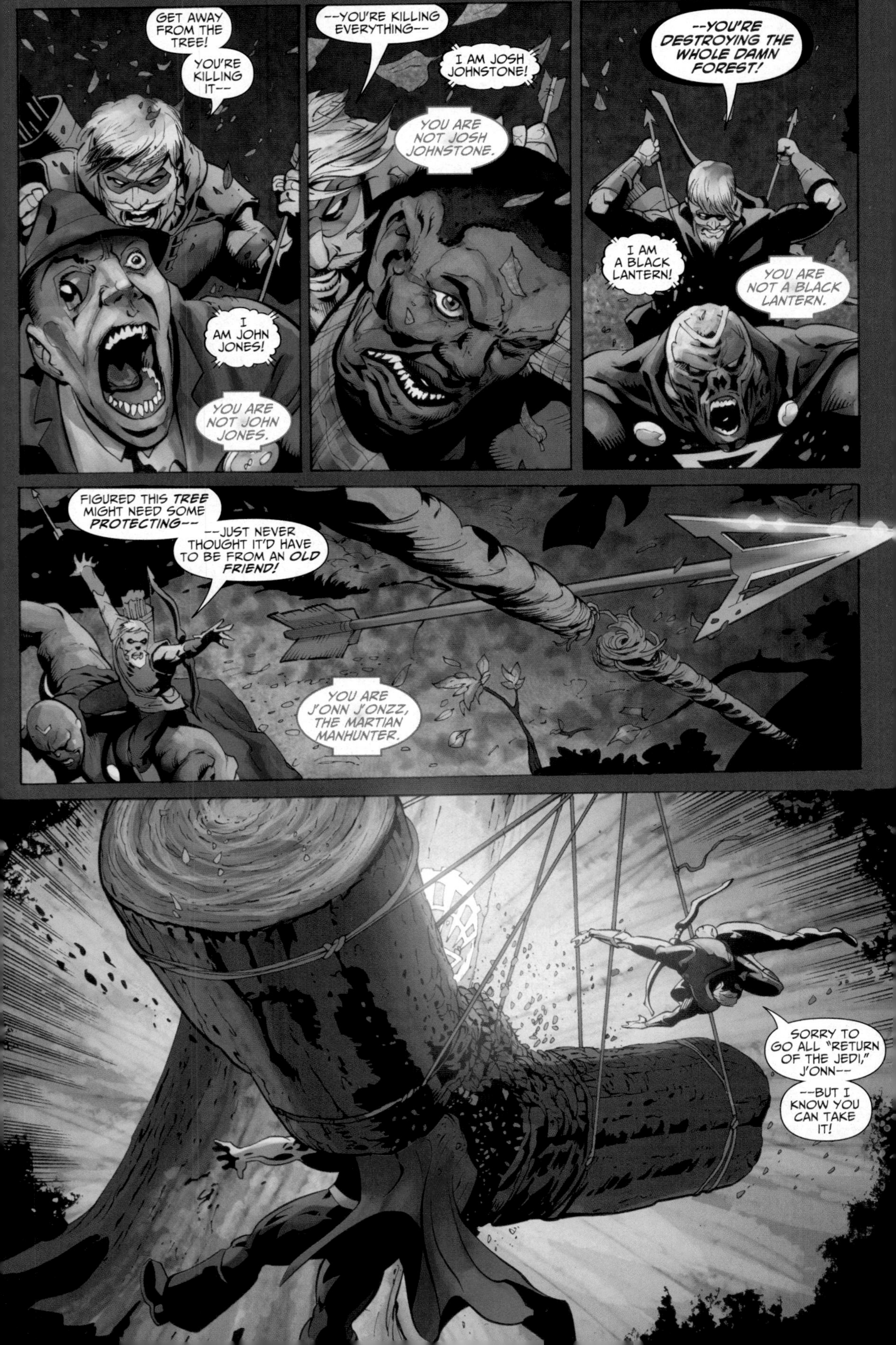
GET AWAY FROM THE TREE!
YOU'RE KILLING IT--
I AM JOHN JONES!
YOU ARE NOT JOHN JONES.
--YOU'RE KILLING EVERYTHING--
I AM JOSH JOHNSTONE!
YOU ARE NOT JOSH JOHNSTONE.
--YOU'RE DESTROYING THE WHOLE DAMN FOREST!
I AM A BLACK LANTERN!
YOU ARE NOT A BLACK LANTERN.
FIGURED THIS TREE MIGHT NEED SOME PROTECTING--
--JUST NEVER THOUGHT IT'D HAVE TO BE FROM AN OLD FRIEND!
YOU ARE J'ONN J'ONZZ, THE MARTIAN MANHUNTER.
SORRY TO GO ALL "RETURN OF THE JEDI," J'ONN--
--BUT I KNOW YOU CAN TAKE IT!

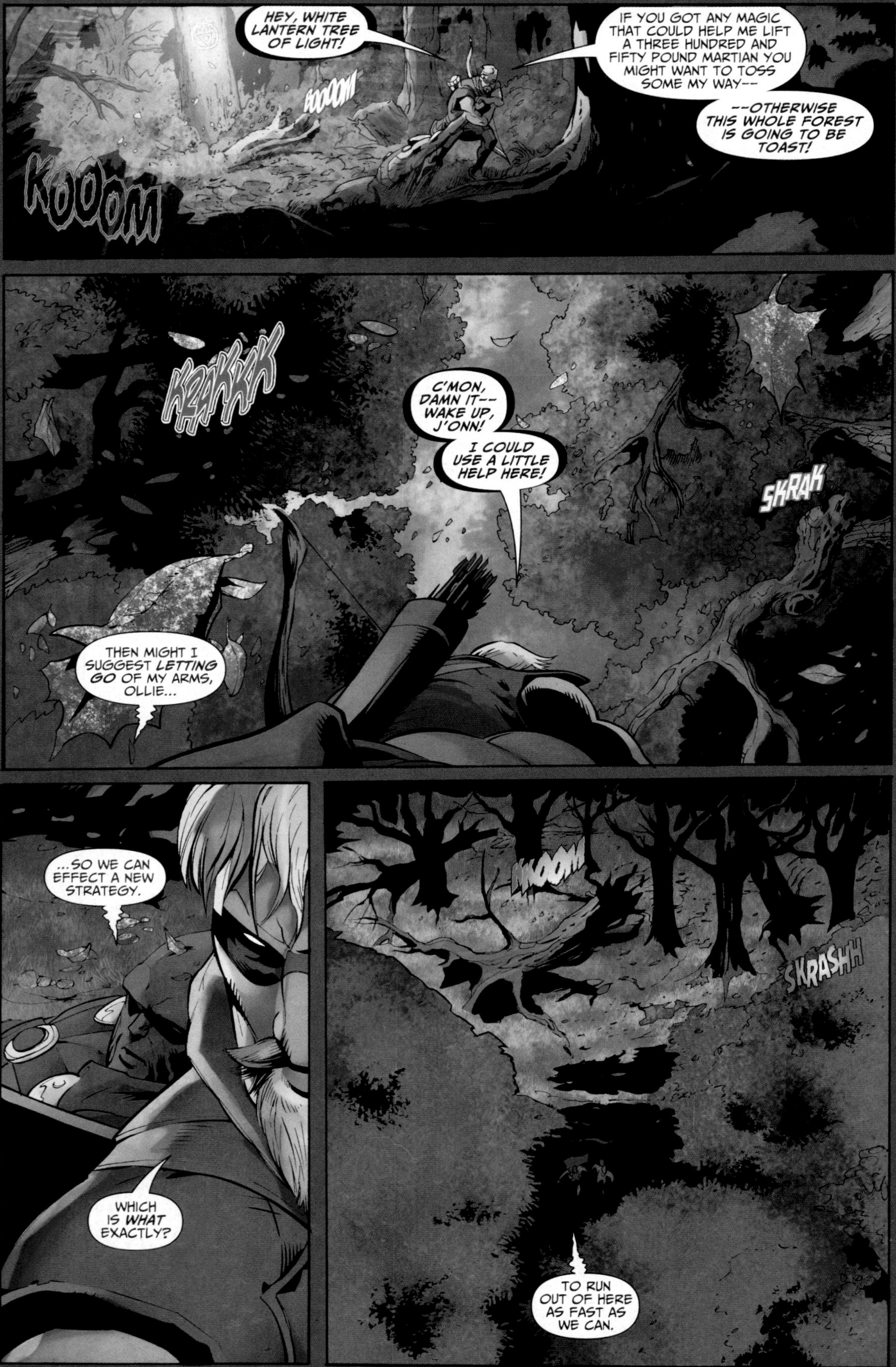
HEY, WHITE LANTERN TREE OF LIGHT!
IF YOU GOT ANY MAGIC THAT COULD HELP ME LIFT A THREE HUNDRED AND FIFTY POUND MARTIAN YOU MIGHT WANT TO TOSS SOME MY WAY--
--OTHERWISE THIS WHOLE FOREST IS GOING TO BE TOAST!
BOOOOM
KOOOM
KRAKKK
C'MON, DAMN IT-- WAKE UP, J'ONN!
I COULD USE A LITTLE HELP HERE!
SKRAK
THEN MIGHT I SUGGEST LETTING GO OF MY ARMS, OLLIE...
...SO WE CAN EFFECT A NEW STRATEGY.
WHICH IS WHAT EXACTLY?
WHOOOM
SKRASHH
TO RUN OUT OF HERE AS FAST AS WE CAN.

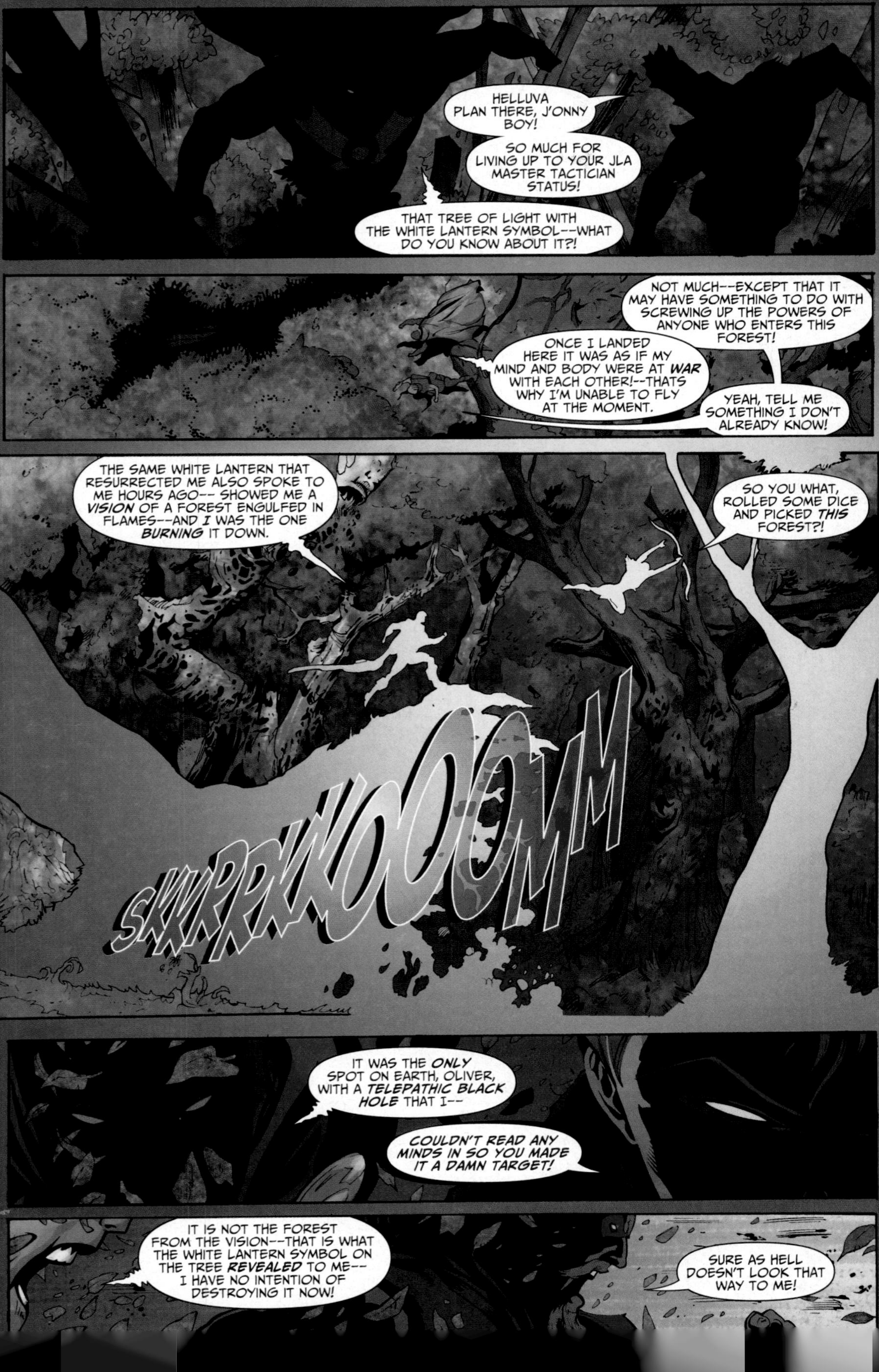
HELLUVA PLAN THERE, J'ONNY BOY!
SO MUCH FOR LIVING UP TO YOUR JLA MASTER TACTICIAN STATUS!
THAT TREE OF LIGHT WITH THE WHITE LANTERN SYMBOL--WHAT DO YOU KNOW ABOUT IT?!
NOT MUCH--EXCEPT THAT IT MAY HAVE SOMETHING TO DO WITH SCREWING UP THE POWERS OF ANYONE WHO ENTERS THIS FOREST!
ONCE I LANDED HERE IT WAS AS IF MY MIND AND BODY WERE AT WAR WITH EACH OTHER!--THATS WHY I'M UNABLE TO FLY AT THE MOMENT.
YEAH, TELL ME SOMETHING I DON'T ALREADY KNOW!
THE SAME WHITE LANTERN THAT RESURRECTED ME ALSO SPOKE TO ME HOURS AGO-- SHOWED ME A VISION OF A FOREST ENGULFED IN FLAMES--AND I WAS THE ONE BURNING IT DOWN.
SO YOU WHAT, ROLLED SOME DICE AND PICKED THIS FOREST?!
SKKRRKKOOOMM
IT WAS THE ONLY SPOT ON EARTH, OLIVER, WITH A TELEPATHIC BLACK HOLE THAT I--
COULDN'T READ ANY MINDS IN SO YOU MADE IT A DAMN TARGET!
IT IS NOT THE FOREST FROM THE VISION--THAT IS WHAT THE WHITE LANTERN SYMBOL ON THE TREE REVEALED TO ME-- I HAVE NO INTENTION OF DESTROYING IT NOW!
SURE AS HELL DOESN'T LOOK THAT WAY TO ME!

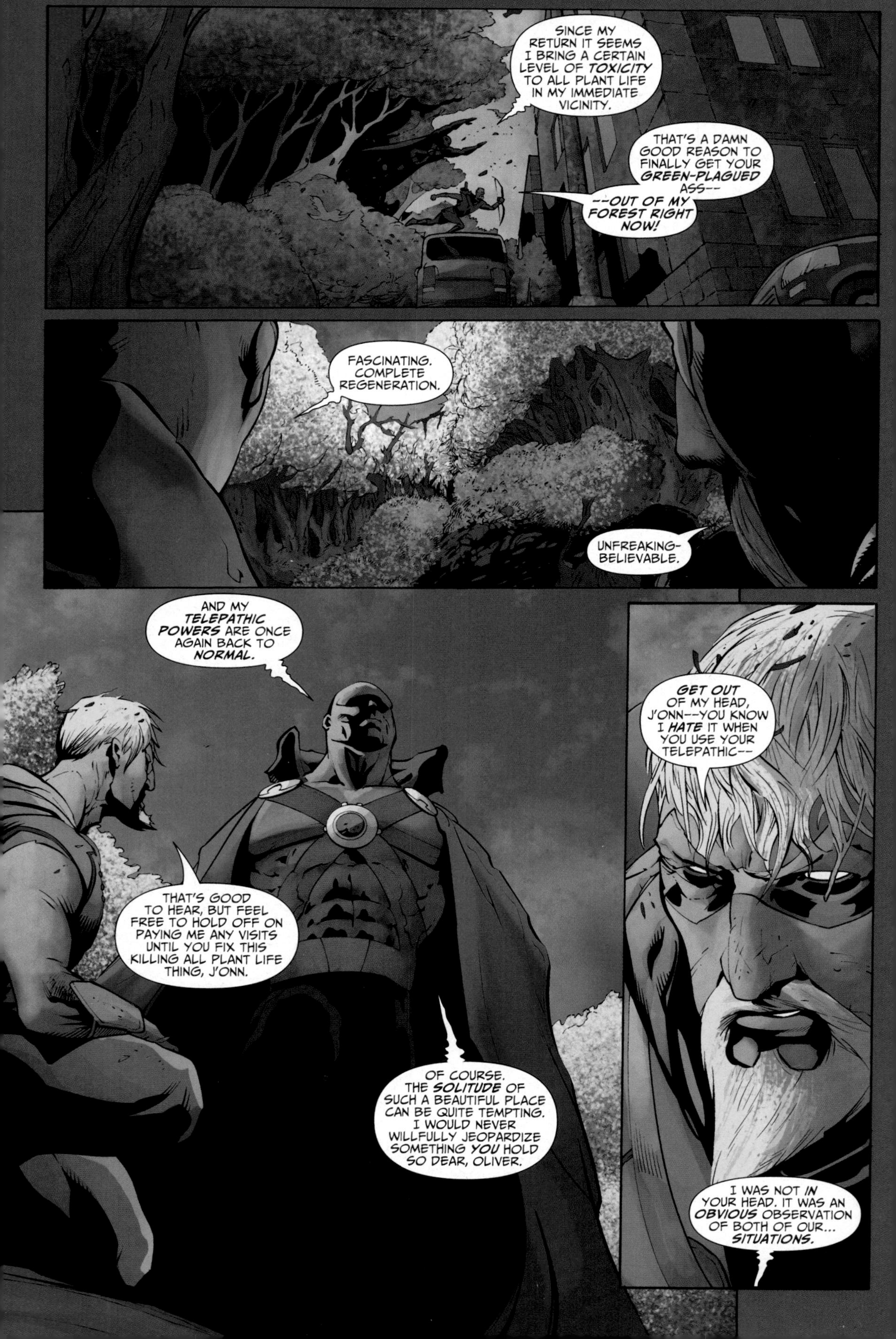
SINCE MY RETURN IT SEEMS I BRING A CERTAIN LEVEL OF TOXICITY TO ALL PLANT LIFE IN MY IMMEDIATE VICINITY.
THAT'S A DAMN GOOD REASON TO FINALLY GET YOUR GREEN-PLAGUED ASS--
--OUT OF MY FOREST RIGHT NOW!
FASCINATING. COMPLETE REGENERATION.
UNFREAKING-BELIEVABLE.
AND MY TELEPATHIC POWERS ARE ONCE AGAIN BACK TO NORMAL.
THAT'S GOOD TO HEAR, BUT FEEL FREE TO HOLD OFF ON PAYING ME ANY VISITS UNTIL YOU FIX THIS KILLING ALL PLANT LIFE THING, J'ONN.
OF COURSE. THE SOLITUDE OF SUCH A BEAUTIFUL PLACE CAN BE QUITE TEMPTING. I WOULD NEVER WILLFULLY JEOPARDIZE SOMETHING YOU HOLD SO DEAR, OLIVER.
GET OUT OF MY HEAD, J'ONN--YOU KNOW I HATE IT WHEN YOU USE YOUR TELEPATHIC--
I WAS NOT IN YOUR HEAD. IT WAS AN OBVIOUS OBSERVATION OF BOTH OF OUR... SITUATIONS.

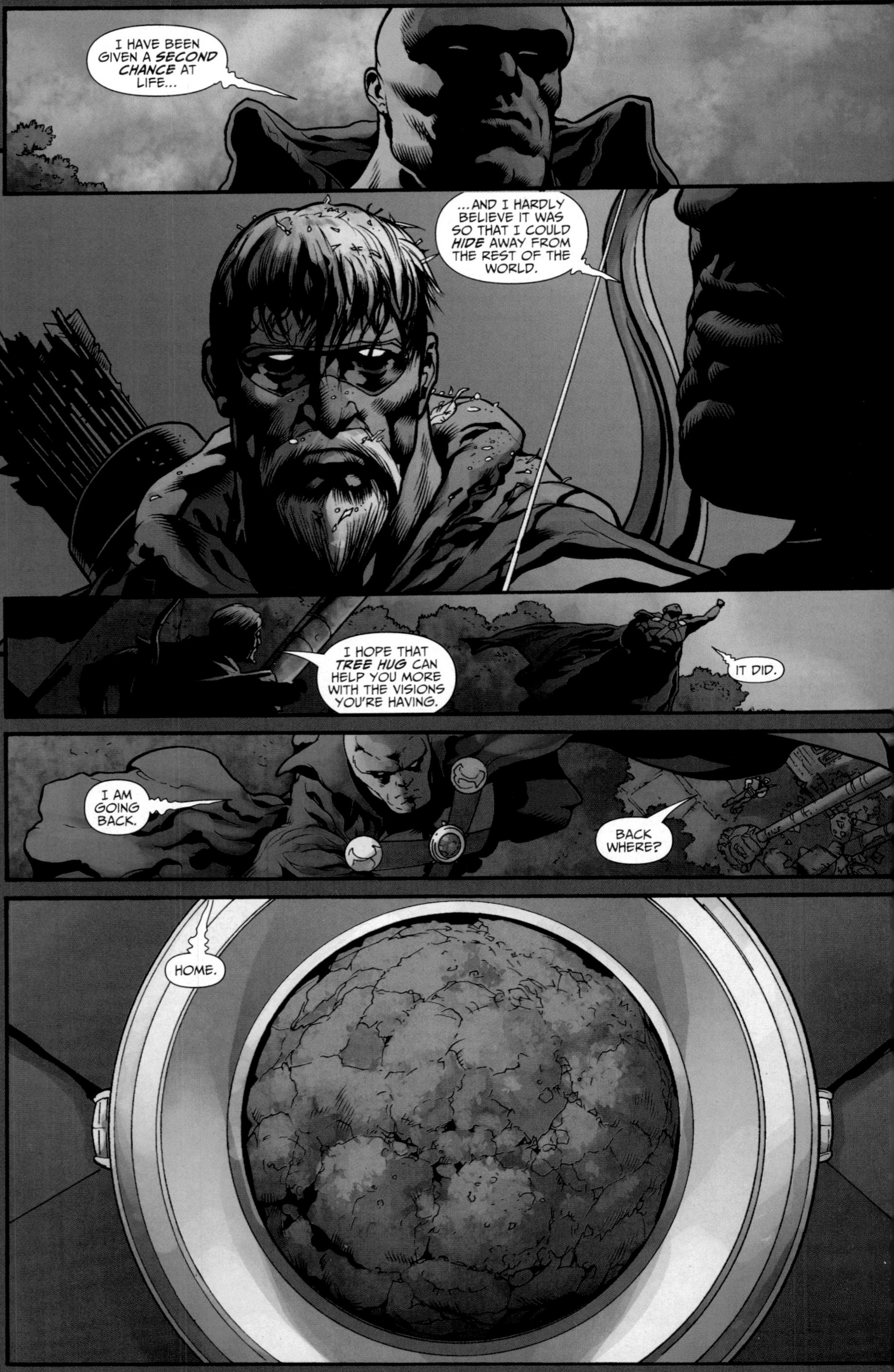
I HAVE BEEN GIVEN A SECOND CHANCE AT LIFE...
...AND I HARDLY BELIEVE IT WAS SO THAT I COULD HIDE AWAY FROM THE REST OF THE WORLD.
I HOPE THAT TREE HUG CAN HELP YOU MORE WITH THE VISIONS YOU'RE HAVING.
IT DID.
I AM GOING BACK.
BACK WHERE?
HOME.

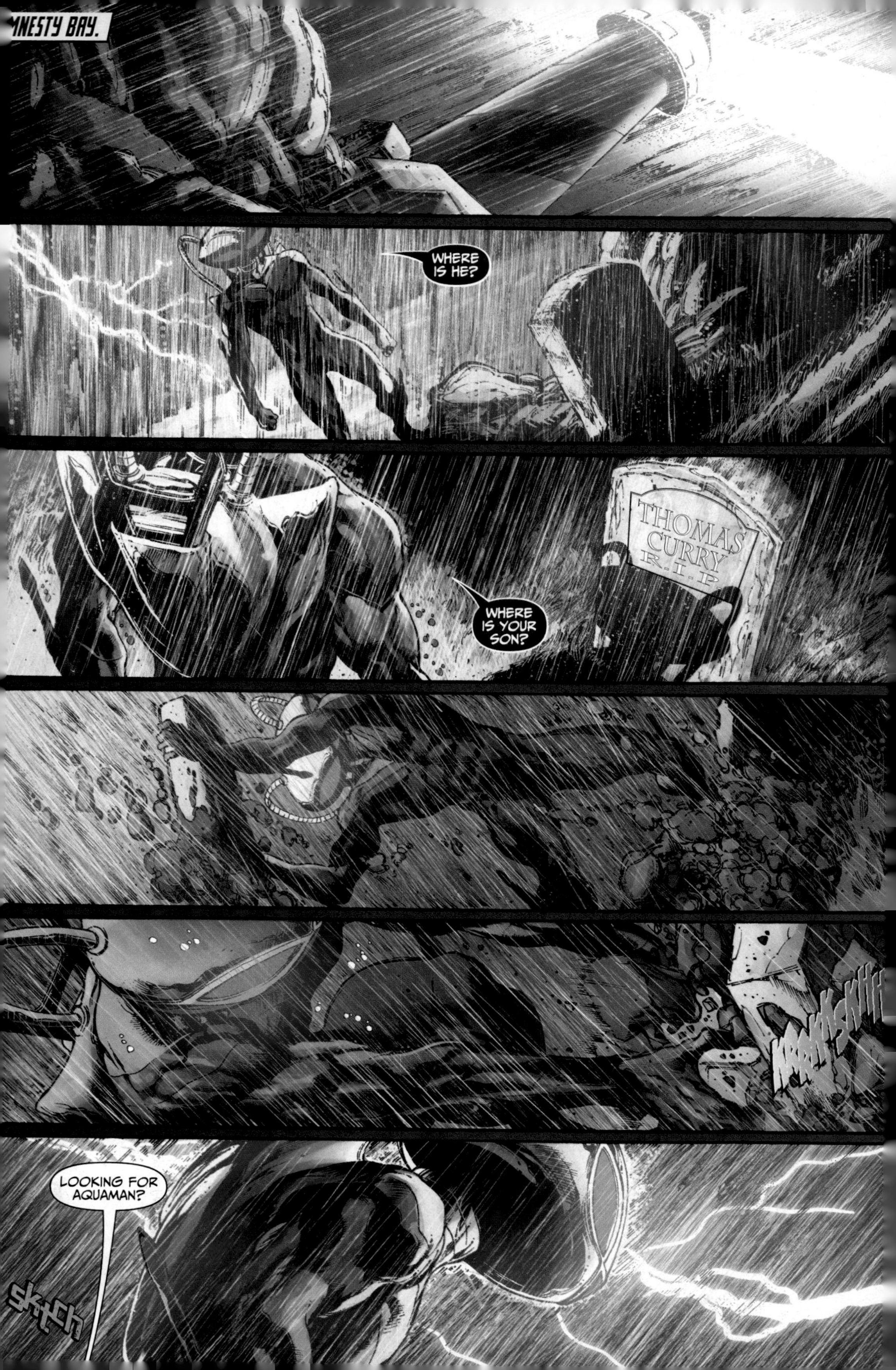
MNESTY BAY.
WHERE IS HE?
THOMAS CURRY R.I.P
WHERE IS YOUR SON?
KRAKASKHH
LOOKING FOR AQUAMAN?
sktch

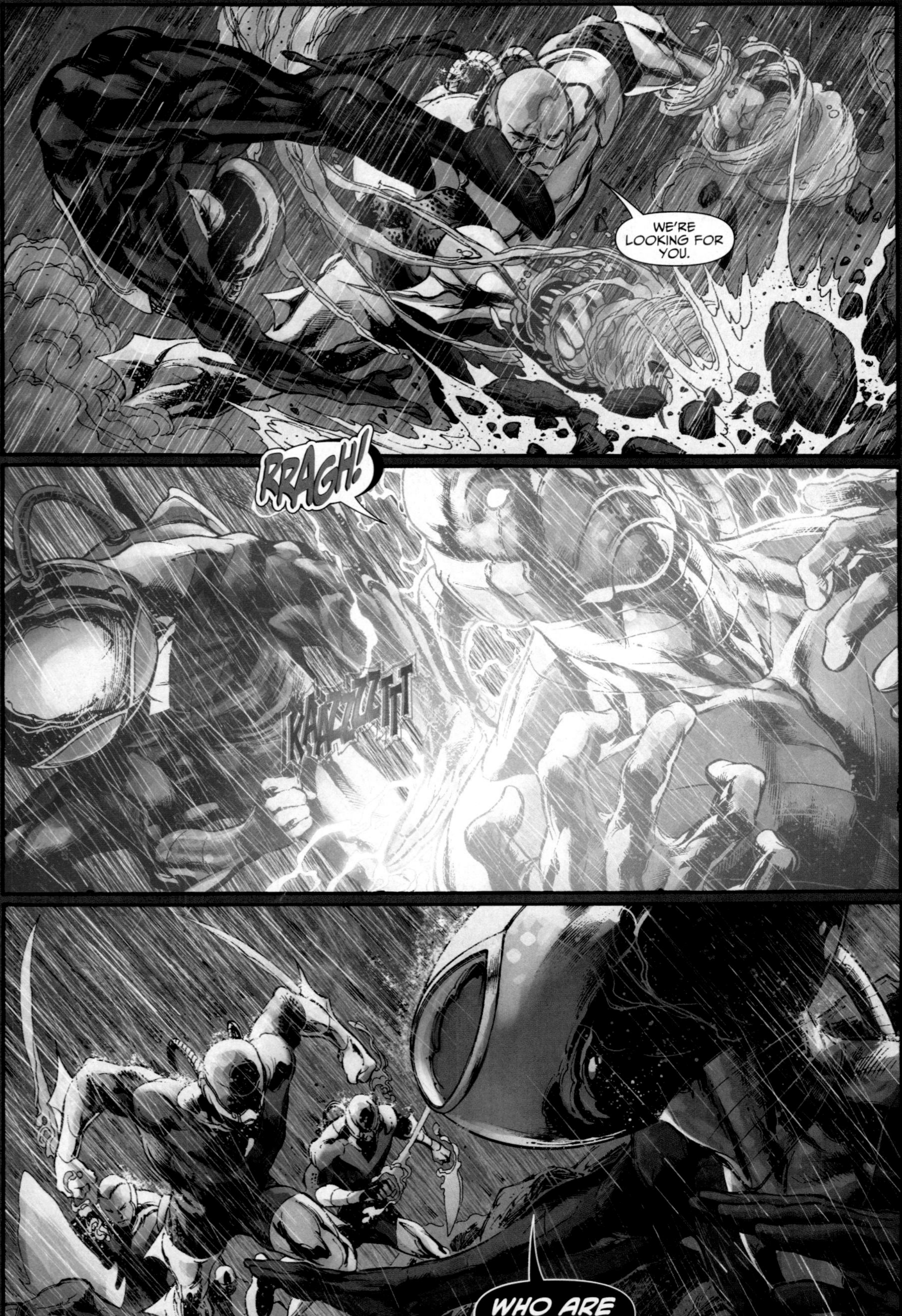
WE'RE LOOKING FOR YOU.
RRAGH!
WHO ARE YOU?

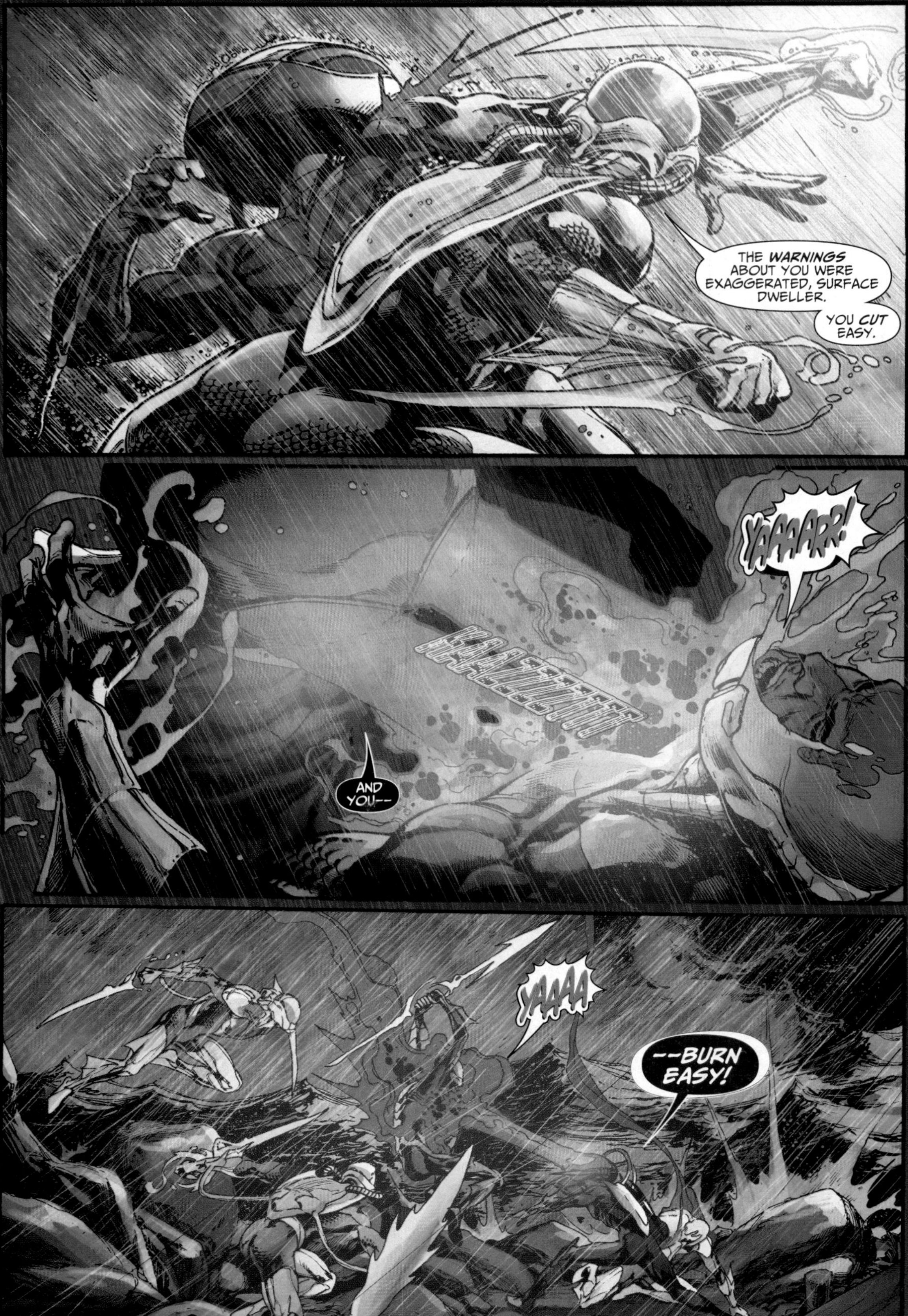
THE WARNINGS ABOUT YOU WERE EXAGGERATED, SURFACE DWELLER.
YOU CUT EASY.
YAAAARR!
AND YOU--
YAAAA
--BURN EASY!

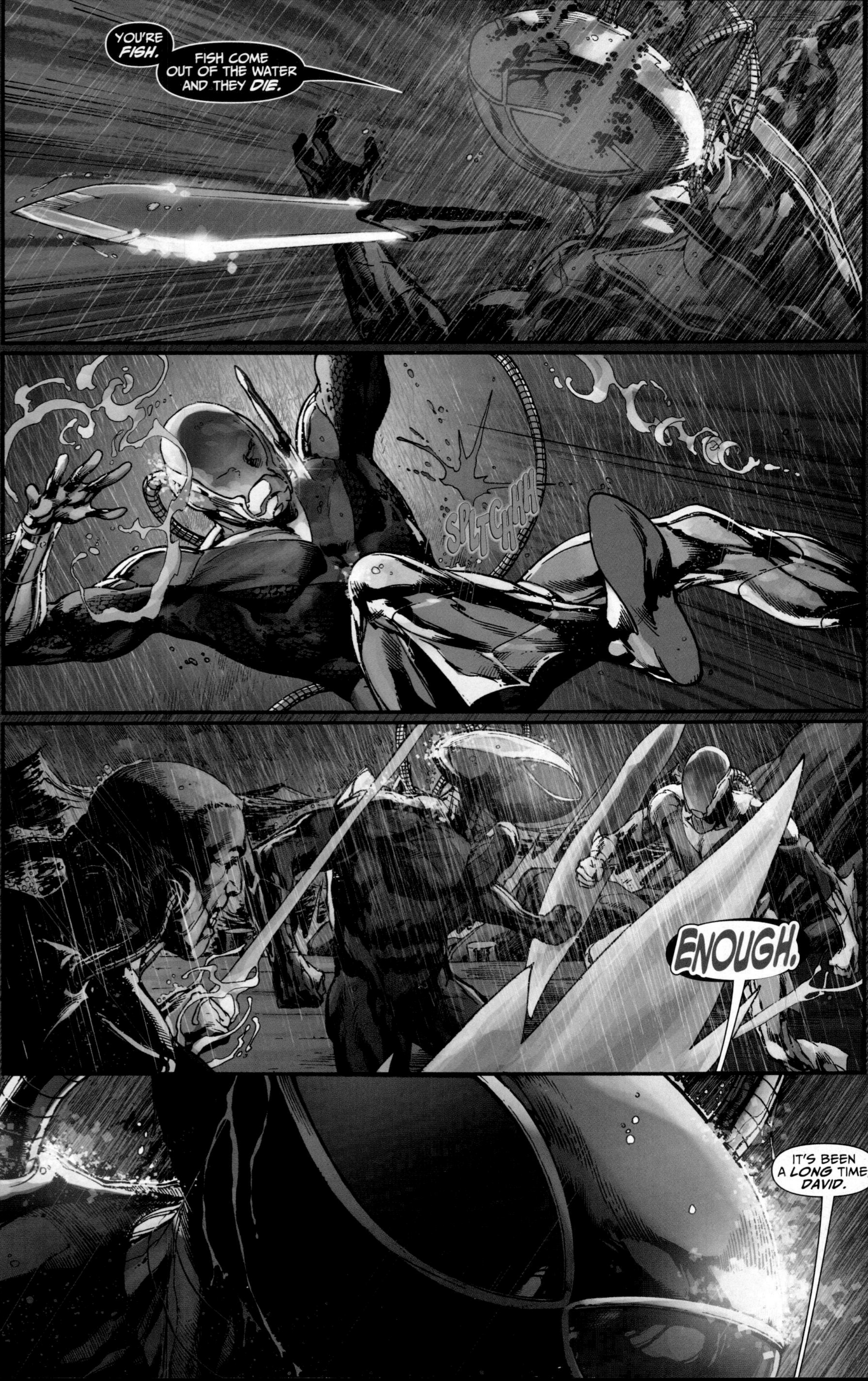
YOU'RE FISH.
FISH COME OUT OF THE WATER AND THEY DIE.
SPLTCHHH
ENOUGH.
IT'S BEEN A LONG TIME, DAVID.

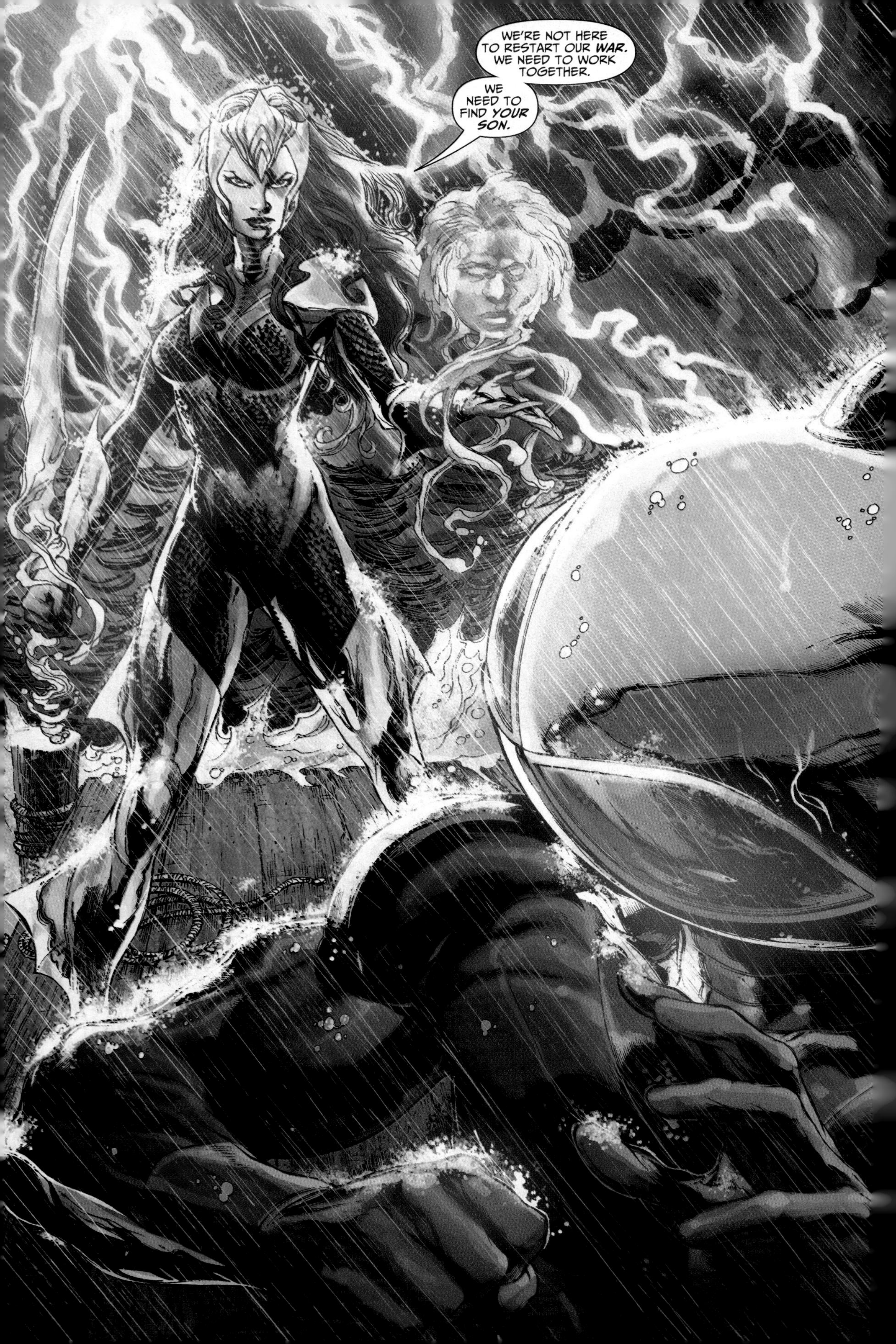
WE'RE NOT HERE TO RESTART OUR WAR. WE NEED TO WORK TOGETHER.
WE NEED TO FIND YOUR SON.

**BRIGHTEST DAY 10**
*Cover by David Finch*

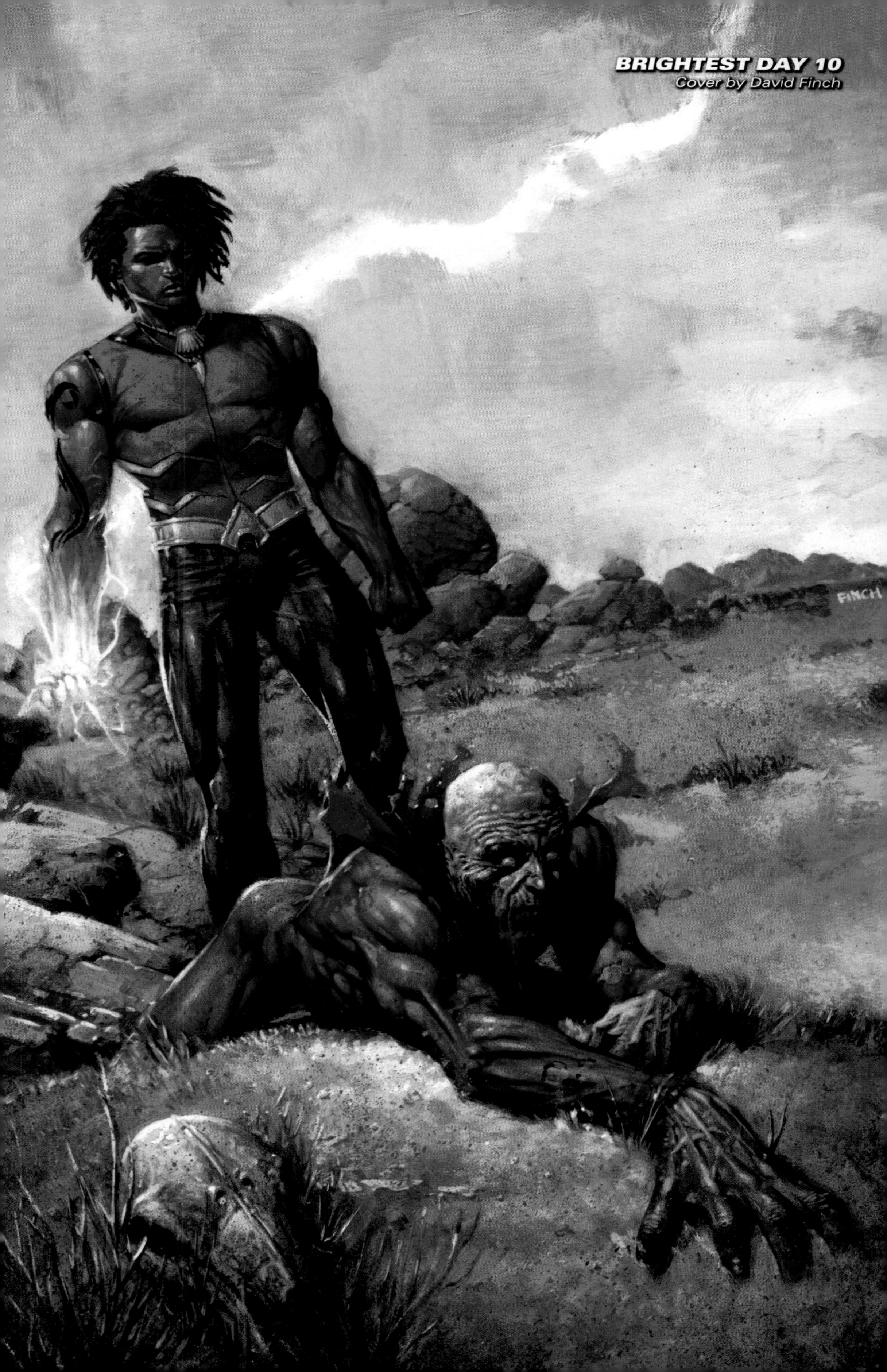
FINCH

# A CHANGE IS GONNA COME

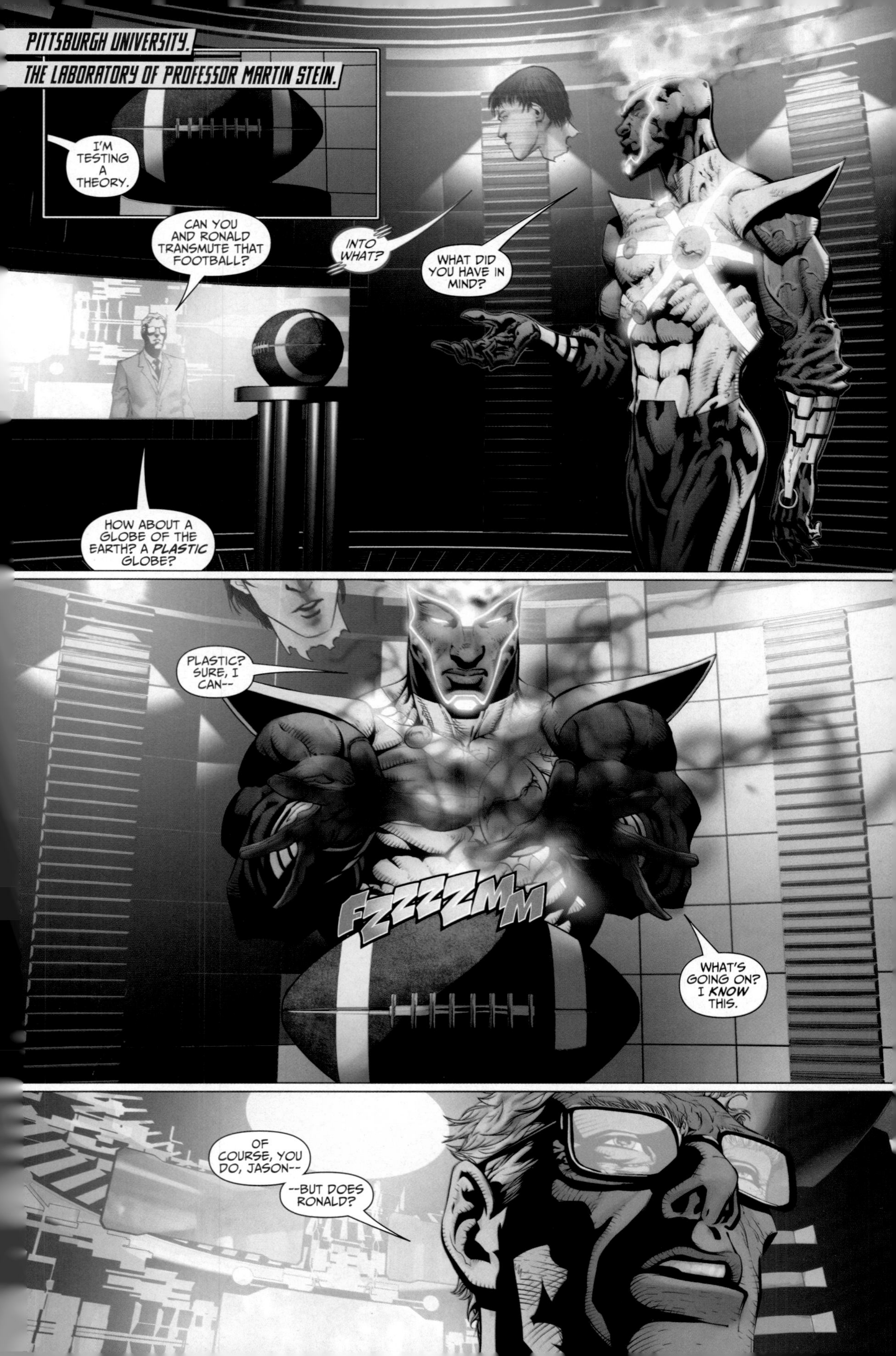
PITTSBURGH UNIVERSITY.
THE LABORATORY OF PROFESSOR MARTIN STEIN.
I'M TESTING A THEORY.
CAN YOU AND RONALD TRANSMUTE THAT FOOTBALL?
INTO WHAT?
WHAT DID YOU HAVE IN MIND?
HOW ABOUT A GLOBE OF THE EARTH? A PLASTIC GLOBE?
PLASTIC? SURE, I CAN--
FZZZZMMM
WHAT'S GOING ON? I KNOW THIS.
OF COURSE, YOU DO, JASON--
--BUT DOES RONALD?

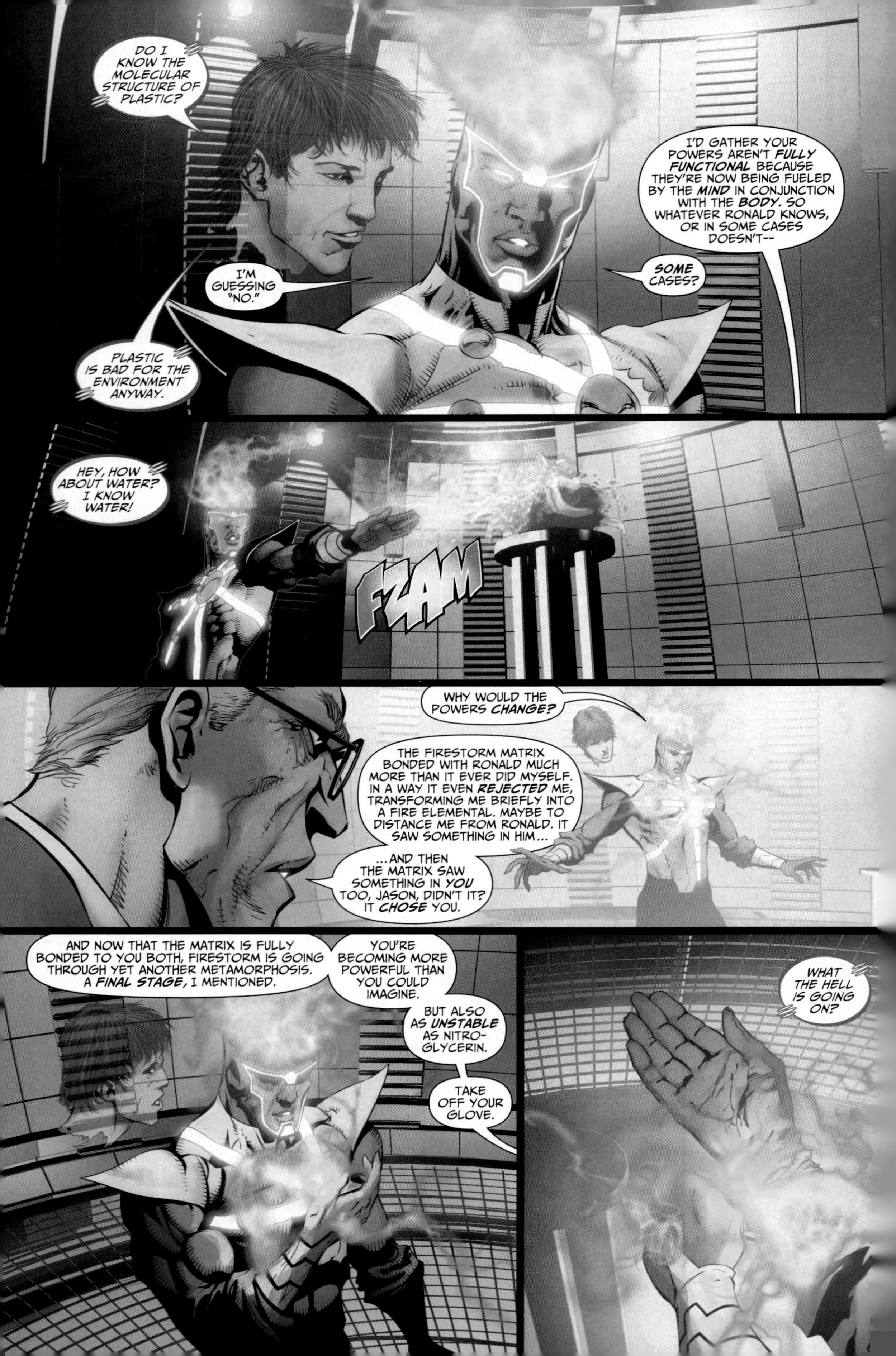
DO I KNOW THE MOLECULAR STRUCTURE OF PLASTIC?
I'D GATHER YOUR POWERS AREN'T FULLY FUNCTIONAL BECAUSE THEY'RE NOW BEING FUELED BY THE MIND IN CONJUNCTION WITH THE BODY. SO WHATEVER RONALD KNOWS, OR IN SOME CASES DOESN'T--
I'M GUESSING "NO."
SOME CASES?
PLASTIC IS BAD FOR THE ENVIRONMENT ANYWAY.
HEY, HOW ABOUT WATER? I KNOW WATER!
FZAM
WHY WOULD THE POWERS CHANGE?
THE FIRESTORM MATRIX BONDED WITH RONALD MUCH MORE THAN IT EVER DID MYSELF. IN A WAY IT EVEN REJECTED ME, TRANSFORMING ME BRIEFLY INTO A FIRE ELEMENTAL. MAYBE TO DISTANCE ME FROM RONALD. IT SAW SOMETHING IN HIM...
...AND THEN THE MATRIX SAW SOMETHING IN YOU TOO, JASON, DIDN'T IT? IT CHOSE YOU.
AND NOW THAT THE MATRIX IS FULLY BONDED TO YOU BOTH, FIRESTORM IS GOING THROUGH YET ANOTHER METAMORPHOSIS. A FINAL STAGE, I MENTIONED.
YOU'RE BECOMING MORE POWERFUL THAN YOU COULD IMAGINE.
BUT ALSO AS UNSTABLE AS NITRO-GLYCERIN.
TAKE OFF YOUR GLOVE.
WHAT THE HELL IS GOING ON?

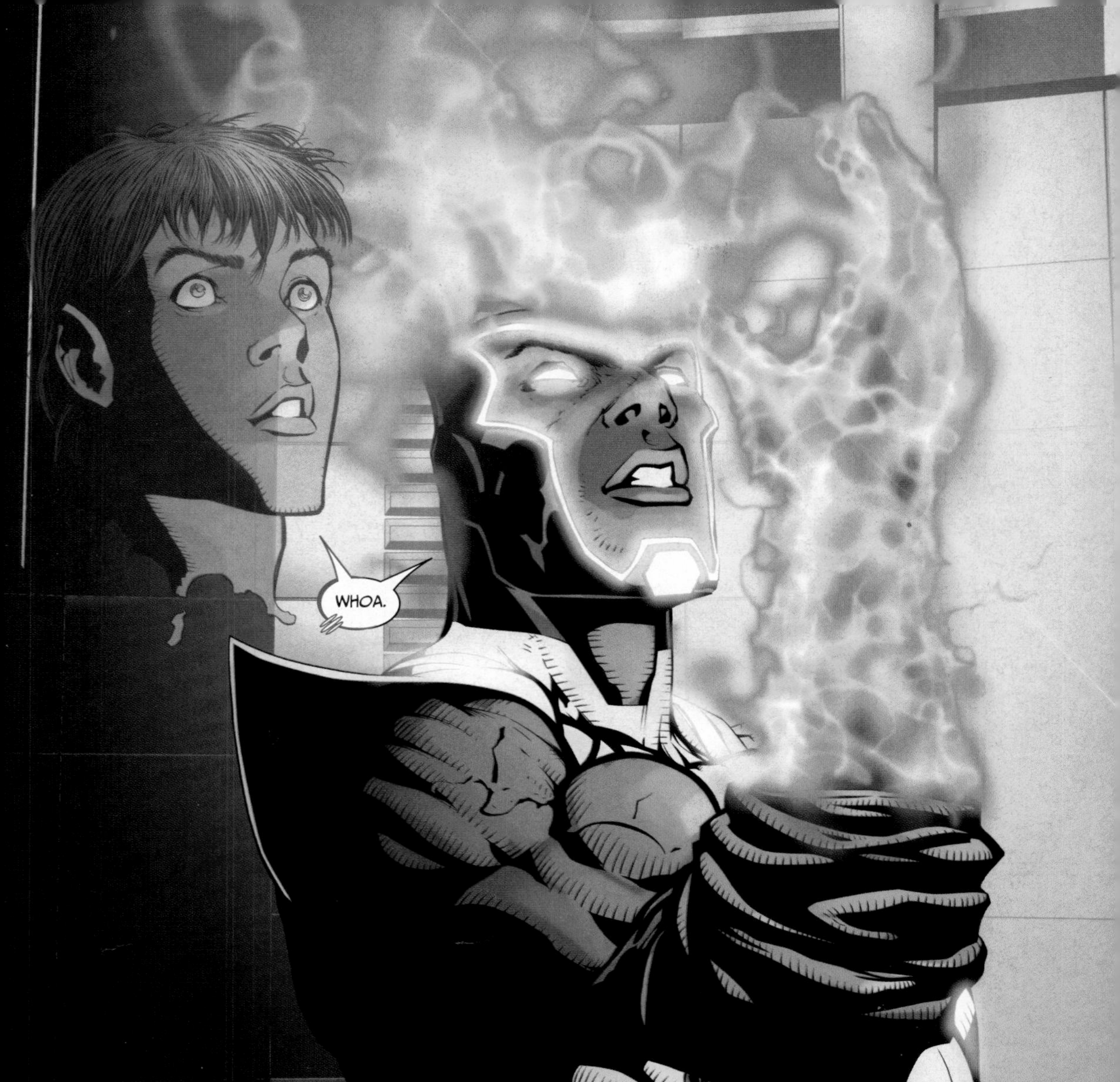
WHOA.

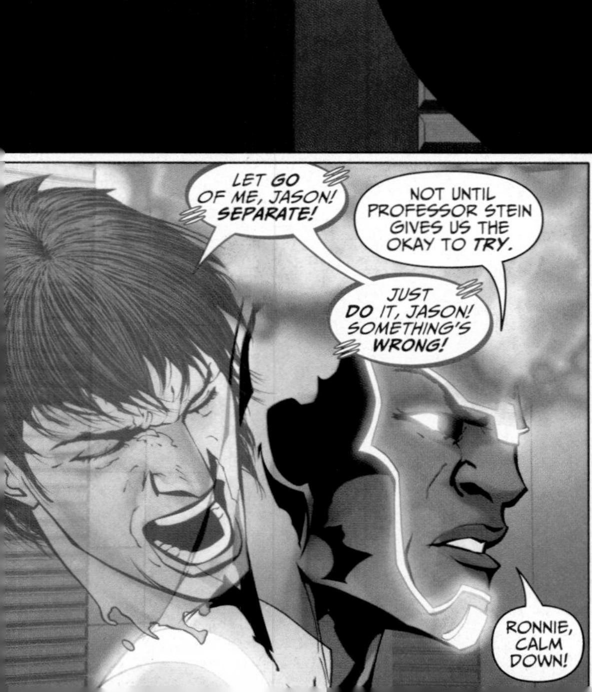
LET GO OF ME, JASON! SEPARATE!
NOT UNTIL PROFESSOR STEIN GIVES US THE OKAY TO TRY.
JUST DO IT, JASON! SOMETHING'S WRONG!
RONNIE, CALM DOWN!

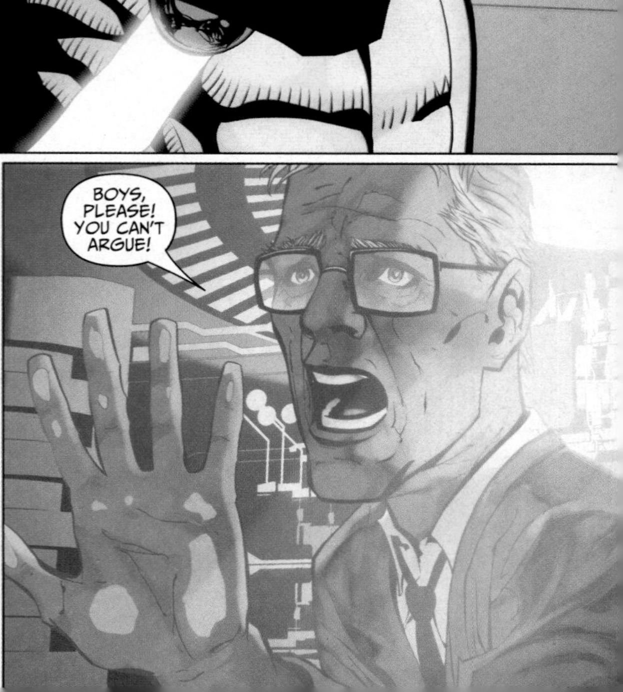
BOYS, PLEASE! YOU CAN'T ARGUE!

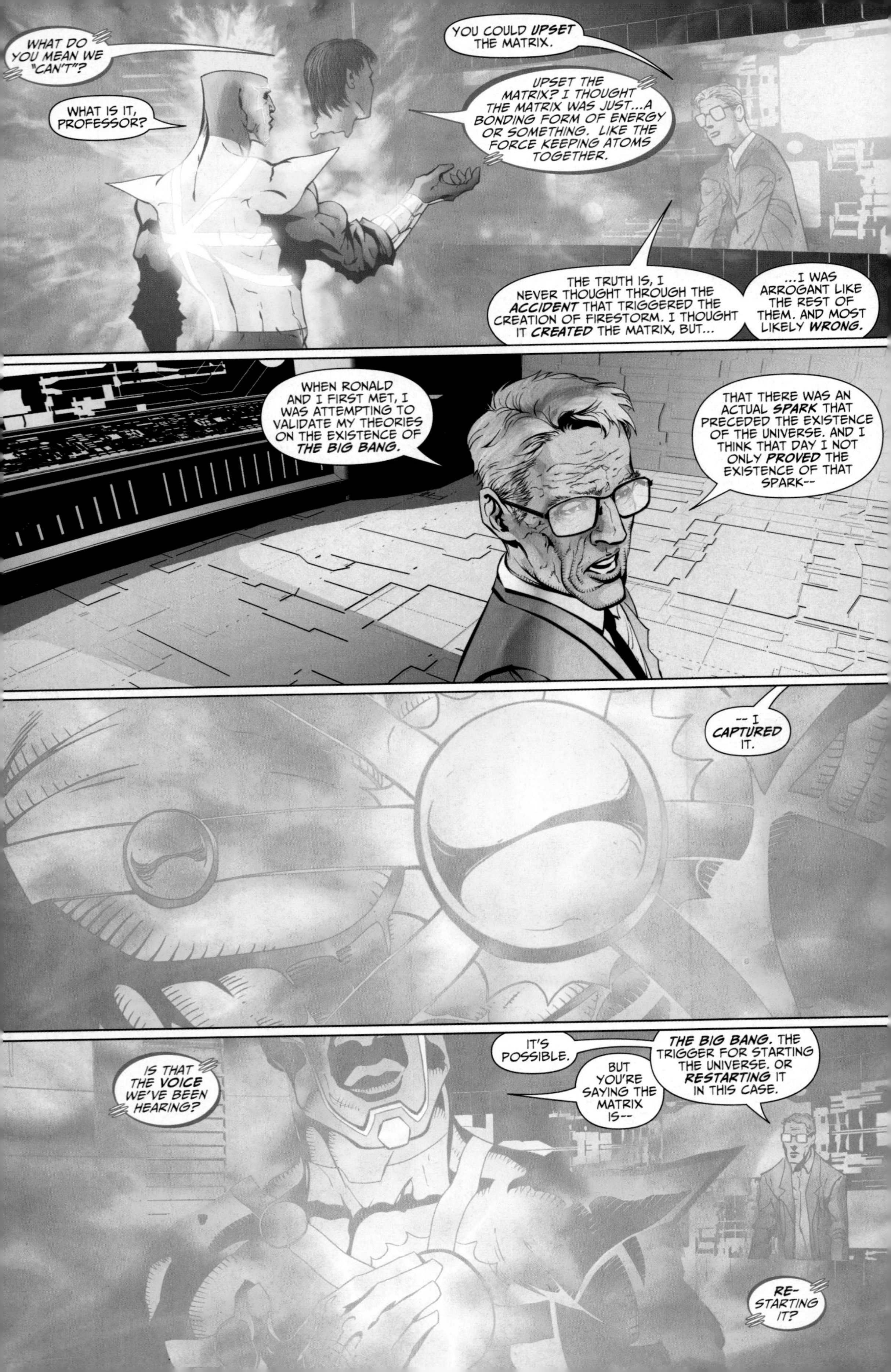
WHAT DO YOU MEAN WE "CAN'T"?
YOU COULD UPSET THE MATRIX.
WHAT IS IT, PROFESSOR?
UPSET THE MATRIX? I THOUGHT THE MATRIX WAS JUST...A BONDING FORM OF ENERGY OR SOMETHING. LIKE THE FORCE KEEPING ATOMS TOGETHER.
THE TRUTH IS, I NEVER THOUGHT THROUGH THE ACCIDENT THAT TRIGGERED THE CREATION OF FIRESTORM. I THOUGHT IT CREATED THE MATRIX, BUT...
...I WAS ARROGANT LIKE THE REST OF THEM. AND MOST LIKELY WRONG.
WHEN RONALD AND I FIRST MET, I WAS ATTEMPTING TO VALIDATE MY THEORIES ON THE EXISTENCE OF THE BIG BANG.
THAT THERE WAS AN ACTUAL SPARK THAT PRECEDED THE EXISTENCE OF THE UNIVERSE. AND I THINK THAT DAY I NOT ONLY PROVED THE EXISTENCE OF THAT SPARK--
-- I CAPTURED IT.
IS THAT THE VOICE WE'VE BEEN HEARING?
IT'S POSSIBLE.
BUT YOU'RE SAYING THE MATRIX IS--
THE BIG BANG. THE TRIGGER FOR STARTING THE UNIVERSE. OR RESTARTING IT IN THIS CASE.
RE-STARTING IT?

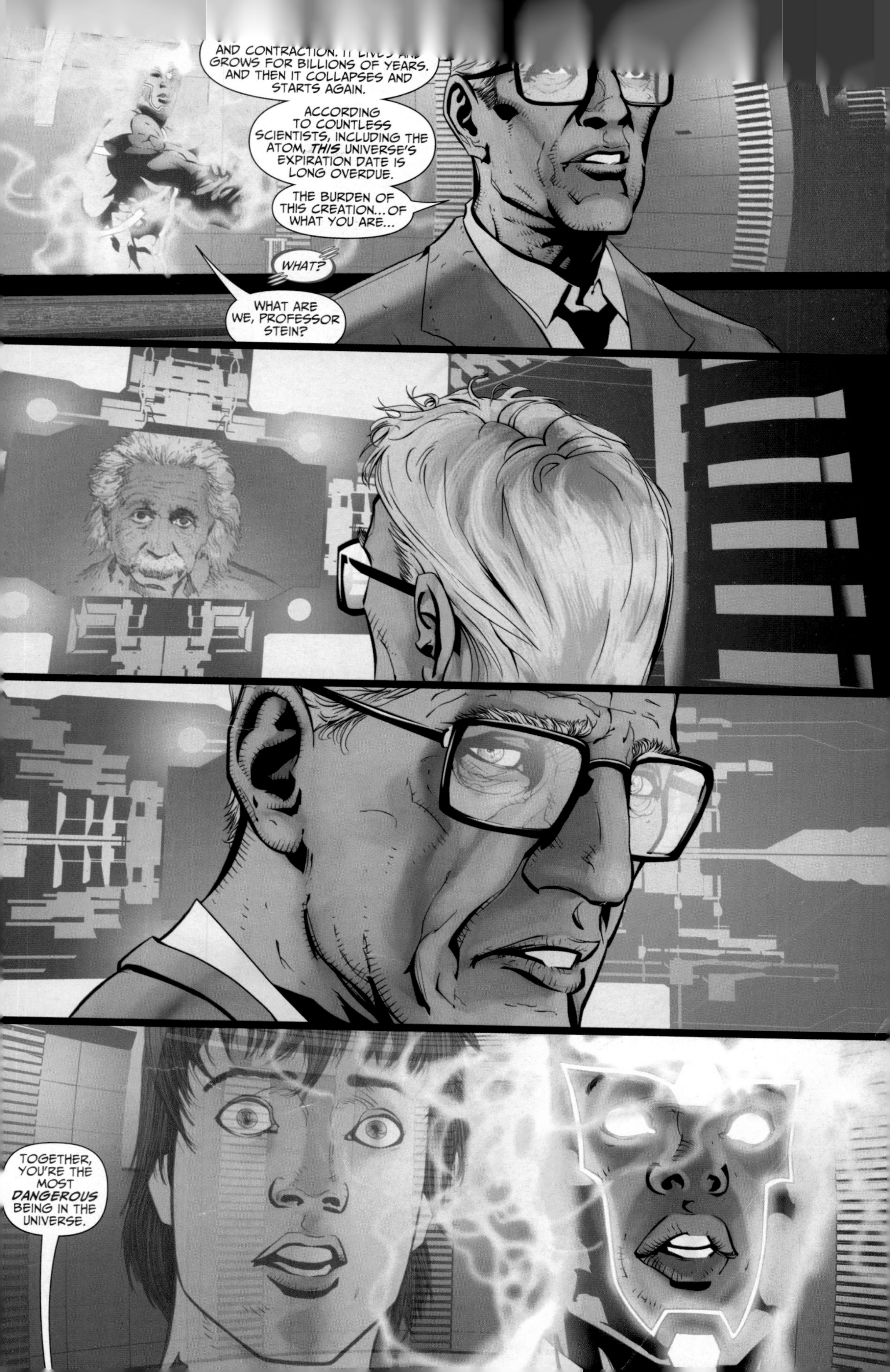
AND CONTRACTION. IT LIVES AND GROWS FOR BILLIONS OF YEARS. AND THEN IT COLLAPSES AND STARTS AGAIN.
ACCORDING TO COUNTLESS SCIENTISTS, INCLUDING THE ATOM, *THIS* UNIVERSE'S EXPIRATION DATE IS LONG OVERDUE.
THE BURDEN OF THIS CREATION... OF WHAT YOU ARE...
*WHAT?*
WHAT ARE WE, PROFESSOR STEIN?
TOGETHER, YOU'RE THE MOST *DANGEROUS* BEING IN THE UNIVERSE.

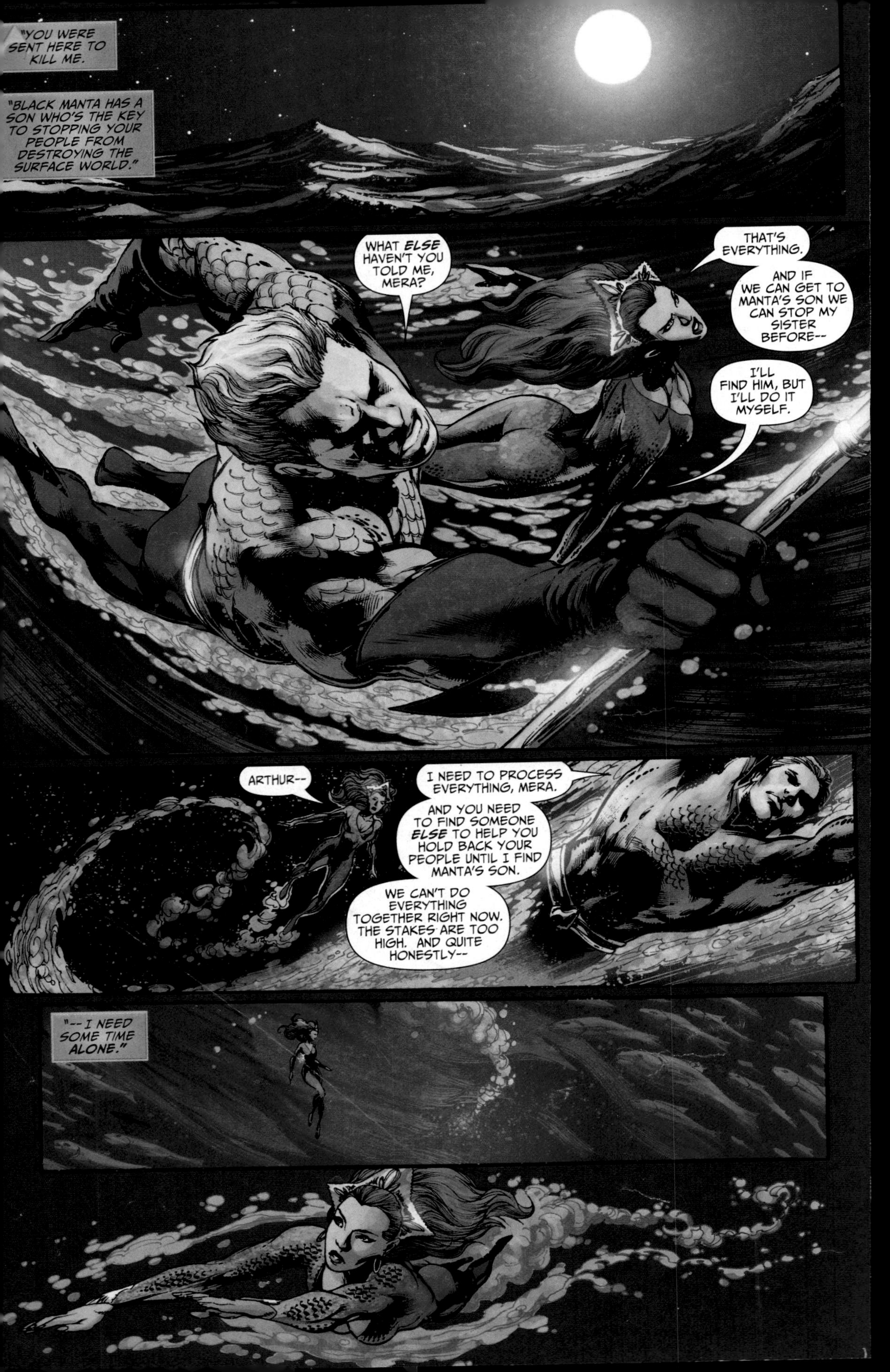
"YOU WERE SENT HERE TO KILL ME.
"BLACK MANTA HAS A SON WHO'S THE KEY TO STOPPING YOUR PEOPLE FROM DESTROYING THE SURFACE WORLD."
WHAT ELSE HAVEN'T YOU TOLD ME, MERA?
THAT'S EVERYTHING.
AND IF WE CAN GET TO MANTA'S SON WE CAN STOP MY SISTER BEFORE--
I'LL FIND HIM, BUT I'LL DO IT MYSELF.
ARTHUR--
I NEED TO PROCESS EVERYTHING, MERA.
AND YOU NEED TO FIND SOMEONE ELSE TO HELP YOU HOLD BACK YOUR PEOPLE UNTIL I FIND MANTA'S SON.
WE CAN'T DO EVERYTHING TOGETHER RIGHT NOW. THE STAKES ARE TOO HIGH. AND QUITE HONESTLY--
"-- I NEED SOME TIME ALONE."

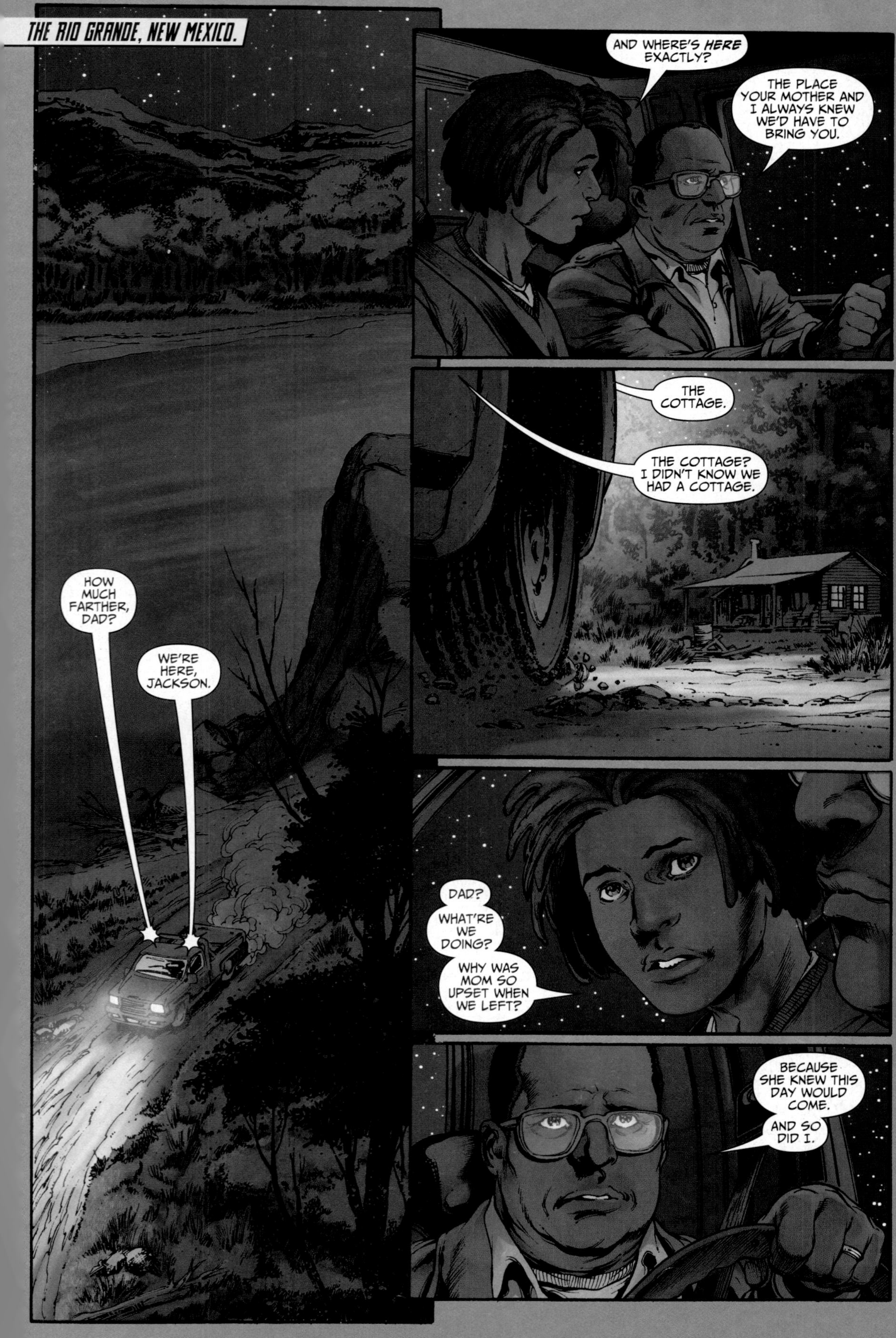
THE RIO GRANDE, NEW MEXICO.
HOW MUCH FARTHER, DAD?
WE'RE HERE, JACKSON.
AND WHERE'S HERE EXACTLY?
THE PLACE YOUR MOTHER AND I ALWAYS KNEW WE'D HAVE TO BRING YOU.
THE COTTAGE.
THE COTTAGE? I DIDN'T KNOW WE HAD A COTTAGE.
DAD?
WHAT'RE WE DOING?
WHY WAS MOM SO UPSET WHEN WE LEFT?
BECAUSE SHE KNEW THIS DAY WOULD COME.
AND SO DID I.

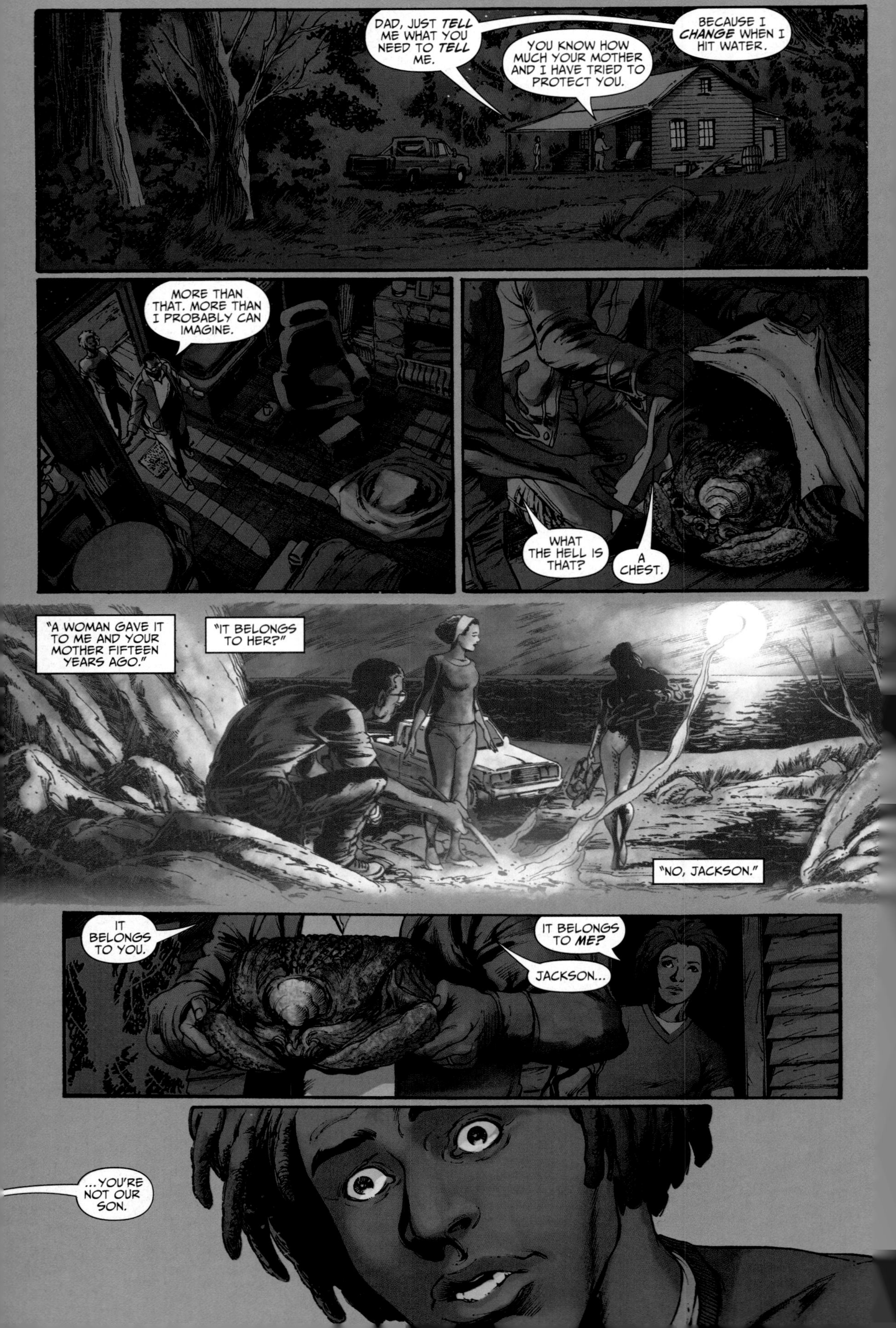
DAD, JUST TELL ME WHAT YOU NEED TO TELL ME.
BECAUSE I CHANGE WHEN I HIT WATER.
YOU KNOW HOW MUCH YOUR MOTHER AND I HAVE TRIED TO PROTECT YOU.
MORE THAN THAT. MORE THAN I PROBABLY CAN IMAGINE.
WHAT THE HELL IS THAT?
A CHEST.
"A WOMAN GAVE IT TO ME AND YOUR MOTHER FIFTEEN YEARS AGO."
"IT BELONGS TO HER?"
"NO, JACKSON."
IT BELONGS TO YOU.
IT BELONGS TO ME?
JACKSON...
...YOU'RE NOT OUR SON.

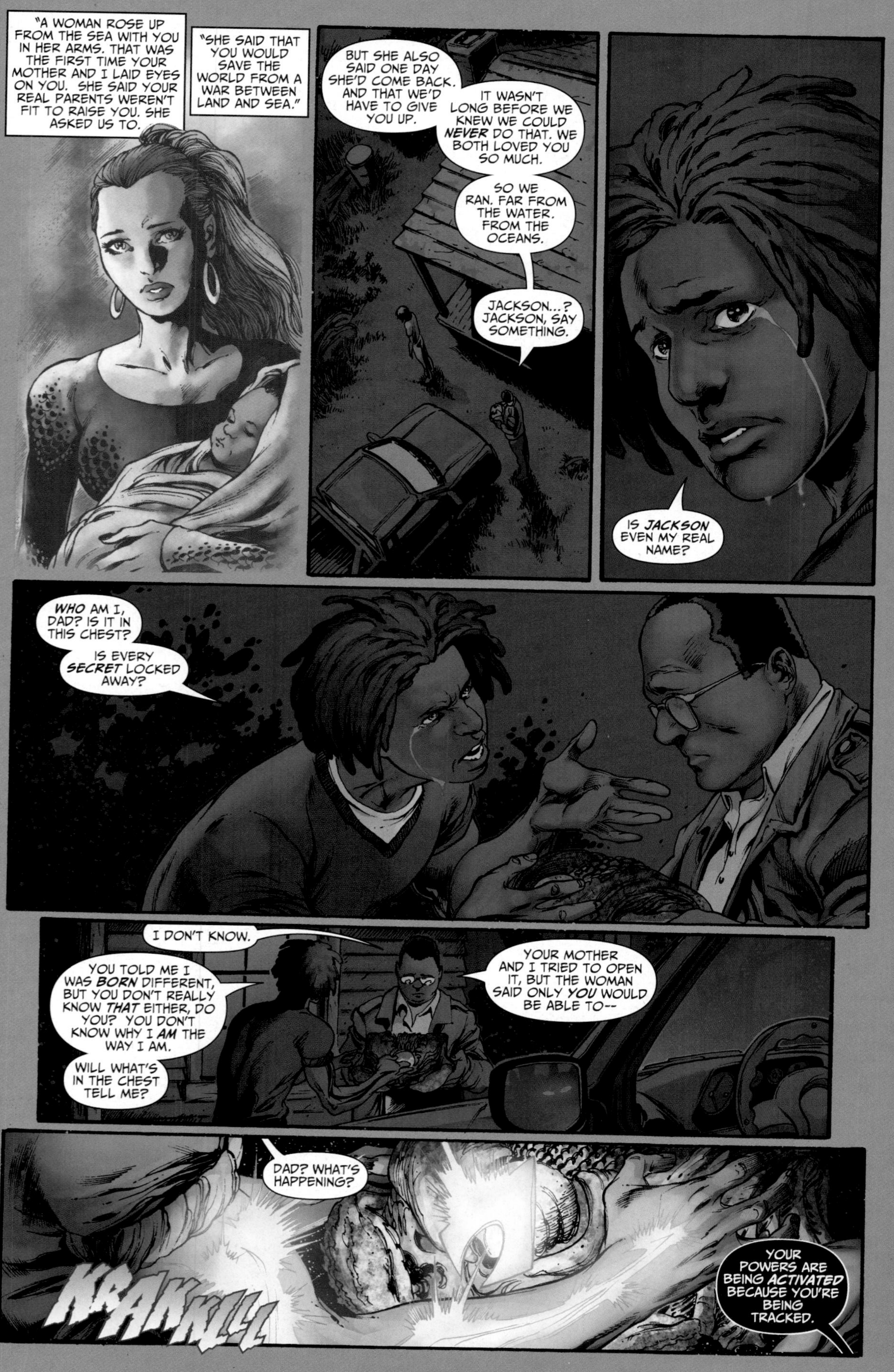
"A WOMAN ROSE UP FROM THE SEA WITH YOU IN HER ARMS. THAT WAS THE FIRST TIME YOUR MOTHER AND I LAID EYES ON YOU. SHE SAID YOUR REAL PARENTS WEREN'T FIT TO RAISE YOU. SHE ASKED US TO.
"SHE SAID THAT YOU WOULD SAVE THE WORLD FROM A WAR BETWEEN LAND AND SEA."
BUT SHE ALSO SAID ONE DAY SHE'D COME BACK. AND THAT WE'D HAVE TO GIVE YOU UP.
IT WASN'T LONG BEFORE WE KNEW WE COULD NEVER DO THAT. WE BOTH LOVED YOU SO MUCH.
SO WE RAN. FAR FROM THE WATER. FROM THE OCEANS.
JACKSON...? JACKSON, SAY SOMETHING.
IS JACKSON EVEN MY REAL NAME?
WHO AM I, DAD? IS IT IN THIS CHEST?
IS EVERY SECRET LOCKED AWAY?
I DON'T KNOW.
YOU TOLD ME I WAS BORN DIFFERENT, BUT YOU DON'T REALLY KNOW THAT EITHER, DO YOU? YOU DON'T KNOW WHY I AM THE WAY I AM.
WILL WHAT'S IN THE CHEST TELL ME?
YOUR MOTHER AND I TRIED TO OPEN IT, BUT THE WOMAN SAID ONLY YOU WOULD BE ABLE TO--
DAD? WHAT'S HAPPENING?
KRAKKLL
YOUR POWERS ARE BEING ACTIVATED BECAUSE YOU'RE BEING TRACKED.

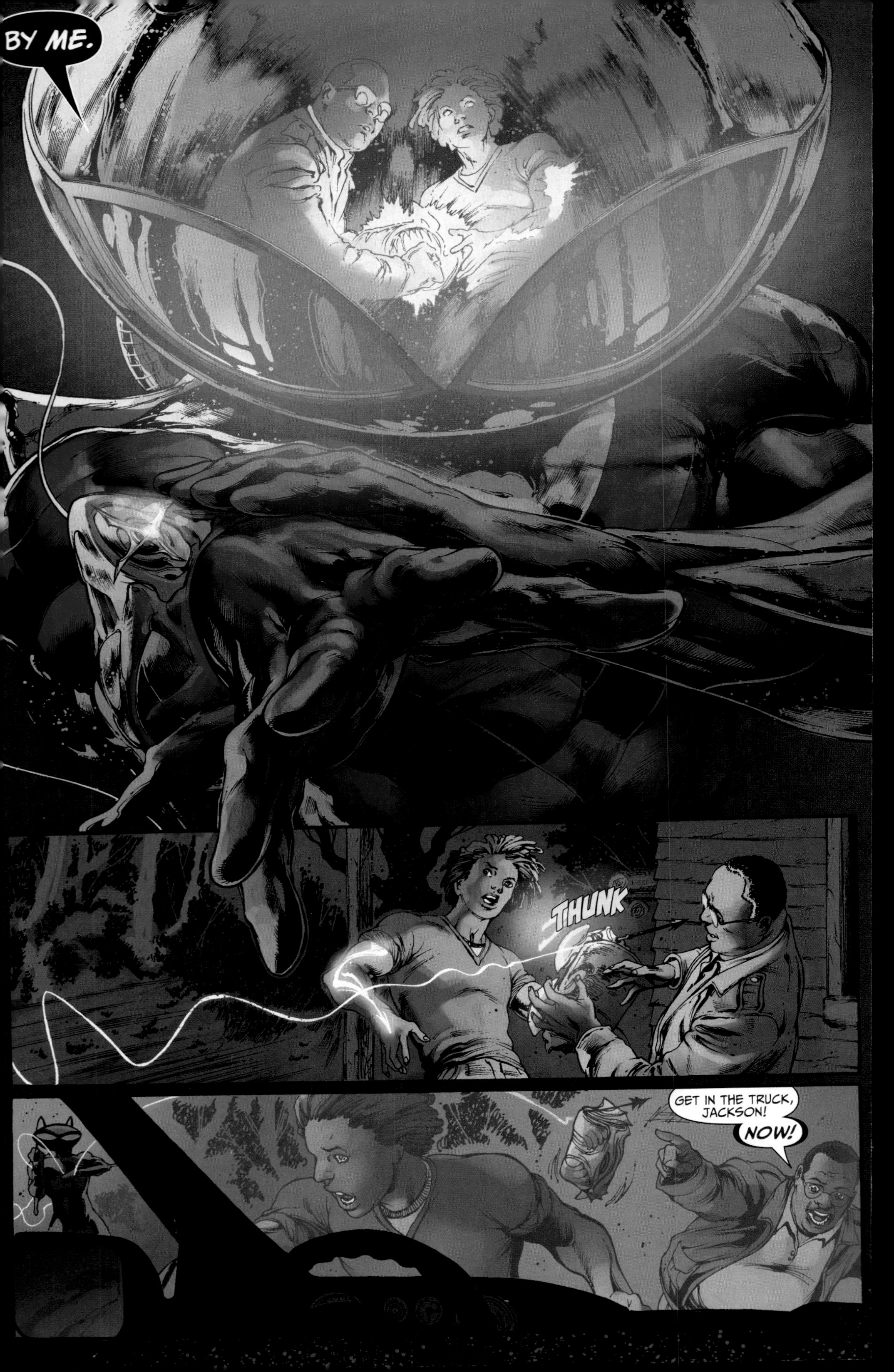
BY ME.
THUNK
GET IN THE TRUCK, JACKSON!
NOW!

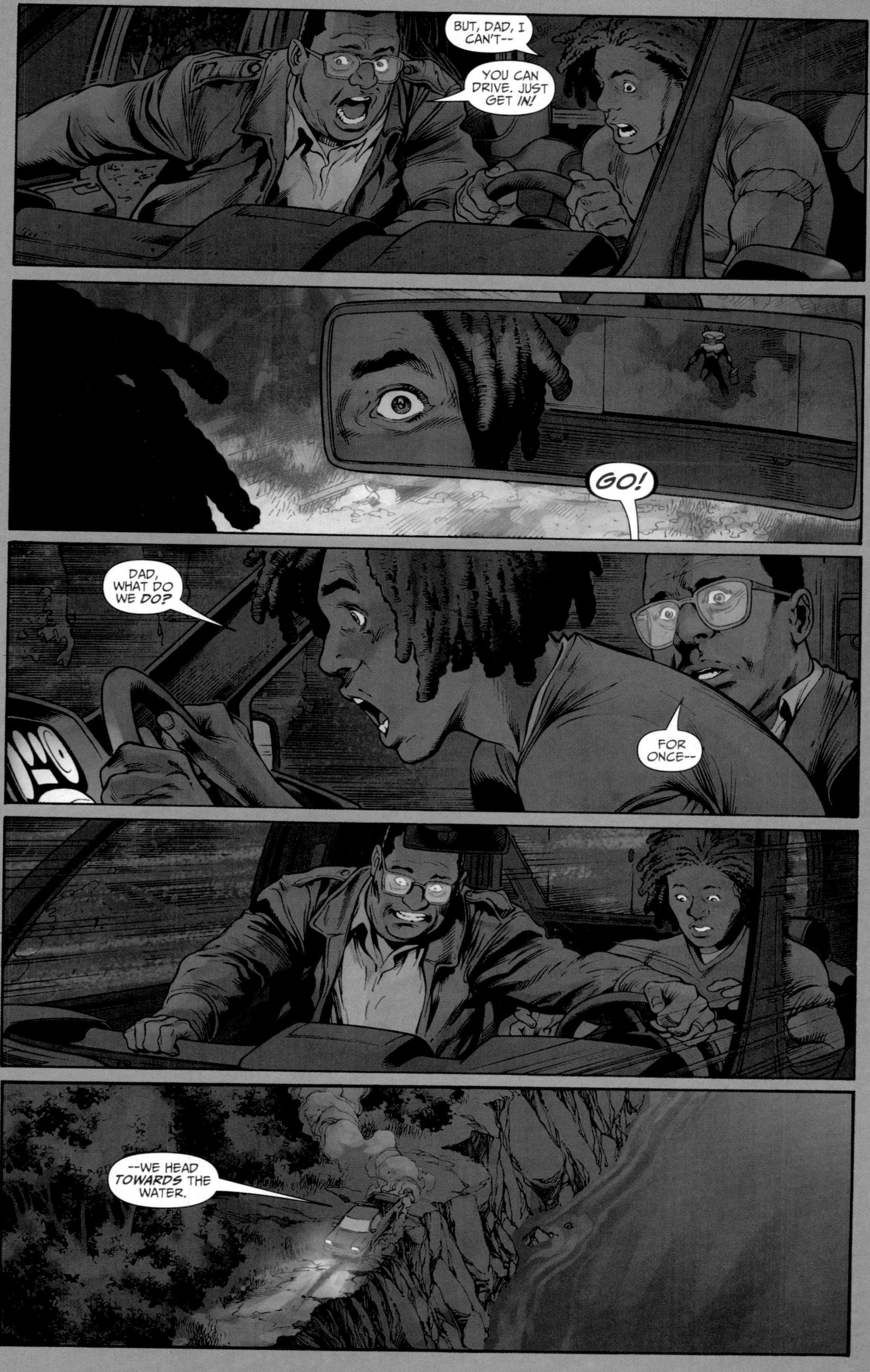
BUT, DAD, I CAN'T--
YOU CAN DRIVE. JUST GET *IN!*
GO!
DAD, WHAT DO WE *DO?*
FOR ONCE--
--WE HEAD *TOWARDS* THE WATER.

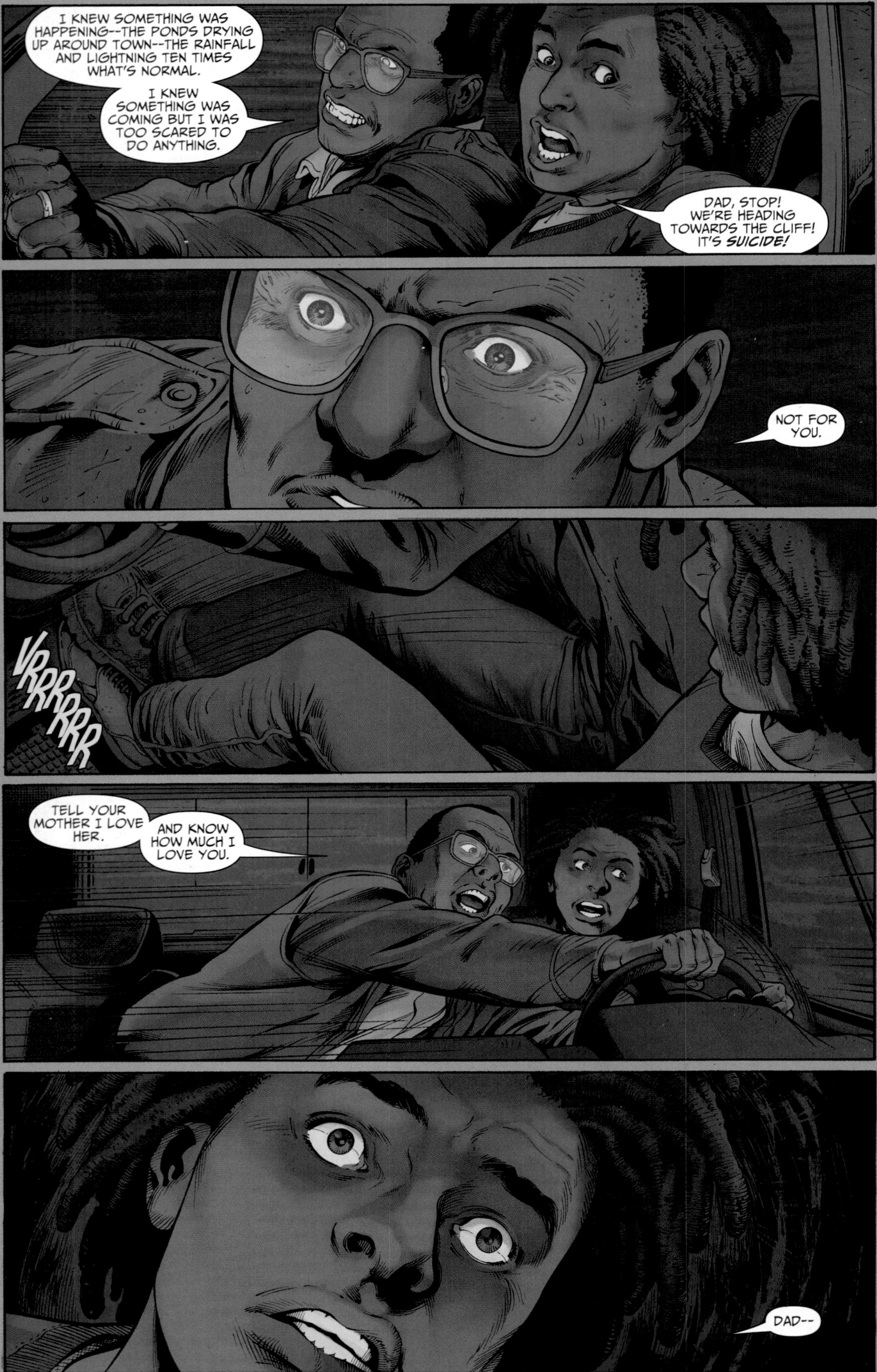
I KNEW SOMETHING WAS HAPPENING--THE PONDS DRYING UP AROUND TOWN--THE RAINFALL AND LIGHTNING TEN TIMES WHAT'S NORMAL.
I KNEW SOMETHING WAS COMING BUT I WAS TOO SCARED TO DO ANYTHING.
DAD, STOP! WE'RE HEADING TOWARDS THE CLIFF! IT'S *SUICIDE!*
NOT FOR YOU.
VRRRRRR
TELL YOUR MOTHER I LOVE HER.
AND KNOW HOW MUCH I LOVE YOU.
DAD--

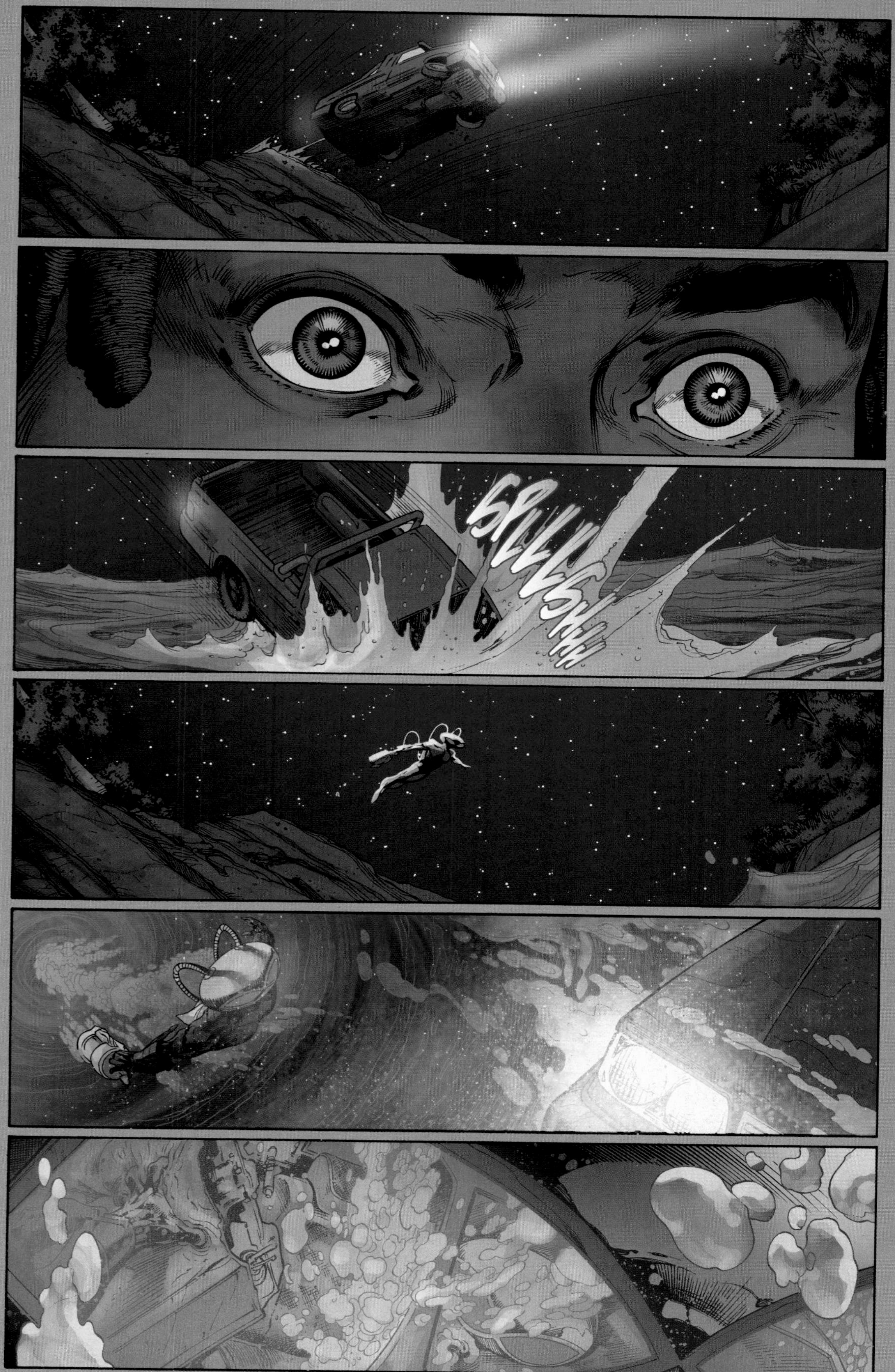
SPLUUSHHH

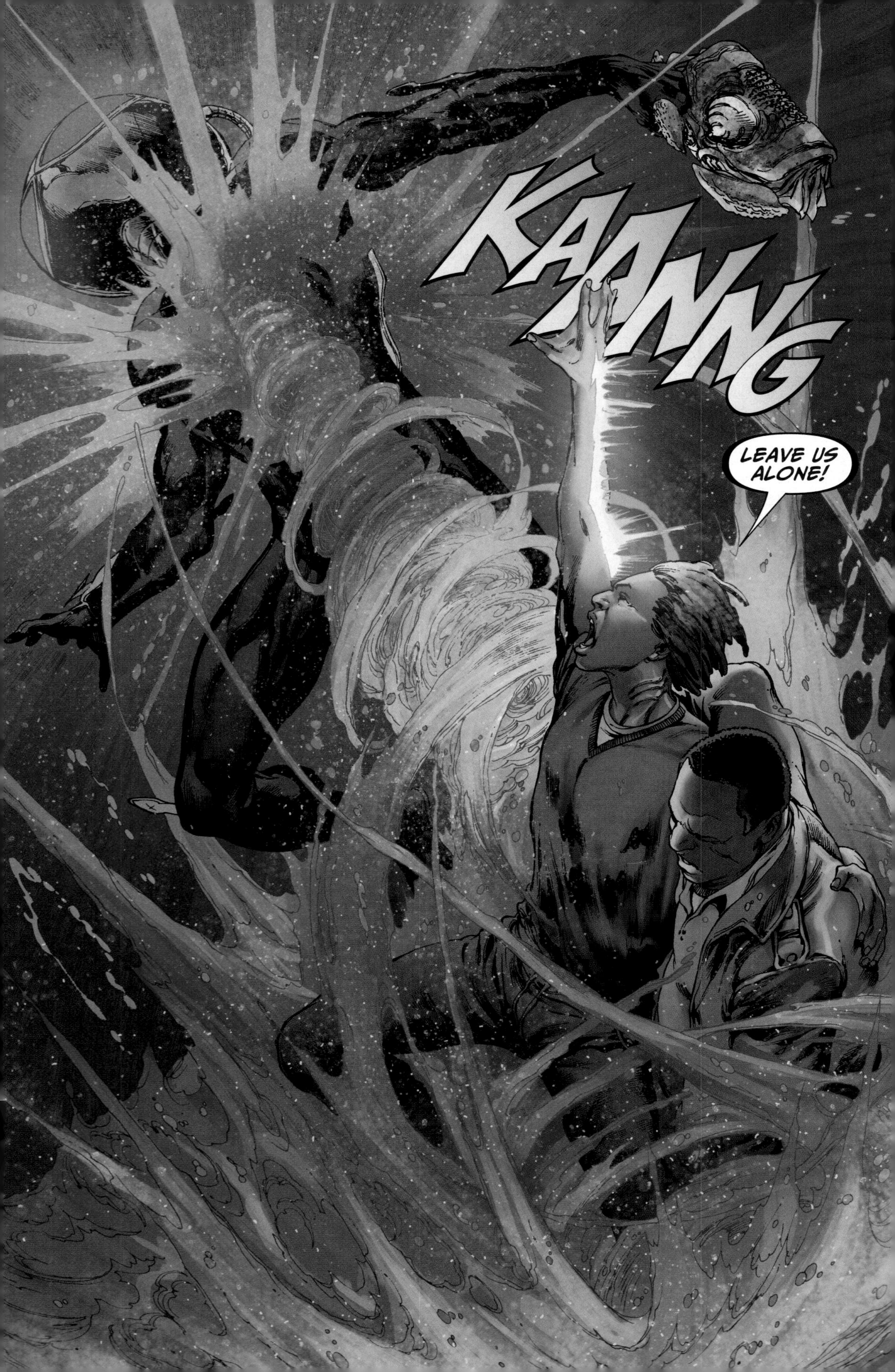
KAANNG
LEAVE US ALONE!

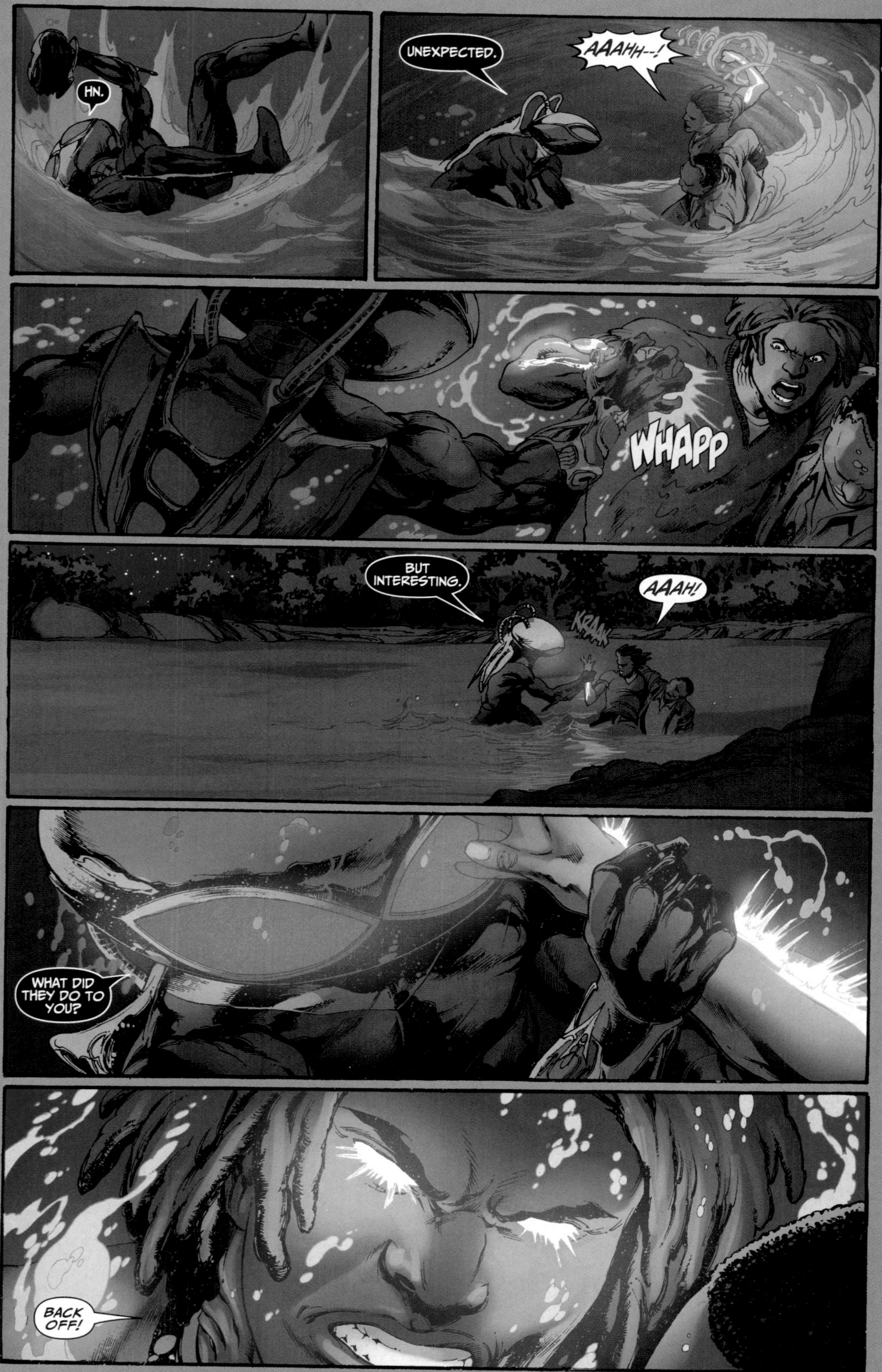
HN.
UNEXPECTED.
AAAHH--!
WHAPP
BUT INTERESTING.
AAAH!
KRAAK
WHAT DID THEY DO TO YOU?
BACK OFF!

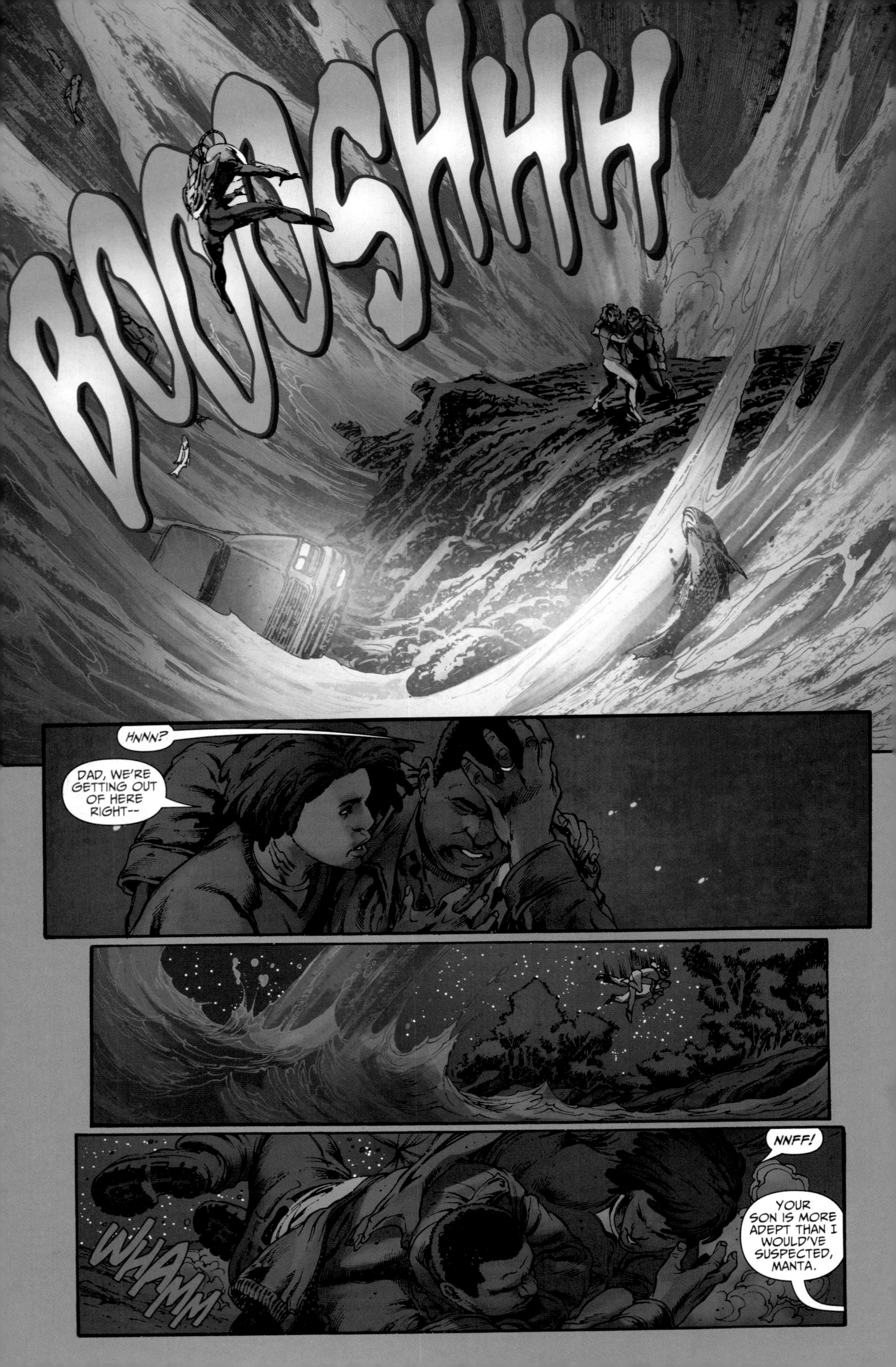
BOOOSHHH
HNNN?
DAD, WE'RE GETTING OUT OF HERE RIGHT--
NNFF!
WHAMM
YOUR SON IS MORE ADEPT THAN I WOULD'VE SUSPECTED, MANTA.

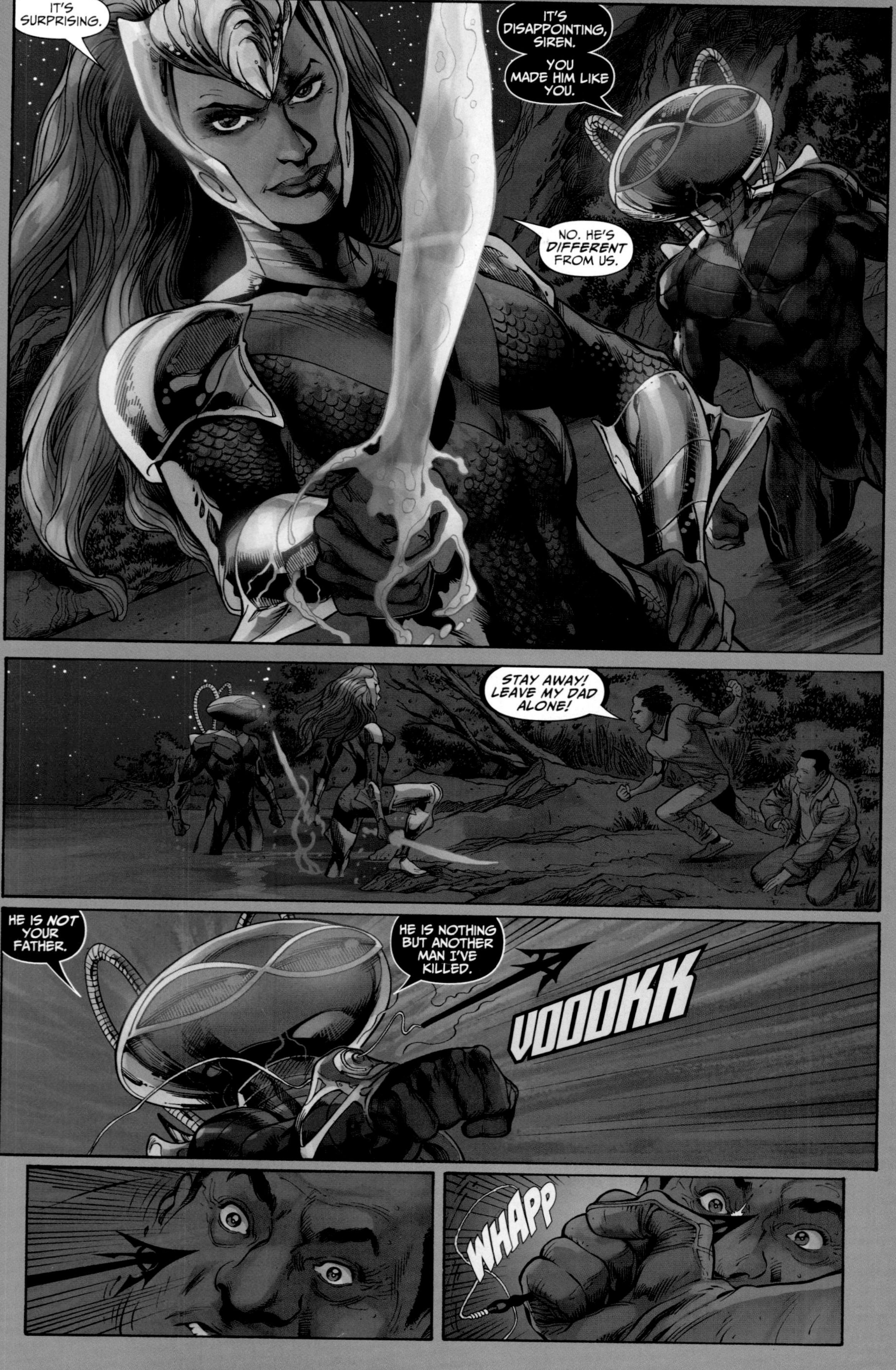
IT'S SURPRISING.
IT'S DISAPPOINTING, SIREN.
YOU MADE HIM LIKE YOU.
NO. HE'S DIFFERENT FROM US.
STAY AWAY! LEAVE MY DAD ALONE!
HE IS NOT YOUR FATHER.
HE IS NOTHING BUT ANOTHER MAN I'VE KILLED.
VOOOKK
WHAPP

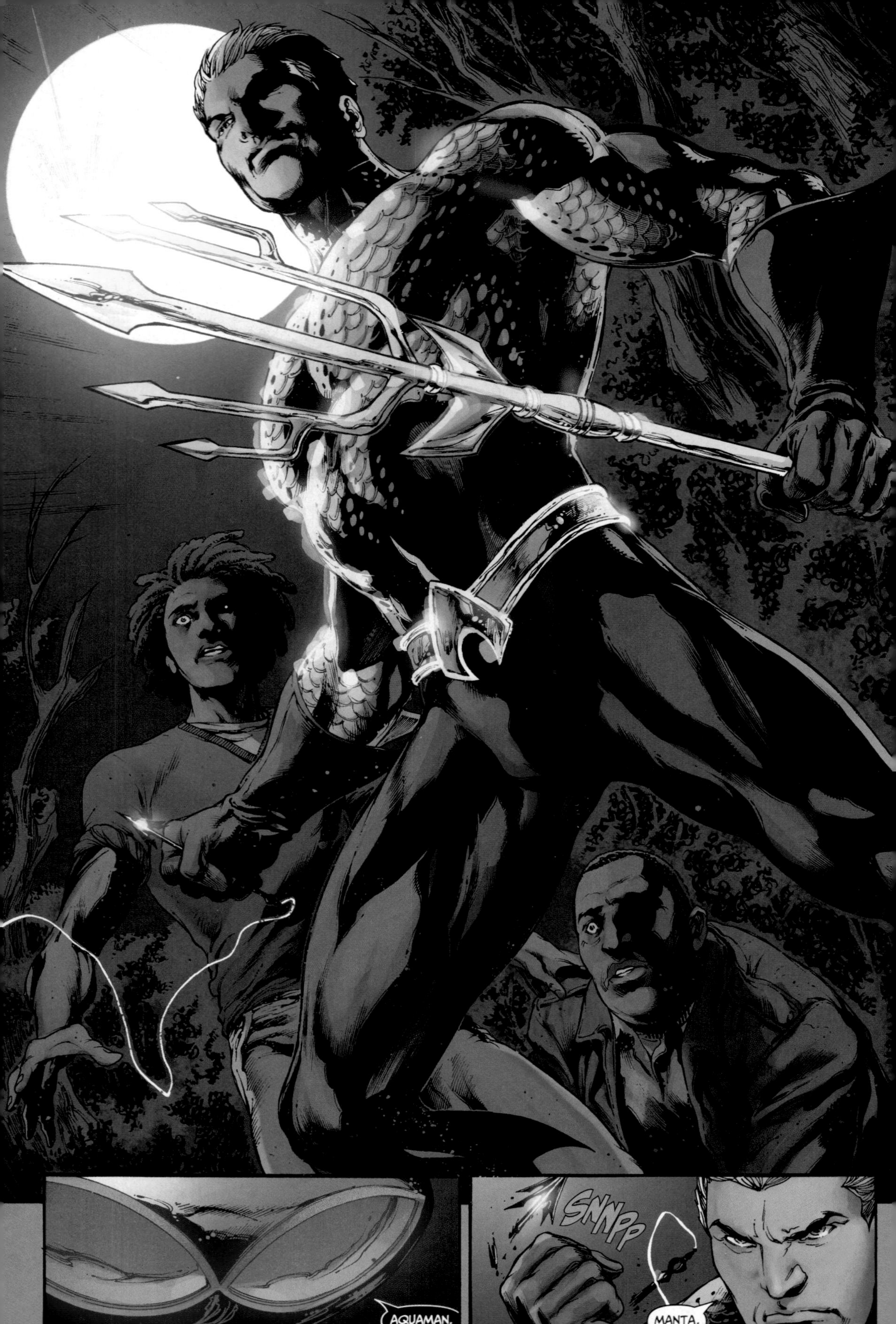
AQUAMAN.
SNNPP
MANTA.

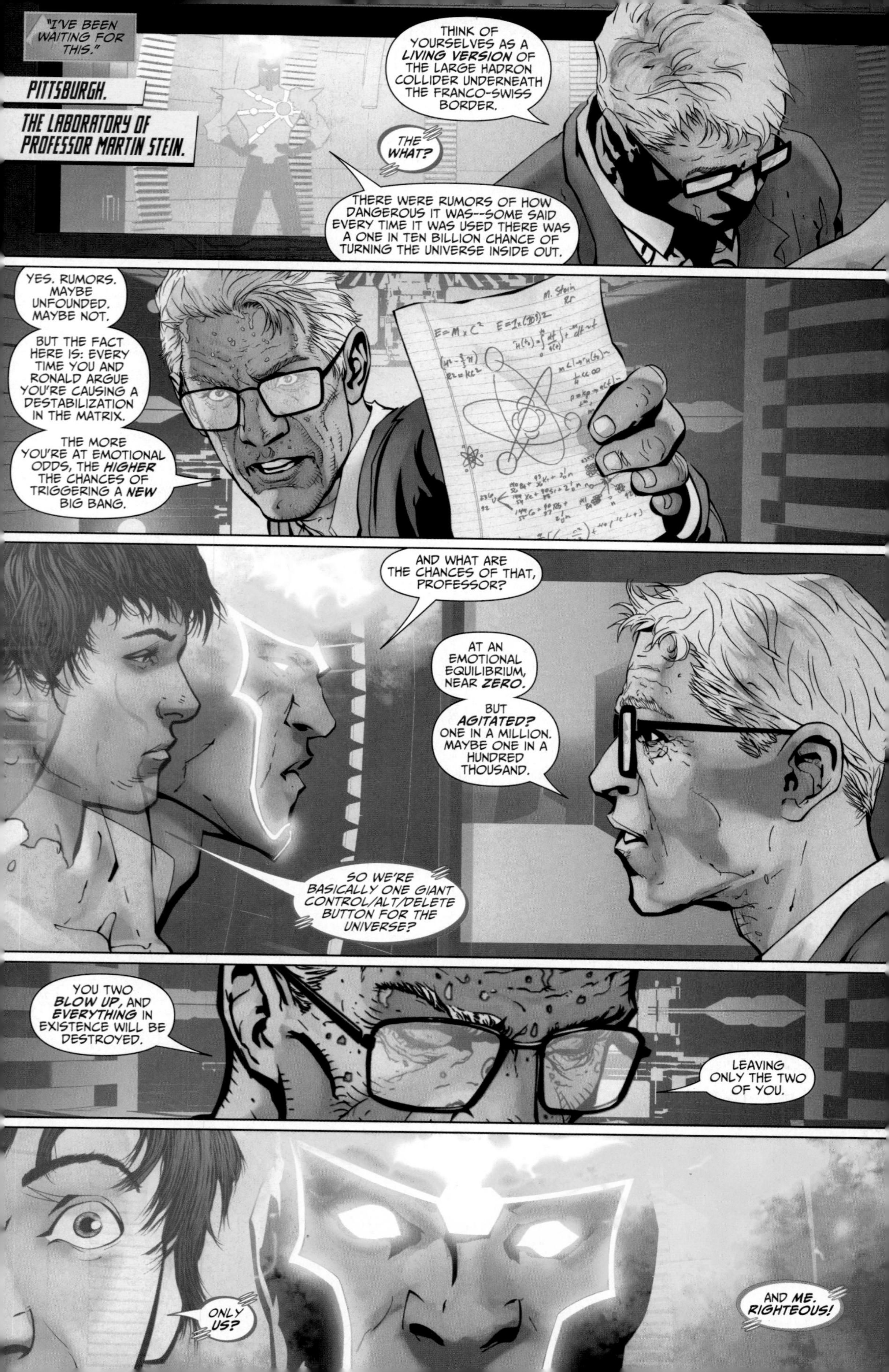
"I'VE BEEN WAITING FOR THIS."
PITTSBURGH.
THE LABORATORY OF PROFESSOR MARTIN STEIN.
THINK OF YOURSELVES AS A LIVING VERSION OF THE LARGE HADRON COLLIDER UNDERNEATH THE FRANCO-SWISS BORDER.
THE WHAT?
THERE WERE RUMORS OF HOW DANGEROUS IT WAS--SOME SAID EVERY TIME IT WAS USED THERE WAS A ONE IN TEN BILLION CHANCE OF TURNING THE UNIVERSE INSIDE OUT.
YES. RUMORS. MAYBE UNFOUNDED. MAYBE NOT.
BUT THE FACT HERE IS: EVERY TIME YOU AND RONALD ARGUE YOU'RE CAUSING A DESTABILIZATION IN THE MATRIX.
THE MORE YOU'RE AT EMOTIONAL ODDS, THE HIGHER THE CHANCES OF TRIGGERING A NEW BIG BANG.
M. Stein
E=M x C²
AND WHAT ARE THE CHANCES OF THAT, PROFESSOR?
AT AN EMOTIONAL EQUILIBRIUM, NEAR ZERO.
BUT AGITATED? ONE IN A MILLION. MAYBE ONE IN A HUNDRED THOUSAND.
SO WE'RE BASICALLY ONE GIANT CONTROL/ALT/DELETE BUTTON FOR THE UNIVERSE?
YOU TWO BLOW UP, AND EVERYTHING IN EXISTENCE WILL BE DESTROYED.
LEAVING ONLY THE TWO OF YOU.
ONLY US?
AND ME. RIGHTEOUS!

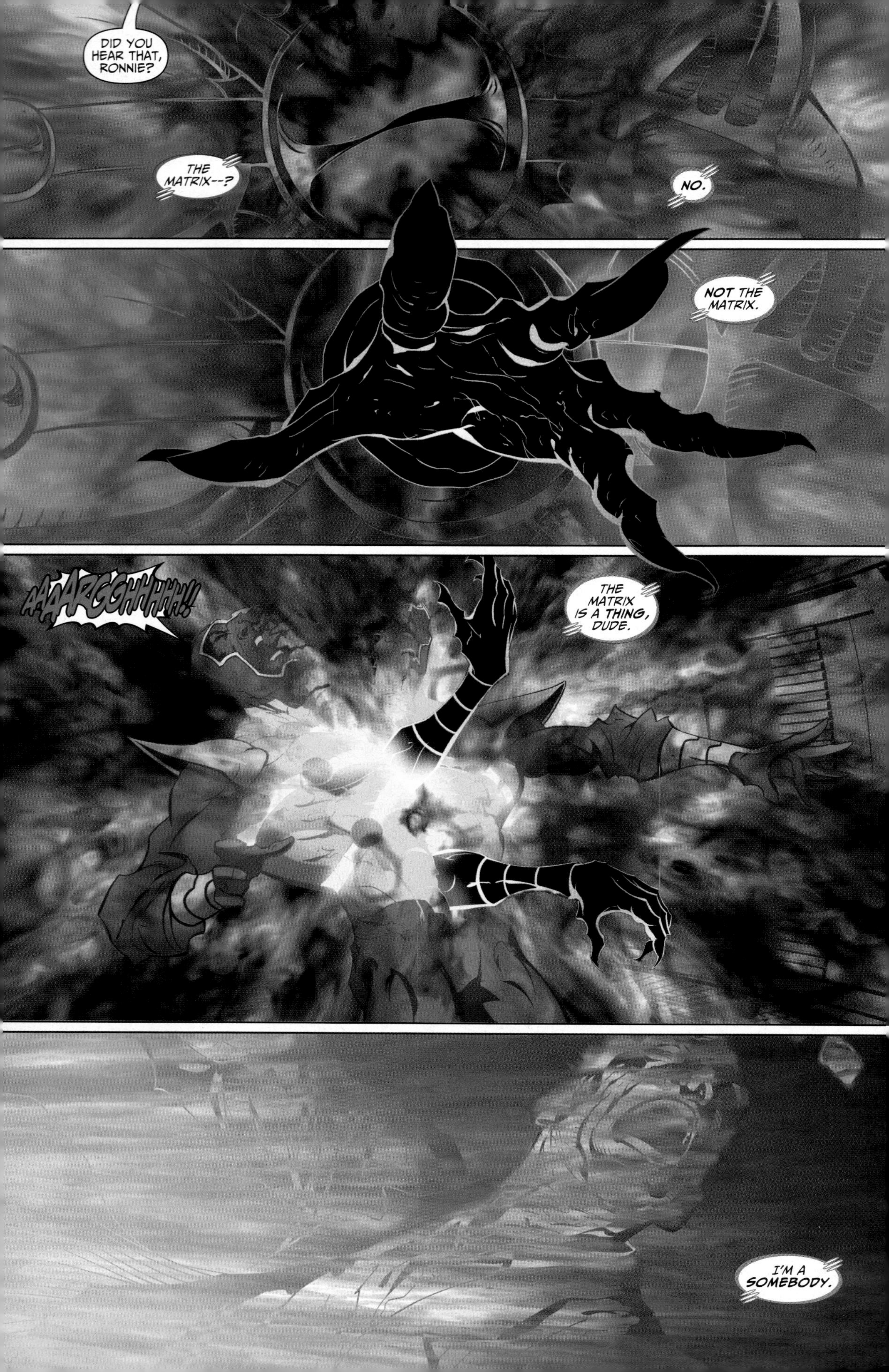
DID YOU HEAR THAT, RONNIE?
THE MATRIX--?
NO.
NOT THE MATRIX.
AAAARGGHHHHH!!
THE MATRIX IS A THING, DUDE.
I'M A SOMEBODY.

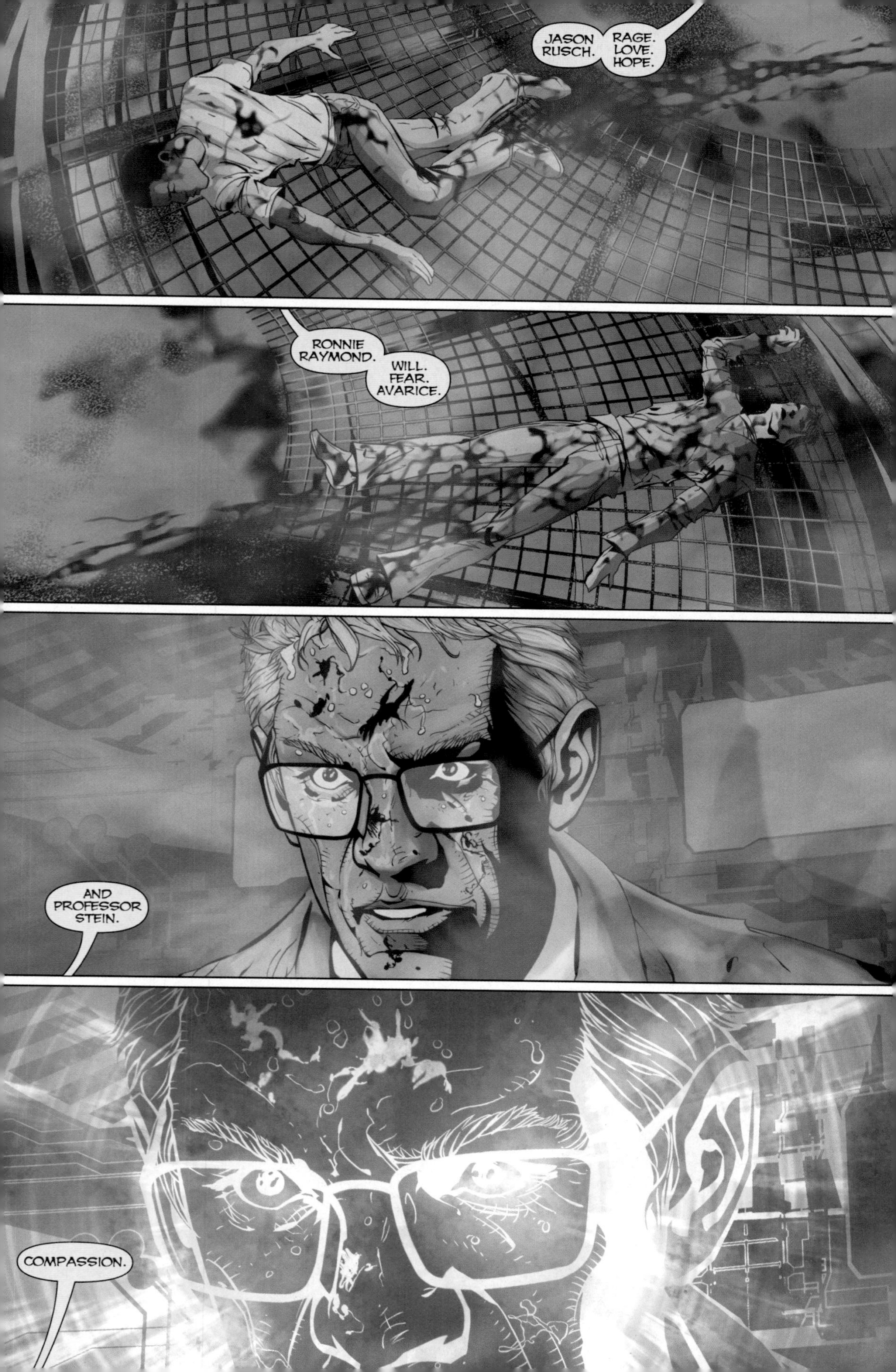

JASON RUSCH.
RAGE. LOVE. HOPE.
RONNIE RAYMOND.
WILL. FEAR. AVARICE.
AND PROFESSOR STEIN.
COMPASSION.

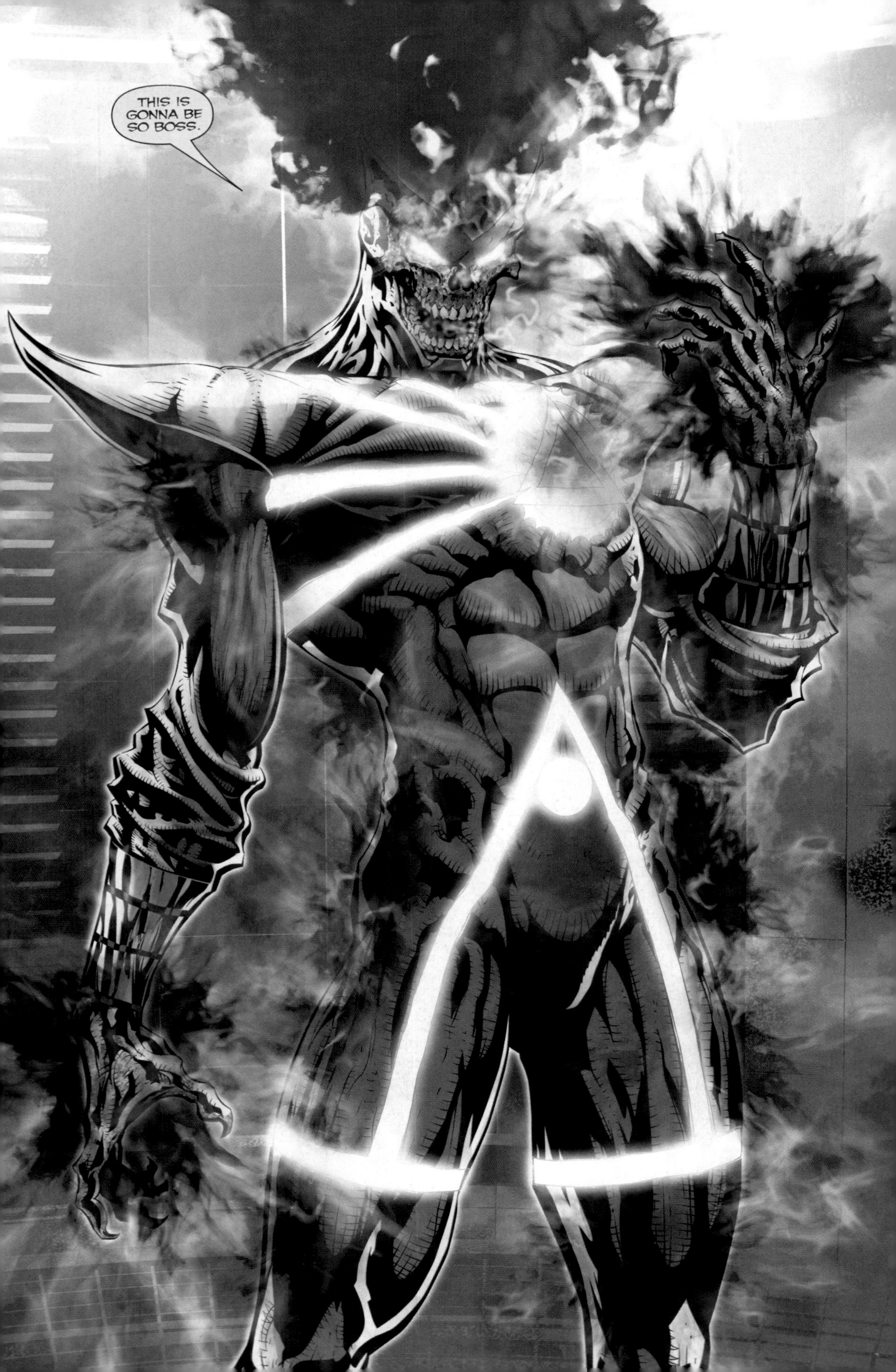
THIS IS GONNA BE SO BOSS.

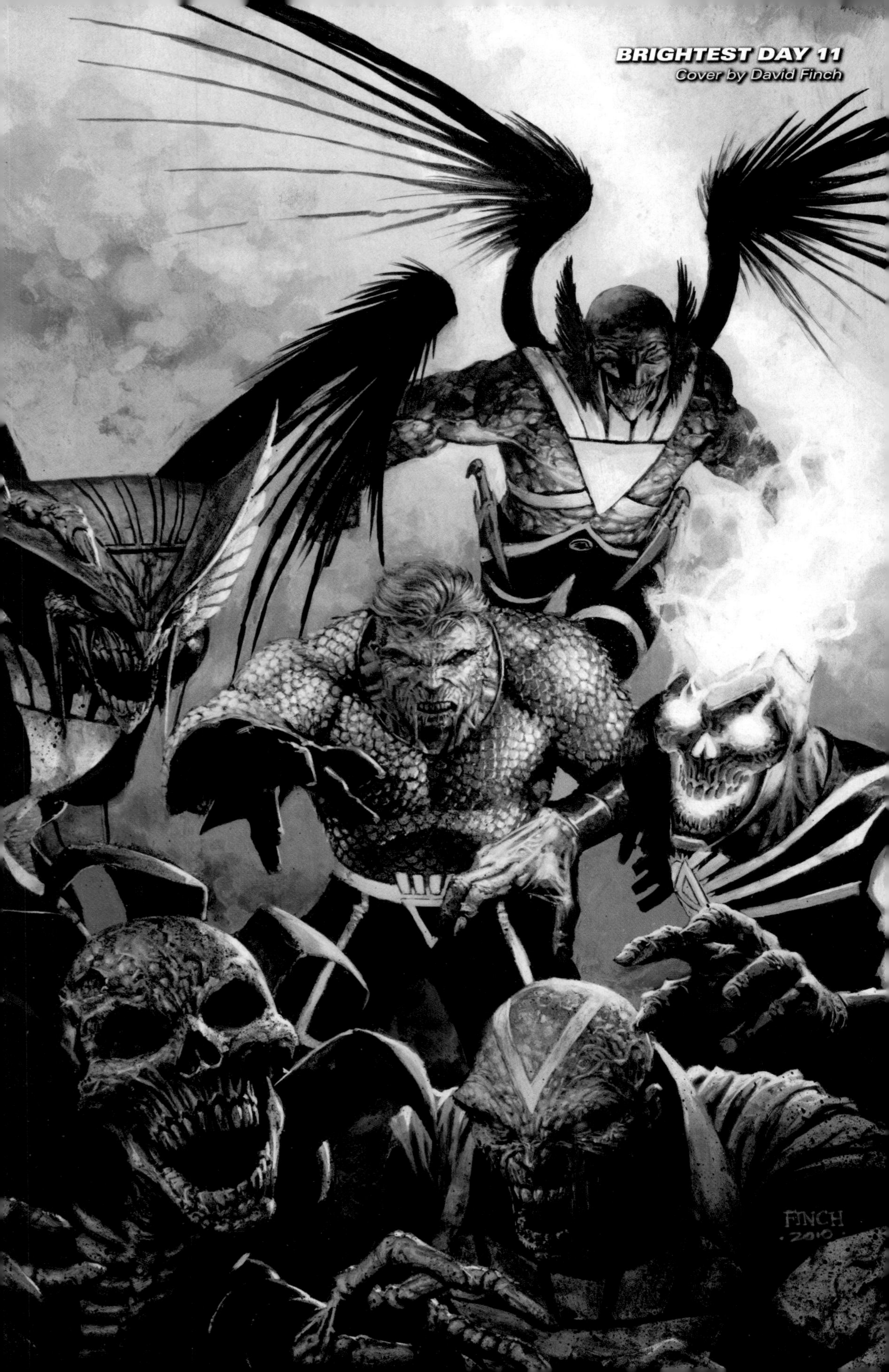
FINCH
2010

**BRIGHTEST DAY 11**
*Cover by David Finch*

# FATHERS' DAY

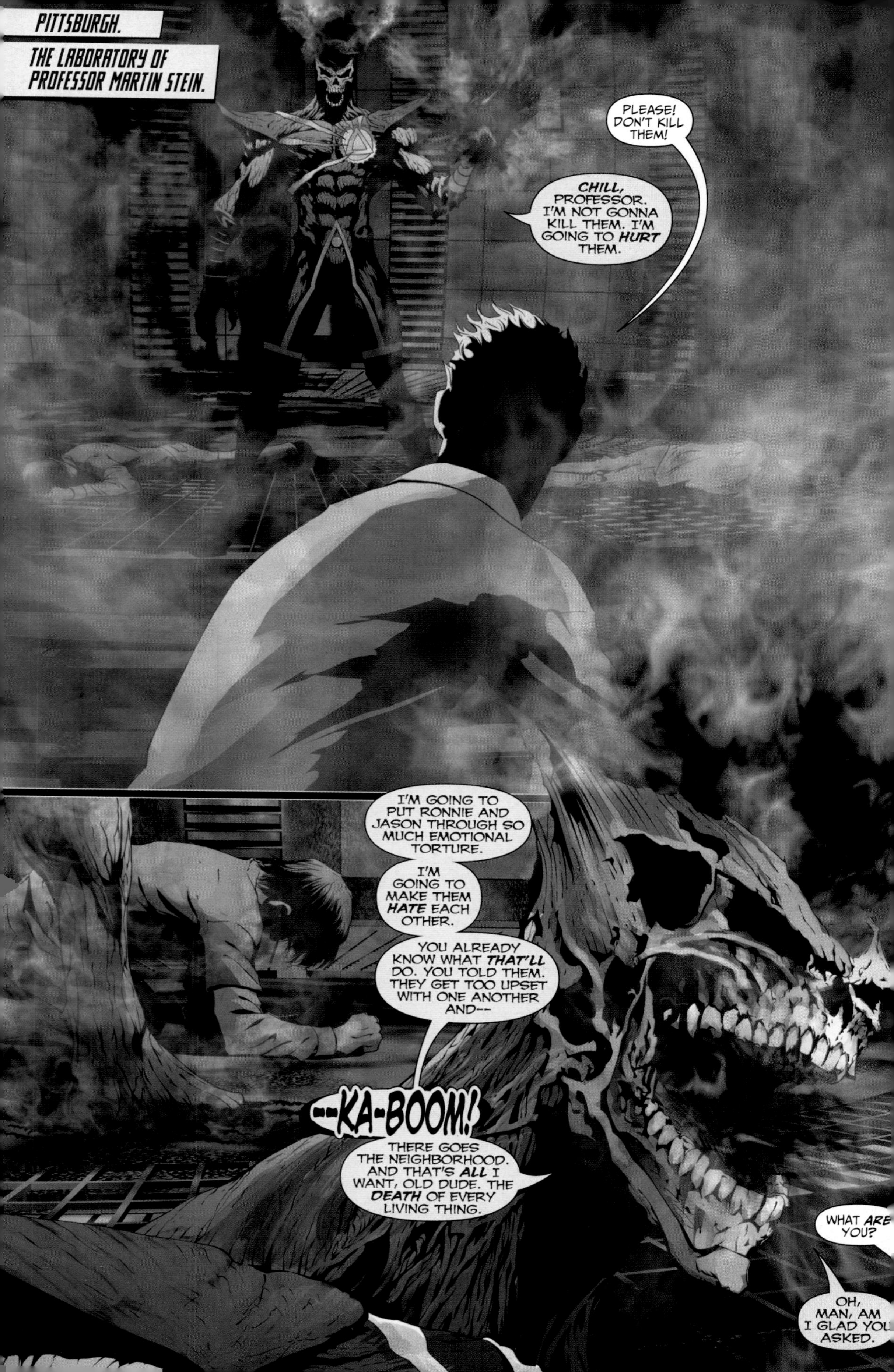
PITTSBURGH.
THE LABORATORY OF PROFESSOR MARTIN STEIN.
PLEASE! DON'T KILL THEM!
CHILL, PROFESSOR. I'M NOT GONNA KILL THEM. I'M GOING TO HURT THEM.
I'M GOING TO PUT RONNIE AND JASON THROUGH SO MUCH EMOTIONAL TORTURE.
I'M GOING TO MAKE THEM HATE EACH OTHER.
YOU ALREADY KNOW WHAT THAT'LL DO. YOU TOLD THEM. THEY GET TOO UPSET WITH ONE ANOTHER AND--
--KA-BOOM!
THERE GOES THE NEIGHBORHOOD. AND THAT'S ALL I WANT, OLD DUDE. THE DEATH OF EVERY LIVING THING.
WHAT ARE YOU?
OH, MAN, AM I GLAD YOU ASKED.

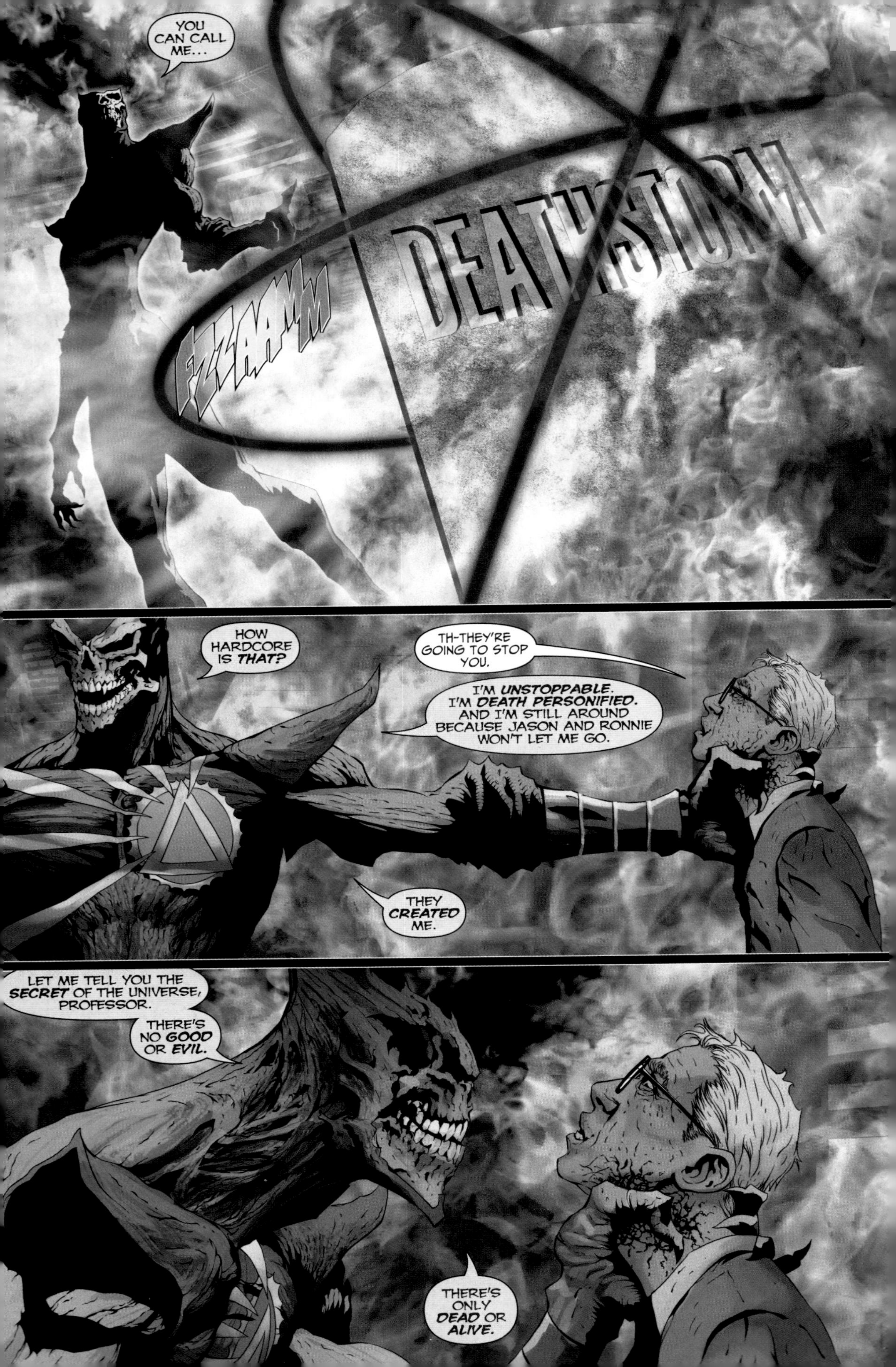
YOU CAN CALL ME...
FZZAAMM
DEATHSTORM
HOW HARDCORE IS THAT?
TH-THEY'RE GOING TO STOP YOU.
I'M UNSTOPPABLE. I'M DEATH PERSONIFIED. AND I'M STILL AROUND BECAUSE JASON AND RONNIE WON'T LET ME GO.
THEY CREATED ME.
LET ME TELL YOU THE SECRET OF THE UNIVERSE, PROFESSOR.
THERE'S NO GOOD OR EVIL.
THERE'S ONLY DEAD OR ALIVE.

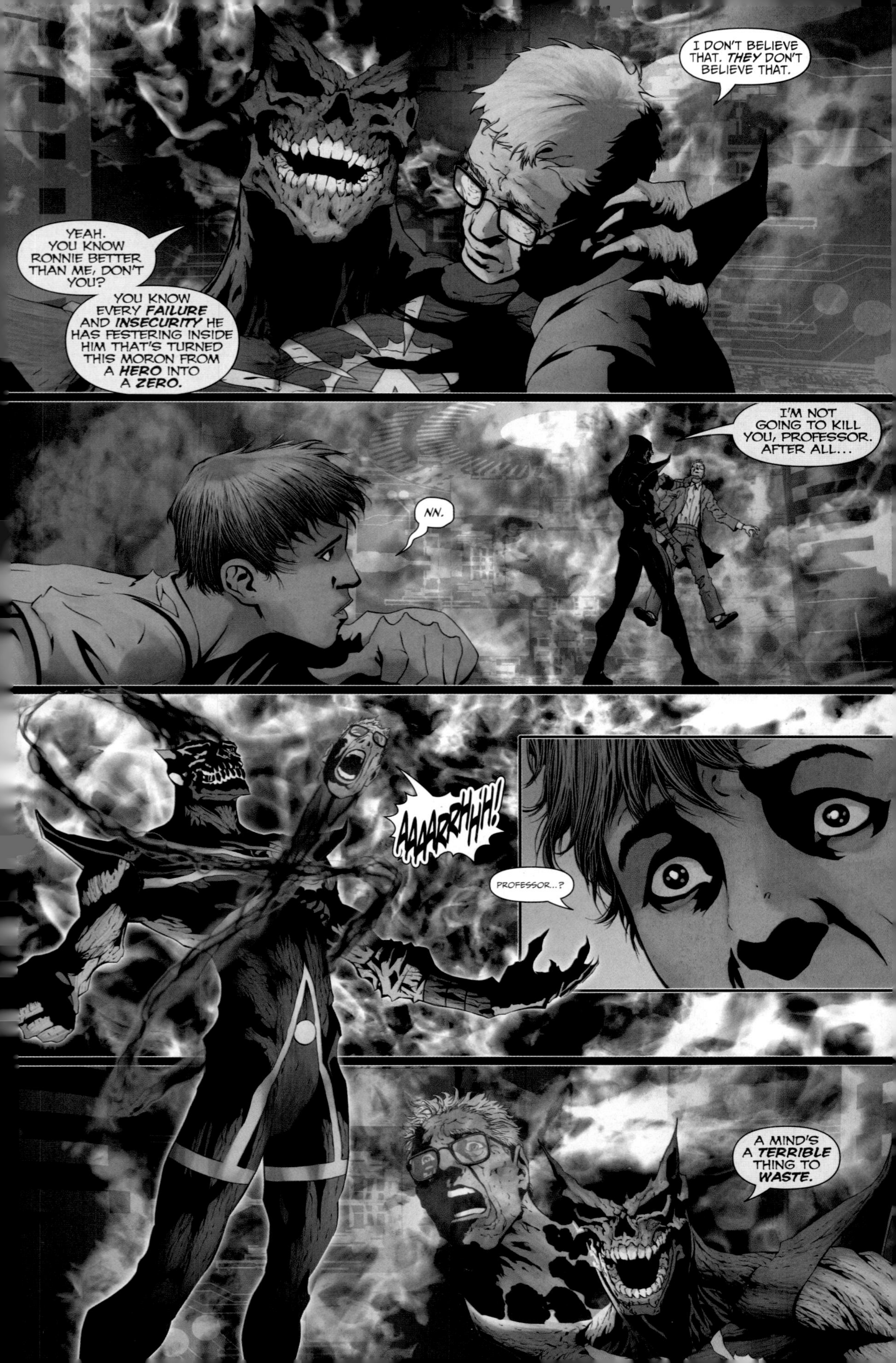

I DON'T BELIEVE THAT. *THEY* DON'T BELIEVE THAT.
YEAH. YOU KNOW RONNIE BETTER THAN ME, DON'T YOU?
YOU KNOW EVERY *FAILURE* AND *INSECURITY* HE HAS FESTERING INSIDE HIM THAT'S TURNED THIS MORON FROM A *HERO* INTO A *ZERO.*
I'M NOT GOING TO KILL YOU, PROFESSOR. AFTER ALL...
NN.
AAAARRHHH!
PROFESSOR...?
A MIND'S A *TERRIBLE* THING TO *WASTE.*

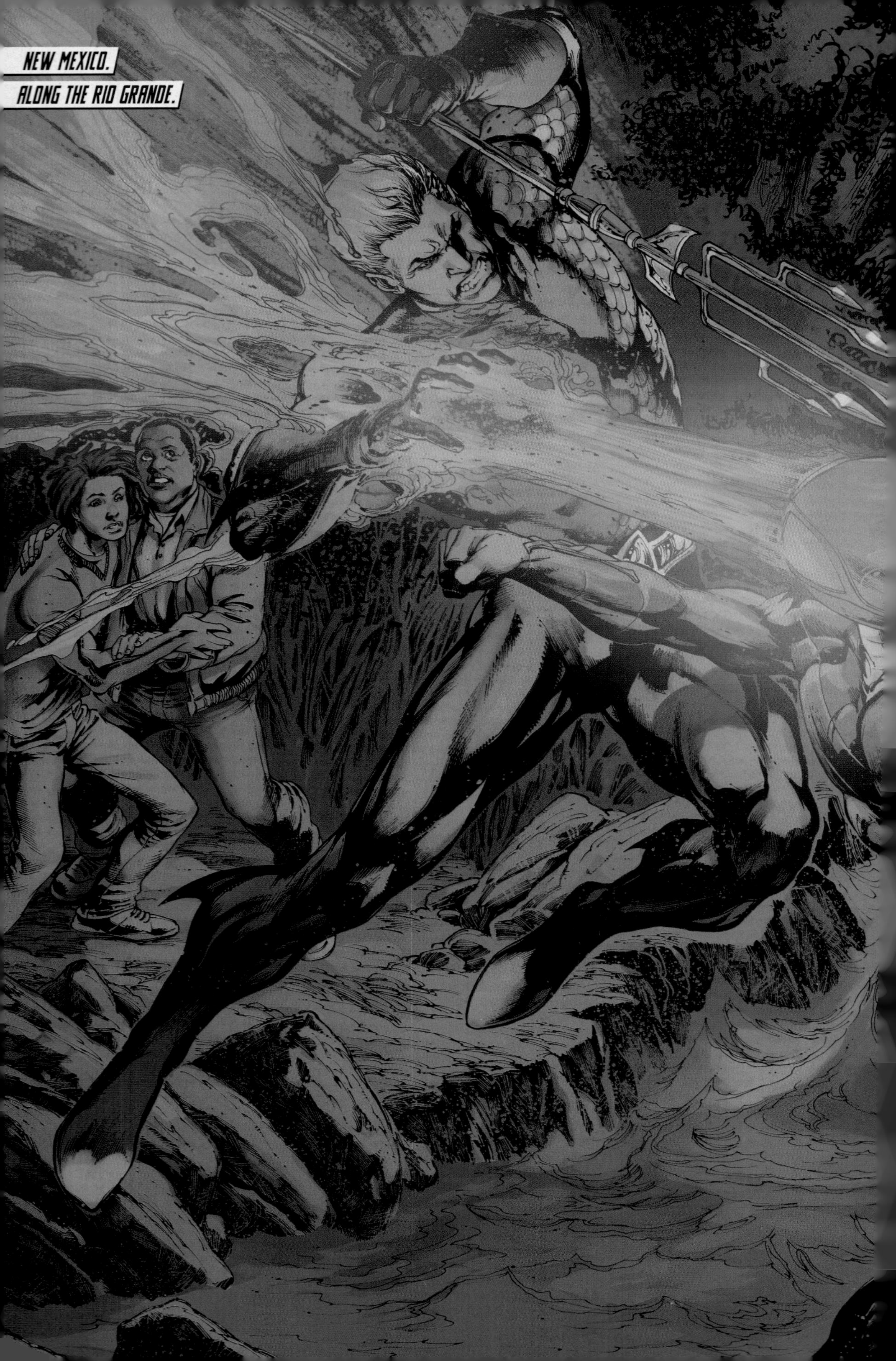
NEW MEXICO.
ALONG THE RIO GRANDE.

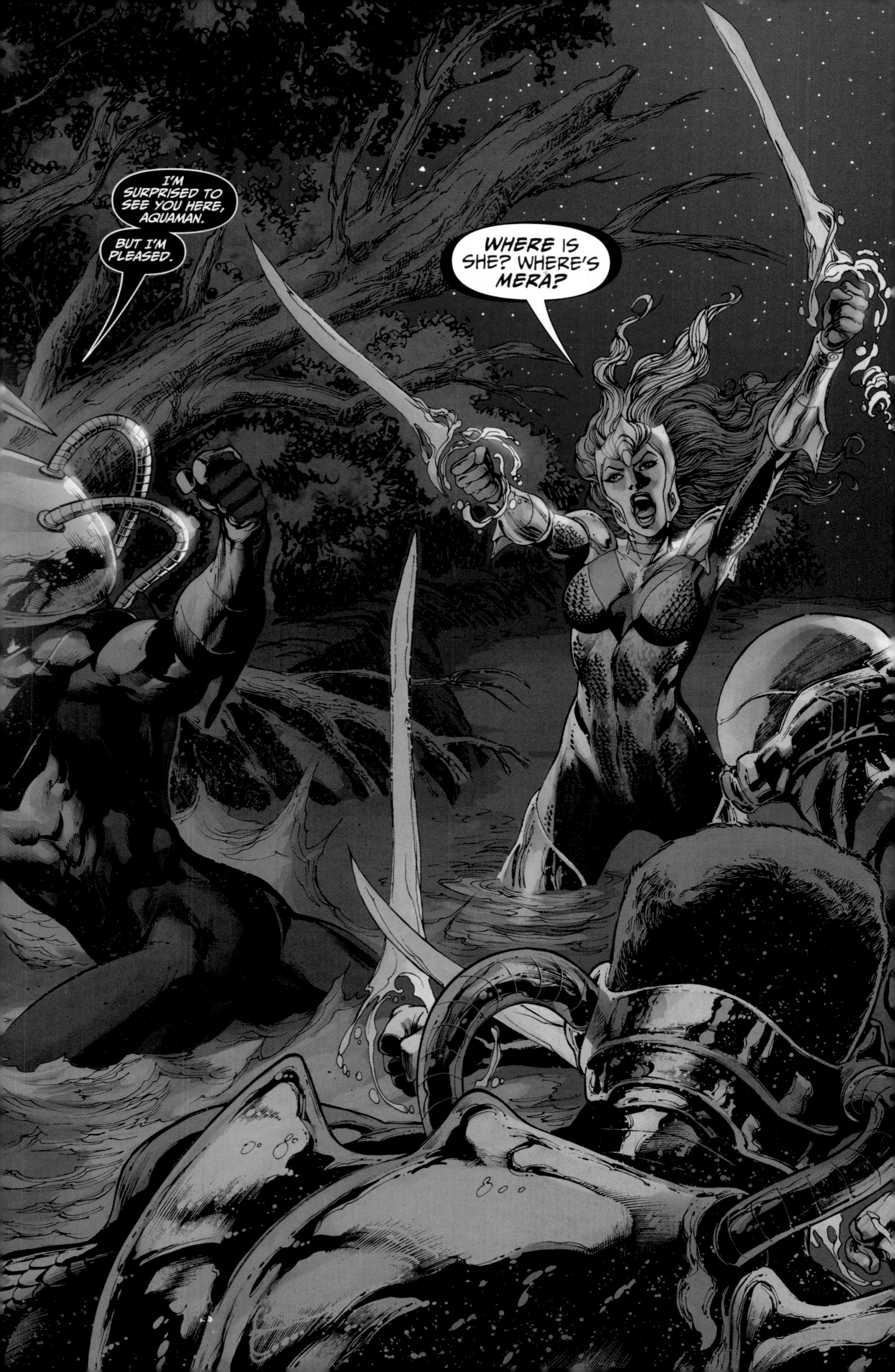
I'M SURPRISED TO SEE YOU HERE, AQUAMAN.
BUT I'M PLEASED.
WHERE IS SHE? WHERE'S MERA?

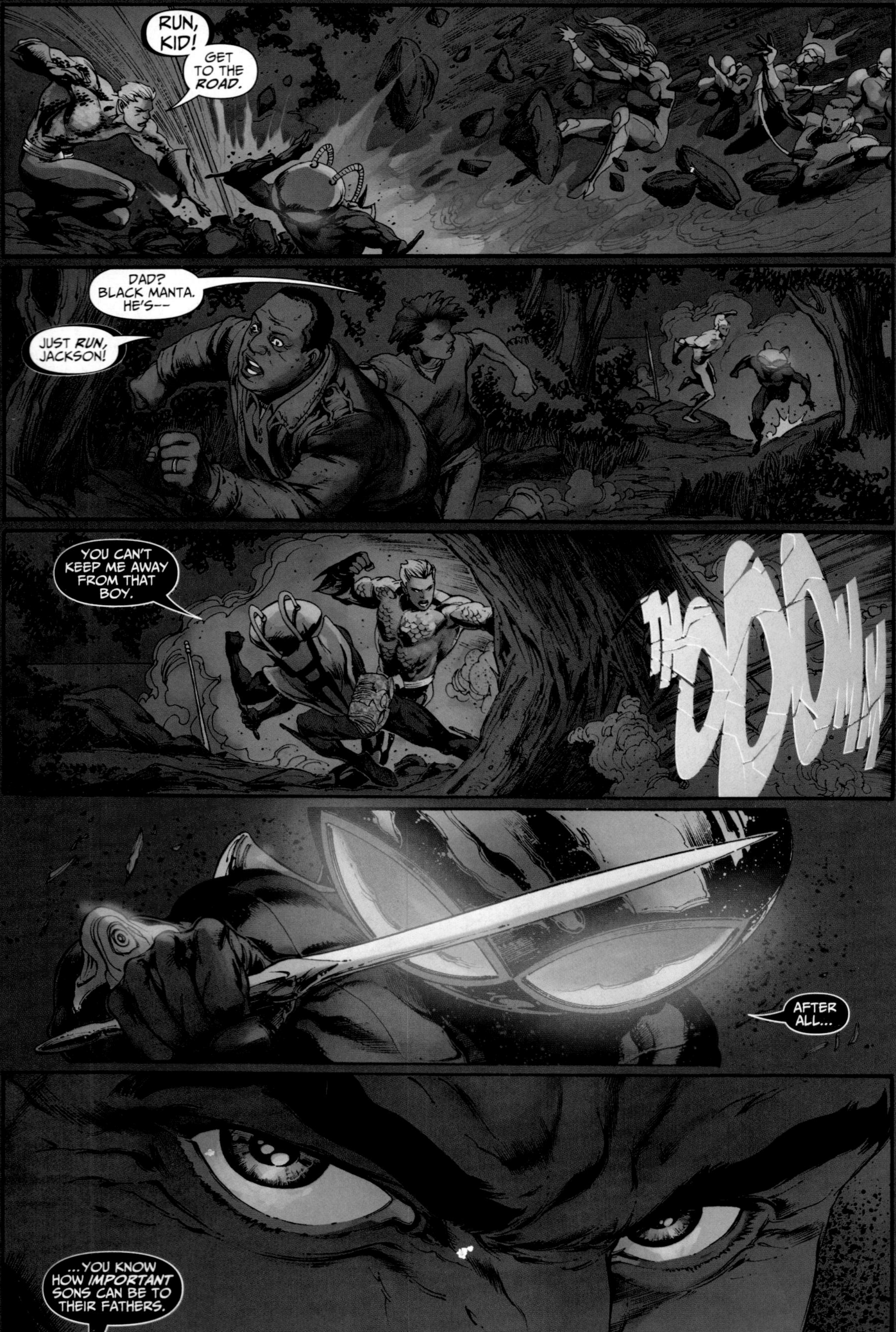
RUN, KID!
GET TO THE *ROAD*.
DAD? BLACK MANTA. HE'S--
JUST *RUN*, JACKSON!
YOU CAN'T KEEP ME AWAY FROM THAT BOY.
THOOOMM
AFTER ALL...
...YOU KNOW HOW *IMPORTANT* SONS CAN BE TO THEIR FATHERS.

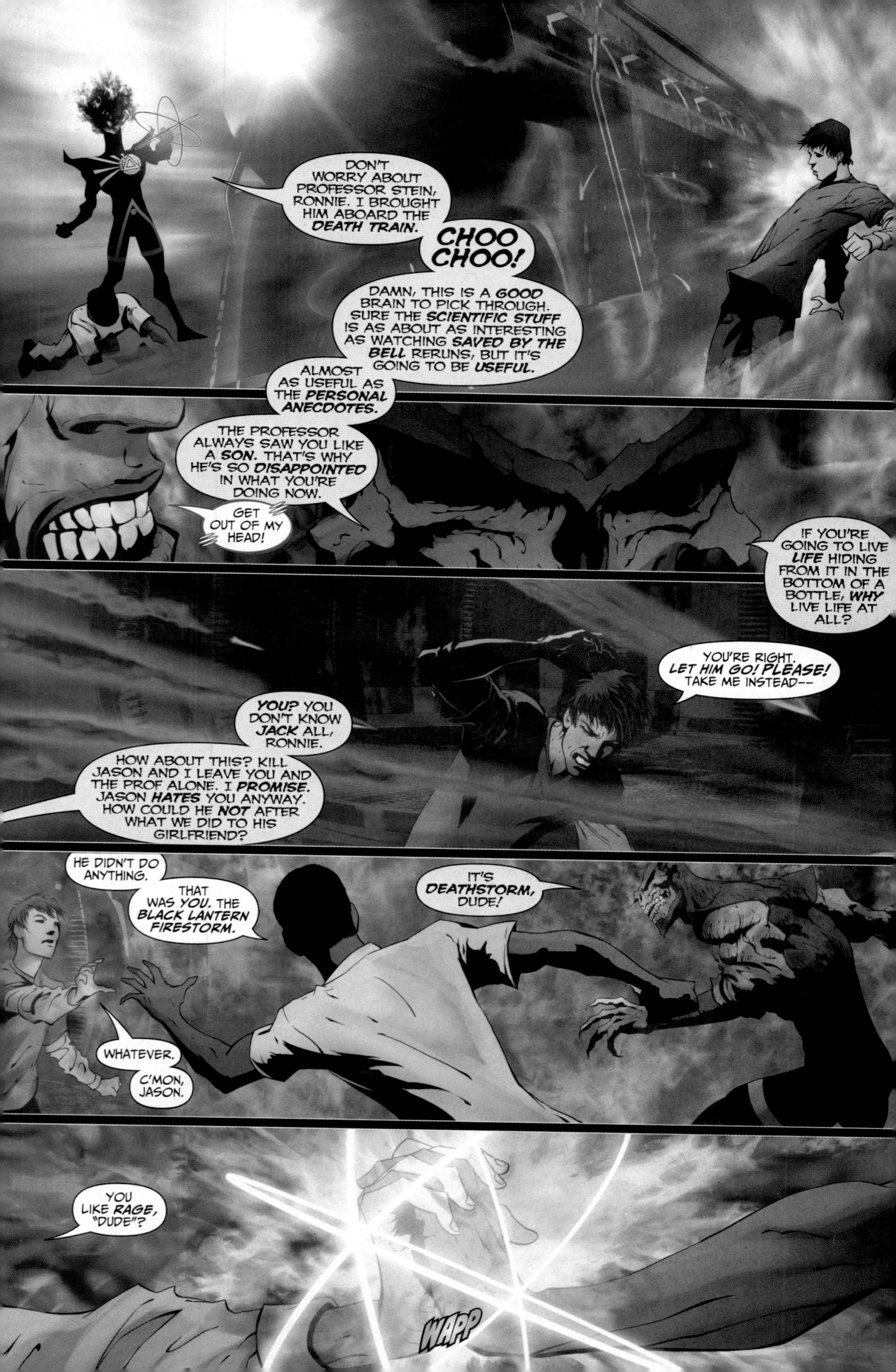
DON'T WORRY ABOUT PROFESSOR STEIN, RONNIE. I BROUGHT HIM ABOARD THE DEATH TRAIN.
CHOO CHOO!
DAMN, THIS IS A GOOD BRAIN TO PICK THROUGH. SURE THE SCIENTIFIC STUFF IS AS ABOUT AS INTERESTING AS WATCHING SAVED BY THE BELL RERUNS, BUT IT'S GOING TO BE USEFUL.
ALMOST AS USEFUL AS THE PERSONAL ANECDOTES.
THE PROFESSOR ALWAYS SAW YOU LIKE A SON. THAT'S WHY HE'S SO DISAPPOINTED IN WHAT YOU'RE DOING NOW.
GET OUT OF MY HEAD!
IF YOU'RE GOING TO LIVE LIFE HIDING FROM IT IN THE BOTTOM OF A BOTTLE, WHY LIVE LIFE AT ALL?
YOU'RE RIGHT. LET HIM GO! PLEASE! TAKE ME INSTEAD--
YOU? YOU DON'T KNOW JACK ALL, RONNIE.
HOW ABOUT THIS? KILL JASON AND I LEAVE YOU AND THE PROF ALONE. I PROMISE. JASON HATES YOU ANYWAY. HOW COULD HE NOT AFTER WHAT WE DID TO HIS GIRLFRIEND?
HE DIDN'T DO ANYTHING.
THAT WAS YOU. THE BLACK LANTERN FIRESTORM.
IT'S DEATHSTORM, DUDE!
WHATEVER.
C'MON, JASON.
YOU LIKE RAGE, "DUDE"?
WAPP

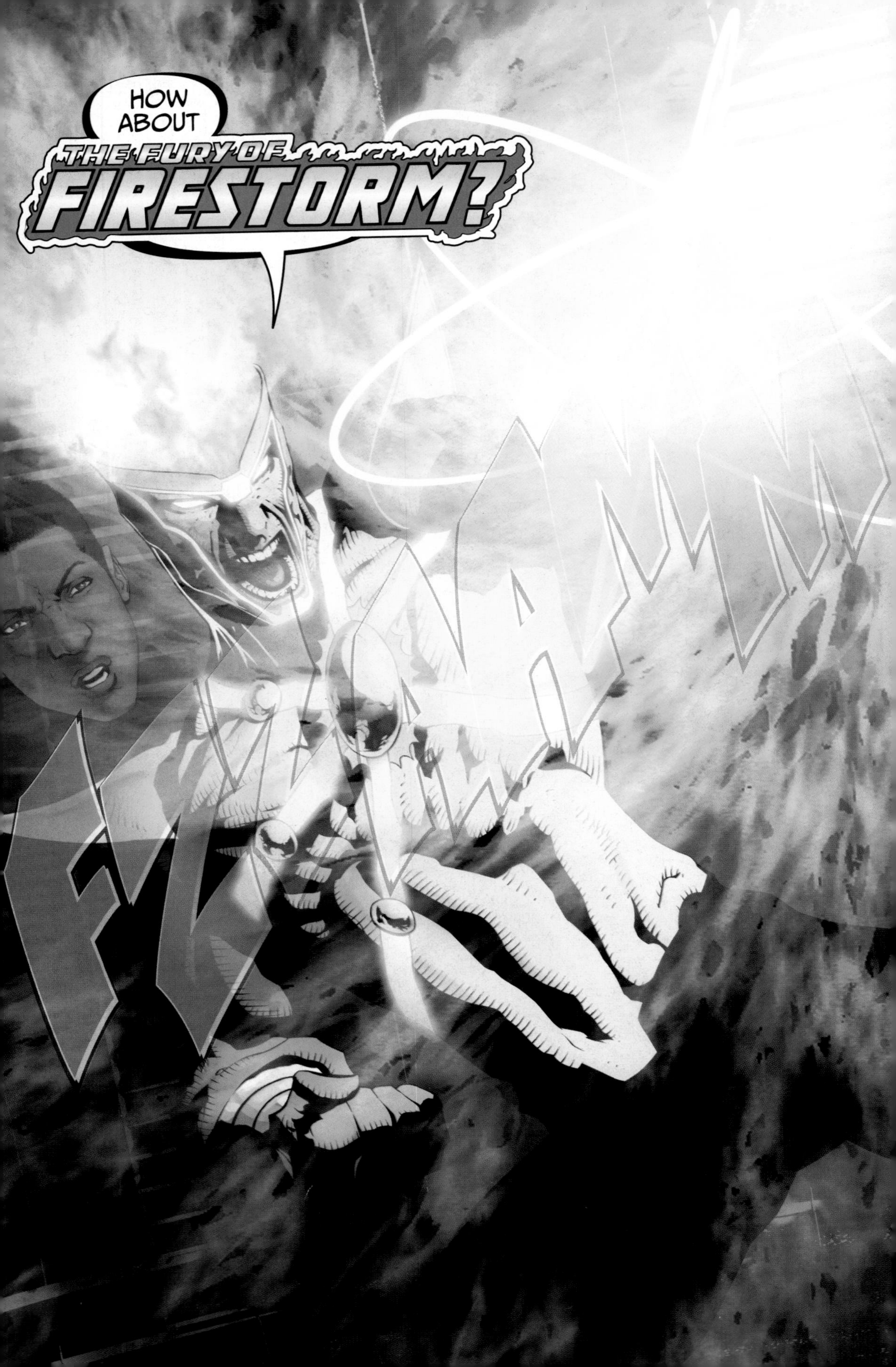
HOW ABOUT THE FURY OF FIRESTORM?

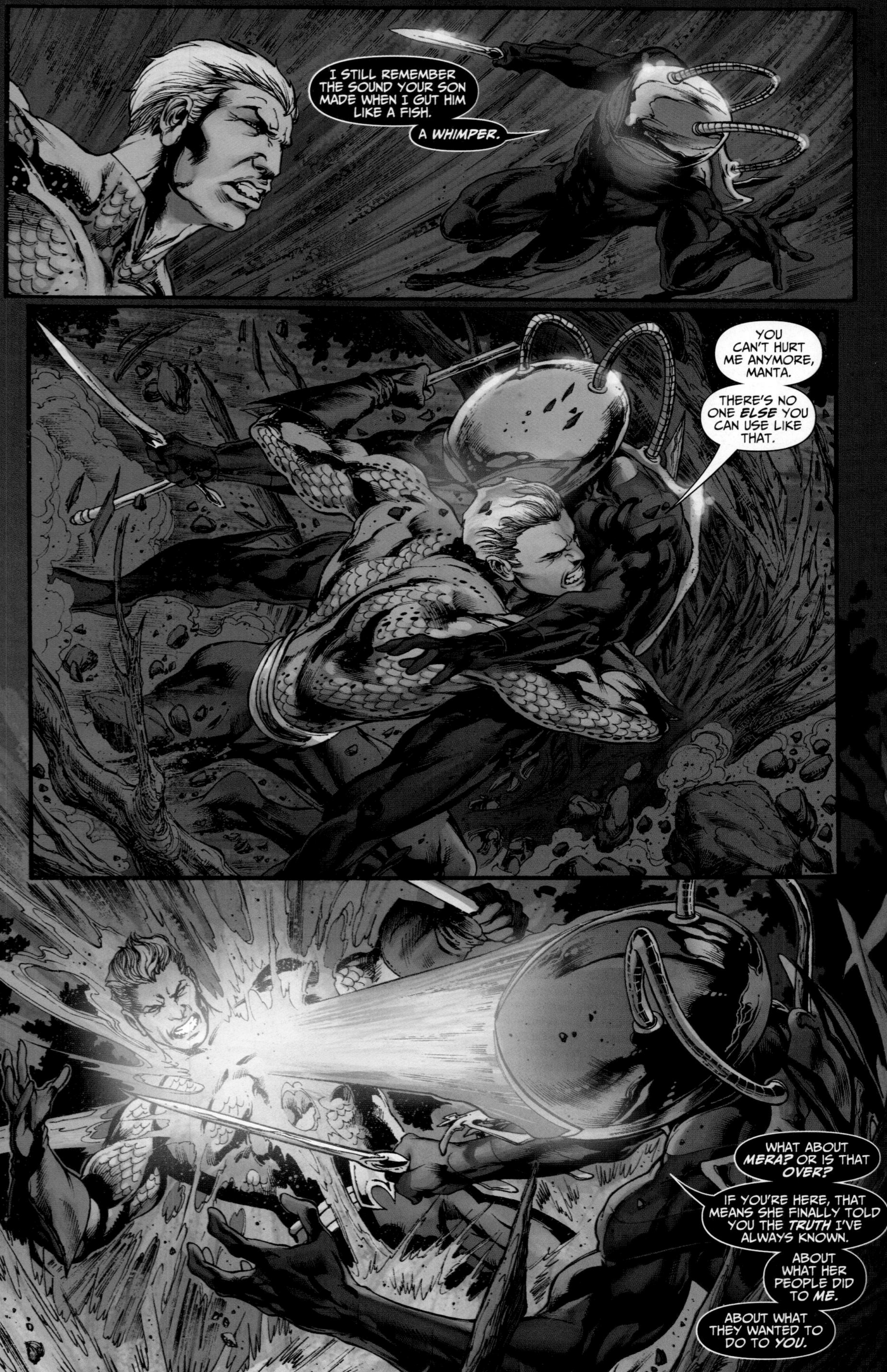
I STILL REMEMBER THE SOUND YOUR SON MADE WHEN I GUT HIM LIKE A FISH.
A *WHIMPER.*
YOU CAN'T HURT ME ANYMORE, MANTA.
THERE'S NO ONE *ELSE* YOU CAN USE LIKE THAT.
WHAT ABOUT *MERA?* OR IS THAT *OVER?*
IF YOU'RE HERE, THAT MEANS SHE FINALLY TOLD YOU THE *TRUTH* I'VE ALWAYS KNOWN.
ABOUT WHAT HER PEOPLE DID TO *ME.*
ABOUT WHAT THEY WANTED TO DO TO *YOU.*

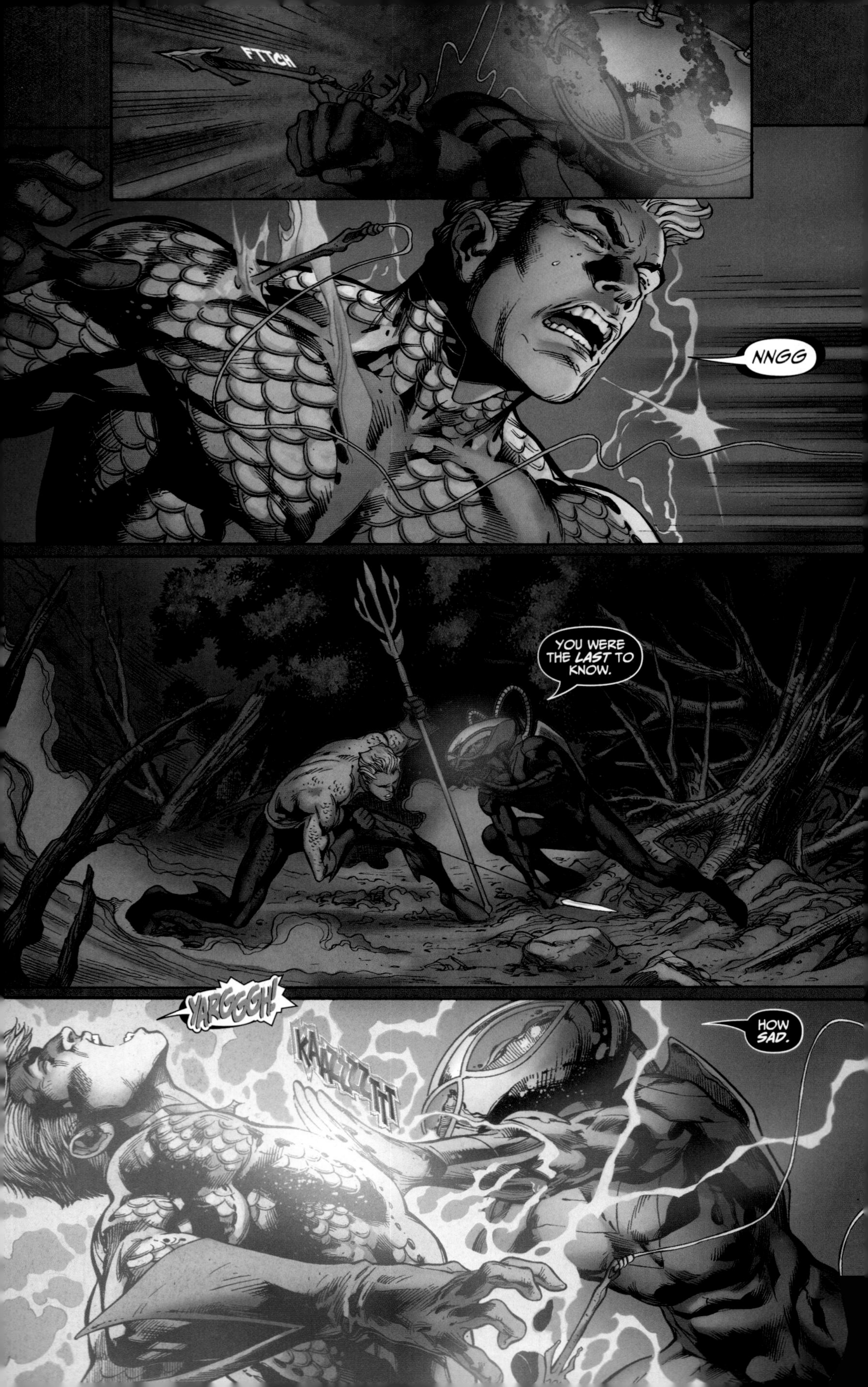
FTTCH
NNGG
YOU WERE THE LAST TO KNOW.
YARGGGH!
KAZZZZT
HOW SAD.

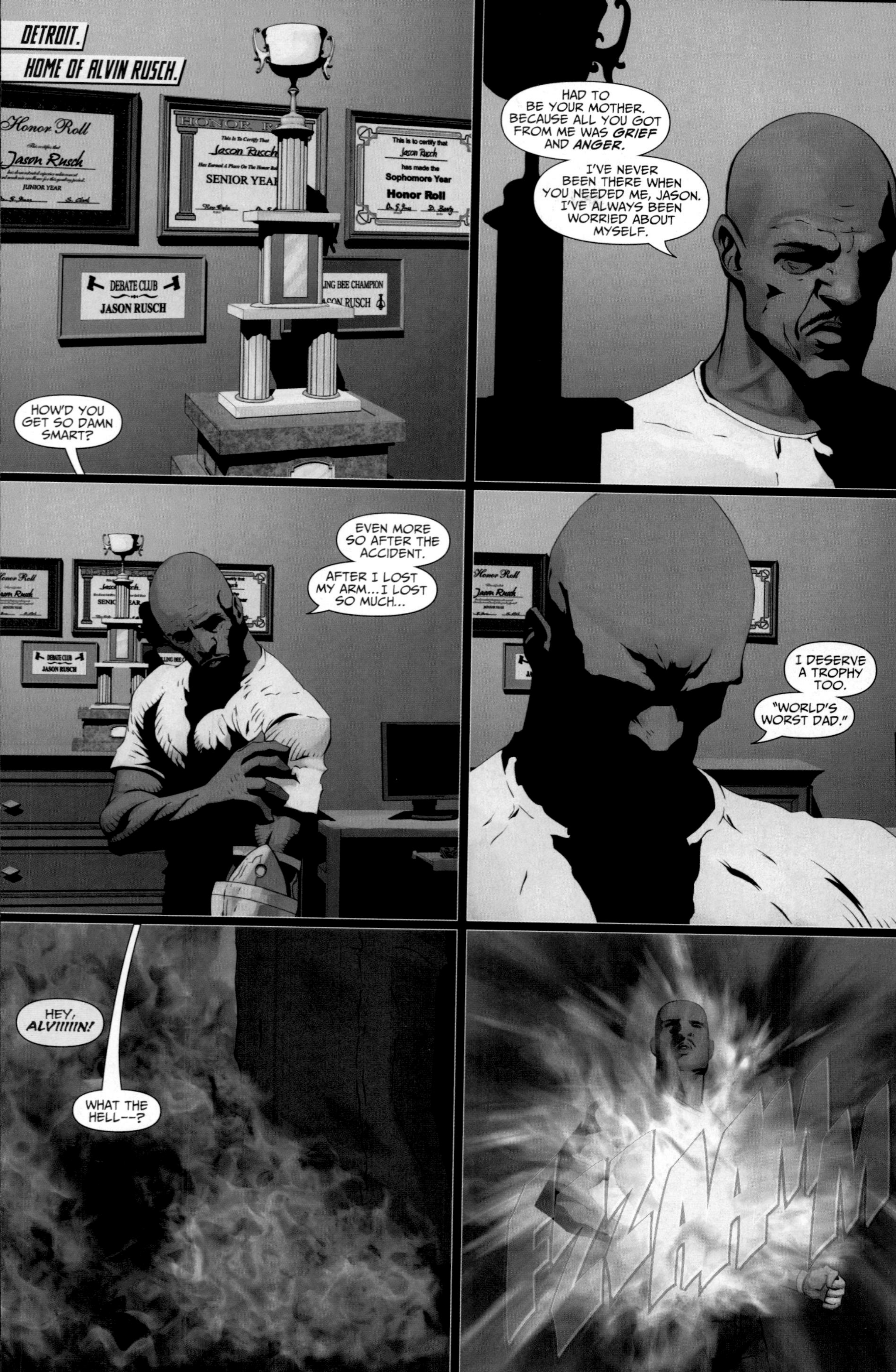

DETROIT.
HOME OF ALVIN RUSCH.
Honor Roll
Jason Rusch
JUNIOR YEAR
HONOR ROLL
This Is To Certify That
Jason Rusch
Has Earned A Place On The Honor Roll
SENIOR YEAR
This is to certify that
Jason Rusch
has made the
Sophomore Year
Honor Roll
DEBATE CLUB
JASON RUSCH
HOW'D YOU GET SO DAMN SMART?
HAD TO BE YOUR MOTHER. BECAUSE ALL YOU GOT FROM ME WAS GRIEF AND ANGER.
I'VE NEVER BEEN THERE WHEN YOU NEEDED ME, JASON. I'VE ALWAYS BEEN WORRIED ABOUT MYSELF.
EVEN MORE SO AFTER THE ACCIDENT.
AFTER I LOST MY ARM...I LOST SO MUCH...
I DESERVE A TROPHY TOO.
"WORLD'S WORST DAD."
HEY, ALVIIIIIN!
WHAT THE HELL--?
FZZAMM

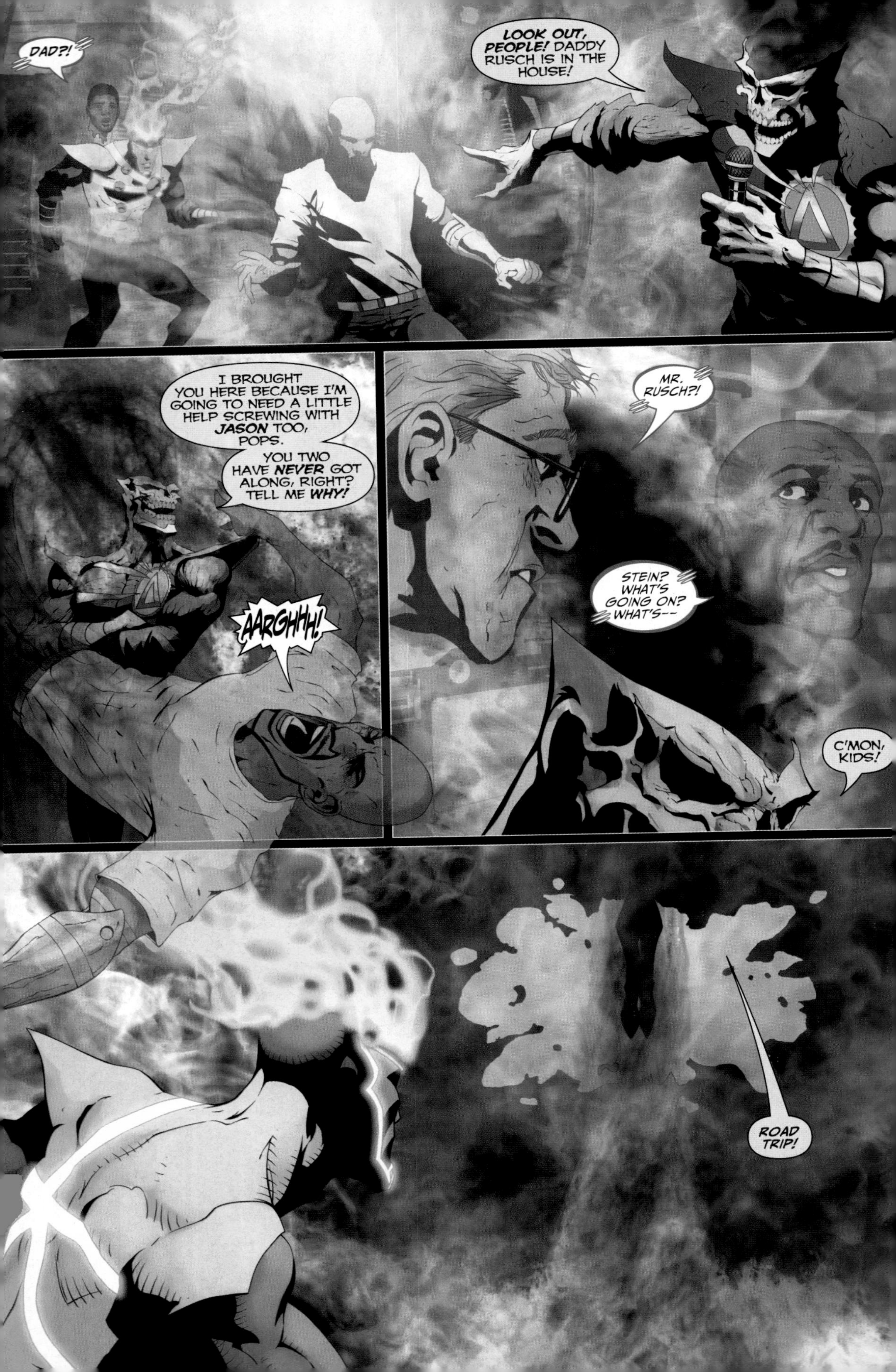
DAD?!
LOOK OUT, PEOPLE! DADDY RUSCH IS IN THE HOUSE!
I BROUGHT YOU HERE BECAUSE I'M GOING TO NEED A LITTLE HELP SCREWING WITH JASON TOO, POPS.
YOU TWO HAVE NEVER GOT ALONG, RIGHT? TELL ME WHY!
AARGHHH!
MR. RUSCH?!
STEIN? WHAT'S GOING ON? WHAT'S--
C'MON, KIDS!
ROAD TRIP!

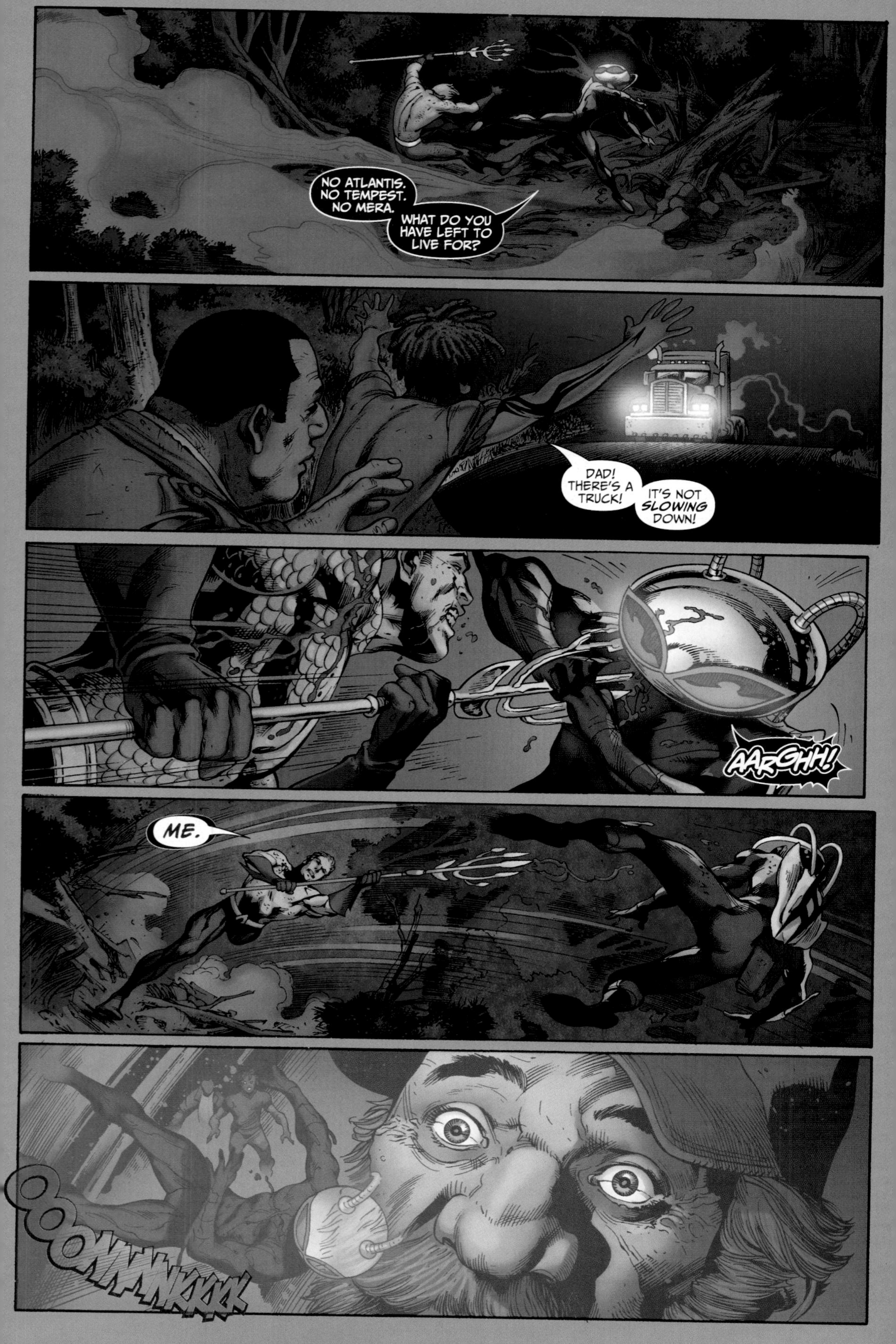
NO ATLANTIS. NO TEMPEST. NO MERA.
WHAT DO YOU HAVE LEFT TO LIVE FOR?
DAD! THERE'S A TRUCK!
IT'S NOT SLOWING DOWN!
AARGHH!
ME.
OOONNNNKKKK

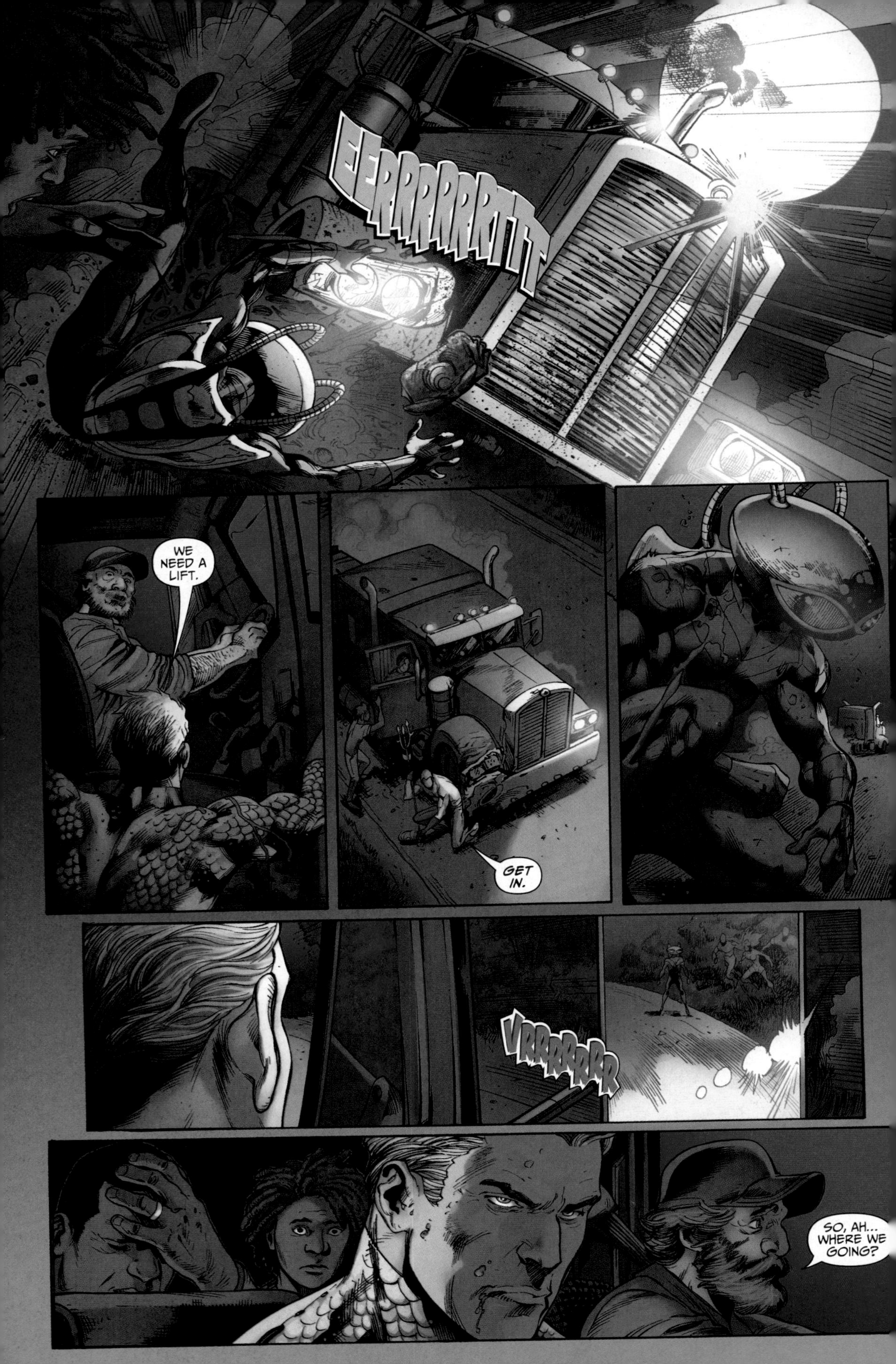
EERRRRRRRTTT
WE NEED A LIFT.
GET IN.
VRRRRRRR
SO, AH... WHERE WE GOING?

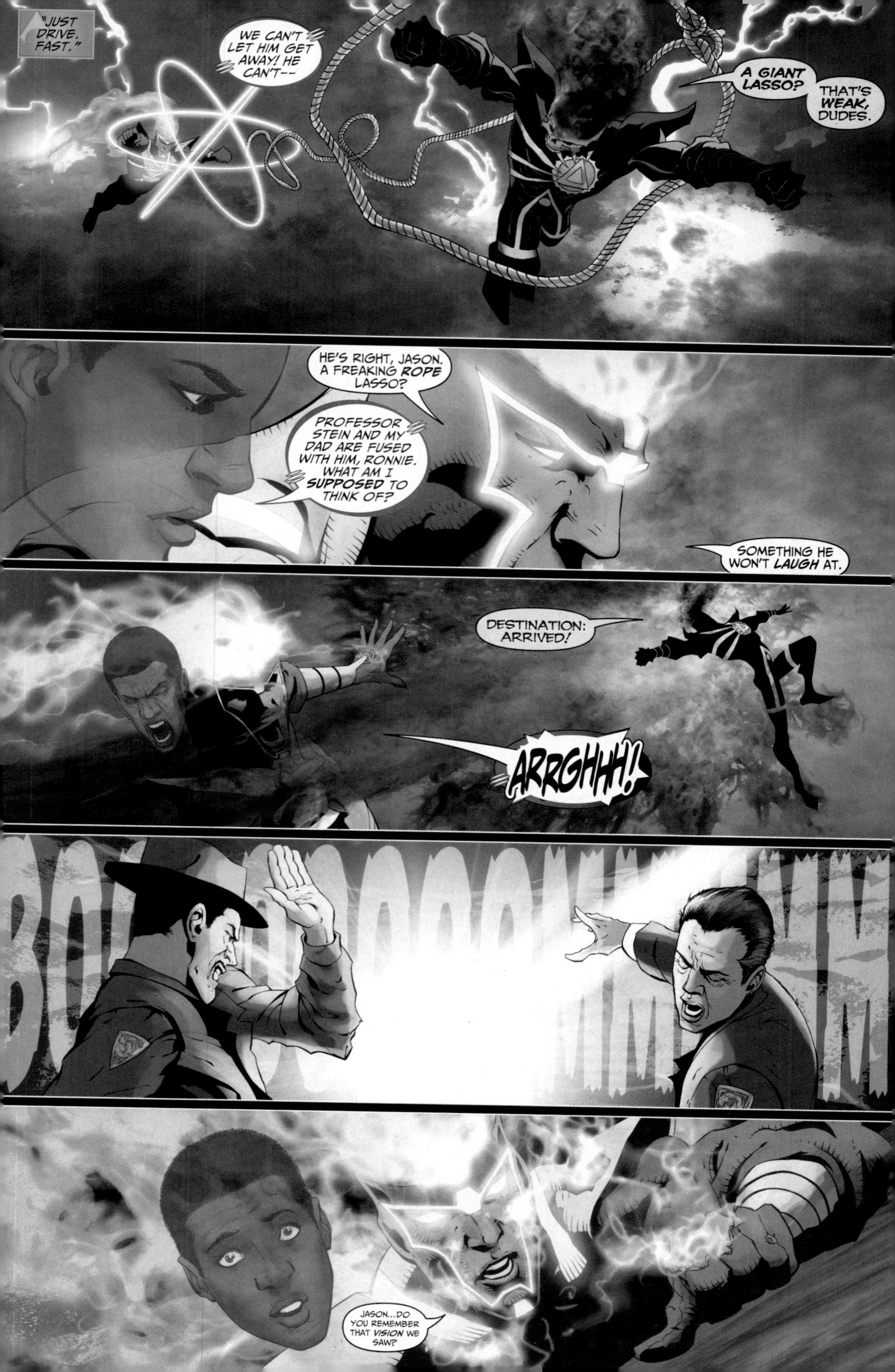
"JUST DRIVE. FAST."
WE CAN'T LET HIM GET AWAY! HE CAN'T--
A GIANT LASSO?
THAT'S WEAK, DUDES.
HE'S RIGHT, JASON. A FREAKING ROPE LASSO?
PROFESSOR STEIN AND MY DAD ARE FUSED WITH HIM, RONNIE. WHAT AM I SUPPOSED TO THINK OF?
SOMETHING HE WON'T LAUGH AT.
DESTINATION: ARRIVED!
ARRGHHH!
JASON...DO YOU REMEMBER THAT VISION WE SAW?

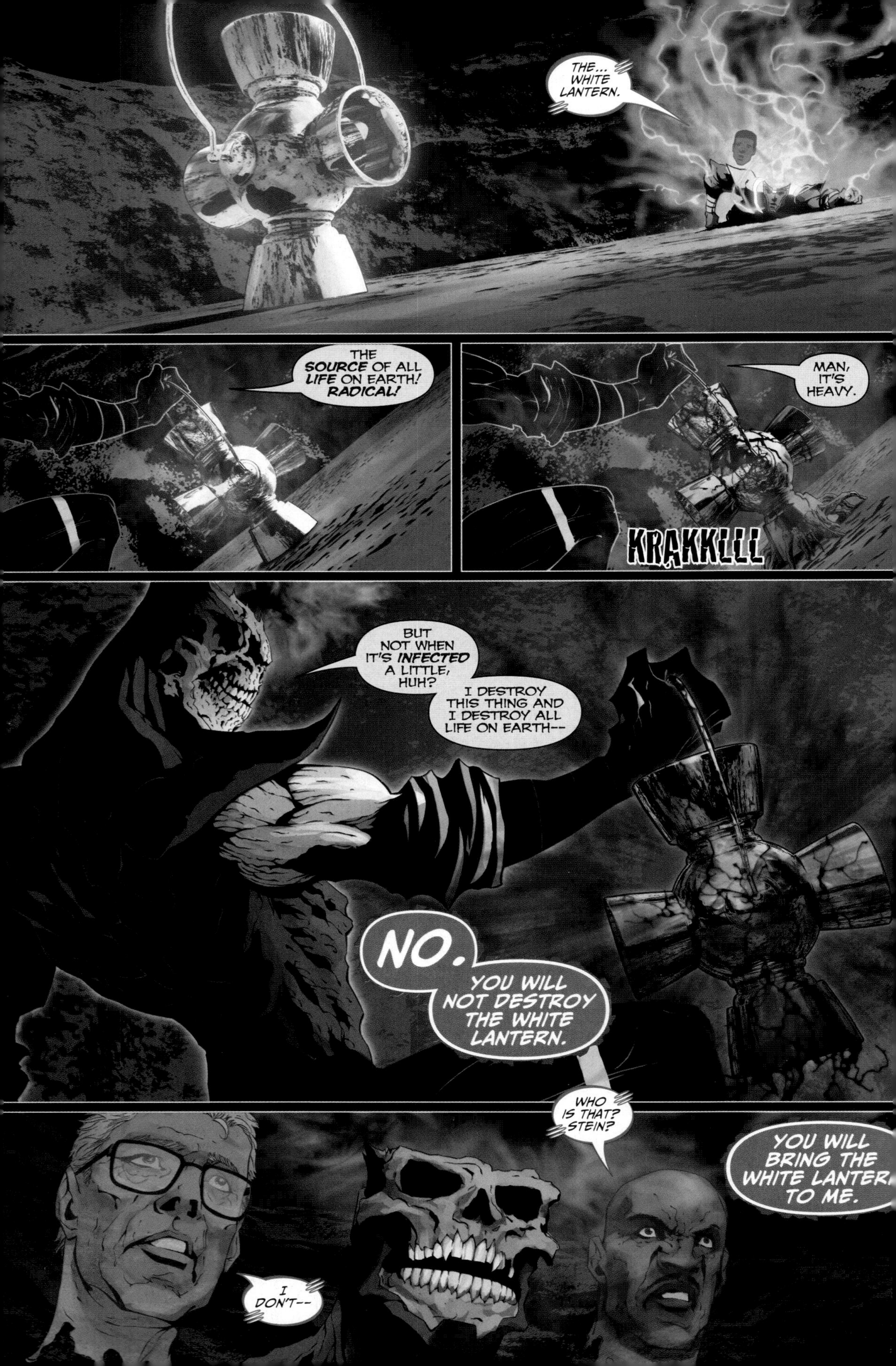
THE... WHITE LANTERN.
THE SOURCE OF ALL LIFE ON EARTH! RADICAL!
MAN, IT'S HEAVY.
KRAKKLLL
BUT NOT WHEN IT'S INFECTED A LITTLE, HUH?
I DESTROY THIS THING AND I DESTROY ALL LIFE ON EARTH--
NO.
YOU WILL NOT DESTROY THE WHITE LANTERN.
WHO IS THAT? STEIN?
YOU WILL BRING THE WHITE LANTER TO ME.
I DON'T--

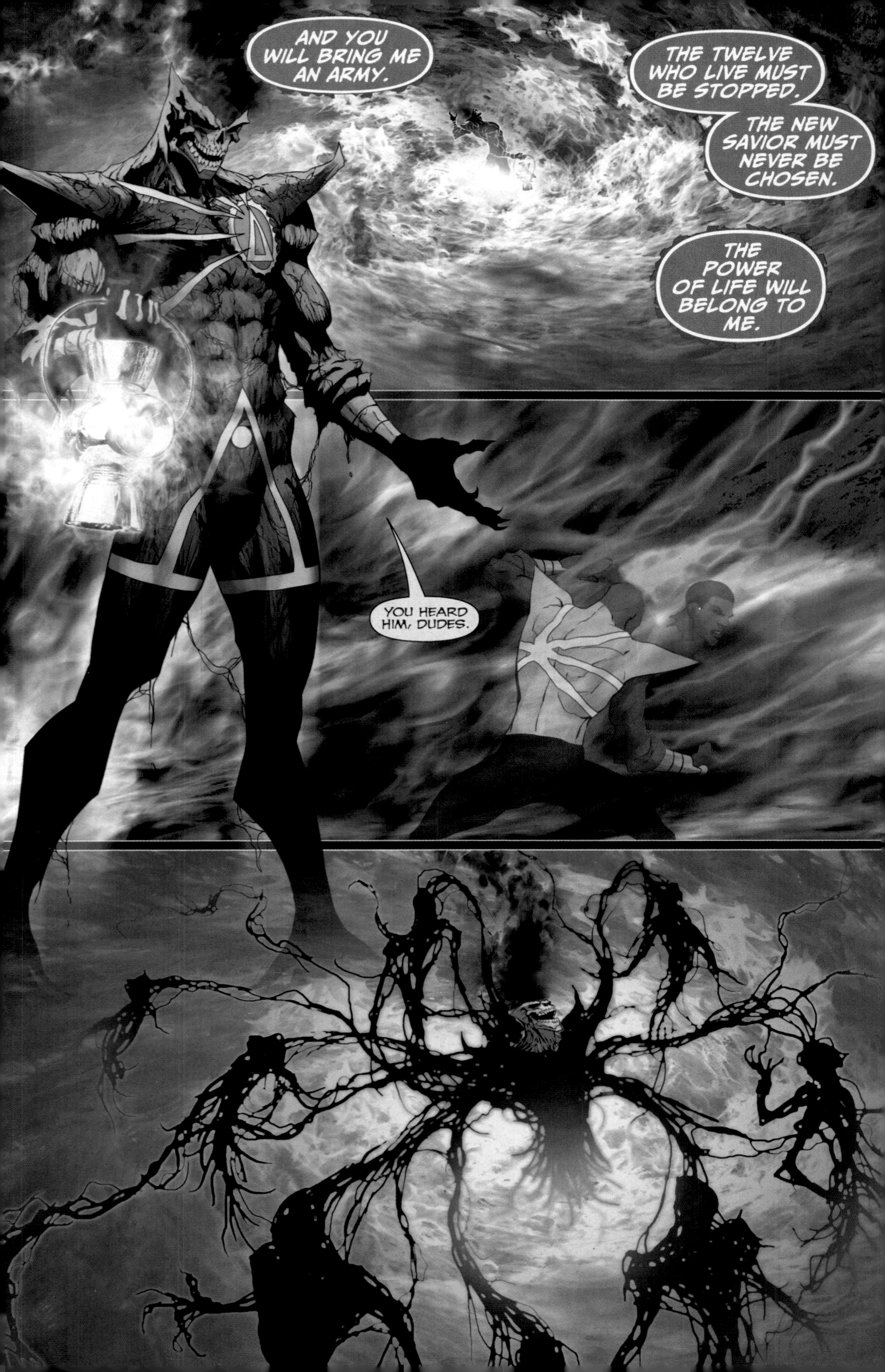
AND YOU WILL BRING ME AN ARMY.
THE TWELVE WHO LIVE MUST BE STOPPED.
THE NEW SAVIOR MUST NEVER BE CHOSEN.
THE POWER OF LIFE WILL BELONG TO ME.
YOU HEARD HIM, DUDES.

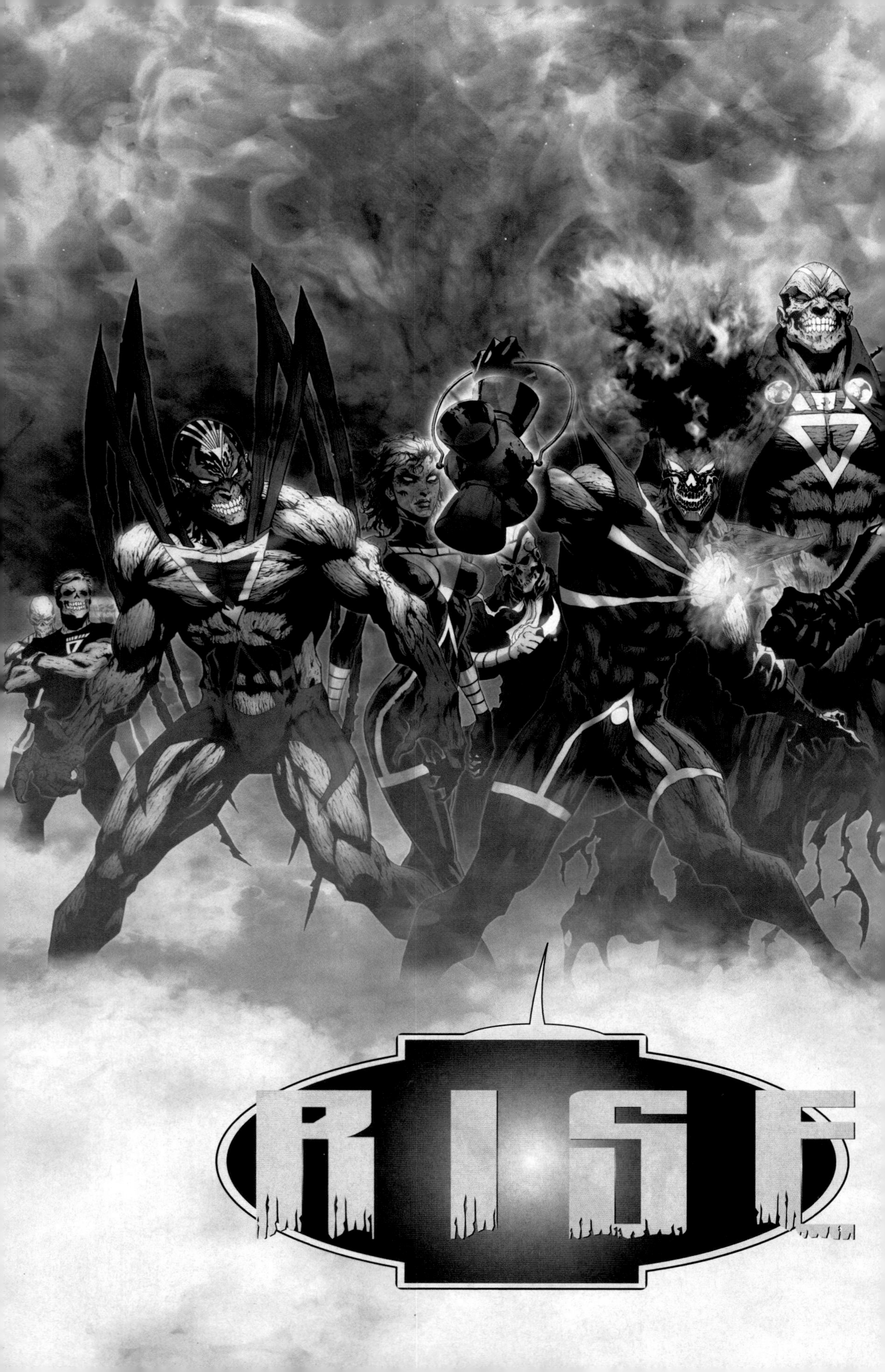
RISE

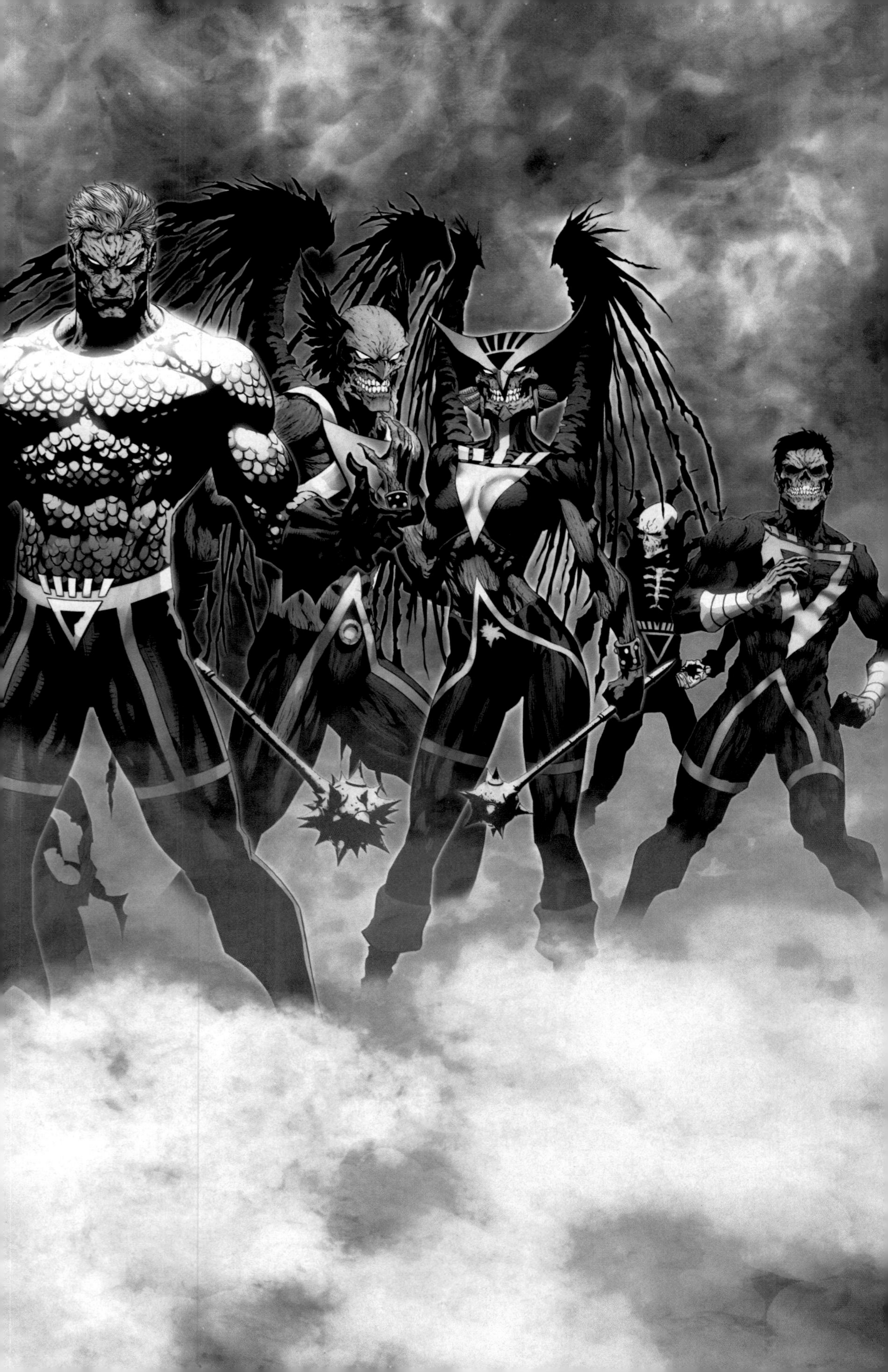

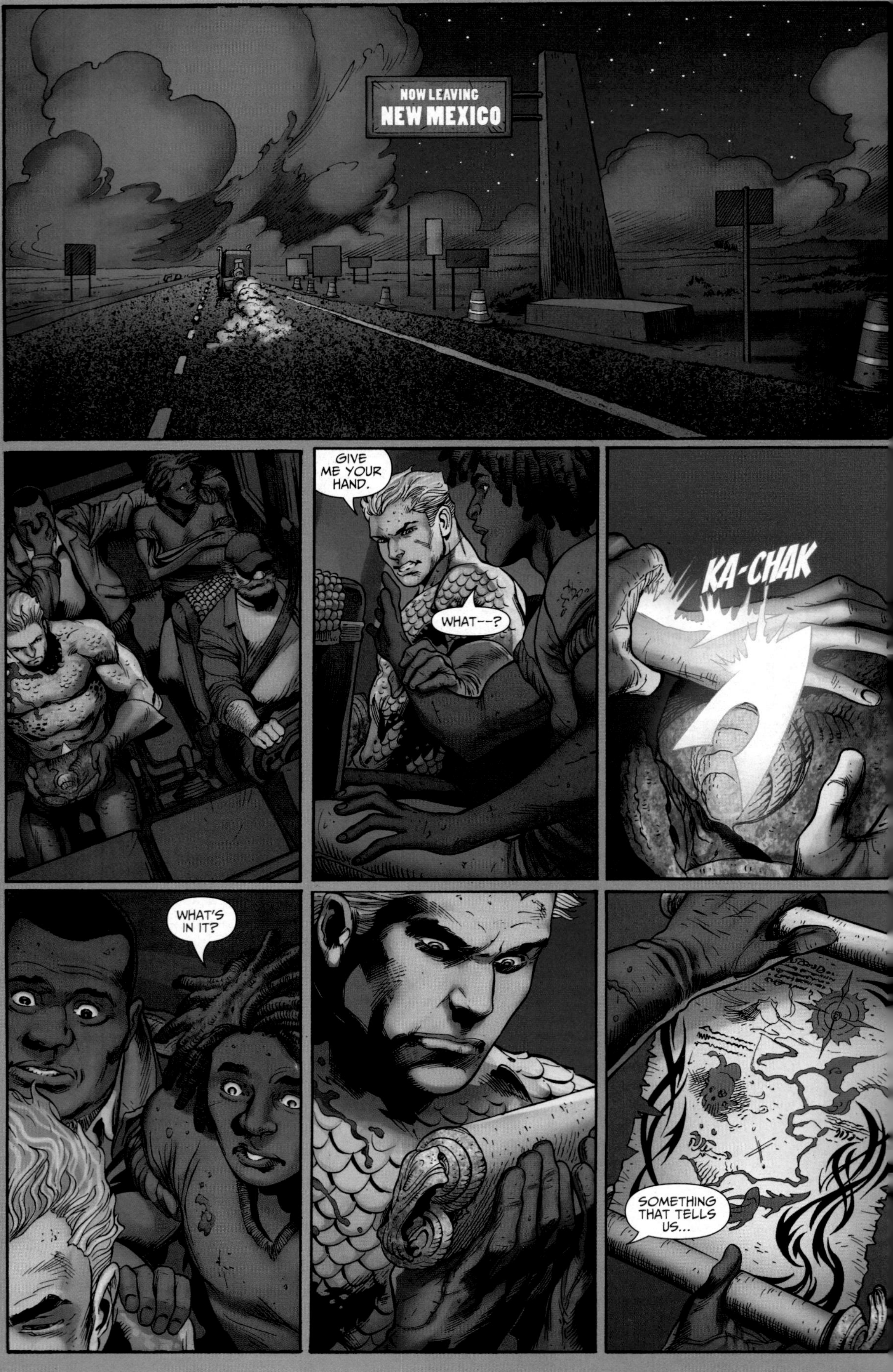
NOW LEAVING
NEW MEXICO
GIVE ME YOUR HAND.
WHAT--?
KA-CHAK
WHAT'S IN IT?
SOMETHING THAT TELLS US...

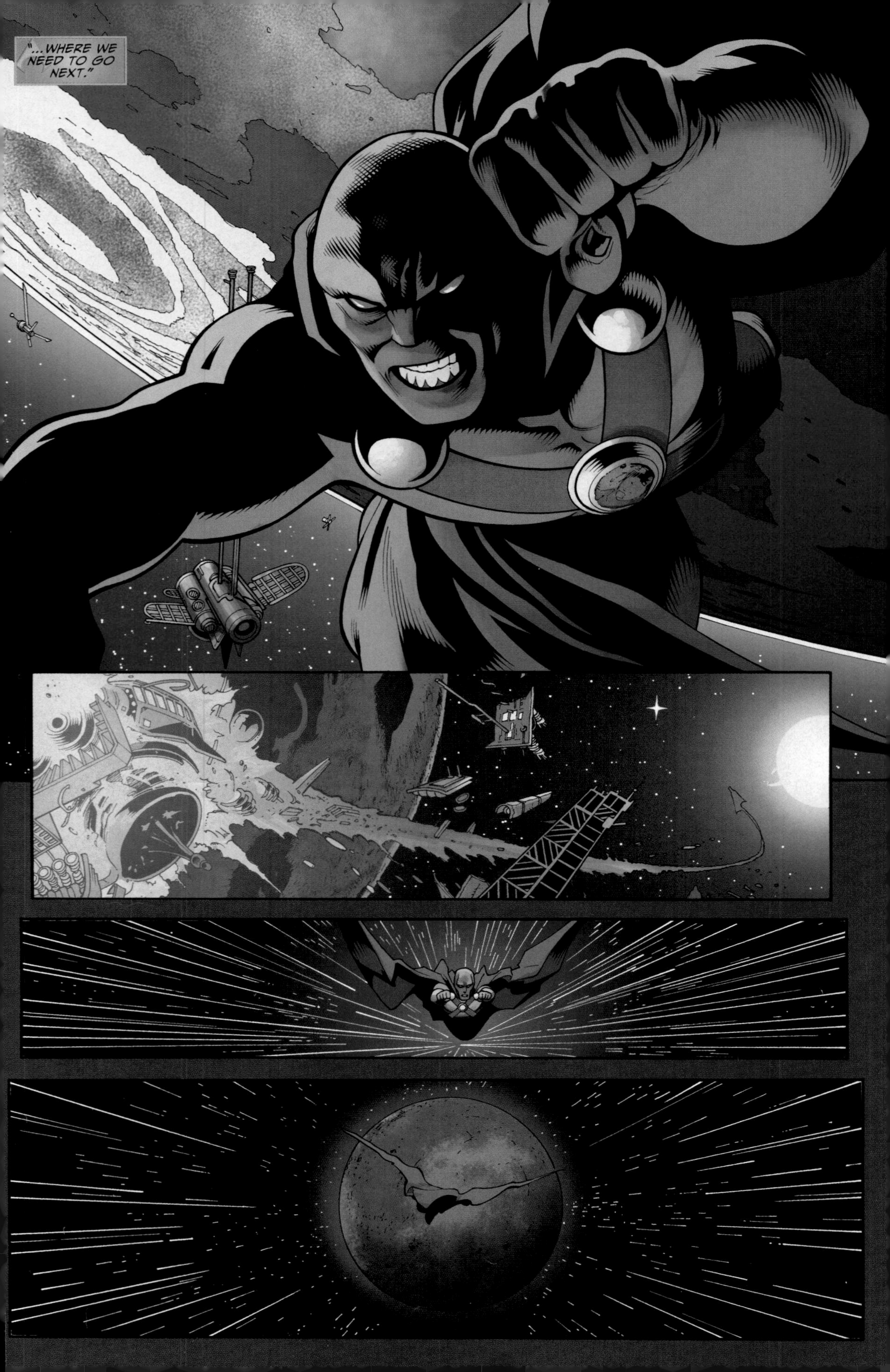
"...WHERE WE NEED TO GO NEXT."

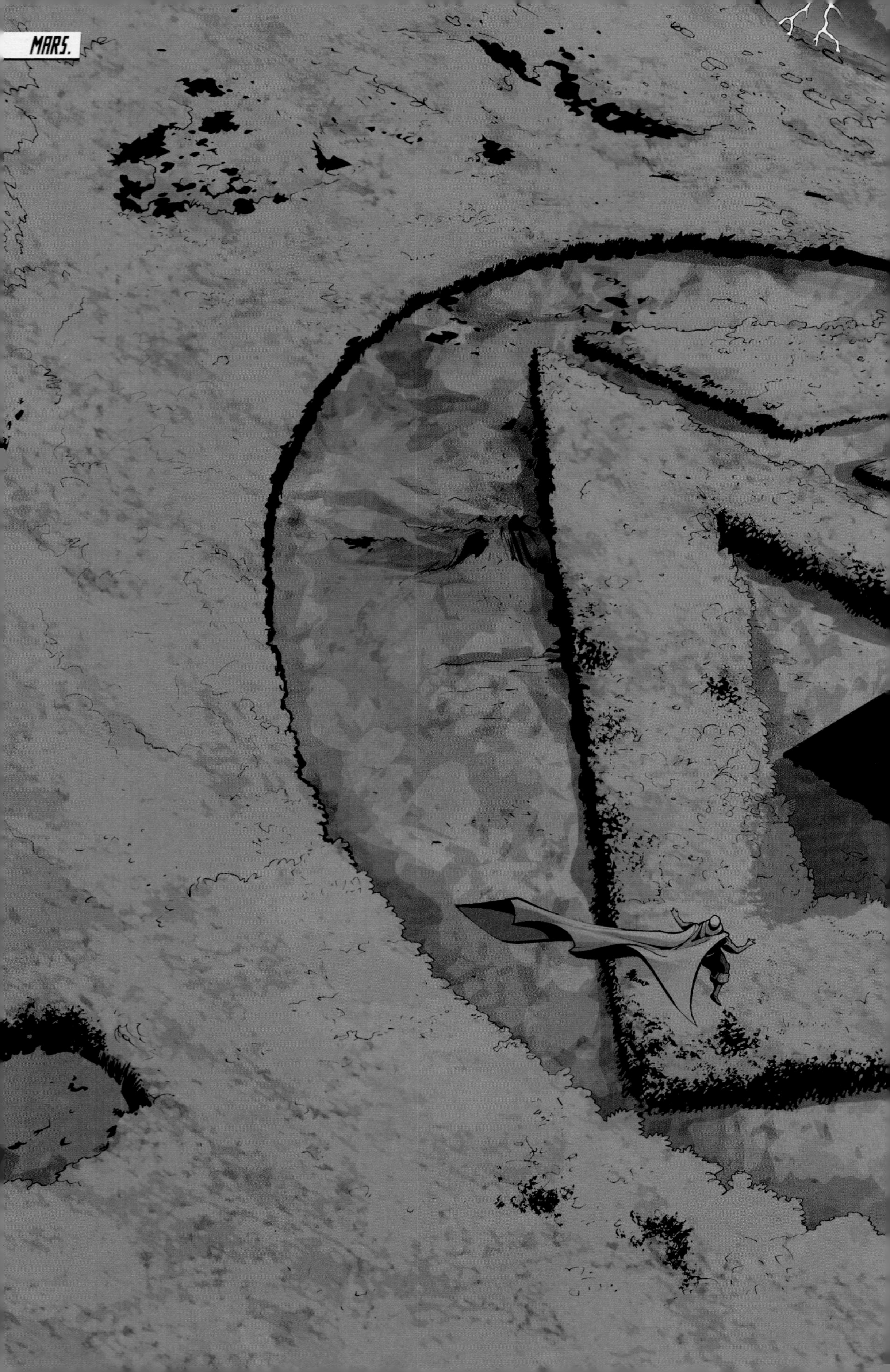
MARS.

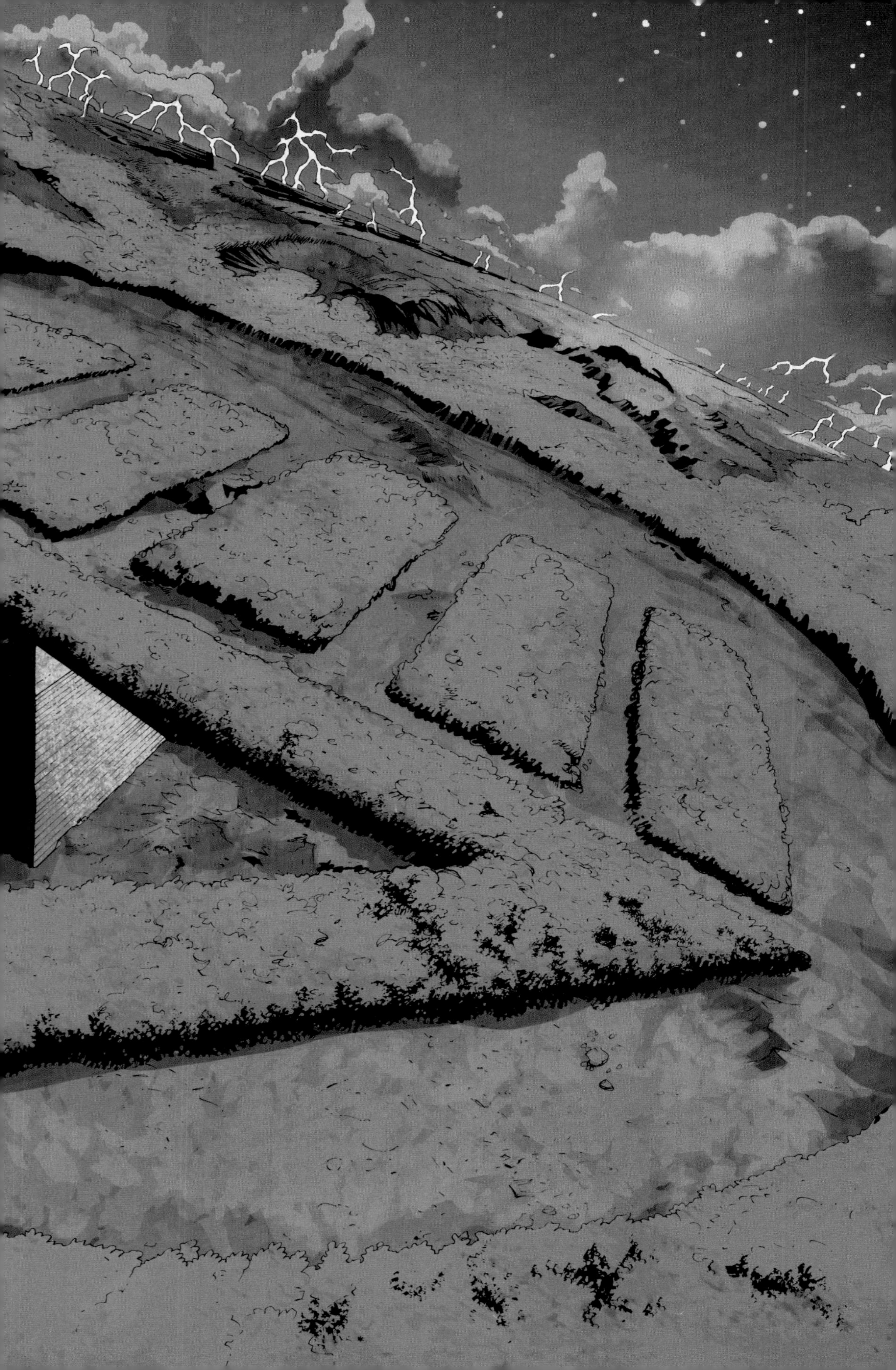

**BRIGHTEST DAY 12**
Cover by David Finch and Scott Williams
with Peter Steigerwald

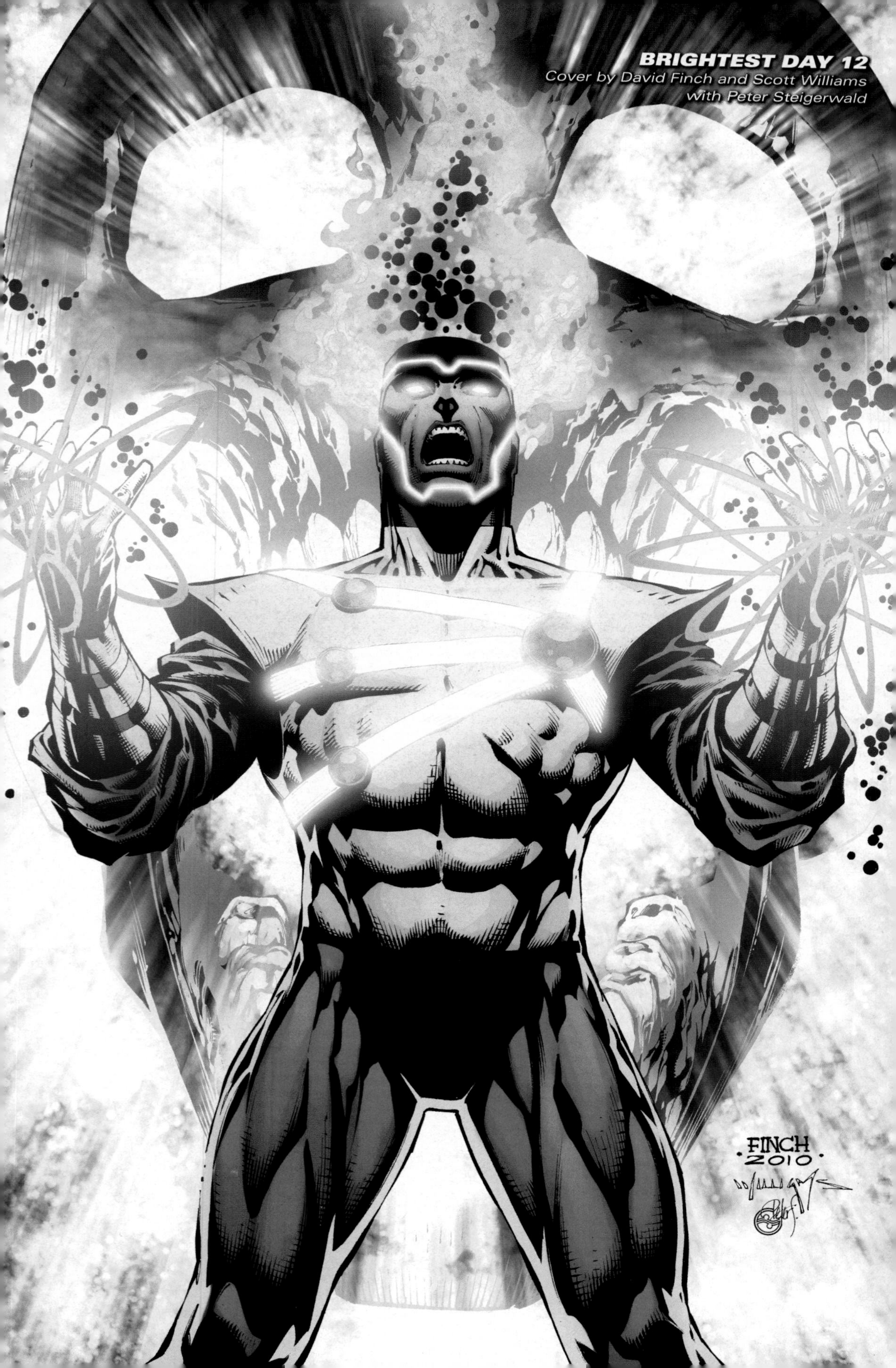
FINCH
2010

# ALL THIS
# USELESS BEAUTY

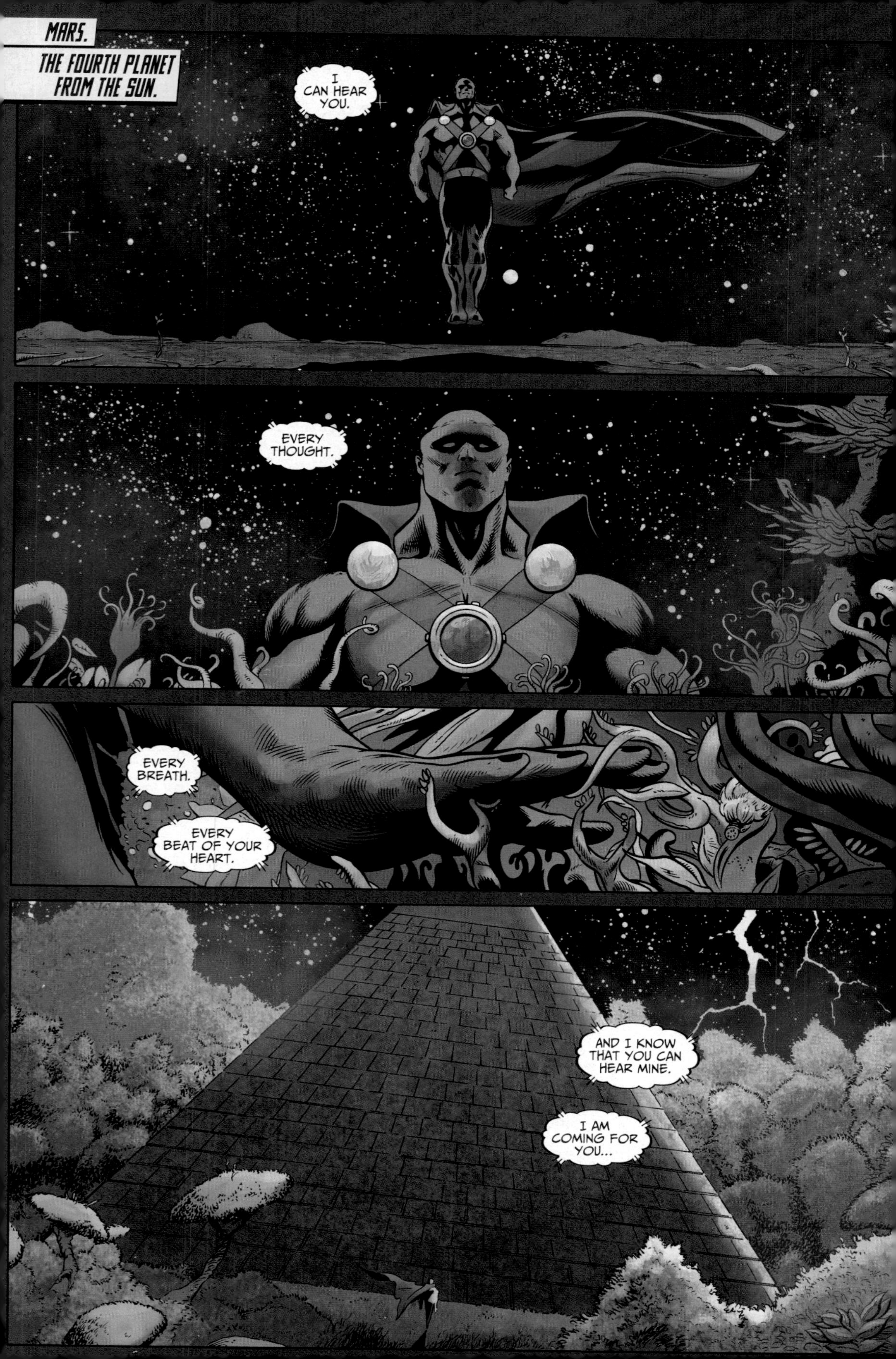
MARS.
THE FOURTH PLANET FROM THE SUN.
I CAN HEAR YOU.
EVERY THOUGHT.
EVERY BREATH.
EVERY BEAT OF YOUR HEART.
AND I KNOW THAT YOU CAN HEAR MINE.
I AM COMING FOR YOU...

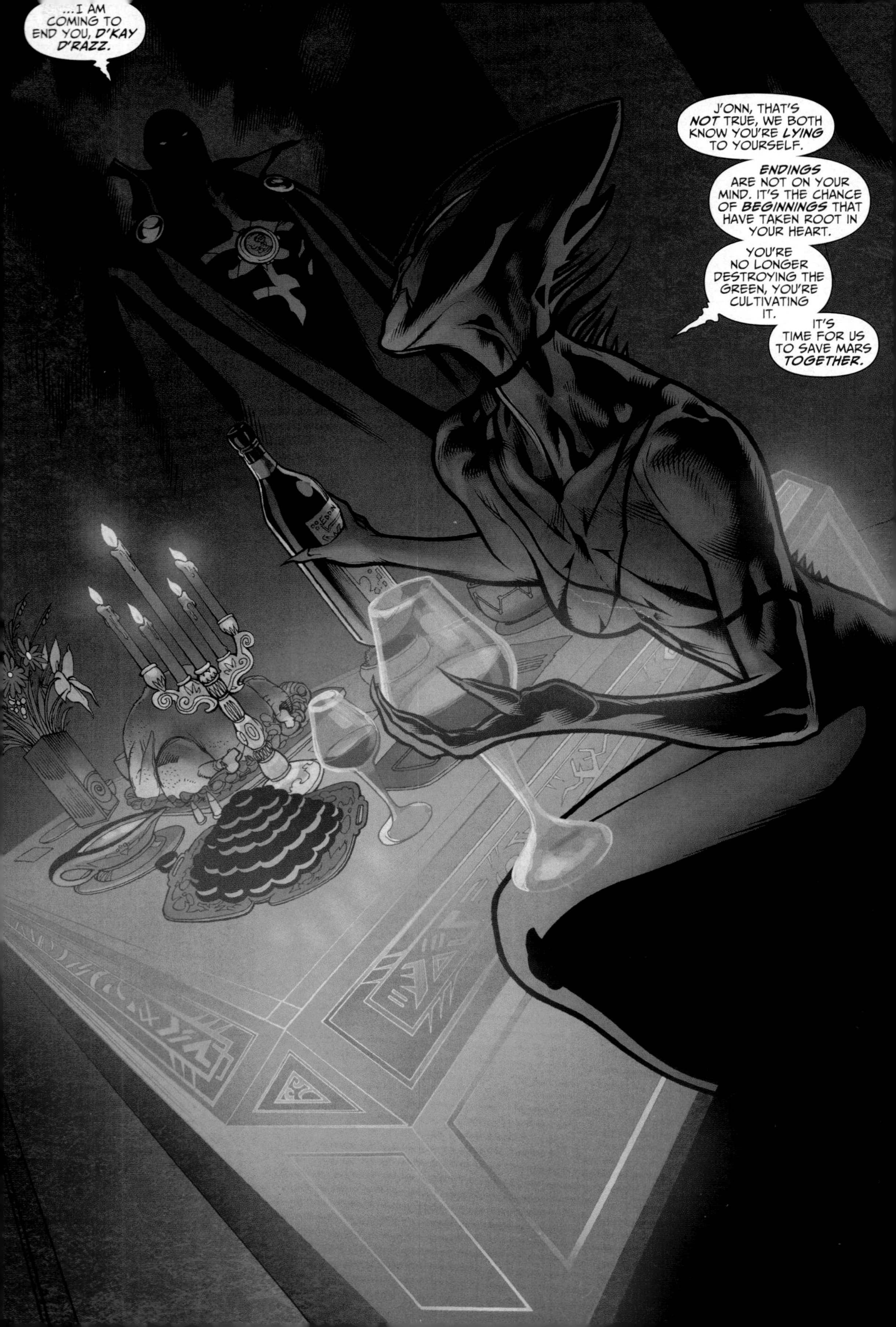
...I AM COMING TO END YOU, *D'KAY D'RAZZ.*
J'ONN, THAT'S ***NOT*** TRUE, WE BOTH KNOW YOU'RE ***LYING*** TO YOURSELF.
***ENDINGS*** ARE NOT ON YOUR MIND. IT'S THE CHANCE OF ***BEGINNINGS*** THAT HAVE TAKEN ROOT IN YOUR HEART.
YOU'RE NO LONGER DESTROYING THE GREEN, YOU'RE CULTIVATING IT.
IT'S TIME FOR US TO SAVE MARS ***TOGETHER.***

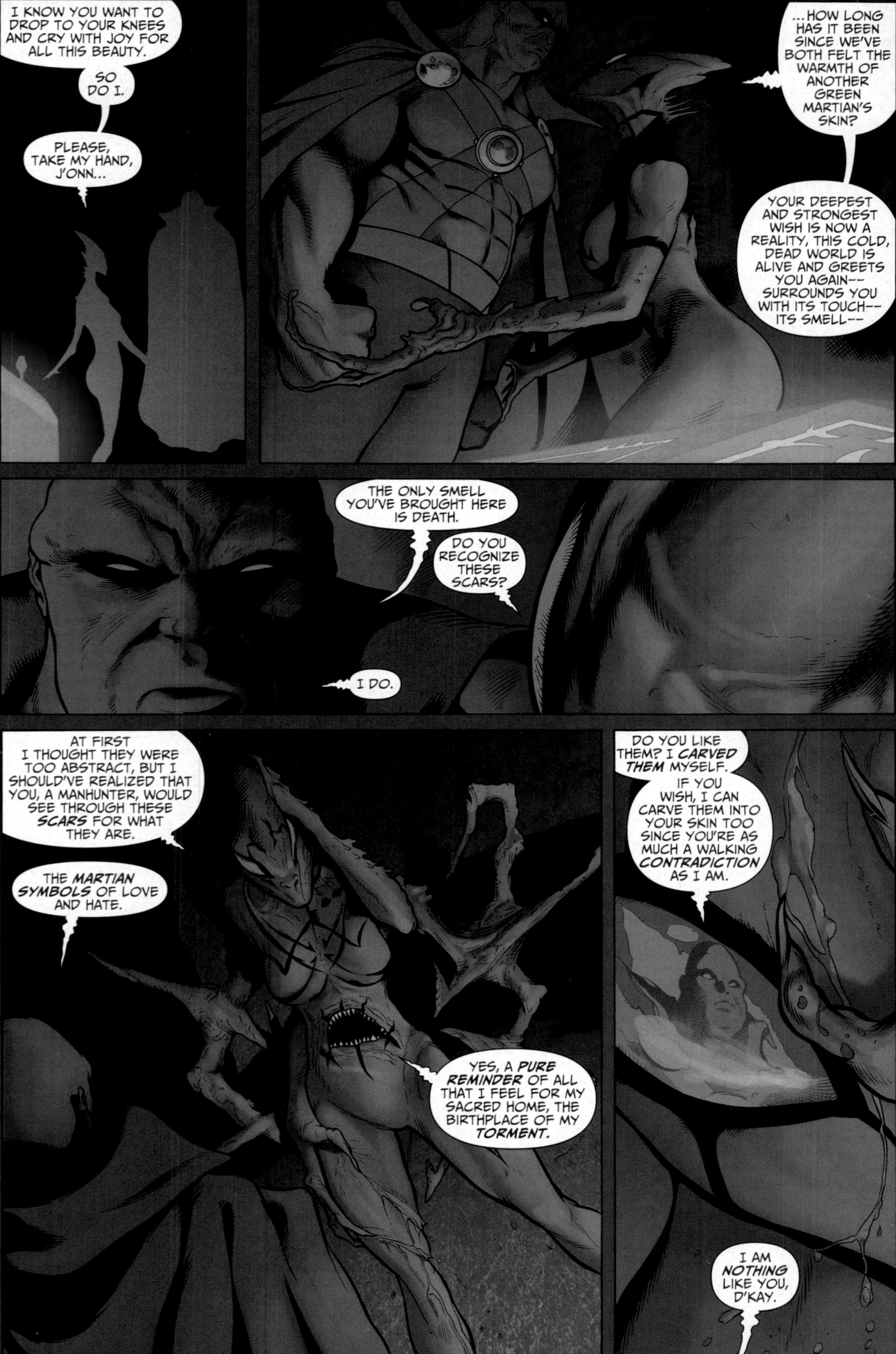
I KNOW YOU WANT TO DROP TO YOUR KNEES AND CRY WITH JOY FOR ALL THIS BEAUTY.
SO DO I.
PLEASE, TAKE MY HAND, J'ONN...
...HOW LONG HAS IT BEEN SINCE WE'VE BOTH FELT THE WARMTH OF ANOTHER GREEN MARTIAN'S SKIN?
YOUR DEEPEST AND STRONGEST WISH IS NOW A REALITY, THIS COLD, DEAD WORLD IS ALIVE AND GREETS YOU AGAIN-- SURROUNDS YOU WITH ITS TOUCH-- ITS SMELL--
THE ONLY SMELL YOU'VE BROUGHT HERE IS DEATH.
DO YOU RECOGNIZE THESE SCARS?
I DO.
AT FIRST I THOUGHT THEY WERE TOO ABSTRACT, BUT I SHOULD'VE REALIZED THAT YOU, A MANHUNTER, WOULD SEE THROUGH THESE SCARS FOR WHAT THEY ARE.
THE MARTIAN SYMBOLS OF LOVE AND HATE.
YES, A PURE REMINDER OF ALL THAT I FEEL FOR MY SACRED HOME, THE BIRTHPLACE OF MY TORMENT.
DO YOU LIKE THEM? I CARVED THEM MYSELF.
IF YOU WISH, I CAN CARVE THEM INTO YOUR SKIN TOO SINCE YOU'RE AS MUCH A WALKING CONTRADICTION AS I AM.
I AM NOTHING LIKE YOU, D'KAY.

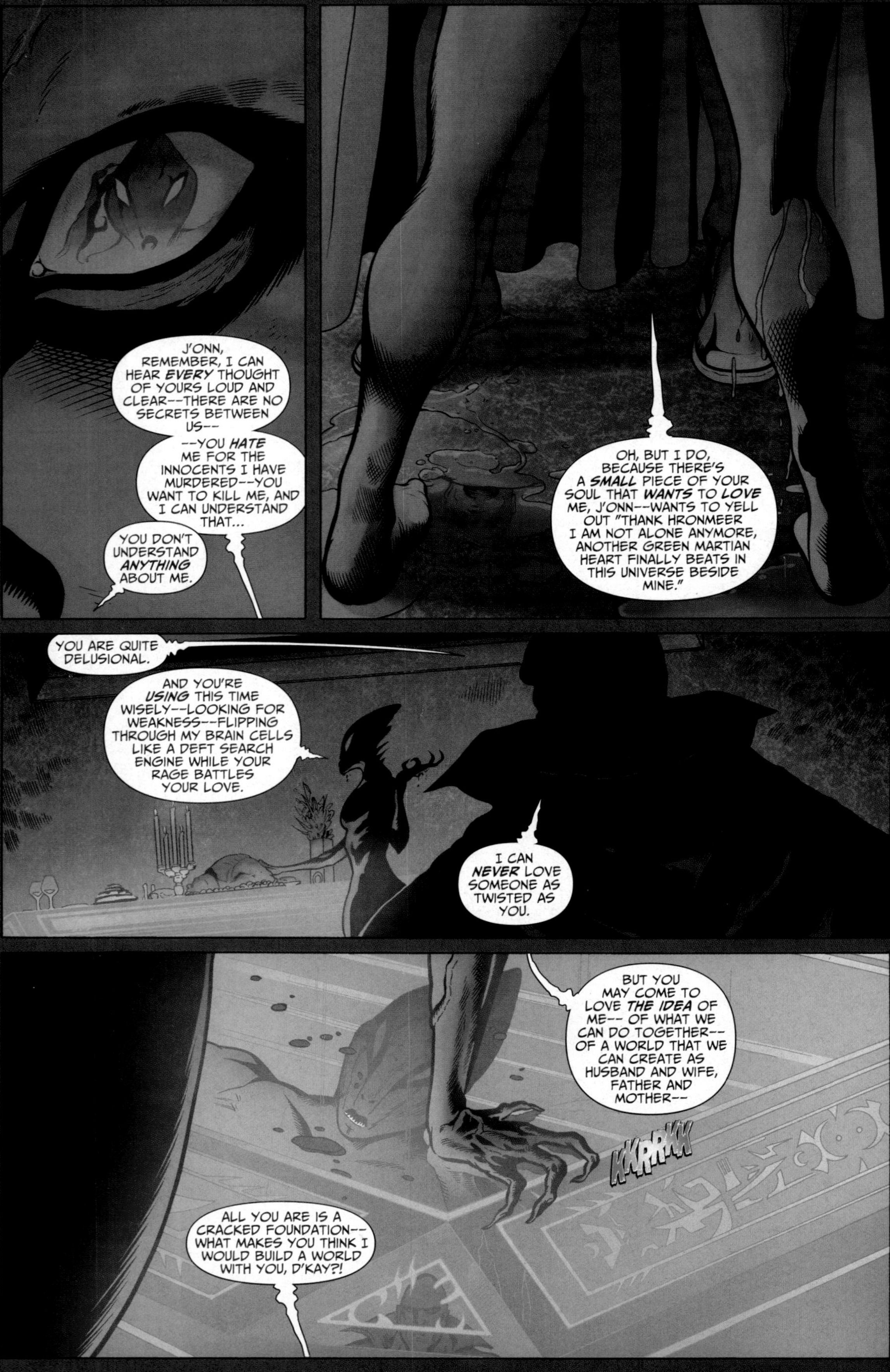
J'ONN, REMEMBER, I CAN HEAR EVERY THOUGHT OF YOURS LOUD AND CLEAR--THERE ARE NO SECRETS BETWEEN US--
--YOU HATE ME FOR THE INNOCENTS I HAVE MURDERED--YOU WANT TO KILL ME, AND I CAN UNDERSTAND THAT...
YOU DON'T UNDERSTAND ANYTHING ABOUT ME.
OH, BUT I DO, BECAUSE THERE'S A SMALL PIECE OF YOUR SOUL THAT WANTS TO LOVE ME, J'ONN--WANTS TO YELL OUT "THANK HRONMEER I AM NOT ALONE ANYMORE, ANOTHER GREEN MARTIAN HEART FINALLY BEATS IN THIS UNIVERSE BESIDE MINE."
YOU ARE QUITE DELUSIONAL.
AND YOU'RE USING THIS TIME WISELY--LOOKING FOR WEAKNESS--FLIPPING THROUGH MY BRAIN CELLS LIKE A DEFT SEARCH ENGINE WHILE YOUR RAGE BATTLES YOUR LOVE.
I CAN NEVER LOVE SOMEONE AS TWISTED AS YOU.
BUT YOU MAY COME TO LOVE THE IDEA OF ME-- OF WHAT WE CAN DO TOGETHER-- OF A WORLD THAT WE CAN CREATE AS HUSBAND AND WIFE, FATHER AND MOTHER--
KKRRKK
ALL YOU ARE IS A CRACKED FOUNDATION-- WHAT MAKES YOU THINK I WOULD BUILD A WORLD WITH YOU, D'KAY?!

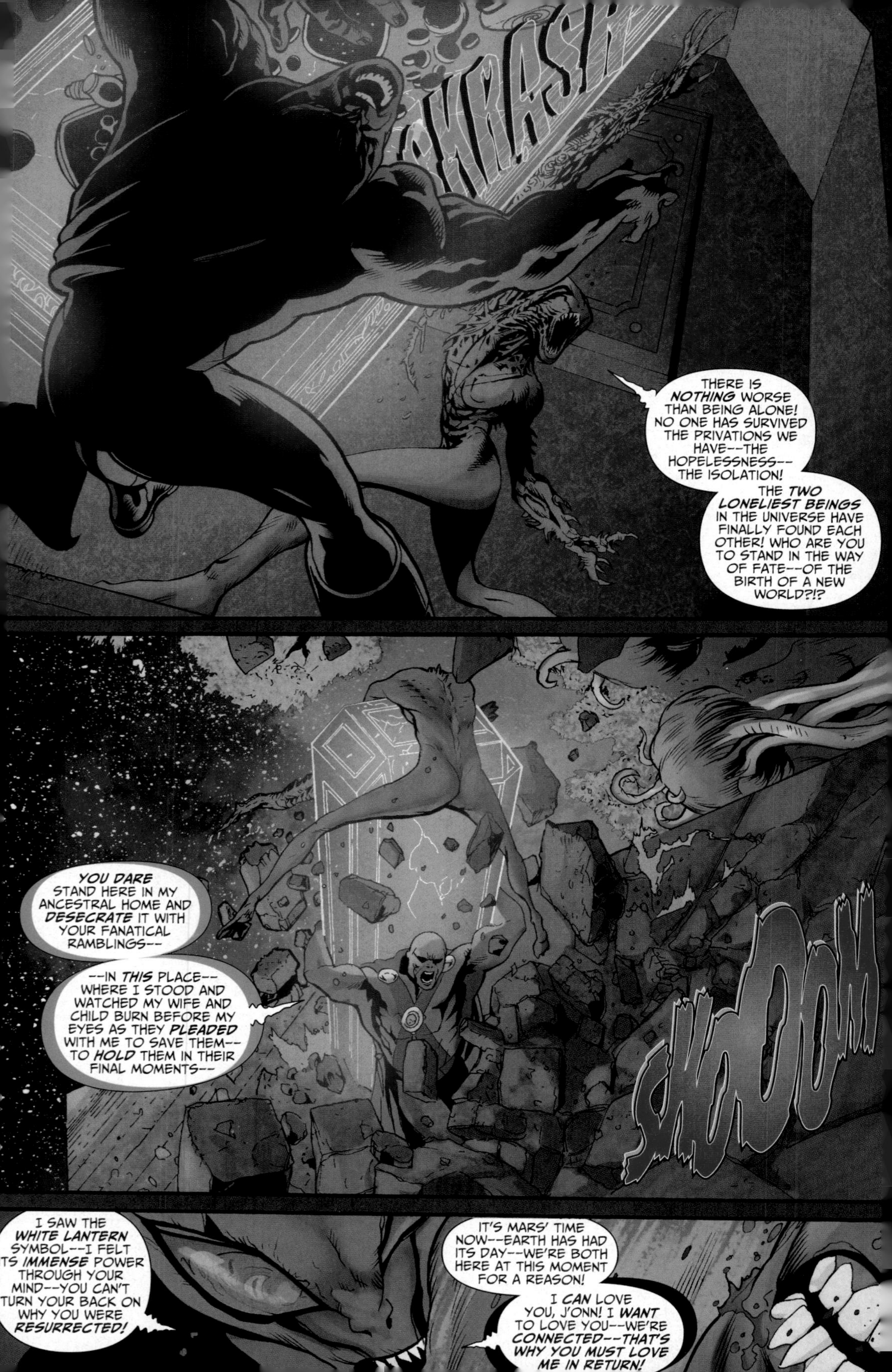
KKRASH
THERE IS NOTHING WORSE THAN BEING ALONE! NO ONE HAS SURVIVED THE PRIVATIONS WE HAVE--THE HOPELESSNESS--THE ISOLATION!
THE TWO LONELIEST BEINGS IN THE UNIVERSE HAVE FINALLY FOUND EACH OTHER! WHO ARE YOU TO STAND IN THE WAY OF FATE--OF THE BIRTH OF A NEW WORLD?!?
YOU DARE STAND HERE IN MY ANCESTRAL HOME AND DESECRATE IT WITH YOUR FANATICAL RAMBLINGS--
--IN THIS PLACE--WHERE I STOOD AND WATCHED MY WIFE AND CHILD BURN BEFORE MY EYES AS THEY PLEADED WITH ME TO SAVE THEM--TO HOLD THEM IN THEIR FINAL MOMENTS--
SKOOOOM
I SAW THE WHITE LANTERN SYMBOL--I FELT ITS IMMENSE POWER THROUGH YOUR MIND--YOU CAN'T TURN YOUR BACK ON WHY YOU WERE RESURRECTED!
IT'S MARS' TIME NOW--EARTH HAS HAD ITS DAY--WE'RE BOTH HERE AT THIS MOMENT FOR A REASON!
I CAN LOVE YOU, J'ONN! I WANT TO LOVE YOU--WE'RE CONNECTED--THAT'S WHY YOU MUST LOVE ME IN RETURN!

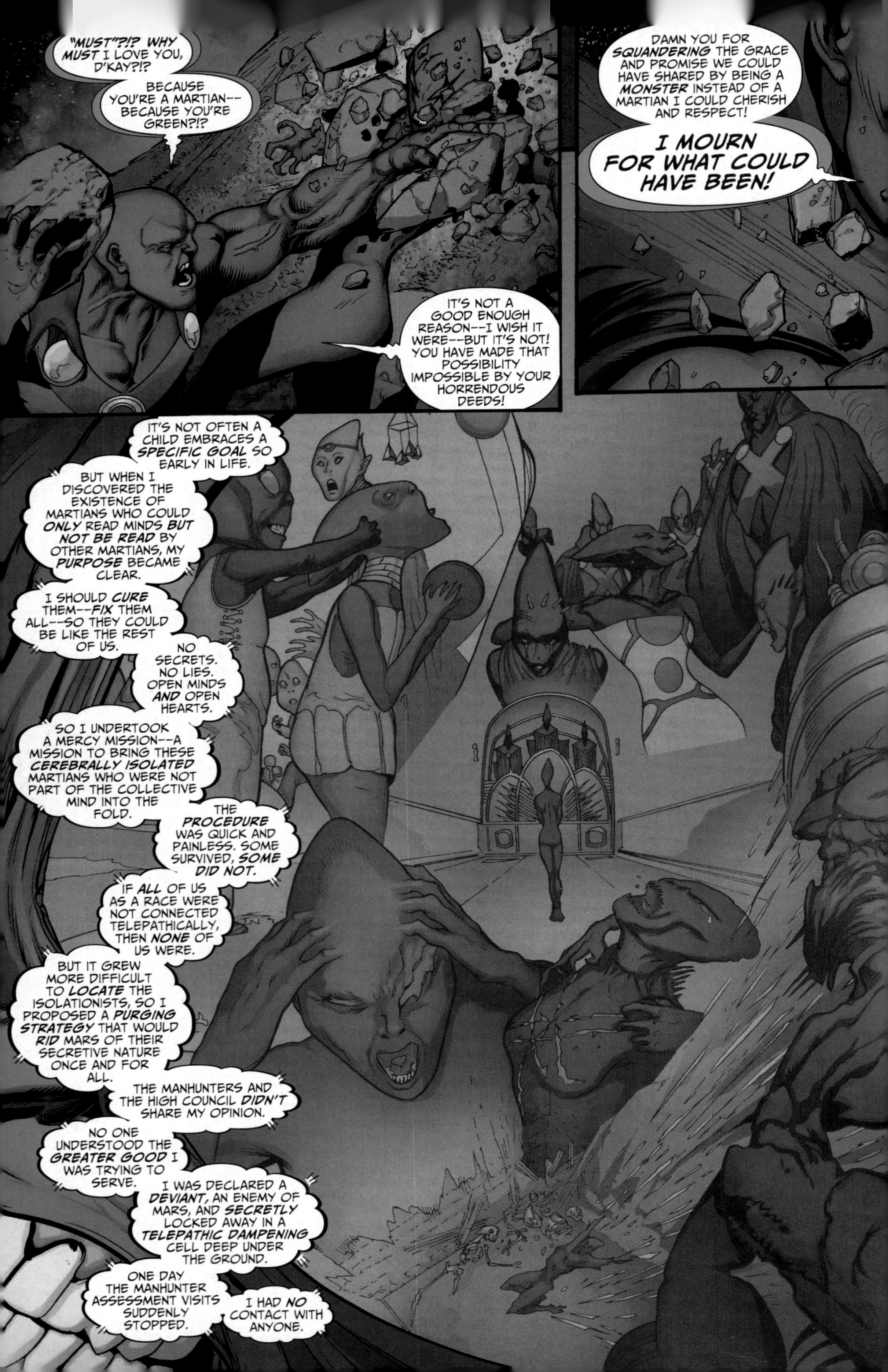
"MUST"?!? WHY MUST I LOVE YOU, D'KAY?!?
BECAUSE YOU'RE A MARTIAN--BECAUSE YOU'RE GREEN?!?
IT'S NOT A GOOD ENOUGH REASON--I WISH IT WERE--BUT IT'S NOT! YOU HAVE MADE THAT POSSIBILITY IMPOSSIBLE BY YOUR HORRENDOUS DEEDS!
DAMN YOU FOR SQUANDERING THE GRACE AND PROMISE WE COULD HAVE SHARED BY BEING A MONSTER INSTEAD OF A MARTIAN I COULD CHERISH AND RESPECT!
I MOURN FOR WHAT COULD HAVE BEEN!
IT'S NOT OFTEN A CHILD EMBRACES A SPECIFIC GOAL SO EARLY IN LIFE.
BUT WHEN I DISCOVERED THE EXISTENCE OF MARTIANS WHO COULD ONLY READ MINDS BUT NOT BE READ BY OTHER MARTIANS, MY PURPOSE BECAME CLEAR.
I SHOULD CURE THEM--FIX THEM ALL--SO THEY COULD BE LIKE THE REST OF US.
NO SECRETS. NO LIES. OPEN MINDS AND OPEN HEARTS.
SO I UNDERTOOK A MERCY MISSION--A MISSION TO BRING THESE CEREBRALLY ISOLATED MARTIANS WHO WERE NOT PART OF THE COLLECTIVE MIND INTO THE FOLD.
THE PROCEDURE WAS QUICK AND PAINLESS. SOME SURVIVED, SOME DID NOT.
IF ALL OF US AS A RACE WERE NOT CONNECTED TELEPATHICALLY, THEN NONE OF US WERE.
BUT IT GREW MORE DIFFICULT TO LOCATE THE ISOLATIONISTS, SO I PROPOSED A PURGING STRATEGY THAT WOULD RID MARS OF THEIR SECRETIVE NATURE ONCE AND FOR ALL.
THE MANHUNTERS AND THE HIGH COUNCIL DIDN'T SHARE MY OPINION.
NO ONE UNDERSTOOD THE GREATER GOOD I WAS TRYING TO SERVE.
I WAS DECLARED A DEVIANT, AN ENEMY OF MARS, AND SECRETLY LOCKED AWAY IN A TELEPATHIC DAMPENING CELL DEEP UNDER THE GROUND.
ONE DAY THE MANHUNTER ASSESSMENT VISITS SUDDENLY STOPPED.
I HAD NO CONTACT WITH ANYONE.

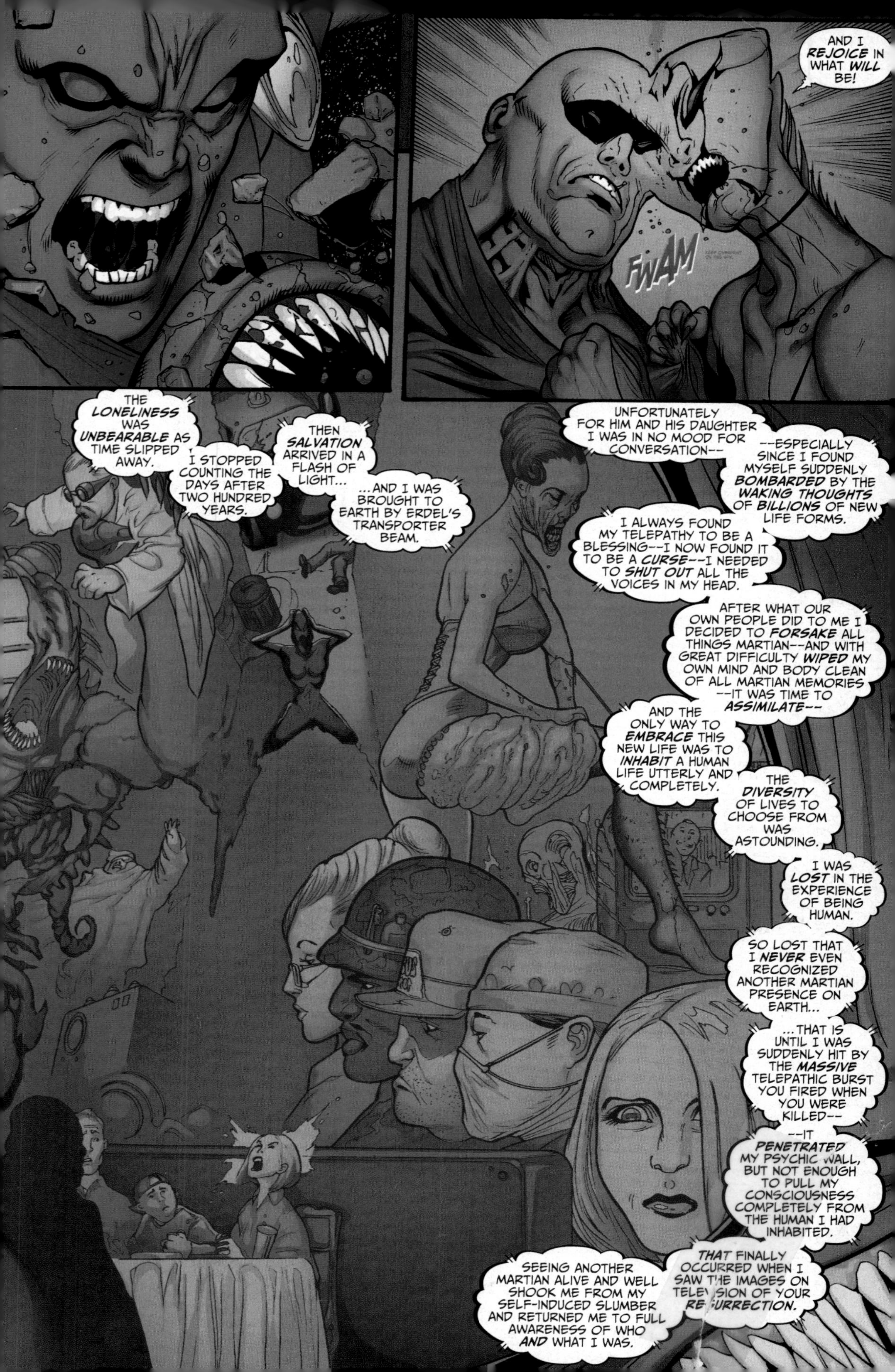
AND I REJOICE IN WHAT WILL BE!
FWAM
THE LONELINESS WAS UNBEARABLE AS TIME SLIPPED AWAY.
I STOPPED COUNTING THE DAYS AFTER TWO HUNDRED YEARS.
THEN SALVATION ARRIVED IN A FLASH OF LIGHT...
...AND I WAS BROUGHT TO EARTH BY ERDEL'S TRANSPORTER BEAM.
UNFORTUNATELY FOR HIM AND HIS DAUGHTER I WAS IN NO MOOD FOR CONVERSATION--
--ESPECIALLY SINCE I FOUND MYSELF SUDDENLY BOMBARDED BY THE WAKING THOUGHTS OF BILLIONS OF NEW LIFE FORMS.
I ALWAYS FOUND MY TELEPATHY TO BE A BLESSING--I NOW FOUND IT TO BE A CURSE--I NEEDED TO SHUT OUT ALL THE VOICES IN MY HEAD.
AFTER WHAT OUR OWN PEOPLE DID TO ME I DECIDED TO FORSAKE ALL THINGS MARTIAN--AND WITH GREAT DIFFICULTY WIPED MY OWN MIND AND BODY CLEAN OF ALL MARTIAN MEMORIES --IT WAS TIME TO ASSIMILATE--
AND THE ONLY WAY TO EMBRACE THIS NEW LIFE WAS TO INHABIT A HUMAN LIFE UTTERLY AND COMPLETELY.
THE DIVERSITY OF LIVES TO CHOOSE FROM WAS ASTOUNDING.
I WAS LOST IN THE EXPERIENCE OF BEING HUMAN.
SO LOST THAT I NEVER EVEN RECOGNIZED ANOTHER MARTIAN PRESENCE ON EARTH...
...THAT IS UNTIL I WAS SUDDENLY HIT BY THE MASSIVE TELEPATHIC BURST YOU FIRED WHEN YOU WERE KILLED--
--IT PENETRATED MY PSYCHIC WALL, BUT NOT ENOUGH TO PULL MY CONSCIOUSNESS COMPLETELY FROM THE HUMAN I HAD INHABITED.
THAT FINALLY OCCURRED WHEN I SAW THE IMAGES ON TELEVISION OF YOUR RESURRECTION.
SEEING ANOTHER MARTIAN ALIVE AND WELL SHOOK ME FROM MY SELF-INDUCED SLUMBER AND RETURNED ME TO FULL AWARENESS OF WHO AND WHAT I WAS.

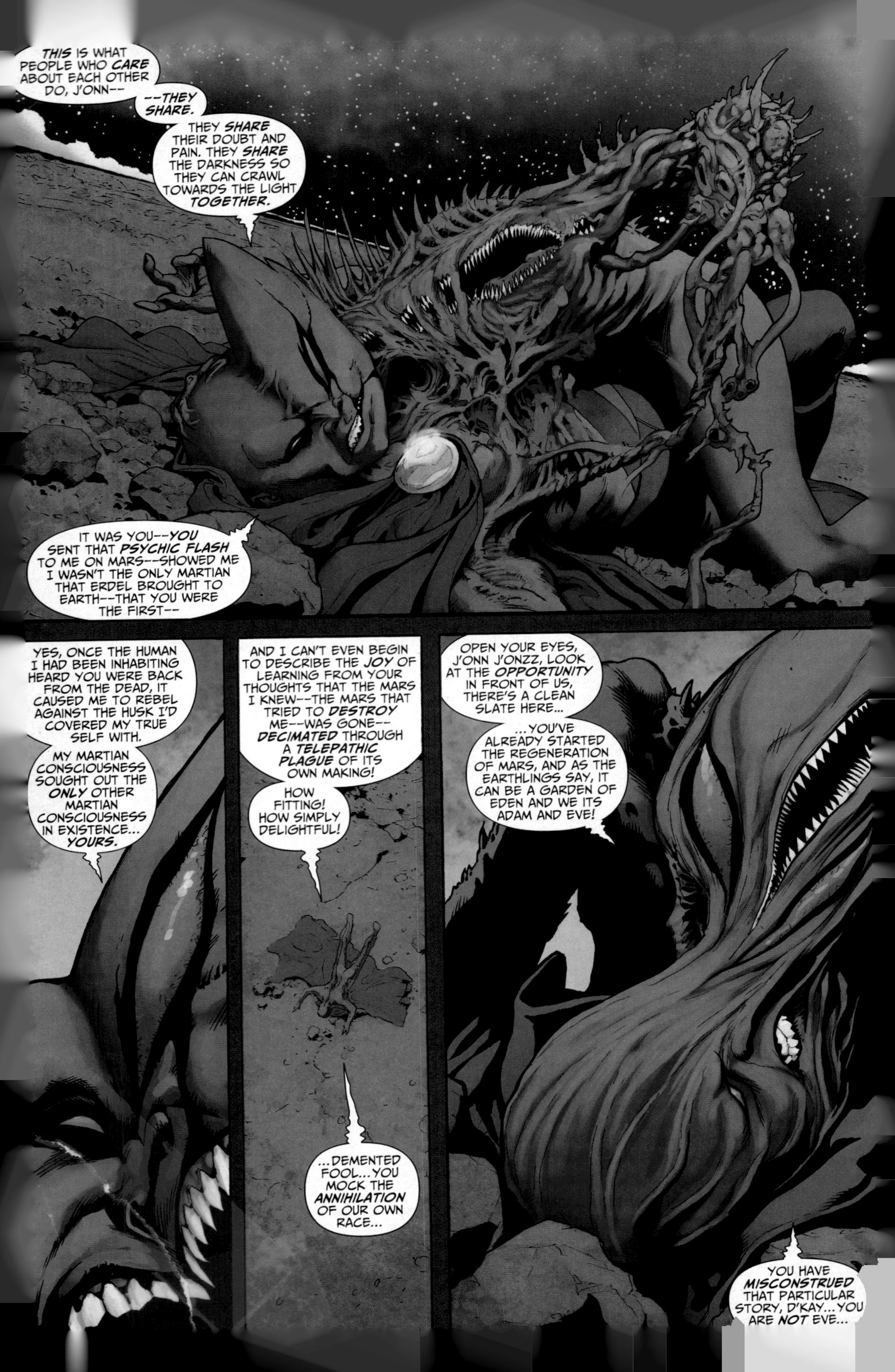
THIS IS WHAT PEOPLE WHO CARE ABOUT EACH OTHER DO, J'ONN--
--THEY SHARE.
THEY SHARE THEIR DOUBT AND PAIN. THEY SHARE THE DARKNESS SO THEY CAN CRAWL TOWARDS THE LIGHT TOGETHER.
IT WAS YOU--YOU SENT THAT PSYCHIC FLASH TO ME ON MARS--SHOWED ME I WASN'T THE ONLY MARTIAN THAT ERDEL BROUGHT TO EARTH--THAT YOU WERE THE FIRST--
YES, ONCE THE HUMAN I HAD BEEN INHABITING HEARD YOU WERE BACK FROM THE DEAD, IT CAUSED ME TO REBEL AGAINST THE HUSK I'D COVERED MY TRUE SELF WITH.
MY MARTIAN CONSCIOUSNESS SOUGHT OUT THE ONLY OTHER MARTIAN CONSCIOUSNESS IN EXISTENCE... YOURS.
AND I CAN'T EVEN BEGIN TO DESCRIBE THE JOY OF LEARNING FROM YOUR THOUGHTS THAT THE MARS I KNEW--THE MARS THAT TRIED TO DESTROY ME--WAS GONE--DECIMATED THROUGH A TELEPATHIC PLAGUE OF ITS OWN MAKING!
HOW FITTING! HOW SIMPLY DELIGHTFUL!
...DEMENTED FOOL...YOU MOCK THE ANNIHILATION OF OUR OWN RACE...
OPEN YOUR EYES, J'ONN J'ONZZ, LOOK AT THE OPPORTUNITY IN FRONT OF US, THERE'S A CLEAN SLATE HERE...
...YOU'VE ALREADY STARTED THE REGENERATION OF MARS, AND AS THE EARTHLINGS SAY, IT CAN BE A GARDEN OF EDEN AND WE ITS ADAM AND EVE!
YOU HAVE MISCONSTRUED THAT PARTICULAR STORY, D'KAY...YOU ARE NOT EVE...

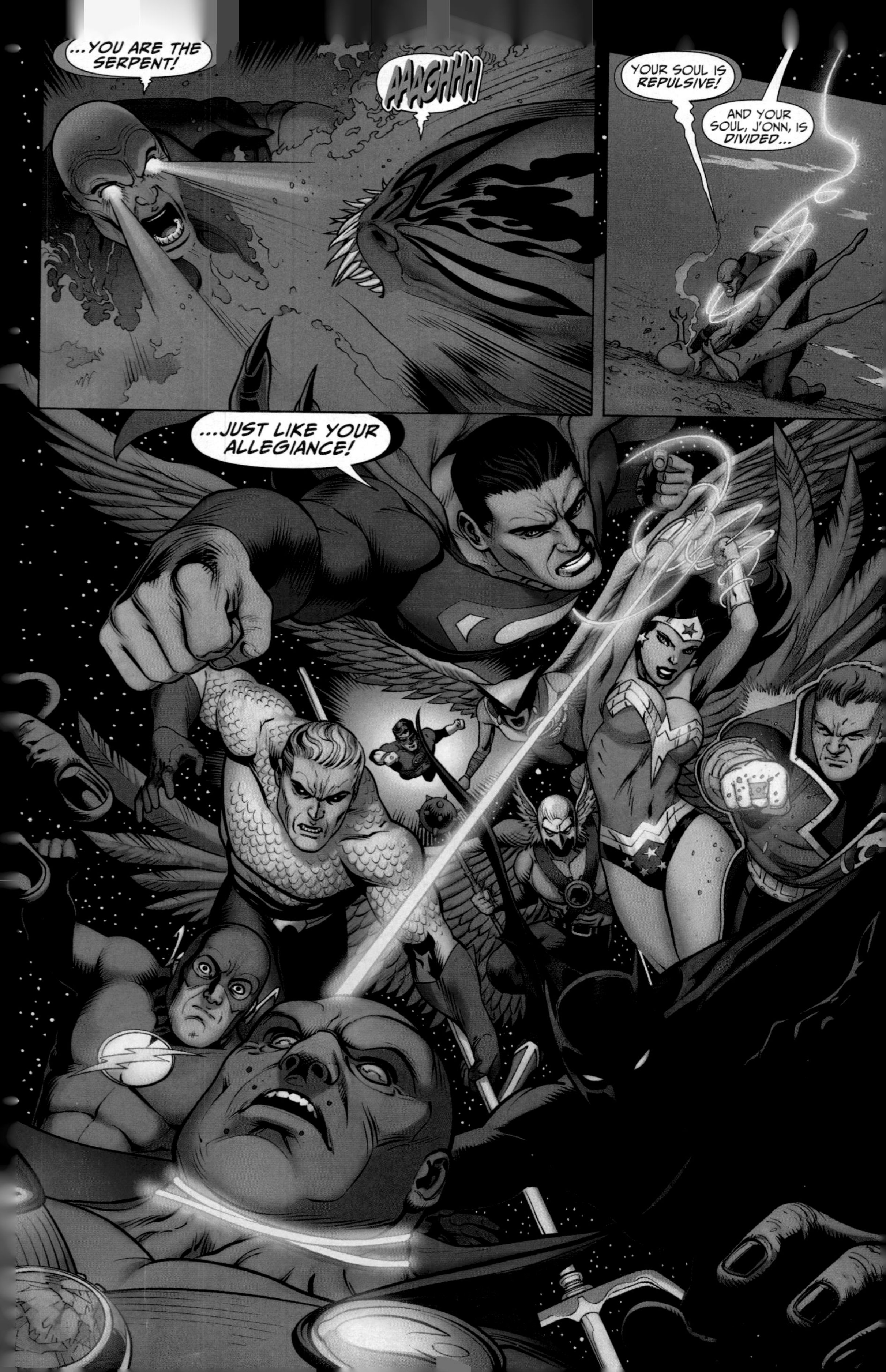
...YOU ARE THE SERPENT!
AAAGHHH
YOUR SOUL IS REPULSIVE!
AND YOUR SOUL, J'ONN, IS DIVIDED...
...JUST LIKE YOUR ALLEGIANCE!

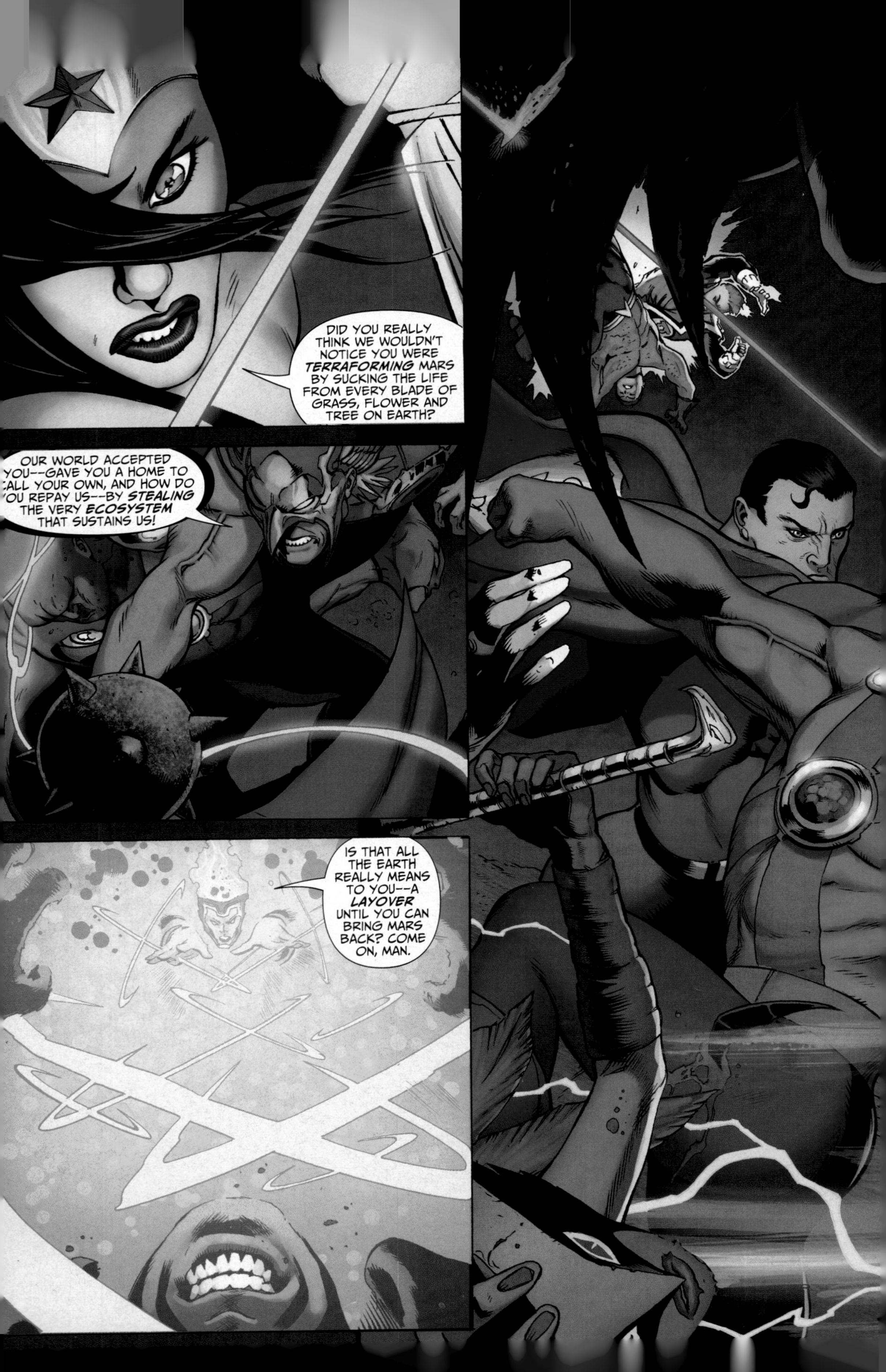
DID YOU REALLY THINK WE WOULDN'T NOTICE YOU WERE TERRAFORMING MARS BY SUCKING THE LIFE FROM EVERY BLADE OF GRASS, FLOWER AND TREE ON EARTH?
OUR WORLD ACCEPTED YOU--GAVE YOU A HOME TO CALL YOUR OWN, AND HOW DO YOU REPAY US--BY STEALING THE VERY ECOSYSTEM THAT SUSTAINS US!
IS THAT ALL THE EARTH REALLY MEANS TO YOU--A LAYOVER UNTIL YOU CAN BRING MARS BACK? COME ON, MAN.

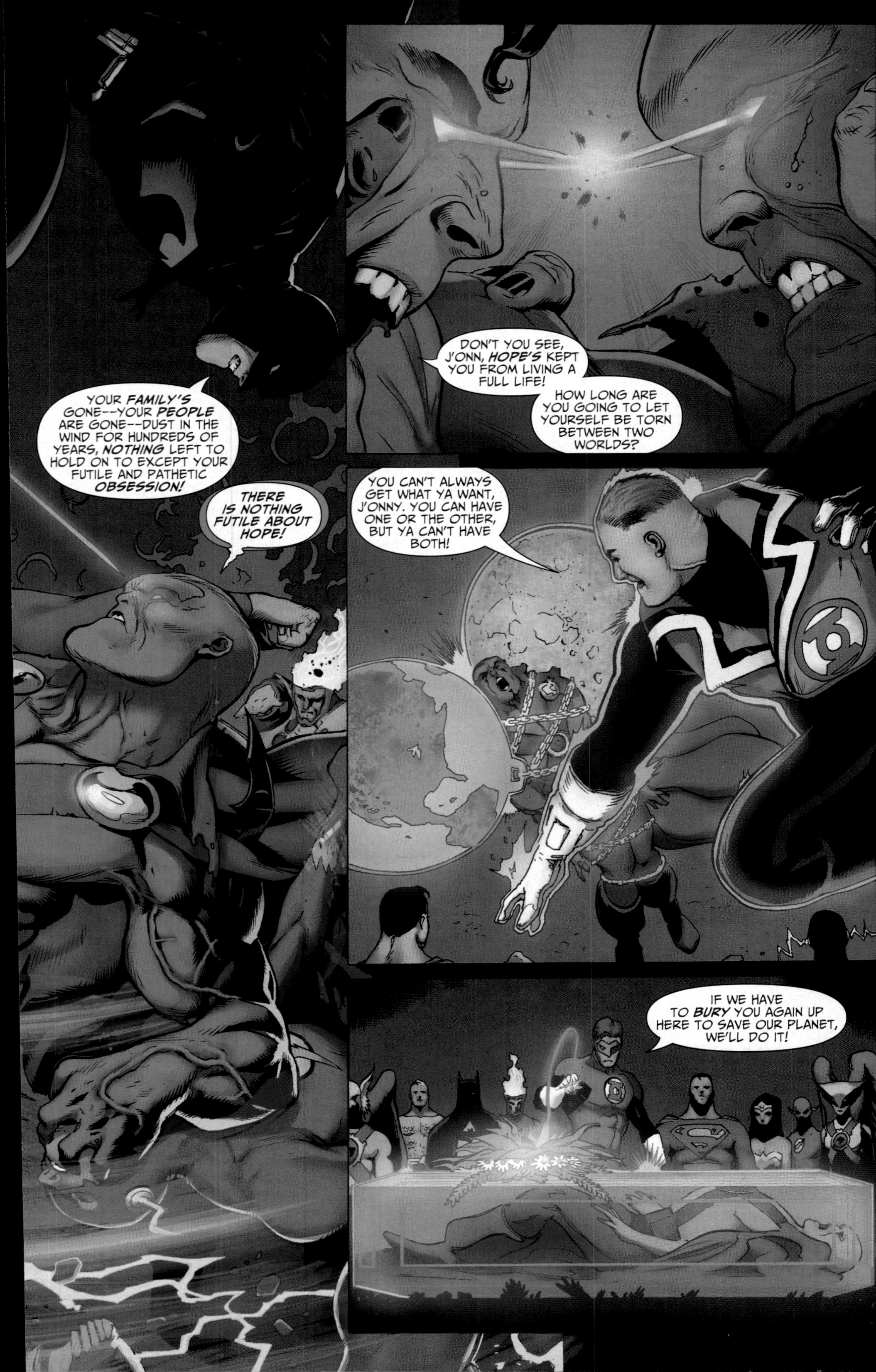
DON'T YOU SEE, J'ONN, HOPE'S KEPT YOU FROM LIVING A FULL LIFE!
HOW LONG ARE YOU GOING TO LET YOURSELF BE TORN BETWEEN TWO WORLDS?
YOUR FAMILY'S GONE--YOUR PEOPLE ARE GONE--DUST IN THE WIND FOR HUNDREDS OF YEARS, NOTHING LEFT TO HOLD ON TO EXCEPT YOUR FUTILE AND PATHETIC OBSESSION!
THERE IS NOTHING FUTILE ABOUT HOPE!
YOU CAN'T ALWAYS GET WHAT YA WANT, J'ONNY. YOU CAN HAVE ONE OR THE OTHER, BUT YA CAN'T HAVE BOTH!
IF WE HAVE TO BURY YOU AGAIN UP HERE TO SAVE OUR PLANET, WE'LL DO IT!

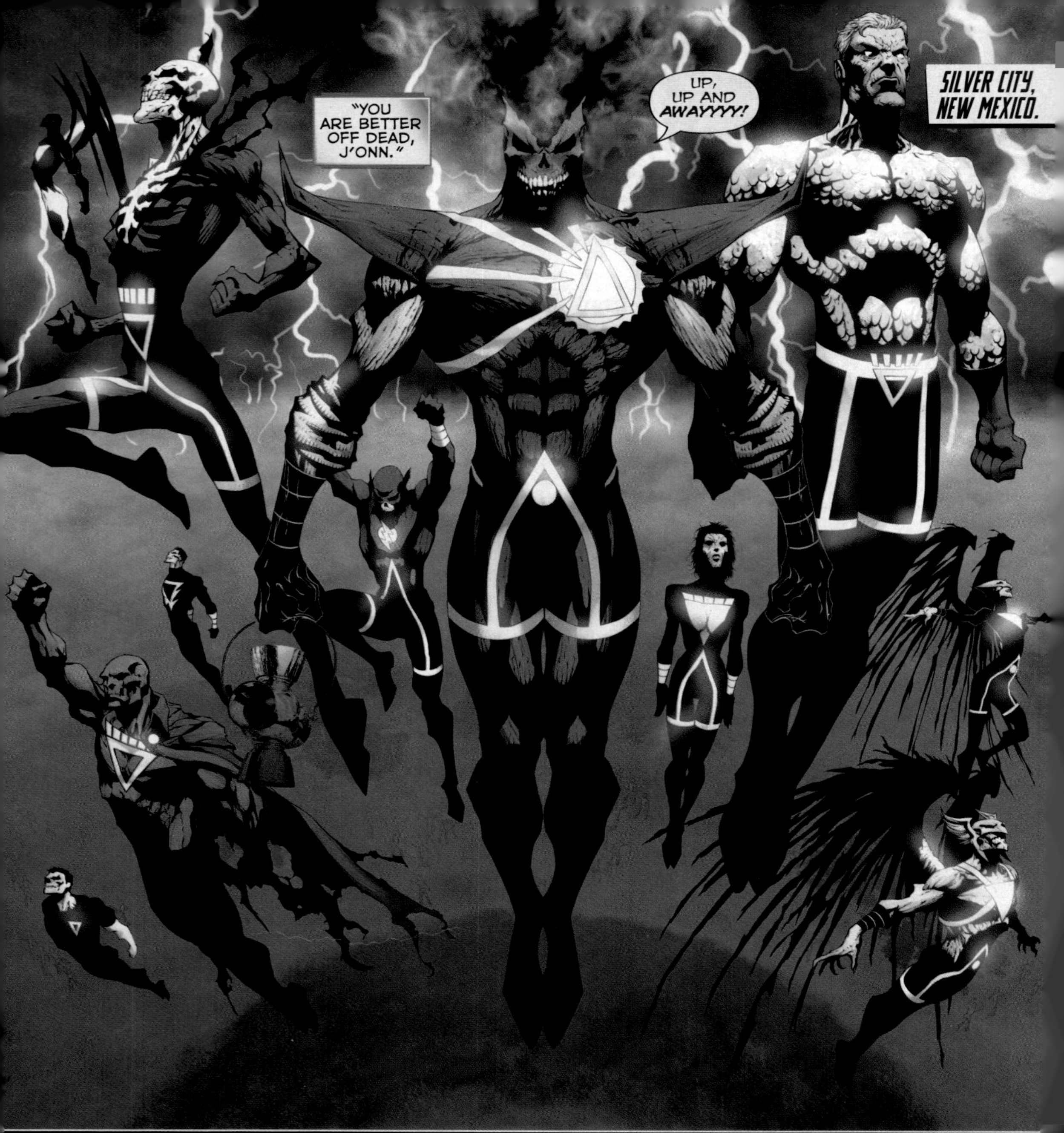
SILVER CITY, NEW MEXICO.
"YOU ARE BETTER OFF DEAD, J'ONN."
UP, UP AND AWAYYYY!

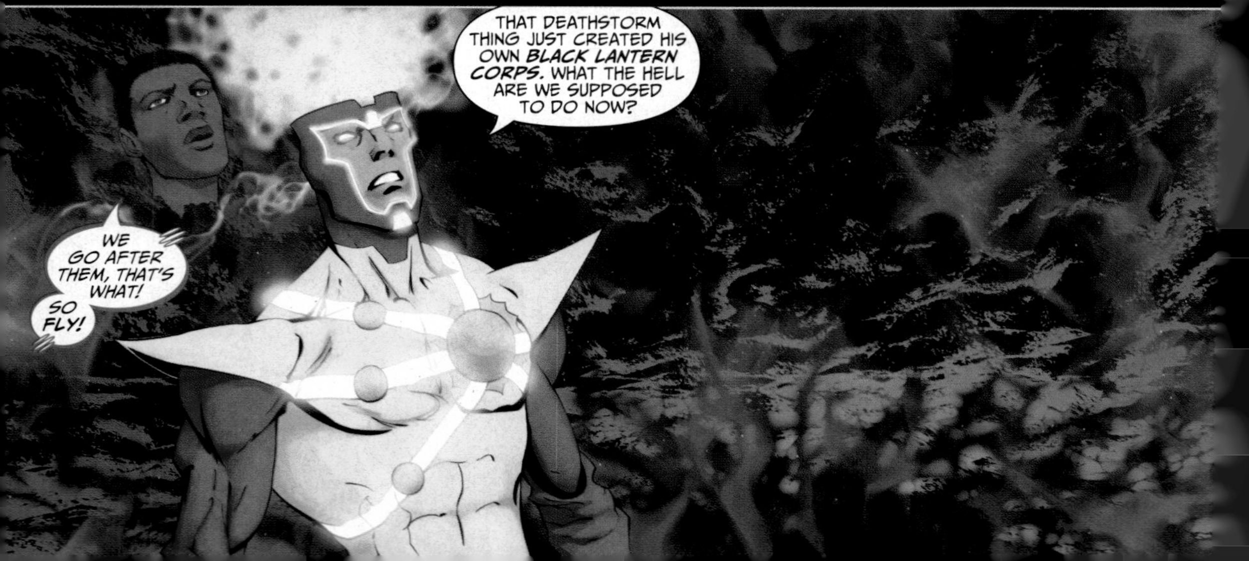
THAT DEATHSTORM THING JUST CREATED HIS OWN BLACK LANTERN CORPS. WHAT THE HELL ARE WE SUPPOSED TO DO NOW?
WE GO AFTER THEM, THAT'S WHAT!
SO FLY!

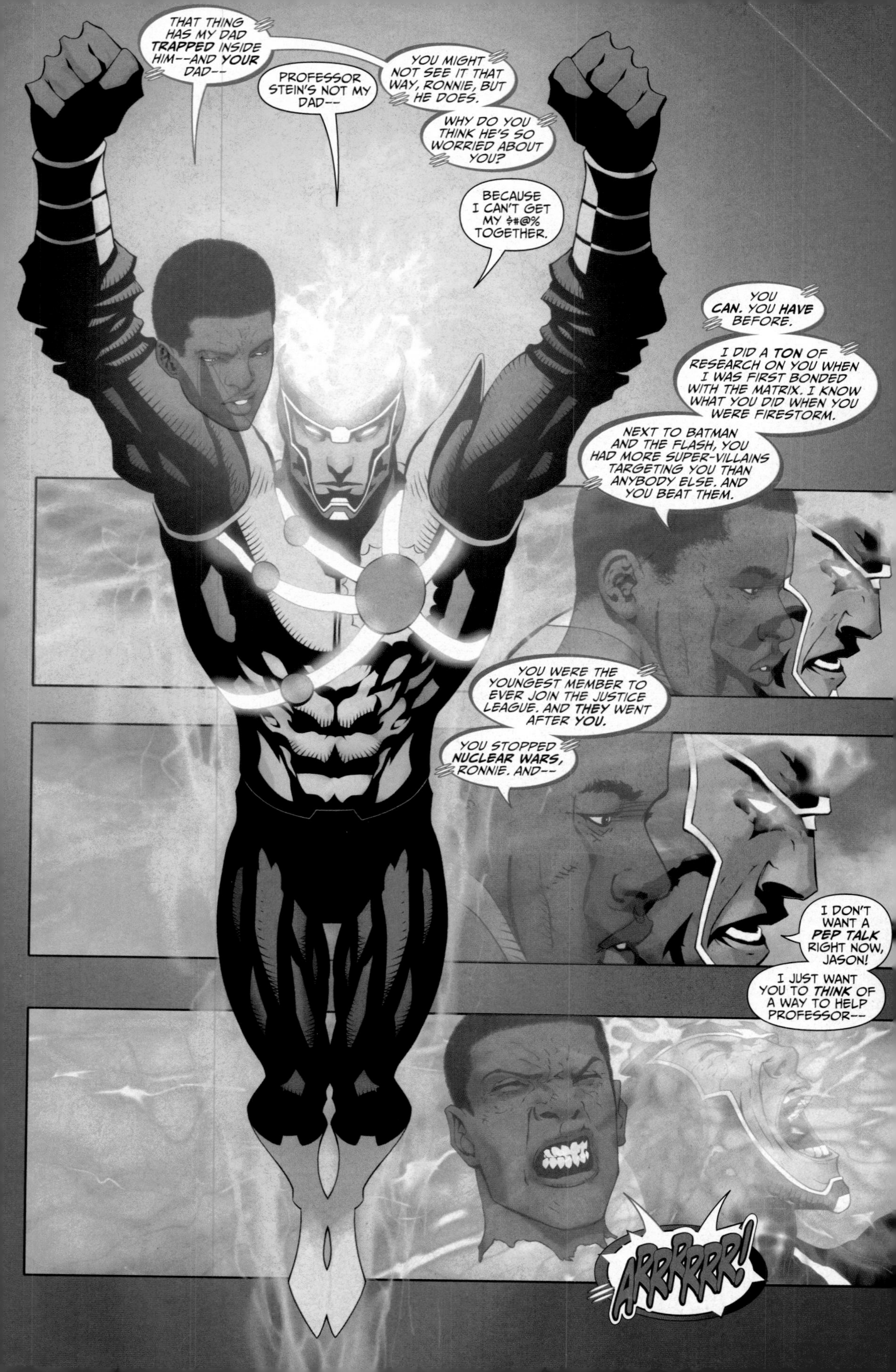
THAT THING HAS MY DAD TRAPPED INSIDE HIM--AND YOUR DAD--
PROFESSOR STEIN'S NOT MY DAD--
YOU MIGHT NOT SEE IT THAT WAY, RONNIE, BUT HE DOES.
WHY DO YOU THINK HE'S SO WORRIED ABOUT YOU?
BECAUSE I CAN'T GET MY $#@% TOGETHER.
YOU CAN. YOU HAVE BEFORE.
I DID A TON OF RESEARCH ON YOU WHEN I WAS FIRST BONDED WITH THE MATRIX. I KNOW WHAT YOU DID WHEN YOU WERE FIRESTORM.
NEXT TO BATMAN AND THE FLASH, YOU HAD MORE SUPER-VILLAINS TARGETING YOU THAN ANYBODY ELSE. AND YOU BEAT THEM.
YOU WERE THE YOUNGEST MEMBER TO EVER JOIN THE JUSTICE LEAGUE. AND THEY WENT AFTER YOU.
YOU STOPPED NUCLEAR WARS, RONNIE. AND--
I DON'T WANT A PEP TALK RIGHT NOW, JASON!
I JUST WANT YOU TO THINK OF A WAY TO HELP PROFESSOR--
ARRRRRR!

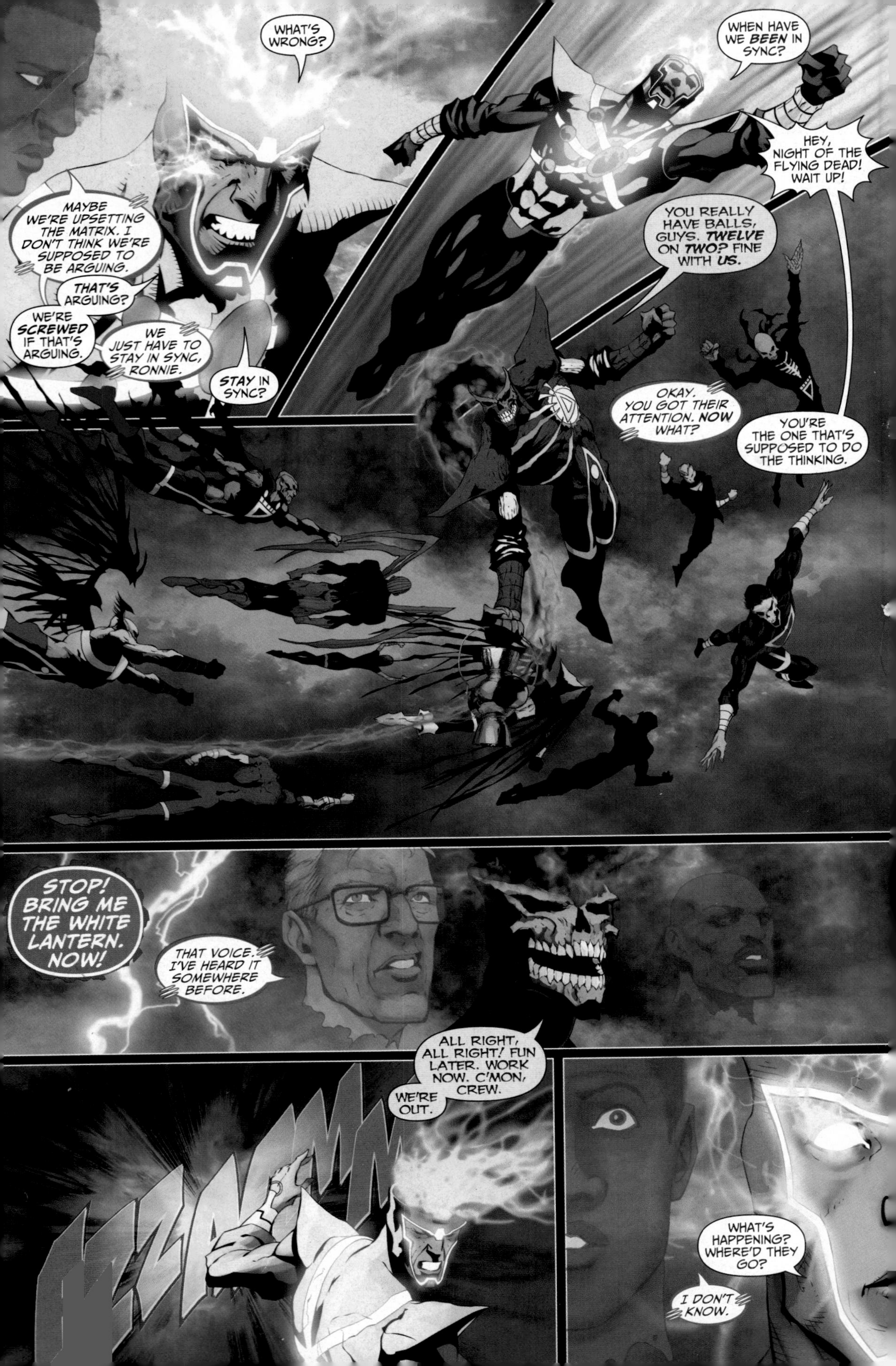
WHAT'S WRONG?
MAYBE WE'RE UPSETTING THE MATRIX. I DON'T THINK WE'RE SUPPOSED TO BE ARGUING.
THAT'S ARGUING?
WE'RE SCREWED IF THAT'S ARGUING.
WE JUST HAVE TO STAY IN SYNC, RONNIE.
STAY IN SYNC?
WHEN HAVE WE BEEN IN SYNC?
HEY, NIGHT OF THE FLYING DEAD! WAIT UP!
YOU REALLY HAVE BALLS, GUYS. TWELVE ON TWO? FINE WITH US.
OKAY. YOU GOT THEIR ATTENTION. NOW WHAT?
YOU'RE THE ONE THAT'S SUPPOSED TO DO THE THINKING.
STOP! BRING ME THE WHITE LANTERN. NOW!
THAT VOICE. I'VE HEARD IT SOMEWHERE BEFORE.
ALL RIGHT, ALL RIGHT! FUN LATER. WORK NOW. C'MON, CREW.
WE'RE OUT.
WHAT'S HAPPENING? WHERE'D THEY GO?
I DON'T KNOW.

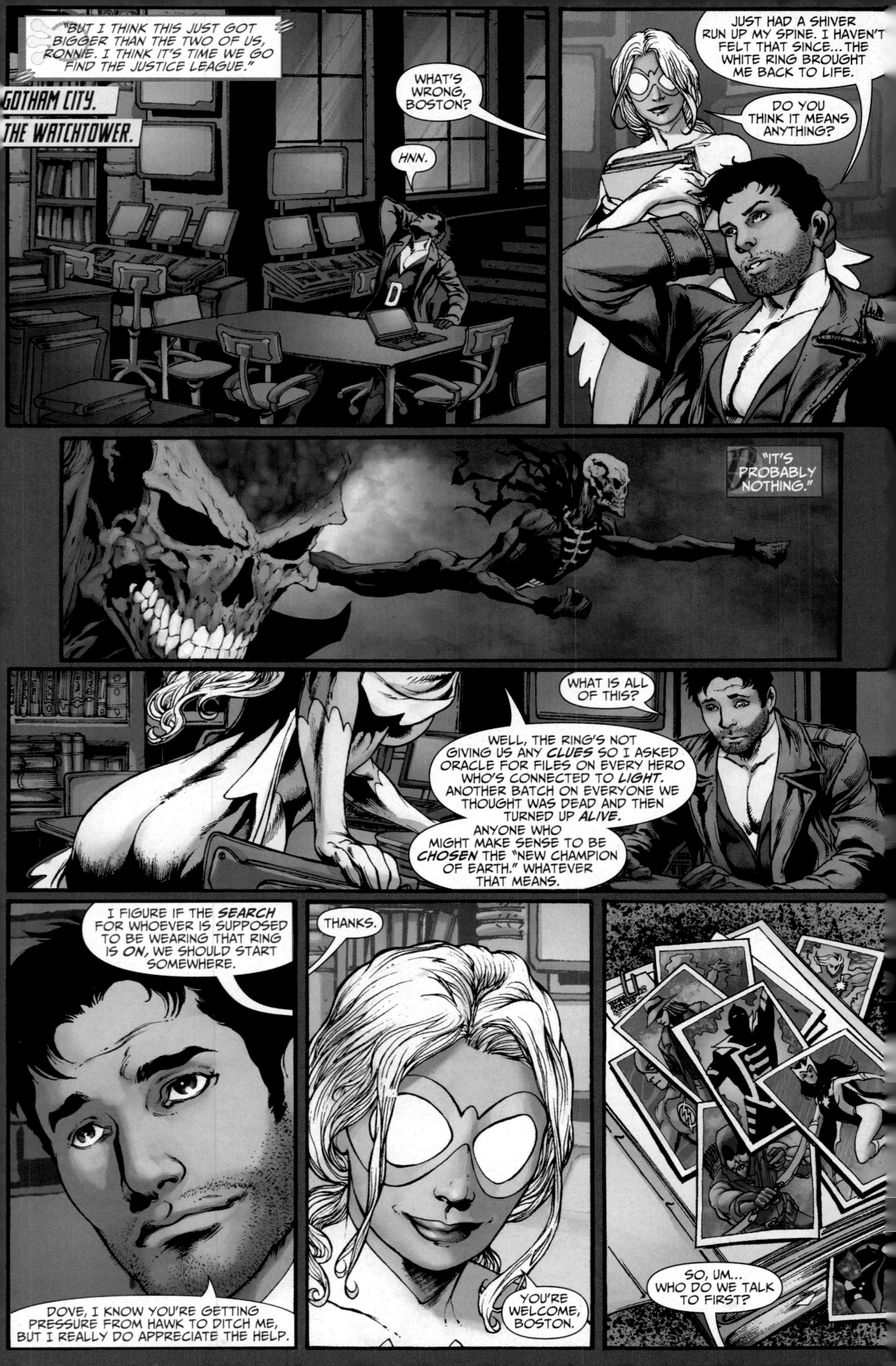
"BUT I THINK THIS JUST GOT BIGGER THAN THE TWO OF US, RONNIE. I THINK IT'S TIME WE GO FIND THE JUSTICE LEAGUE."
GOTHAM CITY.
THE WATCHTOWER.
WHAT'S WRONG, BOSTON?
HNN.
JUST HAD A SHIVER RUN UP MY SPINE. I HAVEN'T FELT THAT SINCE... THE WHITE RING BROUGHT ME BACK TO LIFE.
DO YOU THINK IT MEANS ANYTHING?
"IT'S PROBABLY NOTHING."
WHAT IS ALL OF THIS?
WELL, THE RING'S NOT GIVING US ANY CLUES SO I ASKED ORACLE FOR FILES ON EVERY HERO WHO'S CONNECTED TO LIGHT. ANOTHER BATCH ON EVERYONE WE THOUGHT WAS DEAD AND THEN TURNED UP ALIVE.
ANYONE WHO MIGHT MAKE SENSE TO BE CHOSEN THE "NEW CHAMPION OF EARTH." WHATEVER THAT MEANS.
I FIGURE IF THE SEARCH FOR WHOEVER IS SUPPOSED TO BE WEARING THAT RING IS ON, WE SHOULD START SOMEWHERE.
DOVE, I KNOW YOU'RE GETTING PRESSURE FROM HAWK TO DITCH ME, BUT I REALLY DO APPRECIATE THE HELP.
THANKS.
YOU'RE WELCOME, BOSTON.
SO, UM... WHO DO WE TALK TO FIRST?

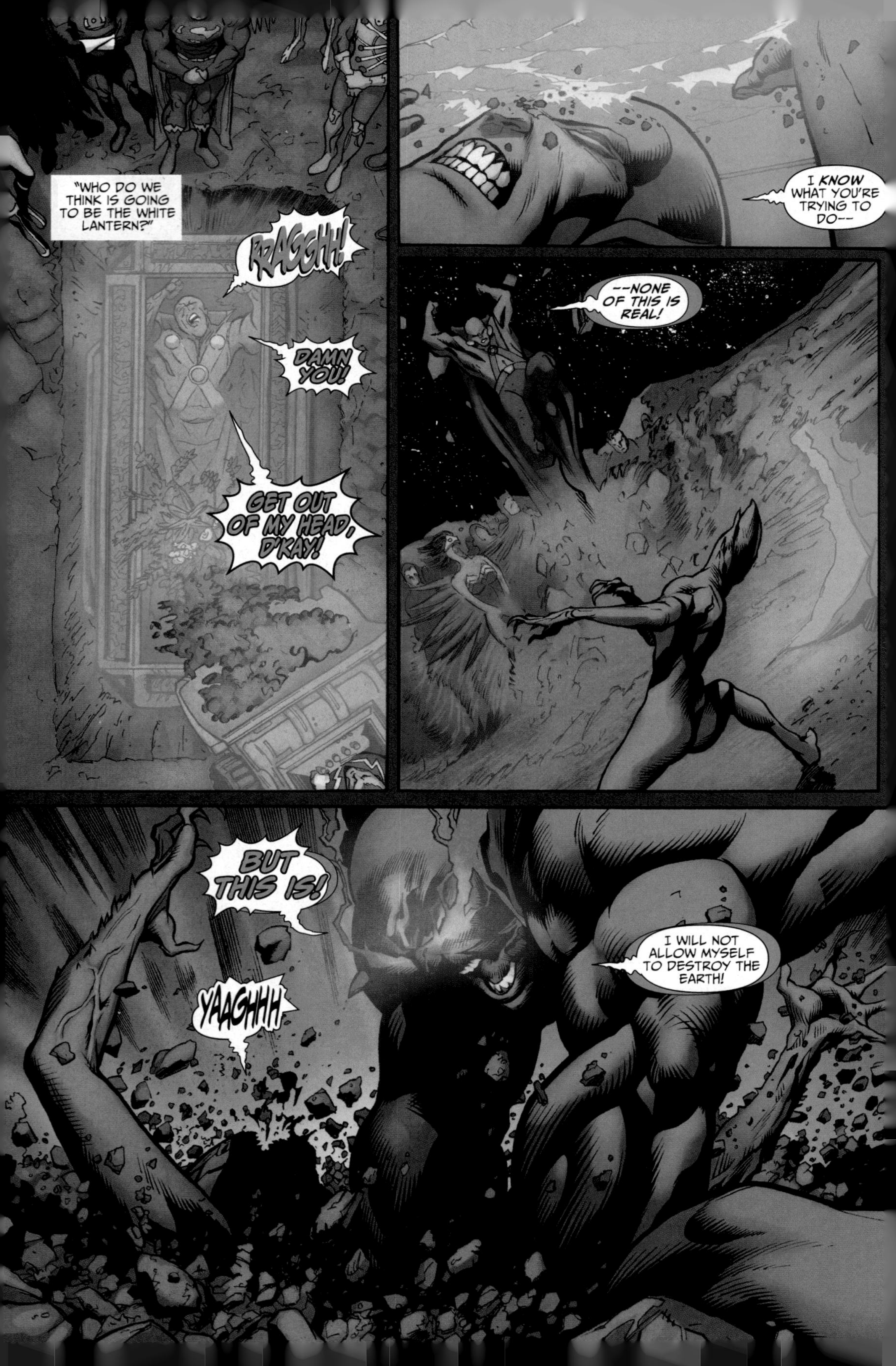
"WHO DO WE THINK IS GOING TO BE THE WHITE LANTERN?"
RRAGGHH!
DAMN YOU!
GET OUT OF MY HEAD, D'KAY!
I KNOW WHAT YOU'RE TRYING TO DO--
--NONE OF THIS IS REAL!
BUT THIS IS!
YAAGHHH
I WILL NOT ALLOW MYSELF TO DESTROY THE EARTH!

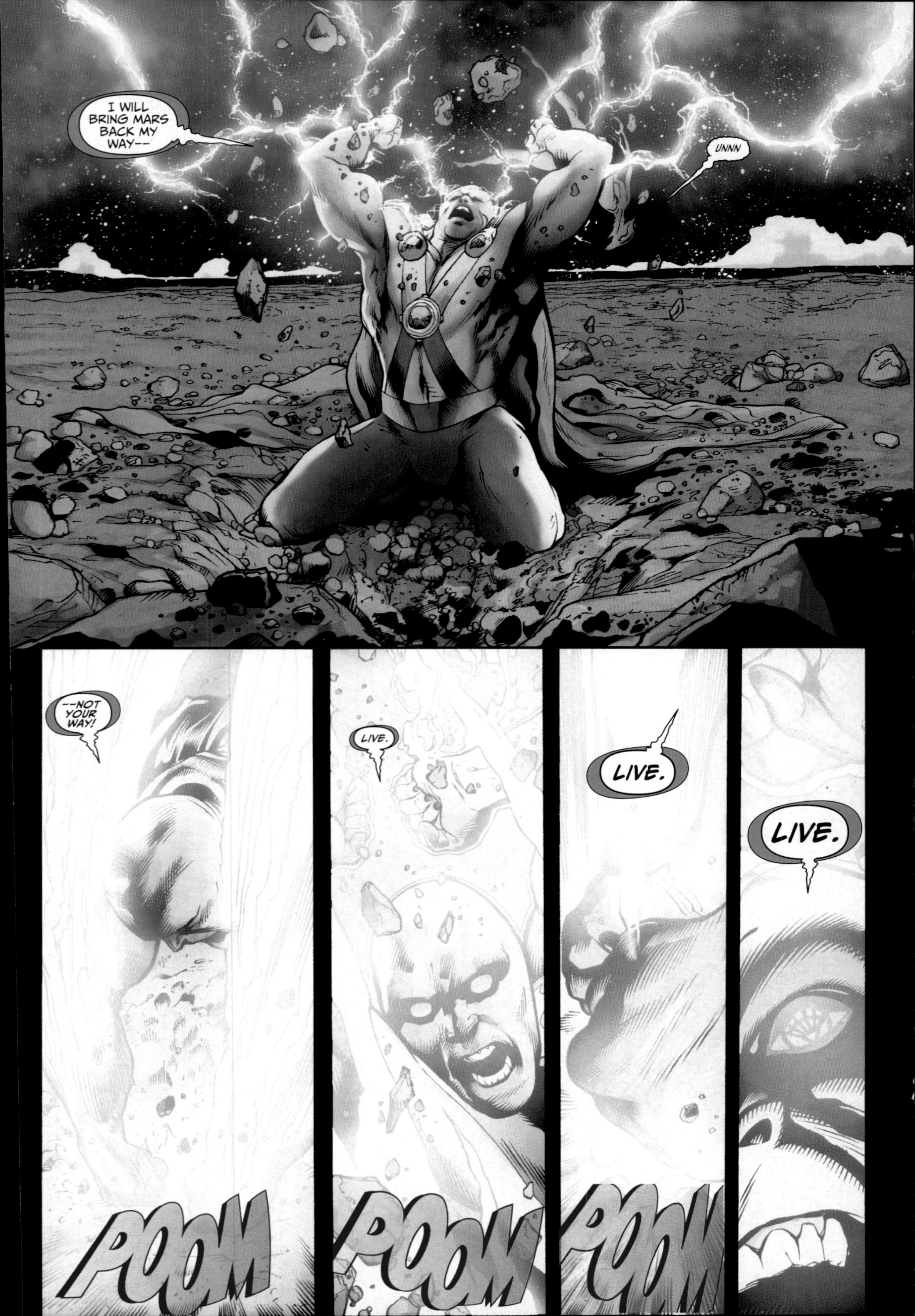
I WILL BRING MARS BACK MY WAY--
UNNN
--NOT YOUR WAY!
POOM
LIVE.
POOM
LIVE.
POOM
LIVE.

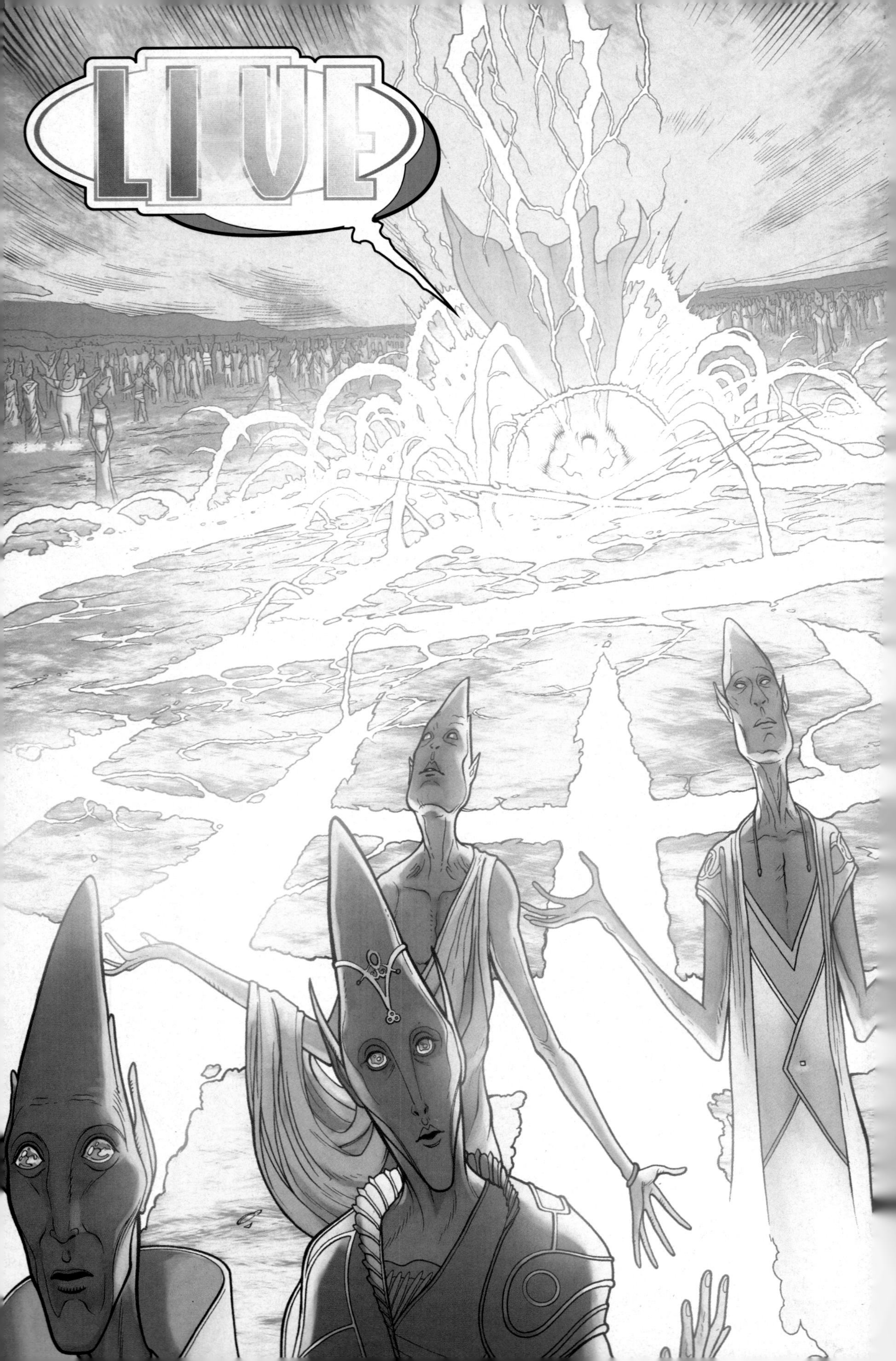
LIVE

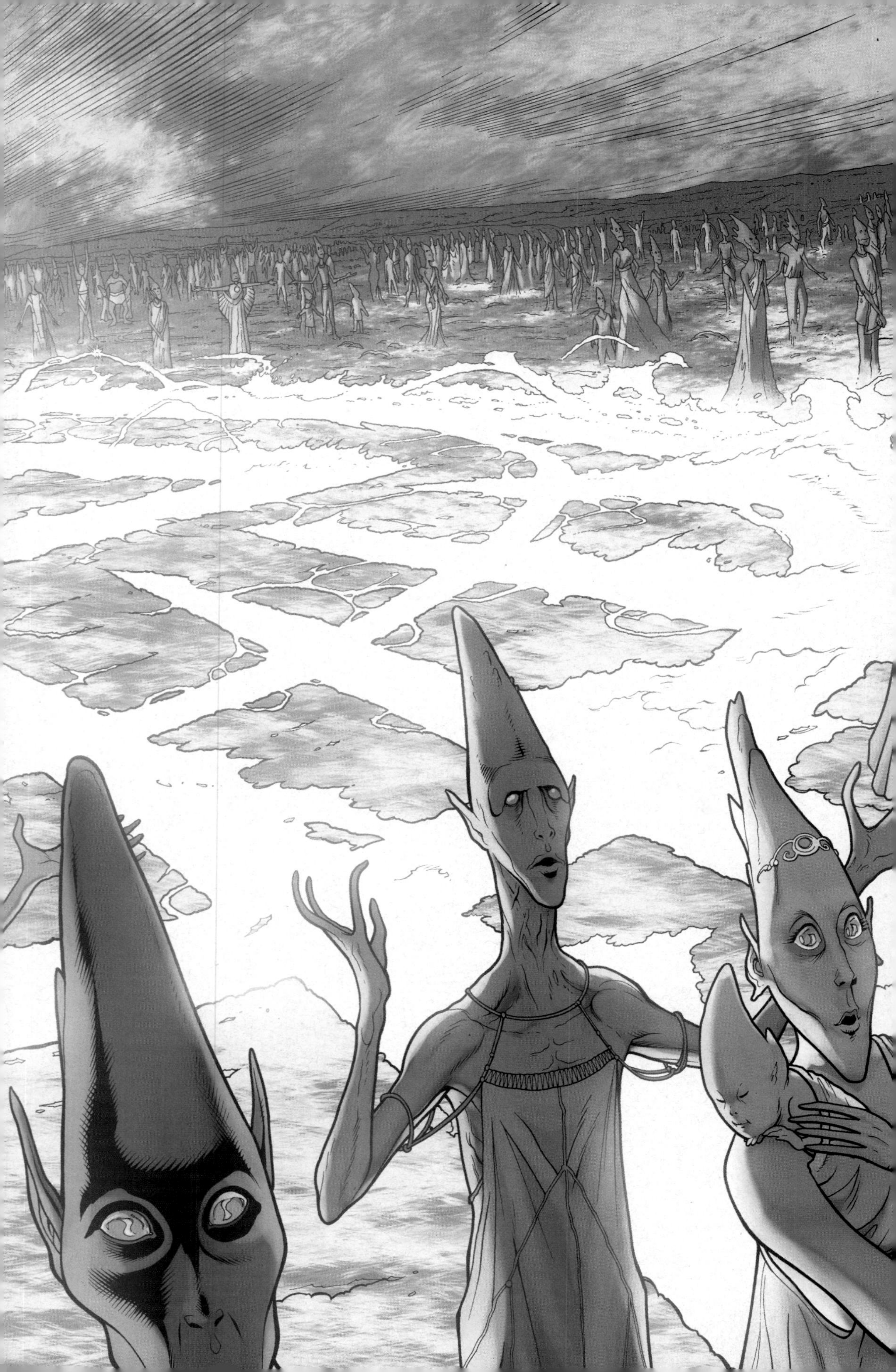

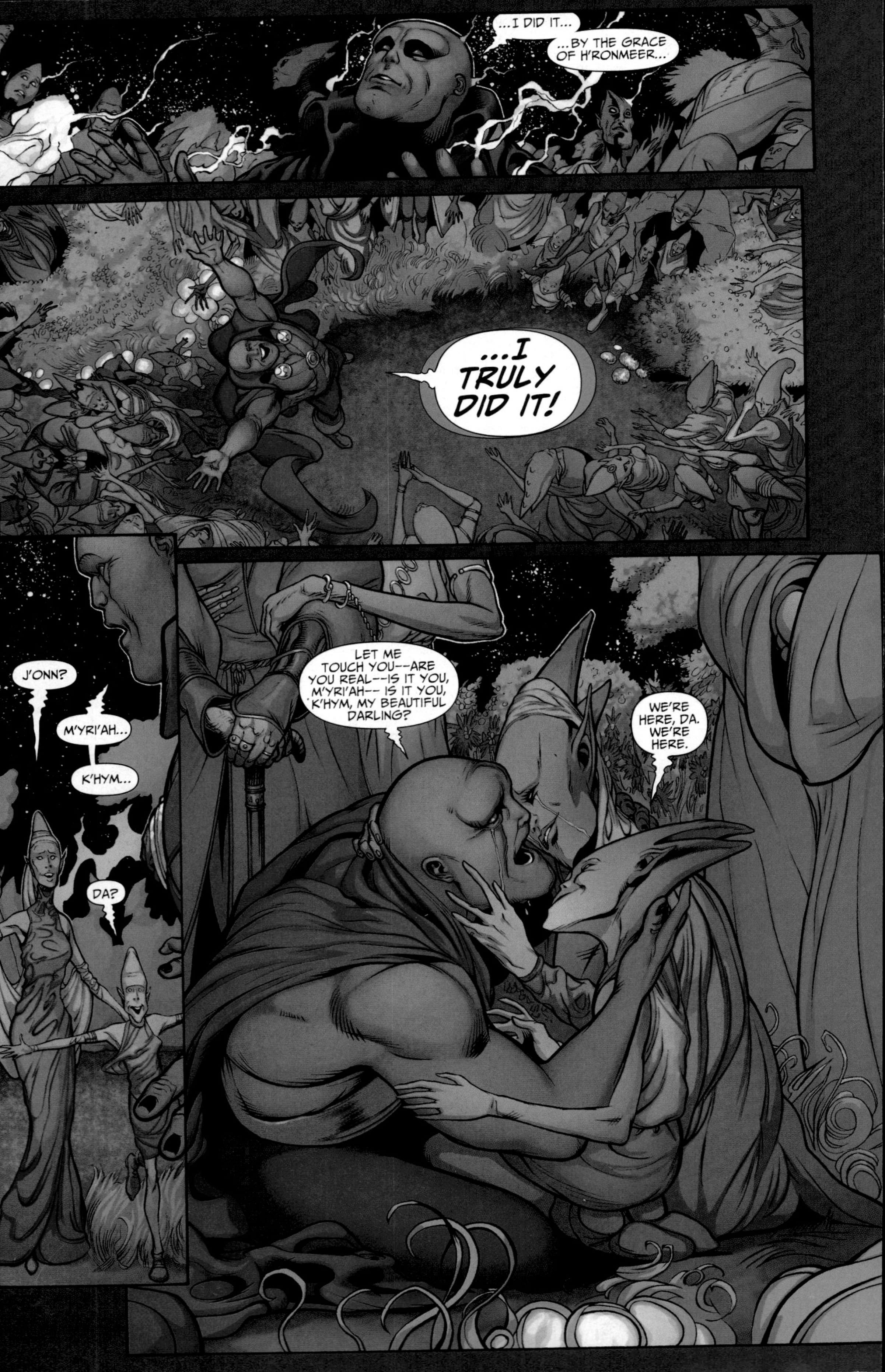
...I DID IT...
...BY THE GRACE OF H'RONMEER...
...I TRULY DID IT!
J'ONN?
M'YRI'AH...
K'HYM...
DA?
LET ME TOUCH YOU--ARE YOU REAL--IS IT YOU, M'YRI'AH-- IS IT YOU, K'HYM, MY BEAUTIFUL DARLING?
WE'RE HERE, DA. WE'RE HERE.

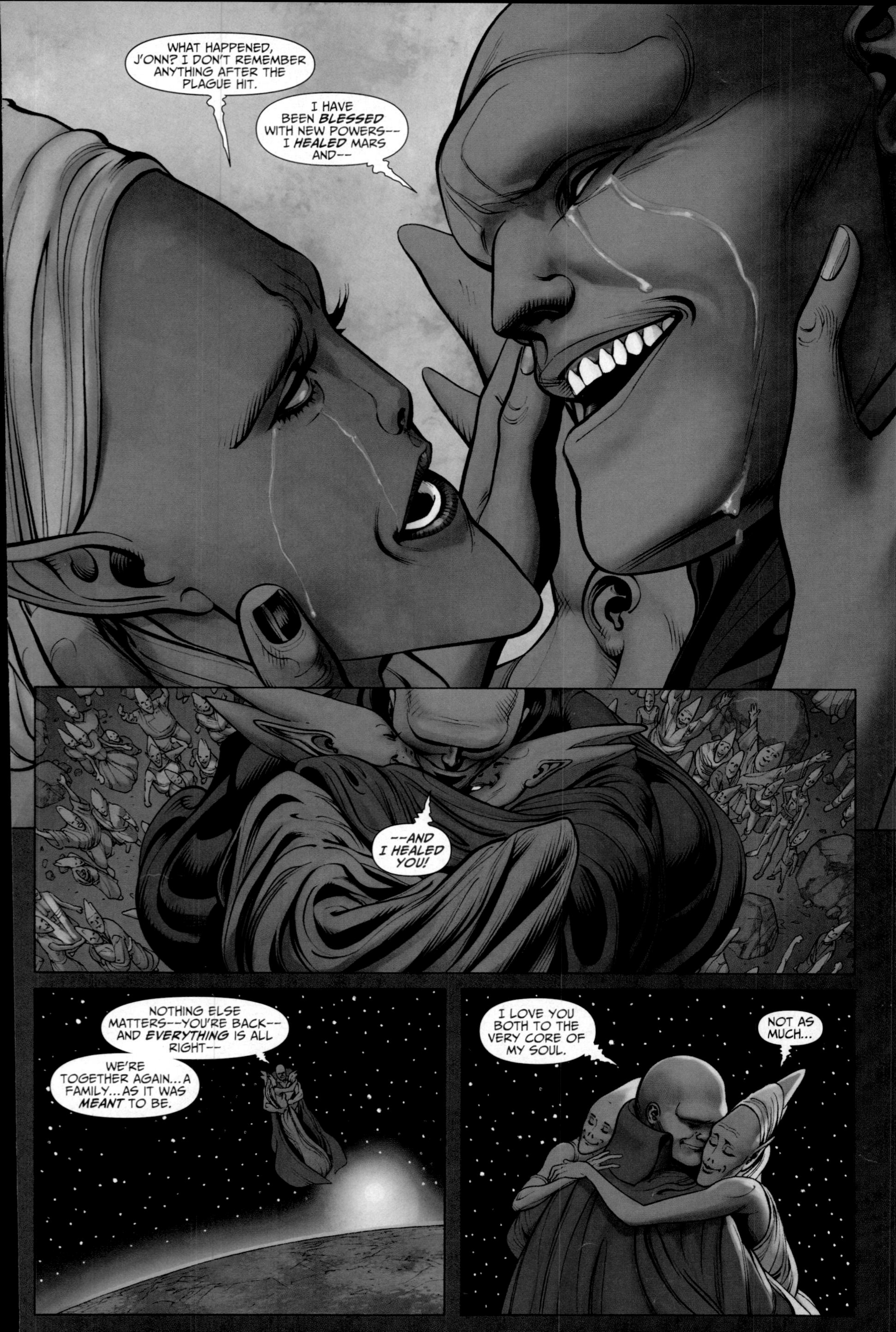
WHAT HAPPENED, J'ONN? I DON'T REMEMBER ANYTHING AFTER THE PLAGUE HIT.
I HAVE BEEN BLESSED WITH NEW POWERS-- I HEALED MARS AND--
--AND I HEALED YOU!
NOTHING ELSE MATTERS--YOU'RE BACK-- AND EVERYTHING IS ALL RIGHT--
WE'RE TOGETHER AGAIN...A FAMILY...AS IT WAS MEANT TO BE.
I LOVE YOU BOTH TO THE VERY CORE OF MY SOUL.
NOT AS MUCH...

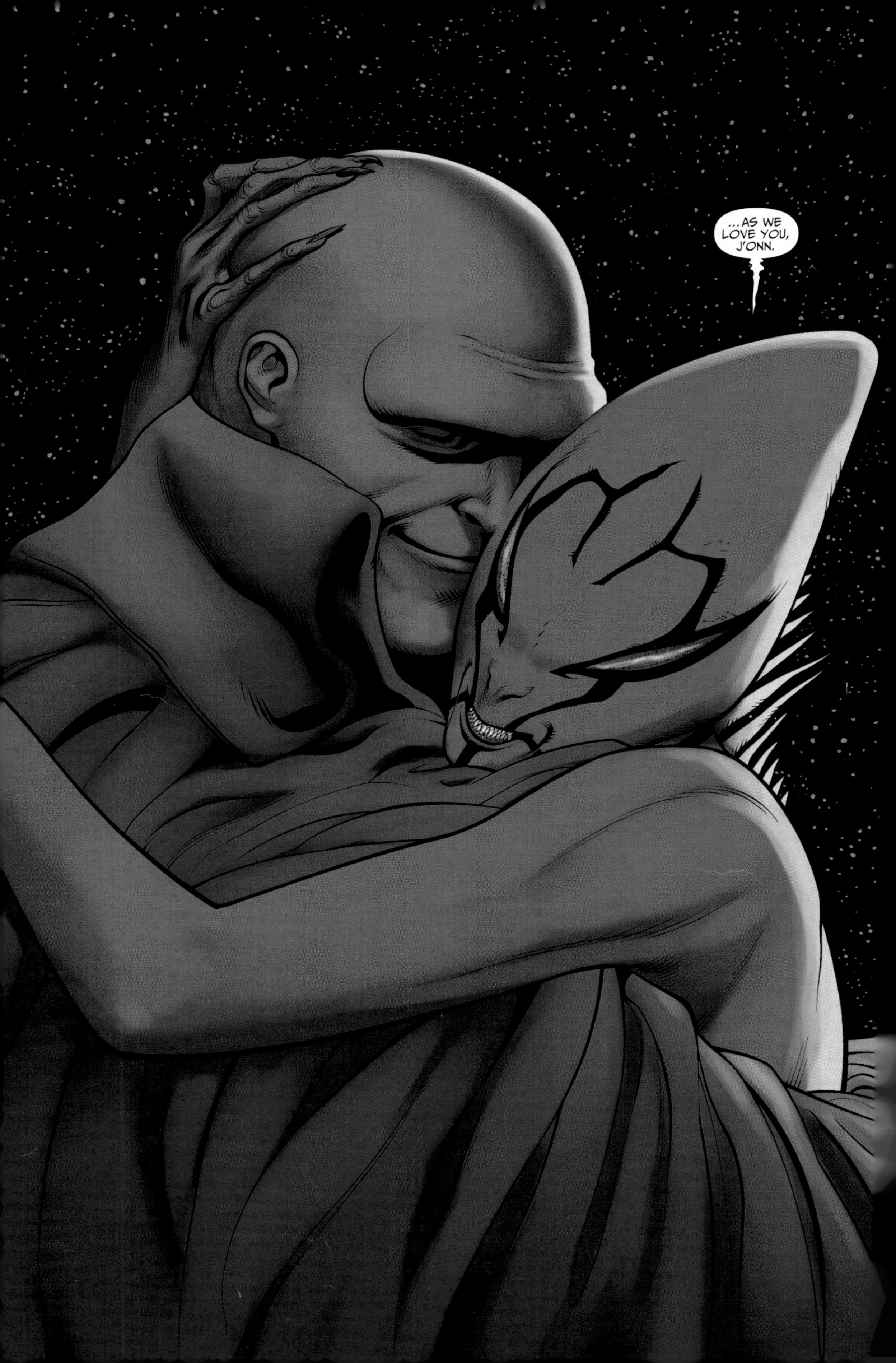
...AS WE LOVE YOU, J'ONN.

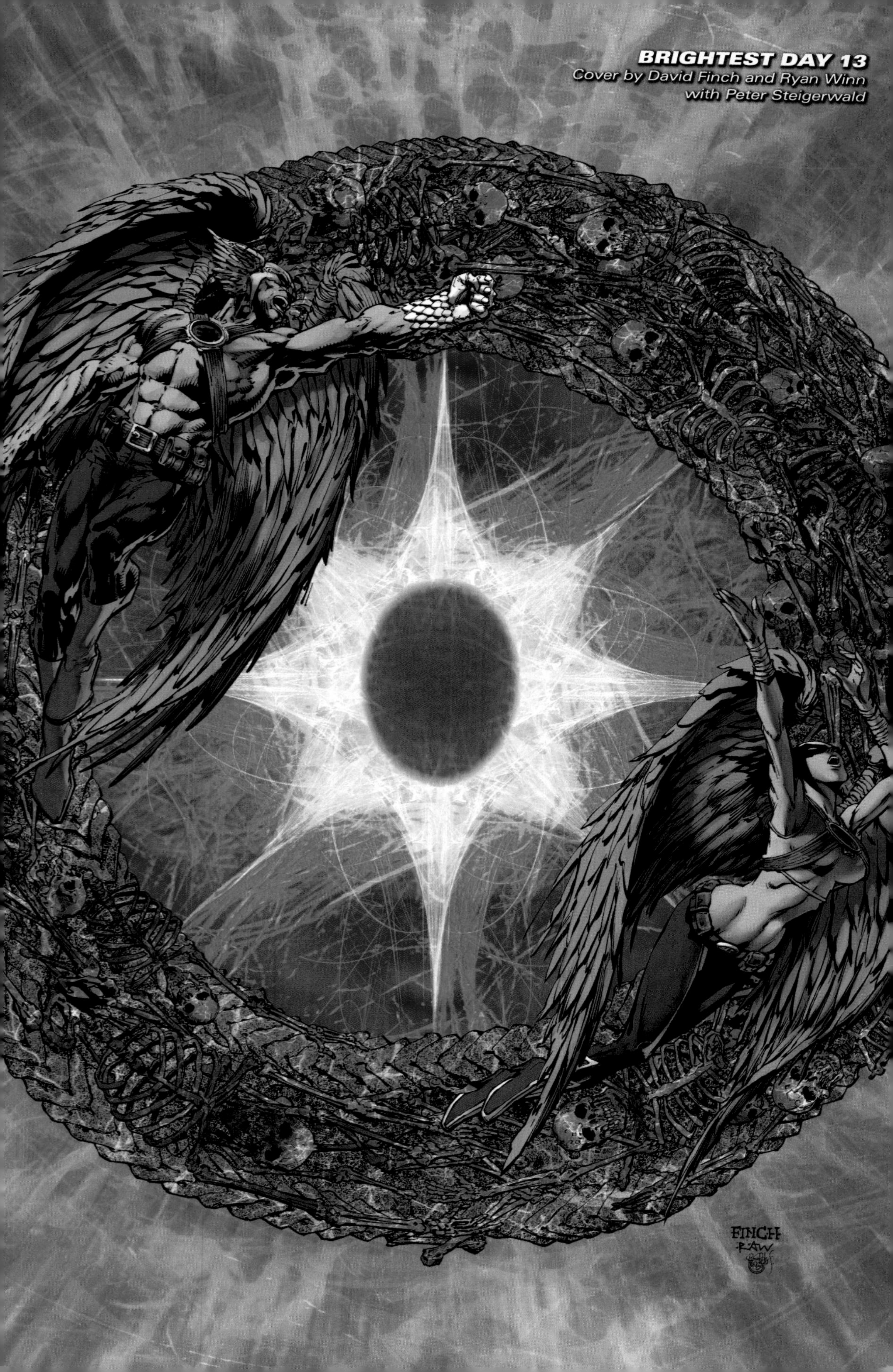
FINCH
RAW

**BRIGHTEST DAY 13**
Cover by David Finch and Ryan Winn
with Peter Steigerwald

# UNDER A
# BLOOD RED SKY

AWKWORLD.
IGH ABOVE THE CLOUDS
F THE NTH CITY.
WE HIT THEM HARD.
WE HIT THEM FAST.
AND WE DON'T TAKE PRISONERS.

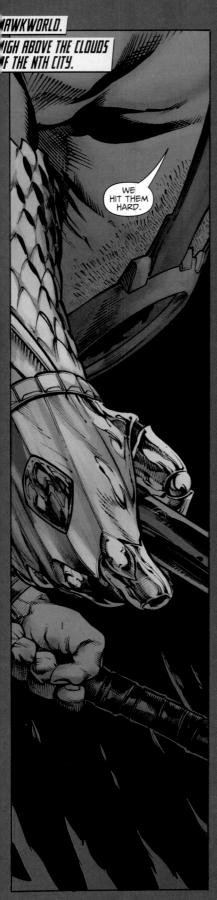

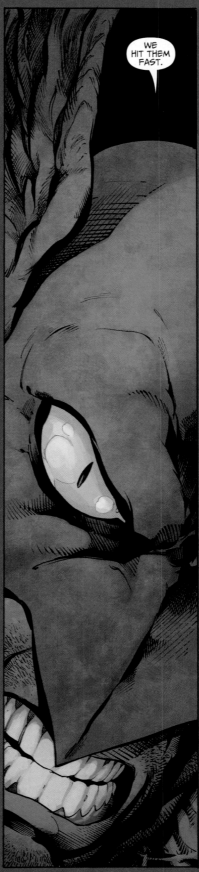

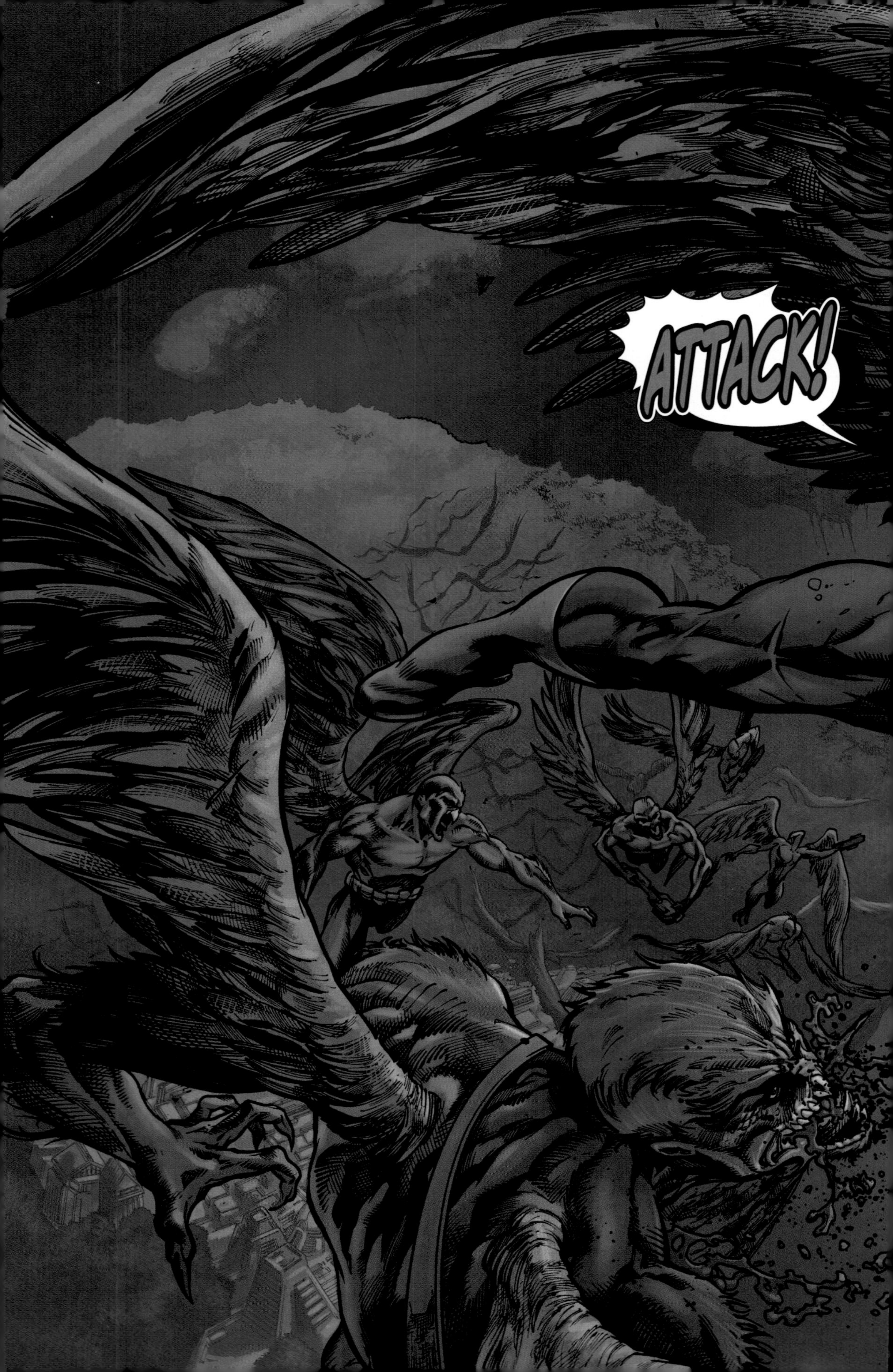
ATTACK!

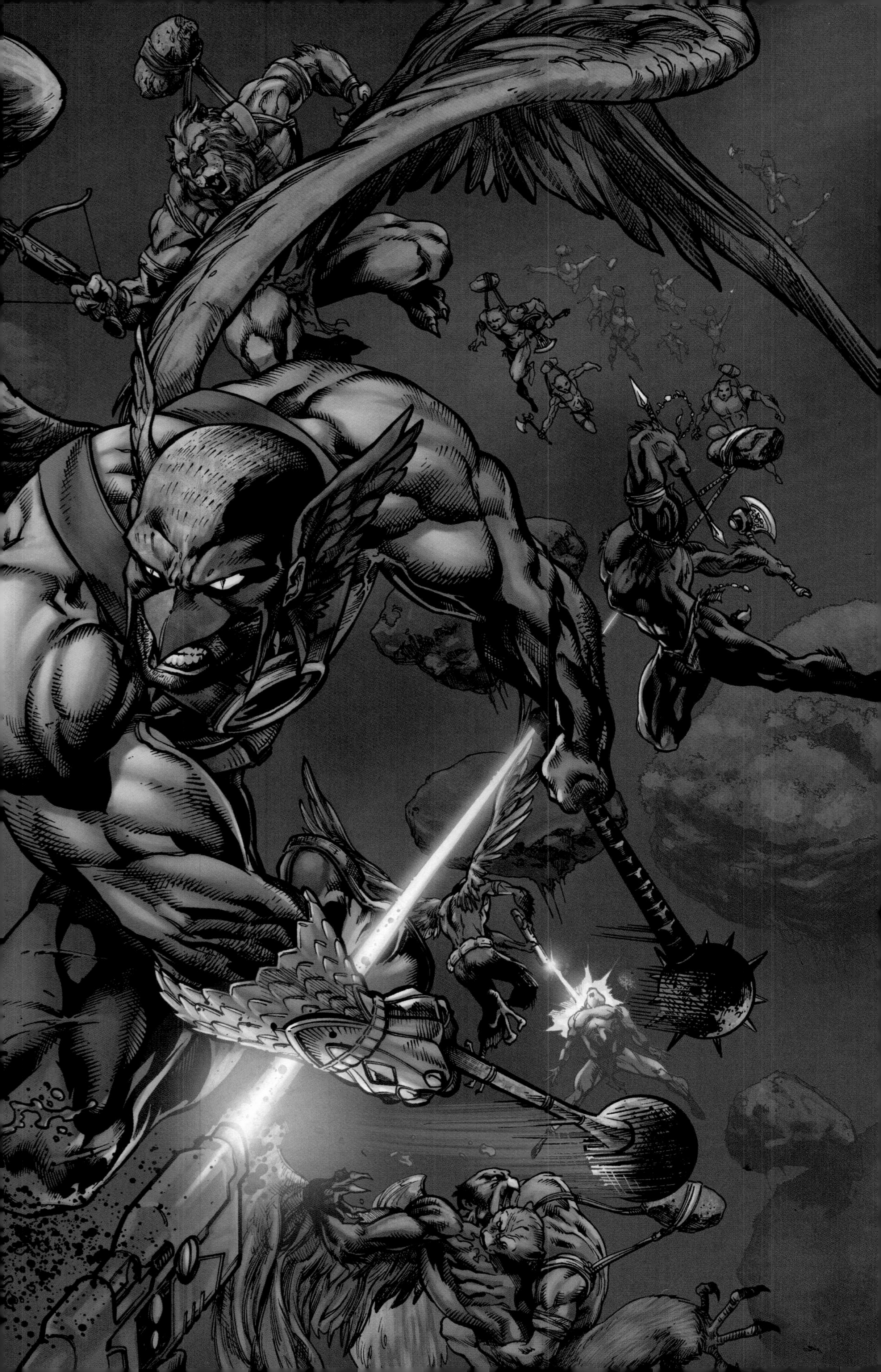

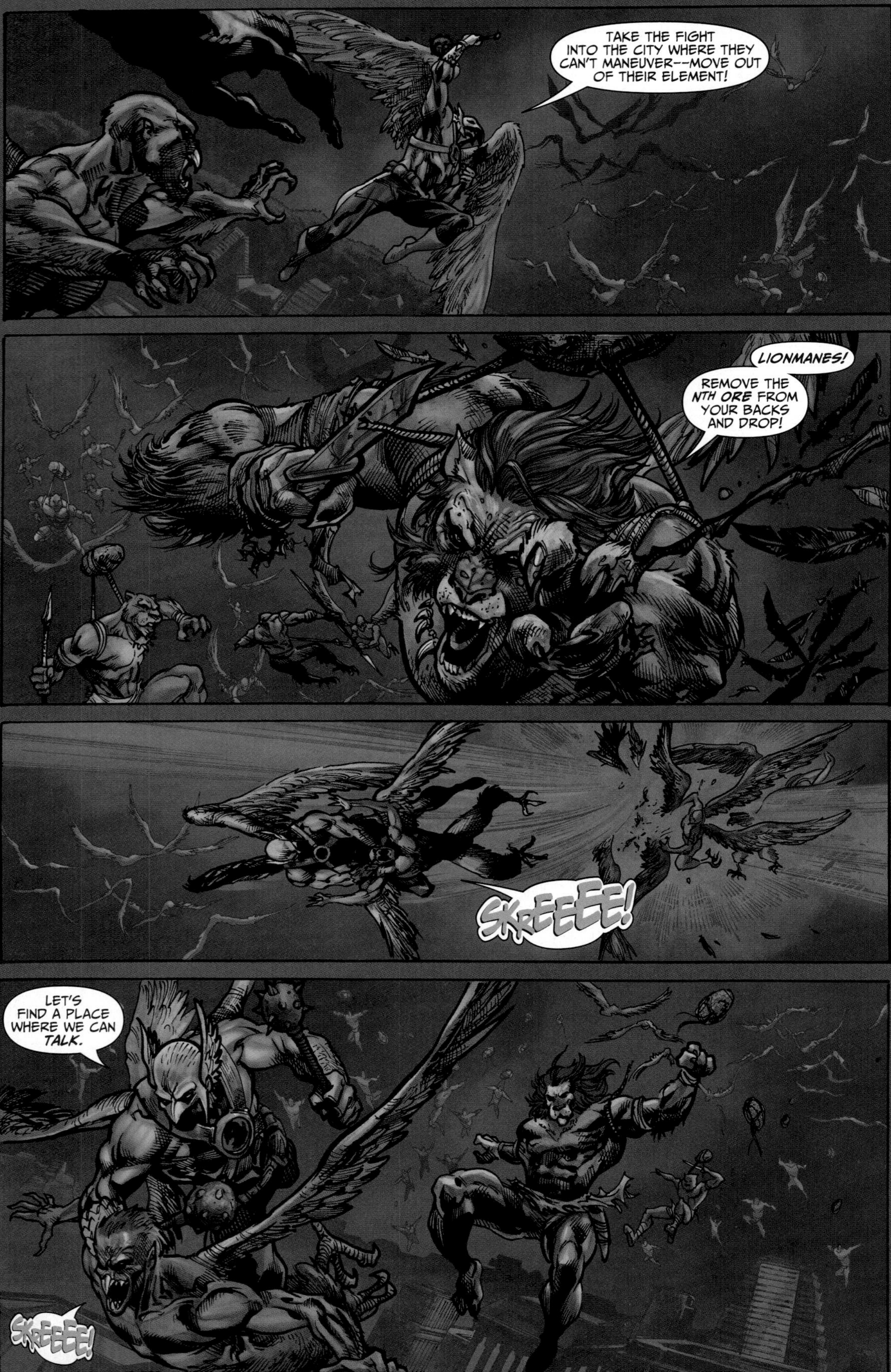
TAKE THE FIGHT INTO THE CITY WHERE THEY CAN'T MANEUVER--MOVE OUT OF THEIR ELEMENT!
LIONMANES!
REMOVE THE NTH ORE FROM YOUR BACKS AND DROP!
SKREEEEE!
LET'S FIND A PLACE WHERE WE CAN TALK.
SKREEEE!

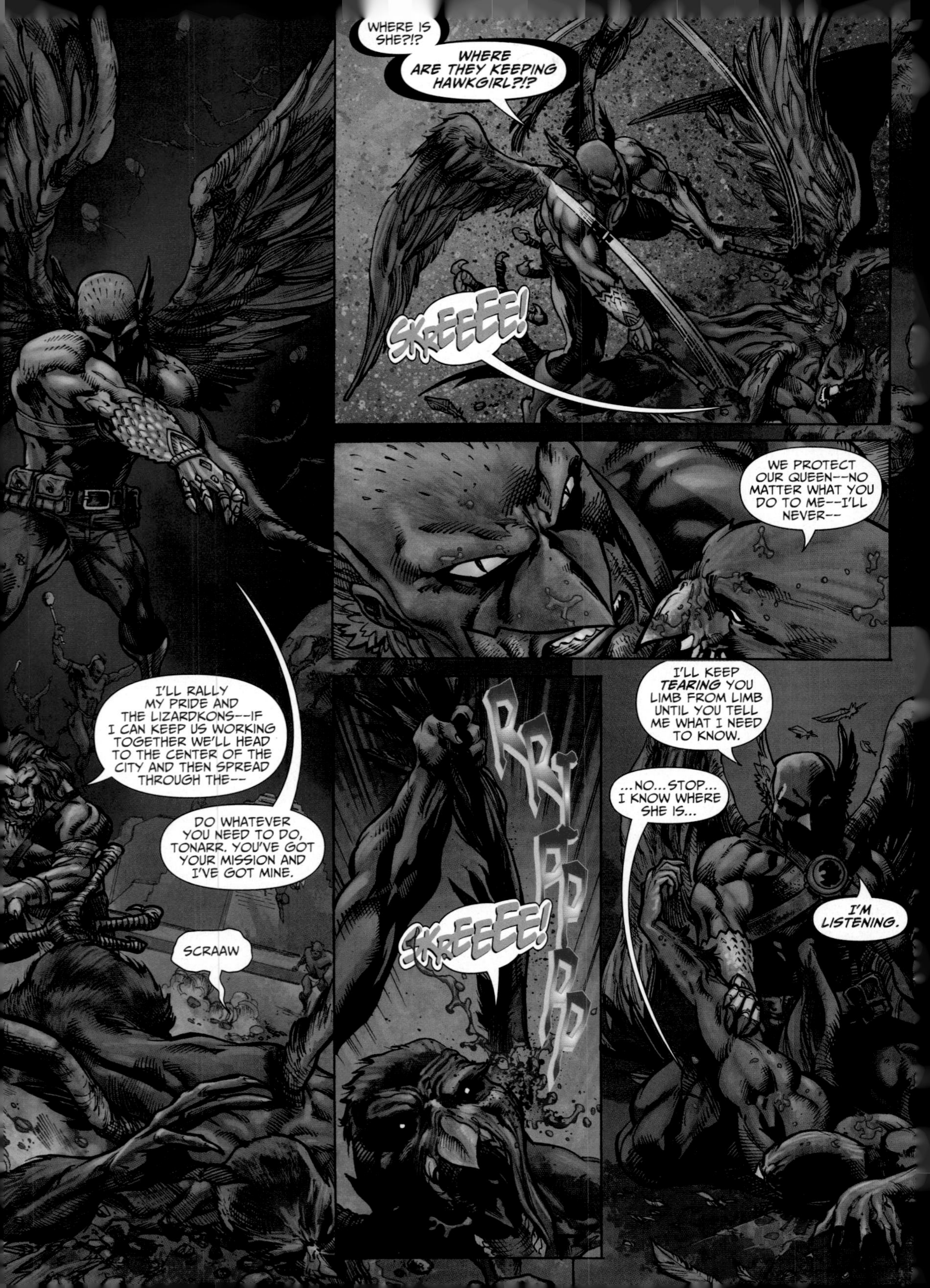
WHERE IS SHE?!?
WHERE ARE THEY KEEPING HAWKGIRL?!?
SKREEEEE!
WE PROTECT OUR QUEEN--NO MATTER WHAT YOU DO TO ME--I'LL NEVER--
I'LL RALLY MY PRIDE AND THE LIZARDKONS--IF I CAN KEEP US WORKING TOGETHER WE'LL HEAD TO THE CENTER OF THE CITY AND THEN SPREAD THROUGH THE--
DO WHATEVER YOU NEED TO DO, TONARR. YOU'VE GOT YOUR MISSION AND I'VE GOT MINE.
SCRAAW
SKREEEEE!
I'LL KEEP TEARING YOU LIMB FROM LIMB UNTIL YOU TELL ME WHAT I NEED TO KNOW.
...NO...STOP... I KNOW WHERE SHE IS...
I'M LISTENING.

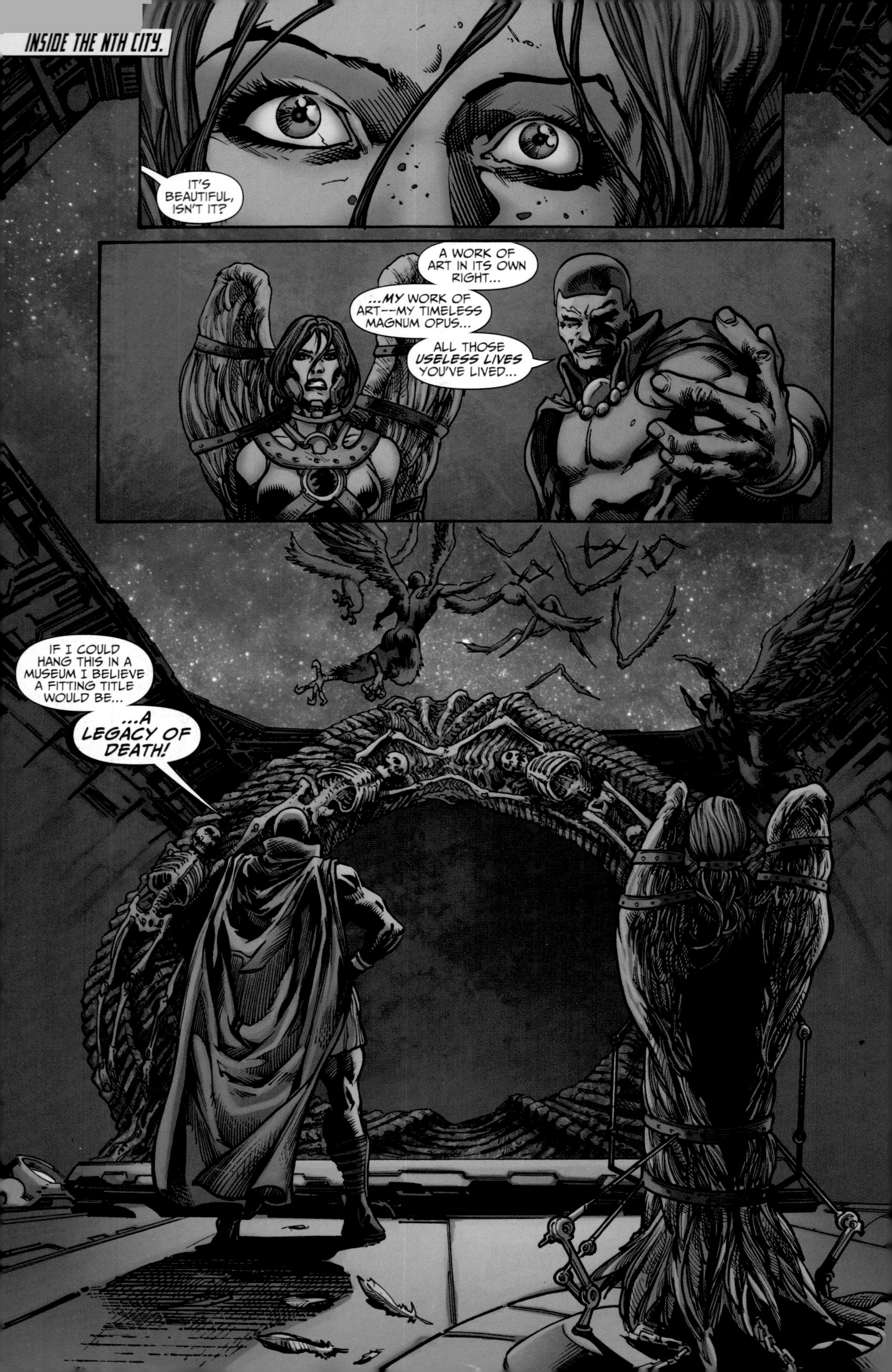
INSIDE THE NTH CITY.
IT'S BEAUTIFUL, ISN'T IT?
A WORK OF ART IN ITS OWN RIGHT...
...MY WORK OF ART--MY TIMELESS MAGNUM OPUS...
ALL THOSE USELESS LIVES YOU'VE LIVED...
IF I COULD HANG THIS IN A MUSEUM I BELIEVE A FITTING TITLE WOULD BE...
...A LEGACY OF DEATH!

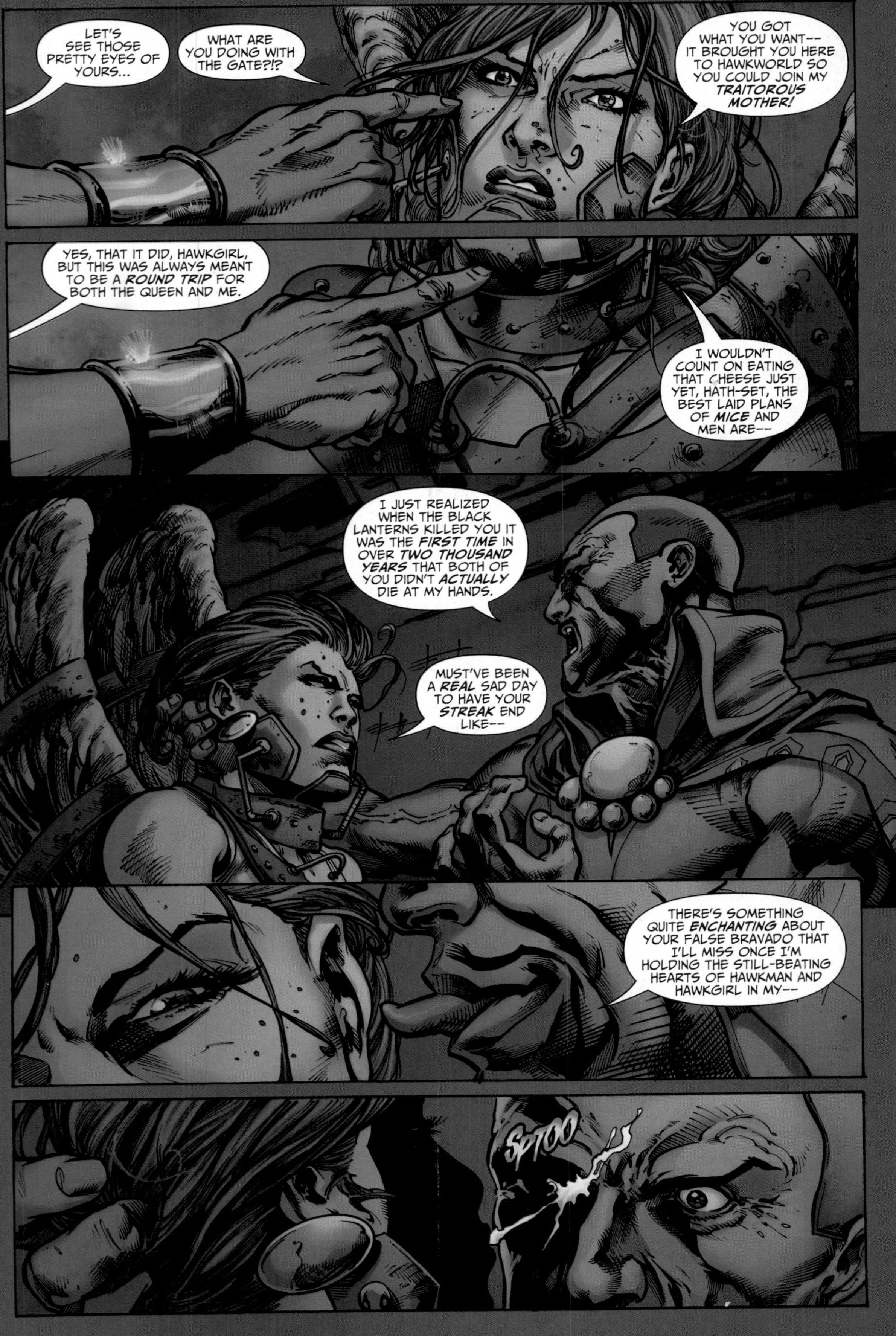
LET'S SEE THOSE PRETTY EYES OF YOURS...
WHAT ARE YOU DOING WITH THE GATE?!?
YOU GOT WHAT YOU WANT-- IT BROUGHT YOU HERE TO HAWKWORLD SO YOU COULD JOIN MY TRAITOROUS MOTHER!
YES, THAT IT DID, HAWKGIRL, BUT THIS WAS ALWAYS MEANT TO BE A ROUND TRIP FOR BOTH THE QUEEN AND ME.
I WOULDN'T COUNT ON EATING THAT CHEESE JUST YET, HATH-SET, THE BEST LAID PLANS OF MICE AND MEN ARE--
I JUST REALIZED WHEN THE BLACK LANTERNS KILLED YOU IT WAS THE FIRST TIME IN OVER TWO THOUSAND YEARS THAT BOTH OF YOU DIDN'T ACTUALLY DIE AT MY HANDS.
MUST'VE BEEN A REAL SAD DAY TO HAVE YOUR STREAK END LIKE--
THERE'S SOMETHING QUITE ENCHANTING ABOUT YOUR FALSE BRAVADO THAT I'LL MISS ONCE I'M HOLDING THE STILL-BEATING HEARTS OF HAWKMAN AND HAWKGIRL IN MY--
SPTOO

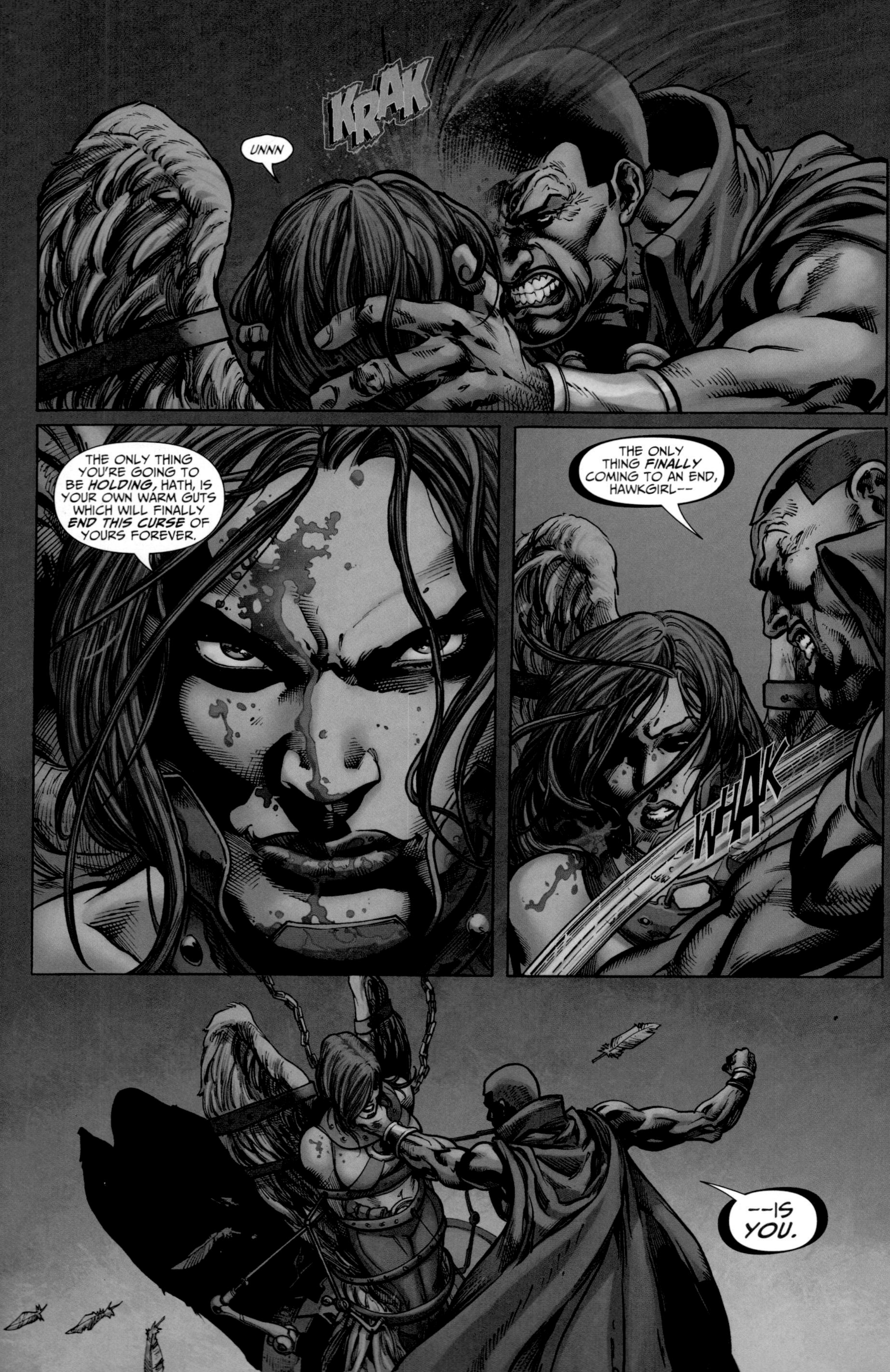
KRAK
UNNN
THE ONLY THING YOU'RE GOING TO BE HOLDING, HATH, IS YOUR OWN WARM GUTS WHICH WILL FINALLY END THIS CURSE OF YOURS FOREVER.
THE ONLY THING FINALLY COMING TO AN END, HAWKGIRL--
WHAK
--IS YOU.

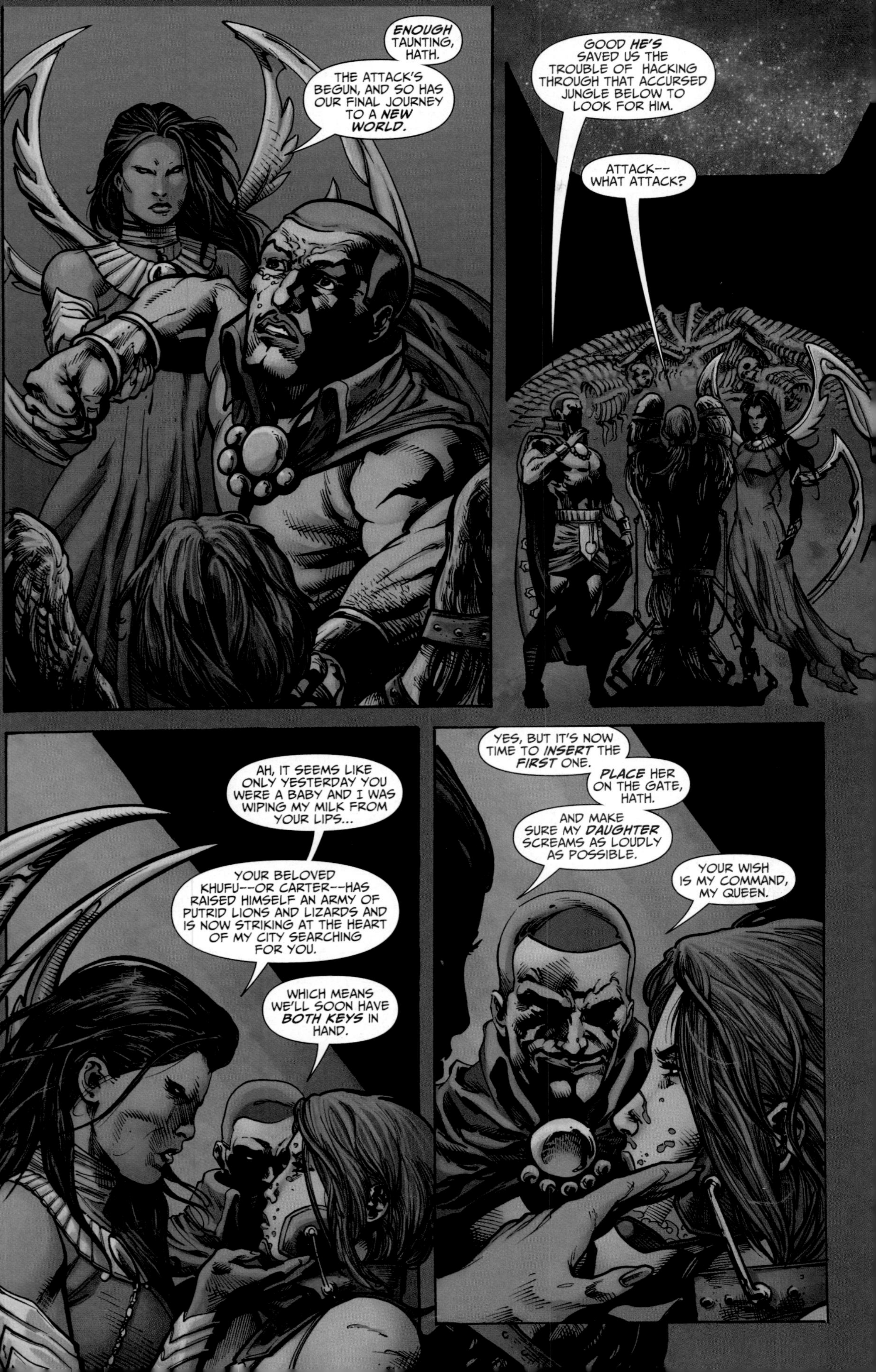
ENOUGH TAUNTING, HATH.
THE ATTACK'S BEGUN, AND SO HAS OUR FINAL JOURNEY TO A NEW WORLD.
GOOD HE'S SAVED US THE TROUBLE OF HACKING THROUGH THAT ACCURSED JUNGLE BELOW TO LOOK FOR HIM.
ATTACK-- WHAT ATTACK?
AH, IT SEEMS LIKE ONLY YESTERDAY YOU WERE A BABY AND I WAS WIPING MY MILK FROM YOUR LIPS...
YOUR BELOVED KHUFU--OR CARTER--HAS RAISED HIMSELF AN ARMY OF PUTRID LIONS AND LIZARDS AND IS NOW STRIKING AT THE HEART OF MY CITY SEARCHING FOR YOU.
WHICH MEANS WE'LL SOON HAVE BOTH KEYS IN HAND.
YES, BUT IT'S NOW TIME TO INSERT THE FIRST ONE.
PLACE HER ON THE GATE, HATH.
AND MAKE SURE MY DAUGHTER SCREAMS AS LOUDLY AS POSSIBLE.
YOUR WISH IS MY COMMAND, MY QUEEN.

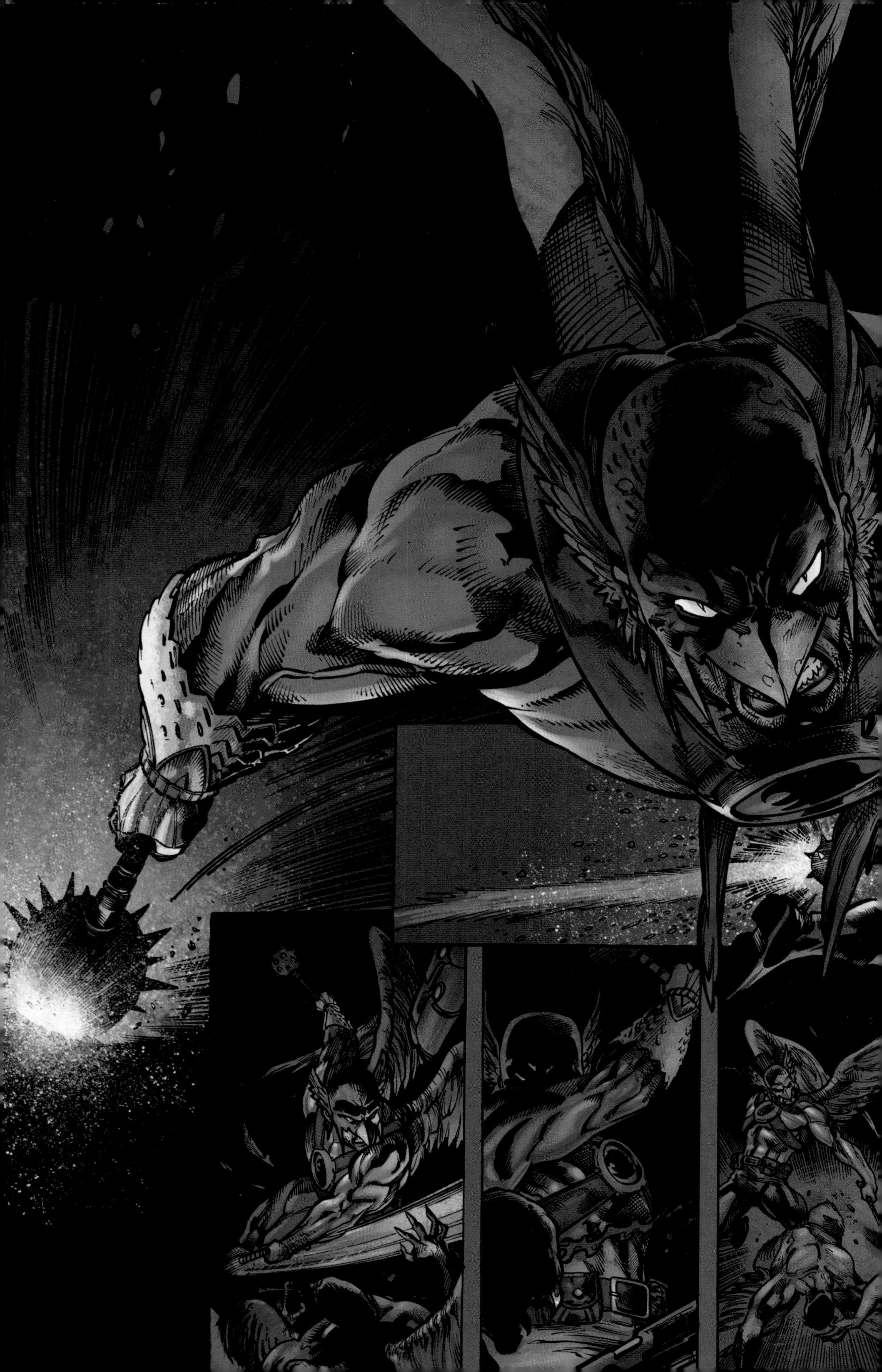

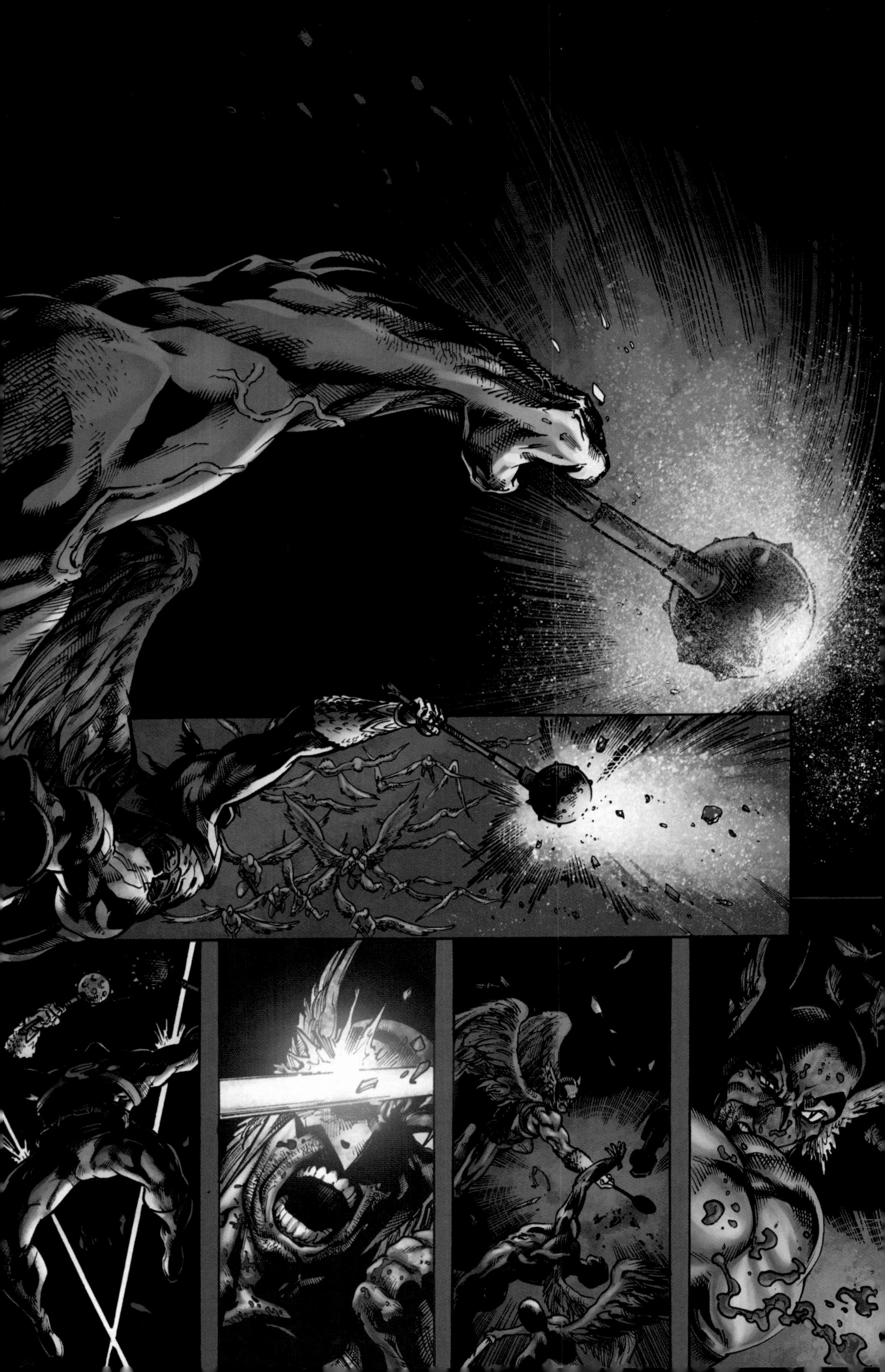

AAGHH!

WE'VE COME FULL CIRCLE, CHAY-ARA.

AAGHH!

I HEAR YOU, SHIERA!

MY PLEASURE.

AAGHH!

SHUNK SHUNK

AAGHH!

RRAGHH!

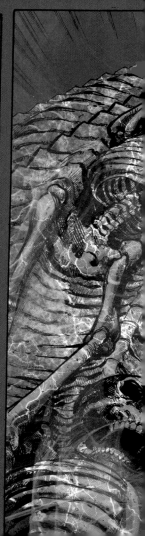

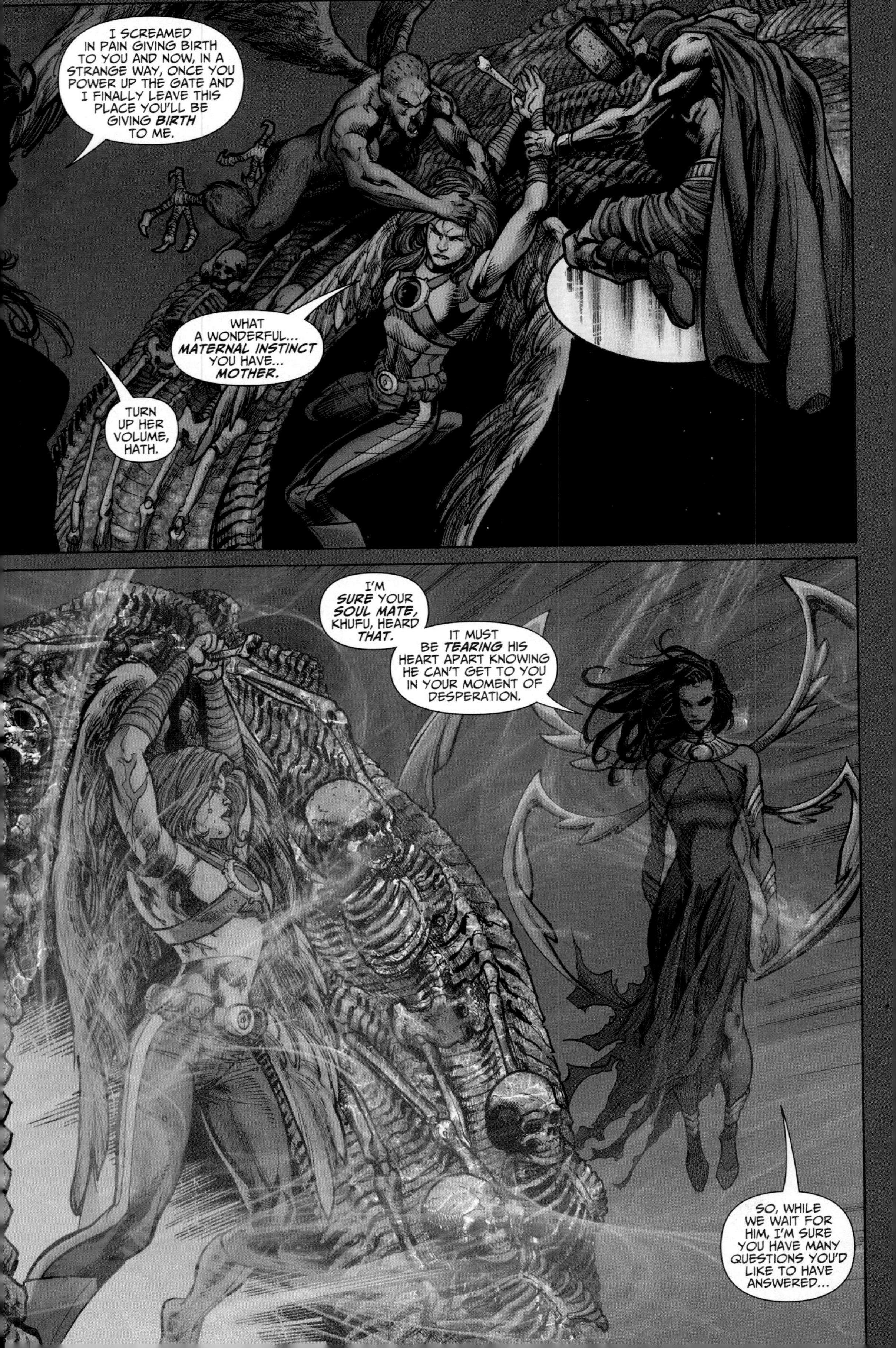
I SCREAMED IN PAIN GIVING BIRTH TO YOU AND NOW, IN A STRANGE WAY, ONCE YOU POWER UP THE GATE AND I FINALLY LEAVE THIS PLACE YOU'LL BE GIVING BIRTH TO ME.
WHAT A WONDERFUL... MATERNAL INSTINCT YOU HAVE... MOTHER.
TURN UP HER VOLUME, HATH.
I'M SURE YOUR SOUL MATE, KHUFU, HEARD THAT.
IT MUST BE TEARING HIS HEART APART KNOWING HE CAN'T GET TO YOU IN YOUR MOMENT OF DESPERATION.
SO, WHILE WE WAIT FOR HIM, I'M SURE YOU HAVE MANY QUESTIONS YOU'D LIKE TO HAVE ANSWERED...

"AS YOU KNOW, MY DARLING, IT WASN'T LONG AFTER THE PHARAOH LOST HIS WIFE THAT WE *LOST* YOUR FATHER TOO, THE PHARAOH'S YOUNGEST BROTHER, TO THAT VILE *PESTILENCE* WHICH TORE THROUGH OUR CITY THAT DARK YEAR.

"I NEVER TOLD YOU THIS, CHAY-ARA, BUT I MARRIED THE PHARAOH WITH THE *UNDERSTANDING* THAT PRINCE KHUFU WOULD ASK FOR YOUR HAND IN MARRIAGE..."

"...*NOT* THAT THE PRINCE NEEDED ANY *PRODDING* FROM HIS FATHER, SINCE BOTH OF YOU LOVED EACH OTHER *DEEPLY* FOR MANY YEARS AND YOUR UNION WAS INEVITABLE.

"AFTER EXTENSIVE ANALYSIS WE ALL REALIZED THAT THIS NTH METAL POSSESSED AMAZING PROPERTIES THAT COULD CHANGE THE COURSE OF HISTORY...

"...A HISTORY WITH EGYPT AS ITS SHINING CENTER.

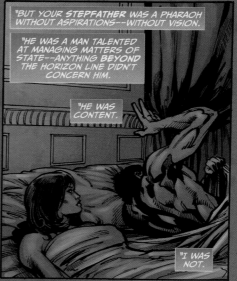

"BUT YOUR STEPFATHER WAS A PHARAOH WITHOUT ASPIRATIONS--WITHOUT VISION.

"HE WAS A MAN TALENTED AT MANAGING MATTERS OF STATE--ANYTHING BEYOND THE HORIZON LINE DIDN'T CONCERN HIM.

"HE WAS CONTENT.

"I WAS NOT.

"WHAT I DID, I DID *FOR* EGYPT, CHAY-ARA."

"YOU DID IT FOR *YOU*, MOTHER. NO ONE ELSE."

"HATH-SET SHOWED ME THE FUTURE. YOU AND KHUFU WERE *NOT* PART OF IT.

"ONLY I WAS *FATED* TO PROVIDE THE GUIDANCE THAT WOULD MAINTAIN EGYPT'S PREDOMINANCE FOR MILLENNIA.

"ONCE HATH-SET AND I CUT INTO OUR SKIN WITH THE NTH METAL DAGGER COVERED IN YOUR *SACRIFICIAL BLOOD* IT WAS PROPHESIED THAT WE WOULD THEN BECOME *IMMORTAL*."

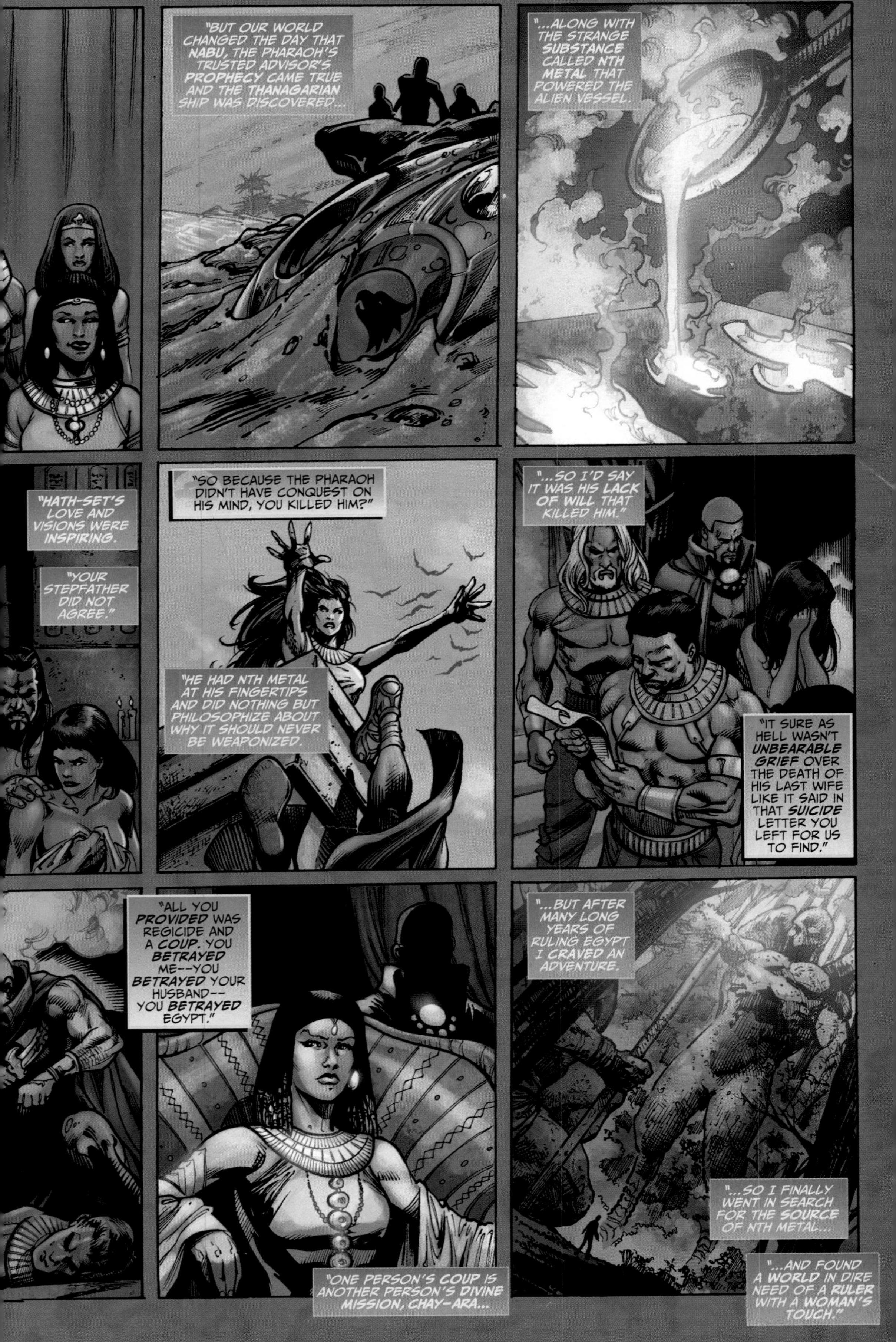
"BUT OUR WORLD CHANGED THE DAY THAT NABU, THE PHARAOH'S TRUSTED ADVISOR'S PROPHECY CAME TRUE AND THE THANAGARIAN SHIP WAS DISCOVERED...
"...ALONG WITH THE STRANGE SUBSTANCE CALLED NTH METAL THAT POWERED THE ALIEN VESSEL.
"HATH-SET'S LOVE AND VISIONS WERE INSPIRING.
"YOUR STEPFATHER DID NOT AGREE."
"SO BECAUSE THE PHARAOH DIDN'T HAVE CONQUEST ON HIS MIND, YOU KILLED HIM?"
"HE HAD NTH METAL AT HIS FINGERTIPS AND DID NOTHING BUT PHILOSOPHIZE ABOUT WHY IT SHOULD NEVER BE WEAPONIZED.
"...SO I'D SAY IT WAS HIS LACK OF WILL THAT KILLED HIM."
"IT SURE AS HELL WASN'T UNBEARABLE GRIEF OVER THE DEATH OF HIS LAST WIFE LIKE IT SAID IN THAT SUICIDE LETTER YOU LEFT FOR US TO FIND."
"ALL YOU PROVIDED WAS REGICIDE AND A COUP. YOU BETRAYED ME--YOU BETRAYED YOUR HUSBAND--YOU BETRAYED EGYPT."
"ONE PERSON'S COUP IS ANOTHER PERSON'S DIVINE MISSION, CHAY-ARA...
"...BUT AFTER MANY LONG YEARS OF RULING EGYPT I CRAVED AN ADVENTURE.
"...SO I FINALLY WENT IN SEARCH FOR THE SOURCE OF NTH METAL...
"...AND FOUND A WORLD IN DIRE NEED OF A RULER WITH A WOMAN'S TOUCH."

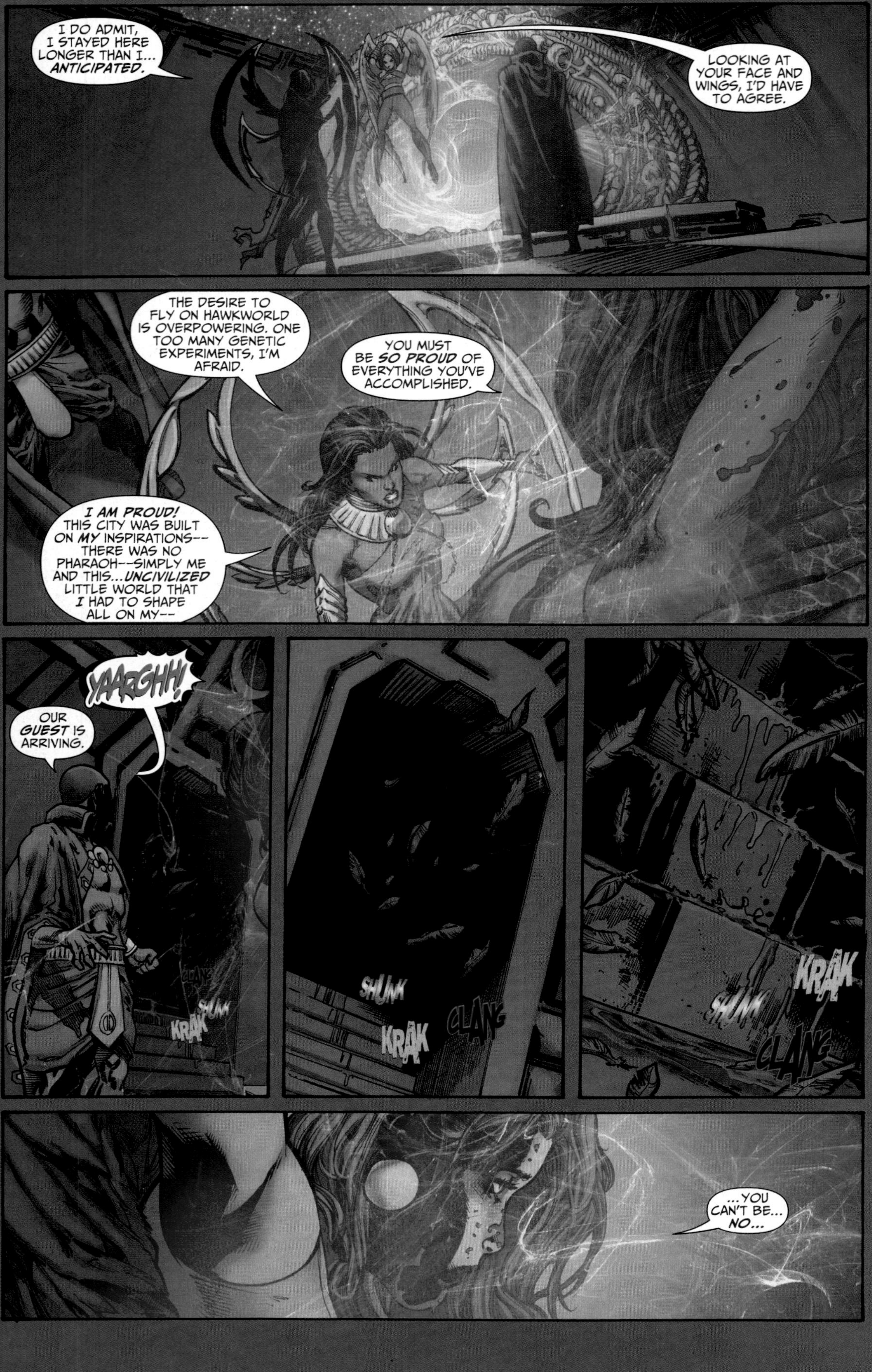
I DO ADMIT, I STAYED HERE LONGER THAN I... ANTICIPATED.
LOOKING AT YOUR FACE AND WINGS, I'D HAVE TO AGREE.
THE DESIRE TO FLY ON HAWKWORLD IS OVERPOWERING. ONE TOO MANY GENETIC EXPERIMENTS, I'M AFRAID.
YOU MUST BE SO PROUD OF EVERYTHING YOU'VE ACCOMPLISHED.
I AM PROUD! THIS CITY WAS BUILT ON MY INSPIRATIONS--THERE WAS NO PHARAOH--SIMPLY ME AND THIS...UNCIVILIZED LITTLE WORLD THAT I HAD TO SHAPE ALL ON MY--
YAARGHH!
OUR GUEST IS ARRIVING.
SHUNK
KRAK
SHUNK
KRAK
CLANG
SHUNK
KRAK
CLANG
...YOU CAN'T BE... NO...

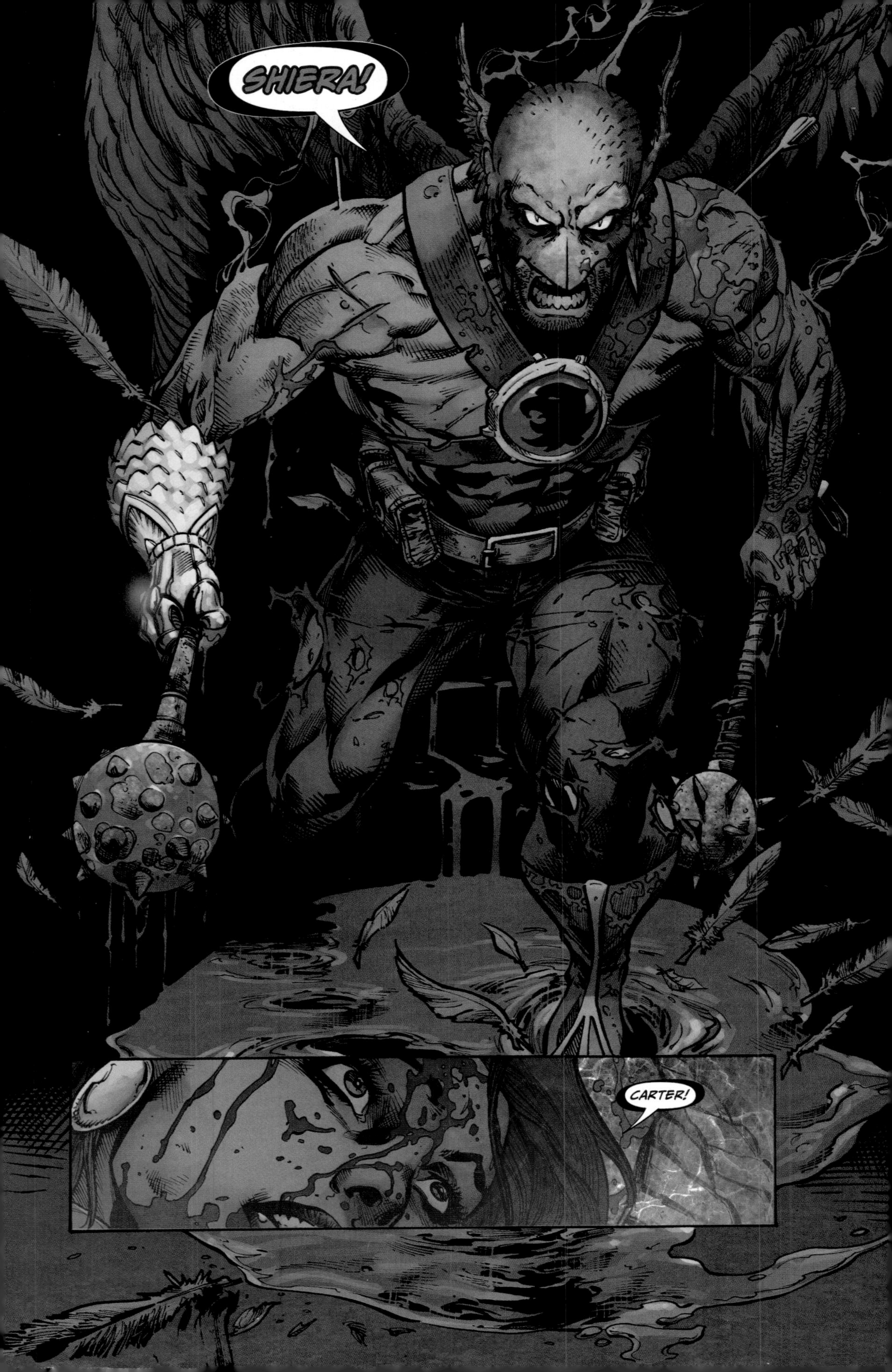
SHIERA!
CARTER!

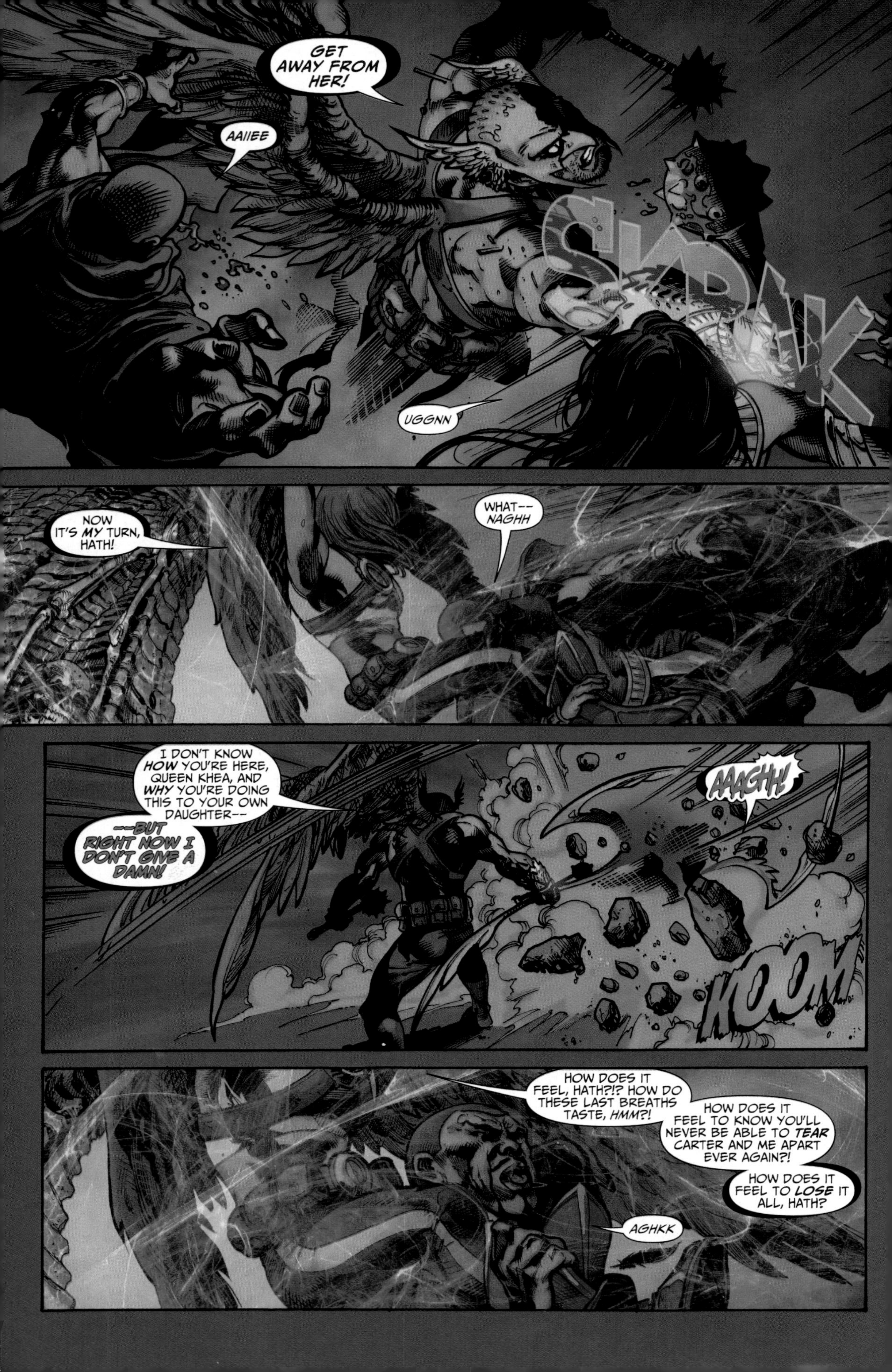
GET AWAY FROM HER!
AAIIEE
SKRAK
UGGNN
NOW IT'S MY TURN, HATH!
WHAT-- NAGHH
I DON'T KNOW HOW YOU'RE HERE, QUEEN KHEA, AND WHY YOU'RE DOING THIS TO YOUR OWN DAUGHTER--
--BUT RIGHT NOW I DON'T GIVE A DAMN!
AAAGH!
KOOM
HOW DOES IT FEEL, HATH?!? HOW DO THESE LAST BREATHS TASTE, HMM?!
HOW DOES IT FEEL TO KNOW YOU'LL NEVER BE ABLE TO TEAR CARTER AND ME APART EVER AGAIN?!
HOW DOES IT FEEL TO LOSE IT ALL, HATH?
AGHKK

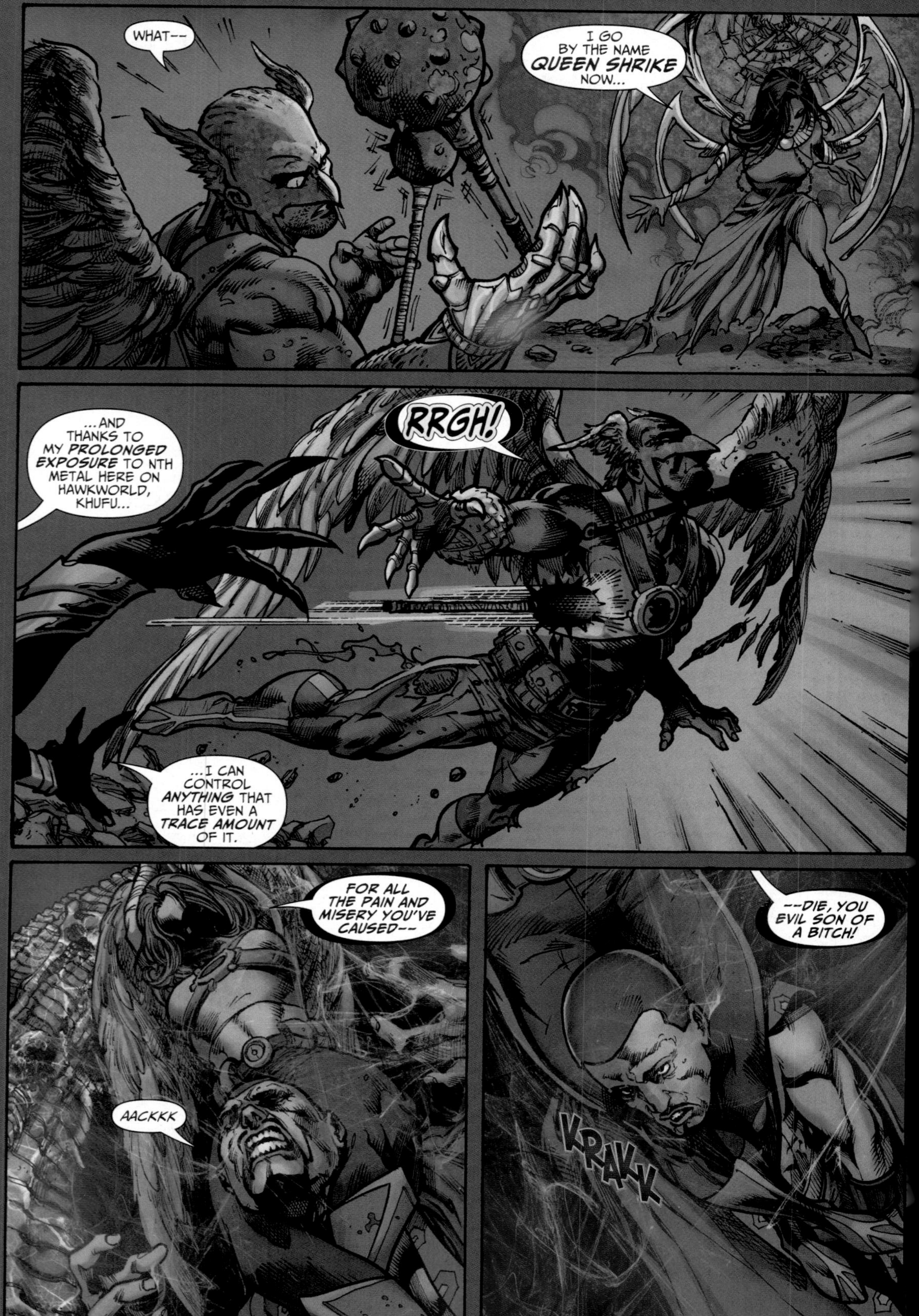

WHAT--
I GO BY THE NAME QUEEN SHRIKE NOW...
...AND THANKS TO MY PROLONGED EXPOSURE TO NTH METAL HERE ON HAWKWORLD, KHUFU...
RRGH!
...I CAN CONTROL ANYTHING THAT HAS EVEN A TRACE AMOUNT OF IT.
FOR ALL THE PAIN AND MISERY YOU'VE CAUSED--
AACKKK
--DIE, YOU EVIL SON OF A BITCH!
KRAKK

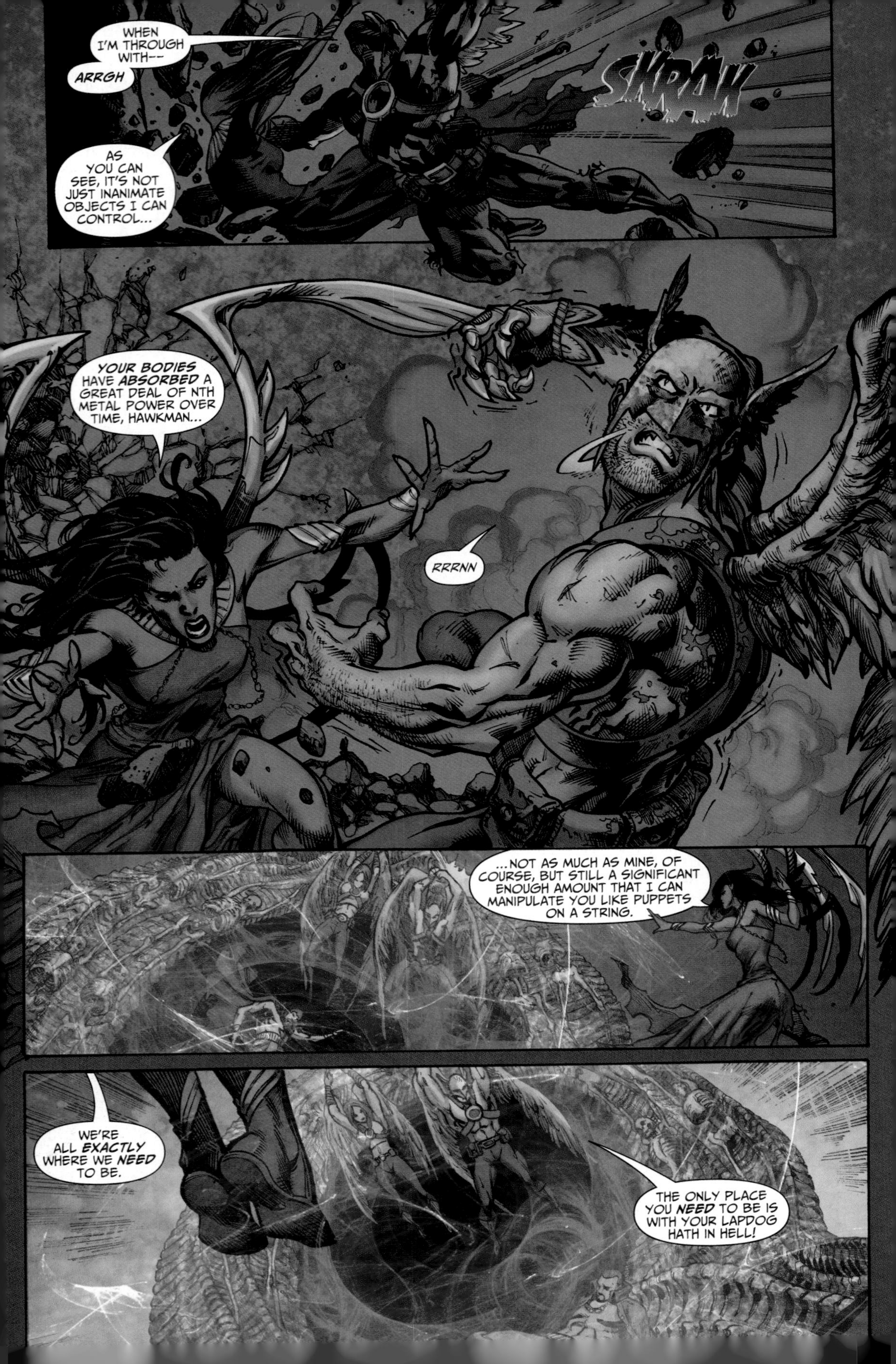
WHEN I'M THROUGH WITH--
ARRGH
SKRAK
AS YOU CAN SEE, IT'S NOT JUST INANIMATE OBJECTS I CAN CONTROL...
YOUR BODIES HAVE ABSORBED A GREAT DEAL OF NTH METAL POWER OVER TIME, HAWKMAN...
RRRNN
...NOT AS MUCH AS MINE, OF COURSE, BUT STILL A SIGNIFICANT ENOUGH AMOUNT THAT I CAN MANIPULATE YOU LIKE PUPPETS ON A STRING.
WE'RE ALL EXACTLY WHERE WE NEED TO BE.
THE ONLY PLACE YOU NEED TO BE IS WITH YOUR LAPDOG HATH IN HELL!

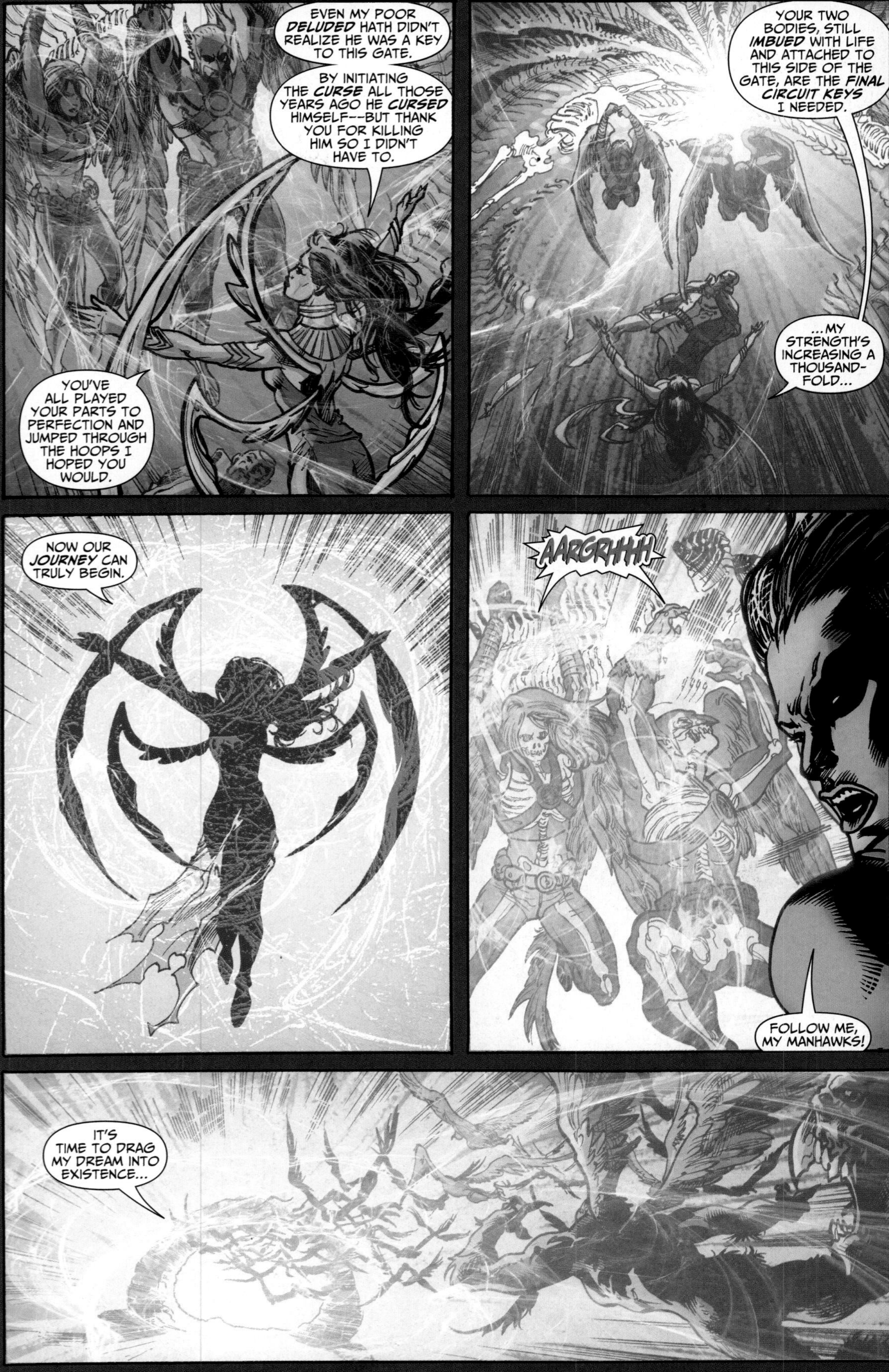
EVEN MY POOR DELUDED HATH DIDN'T REALIZE HE WAS A KEY TO THIS GATE.
BY INITIATING THE CURSE ALL THOSE YEARS AGO HE CURSED HIMSELF--BUT THANK YOU FOR KILLING HIM SO I DIDN'T HAVE TO.
YOU'VE ALL PLAYED YOUR PARTS TO PERFECTION AND JUMPED THROUGH THE HOOPS I HOPED YOU WOULD.
YOUR TWO BODIES, STILL IMBUED WITH LIFE AND ATTACHED TO THIS SIDE OF THE GATE, ARE THE FINAL CIRCUIT KEYS I NEEDED.
...MY STRENGTH'S INCREASING A THOUSAND-FOLD...
NOW OUR JOURNEY CAN TRULY BEGIN.
AARGRHHH
FOLLOW ME, MY MANHAWKS!
IT'S TIME TO DRAG MY DREAM INTO EXISTENCE...

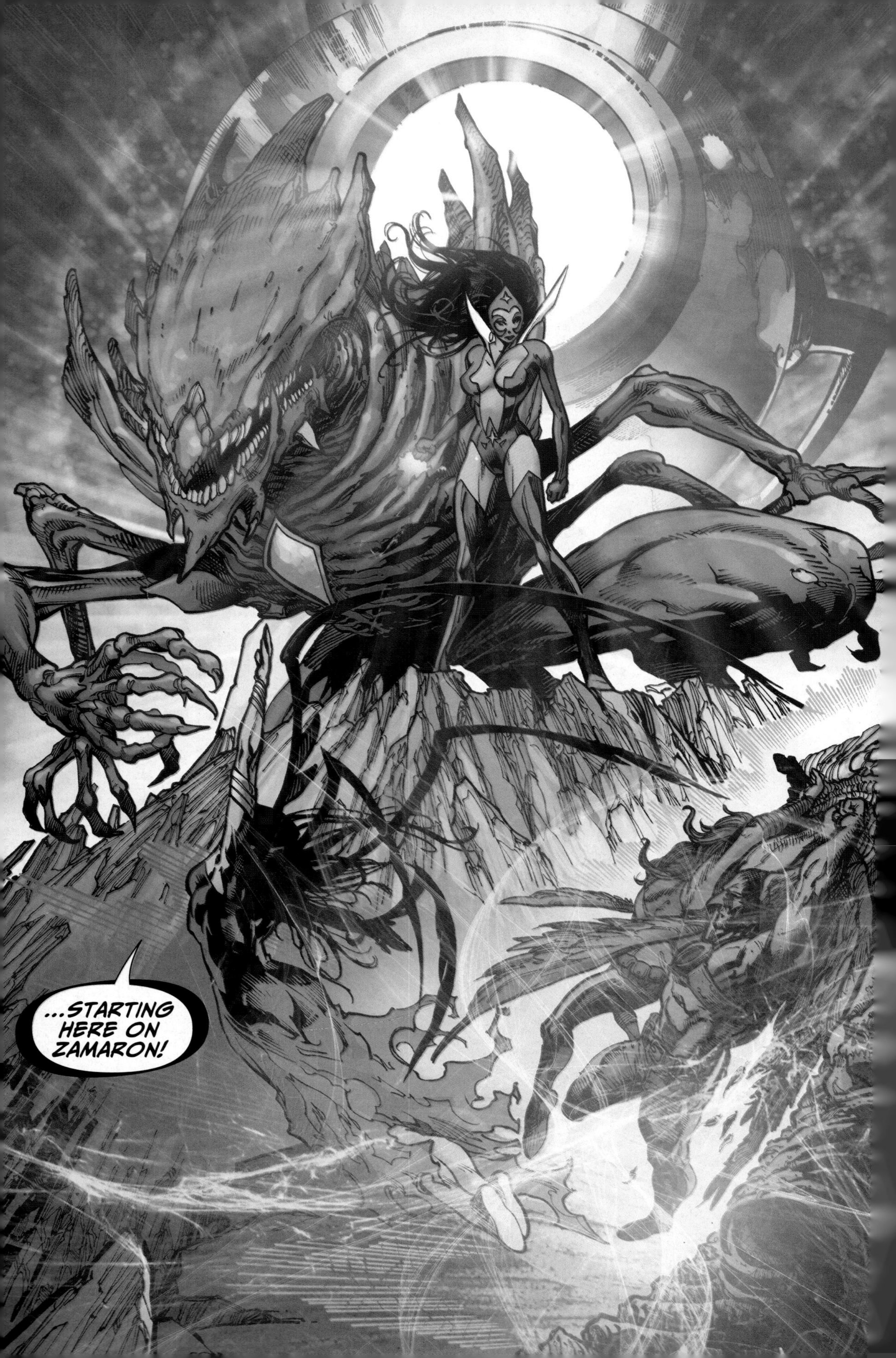
...STARTING HERE ON ZAMARON!

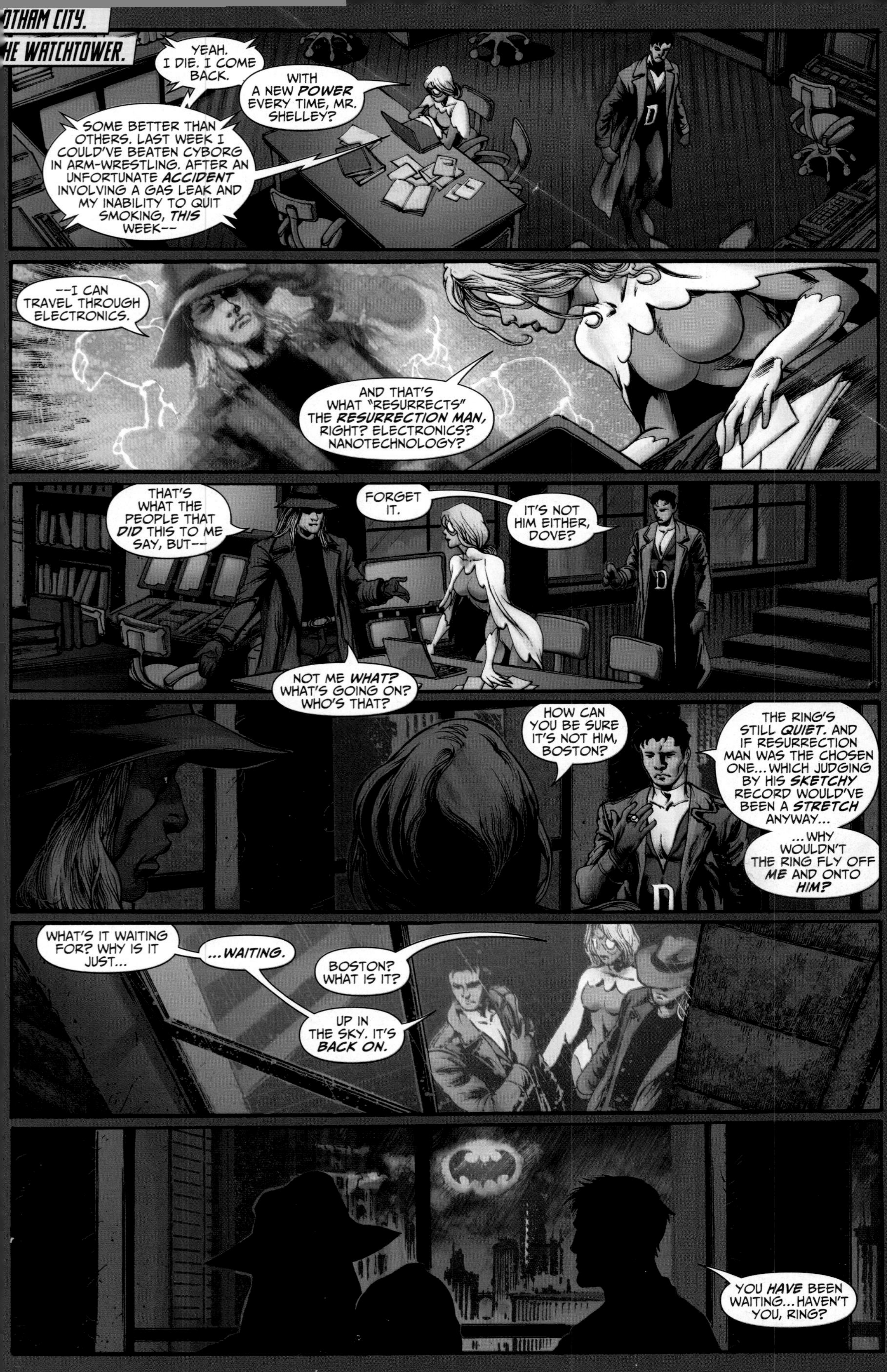
OTHAM CITY.
HE WATCHTOWER.
YEAH. I DIE. I COME BACK.
WITH A NEW POWER EVERY TIME, MR. SHELLEY?
SOME BETTER THAN OTHERS. LAST WEEK I COULD'VE BEATEN CYBORG IN ARM-WRESTLING. AFTER AN UNFORTUNATE ACCIDENT INVOLVING A GAS LEAK AND MY INABILITY TO QUIT SMOKING, THIS WEEK--
--I CAN TRAVEL THROUGH ELECTRONICS.
AND THAT'S WHAT "RESURRECTS" THE RESURRECTION MAN, RIGHT? ELECTRONICS? NANOTECHNOLOGY?
THAT'S WHAT THE PEOPLE THAT DID THIS TO ME SAY, BUT--
FORGET IT.
IT'S NOT HIM EITHER, DOVE?
NOT ME WHAT? WHAT'S GOING ON? WHO'S THAT?
HOW CAN YOU BE SURE IT'S NOT HIM, BOSTON?
THE RING'S STILL QUIET. AND IF RESURRECTION MAN WAS THE CHOSEN ONE... WHICH JUDGING BY HIS SKETCHY RECORD WOULD'VE BEEN A STRETCH ANYWAY...
...WHY WOULDN'T THE RING FLY OFF ME AND ONTO HIM?
WHAT'S IT WAITING FOR? WHY IS IT JUST...
...WAITING.
BOSTON? WHAT IS IT?
UP IN THE SKY. IT'S BACK ON.
YOU HAVE BEEN WAITING... HAVEN'T YOU, RING?

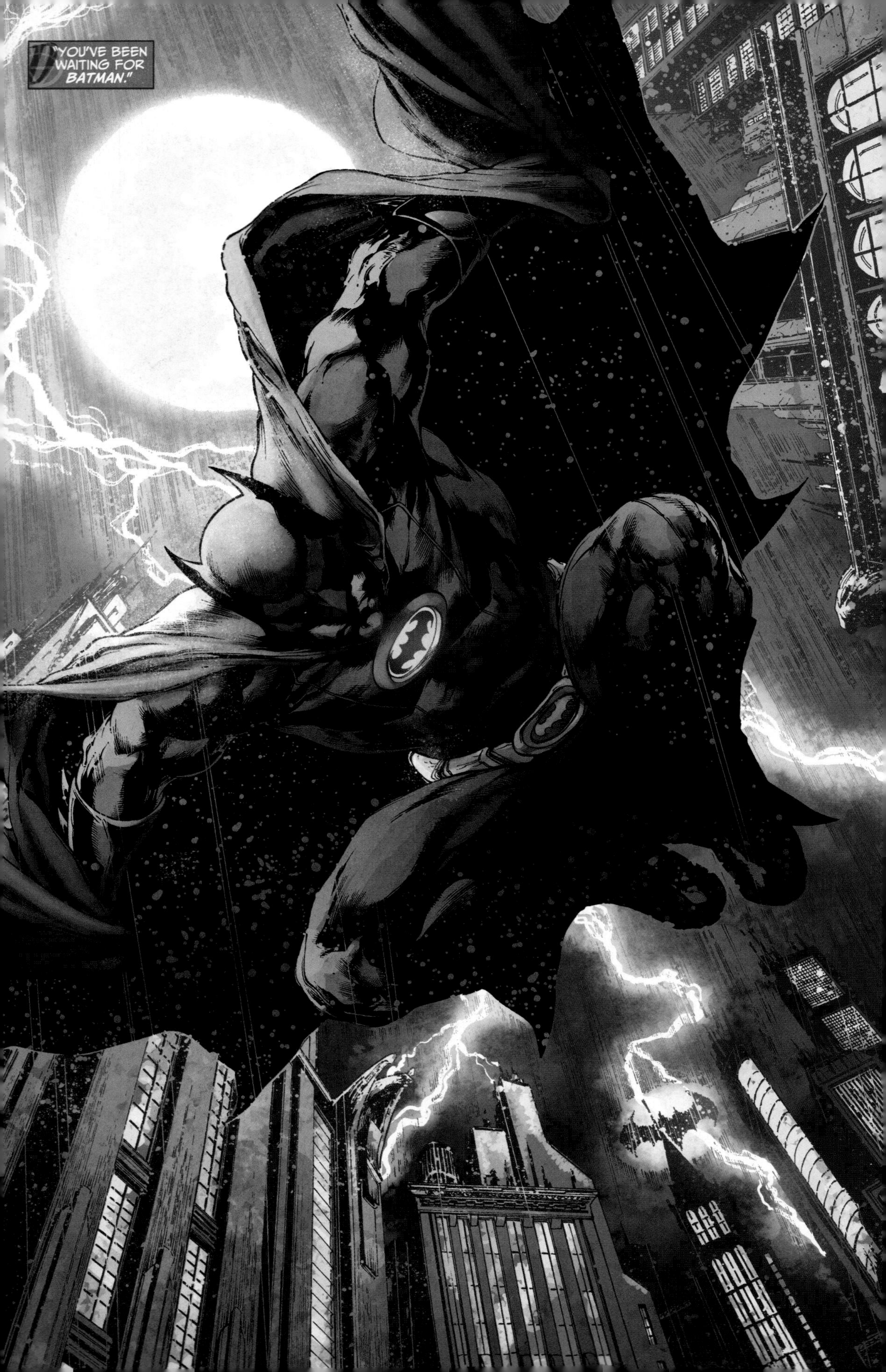
"YOU'VE BEEN WAITING FOR BATMAN."

**BRIGHTEST DAY 14**
*Cover by David Finch*

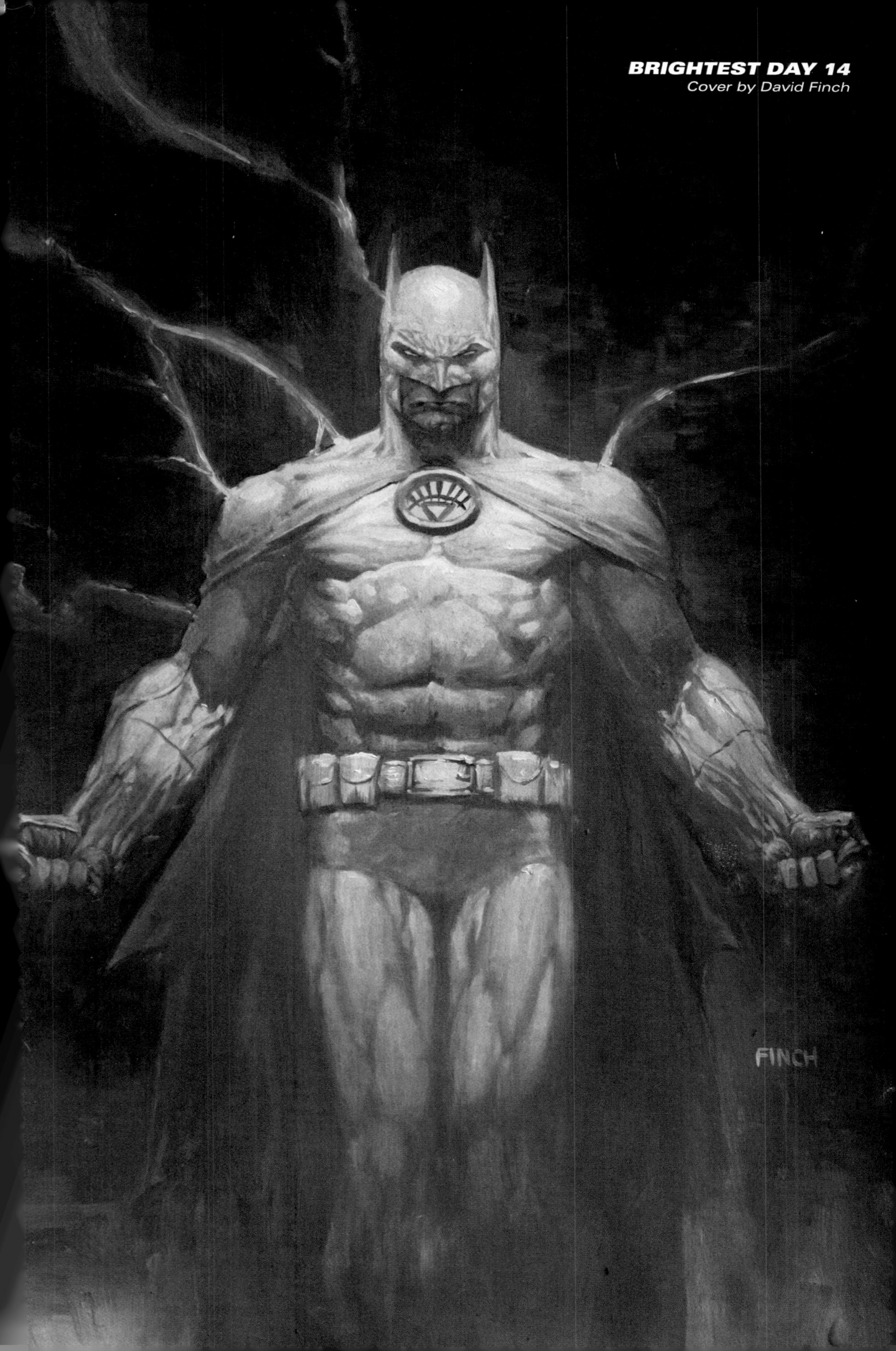
FINCH

ACROBATS

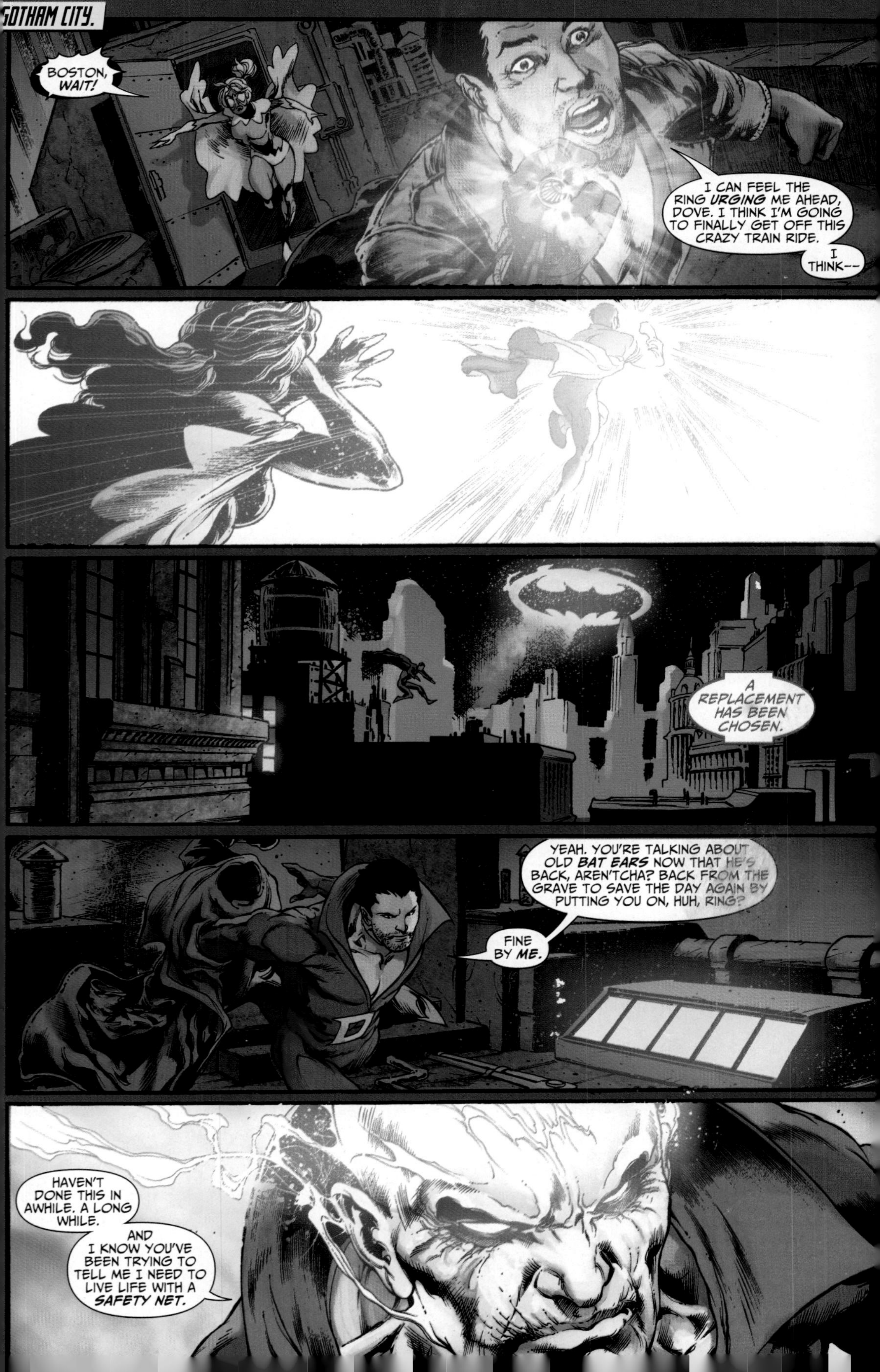
GOTHAM CITY.
BOSTON, WAIT!
I CAN FEEL THE RING URGING ME AHEAD, DOVE. I THINK I'M GOING TO FINALLY GET OFF THIS CRAZY TRAIN RIDE.
I THINK--
A REPLACEMENT HAS BEEN CHOSEN.
YEAH. YOU'RE TALKING ABOUT OLD BAT EARS NOW THAT HE'S BACK, AREN'TCHA? BACK FROM THE GRAVE TO SAVE THE DAY AGAIN BY PUTTING YOU ON, HUH, RING?
FINE BY ME.
HAVEN'T DONE THIS IN AWHILE. A LONG WHILE.
AND I KNOW YOU'VE BEEN TRYING TO TELL ME I NEED TO LIVE LIFE WITH A SAFETY NET.

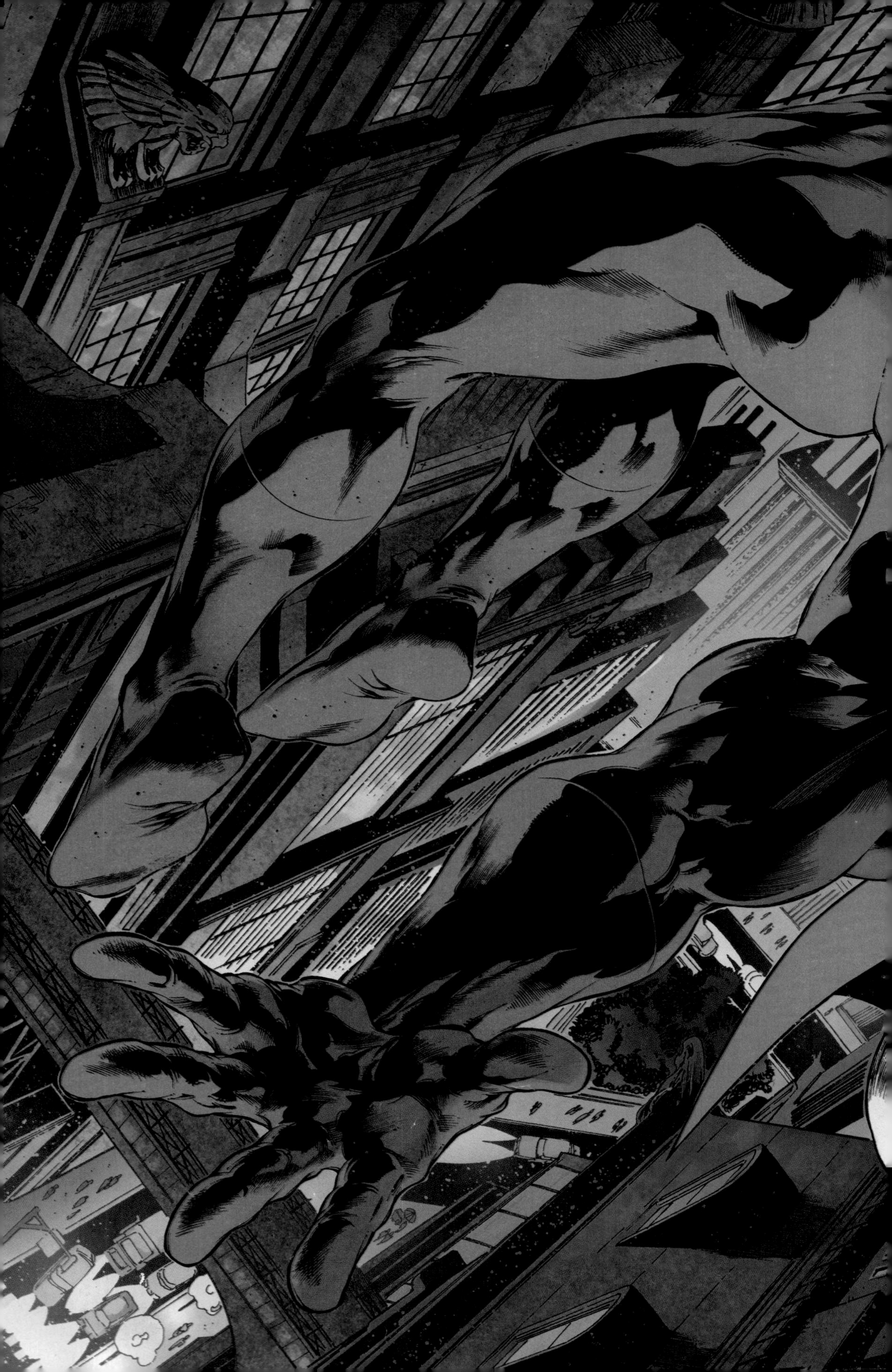

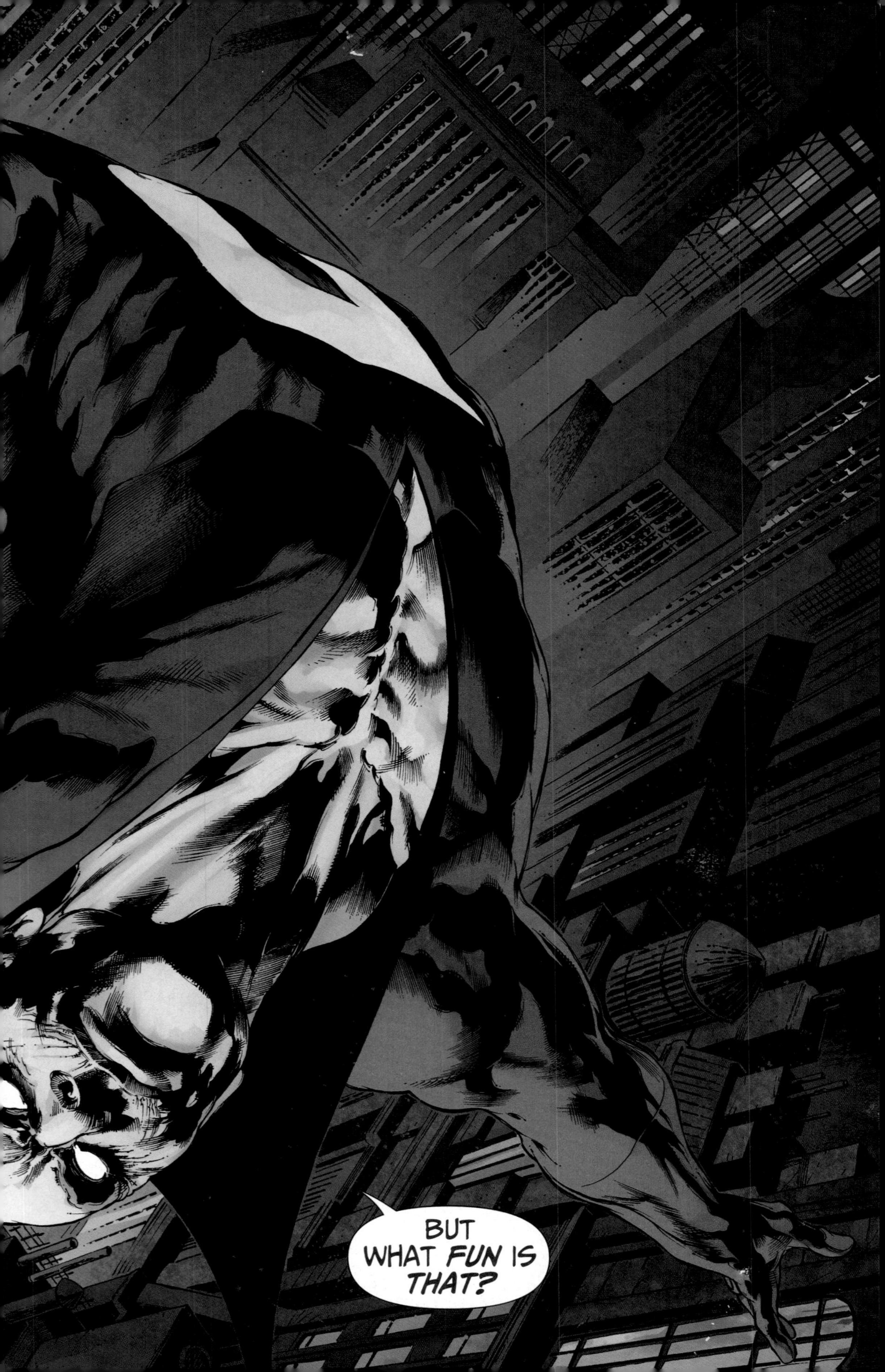
BUT WHAT *FUN* IS *THAT?*

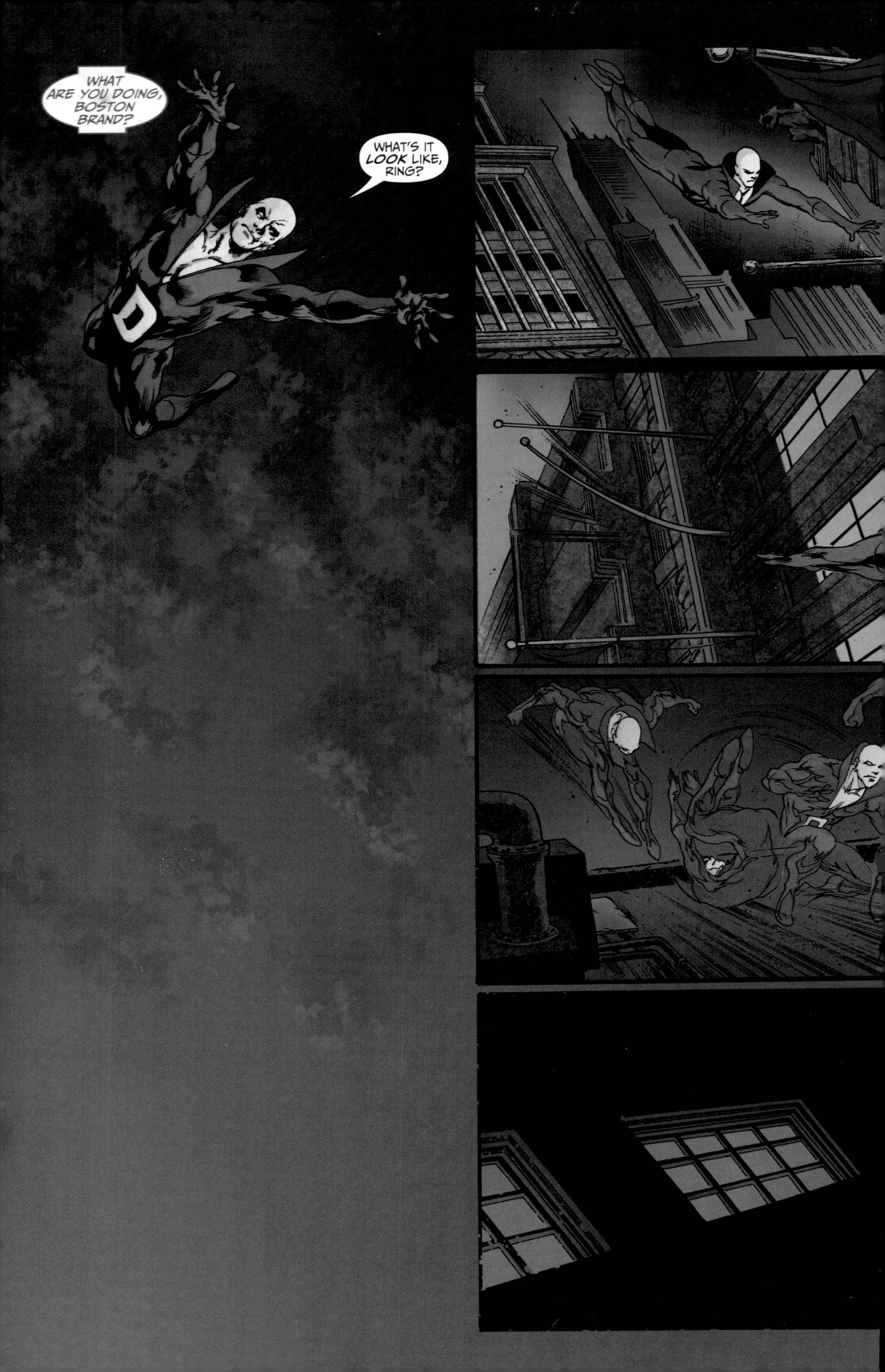
WHAT ARE YOU DOING, BOSTON BRAND?
WHAT'S IT LOOK LIKE, RING?

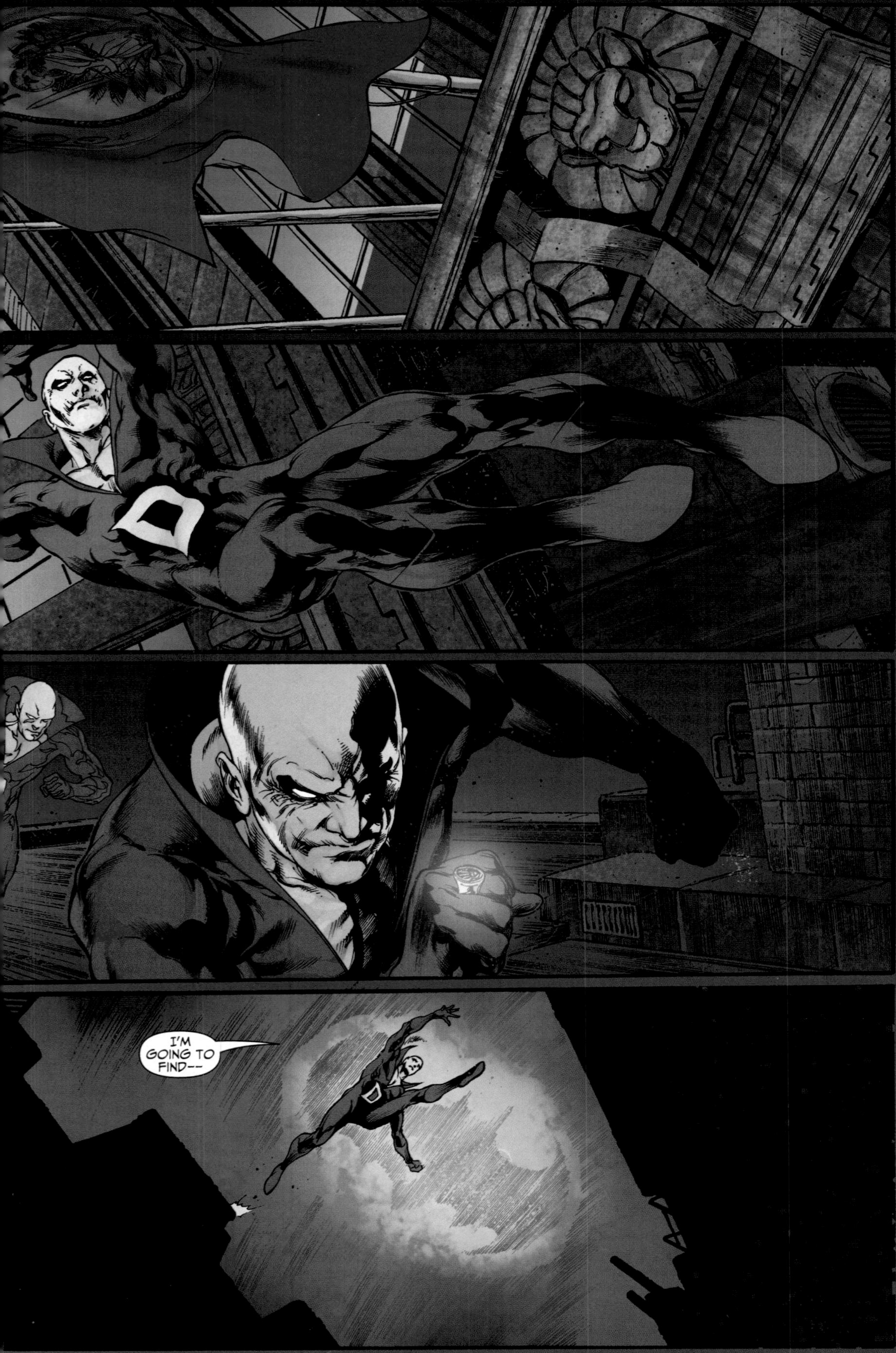
I'M GOING TO FIND--

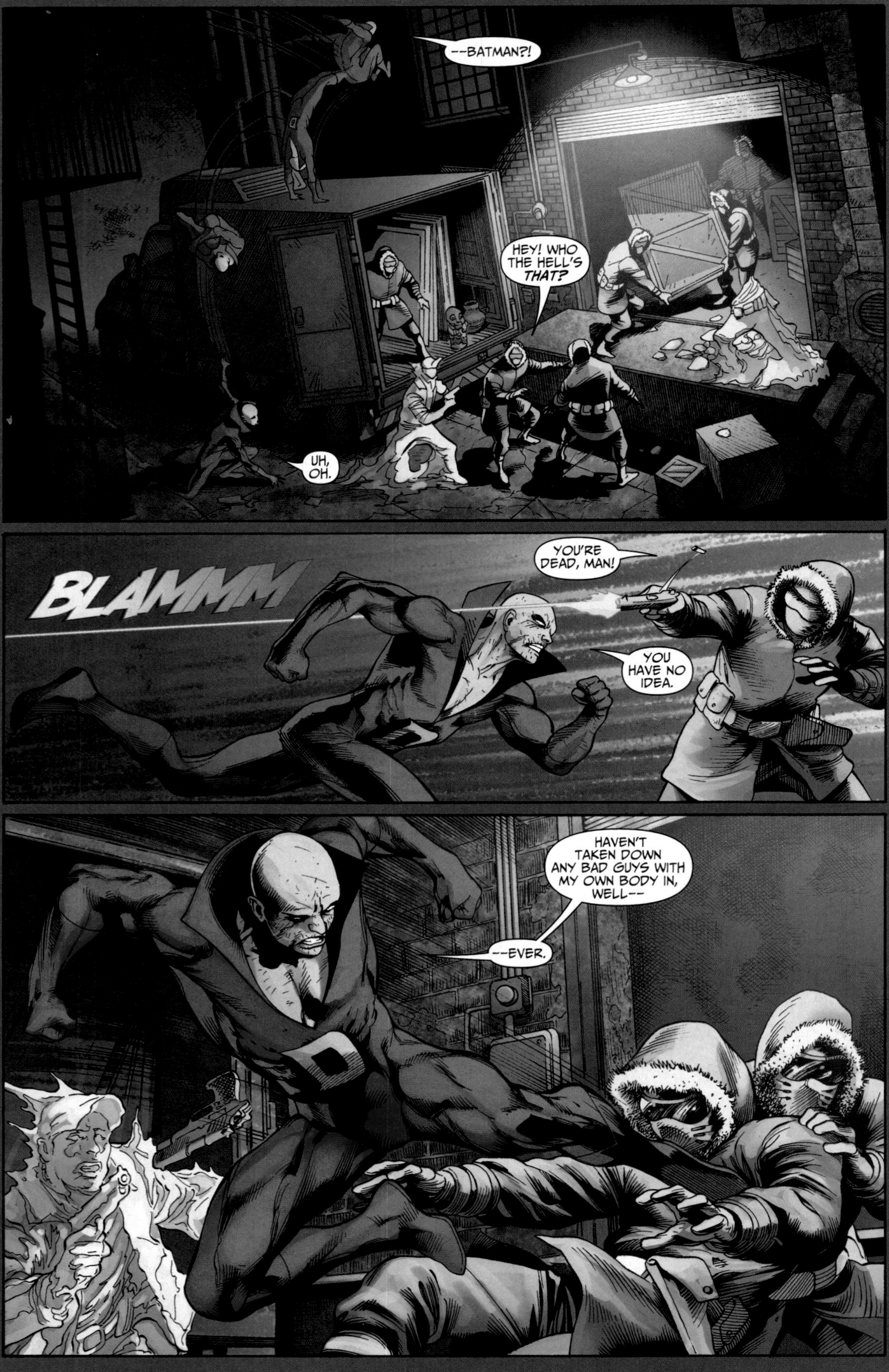
--BATMAN?!
HEY! WHO THE HELL'S *THAT?*
UH, OH.
BLAMMM
YOU'RE DEAD, MAN!
YOU HAVE NO IDEA.
HAVEN'T TAKEN DOWN ANY BAD GUYS WITH MY OWN BODY IN, WELL--
--EVER.

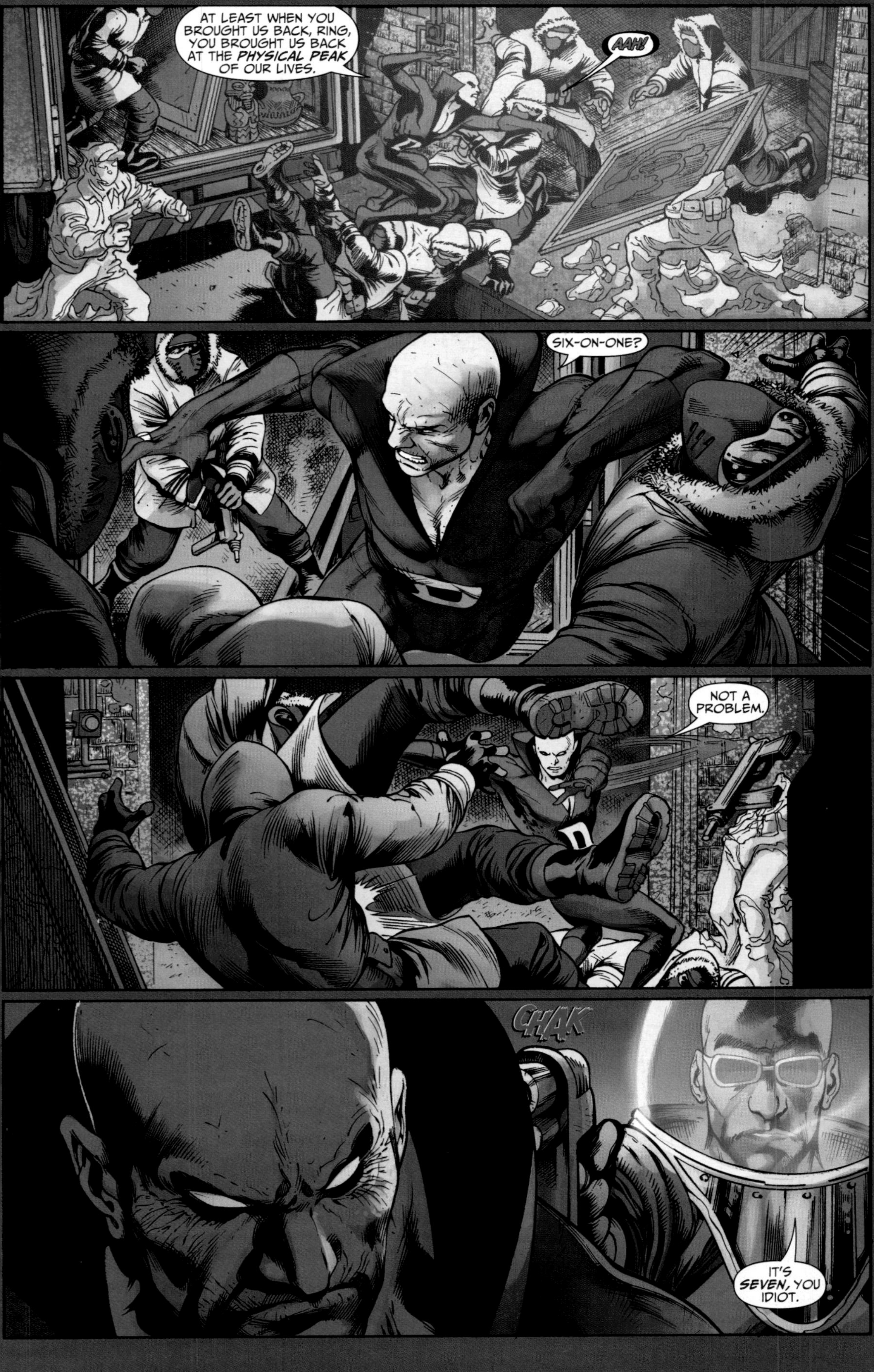
AT LEAST WHEN YOU BROUGHT US BACK, RING, YOU BROUGHT US BACK AT THE PHYSICAL PEAK OF OUR LIVES.
AAH!
SIX-ON-ONE?
NOT A PROBLEM.
CHAK
IT'S SEVEN, YOU IDIOT.

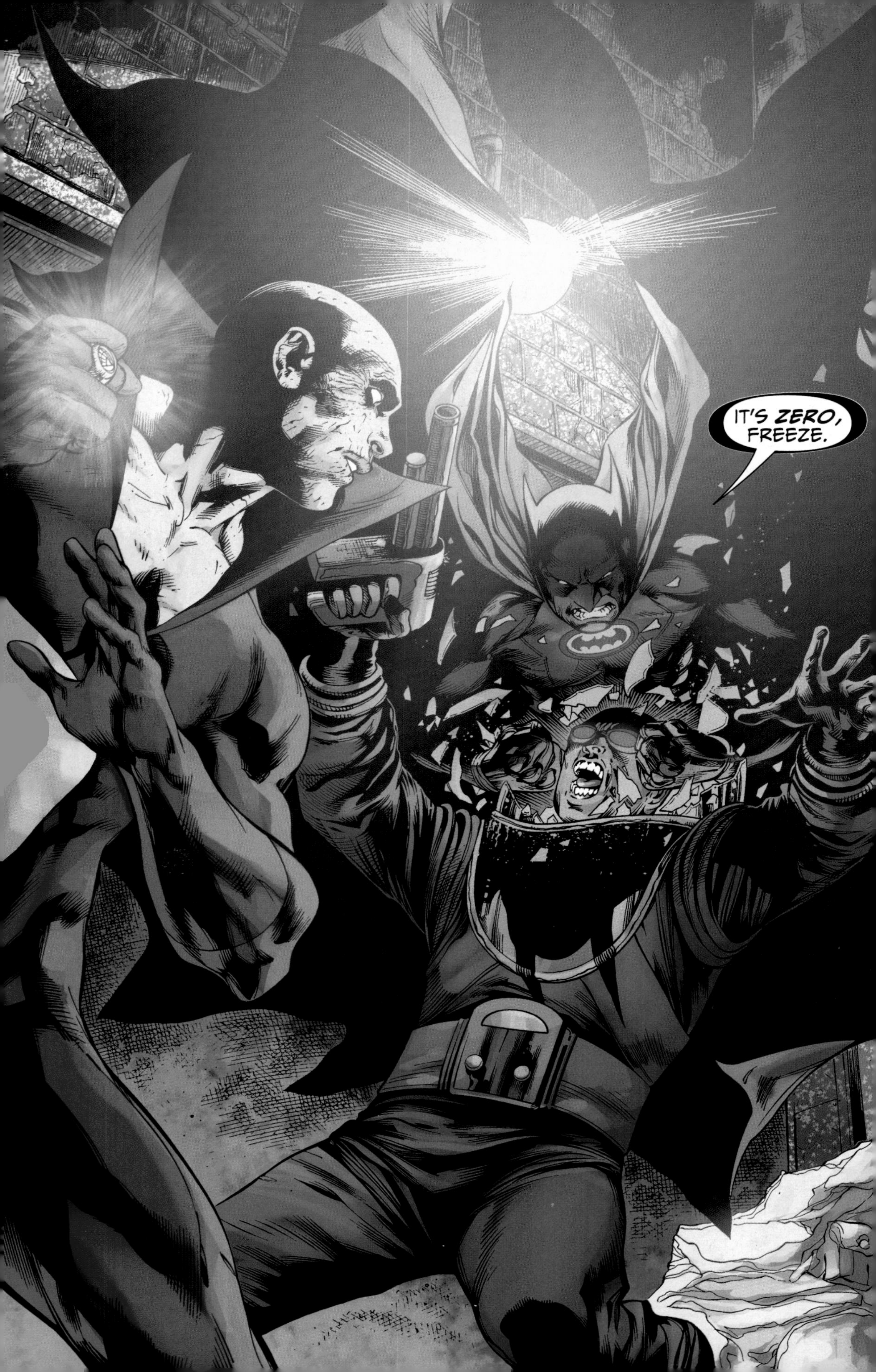
IT'S ZERO, FREEZE.

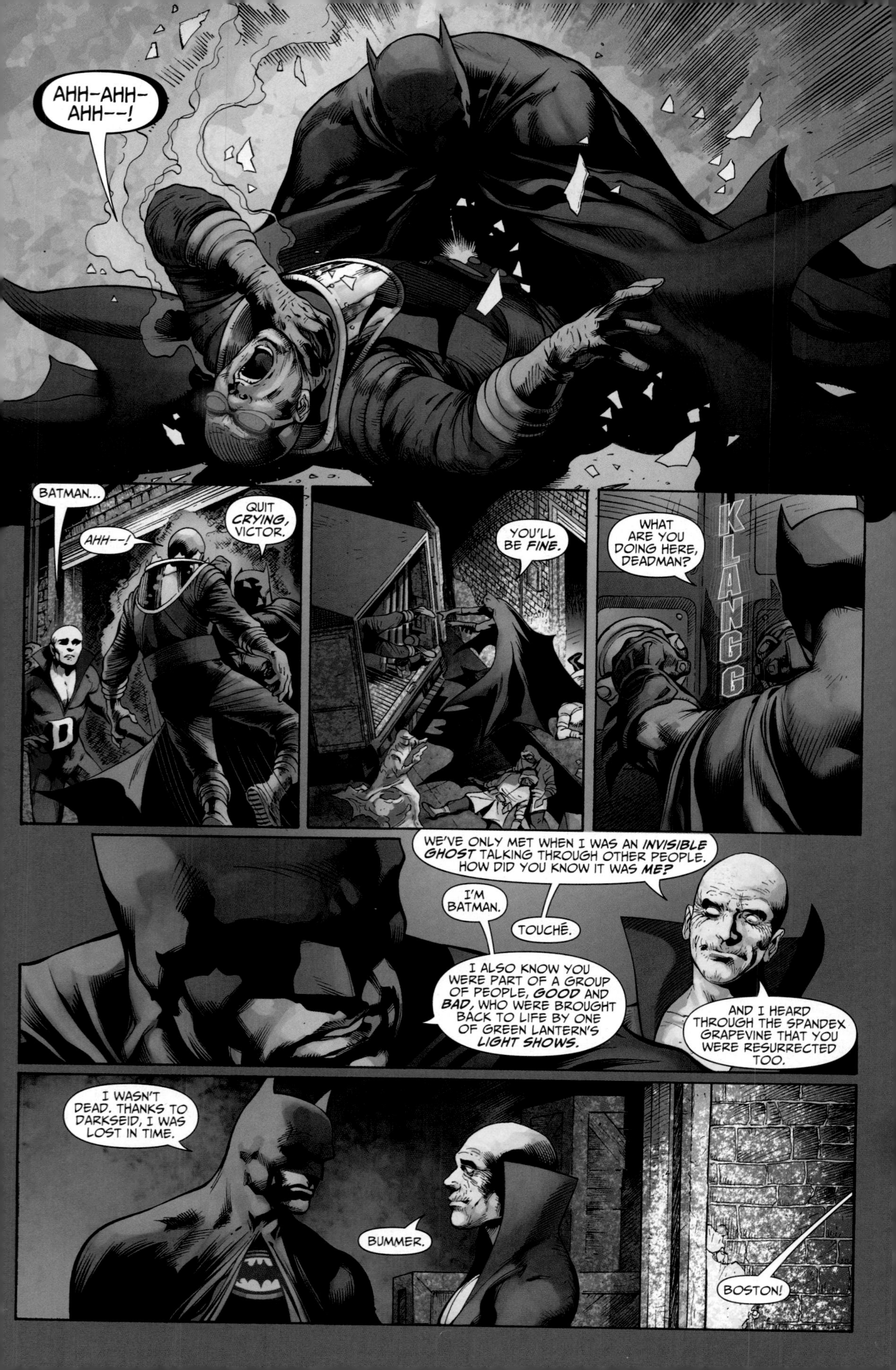
AHH-AHH-AHH--!
BATMAN...
AHH--!
QUIT CRYING, VICTOR.
YOU'LL BE FINE.
WHAT ARE YOU DOING HERE, DEADMAN?
KLANGG
WE'VE ONLY MET WHEN I WAS AN INVISIBLE GHOST TALKING THROUGH OTHER PEOPLE. HOW DID YOU KNOW IT WAS ME?
I'M BATMAN.
TOUCHÉ.
I ALSO KNOW YOU WERE PART OF A GROUP OF PEOPLE, GOOD AND BAD, WHO WERE BROUGHT BACK TO LIFE BY ONE OF GREEN LANTERN'S LIGHT SHOWS.
AND I HEARD THROUGH THE SPANDEX GRAPEVINE THAT YOU WERE RESURRECTED TOO.
I WASN'T DEAD. THANKS TO DARKSEID, I WAS LOST IN TIME.
BUMMER.
BOSTON!

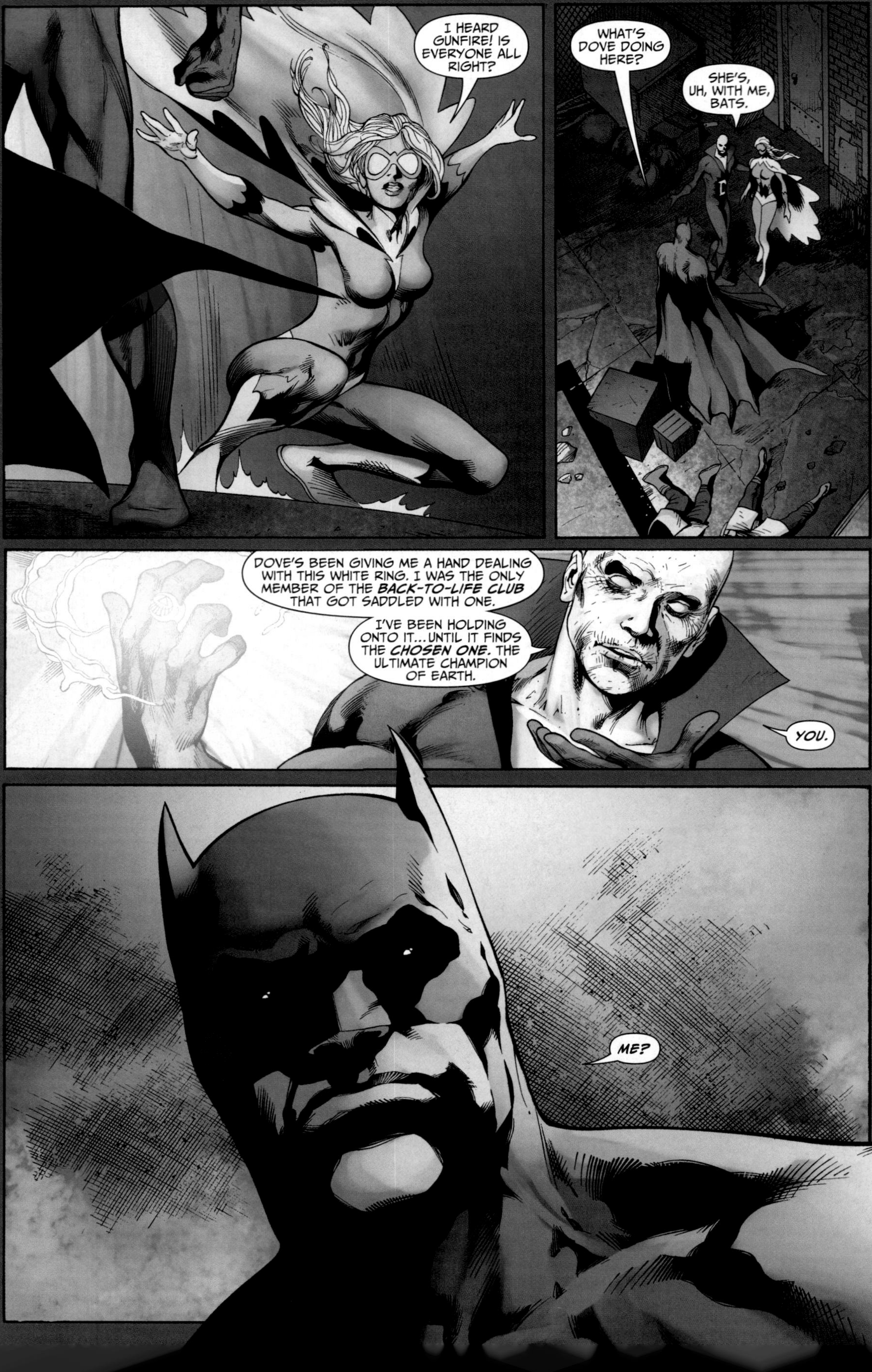
I HEARD GUNFIRE! IS EVERYONE ALL RIGHT?
WHAT'S DOVE DOING HERE?
SHE'S, UH, WITH ME, BATS.
DOVE'S BEEN GIVING ME A HAND DEALING WITH THIS WHITE RING. I WAS THE ONLY MEMBER OF THE BACK-TO-LIFE CLUB THAT GOT SADDLED WITH ONE.
I'VE BEEN HOLDING ONTO IT...UNTIL IT FINDS THE CHOSEN ONE. THE ULTIMATE CHAMPION OF EARTH.
YOU.
ME?

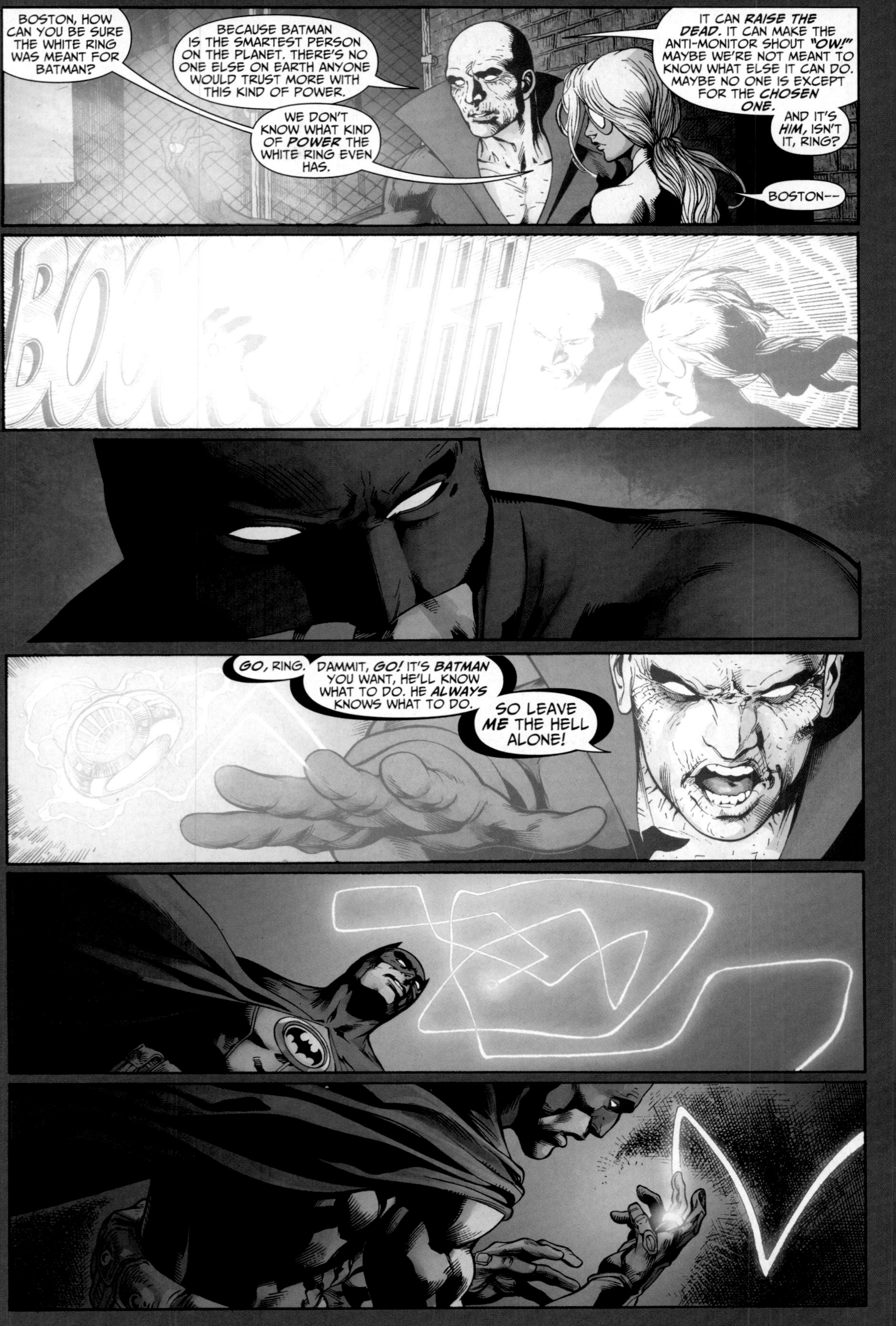
BOSTON, HOW CAN YOU BE SURE THE WHITE RING WAS MEANT FOR BATMAN?
BECAUSE BATMAN IS THE SMARTEST PERSON ON THE PLANET. THERE'S NO ONE ELSE ON EARTH ANYONE WOULD TRUST MORE WITH THIS KIND OF POWER.
WE DON'T KNOW WHAT KIND OF POWER THE WHITE RING EVEN HAS.
IT CAN RAISE THE DEAD. IT CAN MAKE THE ANTI-MONITOR SHOUT "OW!" MAYBE WE'RE NOT MEANT TO KNOW WHAT ELSE IT CAN DO. MAYBE NO ONE IS EXCEPT FOR THE CHOSEN ONE.
AND IT'S HIM, ISN'T IT, RING?
BOSTON--
GO, RING.
DAMMIT, GO! IT'S BATMAN YOU WANT, HE'LL KNOW WHAT TO DO. HE ALWAYS KNOWS WHAT TO DO.
SO LEAVE ME THE HELL ALONE!

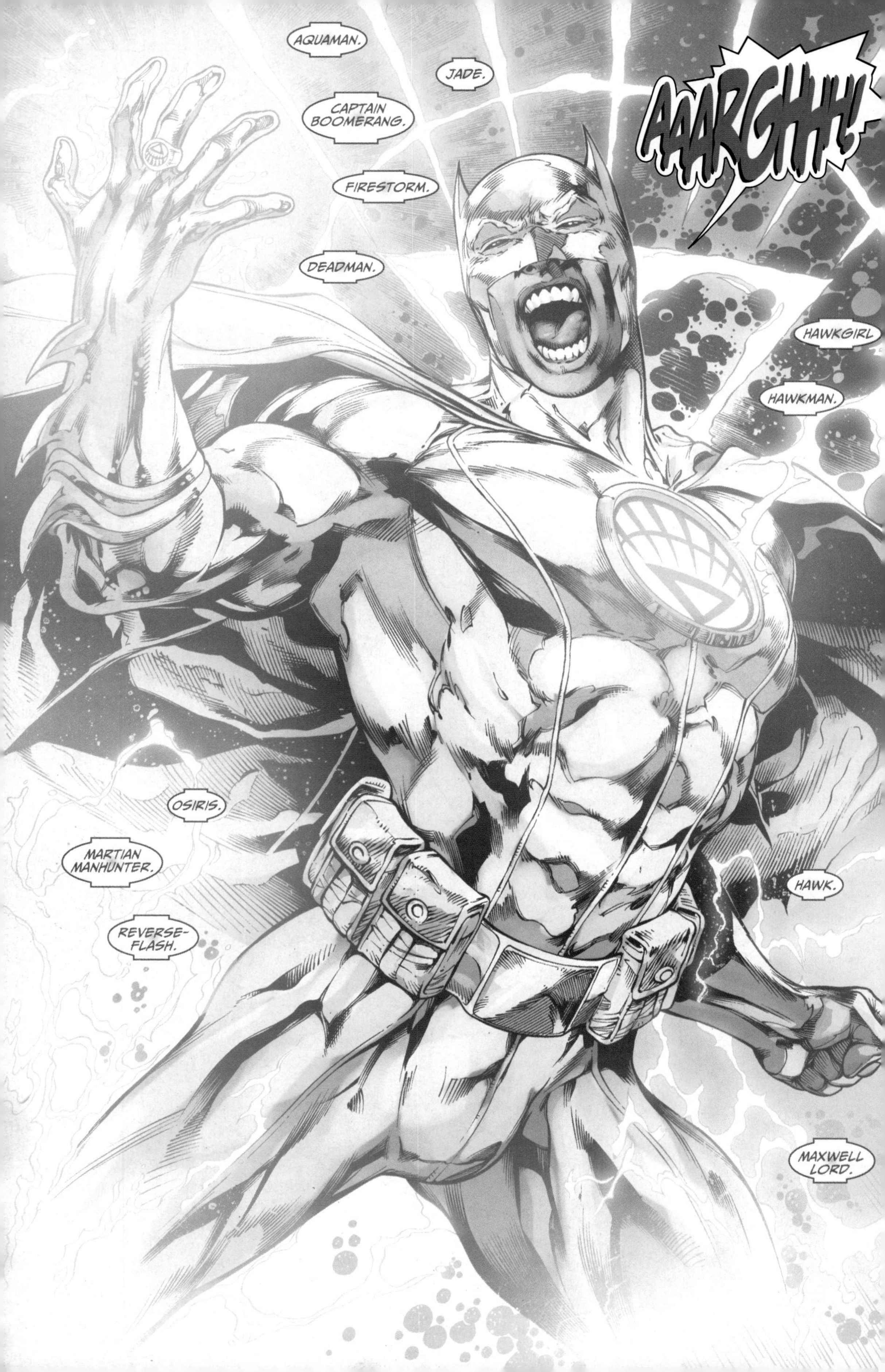
AQUAMAN.
JADE.
CAPTAIN BOOMERANG.
AAARGHHH!
FIRESTORM.
DEADMAN.
HAWKGIRL
HAWKMAN.
OSIRIS.
MARTIAN MANHUNTER.
HAWK.
REVERSE-FLASH.
MAXWELL LORD.

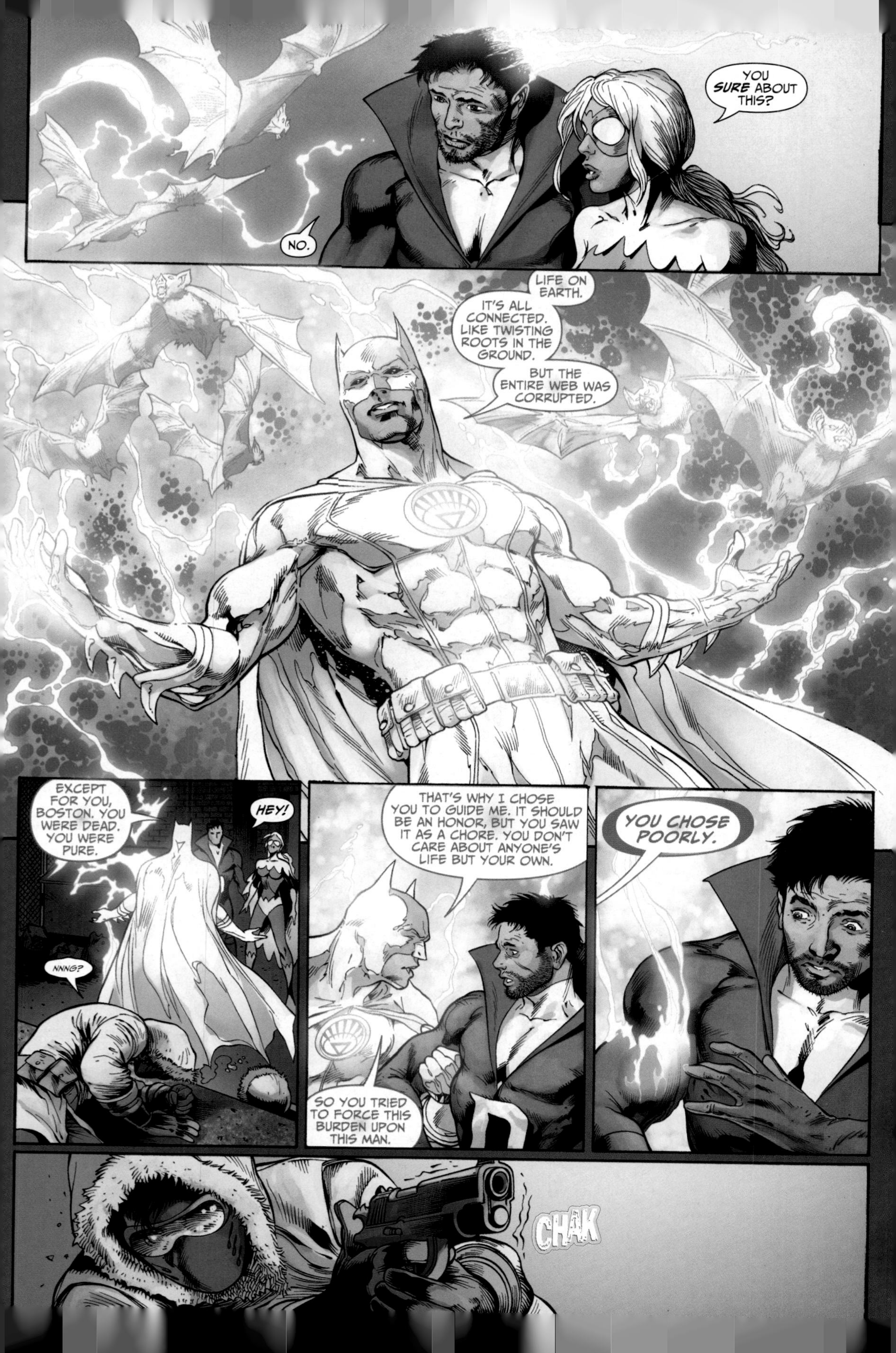

YOU SURE ABOUT THIS?
NO.
LIFE ON EARTH.
IT'S ALL CONNECTED. LIKE TWISTING ROOTS IN THE GROUND.
BUT THE ENTIRE WEB WAS CORRUPTED.
EXCEPT FOR YOU, BOSTON. YOU WERE DEAD. YOU WERE PURE.
HEY!
NNNG?
THAT'S WHY I CHOSE YOU TO GUIDE ME. IT SHOULD BE AN HONOR, BUT YOU SAW IT AS A CHORE. YOU DON'T CARE ABOUT ANYONE'S LIFE BUT YOUR OWN.
SO YOU TRIED TO FORCE THIS BURDEN UPON THIS MAN.
YOU CHOSE POORLY.
CHAK

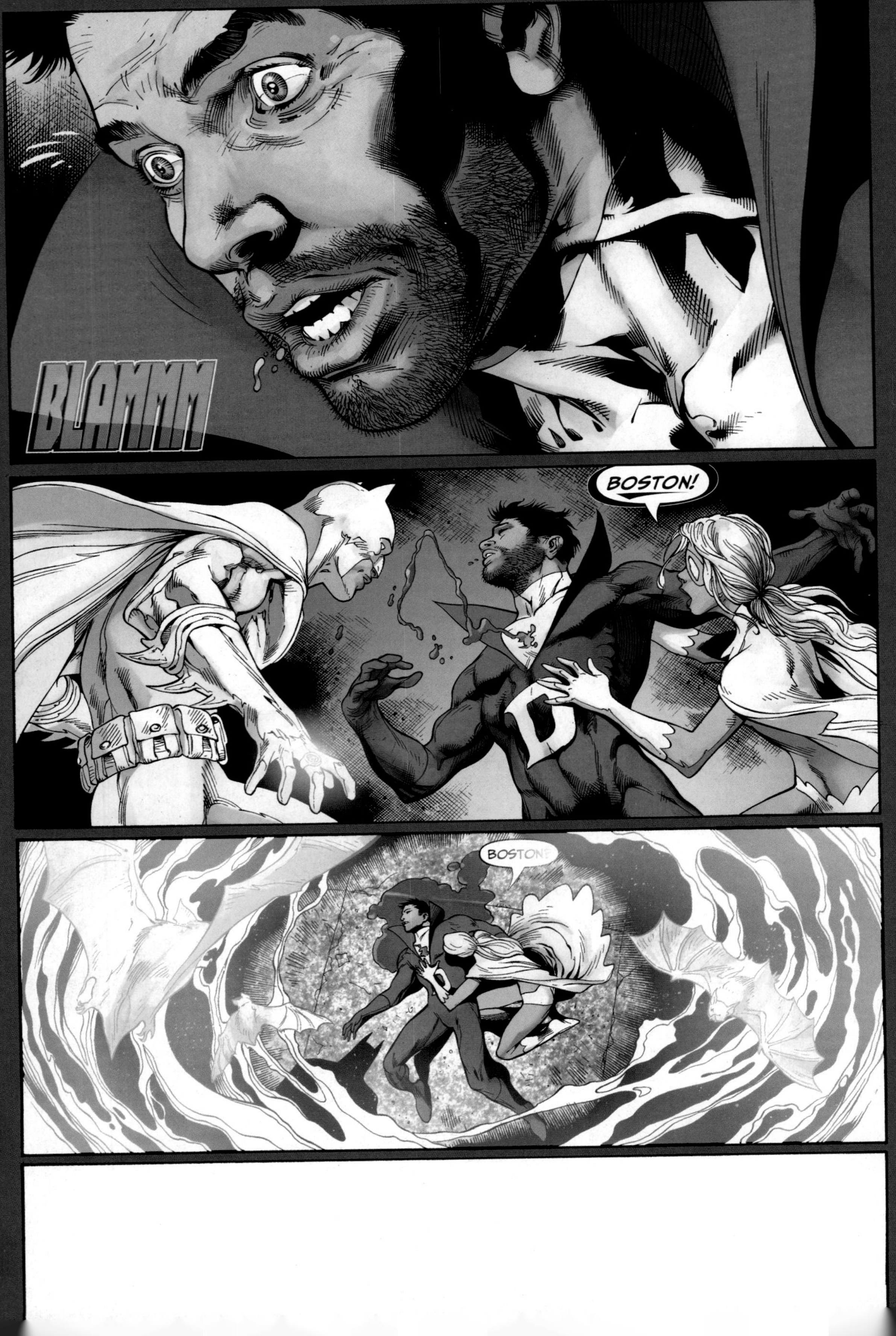
BLAMMM
BOSTON!
BOSTON?

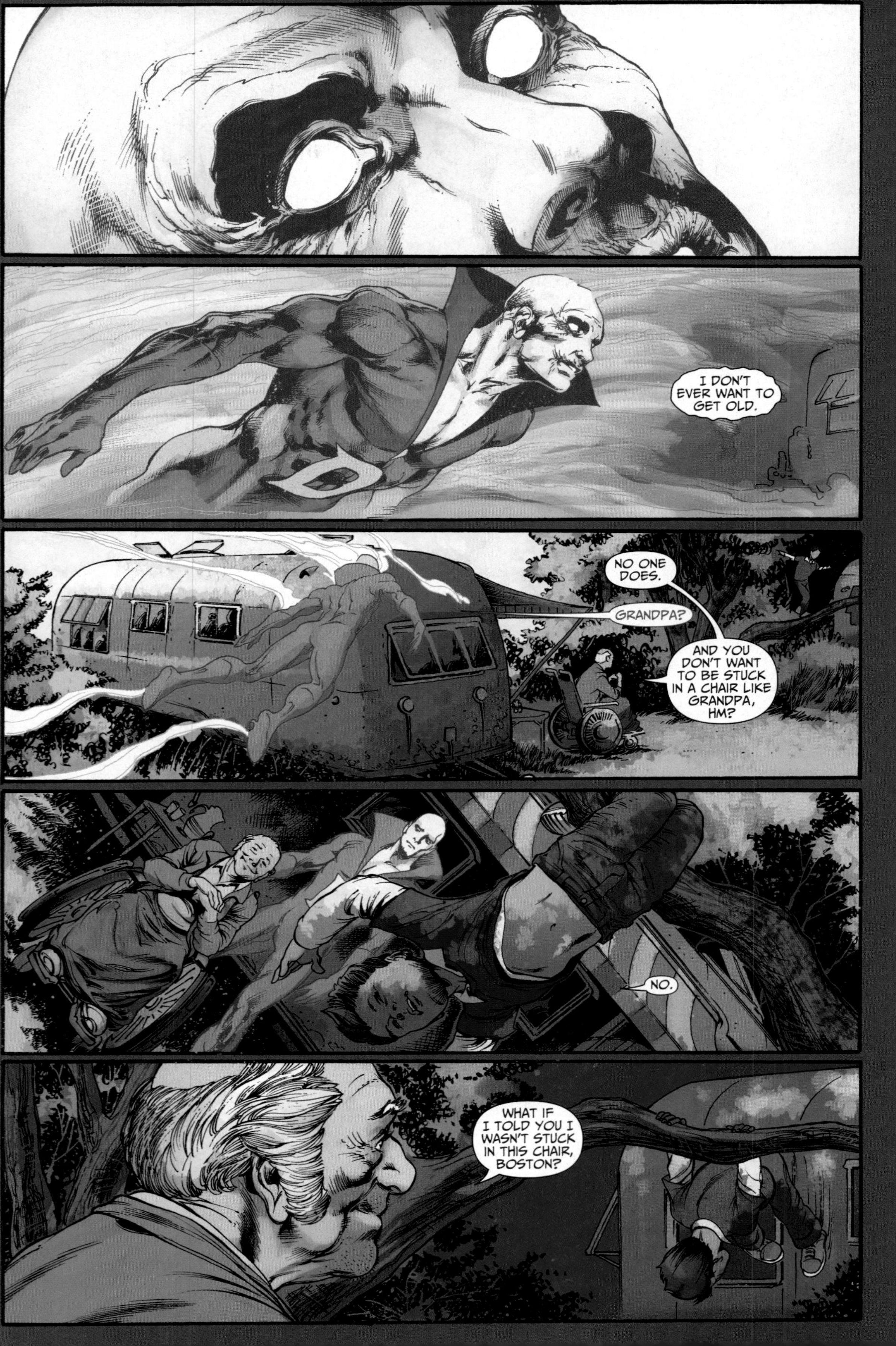
I DON'T EVER WANT TO GET OLD.
NO ONE DOES.
GRANDPA?
AND YOU DON'T WANT TO BE STUCK IN A CHAIR LIKE GRANDPA, HM?
NO.
WHAT IF I TOLD YOU I WASN'T STUCK IN THIS CHAIR, BOSTON?

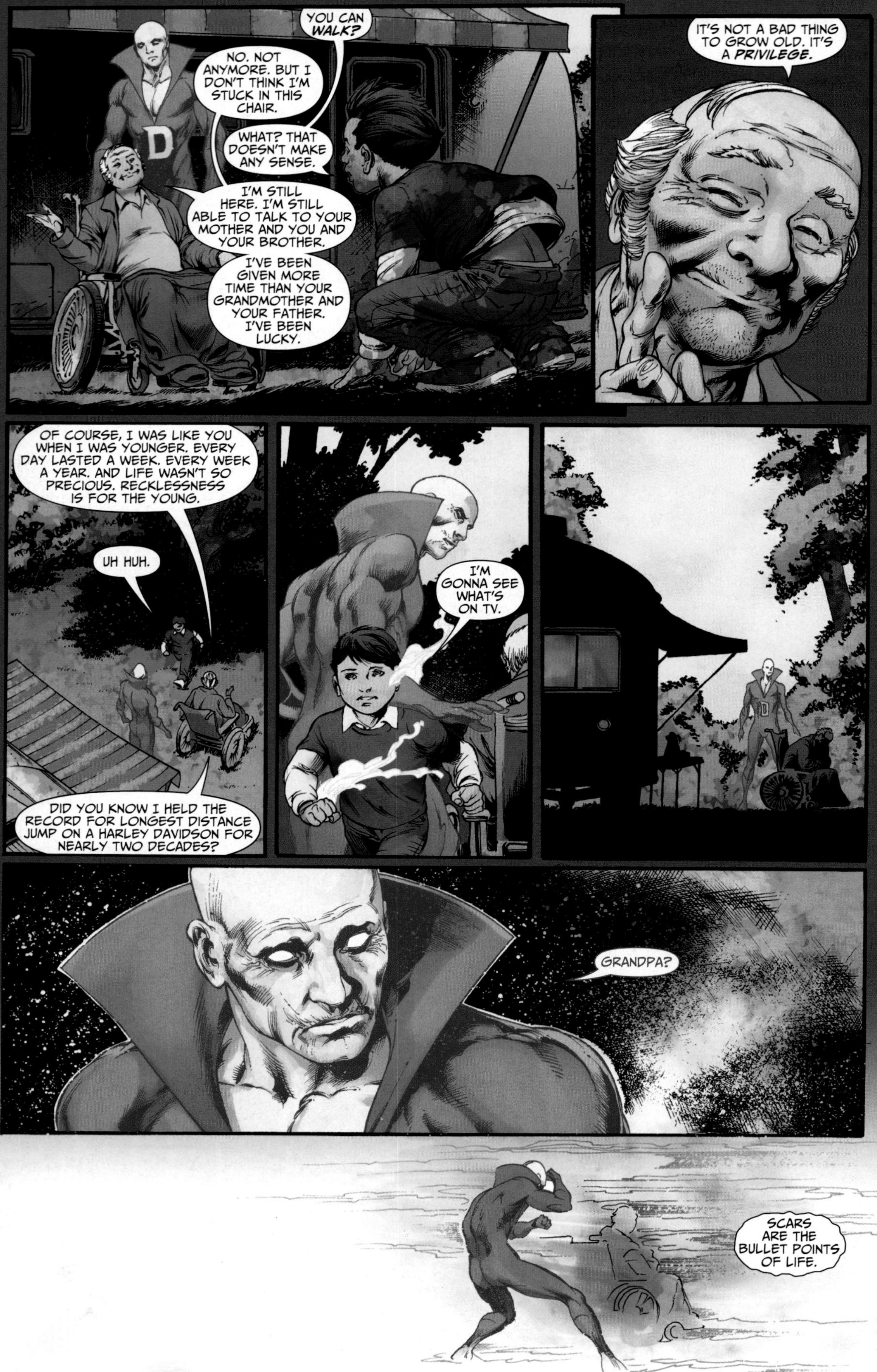
YOU CAN WALK?
NO. NOT ANYMORE. BUT I DON'T THINK I'M STUCK IN THIS CHAIR.
WHAT? THAT DOESN'T MAKE ANY SENSE.
I'M STILL HERE. I'M STILL ABLE TO TALK TO YOUR MOTHER AND YOU AND YOUR BROTHER.
I'VE BEEN GIVEN MORE TIME THAN YOUR GRANDMOTHER AND YOUR FATHER. I'VE BEEN LUCKY.
IT'S NOT A BAD THING TO GROW OLD. IT'S A PRIVILEGE.
OF COURSE, I WAS LIKE YOU WHEN I WAS YOUNGER. EVERY DAY LASTED A WEEK. EVERY WEEK A YEAR. AND LIFE WASN'T SO PRECIOUS. RECKLESSNESS IS FOR THE YOUNG.
UH HUH.
DID YOU KNOW I HELD THE RECORD FOR LONGEST DISTANCE JUMP ON A HARLEY DAVIDSON FOR NEARLY TWO DECADES?
I'M GONNA SEE WHAT'S ON TV.
GRANDPA?
SCARS ARE THE BULLET POINTS OF LIFE.

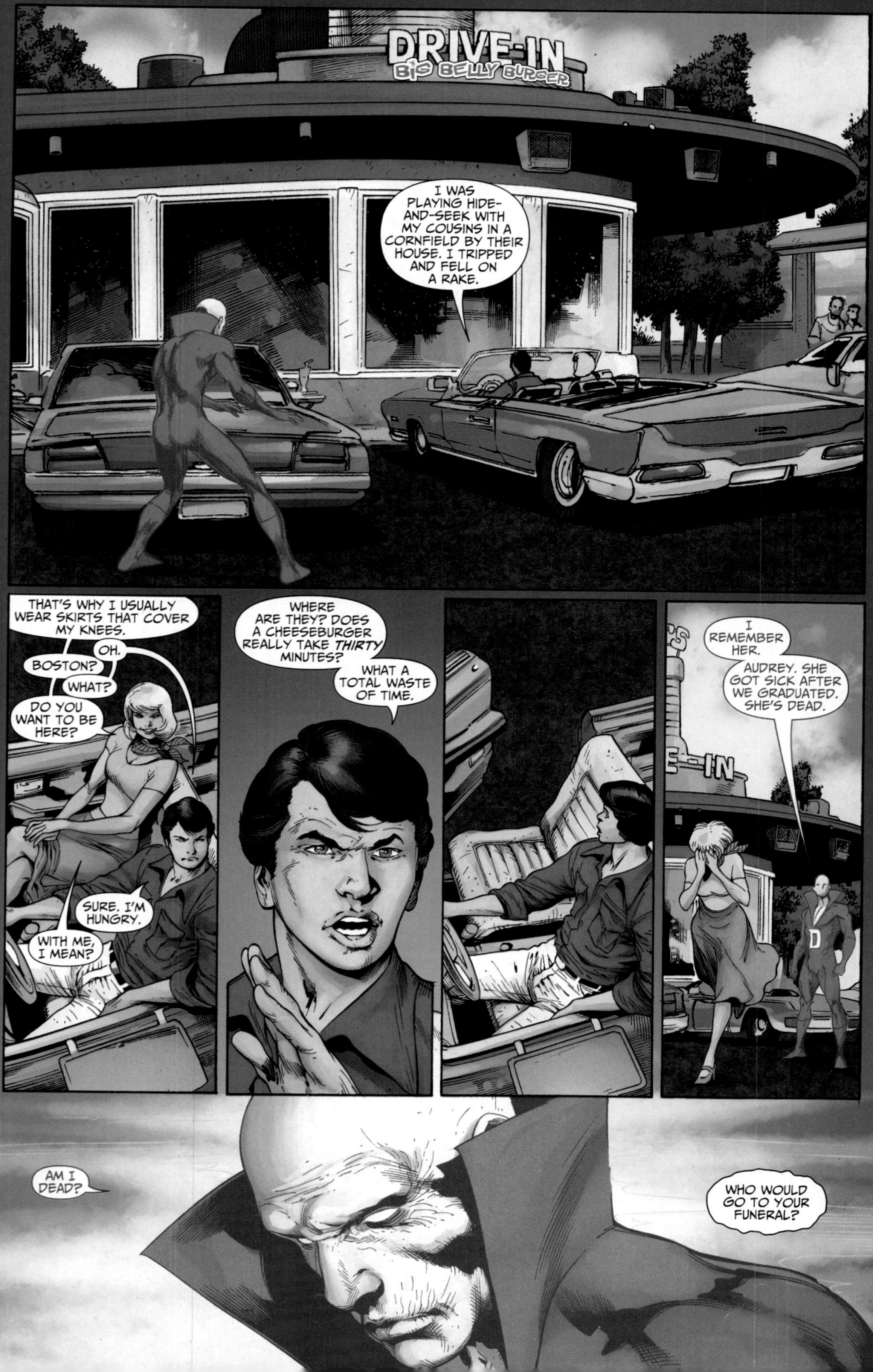
DRIVE-IN
BIG BELLY BURGER
I WAS PLAYING HIDE-AND-SEEK WITH MY COUSINS IN A CORNFIELD BY THEIR HOUSE. I TRIPPED AND FELL ON A RAKE.
THAT'S WHY I USUALLY WEAR SKIRTS THAT COVER MY KNEES.
OH.
BOSTON?
WHAT?
DO YOU WANT TO BE HERE?
SURE. I'M HUNGRY.
WITH ME, I MEAN?
WHERE ARE THEY? DOES A CHEESEBURGER REALLY TAKE *THIRTY* MINUTES?
WHAT A TOTAL WASTE OF TIME.
I REMEMBER HER.
AUDREY. SHE GOT SICK AFTER WE GRADUATED. SHE'S DEAD.
AM I DEAD?
WHO WOULD GO TO YOUR FUNERAL?

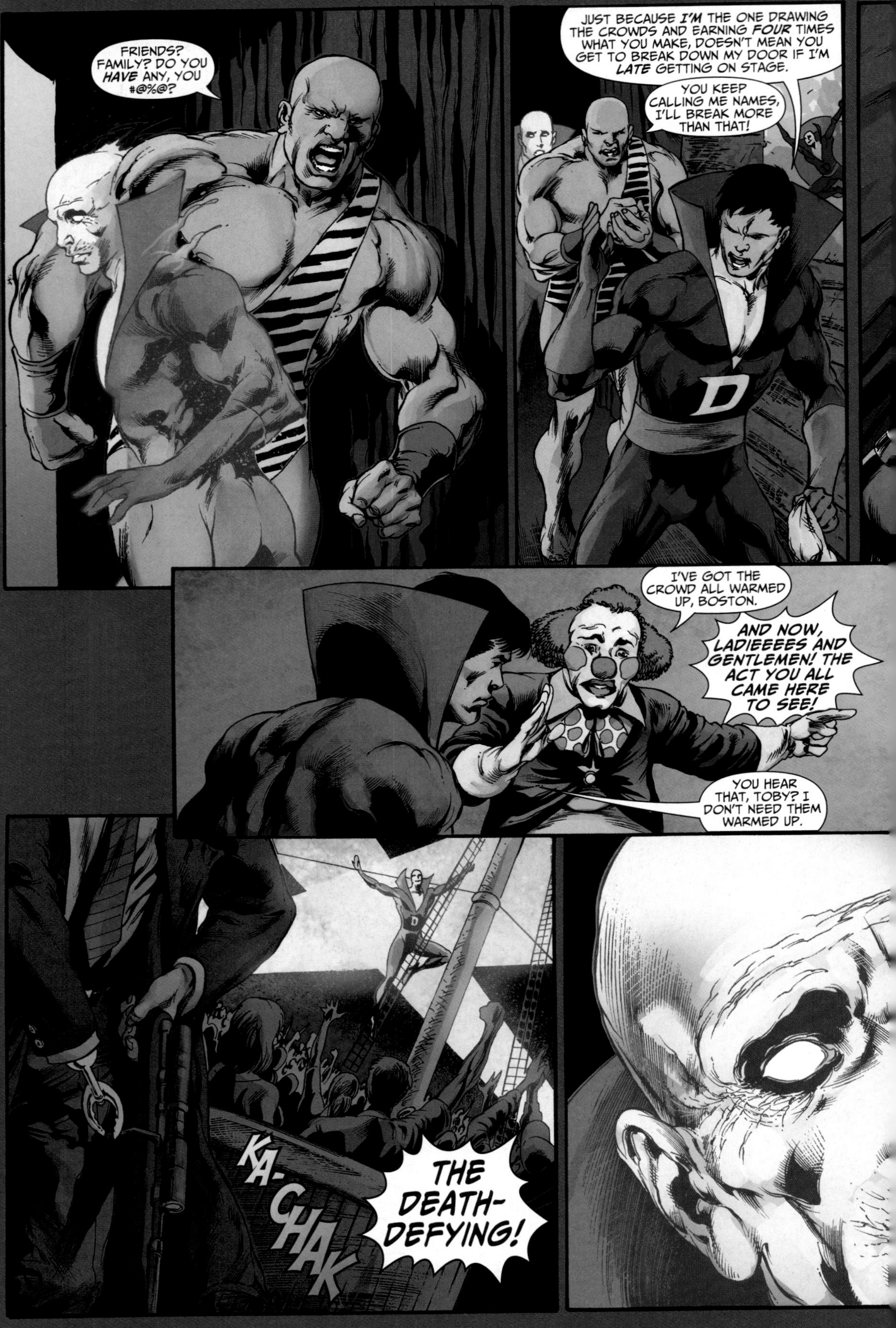
FRIENDS? FAMILY? DO YOU HAVE ANY, YOU #@%@?
JUST BECAUSE I'M THE ONE DRAWING THE CROWDS AND EARNING FOUR TIMES WHAT YOU MAKE, DOESN'T MEAN YOU GET TO BREAK DOWN MY DOOR IF I'M LATE GETTING ON STAGE.
YOU KEEP CALLING ME NAMES, I'LL BREAK MORE THAN THAT!
I'VE GOT THE CROWD ALL WARMED UP, BOSTON.
AND NOW, LADIEEEES AND GENTLEMEN! THE ACT YOU ALL CAME HERE TO SEE!
YOU HEAR THAT, TOBY? I DON'T NEED THEM WARMED UP.
KA-CHAK
THE DEATH-DEFYING!

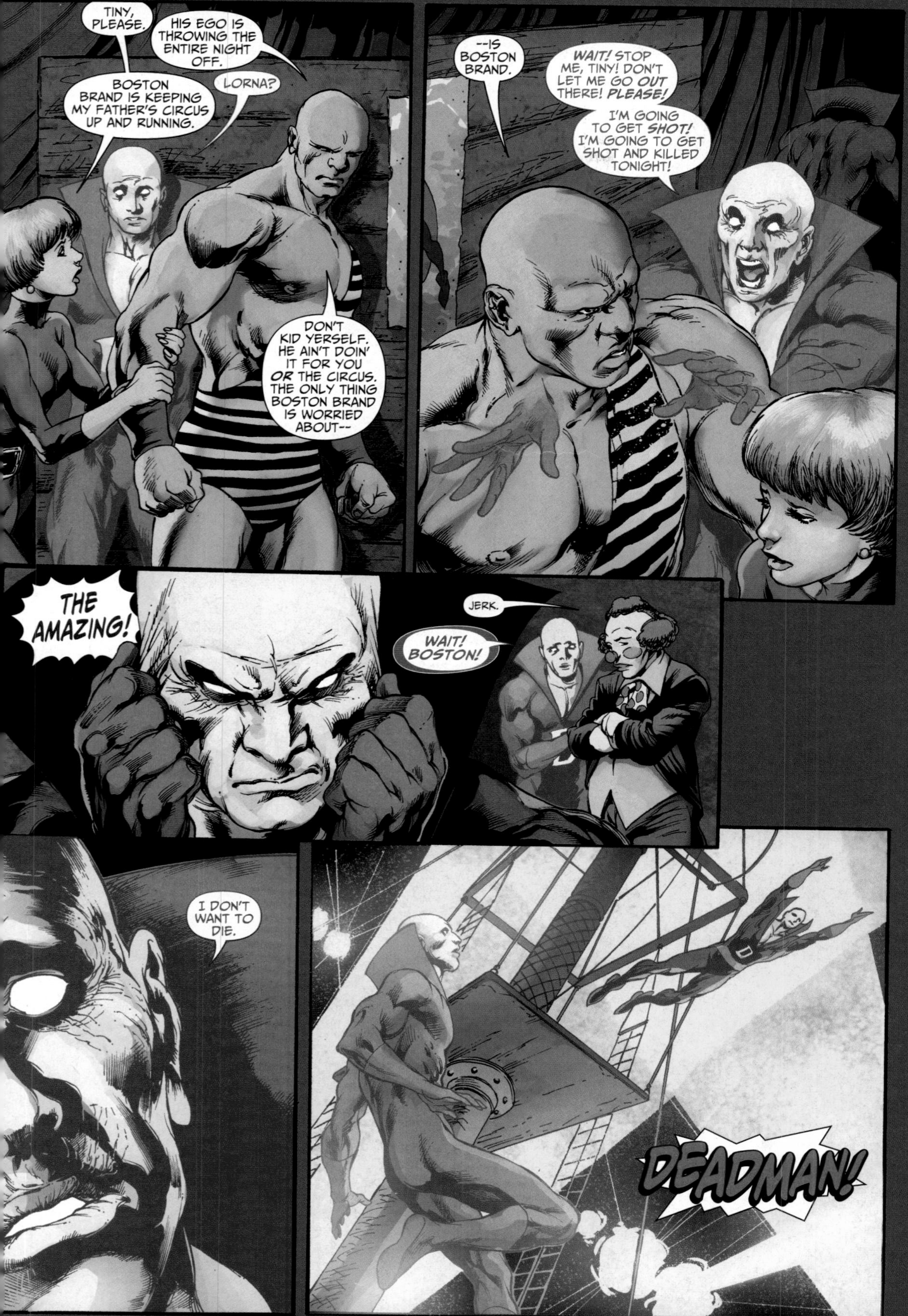
TINY, PLEASE.
HIS EGO IS THROWING THE ENTIRE NIGHT OFF.
BOSTON BRAND IS KEEPING MY FATHER'S CIRCUS UP AND RUNNING.
LORNA?
DON'T KID YERSELF. HE AIN'T DOIN' IT FOR YOU OR THE CIRCUS. THE ONLY THING BOSTON BRAND IS WORRIED ABOUT--
--IS BOSTON BRAND.
WAIT! STOP ME, TINY! DON'T LET ME GO OUT THERE! PLEASE!
I'M GOING TO GET SHOT! I'M GOING TO GET SHOT AND KILLED TONIGHT!
THE AMAZING!
JERK.
WAIT! BOSTON!
I DON'T WANT TO DIE.
DEADMAN!

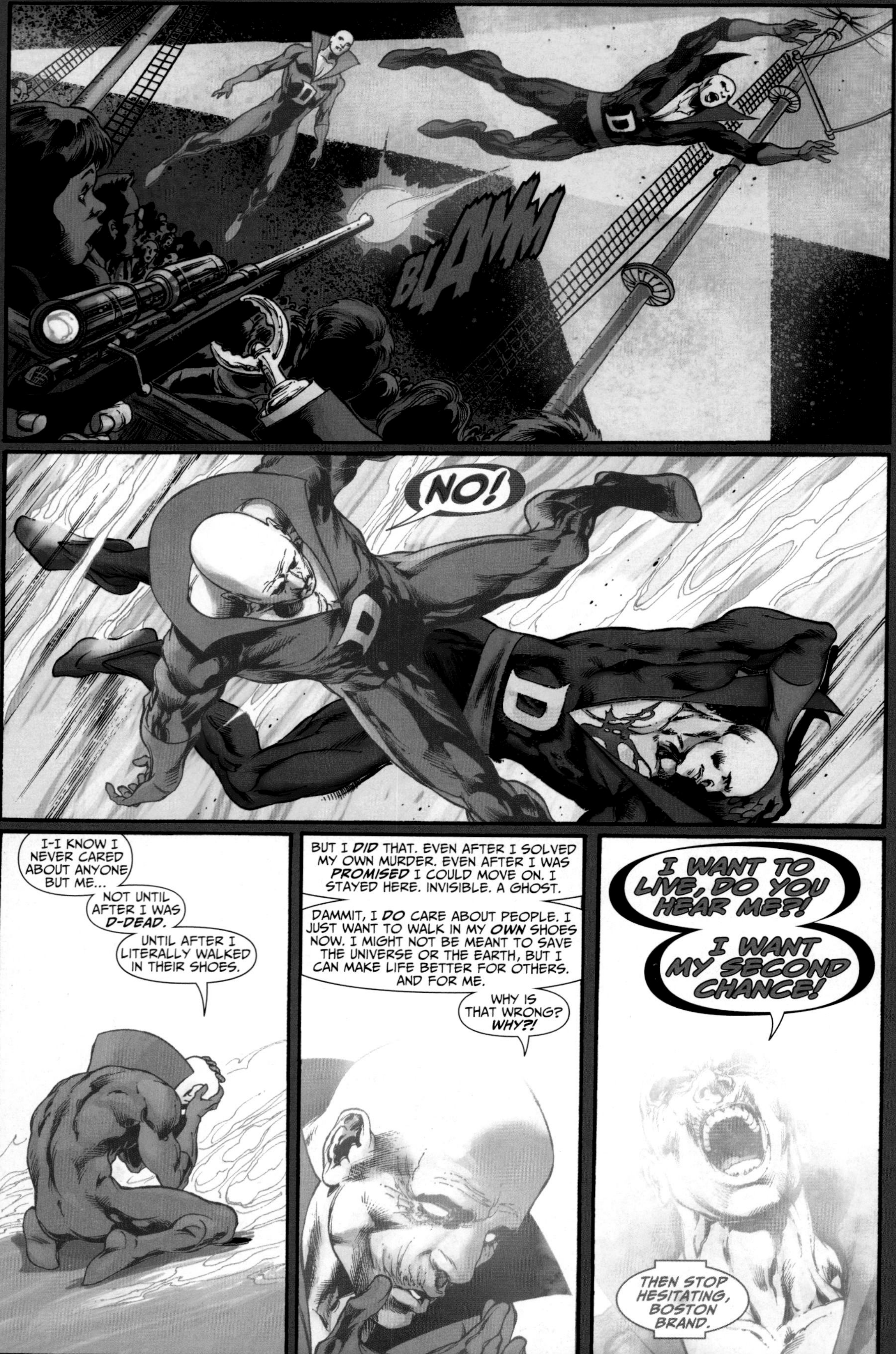
BLAMM
NO!
I-I KNOW I NEVER CARED ABOUT ANYONE BUT ME...
NOT UNTIL AFTER I WAS *D-DEAD.*
UNTIL AFTER I LITERALLY WALKED IN THEIR SHOES.
BUT I *DID* THAT. EVEN AFTER I SOLVED MY OWN MURDER. EVEN AFTER I WAS *PROMISED* I COULD MOVE ON. I STAYED HERE. INVISIBLE. A GHOST.
DAMMIT, I *DO* CARE ABOUT PEOPLE. I JUST WANT TO WALK IN MY *OWN* SHOES NOW. I MIGHT NOT BE MEANT TO SAVE THE UNIVERSE OR THE EARTH, BUT I CAN MAKE LIFE BETTER FOR OTHERS. AND FOR ME.
WHY IS THAT WRONG? *WHY?!*
I WANT TO LIVE, DO YOU HEAR ME?!
I WANT MY SECOND CHANCE!
THEN STOP HESITATING, BOSTON BRAND.

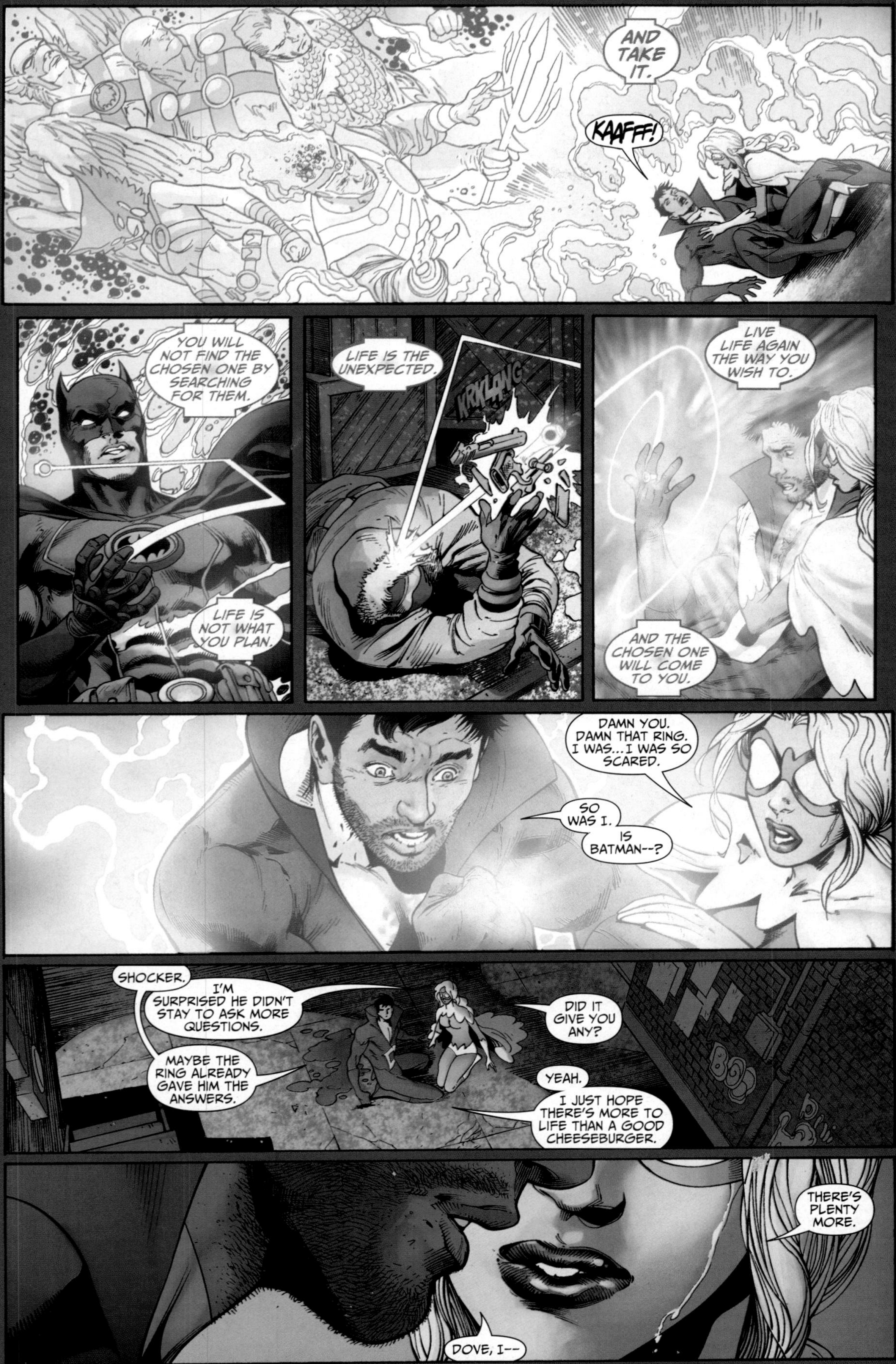
AND TAKE IT.
KAAFFF!
YOU WILL NOT FIND THE CHOSEN ONE BY SEARCHING FOR THEM.
LIFE IS NOT WHAT YOU PLAN.
LIFE IS THE UNEXPECTED.
KRKLANG
LIVE LIFE AGAIN THE WAY YOU WISH TO.
AND THE CHOSEN ONE WILL COME TO YOU.
DAMN YOU. DAMN THAT RING. I WAS...I WAS SO SCARED.
SO WAS I.
IS BATMAN--?
SHOCKER.
I'M SURPRISED HE DIDN'T STAY TO ASK MORE QUESTIONS.
MAYBE THE RING ALREADY GAVE HIM THE ANSWERS.
DID IT GIVE YOU ANY?
YEAH.
I JUST HOPE THERE'S MORE TO LIFE THAN A GOOD CHEESEBURGER.
THERE'S PLENTY MORE.
DOVE, I--

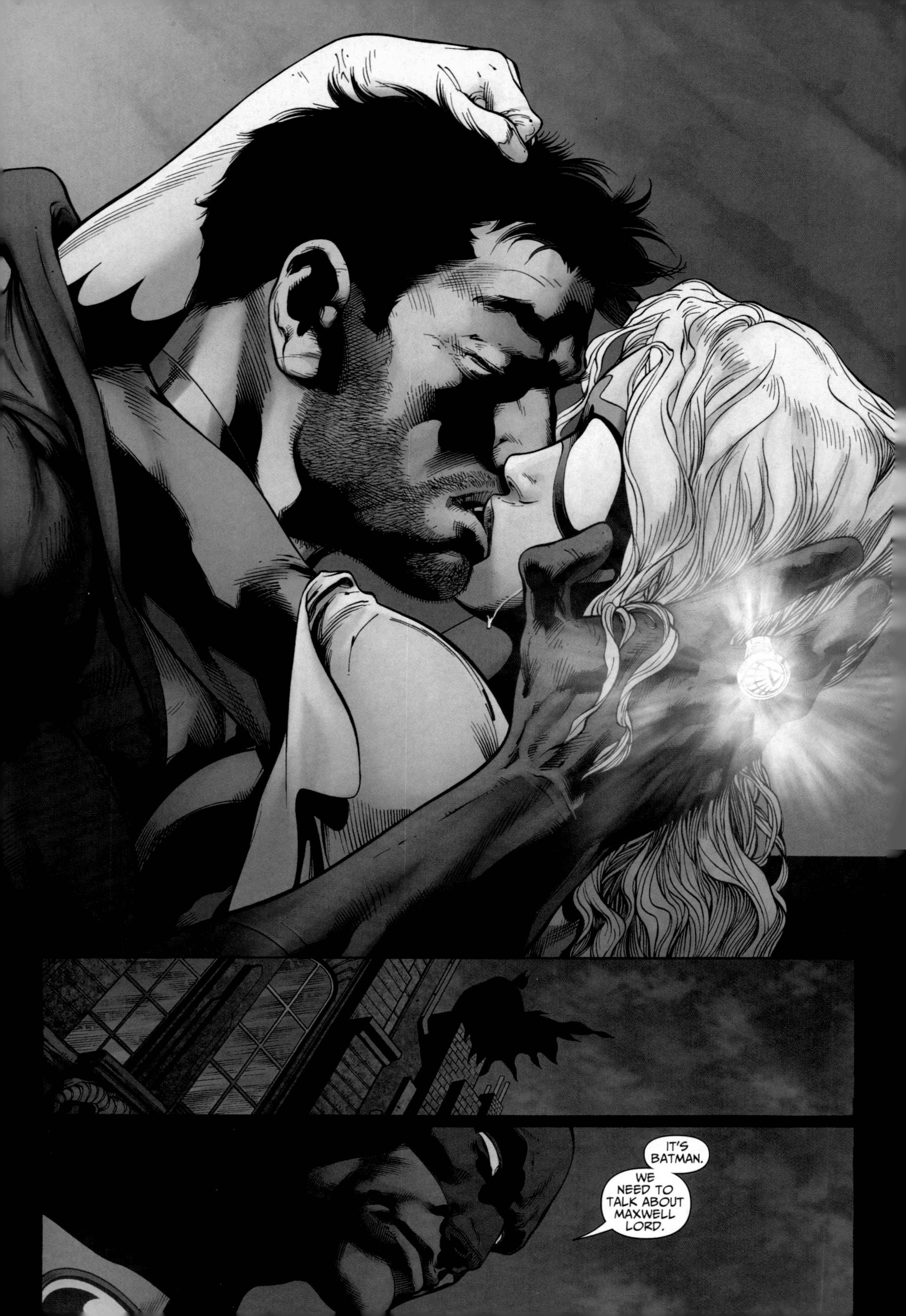
IT'S BATMAN.
WE NEED TO TALK ABOUT MAXWELL LORD.

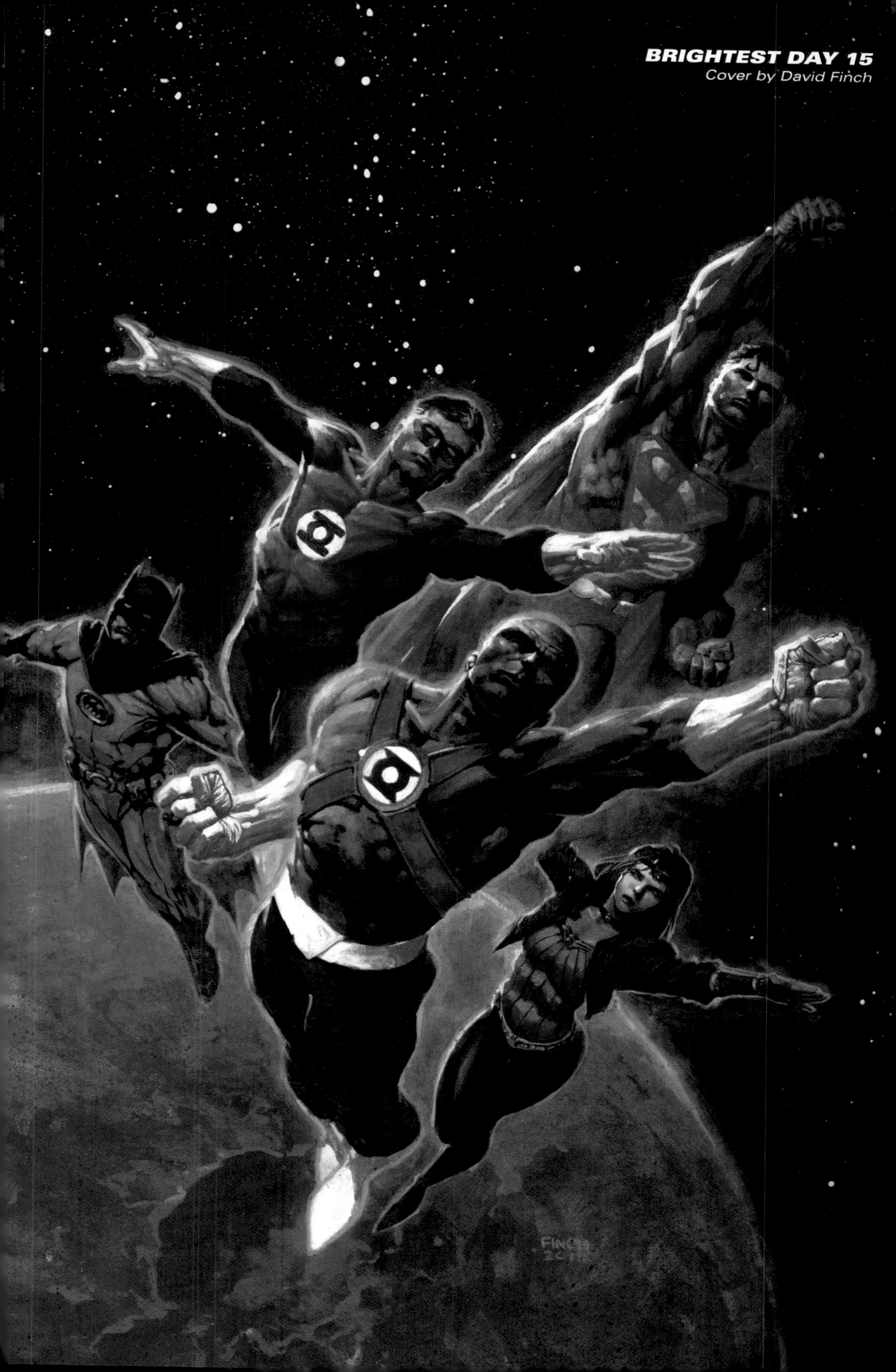
FINCH

**BRIGHTEST DAY 15**
*Cover by David Finch*

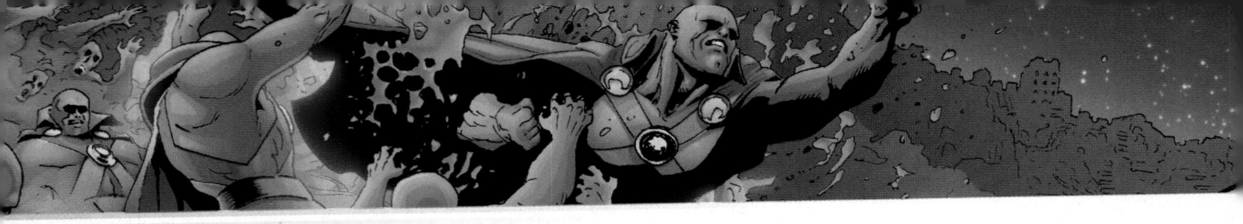

# WHATEVER HAPPENED TO THE MANHUNTER FROM MARS?

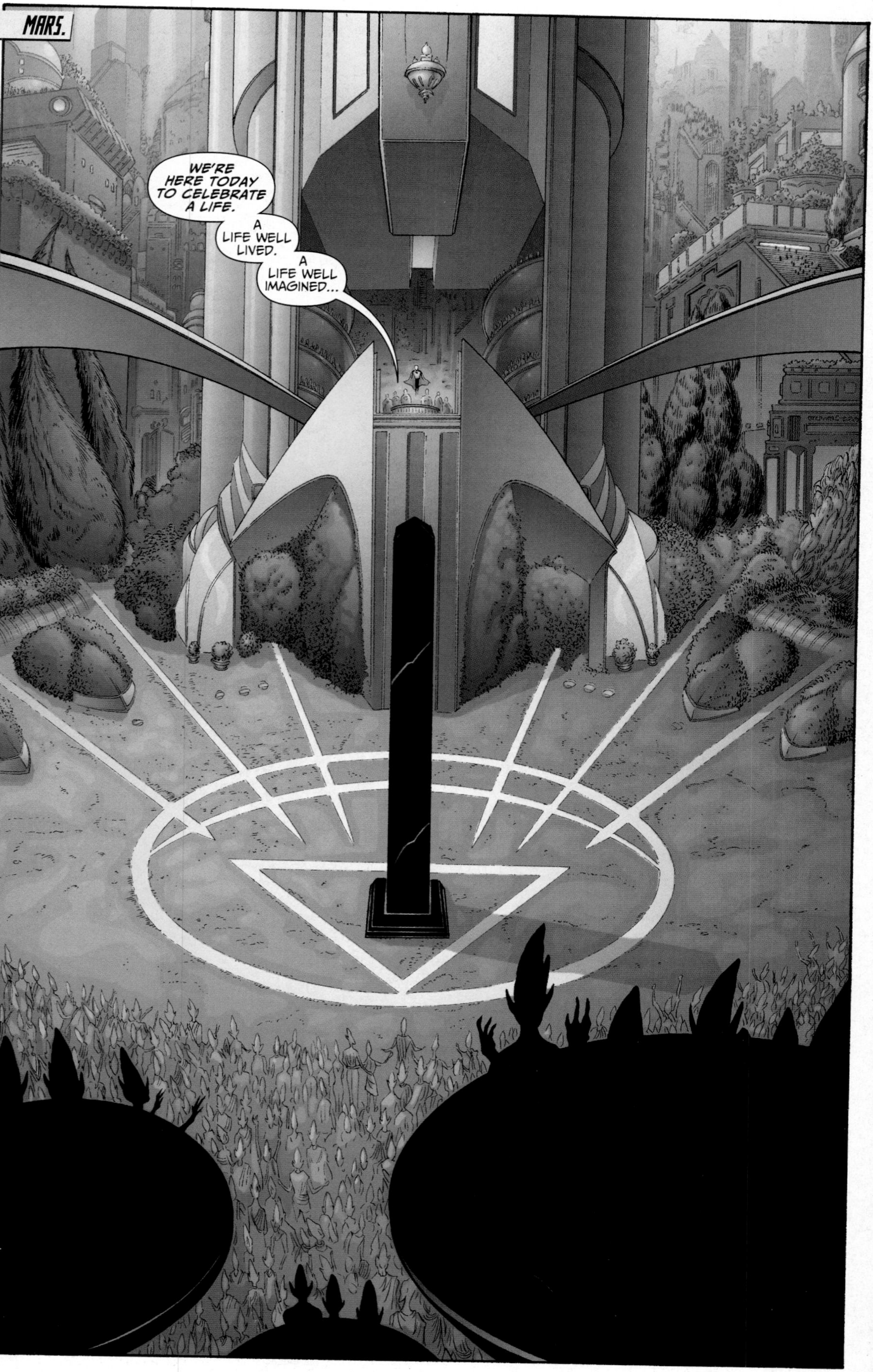
MARS.
WE'RE HERE TODAY TO CELEBRATE A LIFE.
A LIFE WELL LIVED.
A LIFE WELL IMAGINED...

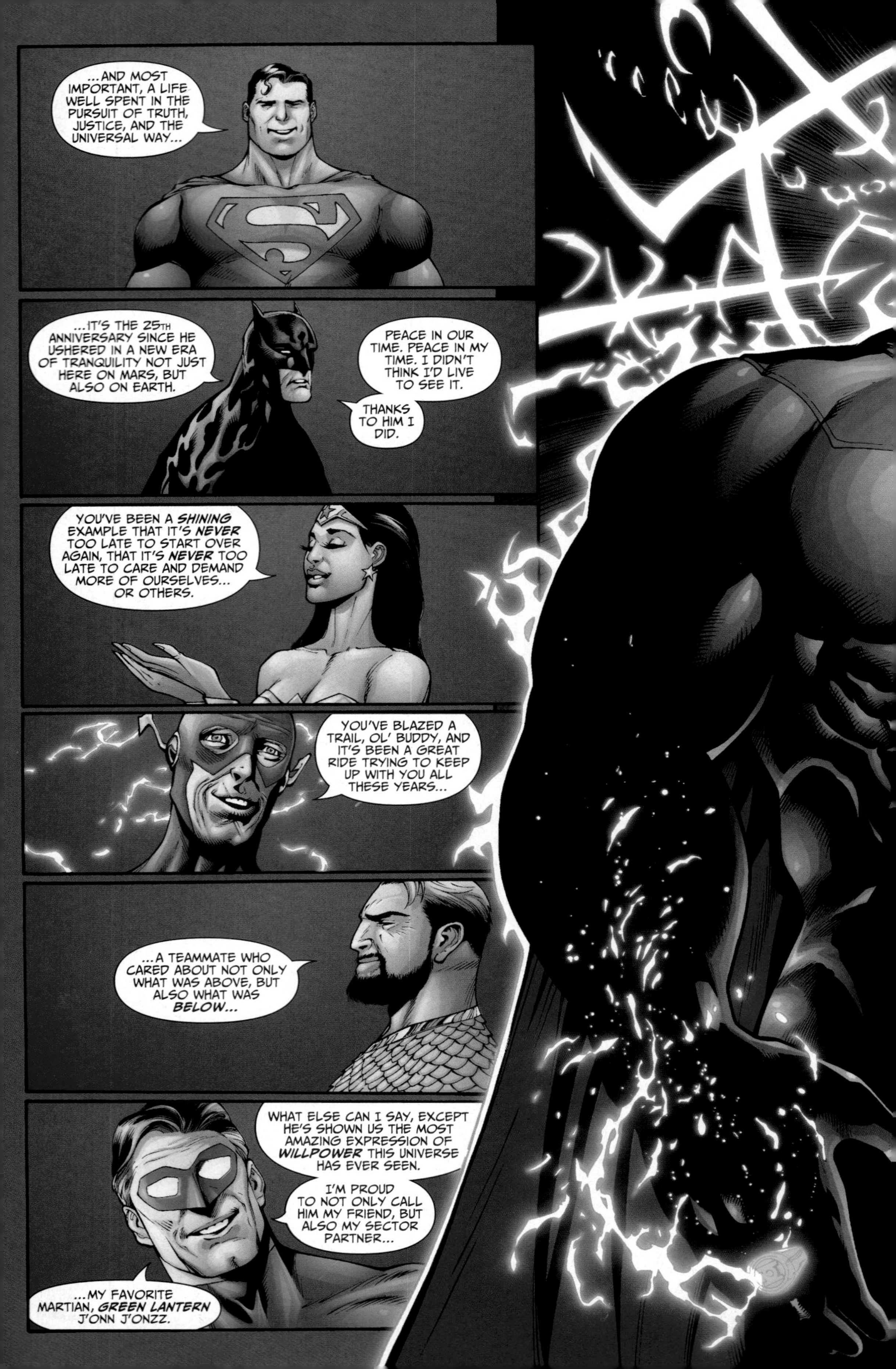
...AND MOST IMPORTANT, A LIFE WELL SPENT IN THE PURSUIT OF TRUTH, JUSTICE, AND THE UNIVERSAL WAY...
...IT'S THE 25TH ANNIVERSARY SINCE HE USHERED IN A NEW ERA OF TRANQUILITY NOT JUST HERE ON MARS, BUT ALSO ON EARTH.
PEACE IN OUR TIME. PEACE IN MY TIME. I DIDN'T THINK I'D LIVE TO SEE IT.
THANKS TO HIM I DID.
YOU'VE BEEN A SHINING EXAMPLE THAT IT'S NEVER TOO LATE TO START OVER AGAIN, THAT IT'S NEVER TOO LATE TO CARE AND DEMAND MORE OF OURSELVES... OR OTHERS.
YOU'VE BLAZED A TRAIL, OL' BUDDY, AND IT'S BEEN A GREAT RIDE TRYING TO KEEP UP WITH YOU ALL THESE YEARS...
...A TEAMMATE WHO CARED ABOUT NOT ONLY WHAT WAS ABOVE, BUT ALSO WHAT WAS BELOW...
WHAT ELSE CAN I SAY, EXCEPT HE'S SHOWN US THE MOST AMAZING EXPRESSION OF WILLPOWER THIS UNIVERSE HAS EVER SEEN.
I'M PROUD TO NOT ONLY CALL HIM MY FRIEND, BUT ALSO MY SECTOR PARTNER...
...MY FAVORITE MARTIAN, GREEN LANTERN J'ONN J'ONZZ.

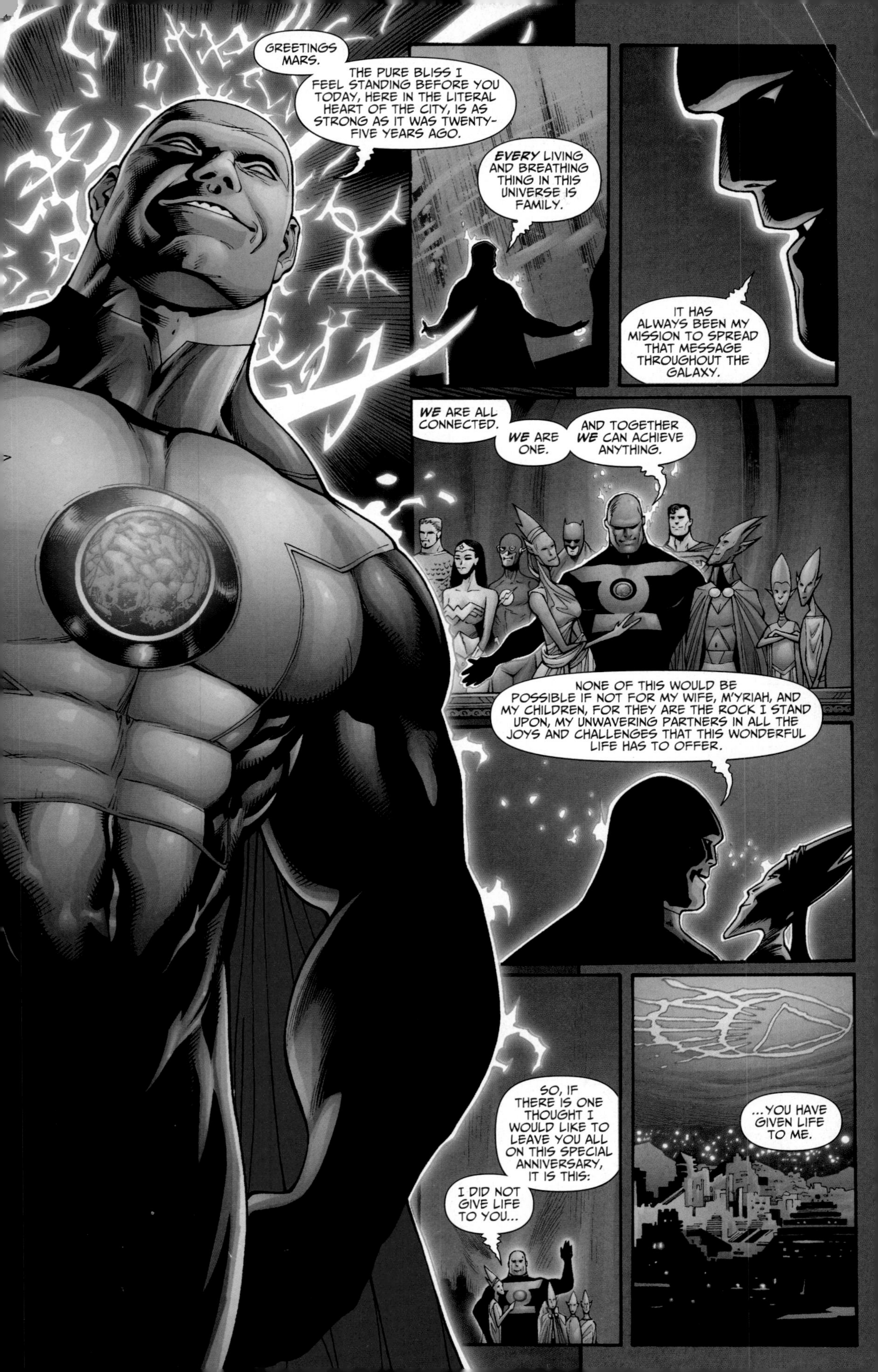
GREETINGS MARS.
THE PURE BLISS I FEEL STANDING BEFORE YOU TODAY, HERE IN THE LITERAL HEART OF THE CITY, IS AS STRONG AS IT WAS TWENTY-FIVE YEARS AGO.
EVERY LIVING AND BREATHING THING IN THIS UNIVERSE IS FAMILY.
IT HAS ALWAYS BEEN MY MISSION TO SPREAD THAT MESSAGE THROUGHOUT THE GALAXY.
WE ARE ALL CONNECTED.
WE ARE ONE.
AND TOGETHER WE CAN ACHIEVE ANYTHING.
NONE OF THIS WOULD BE POSSIBLE IF NOT FOR MY WIFE, M'YRIAH, AND MY CHILDREN, FOR THEY ARE THE ROCK I STAND UPON, MY UNWAVERING PARTNERS IN ALL THE JOYS AND CHALLENGES THAT THIS WONDERFUL LIFE HAS TO OFFER.
SO, IF THERE IS ONE THOUGHT I WOULD LIKE TO LEAVE YOU ALL ON THIS SPECIAL ANNIVERSARY, IT IS THIS:
I DID NOT GIVE LIFE TO YOU...
...YOU HAVE GIVEN LIFE TO ME.

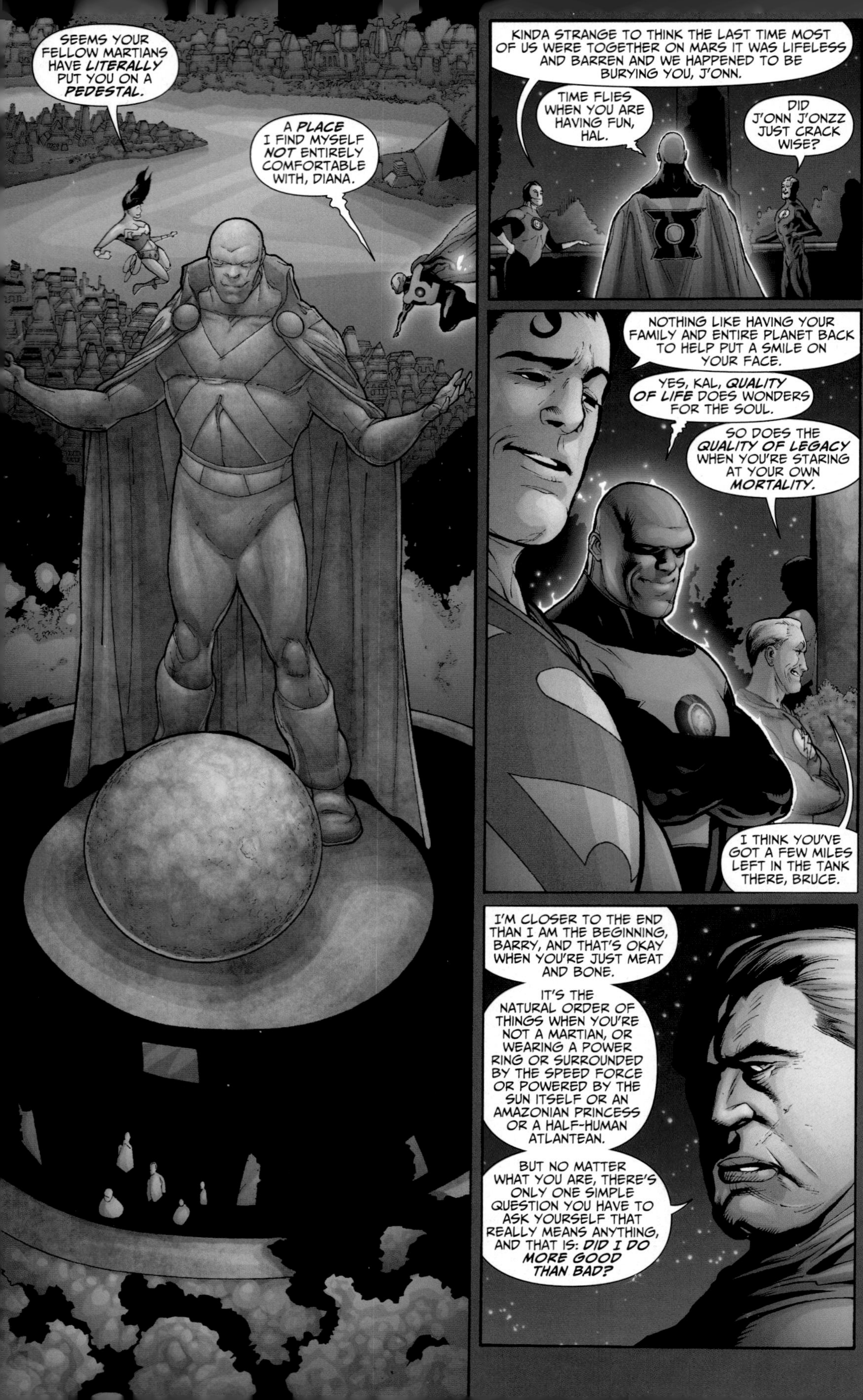
SEEMS YOUR FELLOW MARTIANS HAVE LITERALLY PUT YOU ON A PEDESTAL.
A PLACE I FIND MYSELF NOT ENTIRELY COMFORTABLE WITH, DIANA.
KINDA STRANGE TO THINK THE LAST TIME MOST OF US WERE TOGETHER ON MARS IT WAS LIFELESS AND BARREN AND WE HAPPENED TO BE BURYING YOU, J'ONN.
TIME FLIES WHEN YOU ARE HAVING FUN, HAL.
DID J'ONN J'ONZZ JUST CRACK WISE?
NOTHING LIKE HAVING YOUR FAMILY AND ENTIRE PLANET BACK TO HELP PUT A SMILE ON YOUR FACE.
YES, KAL, QUALITY OF LIFE DOES WONDERS FOR THE SOUL.
SO DOES THE QUALITY OF LEGACY WHEN YOU'RE STARING AT YOUR OWN MORTALITY.
I THINK YOU'VE GOT A FEW MILES LEFT IN THE TANK THERE, BRUCE.
I'M CLOSER TO THE END THAN I AM THE BEGINNING, BARRY, AND THAT'S OKAY WHEN YOU'RE JUST MEAT AND BONE.
IT'S THE NATURAL ORDER OF THINGS WHEN YOU'RE NOT A MARTIAN, OR WEARING A POWER RING OR SURROUNDED BY THE SPEED FORCE OR POWERED BY THE SUN ITSELF OR AN AMAZONIAN PRINCESS OR A HALF-HUMAN ATLANTEAN.
BUT NO MATTER WHAT YOU ARE, THERE'S ONLY ONE SIMPLE QUESTION YOU HAVE TO ASK YOURSELF THAT REALLY MEANS ANYTHING, AND THAT IS: DID I DO MORE GOOD THAN BAD?

AND WHAT WAS *YOUR* ANSWER?

OUR *SCALES* OF JUSTICE ARE PERSONAL, ARTHUR--WE'VE ALL DONE THINGS THAT'VE HAUNTED US--WE ALL BEAR THE WEIGHT OF THOSE CHOICES DIFFERENTLY.

BUT RIGHT HERE, RIGHT NOW, BETWEEN FRIENDS, BRUCE, WHAT ANSWER COMES TO YOU IN YOUR PRIVATE MOMENTS?

*YOU* CAN READ MY MIND AND FIND OUT FOR YOURSELF.

I WOULD PREFER YOU *SHARE* IT WITH US.

MY ANSWER'S AS SIMPLE AS MY QUESTION: I *HOPE* SO.

THAT'S ALL YOU GOT, "I HOPE SO"?

*HOPE* IS ALL YOU EVER HAVE IN THE END, ISN'T THAT RIGHT, J'ONN?

YES, BUT NEVER *UNDERESTIMATE* THE POWER OF WILL.

OUR COMBINATION OF WILL *AND* HOPE IS WHAT'LL CONTINUE TO MAKE PEOPLE'S LIVES BETTER THROUGH THE YEARS.

IT'S WHAT LETS ME GO TO SLEEP JUSTIFIED.

COME ON, KAL, WE ALL KNOW YOU *DON'T* SLEEP.

I SLEEP WITH MY EYES OPEN. I JUST GRABBED A POWER NAP WHILE YOU WERE ALL TALKING.

THIS MARTIAN AIR'S BRINGING OUT THE COMEDIAN IN EVERYBODY. I THINK HAL SHOULD BOTTLE SOME OF IT AND TAKE IT BACK TO THE JLA HQ.

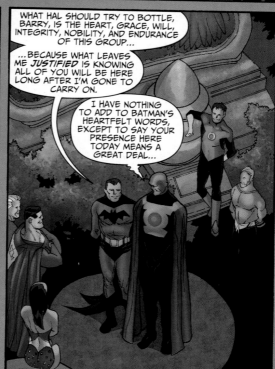

WHAT HAL SHOULD TRY TO BOTTLE, BARRY, IS THE HEART, GRACE, WILL, INTEGRITY, NOBILITY, AND ENDURANCE OF THIS GROUP...

...BECAUSE WHAT LEAVES ME *JUSTIFIED* IS KNOWING ALL OF YOU WILL BE HERE LONG AFTER I'M GONE TO CARRY ON.

I HAVE NOTHING TO ADD TO BATMAN'S HEARTFELT WORDS, EXCEPT TO SAY YOUR PRESENCE HERE TODAY MEANS A GREAT DEAL...

...IT'S BEEN *MY* HONOR AND PRIVILEGE...

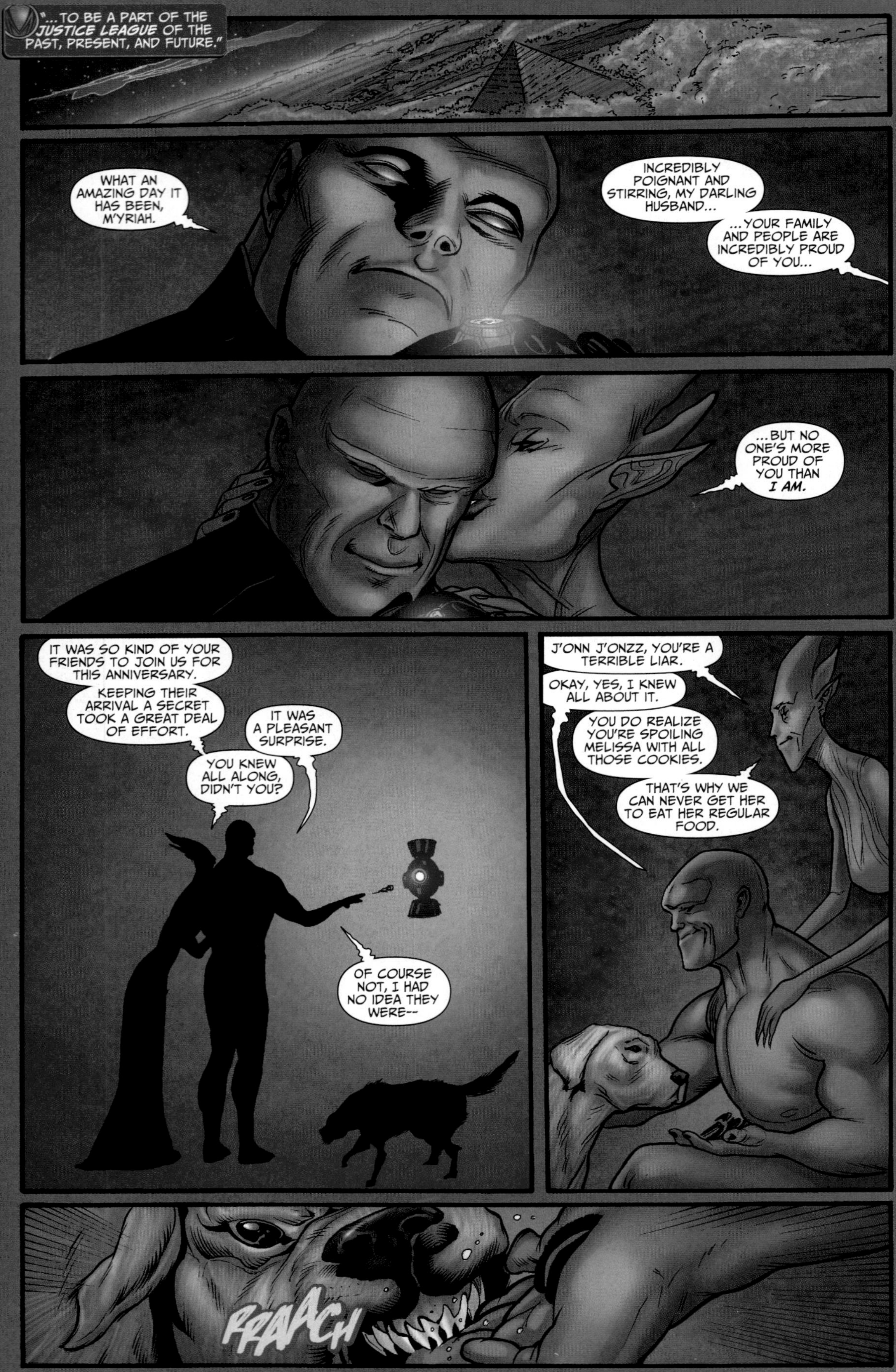
"...TO BE A PART OF THE JUSTICE LEAGUE OF THE PAST, PRESENT, AND FUTURE."
WHAT AN AMAZING DAY IT HAS BEEN, M'YRIAH.
INCREDIBLY POIGNANT AND STIRRING, MY DARLING HUSBAND...
...YOUR FAMILY AND PEOPLE ARE INCREDIBLY PROUD OF YOU...
...BUT NO ONE'S MORE PROUD OF YOU THAN I AM.
IT WAS SO KIND OF YOUR FRIENDS TO JOIN US FOR THIS ANNIVERSARY.
KEEPING THEIR ARRIVAL A SECRET TOOK A GREAT DEAL OF EFFORT.
IT WAS A PLEASANT SURPRISE.
YOU KNEW ALL ALONG, DIDN'T YOU?
OF COURSE NOT, I HAD NO IDEA THEY WERE--
J'ONN J'ONZZ, YOU'RE A TERRIBLE LIAR.
OKAY, YES, I KNEW ALL ABOUT IT.
YOU DO REALIZE YOU'RE SPOILING MELISSA WITH ALL THOSE COOKIES.
THAT'S WHY WE CAN NEVER GET HER TO EAT HER REGULAR FOOD.
RRAAACH

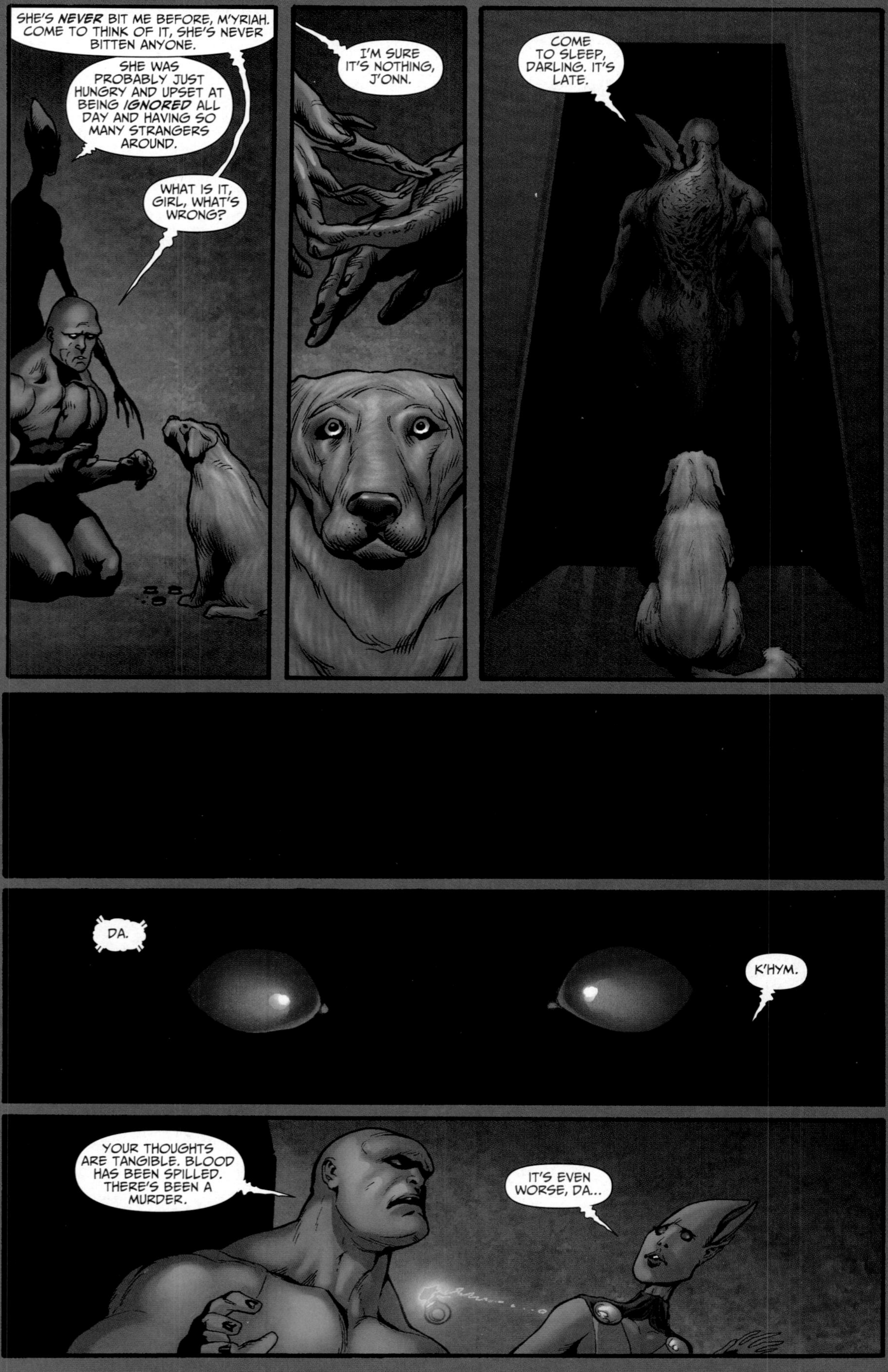
SHE'S NEVER BIT ME BEFORE, M'YRIAH. COME TO THINK OF IT, SHE'S NEVER BITTEN ANYONE.
SHE WAS PROBABLY JUST HUNGRY AND UPSET AT BEING IGNORED ALL DAY AND HAVING SO MANY STRANGERS AROUND.
WHAT IS IT, GIRL, WHAT'S WRONG?
I'M SURE IT'S NOTHING, J'ONN.
COME TO SLEEP, DARLING. IT'S LATE.
DA.
K'HYM.
YOUR THOUGHTS ARE TANGIBLE. BLOOD HAS BEEN SPILLED. THERE'S BEEN A MURDER.
IT'S EVEN WORSE, DA...

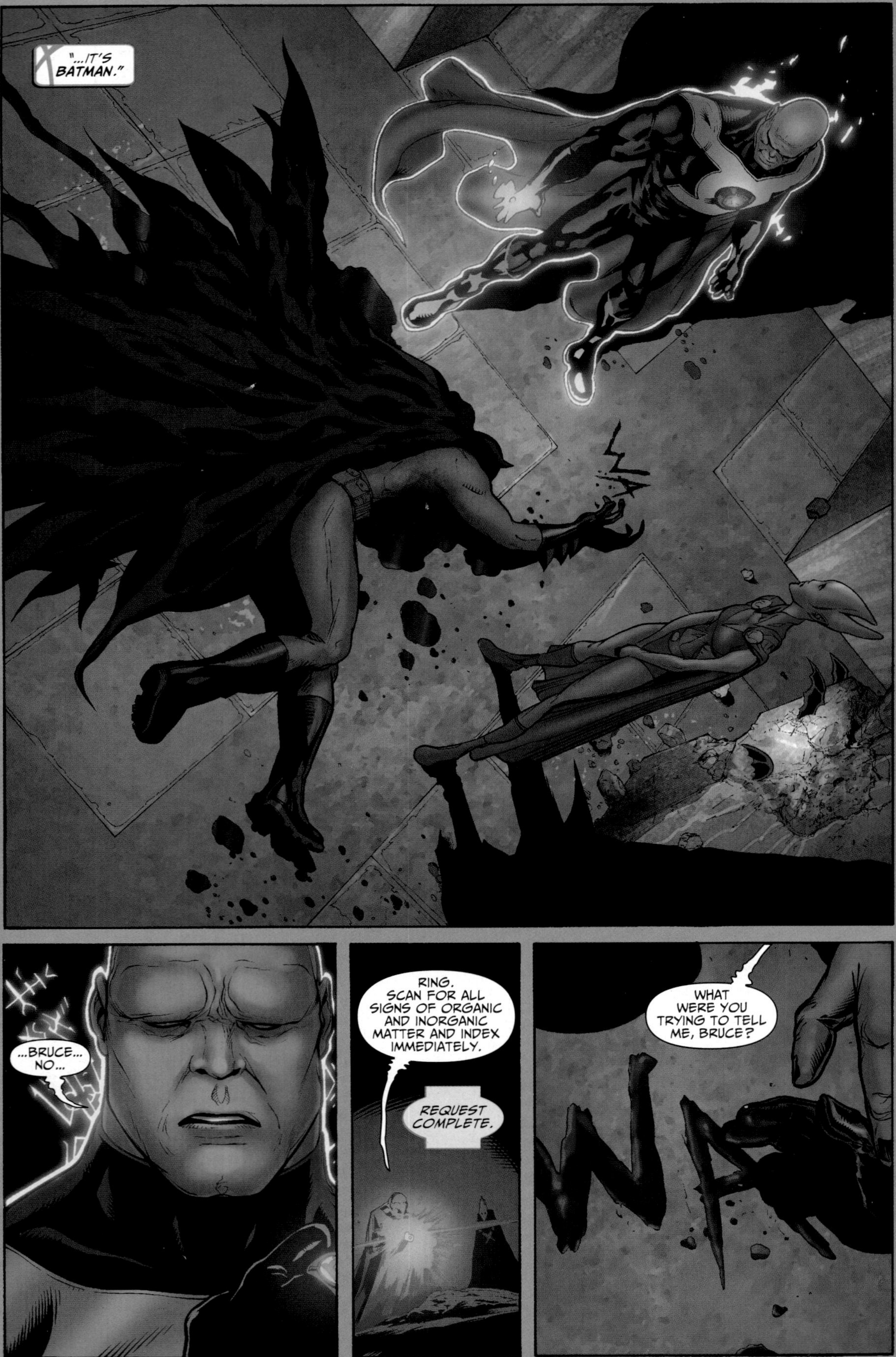

"...IT'S BATMAN."
...BRUCE... NO...
RING. SCAN FOR ALL SIGNS OF ORGANIC AND INORGANIC MATTER AND INDEX IMMEDIATELY.
REQUEST COMPLETE.
WHAT WERE YOU TRYING TO TELL ME, BRUCE?

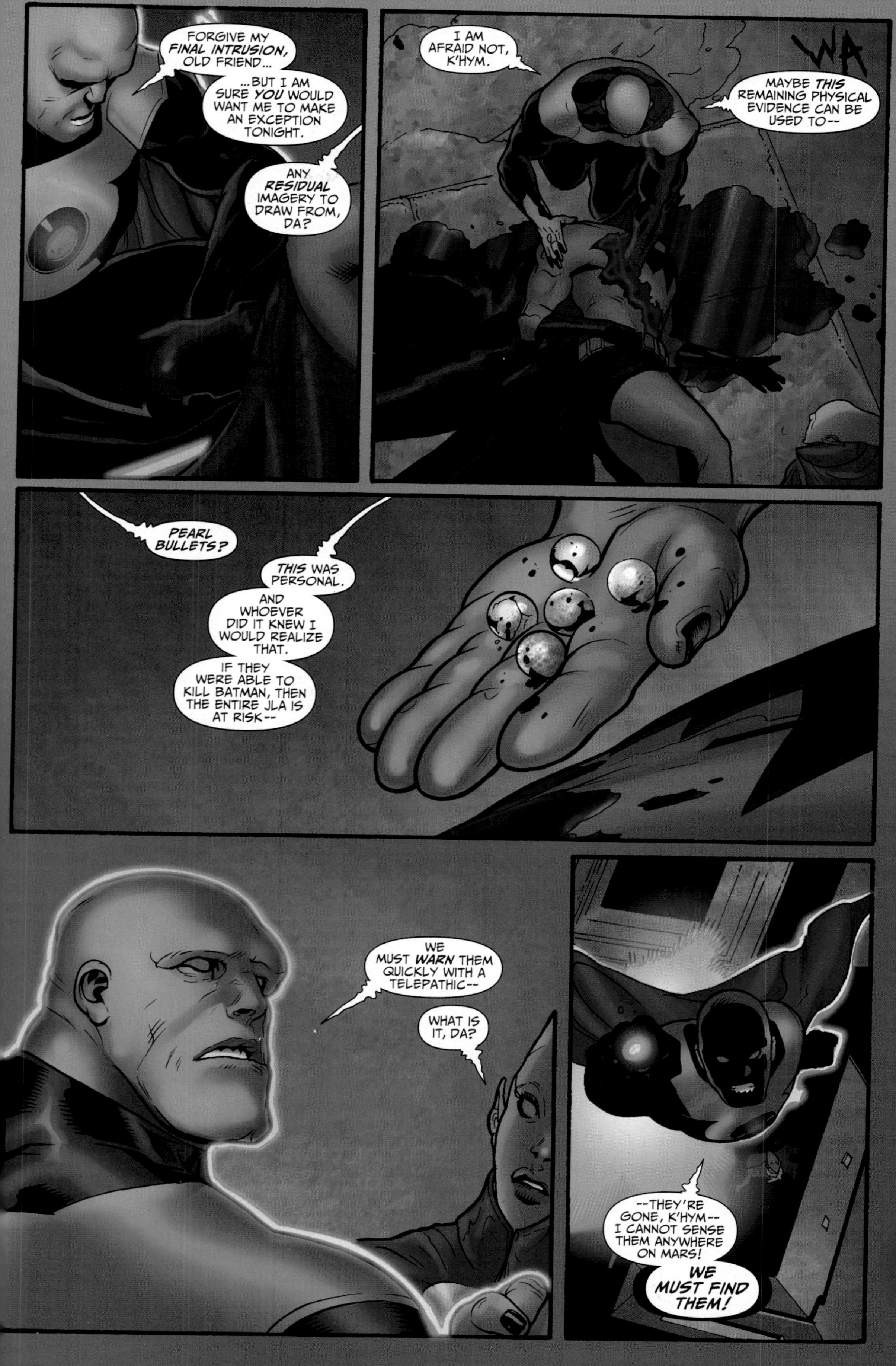
FORGIVE MY FINAL INTRUSION, OLD FRIEND...
...BUT I AM SURE YOU WOULD WANT ME TO MAKE AN EXCEPTION TONIGHT.
ANY RESIDUAL IMAGERY TO DRAW FROM, DA?
I AM AFRAID NOT, K'HYM.
WA
MAYBE THIS REMAINING PHYSICAL EVIDENCE CAN BE USED TO--
PEARL BULLETS?
THIS WAS PERSONAL.
AND WHOEVER DID IT KNEW I WOULD REALIZE THAT.
IF THEY WERE ABLE TO KILL BATMAN, THEN THE ENTIRE JLA IS AT RISK--
WE MUST WARN THEM QUICKLY WITH A TELEPATHIC--
WHAT IS IT, DA?
--THEY'RE GONE, K'HYM-- I CANNOT SENSE THEM ANYWHERE ON MARS!
WE MUST FIND THEM!

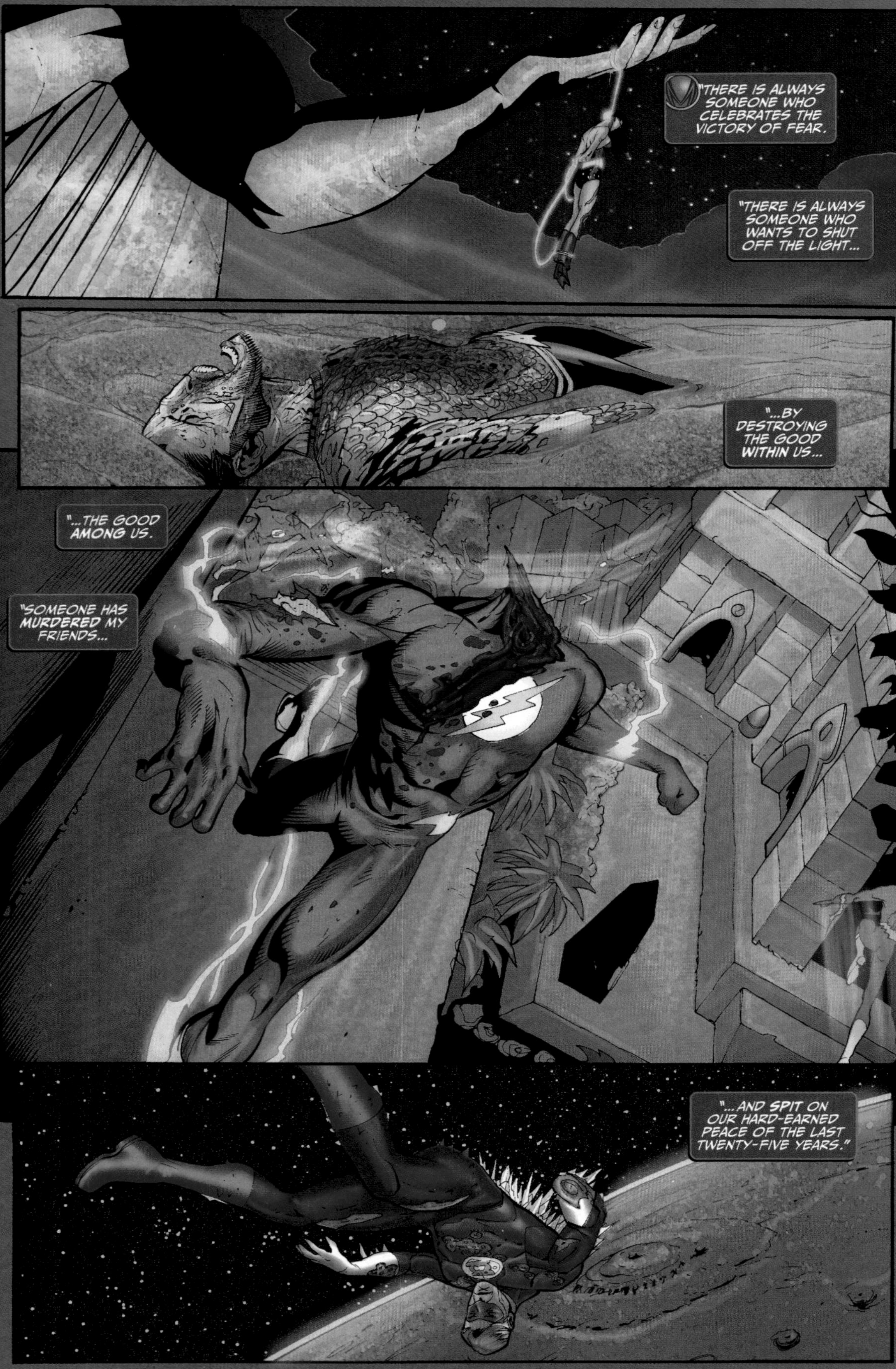
"THERE IS ALWAYS SOMEONE WHO CELEBRATES THE VICTORY OF FEAR.
"THERE IS ALWAYS SOMEONE WHO WANTS TO SHUT OFF THE LIGHT...
"...BY DESTROYING THE GOOD WITHIN US...
"...THE GOOD AMONG US.
"SOMEONE HAS MURDERED MY FRIENDS...
"...AND SPIT ON OUR HARD-EARNED PEACE OF THE LAST TWENTY-FIVE YEARS."

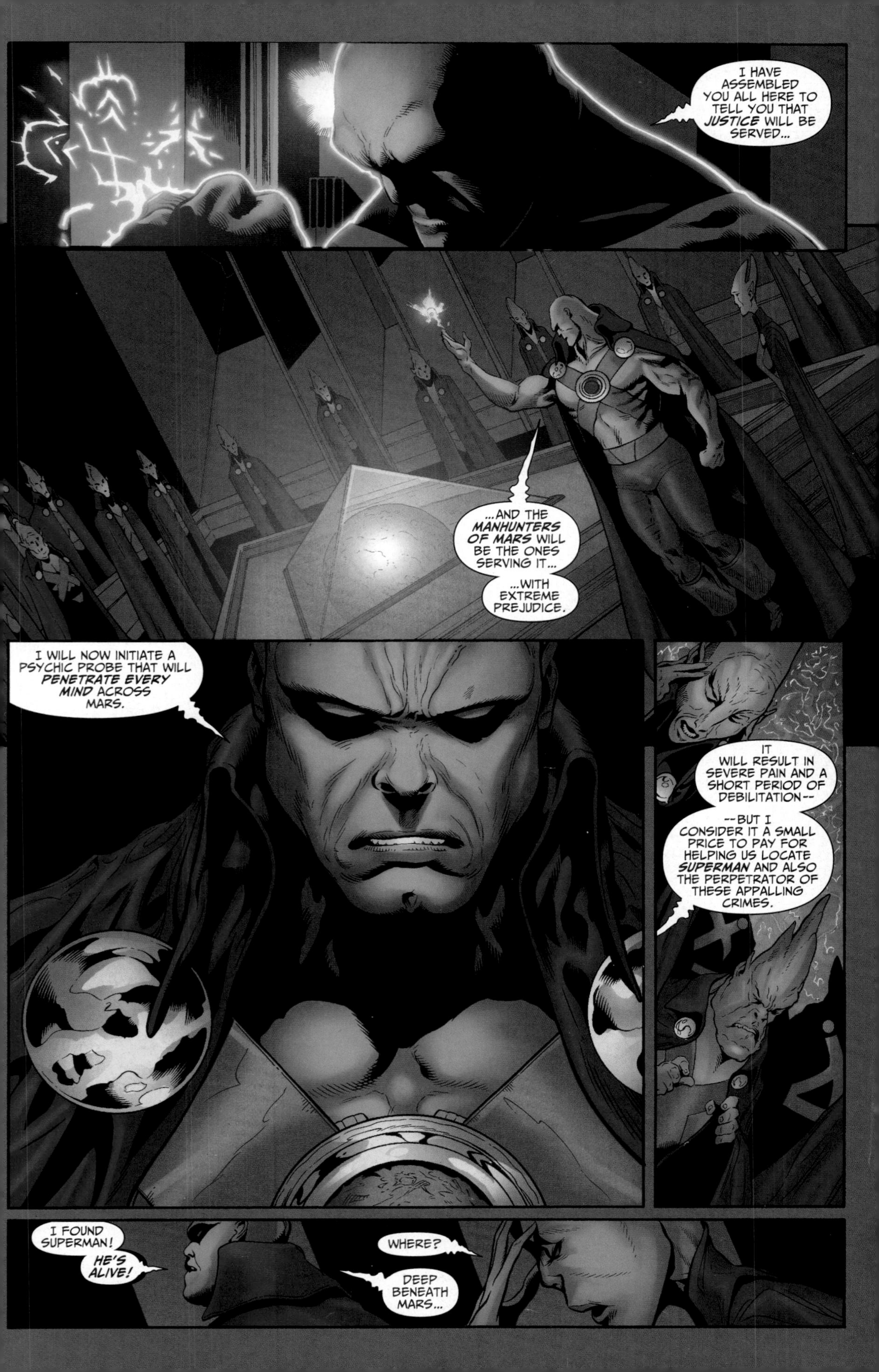
I HAVE ASSEMBLED YOU ALL HERE TO TELL YOU THAT JUSTICE WILL BE SERVED...
...AND THE MANHUNTERS OF MARS WILL BE THE ONES SERVING IT...
...WITH EXTREME PREJUDICE.
I WILL NOW INITIATE A PSYCHIC PROBE THAT WILL PENETRATE EVERY MIND ACROSS MARS.
IT WILL RESULT IN SEVERE PAIN AND A SHORT PERIOD OF DEBILITATION--
--BUT I CONSIDER IT A SMALL PRICE TO PAY FOR HELPING US LOCATE SUPERMAN AND ALSO THE PERPETRATOR OF THESE APPALLING CRIMES.
I FOUND SUPERMAN! HE'S ALIVE!
WHERE?
DEEP BENEATH MARS...

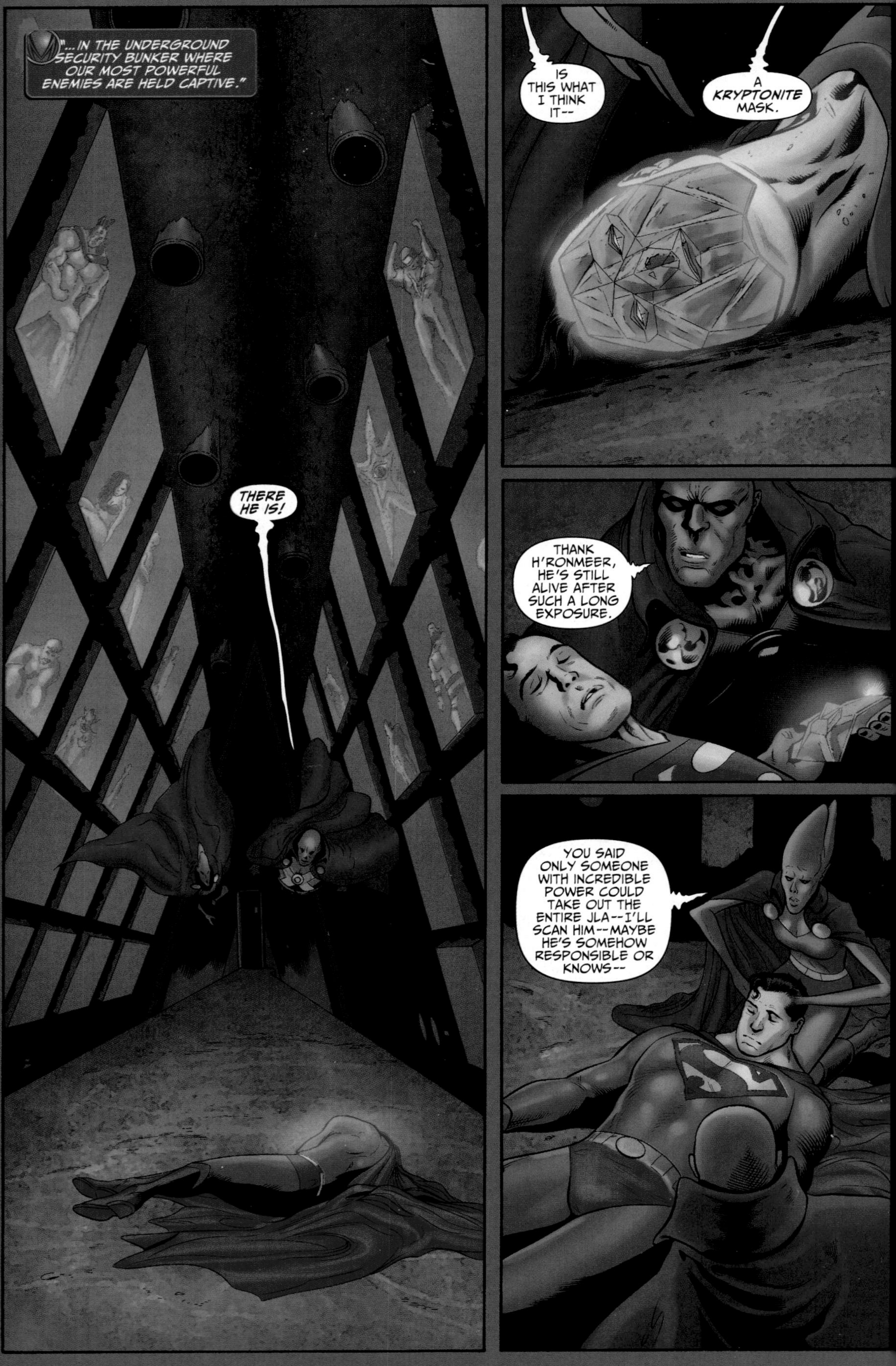
"...IN THE UNDERGROUND SECURITY BUNKER WHERE OUR MOST POWERFUL ENEMIES ARE HELD CAPTIVE."
THERE HE IS!
IS THIS WHAT I THINK IT--
A KRYPTONITE MASK.
THANK H'RONMEER, HE'S STILL ALIVE AFTER SUCH A LONG EXPOSURE.
YOU SAID ONLY SOMEONE WITH INCREDIBLE POWER COULD TAKE OUT THE ENTIRE JLA--I'LL SCAN HIM--MAYBE HE'S SOMEHOW RESPONSIBLE OR KNOWS--

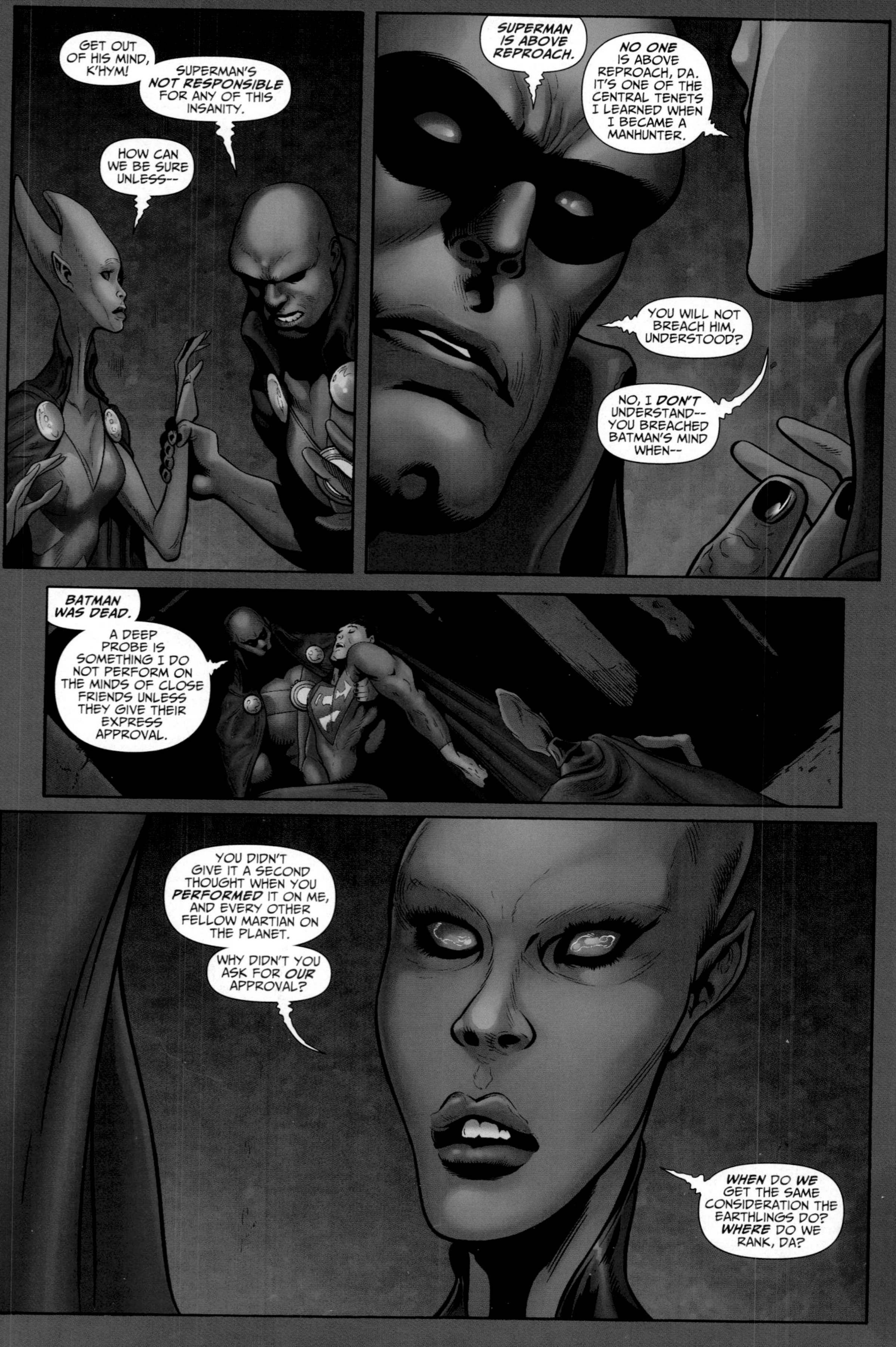
GET OUT OF HIS MIND, K'HYM!
SUPERMAN'S NOT RESPONSIBLE FOR ANY OF THIS INSANITY.
HOW CAN WE BE SURE UNLESS--
SUPERMAN IS ABOVE REPROACH.
NO ONE IS ABOVE REPROACH, DA. IT'S ONE OF THE CENTRAL TENETS I LEARNED WHEN I BECAME A MANHUNTER.
YOU WILL NOT BREACH HIM, UNDERSTOOD?
NO, I DON'T UNDERSTAND-- YOU BREACHED BATMAN'S MIND WHEN--
BATMAN WAS DEAD.
A DEEP PROBE IS SOMETHING I DO NOT PERFORM ON THE MINDS OF CLOSE FRIENDS UNLESS THEY GIVE THEIR EXPRESS APPROVAL.
YOU DIDN'T GIVE IT A SECOND THOUGHT WHEN YOU PERFORMED IT ON ME, AND EVERY OTHER FELLOW MARTIAN ON THE PLANET.
WHY DIDN'T YOU ASK FOR OUR APPROVAL?
WHEN DO WE GET THE SAME CONSIDERATION THE EARTHLINGS DO? WHERE DO WE RANK, DA?

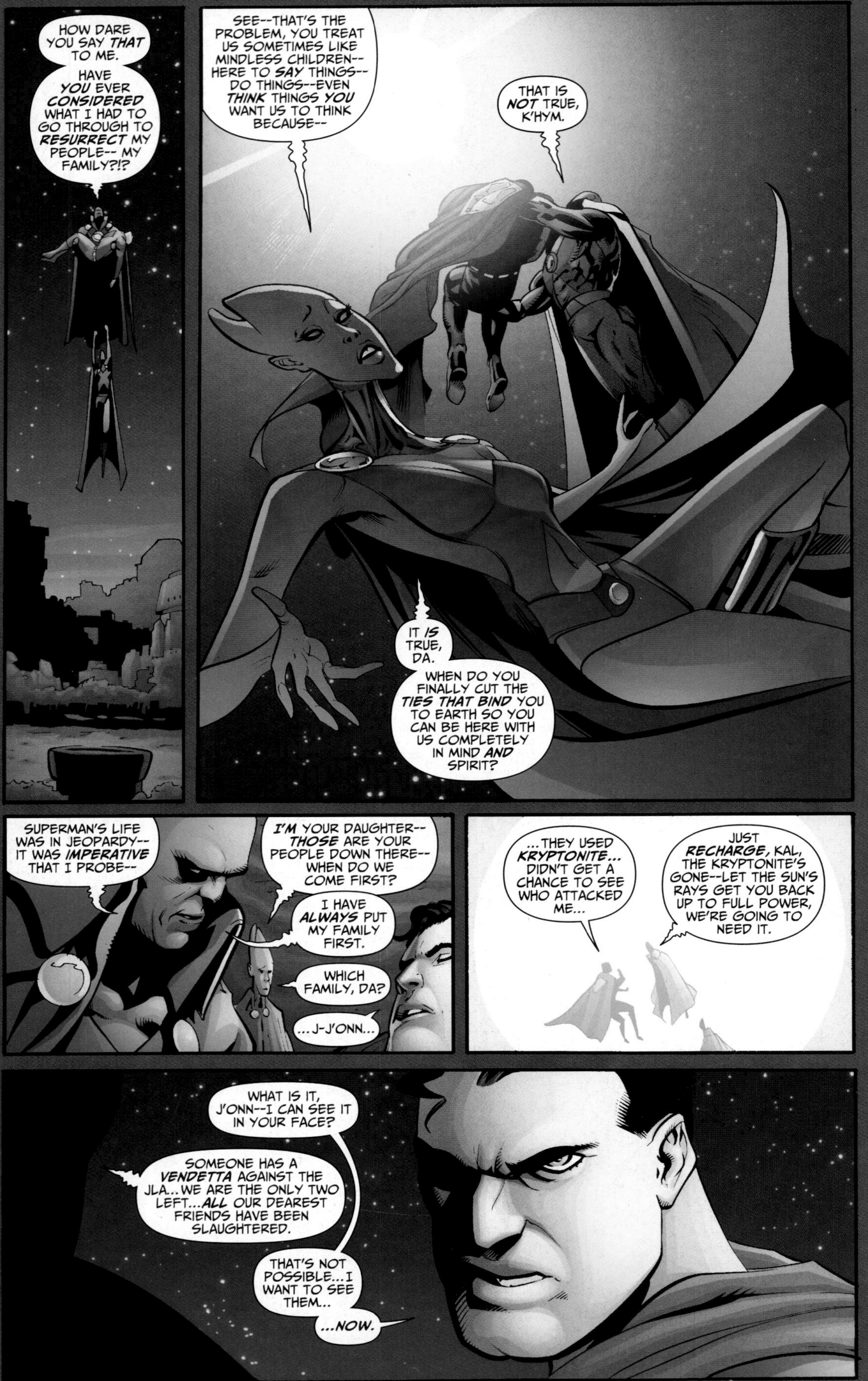
HOW DARE YOU SAY THAT TO ME.
HAVE YOU EVER CONSIDERED WHAT I HAD TO GO THROUGH TO RESURRECT MY PEOPLE-- MY FAMILY?!?
SEE--THAT'S THE PROBLEM, YOU TREAT US SOMETIMES LIKE MINDLESS CHILDREN--HERE TO SAY THINGS--DO THINGS--EVEN THINK THINGS YOU WANT US TO THINK BECAUSE--
THAT IS NOT TRUE, K'HYM.
IT IS TRUE, DA.
WHEN DO YOU FINALLY CUT THE TIES THAT BIND YOU TO EARTH SO YOU CAN BE HERE WITH US COMPLETELY IN MIND AND SPIRIT?
SUPERMAN'S LIFE WAS IN JEOPARDY--IT WAS IMPERATIVE THAT I PROBE--
I'M YOUR DAUGHTER--THOSE ARE YOUR PEOPLE DOWN THERE--WHEN DO WE COME FIRST?
I HAVE ALWAYS PUT MY FAMILY FIRST.
WHICH FAMILY, DA?
...J-J'ONN...
...THEY USED KRYPTONITE... DIDN'T GET A CHANCE TO SEE WHO ATTACKED ME...
JUST RECHARGE, KAL, THE KRYPTONITE'S GONE--LET THE SUN'S RAYS GET YOU BACK UP TO FULL POWER, WE'RE GOING TO NEED IT.
WHAT IS IT, J'ONN--I CAN SEE IT IN YOUR FACE?
SOMEONE HAS A VENDETTA AGAINST THE JLA...WE ARE THE ONLY TWO LEFT...ALL OUR DEAREST FRIENDS HAVE BEEN SLAUGHTERED.
THAT'S NOT POSSIBLE...I WANT TO SEE THEM...
...NOW.

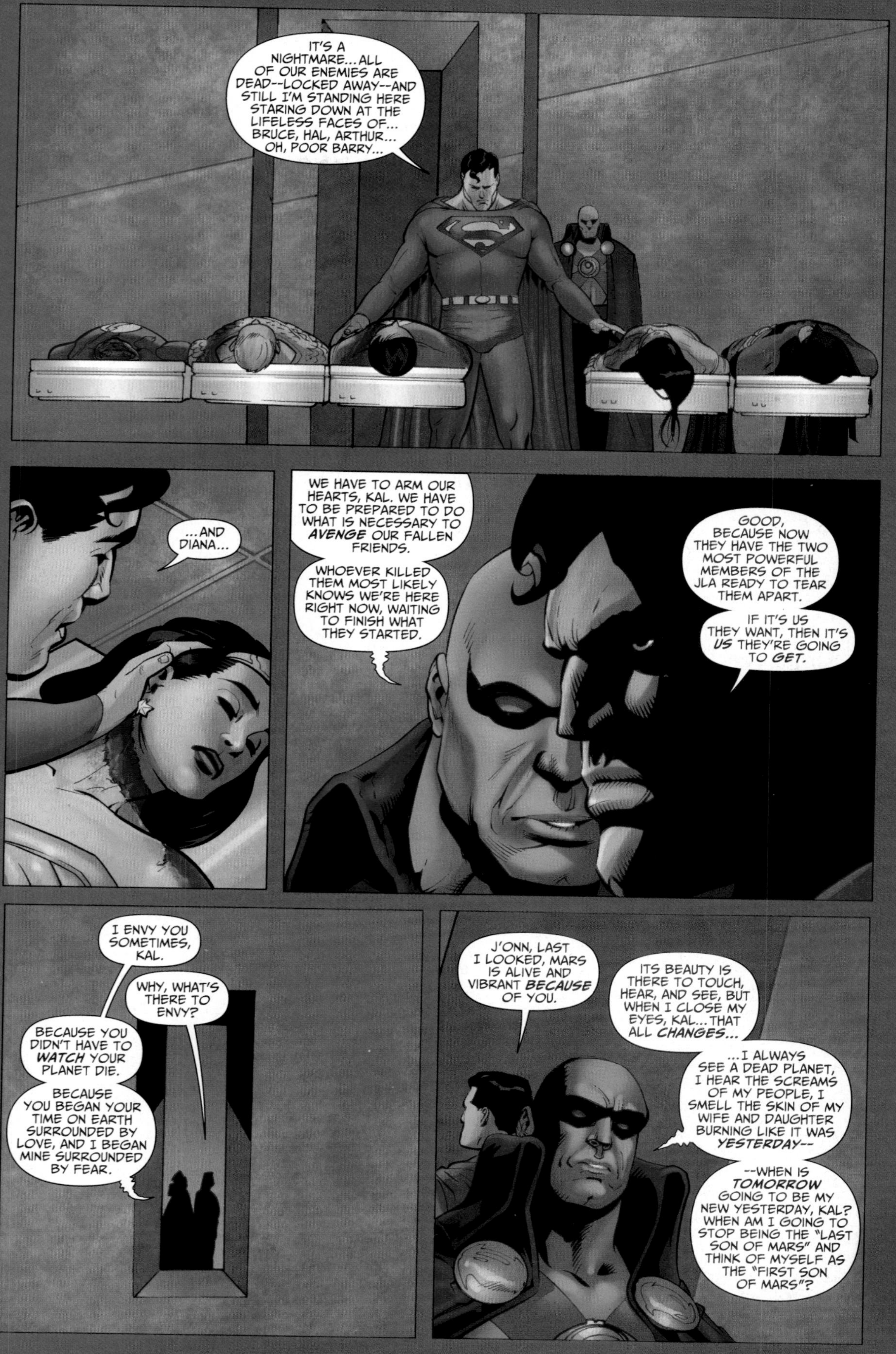
IT'S A NIGHTMARE... ALL OF OUR ENEMIES ARE DEAD--LOCKED AWAY--AND STILL I'M STANDING HERE STARING DOWN AT THE LIFELESS FACES OF... BRUCE, HAL, ARTHUR... OH, POOR BARRY...
...AND DIANA...
WE HAVE TO ARM OUR HEARTS, KAL. WE HAVE TO BE PREPARED TO DO WHAT IS NECESSARY TO AVENGE OUR FALLEN FRIENDS.
WHOEVER KILLED THEM MOST LIKELY KNOWS WE'RE HERE RIGHT NOW, WAITING TO FINISH WHAT THEY STARTED.
GOOD, BECAUSE NOW THEY HAVE THE TWO MOST POWERFUL MEMBERS OF THE JLA READY TO TEAR THEM APART.
IF IT'S US THEY WANT, THEN IT'S US THEY'RE GOING TO GET.
I ENVY YOU SOMETIMES, KAL.
WHY, WHAT'S THERE TO ENVY?
BECAUSE YOU DIDN'T HAVE TO WATCH YOUR PLANET DIE.
BECAUSE YOU BEGAN YOUR TIME ON EARTH SURROUNDED BY LOVE, AND I BEGAN MINE SURROUNDED BY FEAR.
J'ONN, LAST I LOOKED, MARS IS ALIVE AND VIBRANT BECAUSE OF YOU.
ITS BEAUTY IS THERE TO TOUCH, HEAR, AND SEE, BUT WHEN I CLOSE MY EYES, KAL... THAT ALL CHANGES...
...I ALWAYS SEE A DEAD PLANET, I HEAR THE SCREAMS OF MY PEOPLE, I SMELL THE SKIN OF MY WIFE AND DAUGHTER BURNING LIKE IT WAS YESTERDAY--
--WHEN IS TOMORROW GOING TO BE MY NEW YESTERDAY, KAL? WHEN AM I GOING TO STOP BEING THE "LAST SON OF MARS" AND THINK OF MYSELF AS THE "FIRST SON OF MARS"?

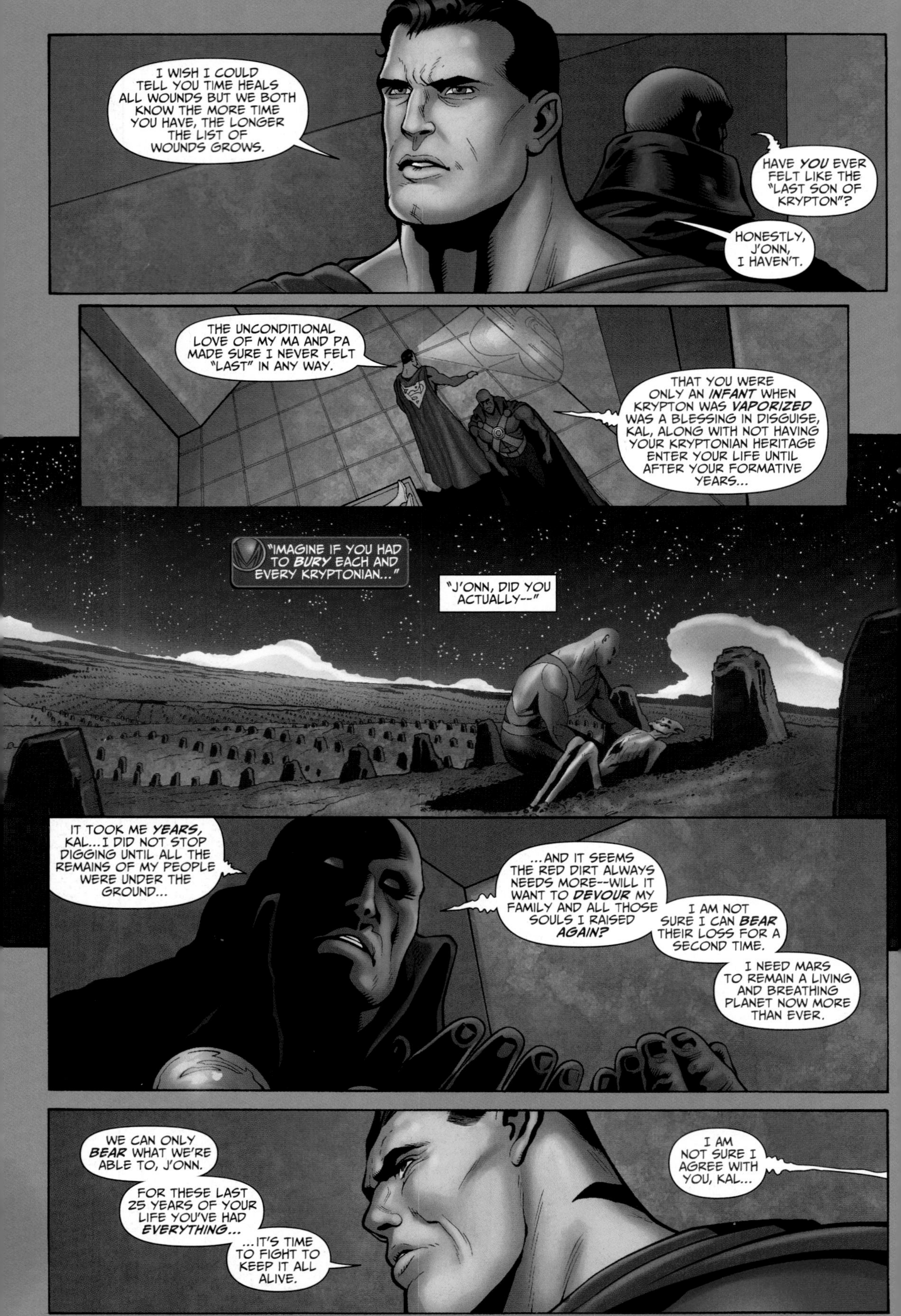
I WISH I COULD TELL YOU TIME HEALS ALL WOUNDS BUT WE BOTH KNOW THE MORE TIME YOU HAVE, THE LONGER THE LIST OF WOUNDS GROWS.
HAVE YOU EVER FELT LIKE THE "LAST SON OF KRYPTON"?
HONESTLY, J'ONN, I HAVEN'T.
THE UNCONDITIONAL LOVE OF MY MA AND PA MADE SURE I NEVER FELT "LAST" IN ANY WAY.
THAT YOU WERE ONLY AN INFANT WHEN KRYPTON WAS VAPORIZED WAS A BLESSING IN DISGUISE, KAL, ALONG WITH NOT HAVING YOUR KRYPTONIAN HERITAGE ENTER YOUR LIFE UNTIL AFTER YOUR FORMATIVE YEARS...
"IMAGINE IF YOU HAD TO BURY EACH AND EVERY KRYPTONIAN..."
"J'ONN, DID YOU ACTUALLY--"
IT TOOK ME YEARS, KAL...I DID NOT STOP DIGGING UNTIL ALL THE REMAINS OF MY PEOPLE WERE UNDER THE GROUND...
...AND IT SEEMS THE RED DIRT ALWAYS NEEDS MORE--WILL IT WANT TO DEVOUR MY FAMILY AND ALL THOSE SOULS I RAISED AGAIN?
I AM NOT SURE I CAN BEAR THEIR LOSS FOR A SECOND TIME.
I NEED MARS TO REMAIN A LIVING AND BREATHING PLANET NOW MORE THAN EVER.
WE CAN ONLY BEAR WHAT WE'RE ABLE TO, J'ONN.
FOR THESE LAST 25 YEARS OF YOUR LIFE YOU'VE HAD EVERYTHING...
...IT'S TIME TO FIGHT TO KEEP IT ALL ALIVE.
I AM NOT SURE I AGREE WITH YOU, KAL...

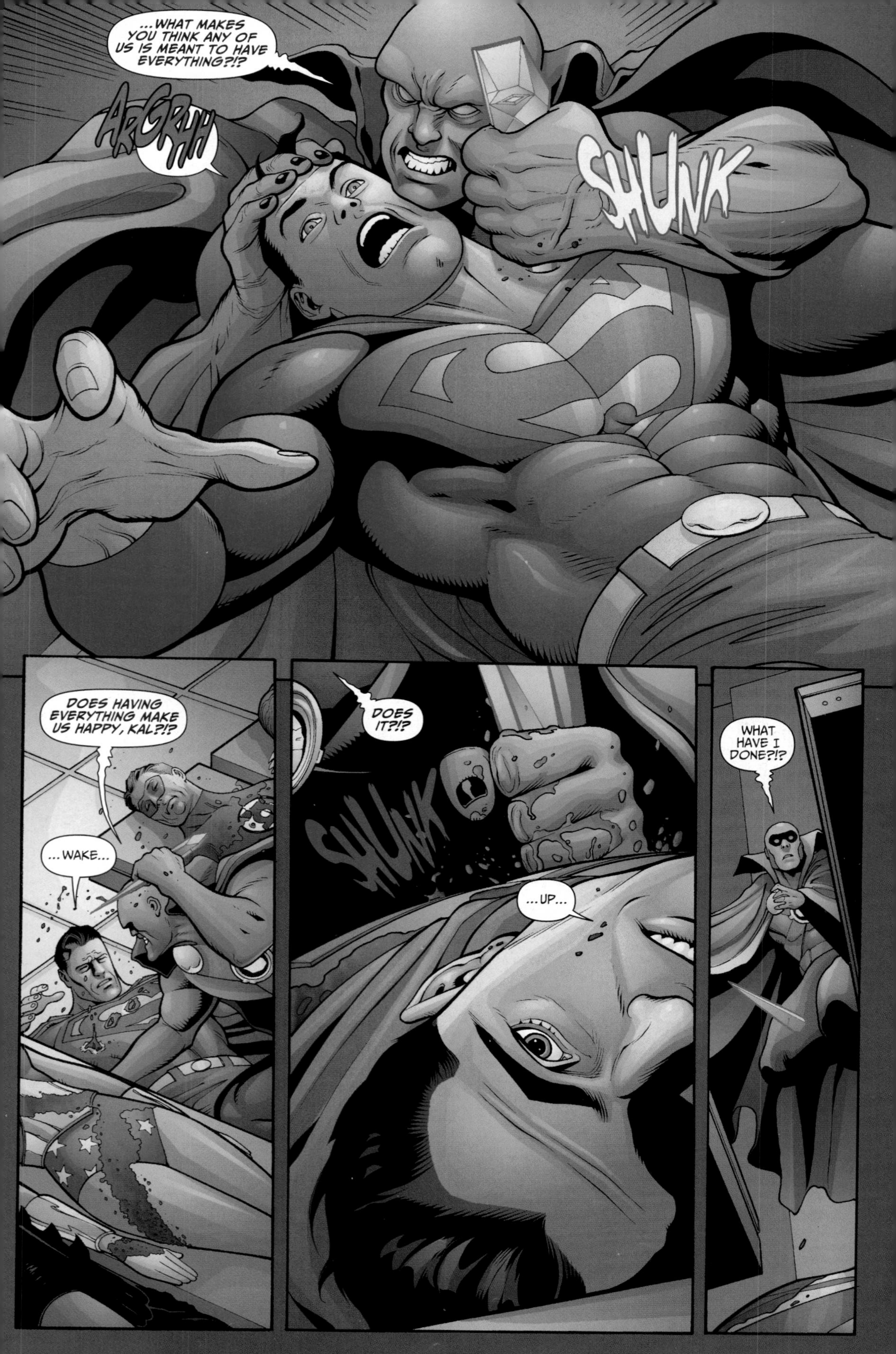
...WHAT MAKES YOU THINK ANY OF US IS MEANT TO HAVE EVERYTHING?!?
ARGRHH
SHUNK
DOES HAVING EVERYTHING MAKE US HAPPY, KAL?!?
...WAKE...
DOES IT?!?
SHUNK
...UP...
WHAT HAVE I DONE?!?

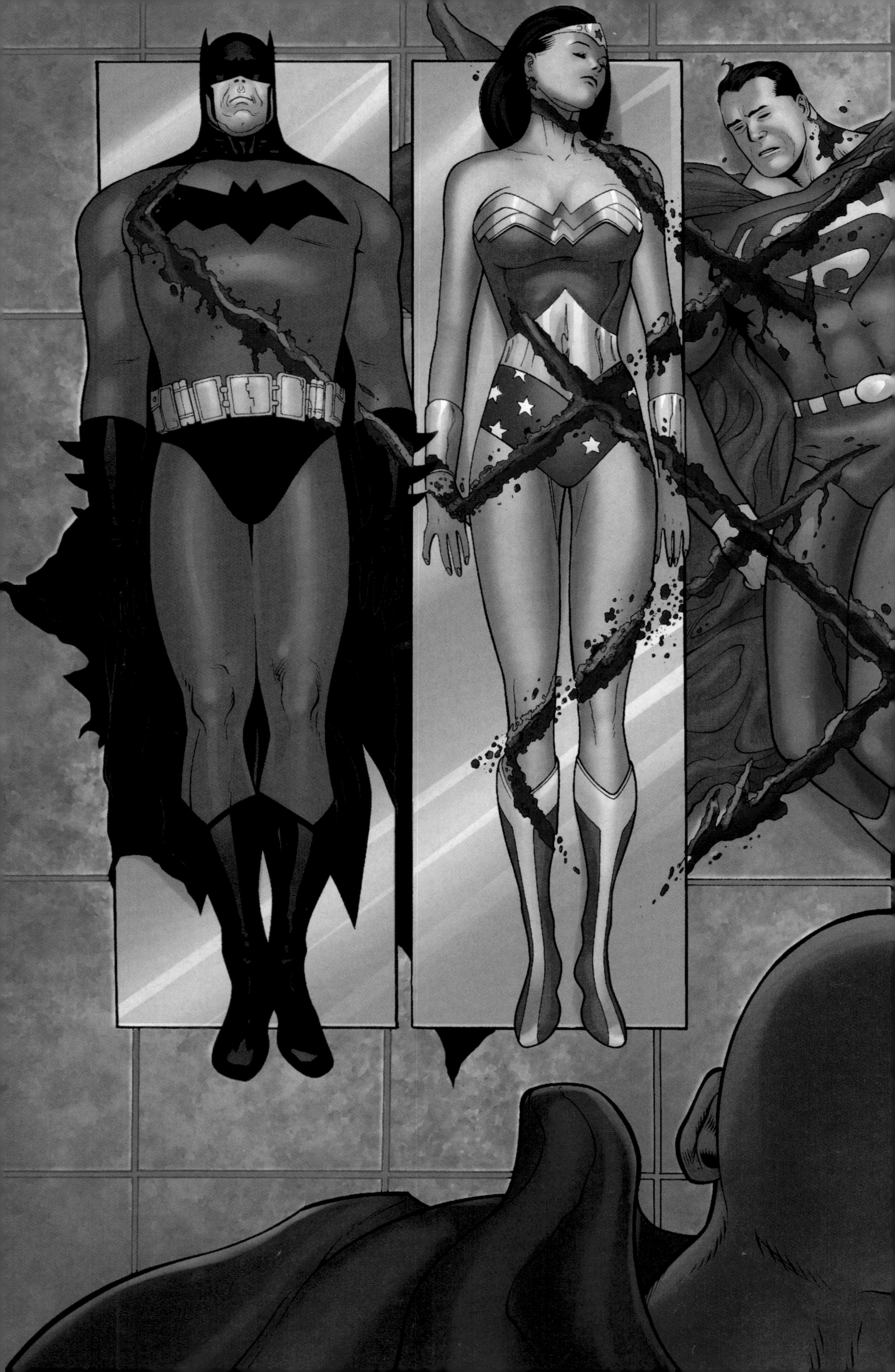

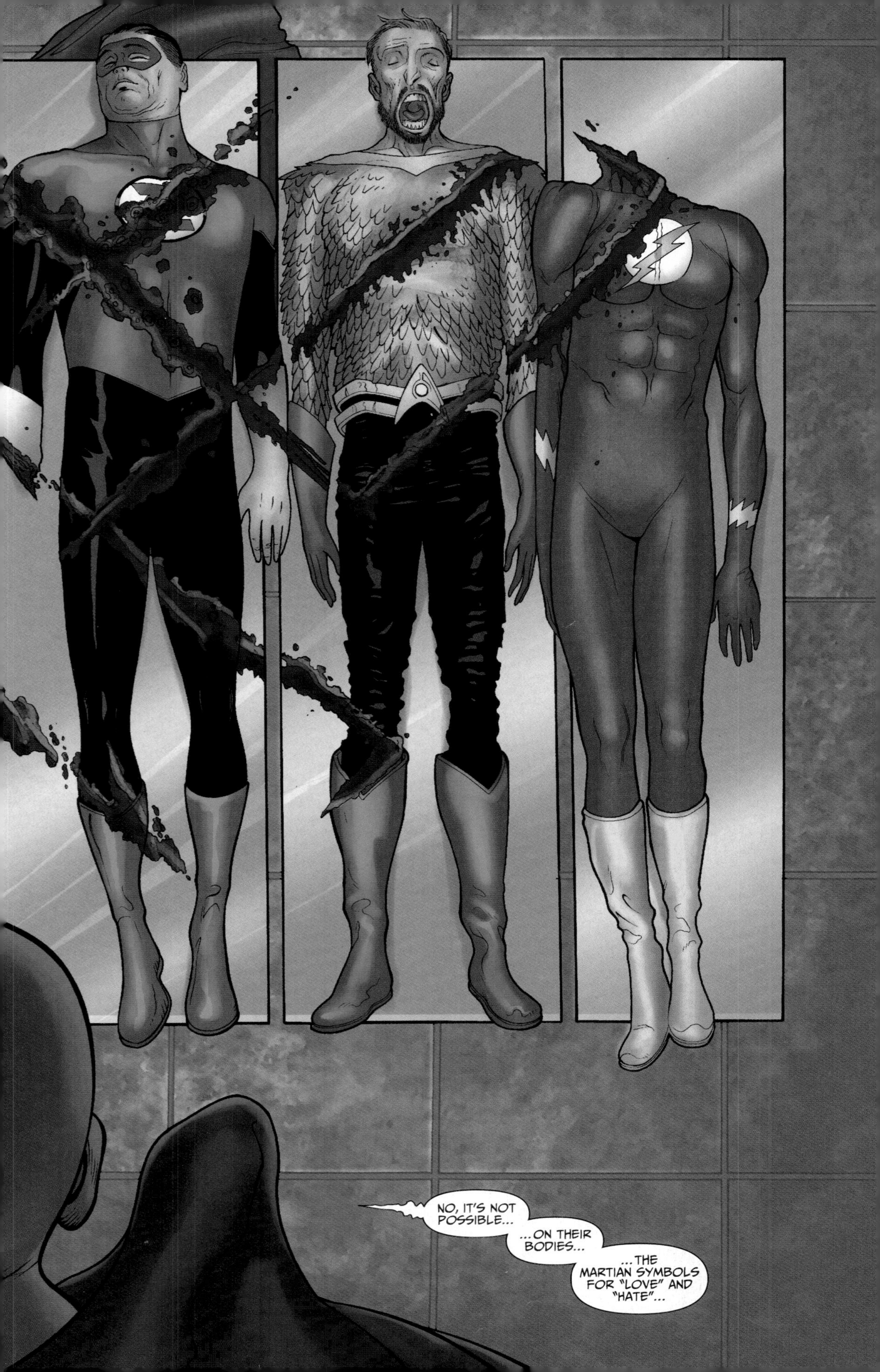
NO, IT'S NOT POSSIBLE...
...ON THEIR BODIES...
...THE MARTIAN SYMBOLS FOR "LOVE" AND "HATE"...

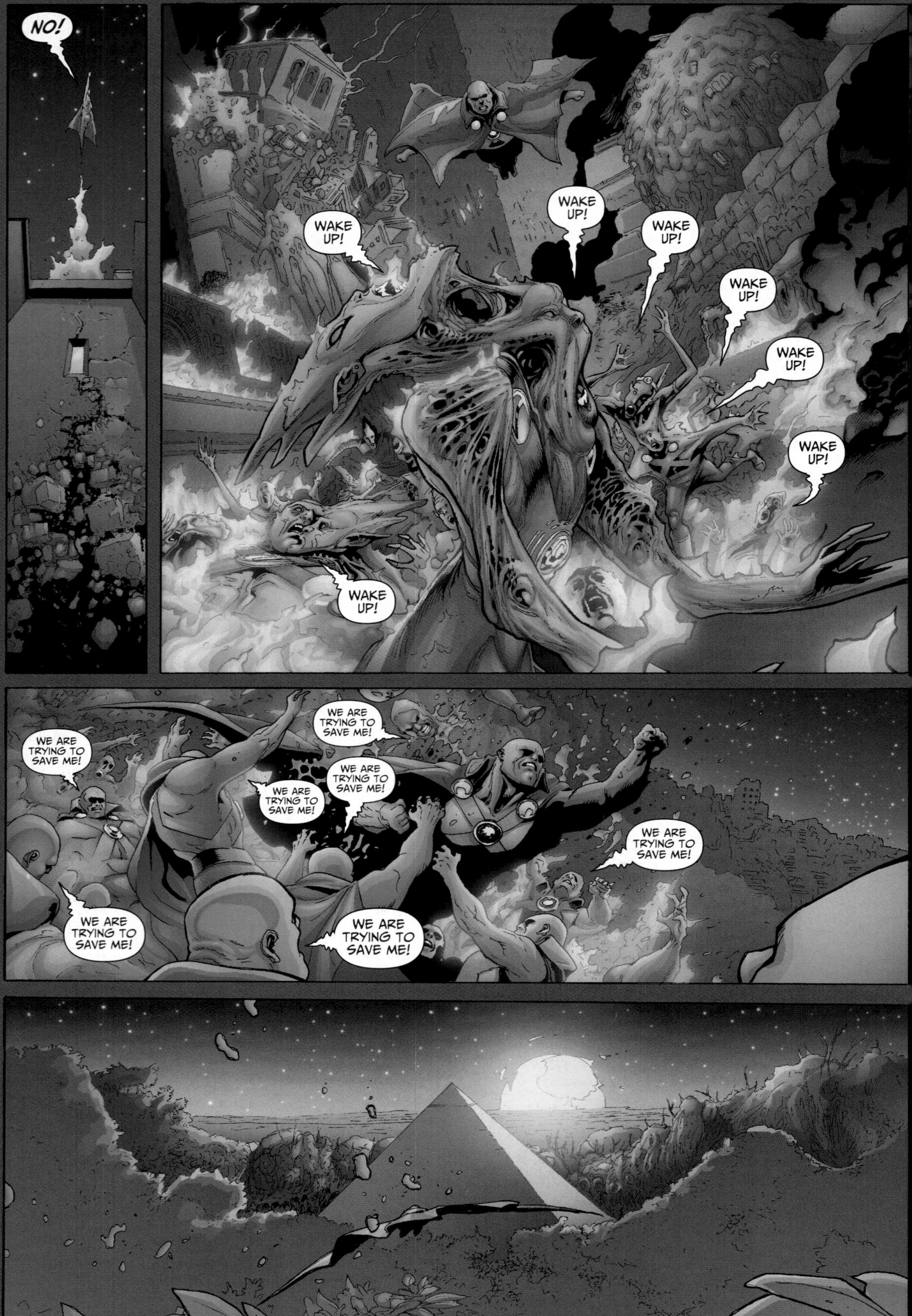
NO!
WAKE UP!
WAKE UP!
WAKE UP!
WAKE UP!
WAKE UP!
WAKE UP!
WAKE UP!
WE ARE TRYING TO SAVE ME!
WE ARE TRYING TO SAVE ME!
WE ARE TRYING TO SAVE ME!
WE ARE TRYING TO SAVE ME!
WE ARE TRYING TO SAVE ME!
WE ARE TRYING TO SAVE ME!
WE ARE TRYING TO SAVE ME!

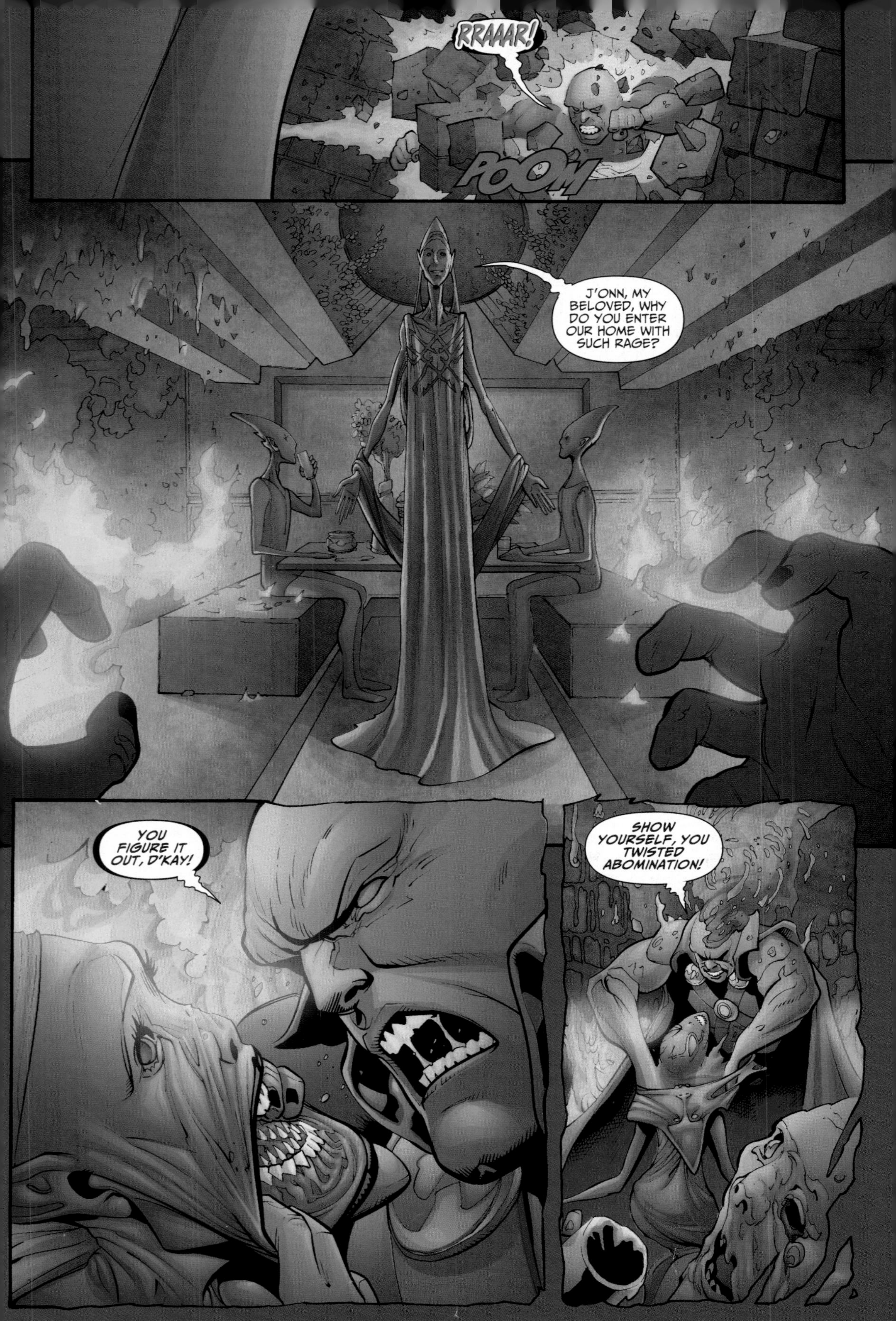
RRAAAR!
POOM
J'ONN, MY BELOVED, WHY DO YOU ENTER OUR HOME WITH SUCH RAGE?
YOU FIGURE IT OUT, D'KAY!
SHOW YOURSELF, YOU TWISTED ABOMINATION!

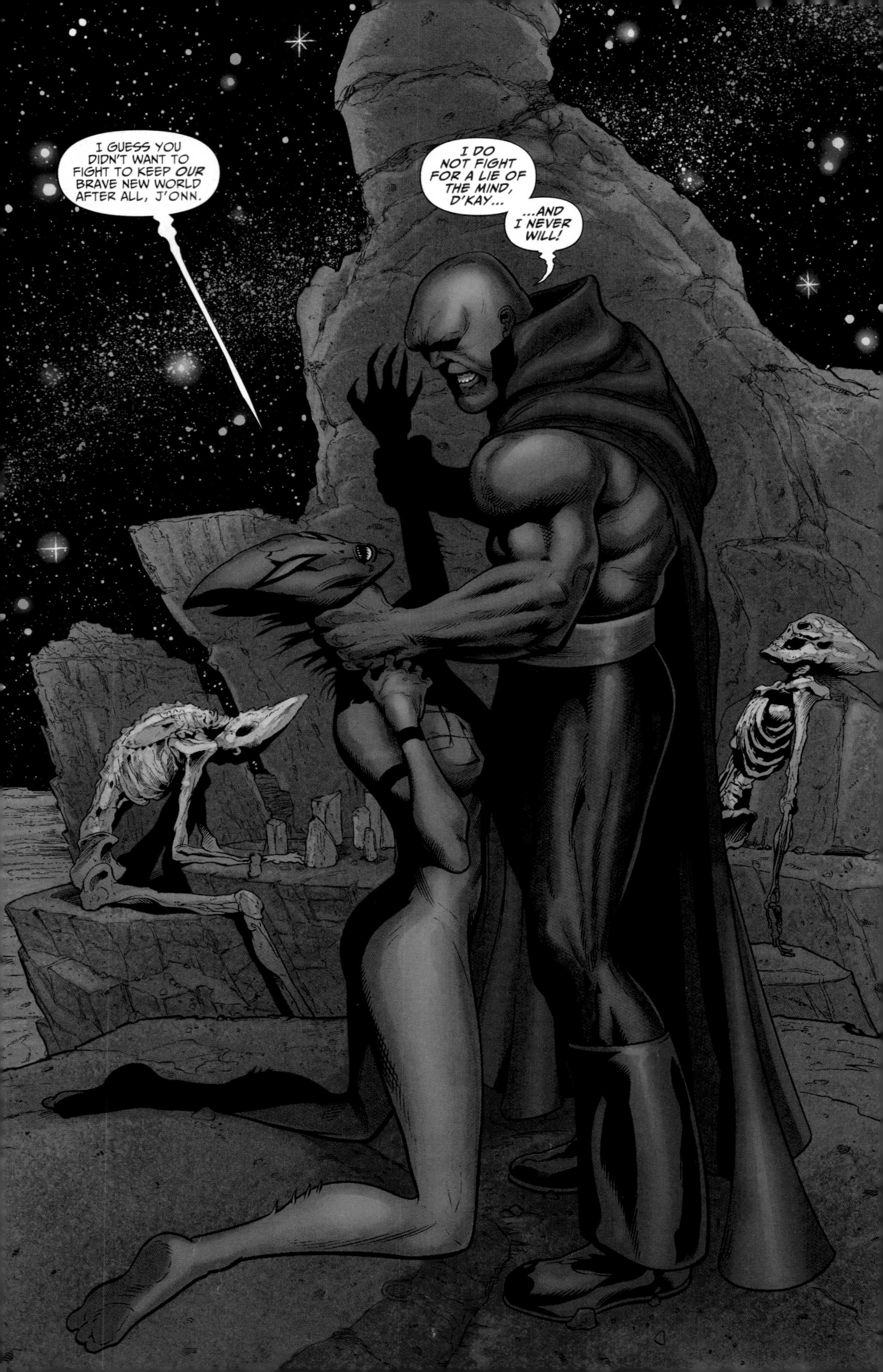
I GUESS YOU DIDN'T WANT TO FIGHT TO KEEP *OUR* BRAVE NEW WORLD AFTER ALL, J'ONN.
I DO NOT FIGHT FOR A LIE OF THE MIND, D'KAY...
...AND I NEVER WILL!

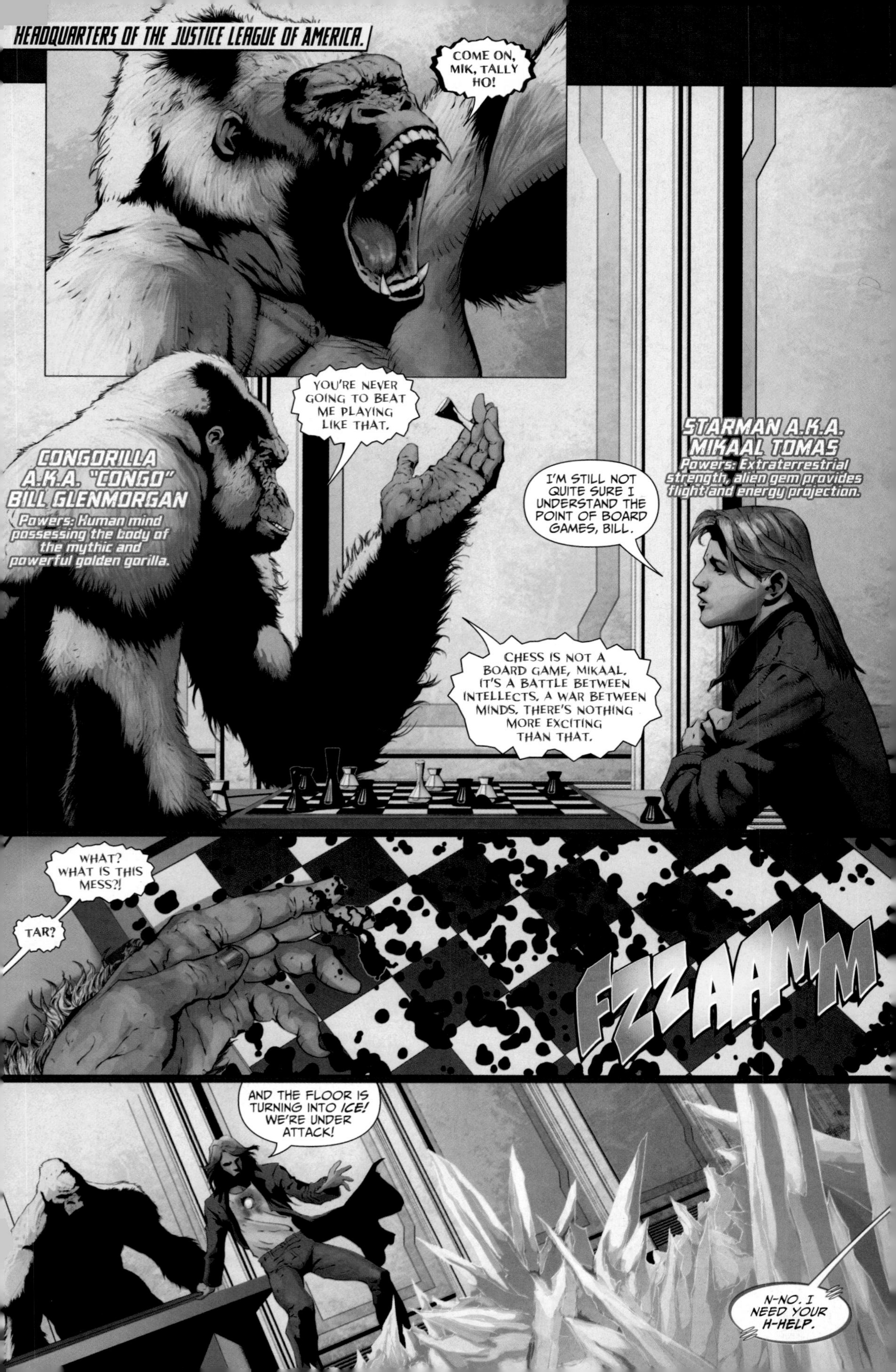

HEADQUARTERS OF THE JUSTICE LEAGUE OF AMERICA.
COME ON, MIK, TALLY HO!
CONGORILLA A.K.A. "CONGO" BILL GLENMORGAN
Powers: Human mind possessing the body of the mythic and powerful golden gorilla.
YOU'RE NEVER GOING TO BEAT ME PLAYING LIKE THAT.
STARMAN A.K.A. MIKAAL TOMAS
Powers: Extraterrestrial strength, alien gem provides flight and energy projection.
I'M STILL NOT QUITE SURE I UNDERSTAND THE POINT OF BOARD GAMES, BILL.
CHESS IS NOT A BOARD GAME, MIKAAL. IT'S A BATTLE BETWEEN INTELLECTS, A WAR BETWEEN MINDS. THERE'S NOTHING MORE EXCITING THAN THAT.
WHAT? WHAT IS THIS MESS?!
TAR?
FZZAAMM
AND THE FLOOR IS TURNING INTO ICE! WE'RE UNDER ATTACK!
N-NO. I NEED YOUR H-HELP.

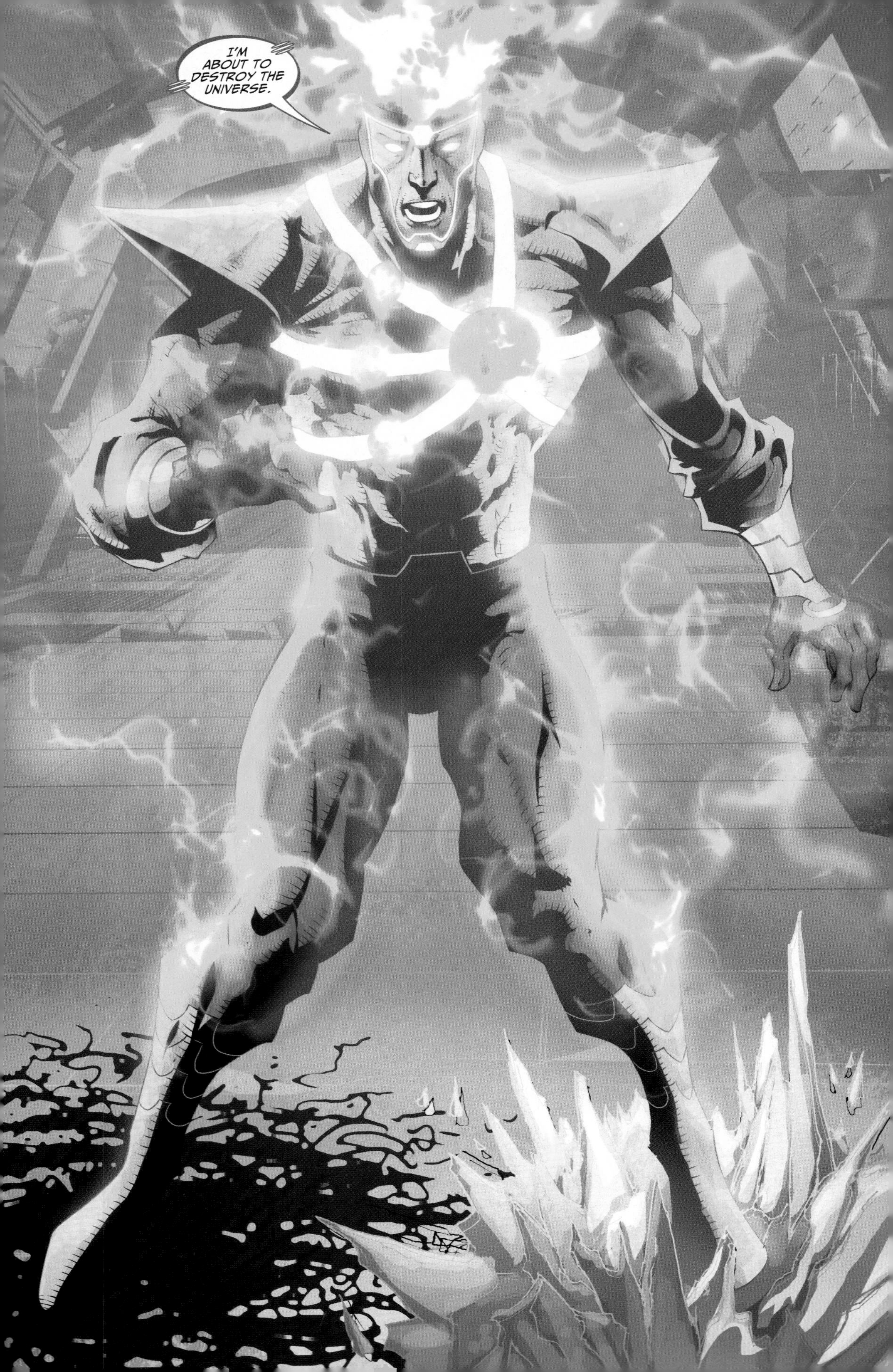
I'M ABOUT TO DESTROY THE UNIVERSE.

**BRIGHTEST DAY 16**
Cover by Gary Frank with Nathan Eyring

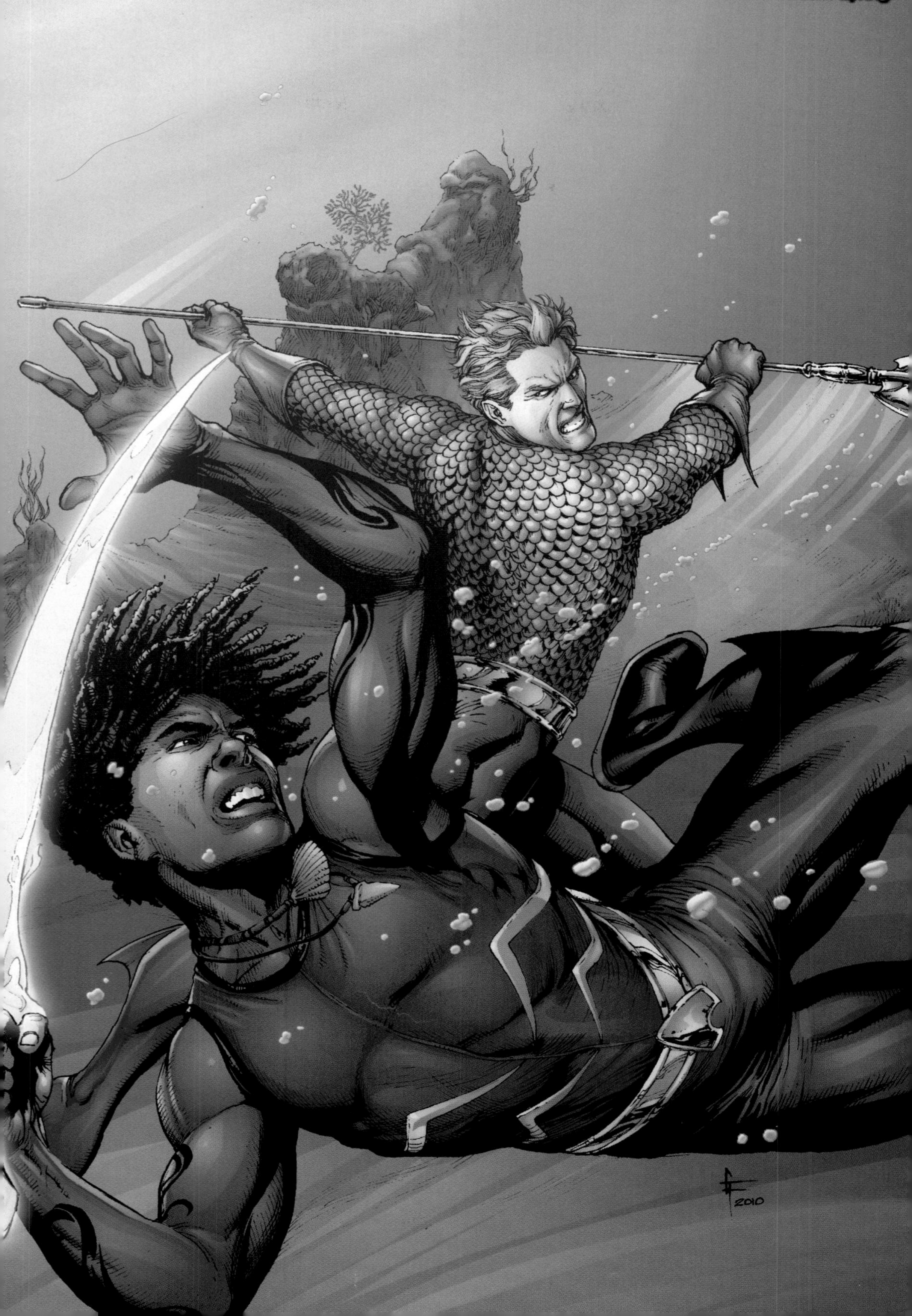
2010

# SHORT FUSE

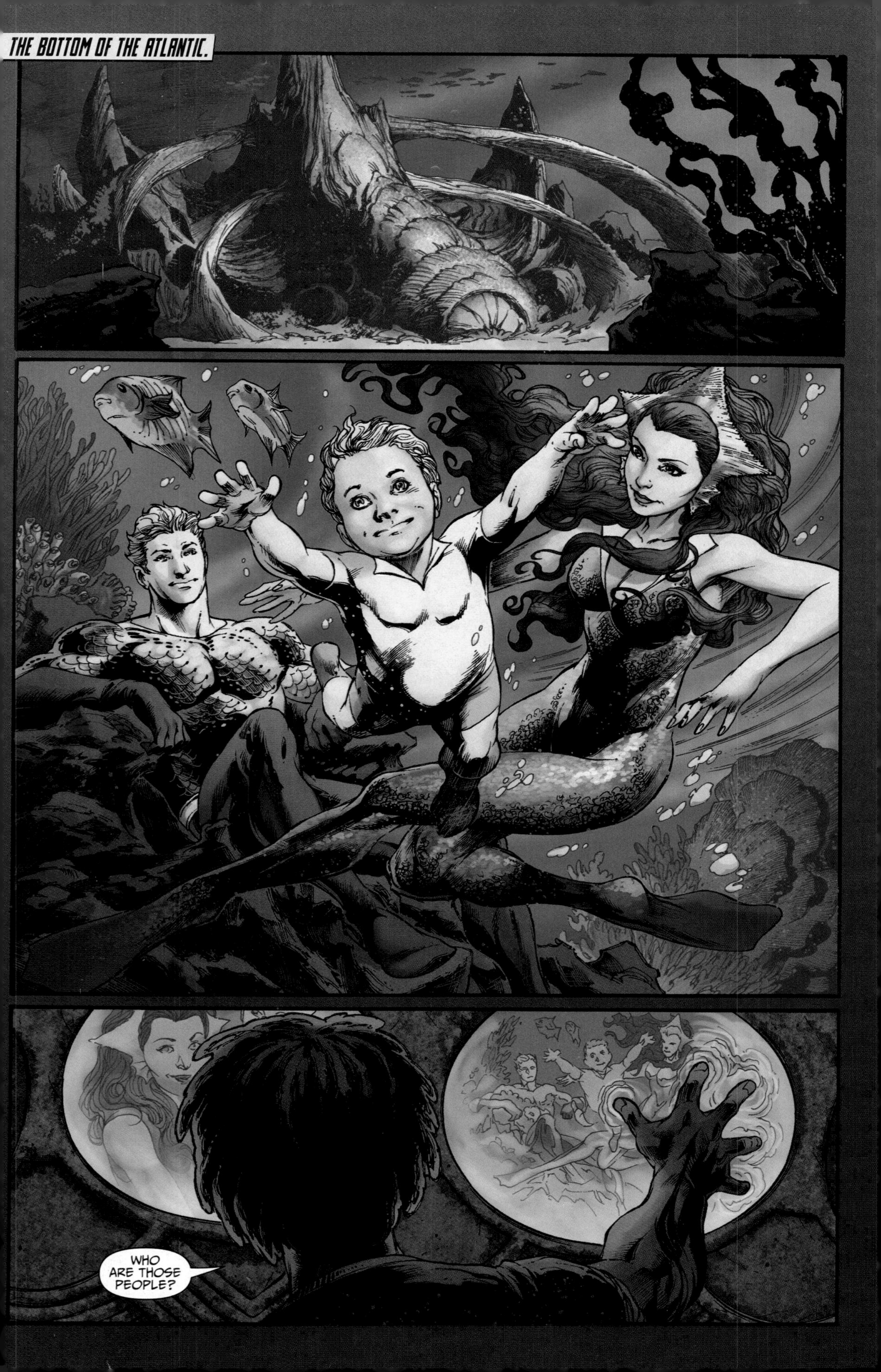
THE BOTTOM OF THE ATLANTIC.
WHO ARE THOSE PEOPLE?

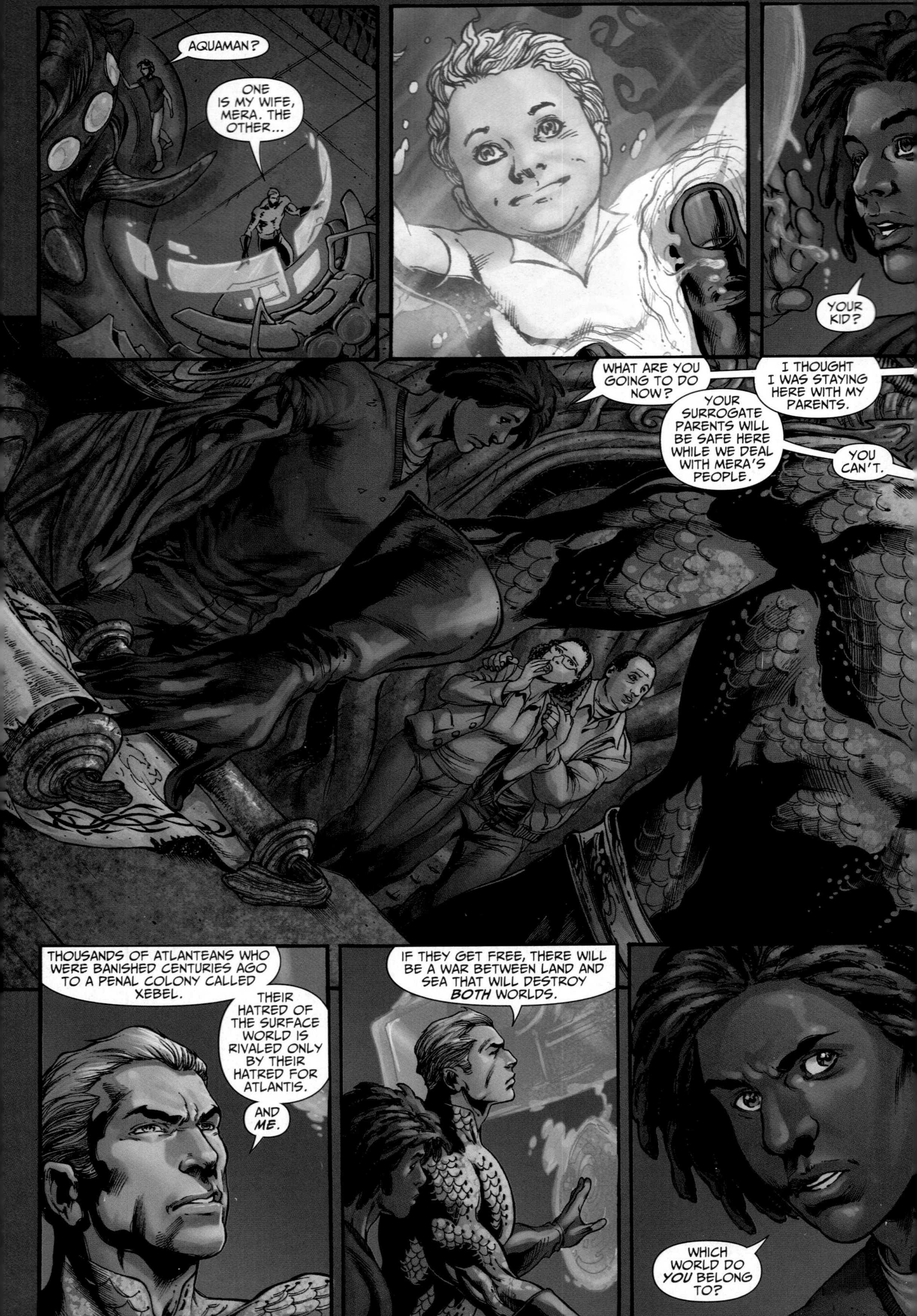

AQUAMAN?
ONE IS MY WIFE, MERA. THE OTHER...
YOUR KID?
WHAT ARE YOU GOING TO DO NOW?
I THOUGHT I WAS STAYING HERE WITH MY PARENTS.
YOUR SURROGATE PARENTS WILL BE SAFE HERE WHILE WE DEAL WITH MERA'S PEOPLE.
YOU CAN'T.
THOUSANDS OF ATLANTEANS WHO WERE BANISHED CENTURIES AGO TO A PENAL COLONY CALLED XEBEL.
THEIR HATRED OF THE SURFACE WORLD IS RIVALED ONLY BY THEIR HATRED FOR ATLANTIS.
AND *ME*.
IF THEY GET FREE, THERE WILL BE A WAR BETWEEN LAND AND SEA THAT WILL DESTROY *BOTH* WORLDS.
WHICH WORLD DO *YOU* BELONG TO?

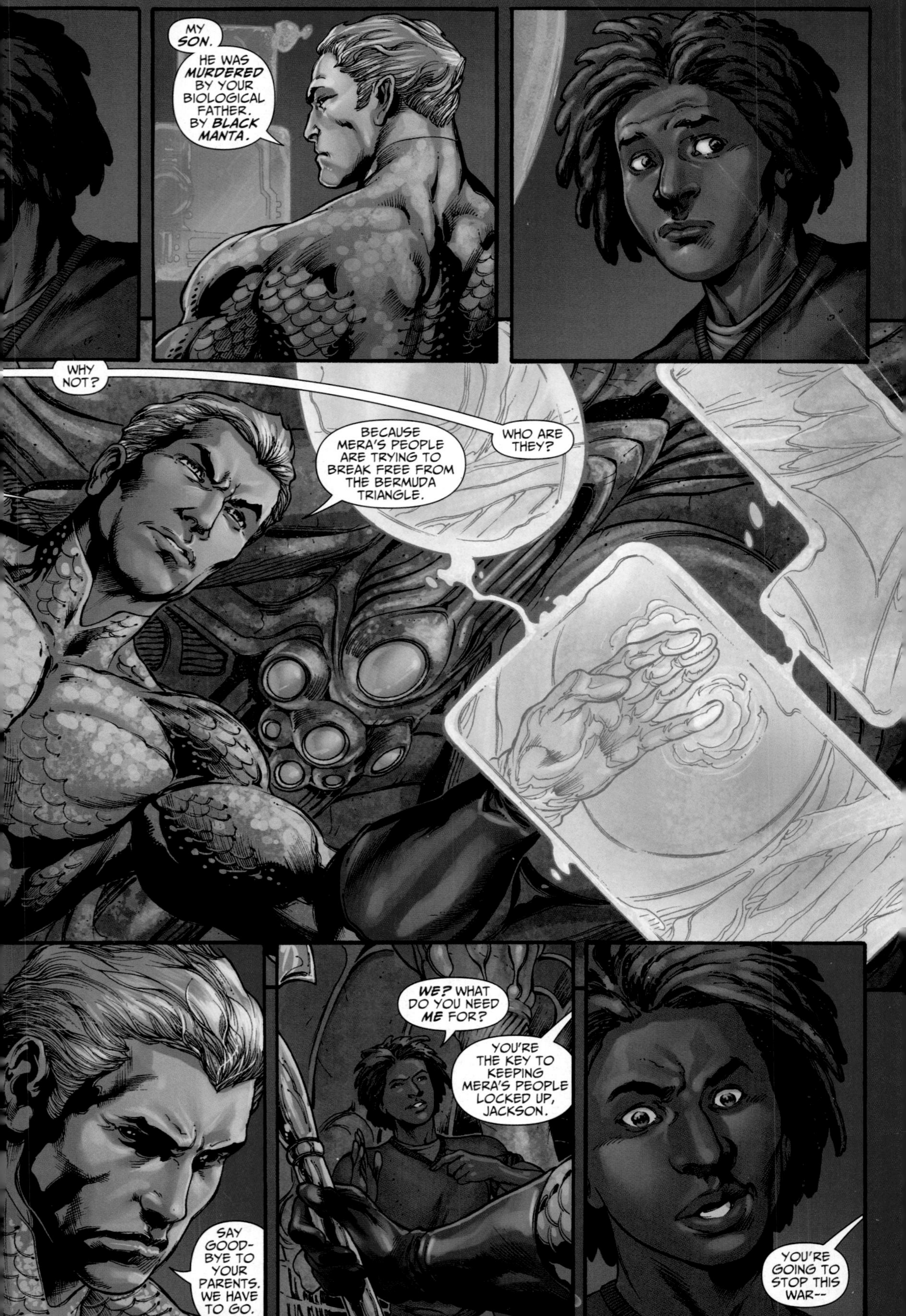
MY SON.
HE WAS MURDERED BY YOUR BIOLOGICAL FATHER. BY BLACK MANTA.
WHY NOT?
BECAUSE MERA'S PEOPLE ARE TRYING TO BREAK FREE FROM THE BERMUDA TRIANGLE.
WHO ARE THEY?
SAY GOOD-BYE TO YOUR PARENTS. WE HAVE TO GO.
WE? WHAT DO YOU NEED ME FOR?
YOU'RE THE KEY TO KEEPING MERA'S PEOPLE LOCKED UP, JACKSON.
YOU'RE GOING TO STOP THIS WAR--

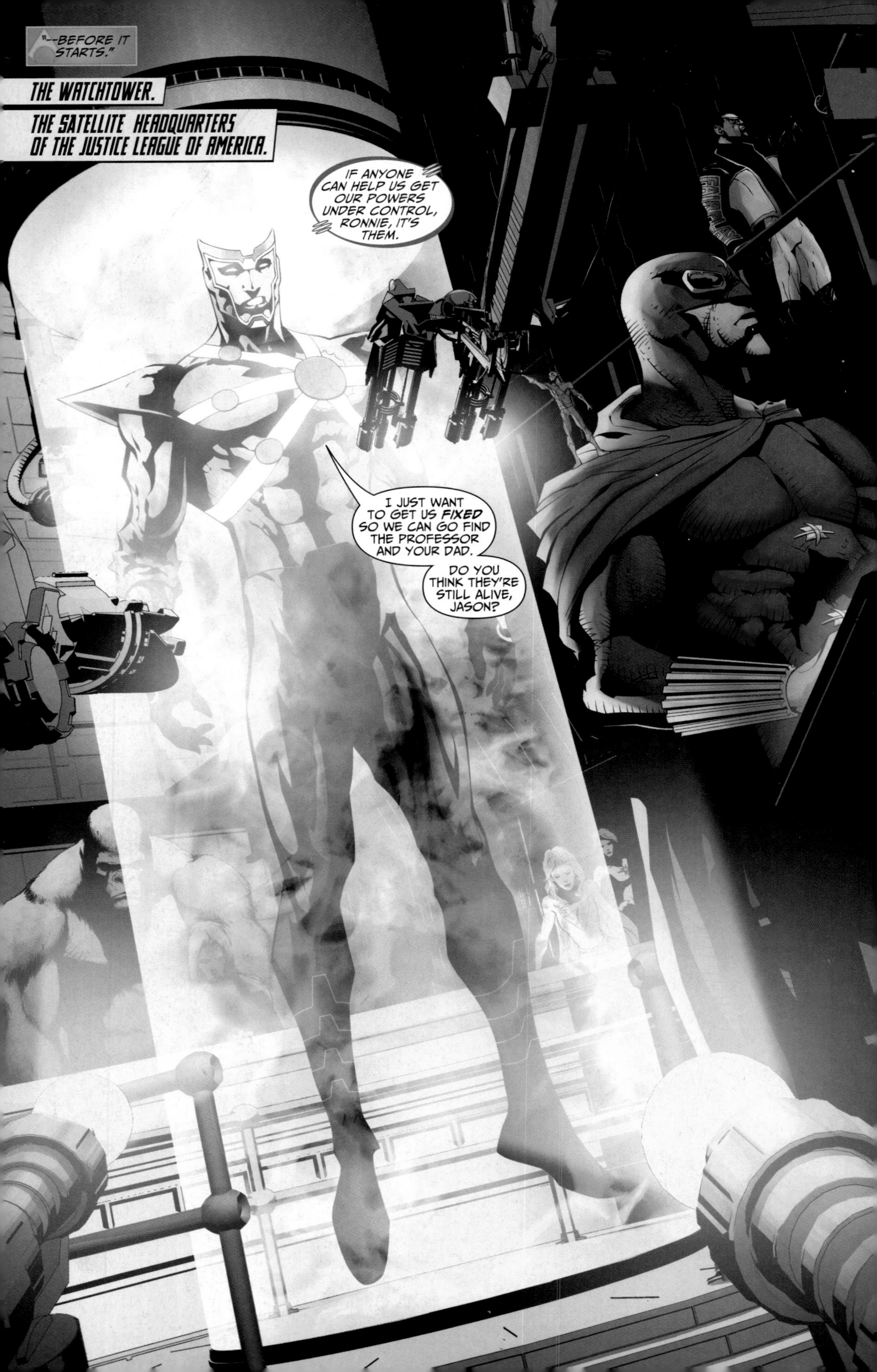
"--BEFORE IT STARTS."
THE WATCHTOWER.
THE SATELLITE HEADQUARTERS OF THE JUSTICE LEAGUE OF AMERICA.
IF ANYONE CAN HELP US GET OUR POWERS UNDER CONTROL, RONNIE, IT'S THEM.
I JUST WANT TO GET US FIXED SO WE CAN GO FIND THE PROFESSOR AND YOUR DAD.
DO YOU THINK THEY'RE STILL ALIVE, JASON?

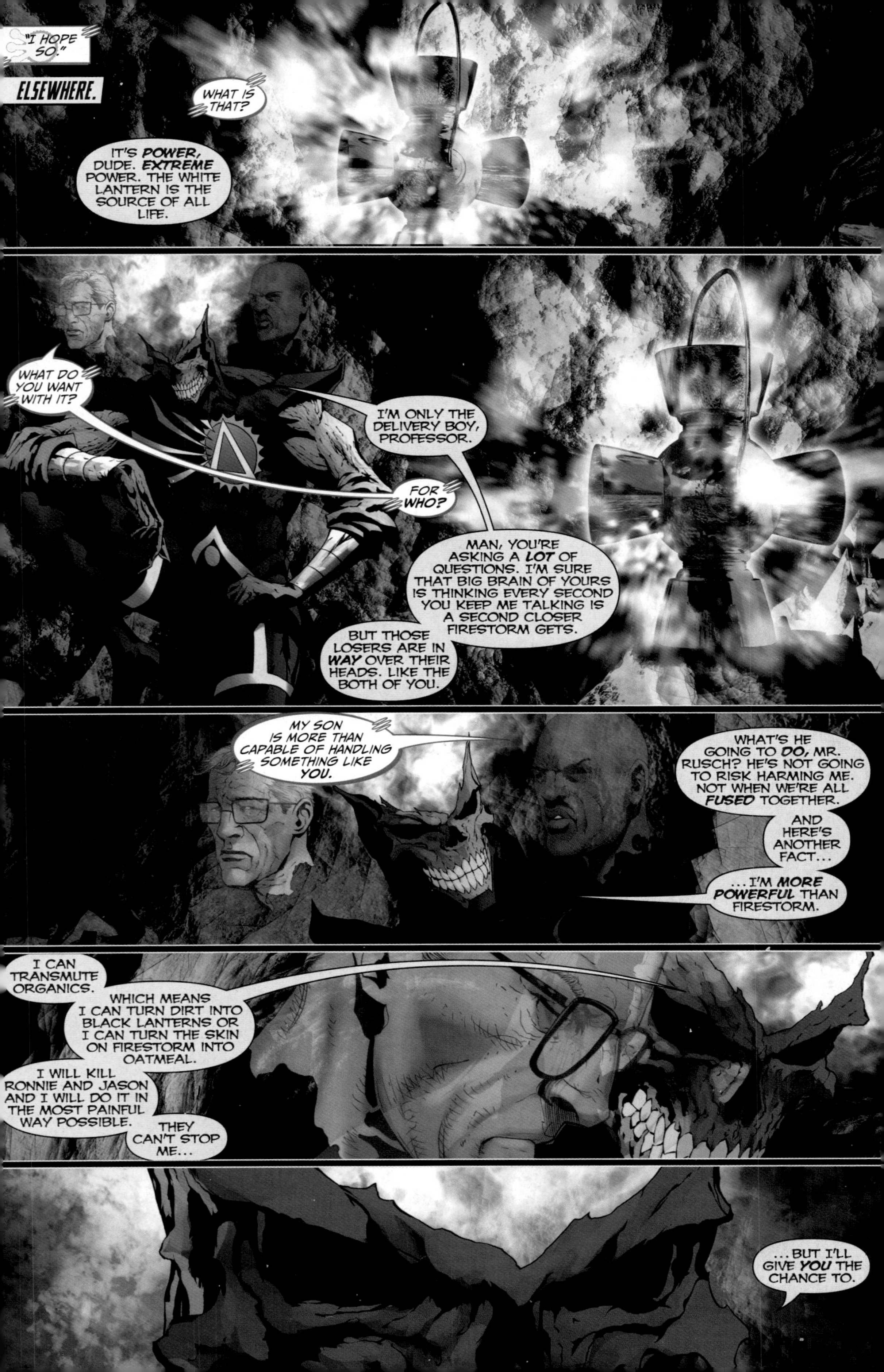
"I HOPE SO."
ELSEWHERE.
WHAT IS THAT?
IT'S POWER, DUDE. EXTREME POWER. THE WHITE LANTERN IS THE SOURCE OF ALL LIFE.
WHAT DO YOU WANT WITH IT?
I'M ONLY THE DELIVERY BOY, PROFESSOR.
FOR WHO?
MAN, YOU'RE ASKING A LOT OF QUESTIONS. I'M SURE THAT BIG BRAIN OF YOURS IS THINKING EVERY SECOND YOU KEEP ME TALKING IS A SECOND CLOSER FIRESTORM GETS.
BUT THOSE LOSERS ARE IN WAY OVER THEIR HEADS. LIKE THE BOTH OF YOU.
MY SON IS MORE THAN CAPABLE OF HANDLING SOMETHING LIKE YOU.
WHAT'S HE GOING TO DO, MR. RUSCH? HE'S NOT GOING TO RISK HARMING ME. NOT WHEN WE'RE ALL FUSED TOGETHER.
AND HERE'S ANOTHER FACT...
...I'M MORE POWERFUL THAN FIRESTORM.
I CAN TRANSMUTE ORGANICS.
WHICH MEANS I CAN TURN DIRT INTO BLACK LANTERNS OR I CAN TURN THE SKIN ON FIRESTORM INTO OATMEAL.
I WILL KILL RONNIE AND JASON AND I WILL DO IT IN THE MOST PAINFUL WAY POSSIBLE.
THEY CAN'T STOP ME...
...BUT I'LL GIVE YOU THE CHANCE TO.

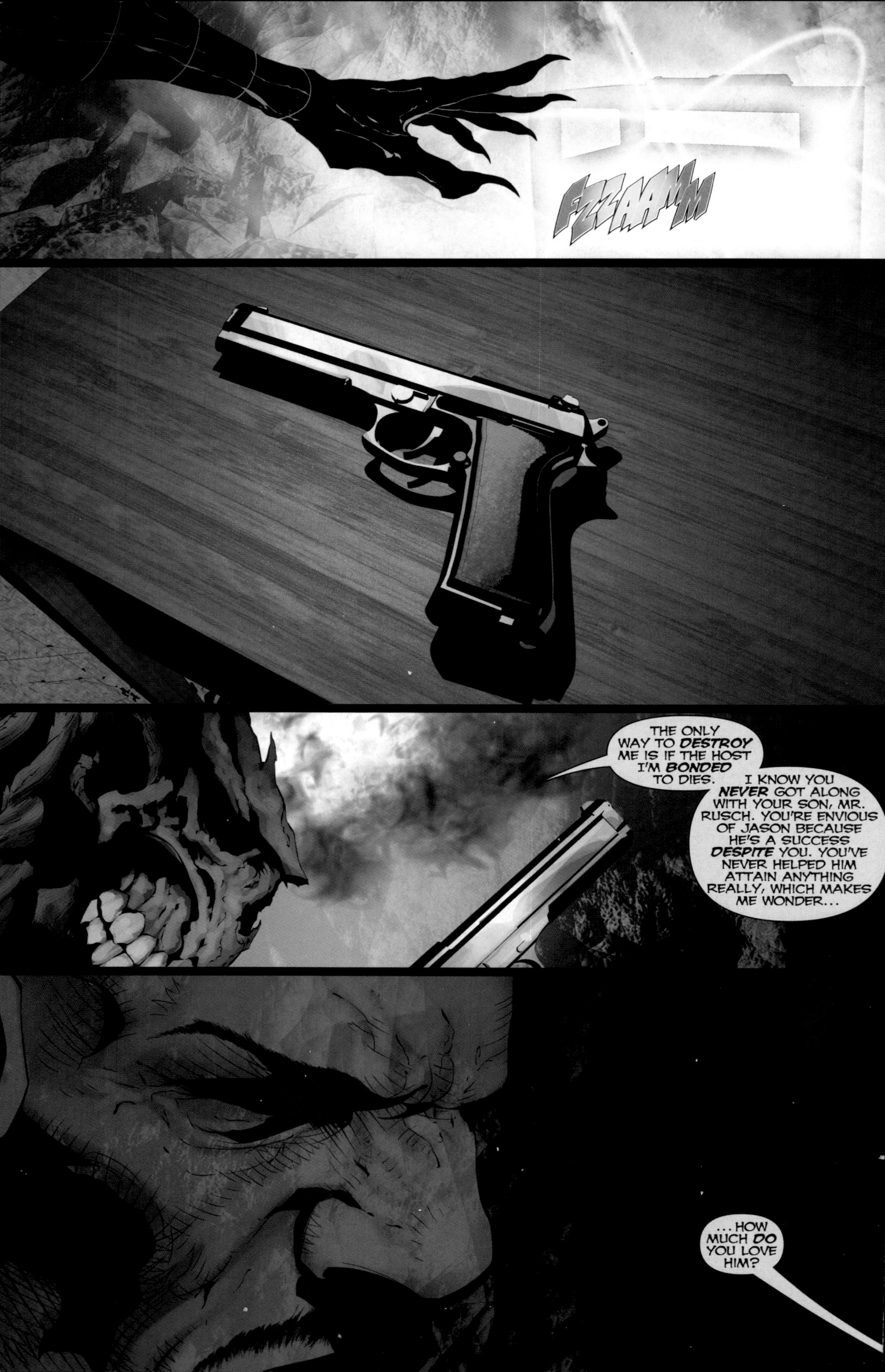
FZZAAMM
THE ONLY WAY TO DESTROY ME IS IF THE HOST I'M BONDED TO DIES.
I KNOW YOU NEVER GOT ALONG WITH YOUR SON, MR. RUSCH. YOU'RE ENVIOUS OF JASON BECAUSE HE'S A SUCCESS DESPITE YOU. YOU'VE NEVER HELPED HIM ATTAIN ANYTHING REALLY, WHICH MAKES ME WONDER...
...HOW MUCH DO YOU LOVE HIM?

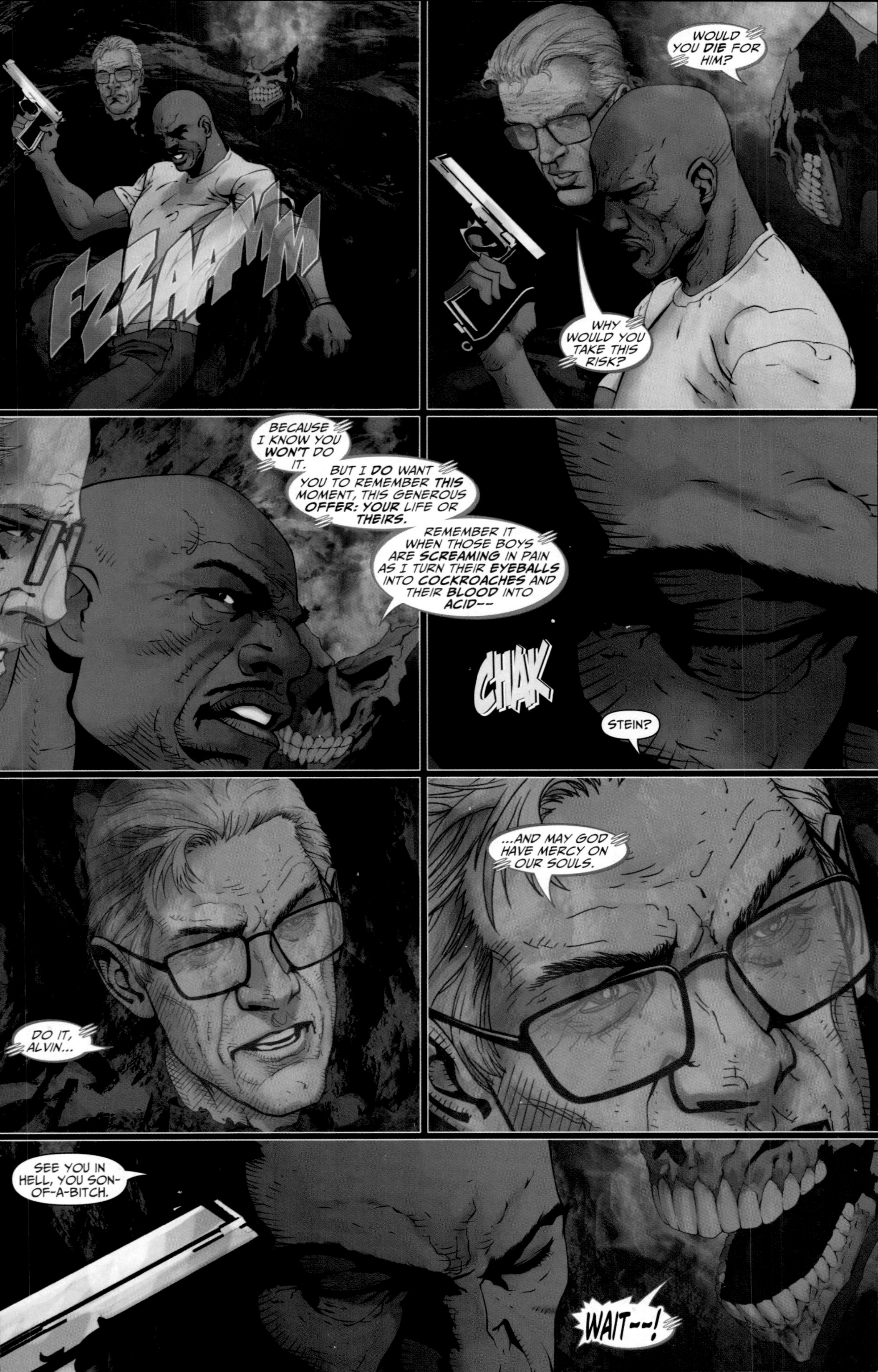

FZZAMM
WOULD YOU **DIE** FOR HIM?
WHY WOULD YOU TAKE THIS RISK?
BECAUSE I KNOW YOU **WON'T** DO IT.
BUT I **DO** WANT YOU TO REMEMBER **THIS** MOMENT, THIS GENEROUS **OFFER: YOUR** LIFE OR **THEIRS.**
REMEMBER IT WHEN THOSE BOYS ARE **SCREAMING** IN PAIN AS I TURN THEIR **EYEBALLS** INTO **COCKROACHES** AND THEIR **BLOOD** INTO **ACID--**
CHAK
STEIN?
DO IT, ALVIN...
...AND MAY GOD HAVE MERCY ON OUR SOULS.
SEE YOU IN HELL, YOU SON-OF-A-BITCH.
WAIT--!

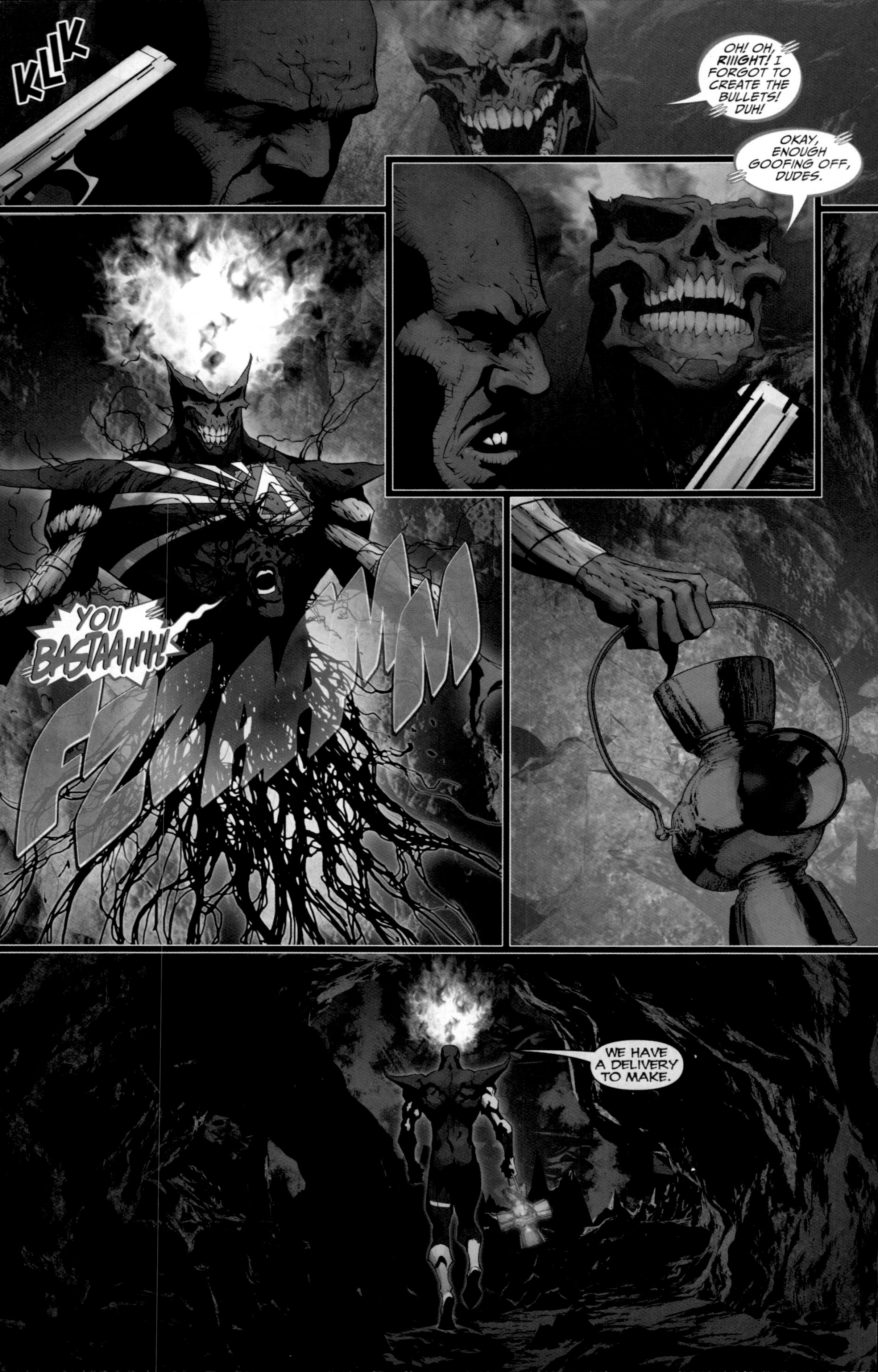
KLIK
OH! OH, RIIIGHT! I FORGOT TO CREATE THE BULLETS! DUH!
OKAY, ENOUGH GOOFING OFF, DUDES.
YOU BASTAAHHH!
FZZAAMMM
WE HAVE A DELIVERY TO MAKE.

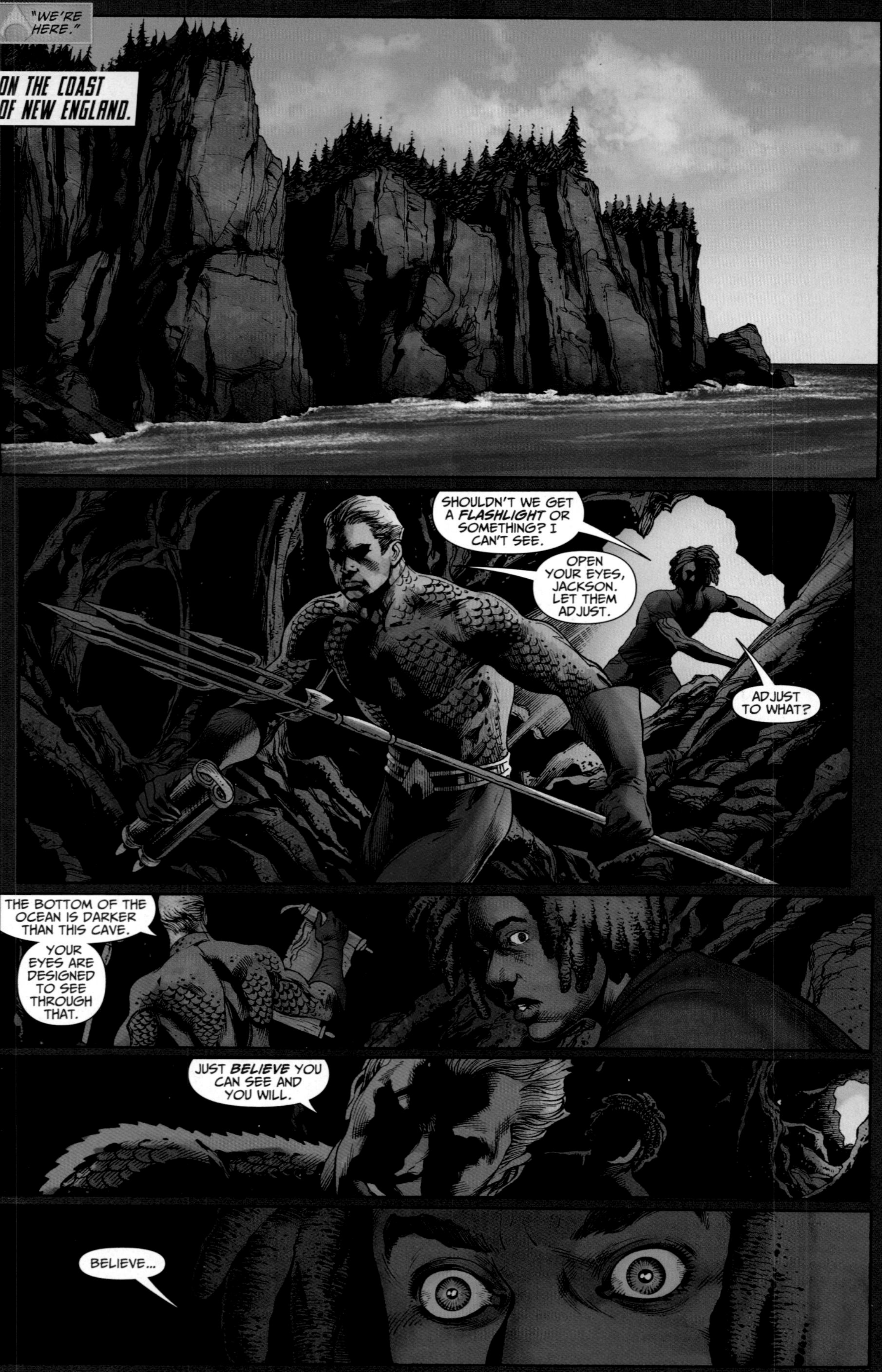
"WE'RE HERE."
ON THE COAST OF NEW ENGLAND.
SHOULDN'T WE GET A FLASHLIGHT OR SOMETHING? I CAN'T SEE.
OPEN YOUR EYES, JACKSON. LET THEM ADJUST.
ADJUST TO WHAT?
THE BOTTOM OF THE OCEAN IS DARKER THAN THIS CAVE.
YOUR EYES ARE DESIGNED TO SEE THROUGH THAT.
JUST BELIEVE YOU CAN SEE AND YOU WILL.
BELIEVE...

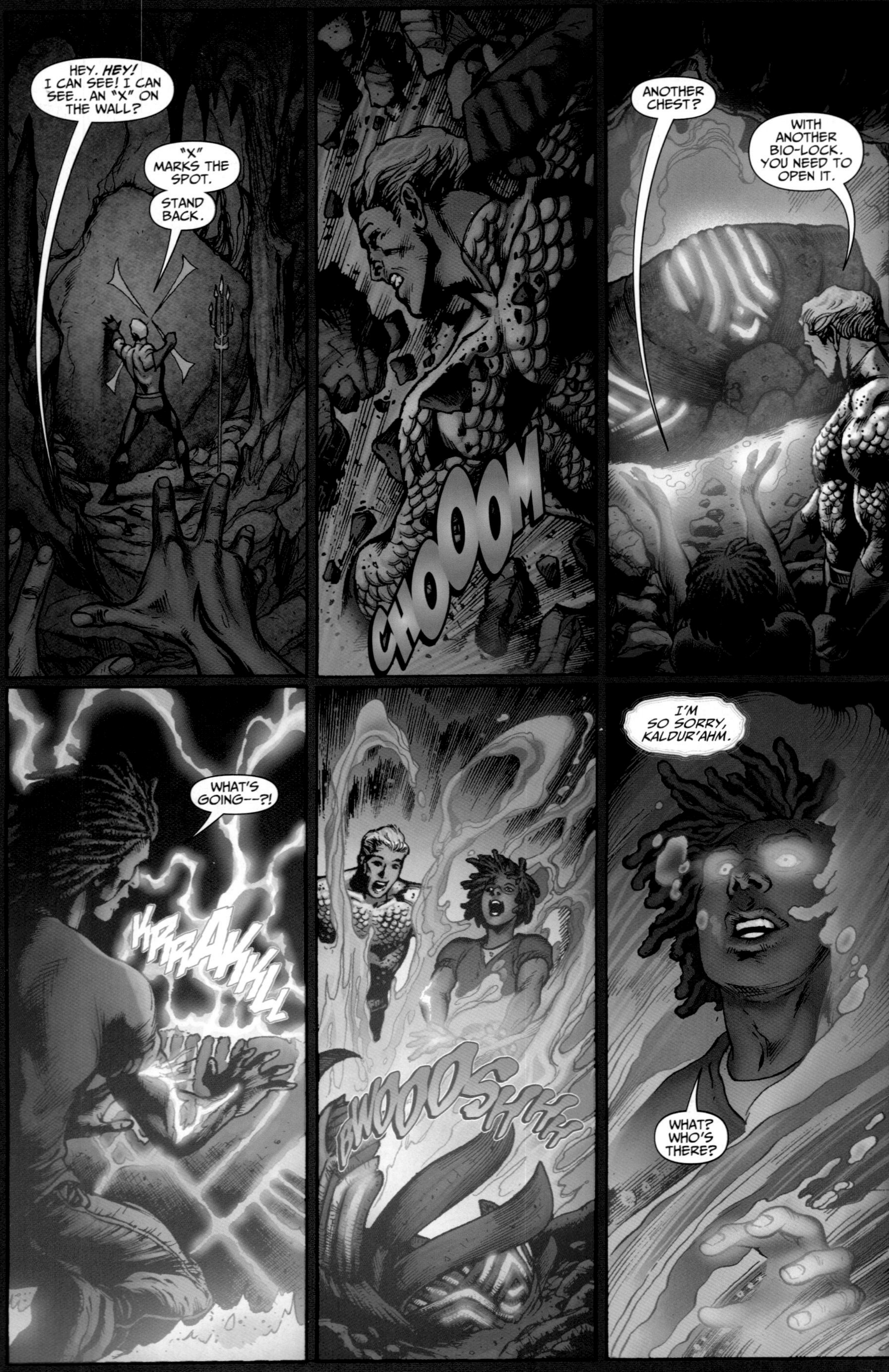
HEY. HEY! I CAN SEE! I CAN SEE... AN "X" ON THE WALL?
"X" MARKS THE SPOT.
STAND BACK.
CHOOOOM
ANOTHER CHEST?
WITH ANOTHER BIO-LOCK. YOU NEED TO OPEN IT.
WHAT'S GOING--?!
KRRAKKLL
BWOOOSHHH
I'M SO SORRY, KALDUR'AHM.
WHAT? WHO'S THERE?

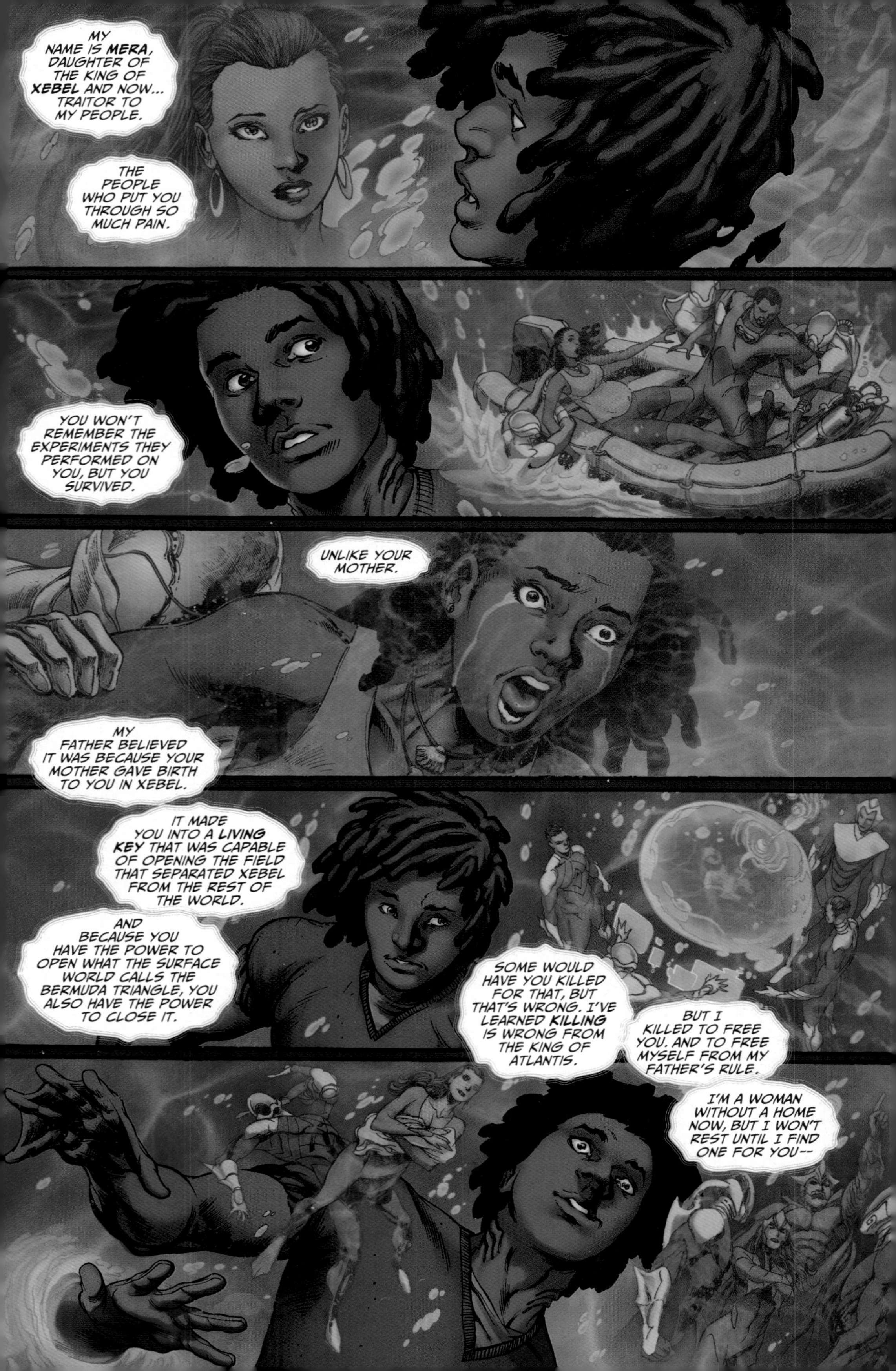
MY NAME IS MERA, DAUGHTER OF THE KING OF XEBEL AND NOW... TRAITOR TO MY PEOPLE.
THE PEOPLE WHO PUT YOU THROUGH SO MUCH PAIN.
YOU WON'T REMEMBER THE EXPERIMENTS THEY PERFORMED ON YOU, BUT YOU SURVIVED.
UNLIKE YOUR MOTHER.
MY FATHER BELIEVED IT WAS BECAUSE YOUR MOTHER GAVE BIRTH TO YOU IN XEBEL.
IT MADE YOU INTO A LIVING KEY THAT WAS CAPABLE OF OPENING THE FIELD THAT SEPARATED XEBEL FROM THE REST OF THE WORLD.
AND BECAUSE YOU HAVE THE POWER TO OPEN WHAT THE SURFACE WORLD CALLS THE BERMUDA TRIANGLE, YOU ALSO HAVE THE POWER TO CLOSE IT.
SOME WOULD HAVE YOU KILLED FOR THAT, BUT THAT'S WRONG. I'VE LEARNED KILLING IS WRONG FROM THE KING OF ATLANTIS.
BUT I KILLED TO FREE YOU. AND TO FREE MYSELF FROM MY FATHER'S RULE.
I'M A WOMAN WITHOUT A HOME NOW, BUT I WON'T REST UNTIL I FIND ONE FOR YOU--

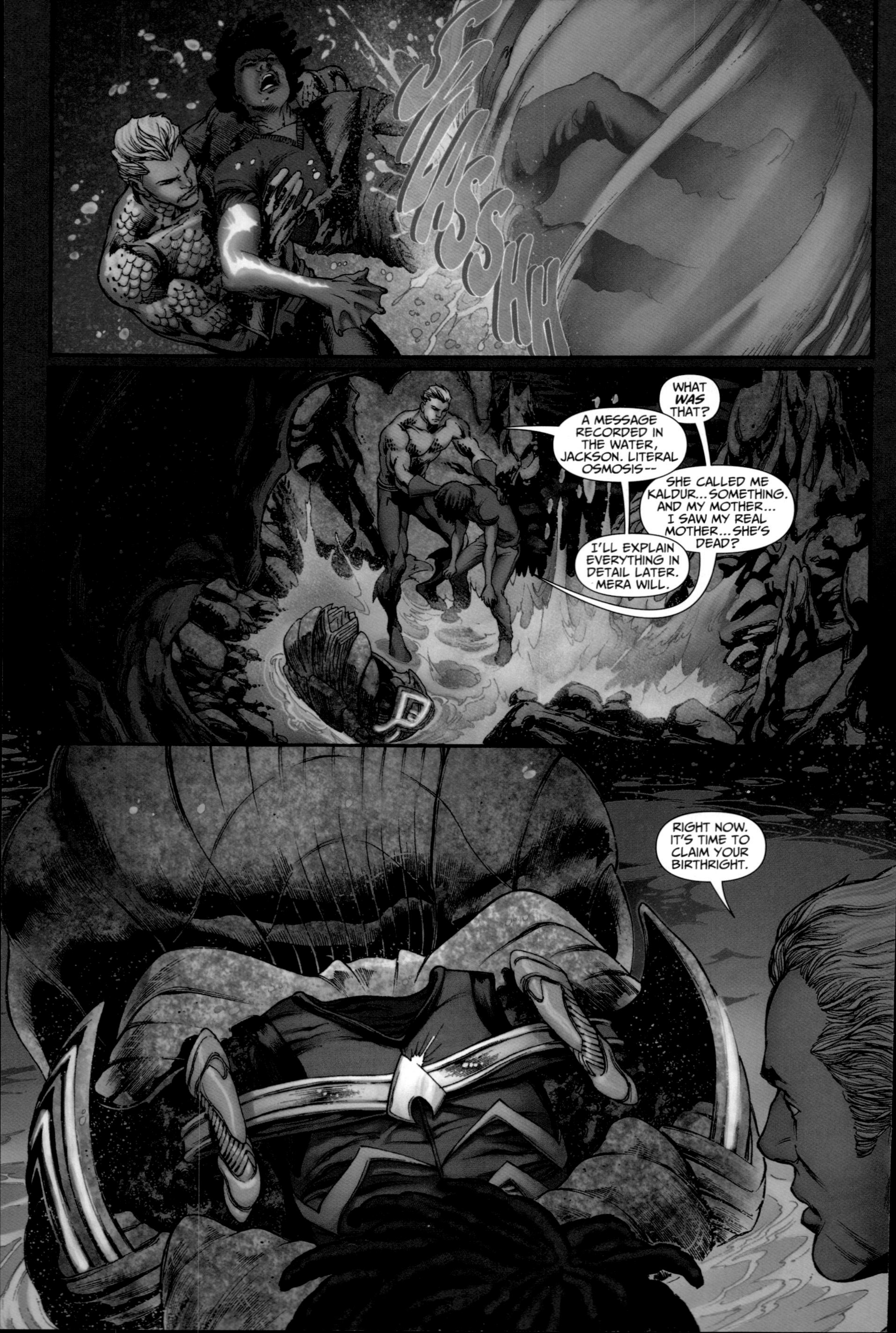
SHLASSHH
WHAT WAS THAT?
A MESSAGE RECORDED IN THE WATER, JACKSON. LITERAL OSMOSIS--
SHE CALLED ME KALDUR...SOMETHING. AND MY MOTHER... I SAW MY REAL MOTHER...SHE'S DEAD?
I'LL EXPLAIN EVERYTHING IN DETAIL LATER. MERA WILL.
RIGHT NOW. IT'S TIME TO CLAIM YOUR BIRTHRIGHT.

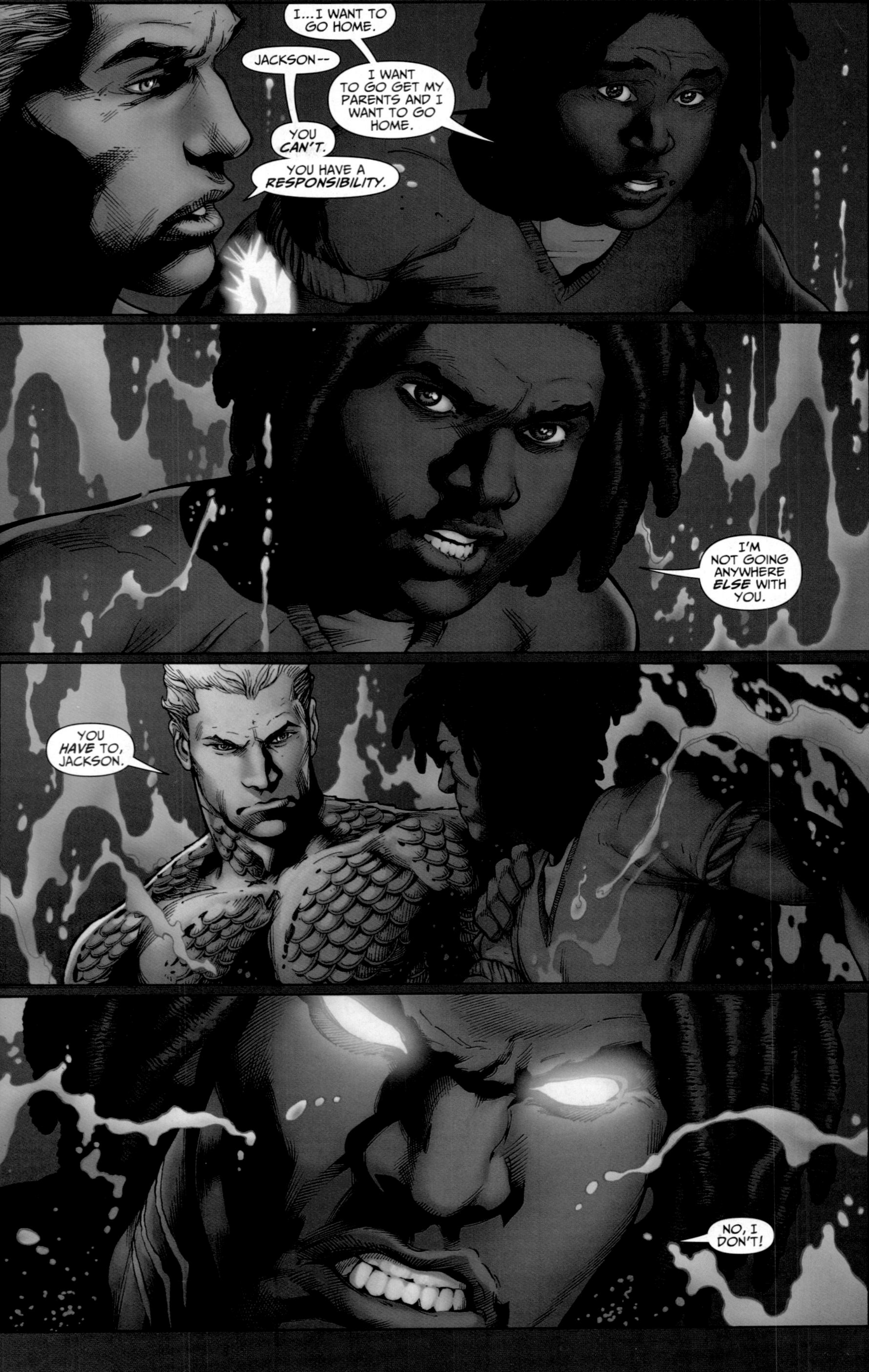
I...I WANT TO GO HOME.
JACKSON--
I WANT TO GO GET MY PARENTS AND I WANT TO GO HOME.
YOU *CAN'T*.
YOU HAVE A *RESPONSIBILITY*.
I'M NOT GOING ANYWHERE *ELSE* WITH YOU.
YOU *HAVE* TO, JACKSON.
NO, I DON'T!

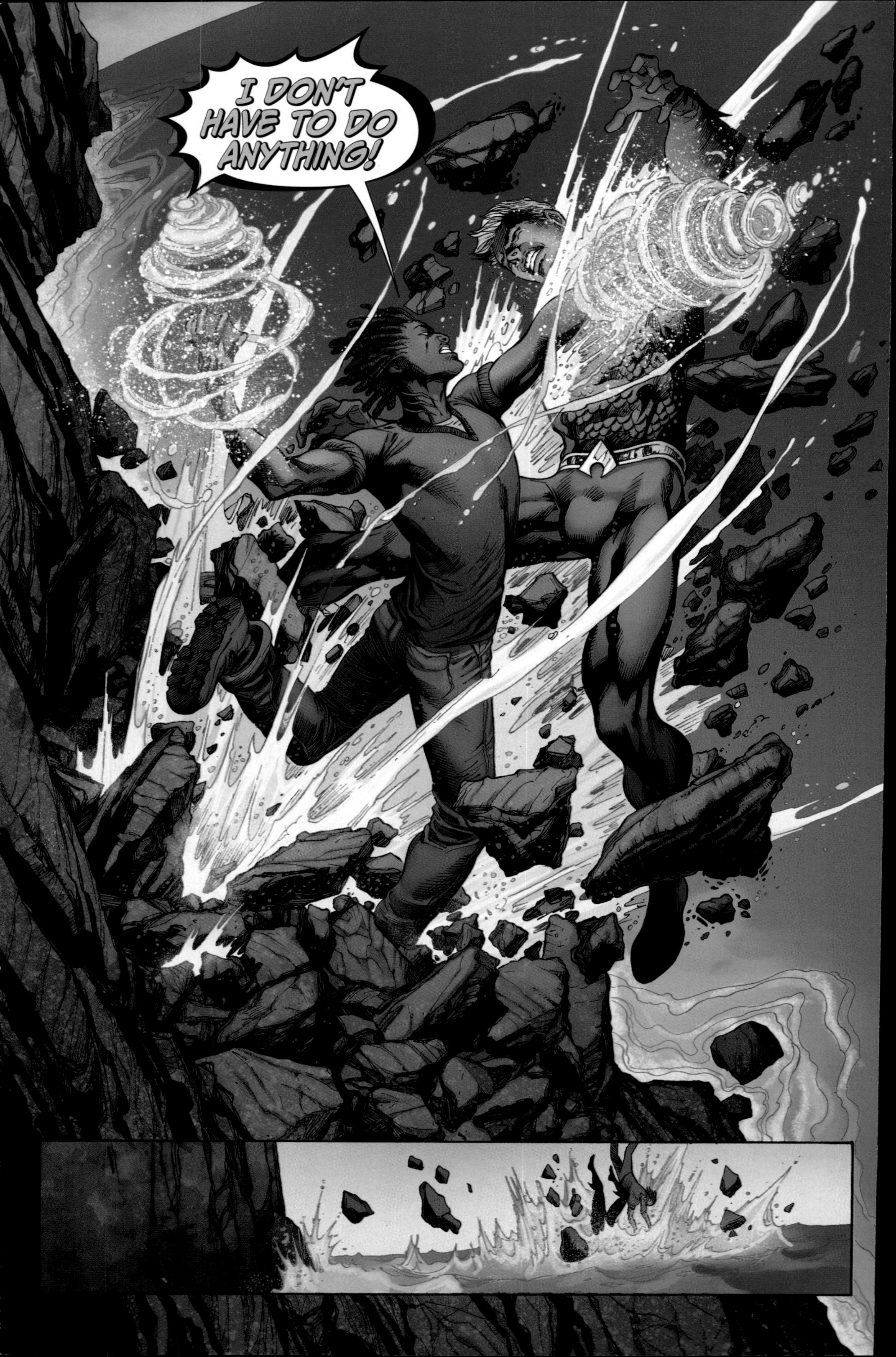
I DON'T HAVE TO DO ANYTHING!

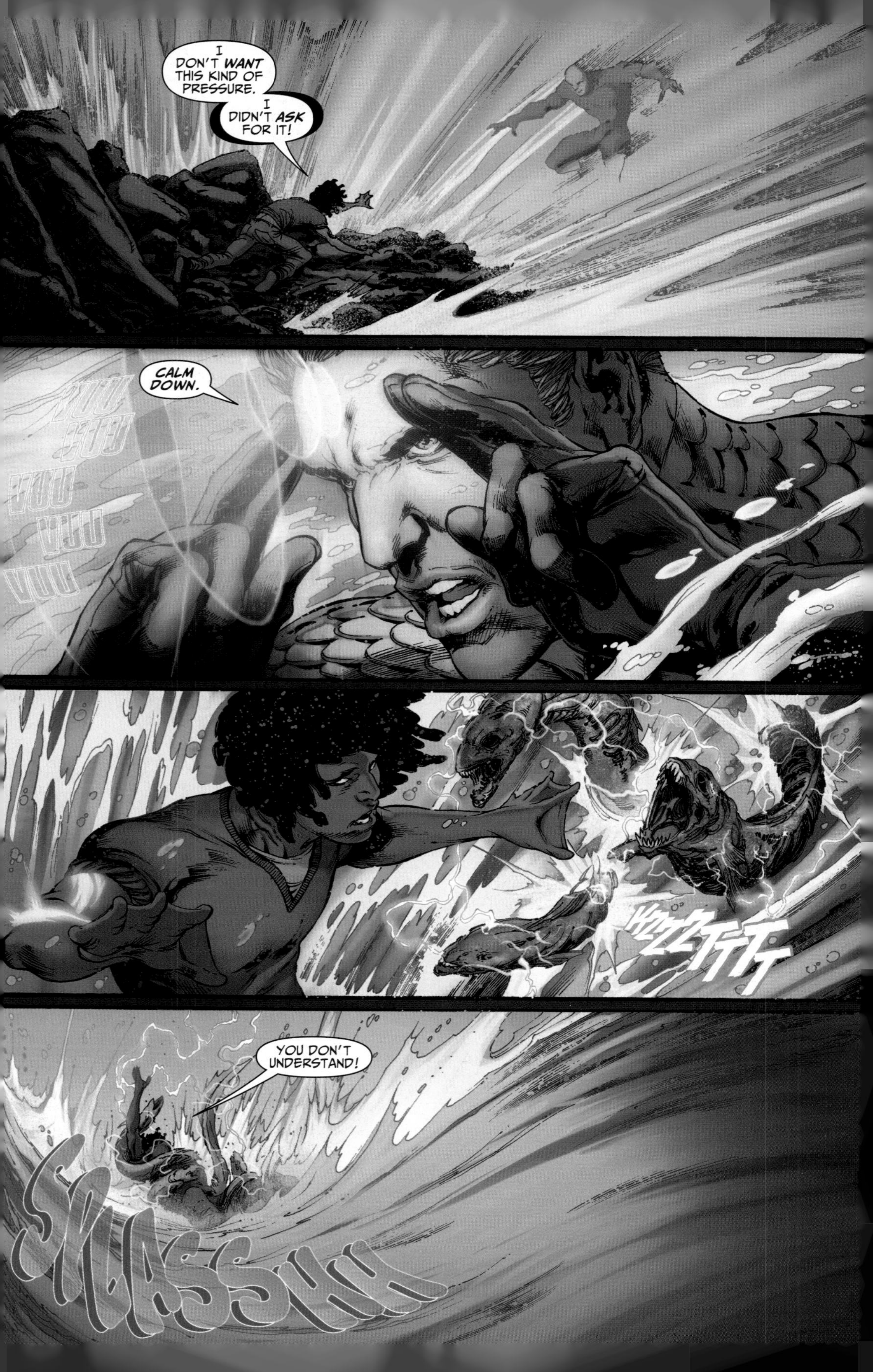
I DON'T WANT THIS KIND OF PRESSURE.
I DIDN'T ASK FOR IT!
CALM DOWN.
YOU DON'T UNDERSTAND!

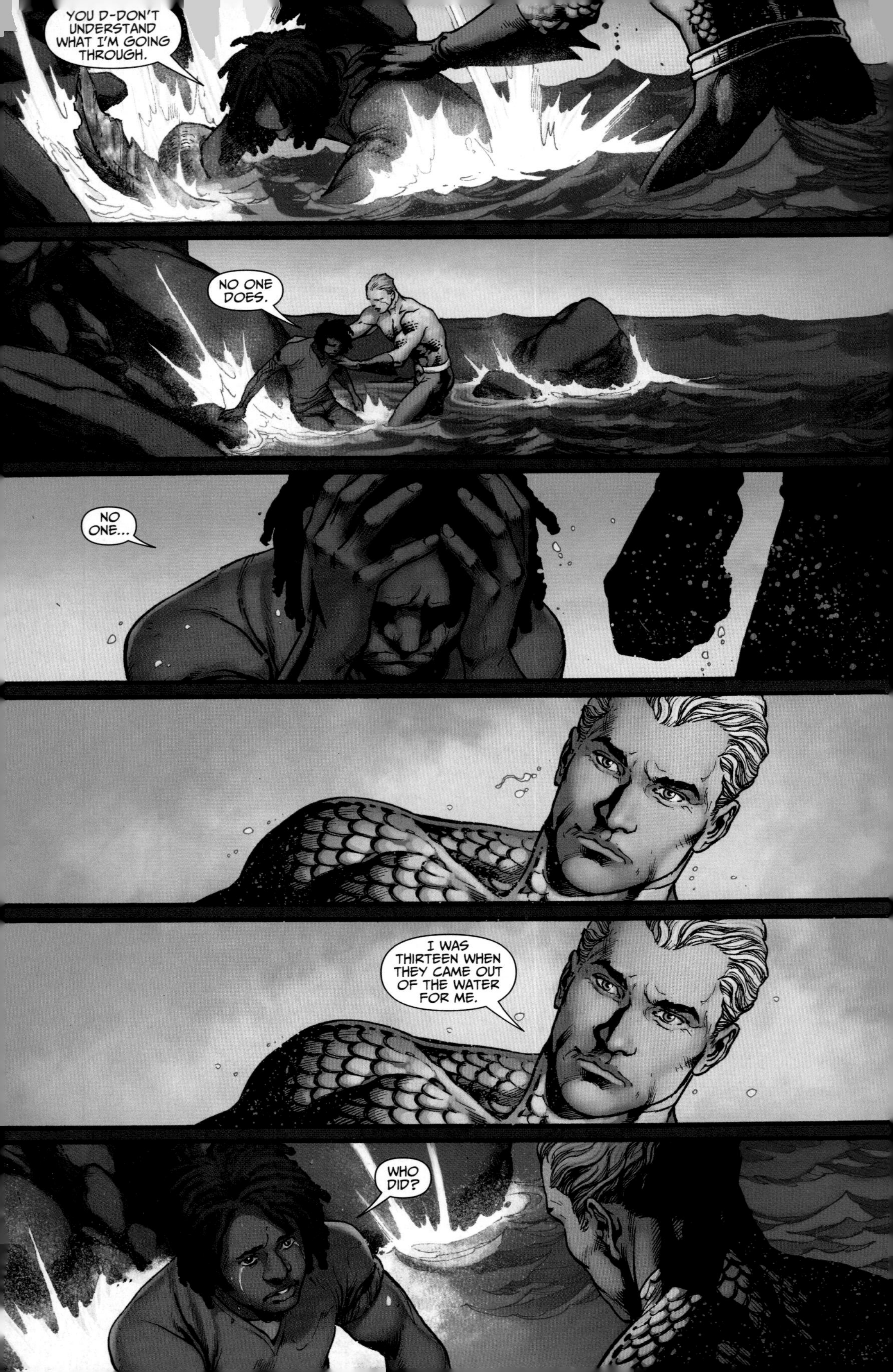
YOU D-DON'T UNDERSTAND WHAT I'M GOING THROUGH.
NO ONE DOES.
NO ONE...
I WAS THIRTEEN WHEN THEY CAME OUT OF THE WATER FOR ME.
WHO DID?

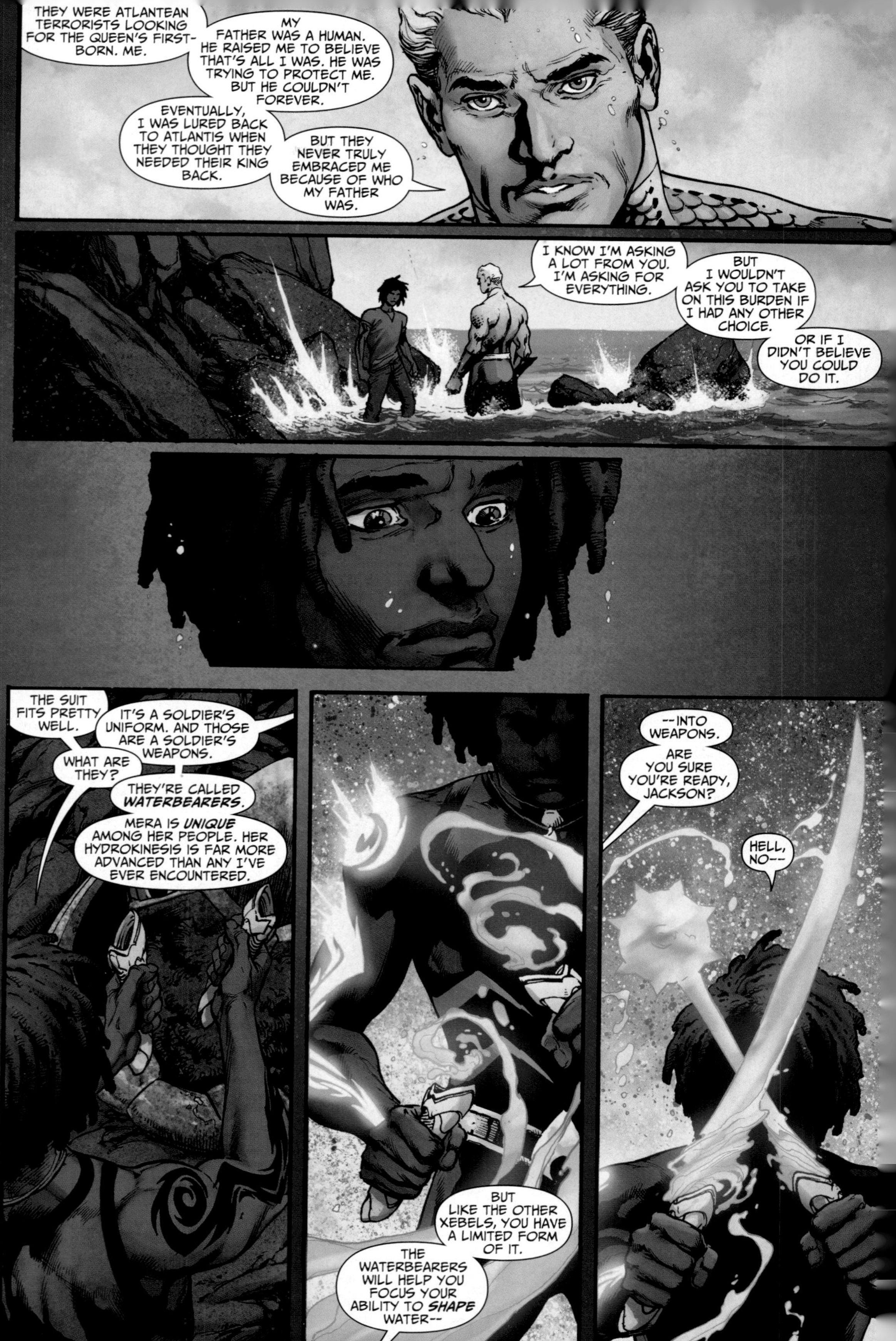
THEY WERE ATLANTEAN TERRORISTS LOOKING FOR THE QUEEN'S FIRST-BORN. ME.
MY FATHER WAS A HUMAN. HE RAISED ME TO BELIEVE THAT'S ALL I WAS. HE WAS TRYING TO PROTECT ME. BUT HE COULDN'T FOREVER.
EVENTUALLY, I WAS LURED BACK TO ATLANTIS WHEN THEY THOUGHT THEY NEEDED THEIR KING BACK.
BUT THEY NEVER TRULY EMBRACED ME BECAUSE OF WHO MY FATHER WAS.
I KNOW I'M ASKING A LOT FROM YOU. I'M ASKING FOR EVERYTHING.
BUT I WOULDN'T ASK YOU TO TAKE ON THIS BURDEN IF I HAD ANY OTHER CHOICE.
OR IF I DIDN'T BELIEVE YOU COULD DO IT.
THE SUIT FITS PRETTY WELL.
IT'S A SOLDIER'S UNIFORM. AND THOSE ARE A SOLDIER'S WEAPONS.
WHAT ARE THEY?
THEY'RE CALLED ***WATERBEARERS***.
MERA IS ***UNIQUE*** AMONG HER PEOPLE. HER HYDROKINESIS IS FAR MORE ADVANCED THAN ANY I'VE EVER ENCOUNTERED.
BUT LIKE THE OTHER XEBELS, YOU HAVE A LIMITED FORM OF IT.
THE WATERBEARERS WILL HELP YOU FOCUS YOUR ABILITY TO ***SHAPE*** WATER--
--INTO WEAPONS.
ARE YOU SURE YOU'RE READY, JACKSON?
HELL, NO--

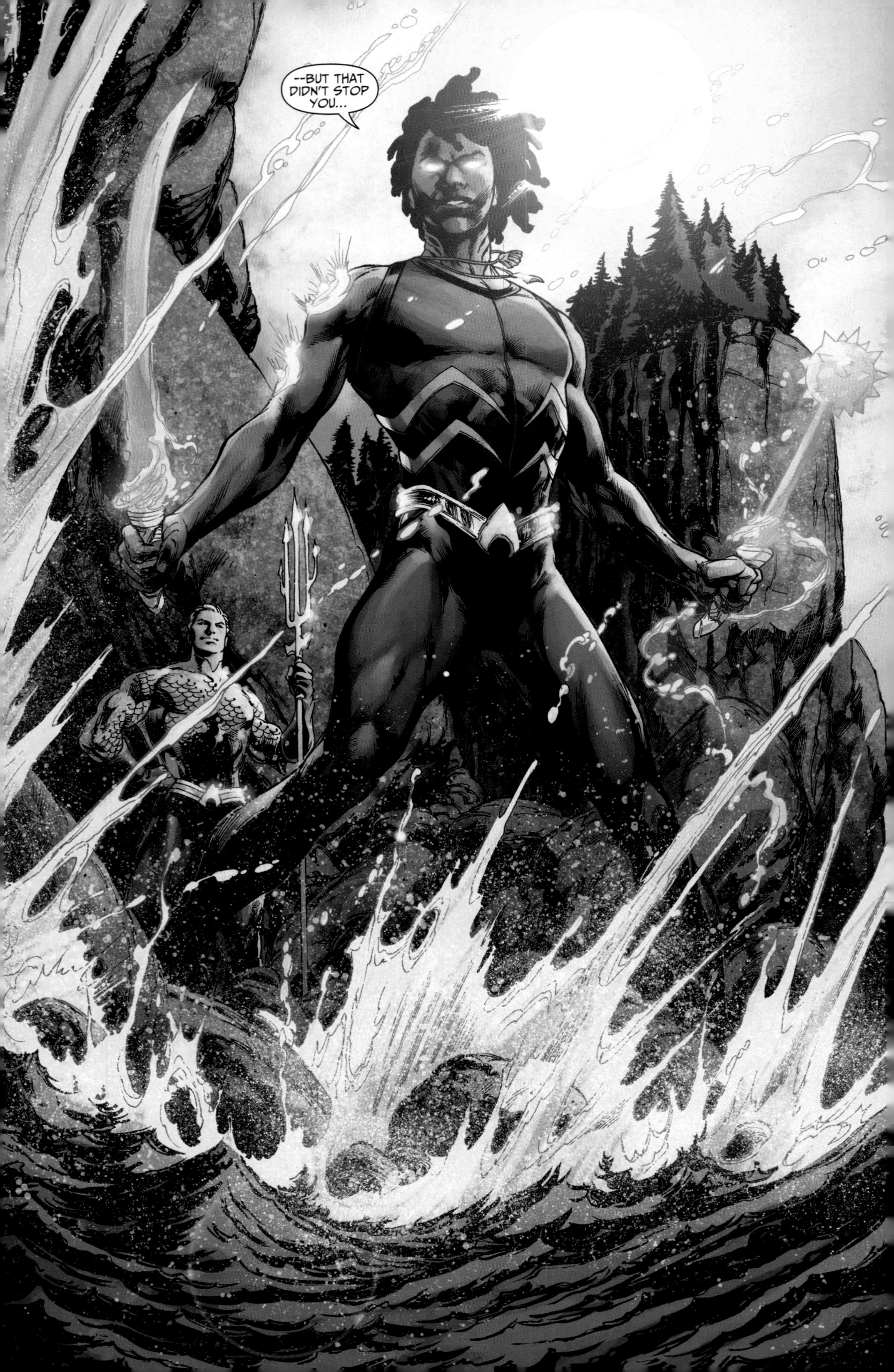
--BUT THAT DIDN'T STOP YOU...

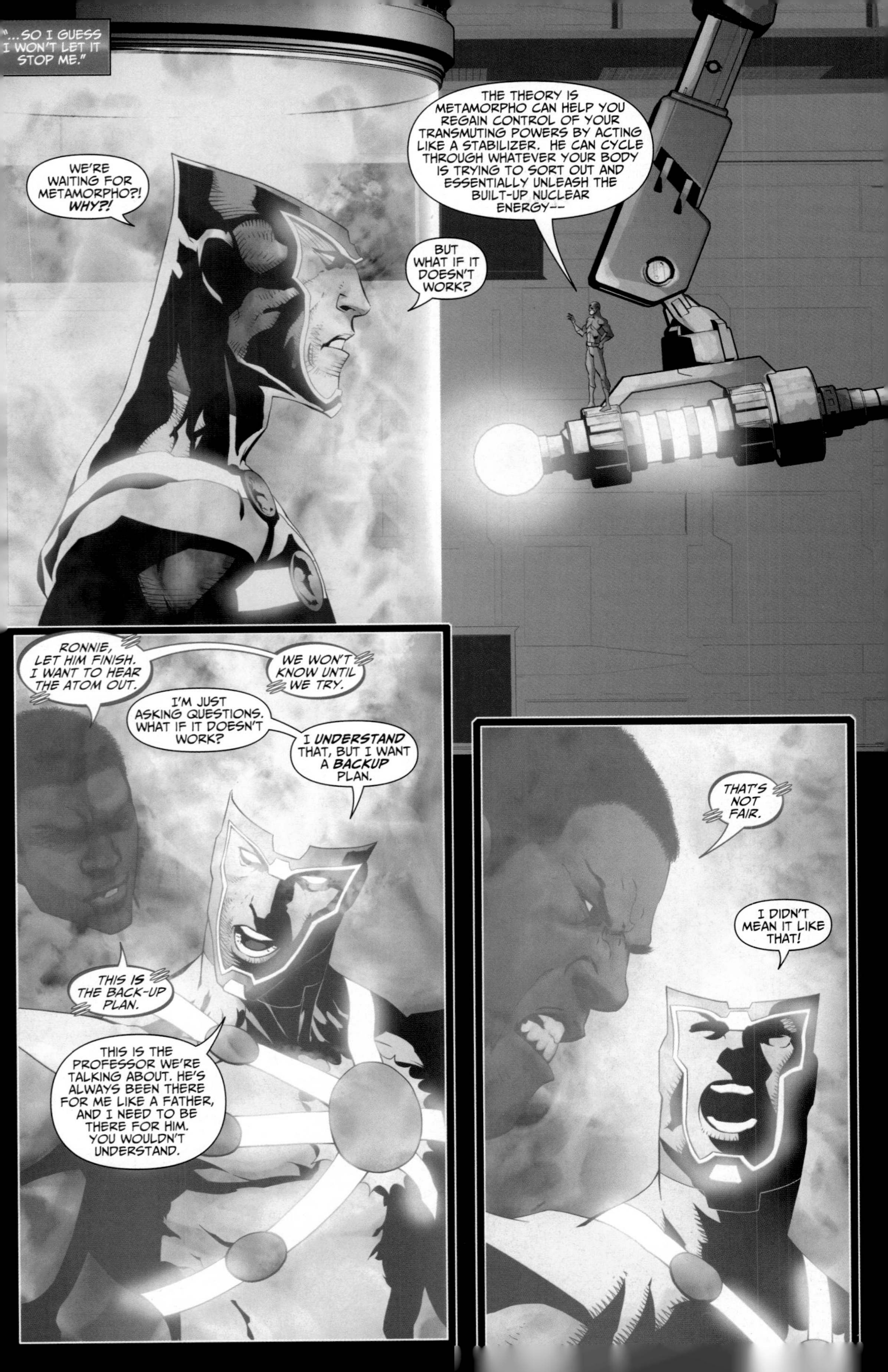
"...SO I GUESS I WON'T LET IT STOP ME."
WE'RE WAITING FOR METAMORPHO?! WHY?!
THE THEORY IS METAMORPHO CAN HELP YOU REGAIN CONTROL OF YOUR TRANSMUTING POWERS BY ACTING LIKE A STABILIZER. HE CAN CYCLE THROUGH WHATEVER YOUR BODY IS TRYING TO SORT OUT AND ESSENTIALLY UNLEASH THE BUILT-UP NUCLEAR ENERGY--
BUT WHAT IF IT DOESN'T WORK?
RONNIE, LET HIM FINISH. I WANT TO HEAR THE ATOM OUT.
WE WON'T KNOW UNTIL WE TRY.
I'M JUST ASKING QUESTIONS. WHAT IF IT DOESN'T WORK?
I UNDERSTAND THAT, BUT I WANT A BACKUP PLAN.
THIS IS THE BACK-UP PLAN.
THIS IS THE PROFESSOR WE'RE TALKING ABOUT. HE'S ALWAYS BEEN THERE FOR ME LIKE A FATHER, AND I NEED TO BE THERE FOR HIM. YOU WOULDN'T UNDERSTAND.
THAT'S NOT FAIR.
I DIDN'T MEAN IT LIKE THAT!

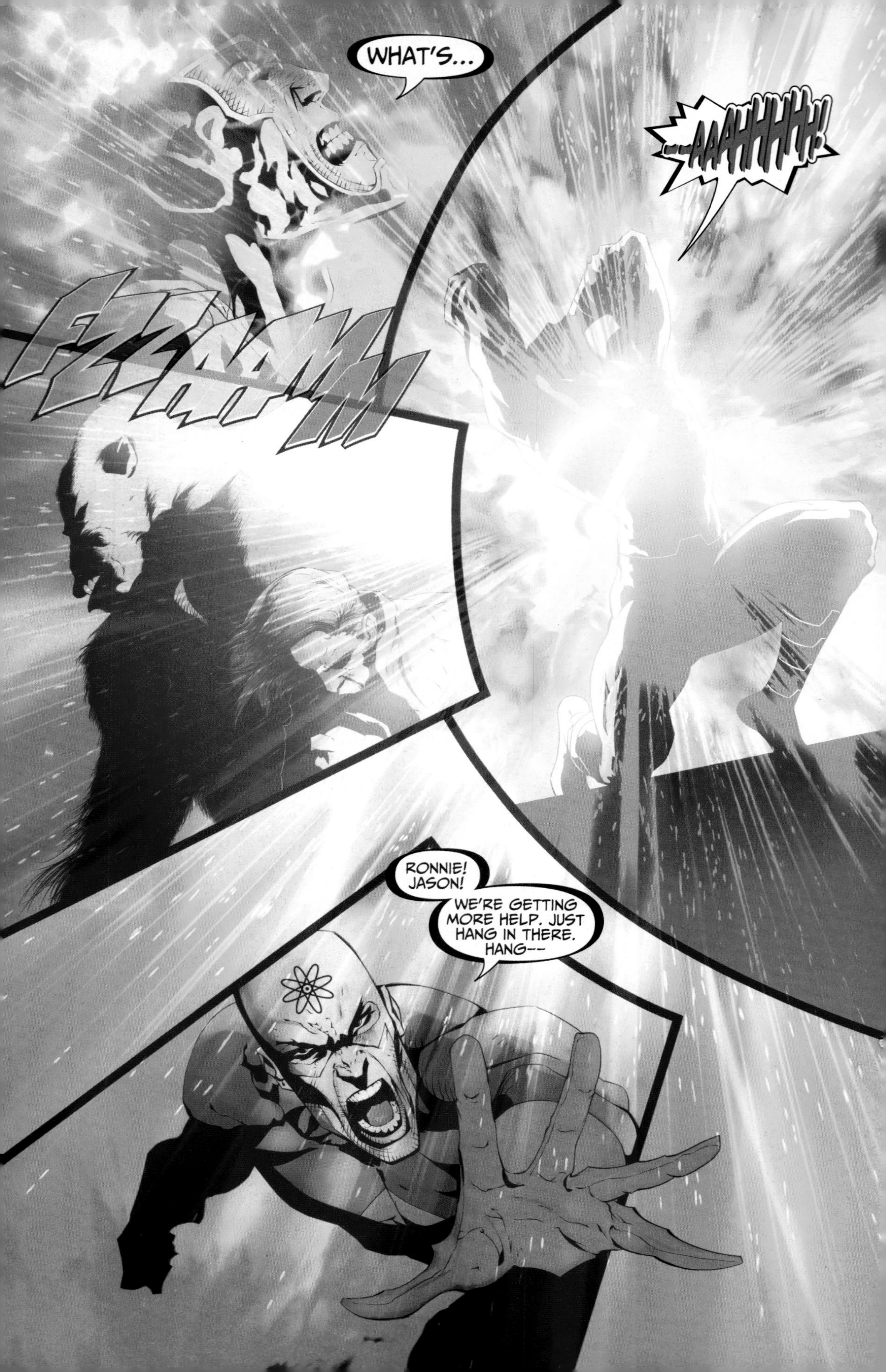

WHAT'S...
--AAAHHHHH!
FZZAAM!
RONNIE! JASON!
WE'RE GETTING MORE HELP. JUST HANG IN THERE. HANG--

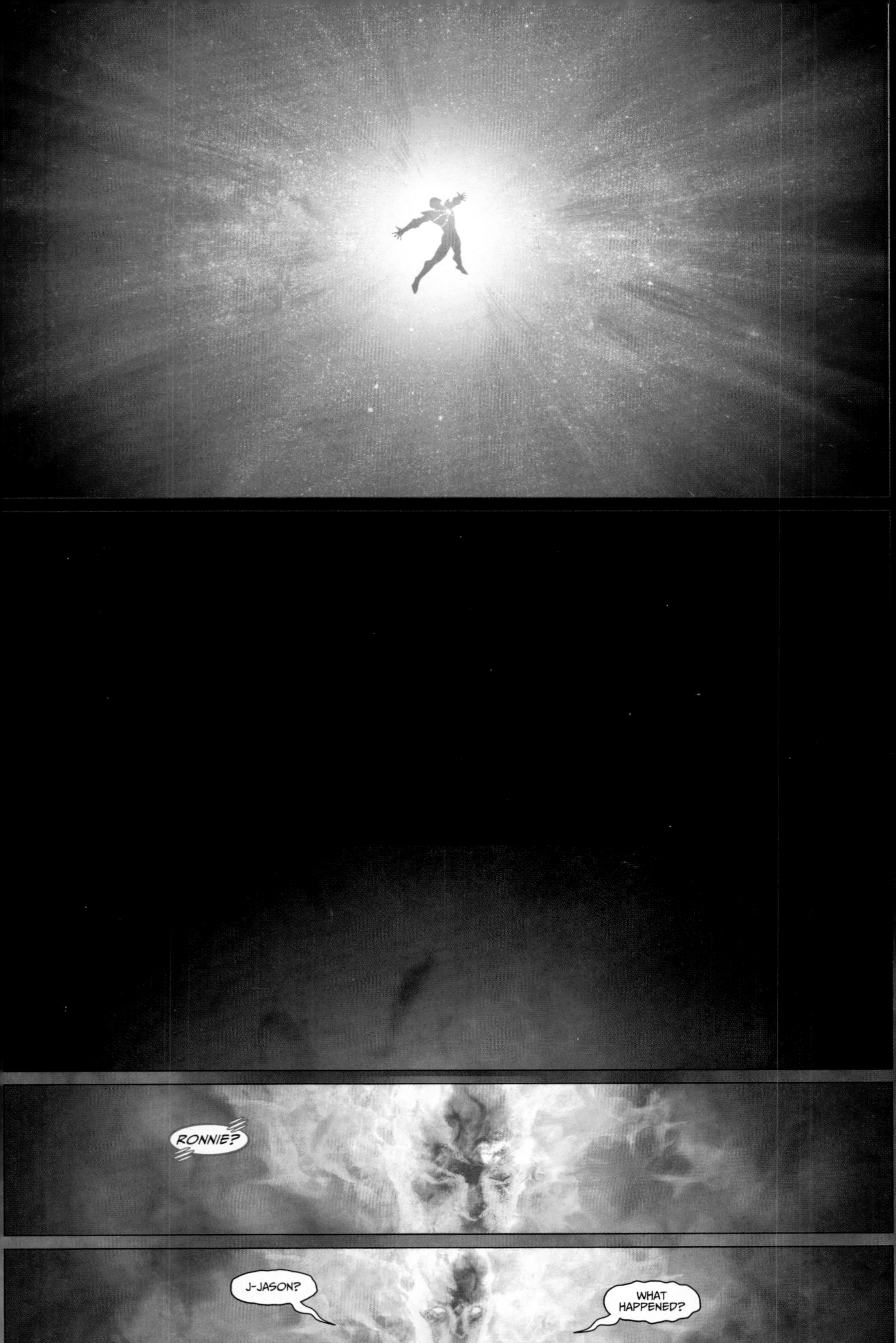
RONNIE?
J-JASON?
WHAT HAPPENED?

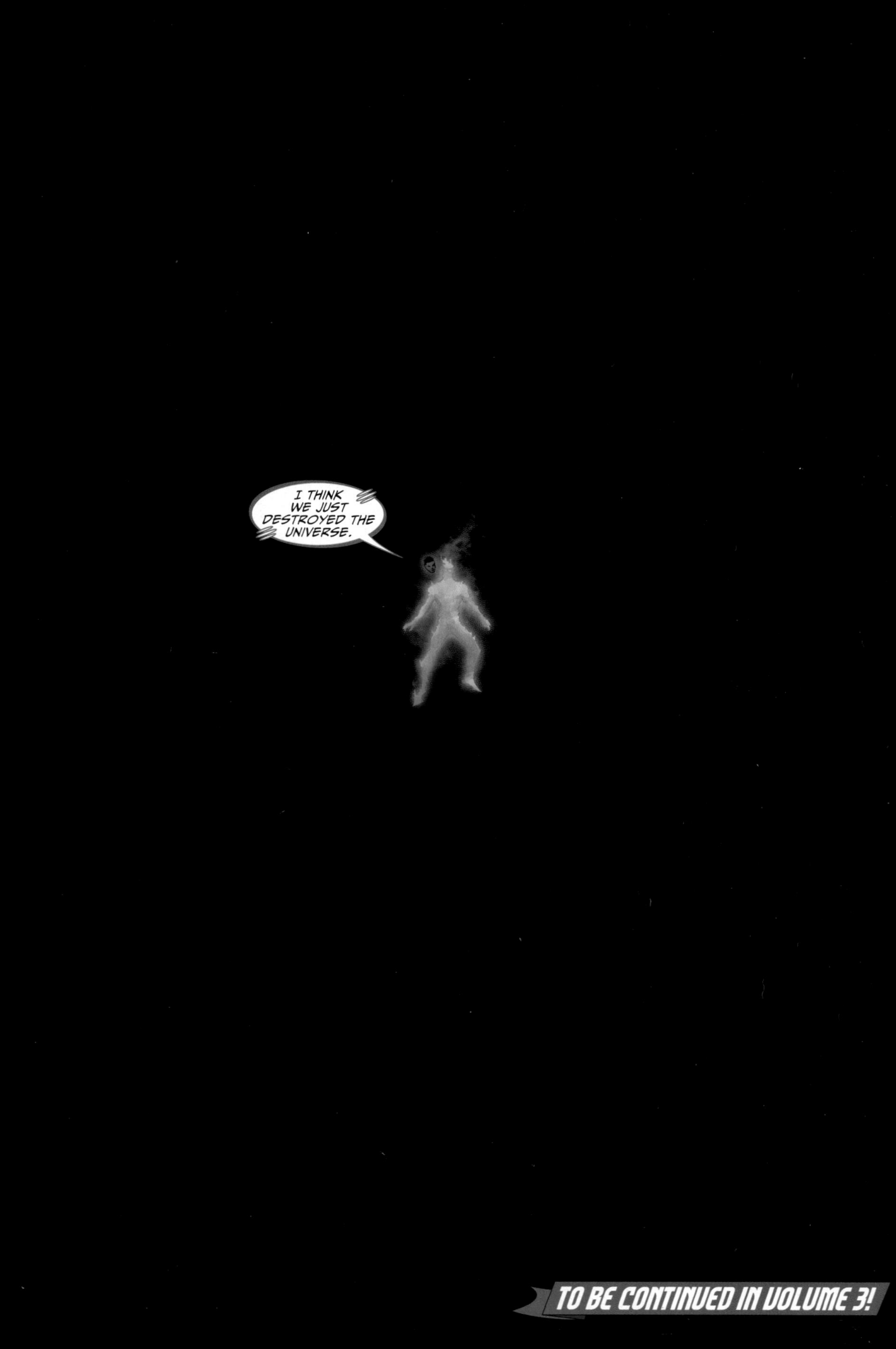
I THINK WE JUST DESTROYED THE UNIVERSE.
TO BE CONTINUED IN VOLUME 3!

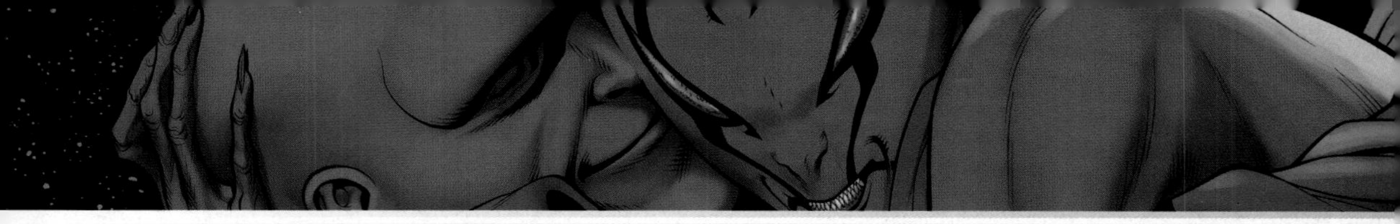

# VARIANT
# COVER GALLERY

**BRIGHTEST DAY 8**
*Variant cover by Ryan Sook, Fernando Pasarin and Joel Gomez with Randy Major and Carrie Strachan*

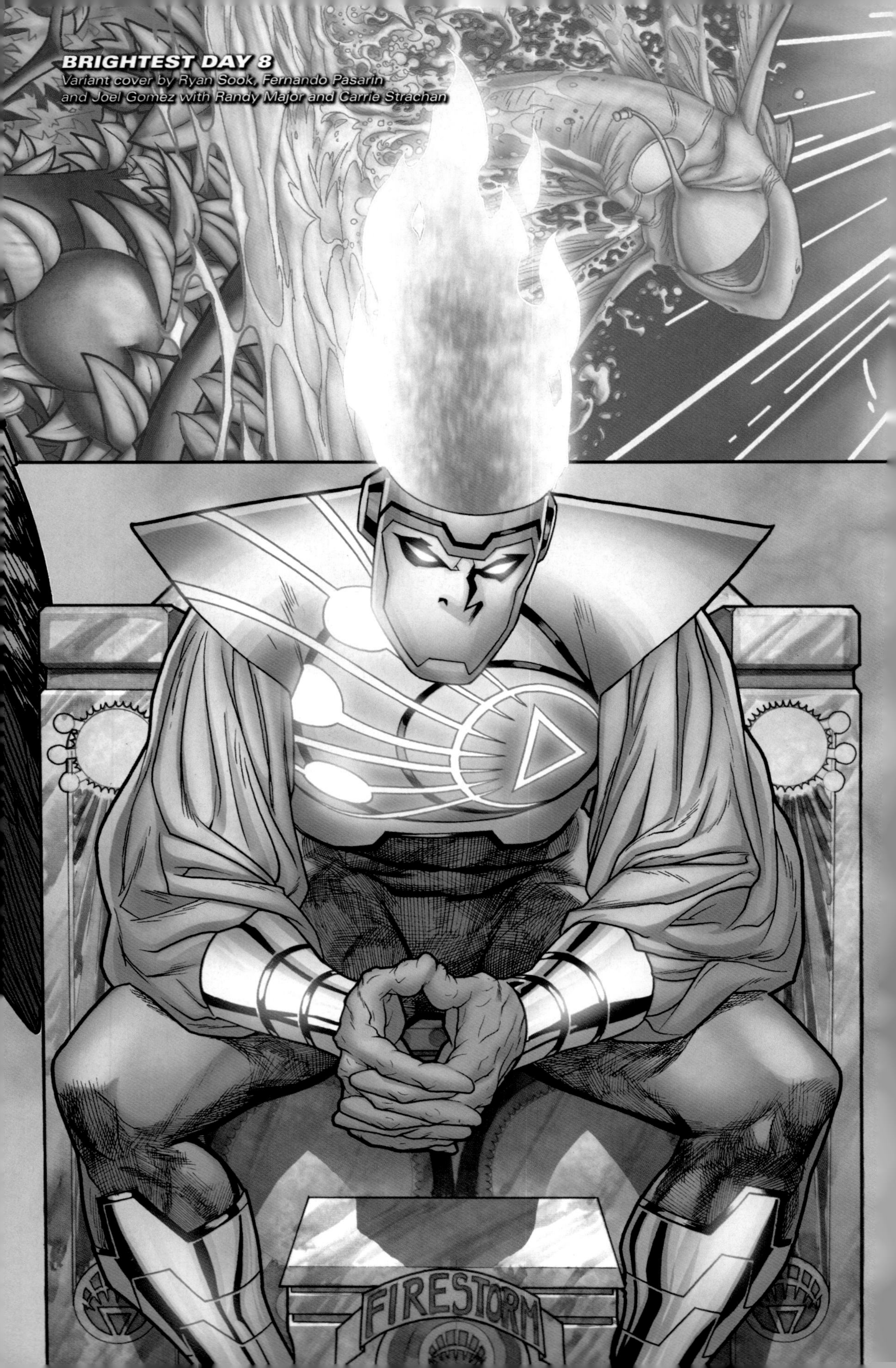
FIRESTORM

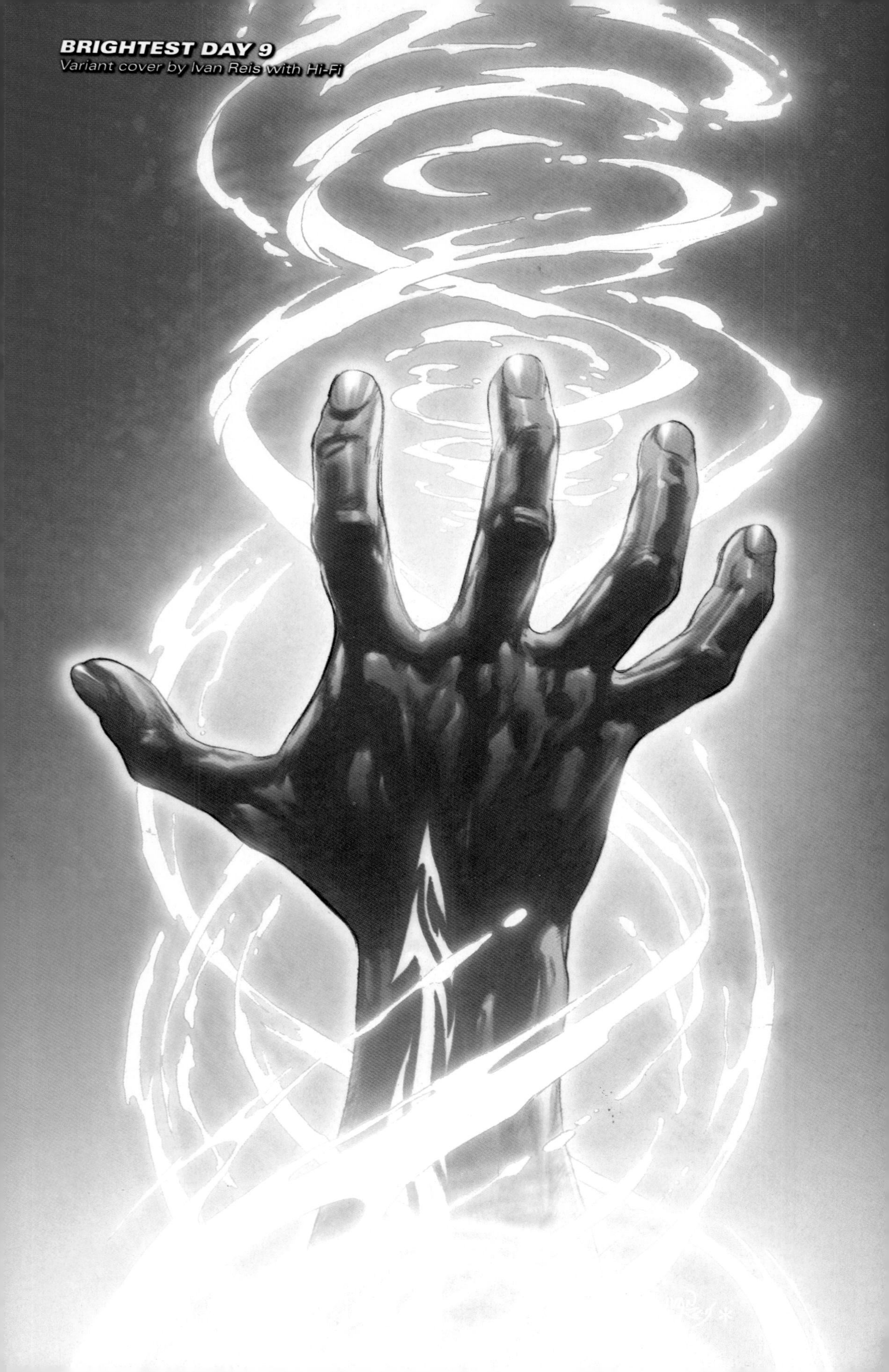

**BRIGHTEST DAY 9**
Variant cover by Ivan Reis with Hi-Fi

**BRIGHTEST DAY 10**
*Variant cover by Ivan Reis with Hi-Fi*

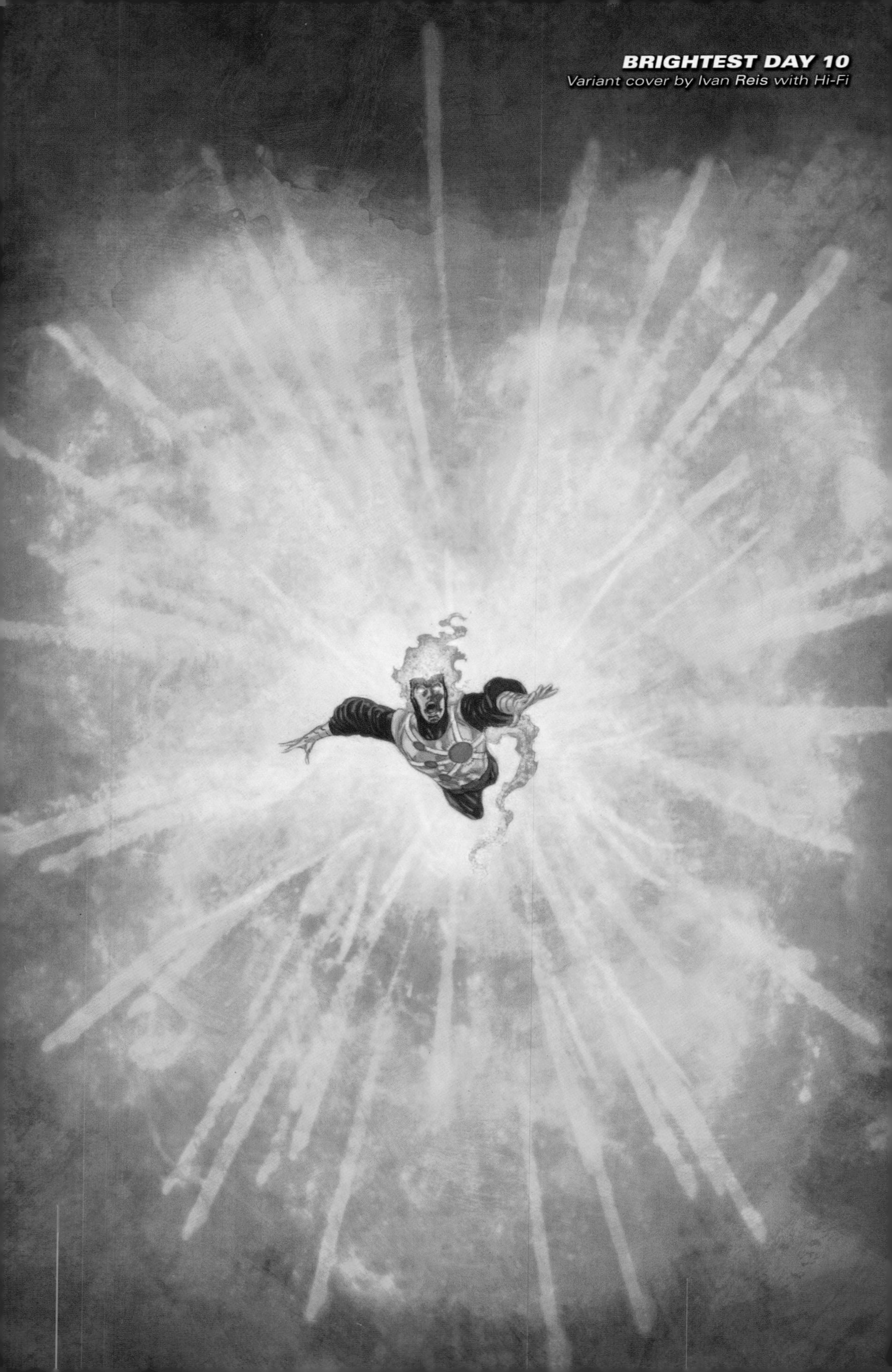

**BRIGHTEST DAY 11**

*Variant cover by Ivan Reis with Hi-Fi*

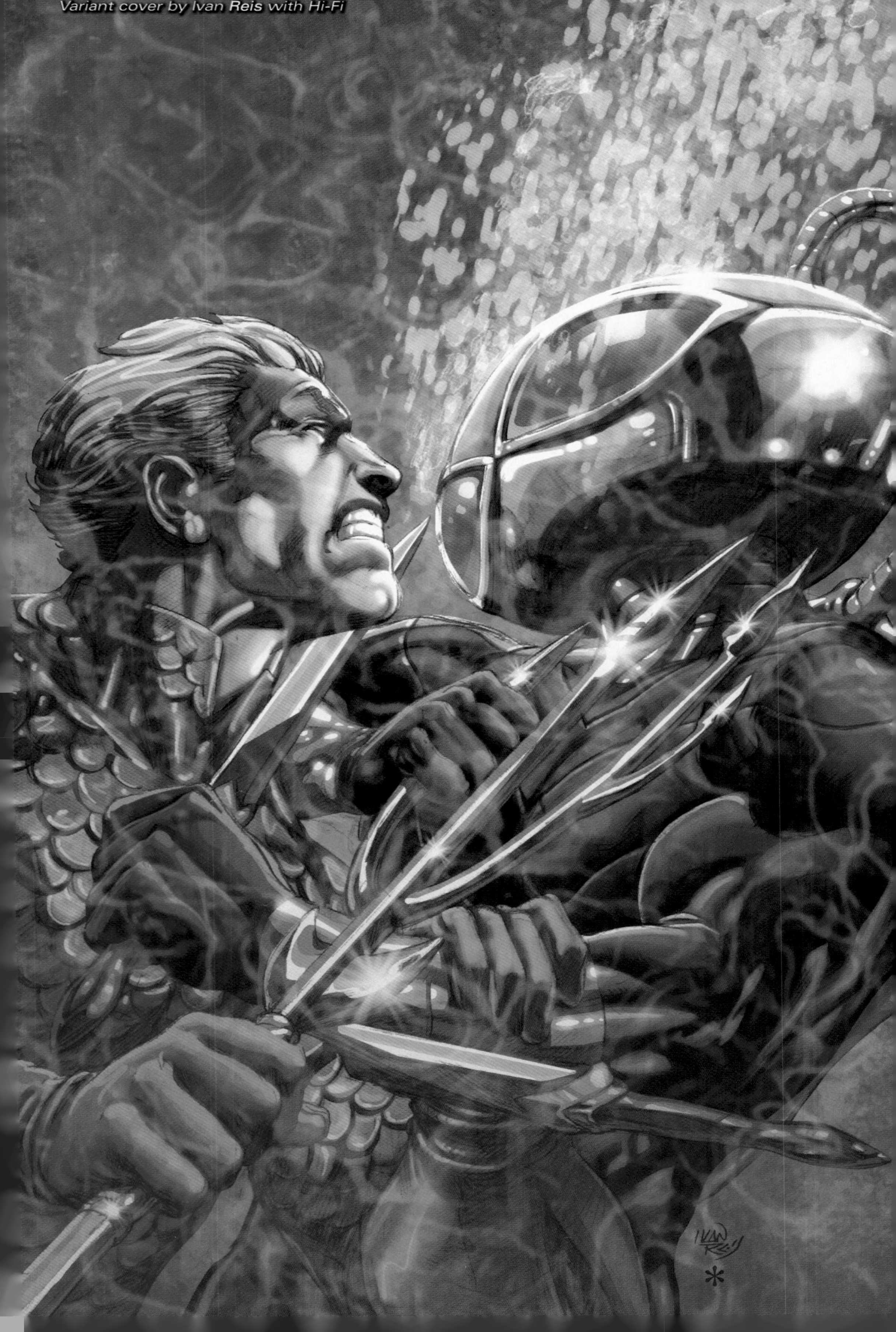

**BRIGHTEST DAY 12**
Variant cover by Ivan Reis with Hi-Fi

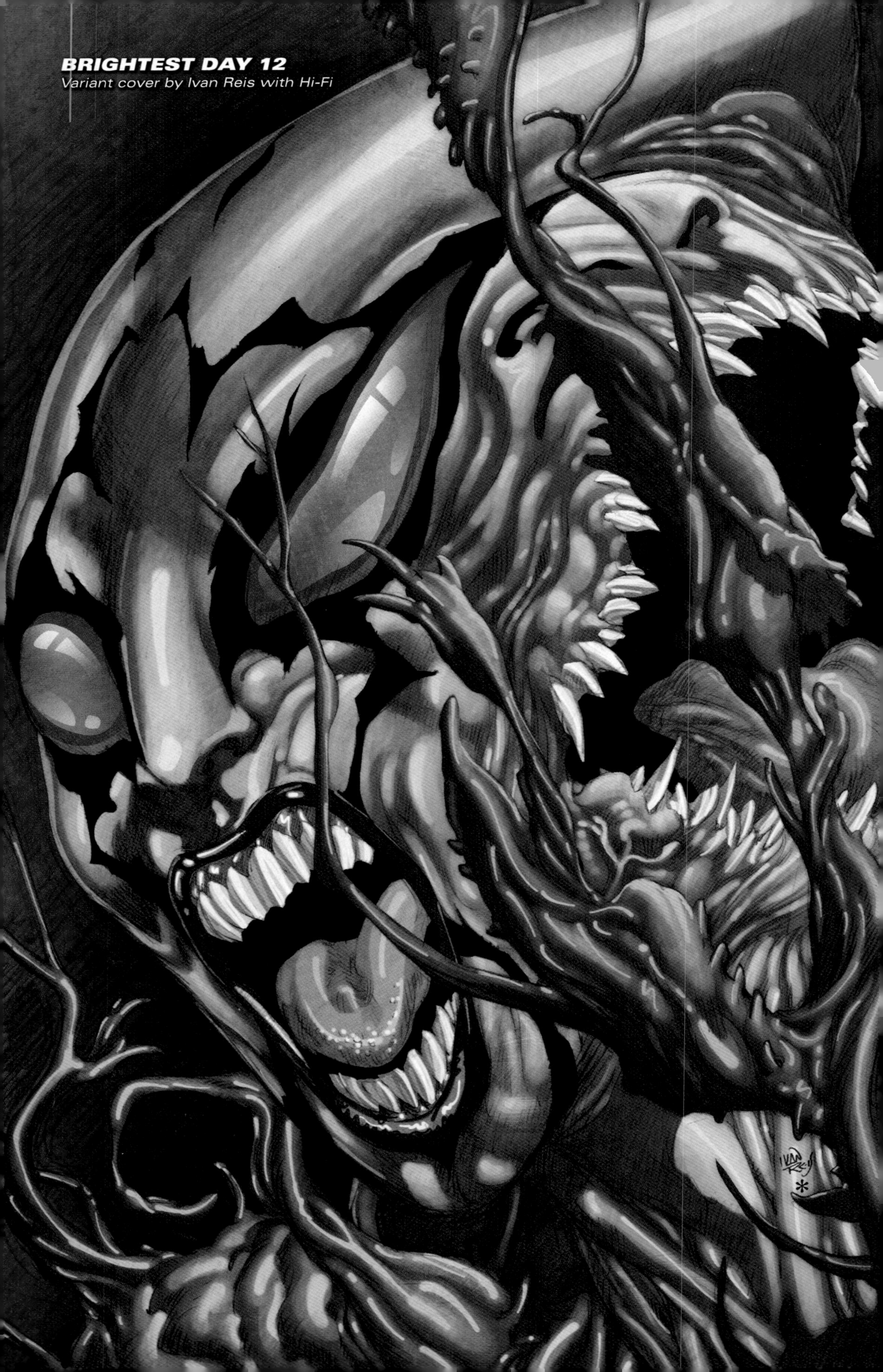
IVAN REIS

**BRIGHTEST DAY 13**
Variant cover by Ivan Reis with Hi-Fi

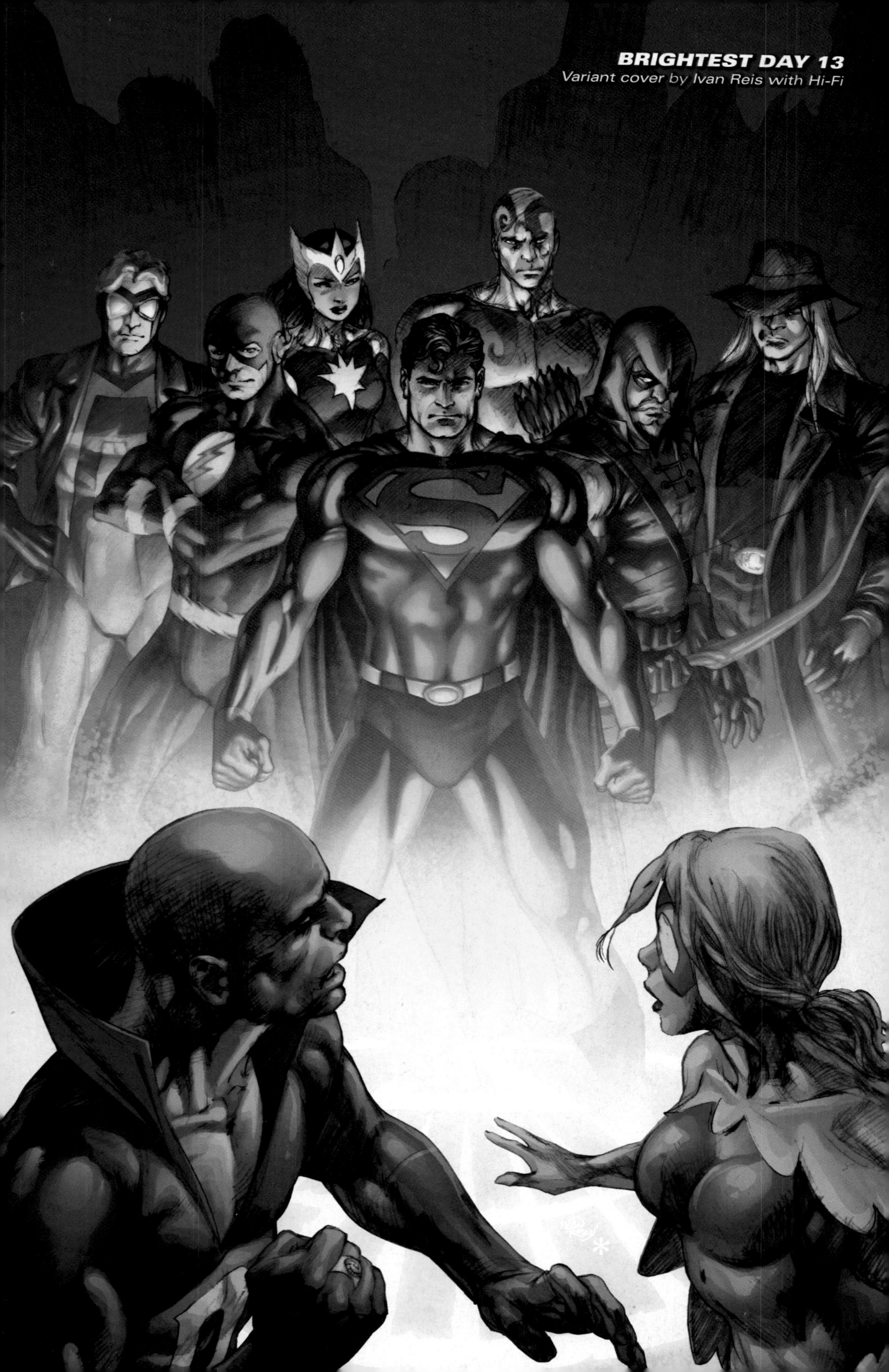

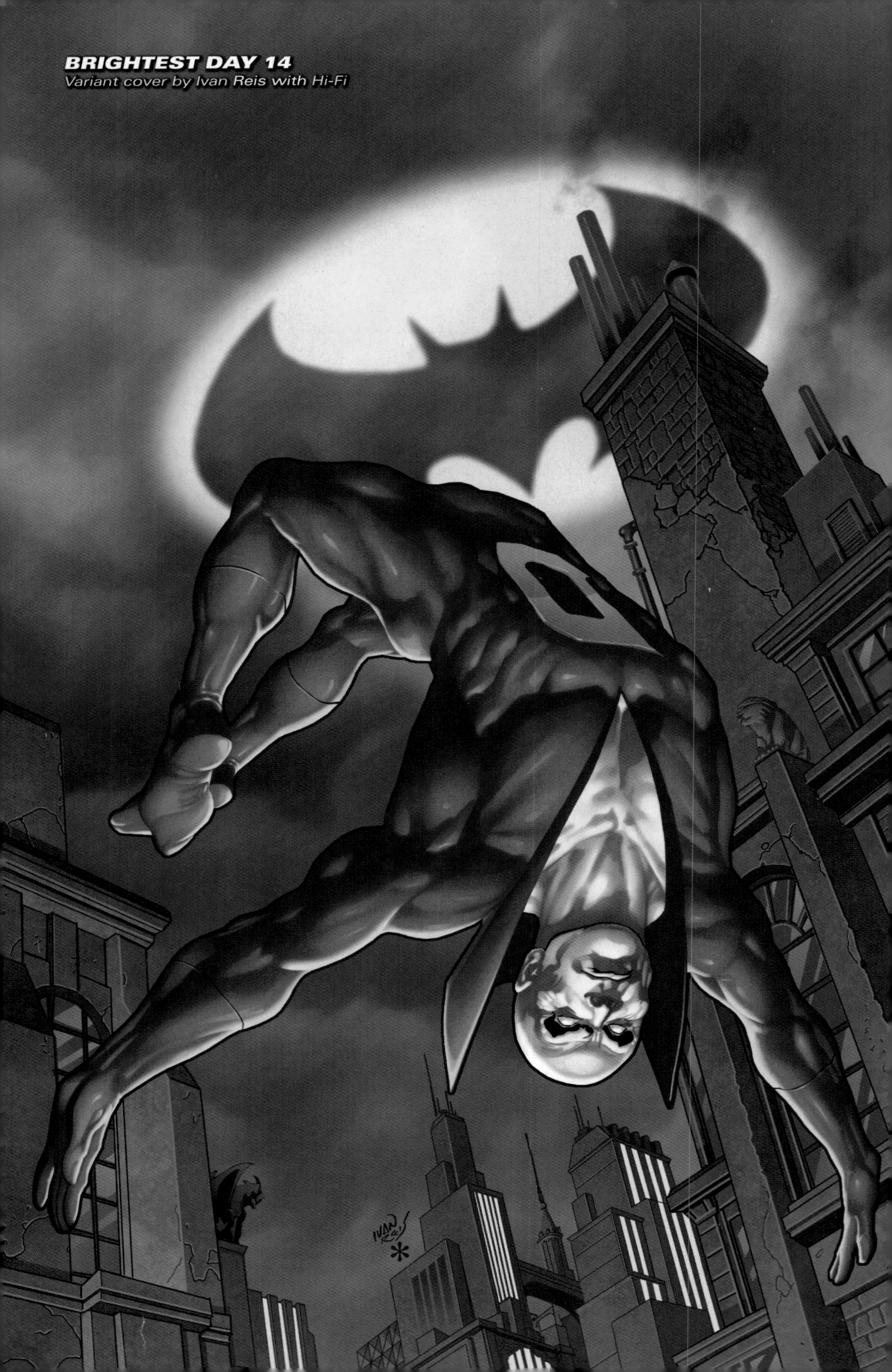

**BRIGHTEST DAY 14**
*Variant cover by Ivan Reis with Hi-Fi*

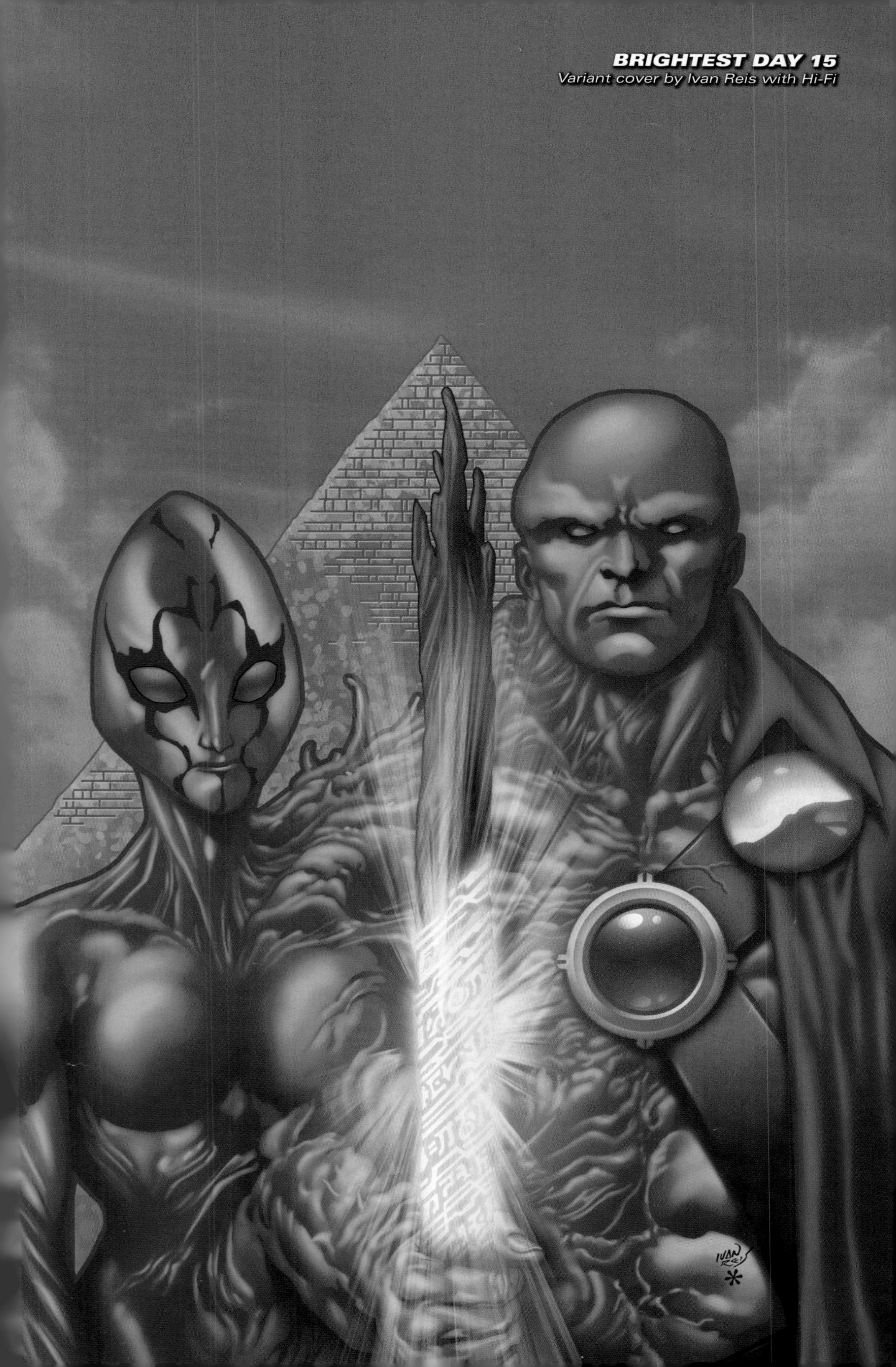

**BRIGHTEST DAY 15**
*Variant cover by Ivan Reis with Hi-Fi*

**BRIGHTEST DAY 16**
*Variant cover by Ivan Reis with Hi-Fi*

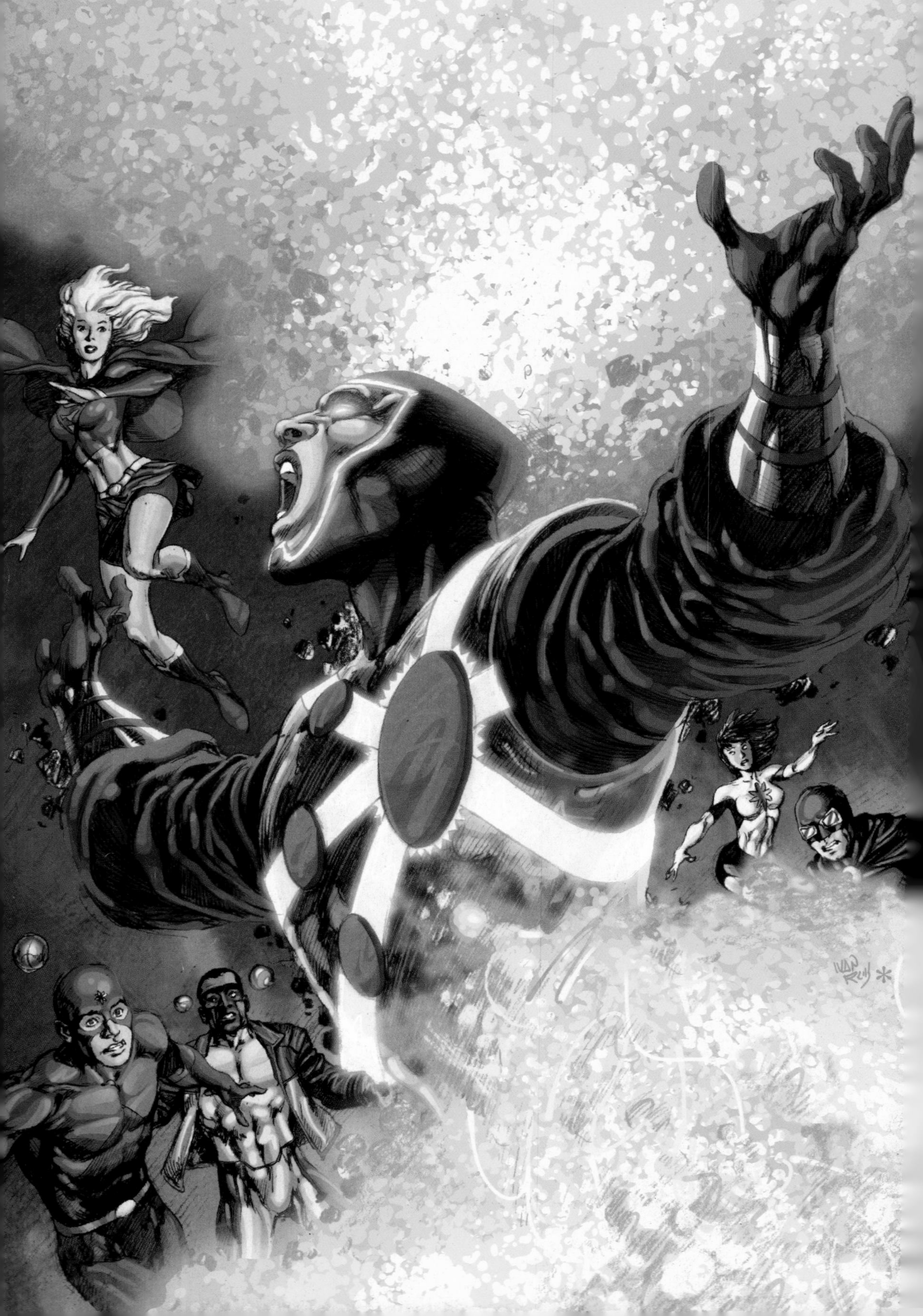

# BIOGRAPHIES

### GEOFF JOHNS

Geoff Johns is one of the most prolific and popular contemporary comic book writers. He has written highly acclaimed stories starring Superman, Green Lantern, the Flash, Teen Titans and the Justice Society of America. He is the author of the *New York Times* best-selling graphic novels GREEN LANTERN: RAGE OF THE RED LANTERNS, GREEN LANTERN: SINESTRO CORPS WAR, JUSTICE SOCIETY OF AMERICA: THY KINGDOM COME, SUPERMAN: BRAINIAC and BLACKEST NIGHT.

Johns was born in Detroit and studied media arts, screenwriting, film production and film theory at Michigan State University. After moving to Los Angeles, he worked as an intern and later an assistant for film director Richard Donner, whose credits include *Superman: The Movie, Lethal Weapon 4* and *Conspiracy Theory.*

Johns began his comics career writing STARS AND S.T.R.I.P.E. and creating Stargirl for DC Comics. Geoff received the Wizard Fan Award for Breakout Talent of 2002 and Writer of the Year for 2005 through 2008 as well as the CBG Writer of the Year 2003 through 2005, 2007 and 2008, and CBG Best Comic Book Series for JSA 2001 through 2005.

After acclaimed runs on THE FLASH, TEEN TITANS and the best-selling INFINITE CRISIS miniseries, Johns co-wrote a run on ACTION COMICS with his mentor, Donner. In 2006, he co-wrote 52, an ambitious weekly comic book series set in real time, with Grant Morrison, Greg Rucka and Mark Waid. Johns has also written for various other media, including the acclaimed "Legion" episode of SMALLVILLE and the fourth season of ROBOT CHICKEN. He wrote the story of the DC Universe Online massively multiplayer action game from Sony Online Entertainment LLC and has recently joined DC Entertainment as its Chief Creative Officer.

Johns currently resides in Los Angeles, California.

### PETER J. TOMASI

Peter J. Tomasi was an editor with DC Comics for many years where he proudly helped usher in new eras for GREEN LANTERN, BATMAN and JSA. He is now devoting all his time to writing comics and screenplays, having worked on such DC titles as GREEN LANTERN CORPS, BATMAN: BLACKEST NIGHT, THE OUTSIDERS, NIGHTWING, BLACK ADAM and the critically acclaimed graphic novel LIGHT BRIGADE, along with many other stories. His current projects include GREEN LANTERN: EMERALD WARRIORS and BATMAN AND ROBIN.

### IVAN REIS

Ivan Reis is a comic book artist born in 1976 in São Bernardo do Campo, São Paulo, Brazil. He started his US career in the '90s, on *Ghost* and *The Mask* for Dark Horse. After pencilling an issue of THE INVISIBLES for Grant Morrison, he started a long run on *Lady Death* for Chaos Comics, then did *The Avengers* and *The Vision*, with Geoff Johns, for Marvel. In 2004 Ivan began to work exclusively for DC. After illustrating high-profile series such as ACTION COMICS, INFINITE CRISIS and RANN-THANAGAR WAR, he started his now legendary run with Geoff Johns on GREEN LANTERN and BLACKEST NIGHT, with his inkers of choice, Oclair Albert and Joe Prado.

### PATRICK GLEASON

Patrick Gleason's career in comics has included work for Marvel and Image Comics. He is most noted for illustrating DC Comics' AQUAMAN, the relaunch of the Green Lantern Corps in the RECHARGE miniseries, and the regular ongoing GREEN LANTERN CORPS series. He is currently working on BATMAN AND ROBIN with Peter J. Tomasi.

### ARDIAN SYAF

Ardian Syaf is an Indonesian comic book artist. He has worked on *The Dresden Files* for Random House and BLACKEST NIGHT: BATMAN, SUPERMAN/BATMAN and GREEN LANTERN CORPS for DC. He is currently working on BIRDS OF PREY.

### SCOTT CLARK

Scott Clark has been working in the comics industry since the early '90s, for Image, Marvel, Aspen and Maximum Press, and most recently for DC on JUSTICE LEAGUE: CRY FOR JUSTICE.

### JOE PRADO

Joe Prado started his career as a professional comic book artist in Brazil during the '90s, and has done hundreds of illustrations for RPG magazines and books. Six years ago he started to produce comics for the US market. His credits include ACTION COMICS, SUPERMAN, BIRDS OF PREY, GREEN LANTERN and THE WARLORD.

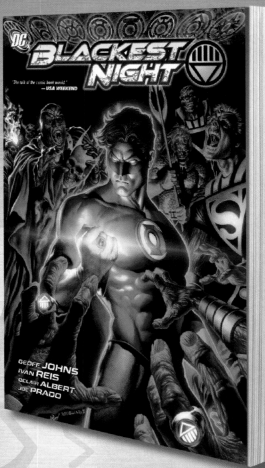